ETERNAL LOVE שיר השירים

RABBI YEHUDA YITZCHOK STEINBERG

ETERNAL LOVE

שיר השירים

A multifaceted commentary on
Shir HaShirim highlighting the
unique love and bond between
HaShem and His People

THE FREIDA COPE EDITION

© Copyright 2024 by Yehuda Steinberg

All questions and for sponsorships please contact the author at:
yehudasteinberg@gmail.com

All rights reserved.

No part of this publication may be translated, reproduced, stored in a retrieval system or transmitted, in a ny form or by means, electronic, mechanical, photocopying, recording or otherwise, even for personal use, without written permission from the copyright holder.

Page layout and design: D Englard
Cover design: D Englard
devorahenglard@gmail.com

הונצח לזכר נשמת

האשה החשובה והצנועה מוכתרת במדות טובות

מרת **פריידא קופ** ע"ה
בת מרדכי חיים ז"ל
אשת ר' מיכאל שמעון הכהן לאי"ט

שעסקה בעניני טהרה בעיר גייטסהעד יותר מעשרים שנה
וגם ביתה היתה פתוחה להרבה נצרכי עירה בעין טובה נפלאה
ותמכה יד בעלה בכל עת לרפואת כל ריעי וקצירי של כלל ישראל
והעמידה באהבה ובחיבה דורות ישרים ומבורכים
העוסקים בתורה ובמעשים טובים

נפטרה בשם טוב יום ד' טבת תשע"ט

ת.נ.צ.ב.ה.

לעילוי נשמת

הרב ברוך שלמה בן הרב דוב דוד שטיינברג ז"ל

נ.ל.ב.ע. ט"ו סיון תשס"ו

ורעיתו מרת אסתר חיה בת החבר ר' חיים שאול ז"ל

נלב"ע כ"ד טבת תשפ"ג

ת.נ.צ.ב.ה.

לעילוי נשמת

ר' חיים משה בן הרב מנחם מנדל ראבערטס זצ"ל

נלב"ע ראש חודש אב תשנ"ט

ת.נ.צ.ב.ה.

לעילוי נשמת

מרת שרה ע"ה

בת יבלחט"א ר' אברהם שיחי'

נלב"ע כ"ה אדר תשע"ג

קדשה שם שמים במעשיה

ת.נ.צ.ב.ה.

לעילוי נשמת

הרב שמואל בן הרב צבי אפרים בלאך ז"ל
נלב"ע ראש חודש שבט תשס"ה

ורעיתו מרת דבורה בת הרב שמשון אליהו ז"ל
נלב"ע כ"ו תמוז תשס"ח

ת.נ.צ.ב.ה.

לעילוי נשמת

הרב יחיאל בן הרב שמואל במברגר זצ"ל
נלב"ע י"ז אלול תשל"ז

ת.נ.צ.ב.ה

רפואה שלמה לכבוד

עקיבא אליהו בן נעמי נ"י

הסכמה מאת אאמו"ר הרה"ג מוהר"ר הרב מרדכי נחום שטיינברג שליט"א

בס"ד

אלול תשפ"ג

אמר רבי עקיבא כל הכתובים קודש ושיר השירים קודש קדשים
Rabbi Akiva says that all of the Scriptures are holy, but Shir HaShirim is the kodesh kodashim, the holy of holies. Mishnayos Yadayim 3:5. But to appreciate the קדושה of שיר השירים a person must first fill his heart and mind with גמרא, פרש"י ותוספות. Only then will he search for the diamonds that lie beneath the surface, and find them.

My son הרב יהודה יצחק שטיינברג is full of תלמוד בבלי, מדרש, וספרי קודש. His main daily efforts are in learning and teaching ש"ס.

But he has seen remarkable סייעתא דשמיא in his elucidation of מגילות רות, איכה ואסתר. And they have been very warmly received.

May his latest effort, to bring the beautiful lessons of שיר השירים to כלל ישראל be crowned with הצלחה.

ברכת אב

מרדכי נחום שטיינברג

מכתב ברכה מאת הרה"ג ראש הישיבה מוהר"ר הרב אברהם גורביץ שליט"א

מכתב ברכה

הובא לפני ספר שלם המבאר כל מגילת שיר השירים לפי פירושו של רש"י ז"ל ומדרשי חז"ל מאת הה"ג ר' יהודה יצחק שטיינברג שליט"א מיושבי אהלי של תורה במנשסתר, ספר הנכתב בלשון ברורה ונעימה. וכשקראתי אותו על אף קוצר הזמן הזמן הפנוי לי נקשתי מאד להניחו באשר מלבד התענוג שהרגשתי בקריאתו הרי היא מעשר הידיעות ומעורר הרגשים לאהבת ה' וליראתו באופן נהדר, והנני לברכו שיזכה להוציאו לאור בקרוב לתועלת הרבים.

אברהם באאמו"ר הגה"צ מוהר"ר ארי' זאב זצוקללה"ה גורביץ

יום ג' לפרשת תולדות תשפ"ג

הסכמה מאת הרה"ג דומ"ץ סאטמאר מוהר"ר הרב ישראל חיים הורוויץ שליט"א

ישראל חיים הורוויץ
הרב דק"ק וויזניץ משה סאטמאר
מאנשעסטער יצ"ו

Y. Ch. Horowitz
Rabbi of Satmar Community
Salford M7 Manchester

בס"ד

חזיתי הגברא רבה תיקון נאה ותמוך על אור השירים אתיקר אצל הרב הגדול
מוה"ר יהודא יצחק שטיינבערג שליט"א והוספות והולפות באולם ש תורה כעורה.
וכבר אתמחי גברא ואתמחי קמיעא בספרו על מגילת רות בפתחתו רבנן
ואצעף גופי' עוד התועלת ורב טוב הצפון בה, ויתאו' לאכול עד עפרי'.
ובעת יעזרהו לברך על הגומר קפל, ובלכתו בדרך הזה, יהא הוא דנו
והדרכה ויגעה לשבת על התורה ועבודת ה' במנוחה לאורך ימים
ושנים טובים עד ביאת גוא"צ בב"א

כו"ח תמוז תש"פ לפ"ק מאנשעסטער יצ"ו
ישראל חיים הורוויץ

בס"ד

חזיתי בקודש חיבור נאה וחשוב על שיר השירים שחיבר מע"כ הה"ג הנעלה מו"ה יהודא יצחק שטיינברג שליט"א מהיושבים באהלה של תורה בעירנו, וכבר איתמחי גברא ואתמחי קמיעא בספרו על מגלת רות ששבחוהו רבנן בהסכמותיהם, כעת מוסיף על הראשונים בחיבורו הלז, אשר כל המעיין ישפוט בצדק גודל התועלת ורב טוב הגנוז בה, ויתאו' לאכול מפרי' ולשבוע מטובה. השי"ת יעזרהו לברך על המוגמר בניקל, ובלכתו בדרך הזה, יהא ה"א עמו וילך מחיל אל חיל לזכות את הרבים. והברכה שיזכה לשבת על התורה ועבודת ה' במנוחה לאורך ימים ושנים טובים עד ביאת גוא"צ בב"א

כו"ח תמוז תש"פ לפ"ק מאנשעסטער יצ"ו

ישראל חיים הורוויץ

הסכמה מאת הרה"ג מרן המשגיח מוהר"ר הרב יהודה ליב וויטלער שליט"א

בס"ד

קיץ תשפ"ג לפ"ק

הנה מגלת שיר השירים היא המגלה שתקנו לנו חכמינו ז"ל עבור זמן חירותינו (ולדעת הגר"א ז"ל גם מברכים על קריאה זו כמו שמברכים על קריאת מגלת אסתר) אבל לא רבים יחכמו להתבונן במגלה זו באותה הדרגה שמתבוננים במגלה האחרת.

והנה ממגלת אסתר אנו שואבים מלא חפנים של דעת בגודל השגחתו ית' על עמו וממגלה זו יודעים על גודל אהבתו ית' אשר "קול דודי הנה זה בא" וגם על גודל אהבתם של סגולתו אשר הם זוכרים תמיד "אהבוך מישרים" שהיא יושר אהבתם בלכתם אחריו ית' למדבר, וגם רואים שם היאך הם מתעוררים מתוך אהבה זו ללימוד תורתו הקדושה "סמכוני באשישות" (הלכות) "רפדוני בתפוחים" (אגדות) "כי חולת אהבה אני" וגם לומדים שם היאך ישראל עם סגולתו מוסרים את נפשם על יחודו ית' בכל דור ודור "כי עזה כמות אהבה" ועוד רבים כהנה. ולמה נגרע מגלה זו ממגלה זו, אין זה כי אם בשביל קושי הלימוד - ללמוד מן המשל אל הנמשל - וגם לתת לב למי הוא המדבר "דודי או רעיתי".

ועל כן בואו ונחזיק טובה לידידי עוז בר אורין ובר אבהן הרב המפואר בתורה ובמעלותיה הרב יהודה שטיינברג שליט"א בן ידידי הג' ר' מרדכי שליט"א אשר ידיו רב לו בהרבצת תורה בכתב ובעל פה. ועכשיו "יבא דודי לגנו" לפרש ולבאר ולפתוח גם את זה כאגרת פתוחה גלוי לכל דורש ומבקש.

הכותב וחותם לכבוד התורה ולומדיה ולכבוד ידיד המחבר שליט"א

יהודה ליב וויטלער

הסכמה מאת הרה"ג רב קלויז טשארטקוב מוהר"ר הרב ישראל פרידמן שליט"א

ב"ה

RABBI Y. FRIEDMAN
12 New Hall Ave Salford
Manchester M7 4JU

ישראל פרידמן
רב קלויז טשארטקוב
מאנשסתר

ט"ו תמוז תש"פ

Chazal tell us (Brochos 57:) "Someone who sees Shir Hashirim in a dream, it is a sign that he is on the way to attaining a very lofty level in avodas Hashem". This new and amazing sefer in English on Shir Hashirim is indeed akin to a dream. Who would have dreamt that it would be possible to translate and to explain such lofty and exalted concepts in such a beautiful and inspiring manner as the reader will see in this sefer.

We owe a great debt of gratitude to the author of this monumental work which is gleaned from the words of Chazal and of the Sages over the centuries. Rav Yehuda Steinberg shlita has already authored a number of important popular english seforim, but this sefer must surely be in a class of its own. Unfortunately, for many people Shir Hashirim has always been regarded as a closed book, a holy work that is recited with great passion, whilst we thought that the holy concepts were beyond us and we could not relate to.

Rav Steinberg's important introduction deserves a special mention, here he explains how we are to understand the choice of words used in Shir Hashirim, and how the secular world of today has unfortunately profaned the purity of the world thus rendering many people to be far removed from these lofty concepts.

In this magnificent sefer, the holy song of Shlomo Hamelech has been opened up for us, allowing us to peek inside and feel the everlasting unbreakable bond between Hashem and Klall Yisroel.

הכותב לכבוד המחבר החשוב וספרו החשוב

ישראל פרידמן

הסכמה מאת הרה"ג מוהר"ר הרב פסח אליהו פאלק זצ"ל

Rabbi E. Falk
146 Whitehall Road
Gateshead, NE8 1TP
England
TEL: 0044-191-4782342

פסח אליהו פאלק
מח"ס שו"ת מחזה אליהו
'זכור ושמור' על הלכות שבת
'עוז והדר לבושה' על צניעות דלבוש
מו"ץ בק"ק גייטסהעד יצ"ו

בס"ד

ערב שבת קודש פרשת וישלח תשע"ה לפ"ק, פה גייטסהעד יצ"ו

מאוד מצא חן בעיני ספרו דמר ידידי הרה"ג ר' יהודה יצחק שטיינברג שליט"א ממנשסתר יצ"ו על מגילת רות. הספר נכתב בשפה ברורה ובנעימה, ומושך את הלב להתעמק בהלימודים הגדולים שאפשר ללמוד מכל פרט ופרט מהמגילה הקדושה הלזו, והספר מקרב דברי אלוקים חיים אלו להחיי יום יום שלנו. במיוחד שם הרה"ג המחבר שליט"א הדגש בהלימודים הנוגעים למדת החסד ומדת הצניעות שעלינו ללמוד ולקרב ללבנו מפעולת האשה הגדולה רות, שנעשית בזכות מעלות אלו לאמה של מלכות. ולכן קרא שם הספר "לב של חסד" באשר הפנימיות המופלגת של רות הביאה להקריב עצמה עבור אחרים ולהתנהג במדת החסד באופן מופלאה, וגם הביאה למדת הצניעות וכדכתיב כל כבודה בת מלך פנימה - היקרות והעדינות של הבת מלך מקורו מהפנימיות שלה. נמצא שנעשית הרכבה מופלאה של חסד וצניעות גם יחד. ובכן שמחה היא לי להשתתף עם מברכים אחרים ולומר שלענ"ד הספר מקנה להקורא הרבה יראת שמים אהבת ה' ומדות טובות, והלואי שנזכה אנו וכל בית ישראל ללכת בדרכי גדולי האומה שכל בית ישראל נשענים עליהם.

ובכן אצא בברכה להמחבר שליט"א שחפץ ה' בידו יצליח ויזכה להוסיף עוד ספרים וכשאר ספרים שכבר זכה להוציא לאור עולם.

החותם לכבוד התורה ולכבוד המשתדלים לקרב התורה ללבן של כלל ישראל.

פסח אליהו פאלק

פסח אליהו פאלק.

REPRINTED FROM PREVIOUS SEFER WITH PERMISSION FROM THE FAMILY

ACKNOWLEDGEMENTS

It is with overwhelming gratitude to Hashem that I complete the writing of this *sefer* on *Shir Hashirim*. There is perhaps no other *sefer* that its central theme is so important: the loving relationship between Hashem and *Klal Yisrael*. I hope and daven to Hashem that this *sefer* facilitates *kiddush Hashem* into the world by illuminating just how much Hashem loves us and by enhancing and deepening our love for Him.

Without the help of many wonderful individuals, this *sefer* would not have been possible. Although I cannot mention them all, I extend my heartfelt thanks to each and every one of them.

I would like to express a special thank-you to the following individuals:

First, my parents: Besides the incalculable debt of gratitude that I owe them for everything that they have done for me, they have also helped me directly with this *sefer*. My father, Rabbi Mordechai Steinberg, *shlita*, reviewed parts of the *sefer* and offered indispensable advice. I am also very grateful for his *haskomo*. Through her love for her family, my mother has always been a role model and reflection of Hashem's love for His children. She is the inspiration for this *sefer*. May they continue to see *Yiddishe nachas* from all their children, grandchildren and future generations.

The constant encouragement and inspiration I receive from my parents-in-law, Rabbi and Mrs. Eliezer Bloch, has given me the strength to continue writing this *sefer* despite the many challenges on the way. May they continue to see *Yiddishe nachas* from all their children and grandchildren and future generations.

I would like to thank Rabbi Avrohom Gurwicz, *shlita*, the Rosh Yeshiva of Gateshead Yeshiva; Rabbi Yisroel Chaim Horowitz, *shlita*, the Satmar Rov; Rabbi Yehuda Leib Wittler, *shlita*, the Rosh Yeshiva of Sharei Chaim; and Rabbi Yisroel Friedman, *shlita*, the Rav of the Tchortkover Kloiz, for taking the time to look through this *sefer* and gracing it with their *haskamos*. I feel tremendous gratitude for having been *zocheh* to receive their *berachos* and encouragement.

In the last conversation I had with Rabbi Pesach Eliyahu Falk, *zt"l*, he told me that he had read parts of my *sefer* and would write an *haskamah*. Unfortunately, he was suddenly *niftar* shortly afterwards. In addition to the great loss for the whole of *Klal Yisrael*, I felt the loss in a personal way because Rabbi Falk had always encouraged me with my *sefarim*. In his great humility, he would tell me how much he enjoyed learning from them, and how much he gained from them. With his family's permission, I have included his *haskamah* from a previous *sefer*.

This *sefer* has been dedicated by my *chavrusah* and good friend, R' Arye Leib HaKohen Cope, *l'ilui nishmas* his mother, Mrs. Freida Cope, *a"h*. It is a privilege that this *sefer* bears the name of such a great *tzadekis*. Besides her countless great deeds and her devotion to *chessed*, she left behind a truly wonderful and kind-hearted family. R' Arye Leib is a true exemplar of this. This is just one of the many wonderful projects he is involved in. May this *sefer* be a true *nachas* and *illui neshamah* for מרת פריידא בת ר' מרדכי חיים קופ ע"ה.

Over the years, Mr. Jan Fidler and Mr. Nathan Marks have provided great assistance with the publishing of my previous sefarim. May they always have much success in their endeavors.

I would like to thank my good friend, R' Pinchos Brandeis, for his help with this *sefer* and previous *sefarim*. May Hashem bless him with much *hatzlachah* in all of his wonderful projects.

I have the great *zechus* of giving the Daf Yomi *shiur* in Beis Yisroel. I am very grateful to the Rav, Rabbi Yehoshua Aharon Sofer *shlita*, and to those who help arrange the *shiur*, and to *shiur* participants for this rewarding opportunity.

Many of the ideas in this *sefer* were first presented at *shiurim* arranged by Mrs. Pamela Katz. Having the opportunity to verbalize these ideas gave them more clarity – and it was her programs that provided the forum. I then had the opportunity to revisit and elucidate these ideas further in *shiurim* on *Nach* arranged by Mr. Leo Stern. I am grateful for their help in being able to present these ideas in front of a live audience.

This *sefer* was first edited expertly by Mrs. Bracha Steinberg. R' Uri Cheskin then revised and edited it again, and his proficiency is clearly evident on every page. Mrs. Devora Montlake skilfully copyedited and proofread the manuscript. Mrs. Devora Englard typeset and did all the graphics for this rather complicated *sefer* – and it is to her credit that it is pleasing to the eye. I am deeply grateful for their dedication and expertise.

Acharon acharon chaviv, I would like to thank my wife. Throughout *Shir HaShirim*, "the wife" – symbolizing *Klal Yisrael* – is praised for her many virtues. These praises aptly describe my wife. Words cannot express my feelings of gratitude for all she does for me, and for her boundless love and devotion to our children.

May we all be *zocheh* to constantly feel close to Hashem – to trust in Hashem, and bask in the warmth of His great love. And may we be privileged to love Hashem, and constantly strive to serve Him better, and to yearn to become closer to Him… until the time when the entire world will stand in awe when they see a glimpse of the Eternal Love that Hashem displays to us – His chosen nation – in the End of Days בביאת גואל צדק במהרה בימינו אמן.

Yehuda Yitzchok Steinberg
Manchester
Nissan 5784

CONTENTS

Foreword 21
Introduction 27
Chapter 1 65
Chapter 2 128
Chapter 3 183
Chapter 4 210
Chapter 5 265
Chapter 6 322
Chapter 7 364
Chapter 8 419
Reciting Shir HaShirim 481
Shir Hashirim Translated 486
Detailed Table of Contents 505
Index 517

FOREWORD

In recent decades, the English-speaking public has shown a growing interest in understanding all of the *Tanach*, and many excellent books have made the *Tanach* much more accessible. But *Shir HaShirim* still remains a closed book for most people. In fact, the enigma of *Shir HaShirim*, the Song of Songs, has fascinated its readers for centuries. The reasons for this are numerous.

Shir HaShirim is an allegory. Therefore, readers face the dual challenge of understanding the allegory and then uncovering the underlying meaning. Unlike most *sefarim* where all one needs to understand are its lessons and teachings, in *Shir HaShirim*, one must first understand the allegory, and only then can he or she begin to fathom its lessons. Additionally, because the content of *Shir HaShirim* seems so mundane, one may wonder about the place in *Tanach* for a song that appears to be lacking any holiness. Furthermore, not only are the words difficult to translate, but the dialogue is complicated. Generally, the dialogue is between Hashem and *Klal Yisrael* (the Jewish People[1]), but *Klal Yisrael*'s friends and enemies also speak. With so many parties involved, it is not always clear who is speaking — and to whom. This must be sorted out verse by verse. Finally, and perhaps most importantly, even after reaching an understanding of the verse, it is still necessary to explore the deeper meaning of its words, and to uncover the valuable lessons here, and understand how they relate to our lives. Of course, these complexities should not deter us from delving into, and understanding, *Shir HaShirim*. Let us make every effort to appreciate this book as one that teaches us how to act and make changes in our lives.

The main theme of *Shir HaShirim* is Hashem's love for us, and our love for Him. The Rambam describes this beautifully in his *Hilchos Teshuvah*:

---

[1] The term "*Klal Yisrael*" is generally used here in this work to signify the Jewish People, although the English term appears as well. Please note that since this work is meant for Jewish readers, the term "we" is also used strategically.

> The appropriate love that one should have for Hashem is…a tremendous, boundless, powerful love, to the point where a person's spirit is bonded with the love of Hashem and he is constantly meditating and thinking about this love. Just as one who has become lovesick is unable to think of anything else… Whether he is sitting, walking, eating, or drinking, his mind is focused only on his love. Even more so should the love of Hashem be within the hearts and minds of those who love Him — to the point where they are possessed by it… The whole of *Shir HaShirim* is an allegory about this idea.[2]

These magnificent words give us a taste of what *Shir HaShirim* is all about and what kind of love for Hashem we should be aspiring to!

As we shall see, the lessons of *Shir HaShirim* are so important that throughout the ages, *Klal Yisrael*, in general, and our great Torah Sages, in particular, have actually treated it with more reverence than any other megillah. Indeed, the messages of *Shir HaShirim* may be even more relevant today than ever before. We live in a world where emotional problems and unhealthy mental attitudes are becoming increasing prevalent. Although society has become more financially and physically secure, unhealthy obsessions, lack of happiness, and even depression have become more prevalent. Even the religiously observant Jewish community has not been spared from a loss of happiness and feelings of love.

The most powerful antidote to all this is a deep appreciation of how meaningful and important our lives are, and how much love Hashem has for us, a love that does not depend on how "superficially successful" we are, but on how intrinsically special we are. This is the essential message of *Shir HaShirim*. Understanding and appreciating it will amplify the love in our lives not just for Hashem, but for ourselves and others.

In the interest of elucidating several other key issues, I would like to take readers behind the scenes for a few moments and say a few words about the genesis of this *sefer*. When I started giving *shiurim* on *Shir HaShirim*, my intent was to make this precious megillah not only understandable, but also inspiring — and to interpret the vital life lessons found here in a way that all could relate to. After giving these *shiurim* for a few years, people encouraged me to write down these ideas for the benefit of others.

That was easier said than done. This *sefer* took me many years to complete, far longer than I anticipated when I first began. I rewrote nearly all of it several times due, in

---

2 *Hilchos Teshuvah* 10:3.

part, to a number of built-in difficulties and even dangers involved in elucidating *Shir HaShirim*.

This megillah portrays one of the deepest, yet most basic concepts, in Jewish belief: Hashem's love for *Klal Yisrael*. On the one hand, we must be careful not to fall into the trap of thinking that we truly grasp Hashem, or even the ways of Hashem. On the other, to feel the love that Hashem has for us, we must begin thinking about Him and His ways. The balance between thinking about Hashem and what He does, without assuming that we actually grasp Him, is a delicate one.

Shlomo HaMelech, the author of *Shir HaShirim*, cloaked his message in an allegory that uses intimate language to express our people's love for Hashem and His love for us. In order to truly appreciate the message of the megillah, one needs to understand the metaphors used. After discussing with my *rabbeim* everything that I had written, I decided to translate every verse as closely as possible to the original Hebrew. Still, in order to uphold the rules of modesty, I did not go into too much detail in the commentary where inappropriate.

Some other basic issues that I had to deal with were these: Should the actual allegory be elucidated, or should the focus be limited to the meaning of the allegory? How much attention should be given to the tremendous wisdom that lies within these verses and how much to the wonderful emotions that these verses invoke?

The answers to many of these questions would depend on who the person reading this book is. I decided to write for the adult reader who has a basic understanding and firm belief in all the principles of Jewish faith. (In any event, *Shir HaShirim* will not be properly appreciated by younger readers.) In addition, some of the ideas presented here can only be understood by someone who has a basic understanding of *Tanach*. Perhaps it goes without saying that the ability to respond to ideas with one's heart, and not just with one's intellect, is imperative for understanding this book. People without these "qualifications" would be better off not reading this book.

In the commentary, I endeavored to make sure that all the ideas are clear, while leaving enough room for these ideas to be thought about and developed further according to each individual's understanding. For this reason, I have held back from plumbing the depths of this megillah so as not to stifle the reader's feelings and thoughts by imposing my own ideas. Since *Shir HaShirim* describes the love Hashem has for every Jewish person and the love every Jewish person is supposed to feel for Hashem, the reader will be able to relate to it in accordance with his life experience and the depth of emotion that he has developed. One who has tangibly felt Hashem's love will understand *Shir HaShirim* differently from one who has struggled to feel His love. One who has enjoyed success and feels a profound appreciation for Hashem will read *Shir HaShirim* differently from one who has suffered greatly and has had to learn to accept the will of Hashem.

It is reported that when the Satmar Rebbe, *zt"l*, saw a book elucidating the prayers, he said, "How can someone explain to me what I am feeling when I am speaking to the One I love?!" A person who has truly developed a relationship with Hashem would find it presumptuous for someone else to tell him what he feels when he is speaking to Hashem, no less than if one would tell a husband what he feels when he is speaking to his beloved wife.

Indeed, one should constantly aspire to having his prayers evolve and deepen throughout his lifetime. The very same prayer that one started saying as a child should take on new meaning later in life because his deeper connection to Hashem influences his feelings and thoughts. Every experience in a person's life should influence his relationship with Hashem and thereby enrich and color his prayers. This applies both when the experience or event is a pleasant one that helps him appreciate Hashem's gifts to him or an upsetting one that prompts him to seek a deeper meaning to his connection to Hashem (other than just receiving all that he desires). It is tragic when one has not developed any real relationship with Hashem and relies completely on others to explain to him how he should feel. I have tried to avoid this. Thus, I have not tried to define the love that my readers have with the One who loves them most. I have, though, tried to provide ideas and insights drawn from *Shir HaShirim* which can help readers appreciate and contemplate Hashem's love for them and their love for Him.

This *sefer* is based on the commentary of Rashi and the allegorical translation is based on his explanations because Rashi has always been considered our foremost commentator. I have, however, included insights from other commentaries when they had particular relevance or offered significant inspiration. Please note that the sources cited often contain only the germ of the insight or idea being developed in the commentary. The reader is thus strongly advised to look up the source for further reference. Any Midrash quoted without a reference is from *Midrash Rabbah* on the verse under discussion. Similarly, any *sefer* quoted without a page or verse reference is a *sefer* on *Shir HaShirim* and is addressing the verse under discussion.

The great Chassidic Rebbe Rabbi Aharon of Karlin, *zt"l*, was once asked by his Chassidim to identify the worst *aveirah* that a Jew can commit. He answered: "The worst thing a Jew can do is to forget that he is a Jew." Out of all the *aveiros*, the Rebbe chose forgetting who we are as being the worst. Why?

I would like to suggest the following: We will learn throughout *Shir HaShirim* how

Hashem loves *Klal Yisrael* more than we can possibly comprehend, and that *Klal Yisrael*'s relationship with Hashem is likened to that of a husband and a wife. Now, if we hear of a couple where the wife, out of anger or spite, walks away from her home, we have reason to hope that her anger will dissipate and that husband and wife will make up. If, however, we hear that a wife, after many years of marriage, forgets that she is married and therefore does not come home, we know that there was something fundamentally wrong with the relationship. A Jew who does an *aveirah* is simply someone whose *yetzer ha'ra* overcame him and got him to follow his desire rather than listen to Hashem. But if a Jew forgets that he is a Jew, this means that his entire relationship with Hashem is so weak that he simply forgets all about it.

Shir HaShirim drives home the message that Hashem loves every Jew, and that every Jew is very precious in the eyes of Hashem. If we forget that, we are forgetting who we really are. Only if we know who we really are will we have the ability to start living the way we are supposed to. Let us proceed now to deepen that knowledge.

INTRODUCTION

Shir HaShirim is a very difficult *sefer* to learn. Although we do not truly understand the full depth of any part of *Tanach*, *Shir HaShirim* is hard to understand even on a simple level. The Introduction that follows is designed to make that challenge a bit easier.[3] It includes background information, an overview, and an introduction to the relevant general concepts.

SHIR HASHIRIM'S CENTRAL THEME

We know that every verse in *Tanach* imparts a number of lessons and that every *sefer* of the *Tanach* touches on numerous subjects. There is, however, always one fundamental theme that every individual *sefer* comes to teach.[4] For example, *Megillas Esther* underscores the fact that Hashem always looks after the Jewish People, and *Megillas Rus* underscores the importance of kindness, and *Mishlei* is all about fear of Hashem.

What is the central message of *Shir HaShirim*? It is the tremendous love that Hashem has for all of us, and the great love that we have, or are supposed to have, for Him.[5] That the whole of *Shir HaShirim* is intended just to teach us this one point gives us a sense of how important this lesson is.

We have to remember that Hashem loves us more than anyone else loves us. He loves us constantly, even if we sin.[6] He loves and cares for us more than we love and care

---

3   It is noteworthy that Rashi felt the need to write an introduction to only one of the twenty-four books of *Tanach*: *Shir HaShirim*. This is due to its great difficulty and to the fact that this book is all a *mashal* (allegory). Furthermore, Rashi departs here from his usual approach of explaining a verse according to its simple meaning (as he often notes is the main aim of his commentary (e.g., *Bereishis* 33:20, *s.v. vayikra*). This approach is not appropriate for *Shir HaShirim*. Therefore, Rashi explains in his introduction how the basic meaning of each verse has to be in accordance with the *nimshal*, the meaning of the allegory (*V'zos L'Yaakov*).

4   Rabbi Hai Gaon and some *Rishonim* had special names for the *sefarim* of *Nach*, depending on their subject (e.g., *Mishlei* was called *Sefer HaChochmah*).

5   The Malbim explains that one reason *Shir HaShirim* is not easily understood is that it is devoted to an emotion: love. Unlike actions or objects, which are relatively easy to describe, emotions are hard to clearly define and explain.

6   Rabbi Shimshon Rafael Hirsh writes that even if a person would sin so much that his parents would reject him, Hashem would still accept and loves him (Commentary on *Tehillim* 27:10).

for ourselves. He loves us infinitely and eternally. Just as we cannot grasp any aspect of Hashem, we cannot grasp His tremendous love for us.

Rabbi Shimshon Pinkus, *zt"l*, once pointed out that if we knew that a cousin or a friend had become extremely wealthy or powerful, we would feel a sense of security that should something go really wrong in our life, we would have someone to fall back on. How much more so should the knowledge that Hashem — to whom all wealth and power belongs — loves us more than anyone else ever loved us, make us feel happy and secure.

Let us try to imagine someone who received a beautiful car as a gift but was unaware that cars are made to move and take us places. He thus used it only for shelter on rainy days. We would pity this fool for missing out on truly benefiting from his car. Similarly, we have this wonderful relationship with Hashem, but if we are not aware of its power and importance — and only during difficult times do we seek His shelter — then we are the fools. We should be connecting to Hashem's love for us not only in times of need, but rather, this should be the main relationship in our lives. What kind of a relationship is it when we only think about Hashem in times of need?!

Of course, we maintain many relationships in our lifetimes, but our closest one should always be our relationship with Hashem. While this might sound very lofty and even a bit difficult to imagine, it is truly part of the essence of being a Jew. And it is not difficult once we get accustomed to it. We should spend more time thinking about what Hashem has done for us and what Hashem wants of us than about what anyone else has done for us or wants of us. We should spend more time talking to Hashem than talking to anyone else. When we do this regularly, we can easily reach a point where the most important relationship we have is with Hashem. Indeed, it should be obvious that this relationship affects our life in every way — both spiritually and physically — more than any other and lasts far longer than any other. Dovid HaMelech expresses this succinctly: "For my father and mother have left me, but Hashem has gathered me in."[7] This means that as wonderful as my relationship with my parents is, it has its limitations. There will be situations, either due to my conduct or to their limitations, when they will abandon me. My closeness to Hashem, however, does not have limitations. Whatever happens and whatever I may do, He will never abandon me. There is much more to be said on this subject, but space limitations preclude doing so here.

The knowledge and feeling that Hashem loves us are fundamental to understanding what it means to be Jewish. It is tragic that these treasures are not an integral part of the lives of many Jews today. Those who do not appreciate this concept and do not have this

---

7 *Tehillim* 27:10.

feeling are truly missing out. Indeed, it is important to learn *Shir HaShirim* just to gain a deeper understanding of how much Hashem loves us!

Immediately before we recite the *Shema* in the morning and evening prayers, we recite a blessing in which we describe how Hashem loves us: *Ahavah Rabbah*[8] / *Ahavas Olam*. This is because the *Shema* is the affirmation of our belief in Hashem. Before we affirm and acknowledge our belief, we express our understanding of what our relationship to Hashem is: a relationship based on love for one another. This can be likened to how we introduce people. Before we tell someone who they are, we indicate what our relationship is to them. We might say, "This is my boss, Mr. So-and-So" or "This is my cousin, Mrs. So-and-So." In a loosely similar way, this blessing is the introduction to the affirmation of our belief in Hashem in the *Shema* prayer: "This is the God who loves us: Hashem who is all-powerful, all-knowing, etc." The fundamental basis of our relationship with Hashem is one of love.

Furthermore, in the *Shema*, we remind ourselves of our obligation to love Hashem. Loving Hashem is one of the highest ideals of a Jew. It is one of the six constant mitzvos.[9] Because feelings are reciprocated, the easiest way to achieve the love of Hashem is by contemplating how much Hashem loves us. As we think about how someone loves us, we come to love him or her.[10] Therefore, in order to enable us to realize the love of Hashem, we focus on how Hashem loves us.

In the blessing *Ahavas Olam*, we speak of the "world of love" that Hashem has for the Jewish People. In Hebrew, the idiomatic expression *"ahavas olam"* actually means "eternal love," i.e., a love that lasts as long as this world. But the deeper meaning is that Hashem's love is greater than all the love in this world. In other words, if we could manage to calculate all the love that has existed in this world from the time of Creation, Hashem loves us even more than that! Let us try to get a feel for the magnitude of this love. We might start by trying to quantify the love we feel for our spouse in a single day. Obviously, emotions cannot be quantified in this way, but imagine that it were possible

---

8   The Ba'al Shem Tov once commented that Mashiach has not come because people do not spend a long time focusing on this wonderful blessing (*Toldos Yaakov Yosef, Parashas Va'era, s.v. va'yedaber*).
     Most people think that he was referring to the part of the blessing in which we pray for success in learning Torah and observing mitzvos. However, Rabbi Elimelech Biderman, *shlita*, points out that the Ba'al Shem Tov might very well have meant that people do not focus on the first words of this blessing which describe Hashem's great love for us. If people would appreciate this, it would change their relationship with Hashem and would bring the Final Redemption. Since all of *Shir HaShirim* revolves around Hashem's love for us, studying this *megillah* can help us achieve the appreciation that we are supposed to derive from this blessing and thus help bring Mashiach (*Be'er HaParashah, Parashas Vayishlach*).

9   See *Biur Halachah* 1:1, *s.v. hu*.

10   See *Mishlei* 27:19 with Rashi and the Vilna Gaon. See also *Chut Hameshulash*, p. 62, in the name of Rabbi Akiva Eiger, *zt"l*.

to add up all the feelings of love that one had for one's spouse in one day and convert that into one intense feeling of love. Then we would have to multiply that love by the total number of days of our marriage, hopefully tens of thousands. But that is only the amount of love from one relationship. Then we would need to add up all the love we feel for each of our children during our entire lives. In addition to that, we would need to figure in all the love we feel for more distant family and our friends. Let us consider this all the love one person has in a lifetime.

But then this sum would have to be multiplied by the number of all those alive around the world today. But this is still only the love of a single generation. Since there have obviously been many generations since Creation, we would need to multiply this by all of the generations since Creation. Imagine adding up all this love into one profoundly intense moment of love. But even all this love does not equal the love that Hashem has for every individual Jew[11] every single moment! Indeed, Hashem loves the Jewish People with a "world of love."[12] How enthusiastically would a person who really feels this go about his service of Hashem! How much joy would he feel! One who meditates on this would be a completely different person!

Once we truly appreciate how very much Hashem loves us, many other fundamental Jewish beliefs come to us more easily. For example:

- The belief in the coming of Mashiach. After all, since Hashem loves us so much, He will surely redeem us.
- The belief that all suffering is for our good. Hashem, who loves us, would not allow us to suffer for no reason.
- The belief that sinning is very harmful. Not only is sinning wrong because it violates Hashem's will, but it is wrong because it does us tremendous harm. Because Hashem loves us so much, it is extremely foolish and harmful to distance ourselves from Him by sinning.
- The belief that doing mitzvos and learning Torah is a privilege and a source of happiness. Since they bring us much closer to Hashem, who loves us, doing

---

11 Many of the verses in *Shir HaShirim* are cast in the singular, partly to teach us that Hashem loves not only the entire nation, but every individual, as will be explained.

12 The truth is that when Hashem created the world and all the wonderful things it contains in order to shower us with His blessings, He also created the feeling of love. And for each and every one of us, He "creates" any number of people who love us. It turns out, then, that all those who love us do so because Hashem loves us. And because Hashem wants us to feel loved by all, He puts it in the hearts of others to love us as well. In short, all love in the world is only a by-product of His love (see *Chovos HaLevavos, Shaar HaBitachon*, ch. 3). It is thus no accident that at every *sheva berachos* following a wedding, we recite a blessing thanking Hashem for "creating love, brotherhood, peace and friendship..."

mitzvos and learning Torah should give us tremendous joy, like bringing a gift to a beloved wife.[13]

- The belief that prayer has such a great impact. Prayer has much deeper meaning when we realize that we are praying to the One who loves us so much.
- Most important of all, love of Hashem becomes more easily attainable, as explained earlier.[14]

There are many other ideas and lessons that can be appreciated only if one has a belief and understanding of how much Hashem loves His people as well as every individual Jew. As important as the beliefs in the list above are, they take second place to the most important and elementary belief of all: that Hashem loves us.

THE GREATNESS OF KLAL YISRAEL

Unfortunately, even some very religious Jews occasionally suffer from the misapprehension that the Jewish People is not particularly special. This mistaken belief stems, in part, from the fact that the Torah and the *Nevi'im* sometimes speak about *Klal Yisrael* very critically. The truth, however, is that *Klal Yisrael* is exceptionally great, the most beautiful, and their conduct is extremely special, and so they are truly deserving of Hashem's love. Two main reasons lie behind the many critical verses about *Klal Yisrael* in *Tanach*. The first is that the Hashem holds *Klal Yisrael* to a very high standard. Just as a perfectly clean tablecloth will be found to have tiny specks of dirt if examined under a microscope, so too *Klal Yisrael* is sometimes found lacking when subjected to the highest level of scrutiny.[15] The second reason is that because Hashem wishes to improve

---

13 In the blessing we recite before performing any mitzvah, the words, "אשר קדשנו במצותיו," are always included. They are commonly understood to mean that we are thanking Hashem for having "sanctified us through His mitzvos." The Avudraham, however, understands the key word "קדשנו" to mean not "sanctified," but "betrothed." He thus explains that the phrase has the same meaning as the words a groom says to his bride under the *chuppah*: "הרי את מקודשת לי" ("Behold, you are betrothed to me"). This means that we are thanking Hashem for taking us as His nation — as if we are His wife — through the mitzvos that we fulfill. Expounding on this concept, the *Tanya* (ch. 46) notes that every single mitzvah creates a bond between a Jew and Hashem far greater than any marriage. In other words, every mitzvah has the potential of creating feelings of happiness and excitement even greater than those felt by a bride and bridegroom under the *chuppah*!

At every *chuppah*, the Rav recites a blessing which concludes "מקדש עמו ישראל על ידי חופה וקידושין." Simply understood, we are thanking Hashem for distinguishing the Jewish People by giving us the special mitzvos and laws relating to the *chuppah* and getting married. The Maharsha (*Kesubos* 7b) adds that included in this blessing is an expression of thanks to Hashem for betrothing us, *Klal Yisrael*, through a "*chuppah*" at Mount Sinai. He explains how *Matan Torah* was a "*chuppah*," and the event was like a marriage between *Klal Yisrael* and Hashem.

14 See *Da'as Chochmah U'Mussar* (vol. 2, ch. 23), quoting the Rambam's *Moreh Nevuchim* (vol. 3, ch. 51), that the **most important mitzvah** is to love Hashem. As we say in the *Shema*: "It shall be, if you continually listen to My commandments that I command you…to love Hashem your God…" (*Devarim* 11:13). This means that heeding the commandments essentially means loving Hashem.

15 We see this, for example, in the way Hashem levels criticism at Moshe Rabbeinu: "You rebelled against My word" (*Bamidbar* 20:24); "You did not believe in Me" (*Bamidbar* 20:12); "You were treacherous to Me" (*Devarim* 32:51). Yet

Klal Yisrael, the *Tanach* focuses on where they could do better and not where they are already perfect. This can be likened to the beautician or dermatologist who looks carefully for spots and other blemishes to eradicate, but does not spend time on areas that do not need enhancing.[16] Parenthetically, let us note that we can learn from this approach in *Tanach* to look for those who can help us improve spiritually and point out our spiritual blemishes, rather than just connecting with those who praise us.

When we hear how our detractors describe *Klal Yisrael*, we get a clear picture of our people's greatness. The wicked Bilaam sang our praises, saying, among many other things, that "Hashem never finds sin in *Klal Yisrael*."[17] Haman told King Achashveirosh about *Klal Yisrael*'s profound and constant devotion to mitzvah observance.[18] There are many other examples of this. These wicked people did not praise *Klal Yisrael* to flatter them, and they did not exaggerate. What they said was the absolute truth.

It is in *Shir HaShirim* that the greatness of *Klal Yisrael* comes to light, and this is one reason why *Shir HaShirim* is so special. A very large portion of *Shir HaShirim* is dedicated to showing how special *Klal Yisrael* is. Indeed, the very fact that the praise of *Klal Yisrael* is so extensive gives us some appreciation of their greatness. *Shir HaShirim* is the place where the truth about the greatness of *Klal Yisrael*, Hashem's beloved nation, is told without reservation. Learning *Shir HaShirim* is to experience, in a very real sense, the beauty of *Klal Yisrael*.[19]

SHIR HASHIRIM'S USE OF ALLEGORY

In his introduction to *Shir HaShirim*, Rashi explains that *Shir HaShirim* is really one long *mashal* (allegory)[20] about a husband and wife who once loved each other very deeply.

---

we know that Moshe Rabbeinu was the greatest of the prophets, a true servant of Hashem.

And regarding *Klal Yisrael* as a whole, we read: "Klal Yisrael has sinned; they have also violated My covenant that I commanded them. They have also stolen and have also denied…" (*Yehoshua* 7:10). This would seem to be a very serious case of a nation sinning in the most terrible manner, yet, as the *Navi* goes on to indicate, the entire sin was that of one individual, Achan, took some spoils. These verses are thus to be understood as Hashem pointing out blemishes that were noticeable only at the highest level of scrutiny. Otherwise, they could not have been seen.

16   See Rabbi Avigdor Miller's *Most Beautiful Nation* for a discussion of the verses in the Torah that are sharply critical of *Klal Yisrael* in light of the true greatness of *Klal Yisrael*. This subject is obviously beyond the scope of our *sefer*.

17   *Bamidbar* 23:21.

18   *Megillah* 13b.

19   The Mishnah tells us that one should be happy with one's portion in life (*Avos* 4:1). *Midrash Shmuel* adds that every good *middah* (character trait) is learned from Hashem, as the Gemara teaches: Just as Hashem is merciful, so should we be etc.… (*Shabbos* 133b). If so, this means that Hashem is also happy with His "portion." But what is Hashem's portion? The Torah tells us that *Klal Yisrael* is Hashem's portion (*Devarim* 32:9). This meaning that Hashem is happy and rejoices in having *Klal Yisrael* as His "portion." Awareness of this truth should fill us with both pride and joy.

20   The words *allegory* and *parable* (*mashal*) are used frequently throughout this *sefer*. This is because, as Rashi explains, the whole of *Shir HaShirim* is an allegory. Let us note the difference between an allegory and a parable. An allegory is a narrative meant to signify or represent another story or set of events. So, *Shir HaShirim*'s narrative about a husband

Then, for a variety of reasons, they were separated from each other. Yet, they both remember with longing the wonderful life they shared, and they are both committed to getting back together. The verses describe their great love for each other and how they find each other so appealing and beautiful. Both husband and wife reminisce about occasions when they did great things, and had wonderful times, together. They also describe how much the two parties still love each other despite the separation, and how much they look forward to being together once again.

In the *nimshal* (the meaning of the allegory), the wife is *Klal Yisrael*, and the husband is Hashem. Because of His wife's (i.e., *Klal Yisrael's*) behavior, Hashem sent her away. Both Hashem and *Klal Yisrael* speak about how much they loved each other and recall the exquisite times they had together (such as at the giving of the Torah at Mount Sinai, etc.). *Klal Yisrael* and Hashem both declare that they still love each other and will continue to do so until Hashem brings *Klal Yisrael* back to Him in the time of Mashiach.

There are others who speak in this allegory. For example, there are "the daughters of Yerushalayim," rivals of the wife (as if other young women are vying for the husband's attention.) In the *nimshal*, these are the other nations of the world. They are given this surprising name because they will eventually view Yerushalayim as their capital.[21]

They are *Klal Yisrael's* rivals in the sense that they are jealous of *Klal Yisrael* and vie for Hashem's attention. But they are eventually forced to admit that *Klal Yisrael* deserves Hashem's love because of their fierce loyalty and their greatness. The fact that even *Klal Yisrael's* opponents recognize this is added confirmation of *Klal Yisrael's* greatness.[22]

To summarize, the whole of *Shir HaShirim* is one long *mashal*, a vivid description of the relationship between a king and his queen, or a husband and his wife: their love, their appreciation of each other's beauty and virtues, and their shared history. The *nimshal* is the relationship between Hashem and the Jewish People.

To understand *Shir HaShirim* properly, we need to understand each verse and how it

---

and wife separating represents *Klal Yisrael* and Hashem separating. In contrast, a parable is usually a brief "story" or vignette which illuminates an idea, concept, behavior, etc., by fleshing it out and depicting it. These are the technical definitions. Since, however, there is some overlap, these terms are used somewhat loosely in the elucidation of this *megillah*.

21   The capital is not necessarily where most of the population lives, but it is where the state's or country's major decisions are made. It is also the powerhouse of the economy. So will Yerushalayim eventually be for the entire world. Not only will all important decisions be made there, but it will also be the powerhouse of both spiritual and physical success for the entire world.

22   See *Yalkut Shimoni* (*Malachi* 580), which notes that the nations' praise for *Klal Yisrael* is like praise from an adversary. This is a great honor, and much greater than praise from a friend, because an adversary never wants to give praise and only does so when it is absolutely clear that the praise is deserved.

fits into the *mashal*, and then we can derive the *nimshal*. Some of those who have written on *Shir HaShirim* have focused almost exclusively on the *nimshal*: the relationship between Hashem and the Jewish People. I, however, feel that it is imperative to explain both the *mashal* and the *nimshal*. Since Shlomo HaMelech chose to render the *mashal* vividly, he obviously felt that this would enhance and underscore the messages contained in this megillah. (Why he chose this particular *mashal* will be discussed later.) If we do not understand the *mashal*, we miss out on all this. Furthermore, as Rashi explains,[23] when a *mashal* is told by a wise person, then simply understanding the *mashal* alone has value. It is for this reason that many of the early commentaries focus on the *mashal* as well as the *nimshal* of *Shir HaShirim*. I will be following in their footsteps.

In *Shir HaShirim*, there is more than one speaker. Indeed, this megillah is a collection of songs/ideas expressed by different "characters" in the *mashal* who generally represent either Hashem, *Klal Yisrael*, their enemies, or their friends. Sometimes these songs are being articulated by *Klal Yisrael* to Hashem, and sometimes vice versa. Some of the verses depict *Klal Yisrael* speaking to the other nations, and some depict *Klal Yisrael* just reminiscing to themselves. Therefore, it is important in every verse to know who is speaking and who is being addressed.

Since *Shir HaShirim* is a full description of the love between *Klal Yisrael* and Hashem, it spans the entire history of the Jewish People. Some verses refer to a period as early as the Exodus from Egypt, while others describe the coming of Mashiach. Some describe the greatness of *Klal Yisrael*, while others the greatness of Hashem. Clearly, then, every verse needs elucidation, not only with regard to who is talking and to whom, but also with regard to the time period or subject at hand.

Following in the footsteps of the Midrash, Rashi often explains a specific verse as referring to one particular moment in history. The Midrash itself, however, sometimes cites a number of different opinions regarding the time period being referred to. In any event, the historical background should not take us away from the beauty and wonder of the verse. Instead, we should be looking at each verse as teaching about a facet of the profound love between Hashem and *Klal Yisrael*. The specific historical event referenced by Rashi or the Midrash is no more than a case in point.

The following Midrash dramatically illustrates why verses in the Torah should not be "straight jacketed":

> When Rabbi Eliezer was deathly ill, his students, including Rabbi Akiva, came to visit him. Rabbi Eliezer began teaching them Kabbalistic

---

23 *Mishlei* 1:6.

ideas so elevated that they caused a fire to break out! Seeing that the fire surrounded only Rabbi Eliezer and Rabbi Akiva, the other students realized that they were not worthy of hearing these teaching and therefore left. Rabbi Eliezer then continued to teach Rabbi Akiva *Shir HaShirim*, explaining each verse in 216 different ways! The tears that began to stream down Rabbi Akiva's face gave way to silent sobbing — out of fear of the Presence of Hashem — until Rabbi Eliezer concluded.[24]

From this episode, we see clearly that the verses of the Torah have many facets, and thus limiting our understanding to one particular event or explanation is incorrect.[25]

Even though the commentators often differ as to the exact meaning of individual verses, almost all of them agree with Rashi that *Shir HaShirim* is a parable reflecting the relationship between Hashem and Klal Yisrael.

We must mention, however, that the Malbim takes a completely different approach. He views *Shir HaShirim* as the framework of Shlomo HaMelech's spiritual life. According to the Malbim, the five meetings between the king and his wife reflect the five times that Shlomo HaMelech received prophecy from Hashem.[26] The Malbim concludes that these correspond to the five times in Jewish history that *Klal Yisrael* reached (or will reach) a special closeness with Hashem, the last being the coming of Mashiach, which is referred to at the conclusion of *Shir HaShirim*. For the sake of clarity and consistency, we have not included the Malbim's fascinating approach in this *sefer*.

LANGUAGE OF THE HEART

In a very real sense, there are two kinds of language: the language of the mind and the language of the heart. If someone asks us for directions to the nearest bus stop, and we reply with a beautifully constructed poem full of superb similes and magnificent metaphors, our response will probably not be appreciated. When one wants information, one wants it to be clear, concise, and exact. This is the language of the mind that processes information. If, however, one is writing a love letter, and suffices

---

24   *Midrash HaNe'elam*, beginning of *Parashas Vayera*.

25   In his introduction to *Shir HaShirim*, Rashi cites the verse, "One thing has Hashem spoken, two have I understood..." (*Tehillim* 62:12). This means, the Gemara tells us (*Sanhedrin* 34a), that every statement from Hashem includes many different meanings and lessons. Rashi notes that this is particularly applicable to *Shir HaShirim*.

26   These are the five occasions: 1) in a dream after bringing a thousand sacrifices in Givon (*Melachim I* 3:5); 2) upon starting to build the Beis HaMikdash (ibid. 6:11); 3) upon completing the building of the Beis HaMikdash (ibid. 9:2; *Divrei HaYamim II* 7:12); 4) when reprimanded by Hashem for marrying too many wives, (*Melachim I* 11:11); 5) after death, when his soul went to Heaven, and Hashem spoke to it as to all righteous souls.

with sentences like, "I really enjoy being with you," the information is clear and concise, but hardly likely to do anything emotionally for the person receiving such a letter. The language of the heart uses words and figures of speech that stir the emotions. The words must be charged, full of descriptions and expressions of emotion. Often, they will be repetitive. The beautiful language and style require contemplation.

Without a doubt, *Shir HaShirim* is written in the language of the heart. We are not merely trying to gain information from it. To actually experience and feel the love of Hashem requires reading *Shir HaShirim* and learning it with an open heart and a readiness to spend time contemplating the power of the words and allowing ourselves to "feel the feelings" behind the messages.[27]

SHIR HASHIRIM'S SONG, WORDS, AND SYMBOLISM

Because *Shir HaShirim* deals with the most powerful emotions a person can feel, it was necessary to convey them in an appropriately compelling manner. The vehicle to transmit these feelings is song. Blissful, joyous emotions are best expressed in song. Both emotions and songs defy easy explanations. They have to be understood and appreciated in all of their complexity.

Shir HaShirim is filled with an array of metaphors and symbols. Since the power of these literary techniques to evoke emotion is much greater than just a simple declaration, Shlomo HaMelech uses many of them. When we wish to describe Hashem as being merciful, for example, we speak of Him as our Father rather than just stating that He is merciful. This is because we know that the image of a father conveys much more than any description can.[28]

Since *Shir HaShirim* is also an allegory, we would do well to familiarize ourselves at the outset with the key symbolic "characters" and articles that we will encounter here. (An elaboration will follow in our commentary on the megillah.) The two main "characters," of course, are "the Beloved" and "the dear one," symbolizing God and the Jewish People, respectively.

These are some of the other symbolic characters who appear in this megillah:

---

27   We would do well to apply this approach to *piyyutim*, *zemiros*, and prayers in general. In our effort to understand the ideas conveyed in all these compositions, we dare not lose the ability to appreciate their profound emotional side. Indeed, this is the main focus of these masterpieces of the language of the heart. Unfortunately, this ability is being lost due to our inclination not to spend time and effort on it in our "instant generation." One of the side benefits of studying *Shir HaShirim* is that one develops the ability to open one's heart to the "language of the heart."

28   The difference between "showing" and merely "telling" can also be seen in the custom that a *kallah* (bride) encircles her *chassan* (groom) seven times under the *chuppah*. The *kallah* thus shows symbolically that she protects him from all sin and all other troubles. Clearly, this is a more powerful way of conveying the idea than merely stating it.

- King Shlomo – whose name derives from the word "peace." This alludes to Hashem, to whom all peace belongs.
- The Friends – generally, alludes to the angels, who are the closest friends of *Klal Yisrael*. They want *Klal Yisrael*'s success and, like us, want to serve Hashem.
- Wine – in general, refers to the Torah, which brings joy to those who imbibe it.
- Pomegranates – are symbolic of the wicked Jewish people, who, though they sin, are filled with merits like a pomegranate is filled with seeds.
- The Guards – represent the evil nations who beat and enslave the Jewish People and are called "guards" because they ensure that we do not sin by making us suffer when we do.
- Breasts – symbolize Moshe Rabbeinu and Aharon HaKohen, who nurtured the Jewish People and took care of them, much like a mother nurses her baby.
- Eyes – refer to the leaders who are able to "see" what is good for the nation and what is harmful.
- Hair – alludes to the lowly Jewish people who lack the ability to act independently. And just as one can manage without hair, so too, *Klal Yisrael* can manage without the lowly Jews. Yet, when they are attached to the main body of *Klal Yisrael* by connecting to the community, they beautify and enhance it.
- Teeth – refers to the powerful Jewish soldiers who are strong and have the ability to consume others.
- Night – refers to the period of exile, a time of darkness and fear.
- The Wedding – generally refers to the day the Torah was given because it was then that Hashem "married *Klal Yisrael*," so to speak, and took the Jewish People as His bride.

Let us note that while these equivalencies generally hold true, there are exceptions. As to the many other symbolic references and allusions, they will be discussed in context.

One character mentioned many times by Rashi is *Knesses Yisrael*, literally, the Congregation of Israel.[29] When describing the Jewish People being praised by Hashem, or the Jewish People praising Hashem, Rashi often calls them *Knesses Yisrael*. There is a profound concept behind this name, one that has been explained memorably by Rabbi Kalonymus Kalman Shapira, *Hy"d*, the Rabbi of Piaseczna:[30]

A stone, when broken in half, remains a stone. Its characteristics do not change. The remainder of the stone remains exactly as it was. Similarly, a plant that is cut back can still be a perfect plant even though there is less of it. In stark contrast, a person who,

---

29 See Rashi on 6:9.

30 *Chovas HaTalmidim, ma'amar* 2.

God forbid, loses a part of his body becomes a different person. His entire being is weakened as a result. His entire body feels the pain of losing just one part of it. It would be ridiculous to suggest that the rest of the body should be happy because only one limb was lost. Similarly, when a person is praised for having skilled hands, only a fool would ask why the person's ears are listening to the praise of a different part of the body, and why his face is smiling. For the entire person is proud of his entire being and concerned lest harm befall any part of himself. Harm to one part is harm to the entire being since a human being is a single unit. Similarly, *Knesses Yisrael* is a single body of the entire nation. What is true for an individual person regarding his own body is true for *Klal Yisrael* as a nation. The phrase *Knesses Yisrael* describes the multitudes of different Jews who all belong to one unified Jewish People. Thus, when *Knesses Yisrael* is praised for having righteous *Kohanim* or great *talmidei chachamim*, the entire nation is praised. It is a compliment to the entire nation that we have been able to produce such tzaddikim. Furthermore, when Hashem says that even the wicked in *Knesses Yisrael* are filled with good deeds, it is praise for the entire nation inasmuch as its weakest parts still wish to do as many things right as possible. Therefore, whenever certain individuals are praised in *Shir HaShirim*, the praise also encompasses the nation as a whole.

To take this analogy one step further, the hand cannot be "proud" that it is so skilled without taking into consideration that the mind controls it, and the heart supplies it with blood enriched with oxygen by the lungs. Clearly, the hand is only as skilled as it is because of the rest of the body. In a similar way, a Jewish person on his own may think that he is highly accomplished, but the truth is that he is only fruitful and effective if the rest of the Jewish People — *Knesses Yisrael* — is functioning well. Only through the rest of the nation is one's own success possible.

Let us consider another facet of this concept with an analogy of a different sort. It takes several different musicians to make a band. The quality of the band is often higher than the quality of any of its members. Now, if each musician is not the world's greatest, but the band *is* the world's greatest, the band is clearly greater than the sum of its parts. No member of the band can be proud that he is best musician in the world, but he can be proud that he belongs to the band that creates the best music in the world. Similarly, *Knesses Yisrael* is much greater than the sum of all of its component parts. Every Jew is unique and is capable of using his talents to achieve great things, but *Knesses Yisrael* as a group is far greater — and only as a unified group is able to fulfill the role that Hashem has designed for us. It turns out that not only is the whole of *Klal Yisrael* greater because we had Moshe Rabbeinu and Aharon HaKohen as part of our nation, but even Moshe and Aharon themselves became greater because they were part of *Klal Yisrael*. When we say that *Klal Yisrael* is perfect and beautiful in every way — and are always vindicated in Divine Judgment — we are referring to the nation as one unit, the unit of *Knesses Yisrael*.

This is the underlying message: We are one unit, as strong as the weakest among us, and as beloved to Hashem as the strongest. We should show care and concern for everyone because neglecting one Jewish person does not just make us a little smaller, but it actually weakens the entire nation. If, *chas v'shalom*, we splinter and divide, we can no longer be described as *Knesses Yisrael*. Furthermore, we should also all be proud of our tzaddikim because they represent the best of us, and Hashem loves us all more because of them.

SHIR HASHIRIM'S PERSPECTIVE

There is another aspect to the unique language and terminology of *Shir HaShirim*. They reflect the work's focus on the love between Hashem and the Jewish People that changes our entire outlook and perspective. *Shir HaShirim* is predicated on the truth that Hashem created the entire world because He loves us. Even when we sin, He continues to love us. Indeed, everyone and everything in the world is put here just to demonstrate how much Hashem loves us. This "viewpoint of love" lies behind the unique language of *Shir HaShirim*. Learning *Shir HaShirim* requires that we learn a new way of looking at things, seeing the world through the lens and the perspective of *Shir HaShirim*. Let us touch on several illustrations. (All will be discussed in our running commentary.)

As mentioned, the wicked are referred to as "pomegranates" because of their merits. Even when we consider the wicked, we focus on the good they have done — what they have done right — and ignore what they have done wrong.[31] The evil nations, who are repeatedly called "our enemies" in *Megillas Eichah* and many other places in *Tanach*, are referred to rather differently here in *Shir HaShirim* as "our guards." This metaphor reflects the role that Hashem gave them: to keep us from sinning and being punished. Through *Shir HaShirim* "lenses," we view them as surgeons who cut a patient, but only for the patient's benefit.

Even the long and bitter exile that has inflicted upon us much suffering is referred to only as "night," a time to "seek our beloved." The "pain and illness" that we suffer is that "we miss Hashem's love." The heathen nations of the world are called the "daughters of Yerushalayim" since, when Mashiach comes, they will recognize Yerushalayim as the capital, and feel a part of it.

Through the lens of *Shir HaShirim*, we are able to see a different world, a world of love between Hashem and the Jewish People. We can see that there are no truly evil

---

31 This is like a couple deeply in love who see one another's deficiencies in a very different light from how others see them.

people in our nation, and that those gentiles who hurt us are really guarding us from our own sins. Our only suffering is the smallest loss of Hashem's love; nothing else upsets us. We also see everyone ultimately perceiving and acknowledging Yerushalayim as the center of the world.

Of course, there are times when we need to put down the "*Shir HaShirim* lens," such as when we contemplate the terrible *churbanos* that took place on Tisha B'Av. Then we have to see our enemies in a different light, as those who wish to destroy us. Another such time is when we are trying to repent on Yom Kippur. Then we realize that even someone who is full of merits must repent lest he be considered wicked. But on Pesach specifically, when our relationship with Hashem began, and on every Erev Shabbos, when we are ready to greet the Shabbos (or at other times when we need to feel uplifted by remembering the love between Hashem and us), we should look through the "*Shir HaShirim* lens" to see things in this unique and elevated perspective.

There is a paradox in *Shir HaShirim* which can inspire us if we appreciate it not just on the intellectual level, but on the emotional level. On the one hand, *Klal Yisrael* is likened in *Shir HaShirim* to Hashem's "wife."[32] This is natural because marriage is the closest relationship of love that can be found in this world. On the other hand, however, *Klal Yisrael* is also likened to: Hashem's flock,[33] His bride,[34] His vineyard,[35] His brother,[36] His sister,[37] His mother,[38] His daughter,[39] and His twin,[40] among others. Each comparison adds another facet to the relationship between Hashem and *Klal Yisrael*. Now, we might ask: "Why not simply work with the closest relationship? Doesn't that encompass all the others?" The answer is that each relationship radiates its own unique beauty and feelings. Obviously, one loves one's daughter more than one's sister, but there is a certain comfortable feeling one has with a sister which is not present with a daughter. One would perhaps accept food and help from a mother in a way one would never accept them from anyone else. A shepherd feels a tenderness to his sheep that does not exist

---

32 1:2.
33 1:7.
34 4:10.
35 8:11.
36 8:1.
37 4:9.
38 3:11.
39 This is not explicit in *Shir HaShirim*, but it is found in *Tehillim* 45:11. See 3:11 here.
40 5:2.

in other relationships. It is not necessary to elaborate here on what is unique in each relationship, as this will be discussed in context. What is important here is the understanding that Hashem's relationship and love for us is all-encompassing. Every kind of loving thought and kind feeling that a person has in any of his relationships, Hashem has towards us, and much, much more.[41] The greatest relationship, and the one which the megillah describes in most detail, is the relationship of marriage. But it is not, by any means, the only one.

ANTHROPOMORPHISM: PORTRAYING GOD AS PHYSICAL

One of the greatest justifiable fears many people have when they learn *Shir HaShirim* is that they might make the terrible mistake of attributing physical aspects to God, since *Shir HaShirim* describes Hashem in so many physical ways. This type of projection is called "anthropomorphism."

One of the Thirteen Principles of Jewish Faith is that God is not physical and has no physical attributes. Anyone who thinks that there is some physical dimension to God is an *apikores* (heretic) and will be denied any reward in the World to Come.[42] Therefore, whenever a verse or an explanation seems to imply that God is physical, one has to be keenly aware that this is not meant literally. It is only an illustration to help us physical beings who need parables in order to grasp and understand lofty ideas.

Although the Torah does not hesitate to describe Hashem in physical terms,[43] *Shir HaShirim* is perhaps the most noticeable example of this use of anthropomorphism. Rabbi Shimshon Rafael Hirsch, *zt"l*, comments on this. His insightful words should be read carefully:

> Let me offer a general observation regarding the many instances where the Torah uses physical descriptions for Hashem. The philosophers have constantly tried to eliminate these descriptions of Hashem so that we should not mistakenly think He is physical. But there is a real danger that Hashem will become an abstract and confusing concept.[44] If this is what the Torah wanted, then it could have easily

---

41   This idea is beautifully encapsulated in one of the *Selichos* recited on Erev Rosh Hashanah which describes the tremendous love that Hashem has for *Klal Yisrael* (No. 25 according to *minhag Polin* and No. 27 according to *minhag Lita*. In the opening phrases, we read: "With every expression of love, brotherhood, and friendship, You have named the nation You have chosen!" See there for further elaboration.

42   Rambam, *Hilchos Teshuvah* 3:7.

43   The expression the "hand of Hashem" is used dozens of times in the Torah. "The breath of Hashem's nostrils" is also used (*Shemos* 15:8) even though Hashem has no physical hands or nostrils. (See Rashi ibid., who explains these anthropomorphisms.)

44   Somewhat like our response to an abstract scientific theory which, even if we understand it, we feel no emotional

avoided using these expressions regarding Hashem. But the second danger [i.e., not perceiving Hashem as a reality] is greater than the first [thinking Hashem is physical]... The belief in Hashem's being is more important than negating his physical attributes.[45]

Rabbi Hirsch's message is that to have a true relationship with Hashem, we need to view Him not as an abstraction but as a reality. That is why the Torah uses anthropomorphic language despite the serious risk of misunderstanding involved.

If we learn *Shir HaShirim* carefully, fully aware that this is only an allegory, we will gain an extremely valuable (according to Rabbi Hirsch, the most valuable) appreciation of Hashem. This will help us love Him more deeply and feel loved by Him. This is far more preferable to spending one's life trying to develop a relationship with a very distant, abstract concept.[46]

There is another danger that we must be aware of when learning *Shir HaShirim*: In the lax society we live in, people often look for excuses to be lax regarding their obligations, especially their obligations towards Hashem.[47] When learning just how much Hashem loves us, we might mistakenly draw the conclusion that it does not really matter if we sometimes commit a small sin. We might tell ourselves, consciously or sub-consciously,

---

connection to it.

45 Commentary on the Chumash, *Bereishis* 6:6.

46 This perspective can be illustrated by an amusing story told by Rabbi Uri Zohar. As is well known, Rabbi Zohar was in the entertainment business before becoming religious. When he decided to leave behind this lifestyle, his irreligious friends asked him to tell one last joke. He obliged them with the following story of a policeman who hated religious people. One day, the policeman saw a religious man riding a motorcycle. He decided to follow him in the hope that he would catch him committing a driving offense and then be able to slap him with a ticket. The policeman tailed the motorcyclist around for a long time, but this man did not break even the smallest law. Eventually, the policeman gave up, stopped the religious fellow, and told him how lucky he was, because he had been just looking for an excuse to give him a ticket.
Answered the religious man, "It was not luck at all. Evidently, Hashem was with me."
"Oh," said the policeman, as he proceeded to write out a ticket with glee. "Two people riding on one motorbike: *that* is an offense!"
Although this was a joke, it should give us pause. Many of us do not think of Hashem as being with us in a real sense.

47 There are many reasons why we sometimes fail to take our obligations towards Hashem seriously enough. These include lack of deep faith and lack of clarity about what is right and what is wrong. There is one reason that is particularly relevant for this discussion. If we hurt someone's feelings, God forbid, we can see the hurt — or at least we have very vivid picture of what we have done. If we show disrespect for a parent or a teacher, we can imagine what it would be like if someone did this to us. This mental picture goes a long way towards deterring us from such behavior in the future. If we disobey Hashem, however — say, by eating non-kosher food — we have no natural feeling of how terrible such a sin is since we have nothing to compare this too. By learning about Hashem and making Him more real in our lives, this difficulty will be somewhat overcome. If we disobey Hashem, *chas v'shalom*, it will feel wrong emotionally, not just intellectually.

that just as a mother forgives and forgets the naughty things her little children do, so will Hashem forgive us. The truth, however, is otherwise. Unless there is repentance for sin, Hashem does not overlook even the smallest sin. On the contrary, we will be punished for every sin, however small. Indeed, as we see in *Mesillas Yesharim*,[48] we will be punished even more severely just for adopting this self-indulgent attitude.

The truth is that Hashem does love us more than any merciful mother. He is exacting in punishment only for our own good — to ensure that we are cleansed of all our sins. Regardless of the fact that Hashem is acting out of love, we must be aware of the fear that this should engender in us and not make the mistake of seeing God as "liberal" or "tolerant."

On the other hand, a person who mistakenly perceives Hashem as full of anger must learn and internalize the message of *Shir HaShirim*. His keen sense of Hashem's exacting justice may diminish a little, but this would be outweighed by the ability to feel a closeness to and love for Hashem that can only come through realizing how much Hashem loves the Jewish People.[49] Indeed, the more prevalent mistake in our community would seem to be that we underestimate Hashem's love and kindness, attributes that are emphasized both in the Torah and the teachings of *Chazal* — and is the underlying theme of *Shir HaShirim*. Of course, if one feels that he is becoming lax due to insufficient appreciation of Hashem's exacting justice, then he would do well to find other inspiration to counterbalance this misperception.

The Talmud Yerushalmi encapsulates this concept in noting that there are two main commandments that deal directly with how to relate to Hashem: The commandment to love Hashem and the commandment to fear Him. One needs to have a balance of both in order to serve Hashem correctly. The Yerushalmi continues that if you serve with love, you will not "hate," and if you serve with fear, you will not "kick."[50] Love and fear are both fundamental emotions and basic motivating forces. If one serves Hashem only out of fear, then he will eventually come to hate Him. If one serves Hashem only out of love, however, he will eventually become lax and not obey the *halachos*. Therefore, we must make sure to have both emotions at the right balance.[51]

Paradoxically, awareness of just how much Hashem loves us should increase our fear of Him. The Gemara tells us that one who sees *Shir HaShirim* in a dream should

---

48 Ch. 4.
49 This is similar to Rabbi Hirsch's comments earlier.
50 *Sotah* 5:5.
51 See Rabbeinu Yonah on *Avos* 3:14, where he discusses this important balance.

anticipate that he will merit piety.[52] Rashi explains that this is because *Shir HaShirim* "is full of fear of Heaven and the love of Hashem in the hearts of *Klal Yisrael*." Now, the love is understandable. That is indeed the theme of this megillah. But where does "fear of Heaven" come up in *Shir HaShirim*?

The Magen Avos[53] tells us that the lowest level of serving Hashem is doing so solely out of fear of being punished. Even though one must rely on this feeling sometimes — especially when one is consumed by a desire to sin — one should aspire to love Hashem and want to serve Him. But the highest level of serving Hashem is to love Him so much that one is fearful of displeasing Him. When one loves someone else intensely, he is constantly trying to please them. For such a person, there is nothing more upsetting than the thought that one may have done the opposite.[54] In light of the comments of the Magen Avos, we can understand that Rashi is telling us that *Shir HaShirim* inspires both fear and love because it inspires us to be fearful lest we displease the One we love. It turns out, then, that *Shir HaShirim* teaches us not only love of Hashem but, perhaps even more so, fear of Hashem.

THE AUTHOR AND TIMEFRAME OF SHIR HASHIRIM

Shir HaShirim was written by Shlomo HaMelech at the time that *Klal Yisrael* was at their very highest level of material and spiritual success. This was the very day that the Beis HaMikdash was completed.[55] Indisputable miracles were occurring every day in the Beis HaMikdash, the Presence of Hashem was felt throughout the land, and every nation recognized the greatness of the Jewish People. The Jewish People could fill their days with service of Hashem and with spiritual advancement. At the time of Shlomo HaMelech, the entire known world was subservient to him. Peace and tranquility reigned, and spiritual elevation was the order of the day. Indeed, this utopian situation will never be matched until the time of Mashiach. Shlomo HaMelech foresaw, however, that things would change. In the future, the Jewish People would live through additional exiles and redemptions. He foresaw many different periods of history in which *Klal*

---

52 *Berachos* 57b.

53 *Avos* 1:3.

54 The Magen Avos points out that when Avraham Avinu completed the last of his ten tests, the *Akeidah*, and prepared to offer his son Yitzchak as a sacrifice, Hashem praised him this way: "Now I know that you are God-fearing" (*Bereishis* 22:12). But this is puzzling. Since Avraham had acted at the highest level of serving Hashem, surely he should be praised as *loving* God — ostensibly a higher level than fearing Him? From Hashem's praise, the Magen Avos proves that the ultimate level is fearing to displease Hashem because one loves him so much.

55 The *Zohar* (beginning of *Parashas Terumah*) teaches that Shlomo HaMelech wrote *Shir HaShirim* on the day the Beis HaMikdash was inaugurated. The Midrash, however, says that he wrote it towards the end of his life. (See Ramban's introduction to *Shir HaShirim*.)

Yisrael's relationship with Hashem would endure many ups and downs. These visions inspired Shlomo HaMelech to write *Shir HaShirim*, in which he relates the passionate yearning of the Jewish People throughout their exiles to return to their original closeness to Hashem.

Paradoxically, Shlomo HaMelech wrote *Shir HaShirim*, which mainly describes periods of exile, at a time when he had just finished building the Beis HaMikdash. This was a time when *Klal Yisrael* was very close to Hashem, and exile was surely not on their minds. The explanation for this would seem to be that *Klal Yisrael* was now feeling strongly how much Hashem loved them. They could see His constant and loving Presence among them in the Beis HaMikdash, where His miracles were on display every day. Through this strength of knowing how much Hashem loves *Klal Yisrael*, Shlomo HaMelech was able to assure *Klal Yisrael* that even in exile, even when it does not feel like it, Hashem loves them. Therefore, this was an ideal time to write about the difficulties ahead from a purely positive perspective.

A more mundane example of this strategy is that the best time to educate a couple about always being kind to one another and always resolving disagreements amicably is close to the wedding. At that time, when they feel so much love for one another, they will firmly resolve to do so. Once the disagreements they thought unimaginable occur, however, it is extremely difficult to establish guidelines regarding how a loving couple should behave towards one another. Similarly, Shlomo HaMelech established at the time of our love how we should always feel towards Hashem — even in exile.

In the Netziv's *sefer* on *Shir HaShirim*, *Rinah shel Torah*, he suggests an alternative explanation as to why Shlomo HaMelech wrote *Shir HaShirim* at this time. Until the Beis HaMikdash was built, one was allowed to build a *bamah* (a private altar) for offering *korbanos* (sacrifices) to Hashem. This meant that at any time and in almost any place, one could bring a *korban*. It is hard for us, who unfortunately are not used to the idea, to appreciate what it was like to bring such sacrifices. We have no idea just how spiritually elevating and enriching this service was. Indeed, our feeling of closeness to Hashem on Yom Kippur does not compare with how a person could feel when he brought a *korban*.

Once the Beis HaMikdash was built, it became forbidden to have a private *bamah*. In order to offer a *korban*, one had to travel to Yerushalayim. This journey was difficult for the majority of people, and they thought that now they would not be able to feel this special closeness to Hashem as often. Most people came to the Beis HaMikdash three times a year at most. There was a real sense of loss that the opportunity to feel very close to Hashem would be limited to very special occasions. This prompted Shlomo HaMelech to write *Shir HaShirim*, in which he taught *Klal Yisrael* that everyone is loved by Hashem and can still draw just as close to Him regularly, even when they could not offer a *korban*.⁵⁶ But how does one experience that special closeness to Hashem without a *korban*? Shlomo HaMelech explains to us throughout *Shir HaShirim* that learning Torah and helping those who learn Torah bring us close to Hashem.⁵⁷ This means that the essential message of *Shir HaShirim* is that any time we wish to get close to Hashem, we can do so through Torah. According to the Netziv, *Shir HaShirim* teaches us that through Torah one reaches the greatest closeness to Hashem, similar to the closeness one achieved by offering a *korban* to Him. That is why the Netziv named his *sefer* on *Shir HaShirim*, *Rinah shel Torah* (*The Song of Torah*). Indeed, he explains how most of the verses in this megillah relate to Torah.

Rashi, in contrast, sees *Shir HaShirim* touching on the many ways in which we feel close to Hashem. As we shall discover, however, that even according to Rashi, a lot of *Shir HaShirim* is about the Torah because that is the best way to genuinely experience closeness to Hashem.

Shir HaShirim describes in great detail many events that happened hundreds of years after Shlomo HaMelech. This can sometimes be confusing because *Shir HaShirim* is generally cast in the past or present tense. We thus have to keep in mind that because Shlomo was able to foresee future events through *ruach hakodesh* (Divine inspiration), he wrote it as if he had actually seen these things occur — as if they had already happened.

The root of the word "*shir*" can also be connected with the concept of seeing, as in the word "*ashurenu*" ("I see it").⁵⁸ The title, "*Shir HaShirim*," can thus be understood to mean

---

56   It is told that a non-Jew approached Rabbi Shimshon Dovid Pinkus a few days before he was to undergo conversion to Judaism and told Rabbi Pinkus that he wanted to offer a sacrifice before converting. He explained that since, according to Jewish law, even though a Jew is not allowed to bring a sacrifice nowadays, a non-Jew may offer a sacrifice privately (even when there is no Beis HaMikdash). He wished to postpone his conversion for a few weeks until he learned how to bring a sacrifice. Once he had brought a sacrifice, he would convert. Although Rabbi Pinkus understood that this very spiritual individual genuinely wished to experience that special and uplifting feeling of offering a sacrifice, he told the prospective convert that he could not advise him on this and that he should do what he thought was best.
   The convert returned a few days later to say that he had changed his mind. He decided that it was not worth losing the privilege of having that extra time as part of the Jewish People and having that special bond with Hashem, despite the closeness one gets through bringing a sacrifice. Rabbi Pinkus commented that this individual truly understood the privilege of being Jewish. Indeed, the feeling of how close Hashem is to every Jewish person is the underlying lesson of *Shir HaShirim*.

57   The Siach Yitzchak notes that the blessings "*Ahavah rabbah*" and "*Ahavas Olam*" begin by stating that Hashem loves *Klal Yisrael* greatly, and immediately continue by saying that He gave them the Torah. He explains the connection this way: Because Hashem loves *Klal Yisrael* so much, He gave them His Torah. This is the best possible gift because it enables us to become close to Him.

58   See *Bamidbar* 24:17 with Rashi.

"The [greatest] vision of [all] visions."[59] This alternative meaning of "*shir*" underscores the fact that *Shir HaShirim* was written through Shlomo HaMelech's extraordinary vision. Not only did he foresee so many different future events clearly, but he also perceived the underlying feelings behind them. Instead of seeing the upcoming exile of *Klal Yisrael* superficially, as Hashem rejecting them or them abandoning Hashem — as superficially, this is what exile seems to be — he saw the true longing and love that existed between them. Shlomo HaMelech was thus able to direct our attention to those deeper, truer feelings, and keep us from being misled. We can liken this, on some level, to a brilliant marriage counselor who sees — and highlights — the yearning for one another's love that lies behind the bickering of the couple he is counseling. Such a counselor has the ability to change the entire course of the marriage. In this sense, *Shir HaShirim* is a precious gift because it helps us "see" the events of Jewish history in the correct perspective and shows us how Hashem always loves us and how we really seek His love, above everything else. Let us treasure this gift because it is truly one that can enhance the future of our relationship with Hashem.

THE SEEMINGLY MUNDANE NATURE OF SHIR HASHIRIM

One of our challenges in appreciating the spiritual greatness of *Shir HaShirim* is that it is written essentially as a love story. The love of Hashem is likened to the love of a husband for his wife. The megillah develops this allegory, describing the Jewish People as a very beautiful woman and Hashem as a handsome man. It even uses expressions which seem to verge on immodesty. This makes it difficult to see *Shir HaShirim* as the very holy and spiritual work that it is.

Why, indeed, did Shlomo HaMelech resort to an allegory, and why this one — an allegory that seems to describe such mundane feelings? Why not, for example, describe the love of a mother for her children? There are obviously many profound ideas here that transcend our understanding, but I would like to suggest a few points to ponder that will help us overcome this difficulty.

First and foremost, parables and symbols give a person the ability to connect with and absorb ideas that he might otherwise not be able to fathom. Furthermore, as we have discussed, allegories and parables have a unique ability to inspire a person and stir his emotions. Knowledge to which one does not connect simply does not influence a person and is thus not true wisdom. At the end of *Koheles*, Shlomo HaMelech is praised for using parables to teach the people: "Even greater than he [Shlomo HaMelech] was

---

59   See our commentary, 1:1.

wise, was his teaching the people knowledge by establishing and explaining many parables."[60] In a loosely similar way, it can be said that many of our mitzvos and customs reinforce, through symbolic means, our knowledge of how to serve Hashem.[61]

The Ben Ish Chai explains that the importance of knowing of Hashem's love for *Klal Yisrael* lies behind the allegory employed in *Shir HaShirim*. Shlomo HaMelech wanted even the simplest person to understand and appreciate this. Furthermore, he wanted learning about this to be stimulating and exciting. He therefore used terminology that anyone can relate to and appreciate, even those who are far removed from spiritual ideas. Had *Shir HaShirim* been written as a dry essay or as a lofty parable, the message would have been lost to some of *Klal Yisrael*. The vital message that Hashem loves us is *so* important that it had to be cast as an allegory that anyone can relate to.[62]

The Ben Ish Chai likens this to the alcoholic drinks given out at a wedding in order to put people in the mood to dance merrily for the newlywed couple. Obviously, the merriment caused by the drinks is not the purpose of the wedding. However, in order to get everyone to join in, it would not be enough to give a deep, philosophical speech about why wedding guests should be happy and dancing. Rather, the simple happiness that comes from the drinks helps everyone feel, and join, the true happiness of the wedding. Similarly, the terms of love used in *Shir HaShirim* are such that anyone can be inspired by them. Of course, one must realize that they are used only to arouse deeper feelings of spiritual love between *Klal Yisrael* and Hashem.

The Tzror HaMor adds that the attitude of the surrounding secular society towards the physical creates an additional obstacle to reading *Shir HaShirim* as Shlomo HaMelech meant it to be read. Since the secular attitude is that physicality is an opportunity to satisfy one's lust through animalistic behavior, we may, at least on some level, be inclined to associate the imagery of *Shir HaShirim* with that behavior. If, for example, we read that someone is very strong, what picture comes to mind? A big brute who beats people up or someone with a lot of self-control who spends his life doing what is right rather than being controlled by his desires? The answer very much depends on us and how we think. If we always think of brute strength as something to admire, then the term "strong" will bring that sort of picture to mind. If, however, we admire unwavering

---

60 *Koheles* 12:9 with Sefornu. Shlomo HaMelech actually composed three thousand parables. See *Melachim I* 5:12.

61 See *Michtav M'Eliyahu*, II:276, about how the emotional dimension is vital in attaining growth in serving Hashem.

62 The Metzudas Dovid observes (1:1) that a *mashal* (parable) need not parallel the *nimshal* (moral/lesson) completely. The importance of attracting the attention and interest of readers is so great that certain details are added to the *mashal* for that purpose alone.

self-control, that is what we will automatically associate with the term "strong." Similarly, the thoughts that the terms and imagery of *Shir HaShirim* bring to mind depend on our outlook.

The Tzror HaMor drives this point home with the following parable of his own.[63] There was once a magnificent building surrounded by exquisite gardens and flowers. An artist was struck by the sight and produced a most enchanting painting of it. People would see this painting in a nearby art gallery and were absolutely enthralled. Sadly, though, one day a deranged person snuck in and threw smelly dirt all over the painting. Now, when people looked at it, they were repulsed. They began thinking of the building as dirty and repulsive because they associated it with the befouled painting.

In a similar way, there are those who have managed to besmirch our picture of marriage as an esteemed and even holy institution. They see it only as a way of fulfilling their most base desires, thereby throwing smelly dirt on the concept. But we must not make the mistake of deriding the lovely building because the picture of it has been soiled. On the contrary, marriage is, and will remain, a pure and spiritual practice. Shlomo HaMelech thus felt justified in using it as the symbol of love between Hashem and us.[64]

There is a deeper level to understanding Shlomo HaMelech's use of this parable. As we pointed out in our earlier discussion on anthropomorphism, we see that the Torah often uses physical terms to describe Hashem, and we explained that these terms are meant only to help us comprehend and appreciate Him. For example, the Torah writes, "*Yemincha Hashem nedari bakoach* — Your right hand, Hashem, is majestic in strength."[65] Our right hands are puny compared to Hashem's great "hand." However, the illustration of our right hand helps us appreciate and connect to Hashem's limitless might. Because we relate easily to terms that we are familiar with in our lives, the Torah uses them. Hence, the physical world helps us develop our appreciation of Hashem.

But it is obviously not the case that the Torah first "saw" our powerful right hand, and then used it as a way of helping us understand Hashem's might. This is because the Torah

---

63 Introduction to his commentary on *Shir HaShirim*.

64 Rabbi Avigdor Miller points out that it is no accident that Rabbi Akiva is the one who describes the greatness of *Shir HaShirim*, calling it "Holy of Holies" (*Mishnayos Yadayim* 3:5) and he would recite it with great devotion (*Midrash HaNe'elam*, beginning of *Parashas Vayera*). Because he experienced first-hand how the great power of marriage saved the Jewish People, he was especially able to see the beauty of the parable of *Shir HaShirim*: marriage. As is well known, it was due to Rachel's stipulating that she would marry the unlearned Akiva only if he goes to learn Torah that he became the greatest sage of his generation. Furthermore, he taught Torah to the entire nation, thereby ensuring the continuation of the Torah for future generations. (See *Yevamos* 62b on how Rabbi Akiva's teaching spread to the entire nation and lasted through the ages.)

65 *Shemos* 15:6.

existed long before the world did, long before any person was aware of the strength of his right hand. Rather, when writing the Torah, Hashem knew that He would create us and how He would create us. He therefore used the metaphor of a right hand, which we would eventually relate to as representing strength, so that we could get some idea of His awesome strength.

On a still deeper level, part of the reason Hashem created us with strong right hands was so that we could understand the concept of His might. Hashem wanted us to be able to connect and draw closer to Him, which is essentially the purpose of Creation. He therefore created us with hands to better appreciate Him and His strength. If we had no strength and never experienced strength, it would be much more difficult, if not impossible, to appreciate His strength. Similarly, every part of our body and all the other physical aspects of our lives which the Torah uses to describe Hashem are only metaphors or illustrations to help us grasp Hashem. He created us with eyes so that we should appreciate how He "sees" us all the time; and He created us with ears so that we should understand that He "listens" to our prayers, etc.[66] Indeed, part of the purpose of our being created with all our physical attributes was so that we should be able to relate to Hashem. He created and gave us a world through which we can — if we make the effort — have some sort of appreciation of Him and His greatness. Since the purpose of Creation was to have us come closer to Hashem, everything that was created could be used to enhance our ability to reach that goal.[67]

As we shall see, Rashi takes this idea even further. The Gemara[68] tells us the now famous story of the convert who requested to learn the entire Torah while standing on one leg. The great Hillel answered him that the Torah can be summed up in one short sentence, "Don't do to your friend that which you wouldn't want to be done to yourself."

A question arises. We know that the Torah is divided mainly into two kinds of mitzvos: interpersonal commandments known as mitzvos *bein adam l'chaveiro* (such as visiting the sick and assisting the poor) and commandments governing the relationship between man and God known as mitzvos *bein adam laMakom* (such as *tefillin* and *tzitzis*). Now, at first glance, it would seem that Hillel's answer only included the interpersonal mitzvos. What about all the mitzvos between man and God? How does Hillel's dictum direct one to put on *tefillin* or pray?

Rashi offers two answers. The first answer is that Hashem can also be considered

---

66 See *Ve'Halacta Bi'Drachav*, page 234, for a discussion of this idea by Rabbi Eliyahu Lopian *zt"l* based on the verse in *Tehillim*, "He who implants the ear, shall He not hear?!" (94:9).

67 This is part of the meaning of the verse, "From my flesh, I see Hashem" (*Iyov* 19:26).

68 *Shabbos* 31a.

"your friend," as it is written, *"Reiacha v'reia avicha al ta'azov* — Do not forsake your friend and the friend of your father" (*Mishlei* 27:10). Rashi tells us that this is a reference to Hashem, who has been a close and loyal friend to us and our fathers and to our forefathers, all the way back to Creation. A person will never have a better friend than Hashem! Therefore, just as one would not want to be betrayed by his friend, so one should not disobey Hashem.[69] This is how Hillel's short summary also includes the mitzvos "between man and God."[70]

We can understand from Rashi's elucidation that one should learn how to relate to Hashem from his relationships with his fellow man. A person who has good friends knows that he should be loyal to them. All the more so should a person be loyal to Hashem, who has always been his most loyal friend. A person's conduct in his relationships with others should teach him how to conduct himself in his most important relationship: with Hashem.

Let us take, for example, one's relationship with one's parents. The love, respect, admiration, etc., one has for them should teach a person how to relate Hashem. And the gratitude one feels to one's parents should help a person understand how much gratitude he owes Hashem.

Not only do these relationships teach us how to relate to Hashem, but they also provide us learning skills and plenty of practical experience for excelling in our most important relationship. Becoming a loyal friend and a good son or daughter trains and teaches a person to serve Hashem faithfully. A selfish person who feels no loyalty to his friends or gratitude toward his parents will not serve Hashem well either.[71] Having good relationships requires learning kindness, appreciation, loyalty, etc., all of which are necessary in serving Hashem as well. Hashem created the world in a way that how a person relates to other people is how he will relate to God. It turns out, then, that these relationships not only teach us by way of comparison, but they also train us to relate to Hashem with loyalty and gratitude.

Since we relate to the physical much more easily than we do to the spiritual, the Torah uses human relationships to help us grasp and relate to Hashem. As explained earlier, it was not that after we were loyal to friends and grateful to parents that the

---

[69] Incidentally, if one is ever unfortunate enough to feel the bitter taste of being betrayed by a trusted friend or colleague, he can use this feeling to increase his devotion to Hashem by meditating on the much greater betrayal of committing a sin.

[70] Rashi's second answer is that the majority of the mitzvos are interpersonal in nature, dealing with conduct between man and his fellow man, and Hillel was referring only to these.

[71] The Gemara (*Kiddushin* 31a) tells us that Hashem opines, *ki'veyachol*, that it is good that His Presence distances itself from a person who does not respect his parents because such a person will not respect Him either.

Torah told us that we should also relate to Hashem this way. Rather, because Hashem wanted us to understand how to relate to Him, He created friends and parents for us. By experiencing and getting a taste of these relationships, we are able to identify with and understand the most important relationship of all: our relationship with Hashem.[72]

This concept, Rabbi Mendel Weinbach, *zt"l*, once pointed out, can help explain why the world as a whole has become so apathetic about serving God. In earlier times, people understood that there was a higher authority that they must heed. Nowadays, people do not necessarily accept that there is a higher authority, let alone that they must obey it. Rabbi Weinbach suggested that the rise of democracy played a significant role in this dramatic change in orientation. In the past, kings and rulers had tremendous power. People knew they had to heed this power. Nowadays, however, democracy occupies a very strong place in people's minds. Most people feel that every citizen has an equal right to do what he wants, and to follow his own beliefs. Indeed, the word "democracy" literally means "the people's power." When there was a king, one had to obey him. People were used to the idea that they had to obey authority. Therefore, when they were told about God's laws, they knew they had to obey. From the mundane world, people learned a mode of behavior that affected their spiritual world. But today, when people are not beholden to any authority that tells them how they are supposed to live in the mundane world, they do not feel the need to listen to a Higher Authority in the spiritual realm either. This explains why the lack of respect for religion is more pronounced in Western society, where democracy is strongest.

The strongest love and closeness (which is also the greatest relationship) that exists in this mundane world is to be found in marriage. One reason that Hashem created the institution of marriage was so that it would serve as a lesson for us. This relationship is, in a sense, a model of how close we can, and should, get to Hashem. Furthermore, a good marriage depends on the spouses' good *middos* (character traits or virtues). These

---

72 This point is exemplified in a touching episode that appears in Ruchama Shain's *All for the Boss*. She describes how her father, Reb Yaakov Yosef Herman, *zt"l*, was living alone in Eretz Yisrael after his wife passed away. His children in America decided to phone him, even though phone calls were difficult and expensive in those days. They sent a telegram that he should be ready to take the call in the post office on a certain day and time. The author looked anxiously forward to hearing her father's voice again after many years. When it was her turn to speak, her father asked her right away how much the phone call would cost them. Her attempt to deflect the question failed, and she revealed that it was quite expensive. R' Herman responded this way: to speak across a few continents to their father who cannot help them, they were willing to pay so much, but to speak to Hashem, their true Father, who is so powerful and is so much further away, they should be willing to pay a lot more. He continued that they get the opportunity to do this three times every day for free! "Do you at least utilize the opportunity?" he asked rhetorically.

good *middos* are essential not only for our relationship with our spouse, but also for our all-important relationship with Hashem. Therefore, marriage is both a model for us to understand our relationship with Hashem and a training ground to develop ourselves to become the kind of person who can have a close relationship with Hashem.

This understanding goes deeper. Generally speaking, there is nothing more important in this world for a person's happiness, success, and health than a good marriage. So, too, there is nothing more important for a person's future in this world and the World to Come than a good relationship with Hashem. And just as a good marriage requires constant attention and care, so does our relationship with Hashem. If we stop focusing on how to cultivate and improve it, this most important of all relationships will also go downhill.

As noted earlier with regard to other mundane matters, it is incorrect to understand that the institution of marriage preceded Hashem's likening His relationship to marriage. On the contrary, because Hashem wanted us to truly grasp how our relationship with Him should be, He created the institution of marriage. He did so to teach us that as close as one can become with his or her spouse, that is how close one should be (and even more so) with Hashem. Indeed, marriage exemplifies our relationship to Hashem in a number of different ways.

Shir HaShirim uses the allegory of marriage because that is the most similar model that we can understand in this world of how we should relate to Hashem.[73] Therefore, when we see that *Shir HaShirim* is written in terms of a very physical love, we have to remind ourselves that this is just an illustration of how great our spiritual love has to be.

Let us keep in mind that at the heart of all relationships is a profound desire for love and closeness. It stems from the soul desiring a relationship with Hashem. All human relationships, regardless of how meaningful they are, cannot completely satisfy this desire. They all pale in comparison to the true love that one can have with Hashem. Of course, this does not mean that one should downplay loving relationships. They are intrinsically important, and, as we mentioned, can be very helpful in learning to connect to Hashem. But it does mean that one should never lose sight of the ultimate goal: to become closer to Hashem. A person may fall in love and become so enthusiastic about the beloved that he or she starts forgetting about Hashem. Ultimately, this relationship will not prove satisfying because it is only a substitute for the real thing. Furthermore, not only will one then fail to connect with Hashem, but he will end up being upset because this relationship is not satisfactory. If a person maintains a correct perspective on all his loving relationships with others, not only will he connect to Hashem, but all

---

73 See *Tomer Devorah* (ch. 9), where the author discusses the likening of our relationship with Hashem to marriage.

his relationships will be vastly improved. He will not harbor the unrealistic expectation that they should be completely satisfying. He will understand that they are wonderful to bolster one's relationship with Hashem — but not replace it. This is part of the meaning of Dovid HaMelech's heartfelt declaration: "My father and mother have abandoned me, but Hashem gathered me in."[74]

THE IMPORTANCE OF SHIR HASHIRIM

Although we obviously cannot rate books of the *Tanach* and say one is more important than the other, *Chazal* give us an inkling of just how extremely important *Shir HaShirim* really is.

Rabbi Akiva commented that all of the Scriptures are holy, but *Shir HaShirim* is *Kodesh Kodashim*, the Holy of Holies.[75]

The *Targum*, based on the *Yalkut Shimoni*, says that of all the ten immortal songs that have been and will be sung to Hashem, *Shir HaShirim* is the greatest of them all.[76] This means that *Shir HaShirim* is a greater song even than the song that will be sung in the time of Mashiach!

The *Zohar* teaches that no praise is as precious and as great in Hashem's eyes as the praise in *Shir HaShirim*. It reveals that Hashem's greatest joy and *nachas* is to hear us recite it, and His happiest day was the day that Shlomo wrote *Shir HaShirim*.[77] Furthermore the *Zohar* tells us that *Shir HaShirim* eradicates the power of the *yetzer ha'ra*.[78]

Earlier, we mentioned the Midrash that describes Rabbi Eliezer teaching Rabbi Akiva *Shir HaShirim* on the day of the former's death and the fire that surrounded them during this session.

The Ramban writes that Hashem recites *Shir HaShirim* every day.[79] Shlomo HaMel-

---

74   *Tehillim* 27:10.

75   *Yadayim* 3:5. Rabbi Yisrael Salanter explained Rabbi Akiva's comment in the following way: All parts of Torah can be understood on four levels: *peshat* — the simple explanation; *remez* — the hidden messages; *derush* — the deeper meaning; and *sod* — the esoteric or mystical meaning. But in *Shir HaShirim*, those who look only at the simple, literal, meaning may think of it as merely a lowly love song. Thus, *Shir HaShirim* is the "Holy of Holies" in the sense that even its simple meaning needs to be understood in the truly holy fashion that was intended (*Ke'Motzei Shlal Rav*).

76   The ten songs are: 1) Adam HaRishon's *Song of Shabbos*; 2) Moshe Rabbeinu's *Song of the Splitting of the Sea of Reeds*; 3) *Klal Yisrael's Song of the Well*; 4) Moshe Rabbeinu's *Song of Ha'azinu*; 5) Yehoshua's *Song of the Stopping of the Sun*; 6) Devorah HaNeviah's *Song of Victory against Sisra*; 7) Chana's song upon bringing her son, Shmuel, to Eli HaKohen; 8) Dovid HaMelech's song upon winning all his battles; 9) Shlomo HaMelech's *Shir HaShirim*; and 10) *Klal Yisrael's* future song at the time of the coming of Mashiach.

77   See *Tikkunei Zohar*, 10 (24b), and *Zohar, Parashas Terumah* 143b-144a.

78   *Zohar Chadash, Rus* 83.

79   Introduction to *Shir HaShirim*. The Ramban derives this from the first verse, which he understands to mean: "The song of songs of Hashem, [the God] of peace" — the song that Hashem Himself sings.
See the introduction to *Ani L'Dodi* by Rabbi Shmuel Hominer, *zt"l*, for much more on the power and greatness of *Shir*

ech himself points out the greatness of *Shir HaShirim* at the very beginning of *Shir HaShirim* by calling it the "song of [all] songs."

Let us try to zero in, now, on its greatness. In his commentary on the very first verse of *Shir HaShirim*, Rashi addresses this issue by quoting Rabbi Akiva's statement that *Shir HaShirim* is the "Holy of Holies" and then goes on to cite a parable told by Rabbi Elazar ben Azaryah intended to help us understand its uniqueness. The parable is about a king who brings a large amount of wheat to a baker and instructs him to sift the flour meticulously and then bake a small, refined piece of bread from the finest of the flour. So too, says Rashi *Shir HaShirim* is "holy of holies."

At first glance, this parable is very puzzling. How is the delectable piece of bread similar to *Shir HaShirim*? If *Shir HaShirim* had contained all of the *special* verses taken from the other *sefarim* in *Kesuvim*, then we could understand that *Shir HaShirim* is the fine flour sifted and separated from the rest. However, *Shir HaShirim* has not been sifted from anywhere; it is about a separate subject entirely.

We can understand the parable as well as Rashi's intent in the following way: When a parent engages in an activity with a child, such as playing a game or shopping, the child may mistakenly believe that all the parent wants is for the activity to be successfully completed, e.g., by giving the child a good time or buying something that he needed. The truth, however, is that the parent has a far more fundamental and important mission in mind: to develop a close relationship with the child. Obviously, when playing a game with a child, the parent has no real interest in the game other than to bond with the child. But even when eating and shopping together, for example, the real desire of the parent is to be kind to the child and draw him or her closer. Similarly, Hashem gave us many different tasks and responsibilities. From *Megillas Rus*, we learn to do *chessed*; from *Megillas Esther*, we learn to trust in Hashem, and so forth. But if we were to try to understand the main goal and objective of all of this, our conclusion would be that they are all designed to help us develop our relationship with Hashem, and become closer to Him.[80] For instance, doing *chessed* helps a person become more similar to Hashem, and

---

HaShirim. Rabbi Hominer also quotes Rabbi Tzvi of Zidthov, *zt"l*, as saying that whenever he was going through a *nisayon* (trial), he would remind himself of the time he heard Rabbi Baruch of Mezhibuz, *zt"l*, reciting *Shir HaShirim* with intense devotion which made it impossible for him to sin. See there for other descriptions of how great people would recite *Shir HaShirim* with complete devotion.

80   The Ramchal elaborates on this idea in the introduction to his *Mesillas Yesharim*. He explains that the purpose of Creation is to come close to Hashem, which is the greatest kindness that Hashem could give mankind. The place of this ultimate closeness is in the World to Come. To achieve this closeness in the next world, however, one has to earn it here in our mundane world. This is achieved by trying, out of one's own free choice, to develop this closeness to Hashem, and not letting all of this world's allures pull one away from this goal. The reward and closeness to Hashem granted in the next world is proportional to how much a person was able to get close to Hashem in this world. Clearly, becoming close to Hashem is the ultimate goal.

helps him recognize Hashem's abundant *chessed*; trusting in Hashem brings a person closer to Him, and so forth. All the *sefarim* in *Tanach* teach us many different lessons. However, the ultimate purpose of them all is to help us get closer to Hashem. As the Ramchal writes in *Mesillas Yesharim*, the purpose of Creation is to become close to Hashem.[81] Hashem put us in a world full of challenges and distractions in order that we become close to Him through our efforts, and thus earn the reward of being close to Him in the World to Come.[82]

Since *Shir HaShirim* describes our relationship with Hashem and teaches us how to get close to Him, it is presenting the essence of all of the different lessons that we learn from all of the other *sefarim*. Indeed, as Rabbi Akiva said, "all the *sefarim* are holy" because they all teach us how to connect to Hashem through different pathways, but "*Shir HaShirim* is the "Holy of Holies" because it deals only with the actual closeness, the actual relationship with Him. Returning now to Rabbi Elazar's parable, *Shir HaShirim* is really like the small, immaculate piece of bread which is the final outcome of all the refining that was done with the flour. *Shir HaShirim* is the finest outcome that we get from all the other *sefarim* together.

We are now in exile, which is a punishment for sin. The seed for our exile was the Sin of the Spies who came back from Eretz Yisrael with a negative and frightening report about the Land. When we cried that night — the night of Tisha B'Av — Hashem said: "Because you cried in vain, I will establish this night as a night for crying in the future." And, indeed, our suffering as a nation has given us reason to cry on that night for close to two thousand years. But what was the underlying cause for the unwarranted crying back in the Wilderness? The Torah tells us that it was the people's feeling that Hashem hated them.[83] Of course, Hashem never hated them at all, but they wept because they mistakenly thought so.[84] Now, we know that the rewards Hashem awards are 500 times greater than the punishments He metes out.[85] If after complaining in vain that Hashem hated us, we were punished to this extent, let us imagine how much reward we will receive for praising Hashem for His love. One is greatly rewarded for feeling gratitude and

---

81 Ch. 1.

82 The Ramchal quotes the verse in *Tehillim* (73:28): ואני קרבת אלוקים לי טוב. This literally means that being close to Hashem is good, but, as the Ramchal explains, the import is that the only true good thing is to be close to Hashem and that everything else is not good.

83 *Devarim* 1:27.

84 Rashi, ibid.

85 Rashi *Shemos* 20:6, *s.v. v'notzeir chessed*; see also *Yoma* 76a.

love towards Hashem. If we recall Hashem's love and thank Him for all of His kindness even when we might mistakenly feel that He does not love us and even when we are suffering and do not readily feel the blessings He has bestowed upon us, our reward will be tremendous! Just contemplating it will make us feel like singing to Hashem in praise.

SHIR HASHIRIM AND PESACH

There is a very old custom, mentioned in halachah, to read *Shir HaShirim* after the Pesach Seder[86] and to read it again in shul on Shabbos during Pesach.[87] Let us consider the connection between re-experiencing the Exodus from Egypt on Pesach and *Shir HaShirim*.

The Avudraham notes that since *Shir HaShirim* deals, in part, with the redemption from Egypt — which is the focus of Pesach — it is appropriate to read it on Seder Night.[88] The *Sefer HaMata'amim*[89] points out that *Klal Yisrael* was redeemed from Egypt in the merit of their faith in Hashem which is lovingly expressed in *Shir HaShirim*. To recall that merit, we read *Shir HaShirim*. Furthermore, Pesach is the time when Hashem showed us and the entire world that He chose us as His beloved nation. It is fitting that we should read about our loving relationship on the anniversary of the beginning that relationship. Pesach is also a time that is ripe for the Final Redemption. Since *Shir HaShirim* portrays the coming of Mashiach, it is appropriate to study it at this time, and thus to prepare for, and anticipate, the Redemption.

The Sefas Emes adds another dimension. He says that to understand *Shir HaShirim* correctly, we should view everything in this world as only a symbol of the real world of spirituality. For example, the love between husband and wife is an allegory of the love between *Klal Yisrael* and Hashem. Only on Pesach, when we are on an elevated spiritual plane, can we see this clearly. Indeed, this perspective correlates with a key lesson of Pesach. Pesach teaches us that this world is, in a sense, no more than an allegory. Pharaoh and the Egyptians thought they were in control when, in reality, everything was being controlled by Hashem. He was merely using them to illustrate His Power. Had Hashem wanted to, He could have gotten rid of them from the first moment, but He let them live

---

86   This custom is first mentioned in *Maseches Sofrim* (14:18) and quoted by the Rema (*Orach Chaim* 490:9).
     The Vilna Gaon would send everyone out of the room when he recited *Shir HaShirim* at the end of the Seder. One year, a relative found somewhere to hide in order to witness this spectacle. After a few moments, however, the relative was overcome with fear when he felt the intense holiness surrounding the Vilna Gaon as he was reciting *Shir HaShirim* and was forced to flee (*Menuchah U'Kedushah*, p. 32).

87   Outside of Eretz Yisrael, where two days of Pesach sometimes fall on Shabbos (i.e., the first day and eighth day), *Shir HaShirim* is read on the eighth day.

88   *Mishnah Berurah* 490:17.

89   *Pesach* 52.

and punished them to display His Power and thus teach the world a lesson. Pesach reminds us that we should look beyond the facade of events and understand that there is a deeper existence to discover. If we approach *Shir HaShirim* with that mindset, we will be able to learn *Shir HaShirim* properly. We will thus be open to understanding that the entire story is about the deep, loving relationship between *Klal Yisrael* and Hashem.[90]

As with all of *Klal Yisrael*'s ancient customs, the custom of reading and studying *Shir HaShirim* on Pesach teaches a variety of important lessons. It is beyond the scope of this work to review them all. Suffice it to say that *Chazal* wanted our Pesach to be enhanced by understanding the lessons of love from *Shir HaShirim* and our understanding of *Shir HaShirim* to be influenced and colored by our Pesach. Those who have striven to connect deeply with these two delightful events and have experienced the wonderful feelings that they both engender, will find additional, subtle links between the two which have not been enumerated here but are no less valid.

SHIR HASHIRIM AND SHALOM BAYIS

Although the primary purpose of learning *Shir HaShirim* is to gain a deeper understanding of our relationship with Hashem, the allegory of a loving marriage contains many details that can help us enhance our own marriages. Indeed, Rashi himself tells us that there is value in understanding the surface meaning of a *mashal* told by a wise person.[91] *Shir HaShirim*'s many descriptions of how Hashem loves us and forgives us and how we admire Hashem and are loyal to him, can be used as a gauge to make sure that our marriage is of a similar high caliber. We will be taking note of this type of thing from time to time in our running commentary. We mention it here in the Introduction only to alert readers so that when a verse or idea arouses a feeling of "Yes, this is how I ought to conduct myself with my spouse," it should be viewed as one of the valuable lessons found in *Shir HaShirim*.

The very fact that Shlomo HaMelech used the parable of a loving marriage to speak about our relationship with Hashem tells us a great deal about how highly he viewed marriage. Viewed in this way, the megillah can also be seen as an appeal for increased *shalom bayis*.

There is, however, one point that should be spotlighted here since it is not limited to any one verse of *Shir HaShirim* but emerges from the entire *sefer*: A truly good marriage is built through many different bonds.[92] We can see this in *Shir HaShirim* through the

---

90   *Pesach* 631.

91   *Mishlei* 1:6.

92   One of the greatest strengths of a religious Jewish marriage is that there is a shared goal and common meaning in the marriage. Since both spouses' greatest aspiration is to serve Hashem and since they both know that marriage is a means

variety of terms used to describe Hashem's love for *Klal Yisrael*, each one depicting another facet of our relationship. Let us cite a few examples to underscore this point, and to illustrate how it can enhance our *shalom bayis* (marital harmony). Hashem calls *Klal Yisrael* My flock,[93] My bride,[94] My vineyard,[95] My brother,[96] My sister,[97] My mother,[98] My daughter,[99] My perfection, My dove, My beloved, My Friend,[100] and My beauty.[101] Each metaphor suggests another facet of the relationship between Hashem and *Klal Yisrael*, and thus another dimension of a healthy marriage.

"My beloved" tells us that there must be endearment for there to be a bond. One should aim to always be heartwarming to his or her spouse. Through endearment, the couple generates the love and affection that bring them to true oneness for a lifetime. This is accomplished mainly by each one looking out for and contributing to the good and happiness of the other. "My beauty" tells us that one should be attracted to one's spouse.

How does "My perfection" relate to marriage? After all, no one is absolutely pure and faultless. The point is that we can accept our spouse and be satisfied as if he or she were pure and perfect by overlooking faults, hang-ups, shortcomings, quirks, and the like, and by appreciating wholeheartedly the qualities that make the spouse special, precious, beautiful, and unique. This is as if to say, "With all your faults, I love you no less than if you would be perfect."

"My dove" points to a member of the animal kingdom who remains loyal to its mate for a lifetime. The use of this term in *Shir HaShirim* teaches us that our commitment and loyalty to our spouse should be forever.[102]

"My sister" connotes a close, deep, familial bond that is free of the confusion that may arise out of purely romantic emotions. The bond is that of one's flesh and blood. It

---

       to reach that goal, they have the extra bond that they work together as a team for this highest of goals.

93   1:7.

94   4:10.

95   8:11.

96   8:1.

97   4:9.

98   3:11.

99   Interestingly, there is no explicit comparison in *Shir HaShirim* to this, but it is found in *Tehillim* 45:11. See further 3:11.

100 5:2.

101 2:10.

102 See our commentary on 1:15. It should be noted that the bonds of a truly committed Jewish marriage continue into the World to Come, not just "until death do us part." This is evidenced by the Gemara's description of how the great tzaddik Rabbi Chanina ben Dosa sat next to his wife in Gan Eden (*Ta'anis* 25a). Contemplating the eternity of the relationship should help inspire us to make sure it is a truly worthy one.

provides the unconditional, non-physical, and constant element of a love-relationship that a physical relationship lacks. "My friend" implies that a spouse should first and foremost be a friend. We all strive to treat friends in a kind manner and are always careful to avoid insulting them or belittling them. We also maintain a healthy amount of respect and try not to overstep boundaries. This is just as important in a marriage where, unfortunately, familiarity can make a person forget this precaution. Finally, "My bride" clearly connotes the male/female aspect of marriage, as well as the passionate and even physical side — all of which are integral to marriage. Clearly, we can learn much from *Shir HaShirim* about how an ideal marriage should be!

It is imperative that we guard against getting so involved in the intricacies and profound ideas of *Shir HaShirim* that we lose sight of its main message. Through *Shir HaShirim*, we learn about the greatest love story of all time: the relationship between Hashem and every single Jew, including ourselves. Thus, while engrossed in *Shir HaShirim*, we should be feeling: "I love Hashem, and Hashem loves me!" Indeed, this feeling should remain with us forever.

A NOTE REGARDING THE CHAPTERS DIVISIONS

While it is always interesting to discover a new explanation of a particular verse, to truly understand *Shir HaShirim*, we have to view it as an edifice of ideas and messages carefully built to give us a true appreciation of our relationship with Hashem. To fully appreciate the beauty and lessons contained here, we have to understand how each verse follows from the previous one, and how one topic connects with the next. This requires effort, but it is truly worthwhile if one sincerely wishes to understand *Shir HaShirim*. I have made every effort to explain the flow of the verses, and how each topic leads on to the next. Readers of this work will see clearly that *Shir HaShirim* is not just an assortment of inspirational ideas, but like any great *sefer*, a methodical work with great lessons to teach.

Chapters are often used to help one navigate through the lessons of a *sefer*. We must be aware, however, that the chapter divisions in the printed versions of *Shir HaShirim* are unreliable. As is well known, the original printers were not learned people. In fact, oftentimes, they were not even Jewish.[103] Clearly then, using a chapter division as a signpost of a new subject is incorrect. Indeed, we find new chapters suddenly beginning in the middle of a subject!

---

103 See Abarbanel, beginning of *Shmuel I*.

According to the Malbim and other commentators, *Shir HaShirim* has only five chapters.[104] The first chapter ends with the verse beginning הִשְׁבַּעְתִּי אֶתְכֶם —"I adjure you..." (2:5). The second chapter ends with the verse beginning צְאֶנָה וּרְאֶינָה בְּנוֹת צִיּוֹן — "Go forth, daughters of Zion..." (3:11). The third chapter ends with בָּאתִי לְגַנִּי—"I have come into my garden..." (5:1). The fourth chapter ends with חִכּוֹ מַמְתַקִּים—"His mouth is most sweet..." (5:16). The fifth chapter ends with the verse מַיִם רַבִּים — "Many waters..." (8:7). From there until the end of *Shir HaShirim* are a few concluding verses. To understand the flow and the continuation of the verses, it is sometimes necessary to keep in mind the breaks of these five chapters. For the sake of simplicity, however, our commentary uses the standard chapter numbers assigned by the printers.[105]

---

104 This division fits in well according to Rashi and the Midrash. It also follows, to a large extent, the breaks in a hand-written *Shir HaShirim* scroll.

105 Rabbi Chaim Kanievsky suggests that *Shir HaShirim* can indeed be divided into eight parts, corresponding to the chapters assigned by the printers: 1) *Klal Yisrael* in Egypt; 2) *Klal Yisrael* coming out of Egypt and receiving the Torah; 3) *Klal Yisrael*'s entry into Eretz Yisrael; 4) The building of the first Beis HaMikdash; 5) The destruction of the first Beis HaMikdash; 6) The Second Beis HaMikdash; 7) Our long exile; 8) The Final Redemption. As he notes, however, this can only be seen as a very general guide.

RASHI'S INTRODUCTION

אחת דבר אלהים שתים זו שמעתי[106], מקרא אחד יוצא לכמה טעמים וסוף דבר אין לך מקרא יוצא מידי פשוטו [ומשמע ואף על פי שדברו הנביאים דבריהם בדוגמא צריך ליישב הדוגמא על אופניה ועל סדרה כמו שהמקראות סדורים זה אחר זה וראיתי לספר הזה כמה מדרשי אגדה יש סודרים כל הספר הזה במדרש אחד, ויש מפוזרים בכמה מדרשי אגדה מקראות לבדם ואינם מתיישבים על לשון המקרא וסדר המקראות, ואמרתי בלבי לתפוש משמעות המקרא ליישב ביאורם על סדרם והמדרשות מרבותינו אקבעם מדרש ומדרש איש איש במקומו.]

ואומר אני שראה שלמה ברוח הקדש שעתידין ישראל לגלות גולה אחר גולה חורבן אחר חורבן ולהתאונן בגלות זה על כבודם הראשון ולזכור חבה ראשונה אשר היו סגולה לו מכל העמים לאמר אלכה ואשובה אל אישי הראשון כי טוב לי אז מעתה[107] ויזכרו את חסדיו ואת מעלם אשר מעלו[108] ואת הטובות אשר אמר לתת להם באחרית הימים.

ויסד ספר הזה ברוח הקדש בלשון אשה צרורה אלמנות חיות[109] משתוקקת על בעלה מתרפקת על דודה מזכרת אהבת נעורים אליו ומודה על פשעה אף דודה צר לו בצרתה[110] ומזכיר חסדי נעוריה ונוי יופיה וכשרון פעליה בהם נקשר עמה באהבה עזה להודיעם כי לא מלבו ענה[111] ולא שילוחיה שילוחין כי עוד היא אשתו והוא אישה והוא עתיד לשוב אליה.

FREE TRANSLATION

From even so much as a single word uttered by Hashem, we can learn many lessons. Yet every verse must also be understood according to its simple meaning. Many interpretations have been given to this *sefer*, *Shir HaShirim*, but I [Rashi] seek to find an interpretation that accords with the simple meaning of the individual verses as well as the order of all the verses and the explanations of *Chazal*.

Therefore, I explain that Shlomo HaMelech foresaw through *ruach hakodesh* that *Klal Yisrael* was destined to suffer a series of exiles and devastations. They would come to lament, nostalgically recalling their former status as God's chosen beloved and say: "I will return to my first Husband, for it was better for me then than now." *Klal Yisrael* would remember His kindness as well as their rebellious sins. Then they will recall the goodness that He promised them in the End of Days.

---

106 *Tehillim* 62:12.
107 *Hoshea* 2:9.
108 *Vayikra* 26:40.
109 *Shmuel II* 20:3.
110 *Yeshayahu* 63:9.
111 *Eichah* 3:33.

Shlomo composed *Shir HaShirim* in the form of an allegory of a woman deserted by her husband, yearning for him and seeking to endear herself to him once more. She seeks her husband's love by reminding him of her youthful love to him and by admitting her guilt. He, too, is pained by her afflictions. He recalls the kindness of her youth, her beauty, and her wonderful deeds through which he attached himself to her with a bond of intense love. He thereby lets her know that he has not afflicted her without purpose, and that **their parting ways is not permanent because she is still his wife, and he remains her husband, and that he will yet return to her.**

פרק א׳
CHAPTER 1

> שִׁיר הַשִּׁירִים, אֲשֶׁר לִשְׁלֹמֹה.
>
> *The song of [all] songs that is [dedicated] to Hashem, [the God] of peace.*
>
> א 1

Allegorical Translation — The greatest of songs: the one sung to Hashem by His chosen nation, *Klal Yisrael*.

Subject of the Verse — The author, Shlomo HaMelech, introduces the song.

This verse tells us the importance of *Shir HaShirim*: It is the "song of songs," the choicest song ever composed.[1] And it tells us who it was written for: Hashem.

THE SONG OF SONGS

This verse introduces *Shir HaShirim*. The Vilna Gaon notes at the beginning of his commentary on *Mishlei* that the first few verses of every *sefer* in *Tanach* are a short summary of the entire *sefer*. As we shall see, the first few verses of *Shir HaShirim* give us the entire picture of *Shir HaShirim*.

THE SONG OF SONGS

As we have noted in the Introduction, Rashi explains this phrase to mean "choicest of all songs." This is similar, grammatically, to the expressions *raz she'barazim* ("the deepest of all secrets"), and *chacham she'bachachamim* ("the wisest of the wise"). Thus, "*shir*

---

1   As explained in the Introduction.

ha'shirim" means "the choicest [or greatest] song of all songs."[2]

The Chasam Sofer explains these words differently.[3] Just as we find that *Shiras HaBe'er* ("the Song of the Well") means that it was the song of thanks to Hashem for the well, and *Shiras HaYam* ("the Song of the Sea") means that it was the song of thanks to Hashem for the miracles at the sea, so *Shir HaShirim* ("the Song of the Songs") means that it is a song of thanks to Hashem for the privilege of singing songs to Him.[4] We should feel gratitude and joy over this privilege, so much so that it should inspire us to sing![5]

When a person does a mitzvah, part of the reward is that Hashem helps him[6] do additional mitzvos because "the reward of a mitzvah is a mitzvah."[7] So, too, when a person sings to Hashem, part of the reward is that Hashem gives him more reasons to sing: more blessings and a greater appreciation of Hashem's love and kindness. Thus, one single song can bring about many songs. Looked at from this standpoint, the expression "song of songs" connotes "a song which leads to more songs." There is nothing more capable of bringing a person closer to Hashem and cleansing him from sin than singing to Him.[8] A song to Hashem which leads to many such songs then brings one to perfection. Indeed, since the concluding word of this verse, "*shlomo*," can also mean "perfection," the entire verse can be understood to mean: "The song of songs that [brings one] to perfection."

The Ohr HaChaim takes a very different approach to the words "the song of songs."[9] Because his explanation helps us understand the whole of *Shir HaShirim*, I will elaborate on it. The Ohr HaChaim offers a parable about a most kind and majestic king and his beautiful and loving queen. They enjoy a wonderful marriage and rule over a grand kingdom. Their noble son has all the qualities of a great prince. One day, the queen is rumored to have betrayed her husband, and he sends her away. Everyone in the kingdom is devastated by this separation, but no one is as upset as their son, the prince, whose

---

2   See *Metzudas Tzion*.
    The Rambam writes that this grammatical construction — a singular noun followed by the definite article and then the same noun in the plural — is used to include everything of this sort. Accordingly, "*Shir HaShirim*" means that this song includes all songs (*Peirush HaMishnayos, Nedarim* 6:4).

3   *Haggadas Chasam Sofer* and *Derashos Chasam Sofer* (vol. 2, p. 265).

4   The beginning of the *Aleinu* prayer teaches us this idea.

5   I recall that at the wedding of the grandson of Rabbi Moshe Shmuel Shapiro, *zt"l*, there was a tremendously long line of people who wanted to wish *Mazal Tov* to this *Gadol*. Indeed, the crowd was so large that many were not able to get in. Now, if we can appreciate what a privilege it is to greet a *Gadol HaDor*, how much more so is it a privilege to sing to Hashem, the King of Kings.

6   The masculine pronoun is used for convenience. The intent, of course, is "him or her."

7   *Avos* 4:2.

8   *Sefer Chareidim*, ch. 73. See also Rashi on *Shoftim* 6:1.

9   In his *Rishon L'Tzion* on *Shir HaShirim*.

life has been ruined. Then one day, the prince hears his father singing about how wonderful, attractive, and desirable the queen was and how much he still loves her, and how he looks forward to rejoining her every moment of every day. Later, when the prince passes his mother's house, he hears her singing the same type of song about the king. After hearing these two songs, the prince realizes, based on the strength of the love they have for each other, that they will eventually get back together. Then the prince himself starts singing a new song of the wonderful time to come when his parents will be together again. But the people around the prince mock him, and tell him that he is dreaming, that the relationship is dead, and that he has to get used to it. They tell him, "The separation is final, and they will never get back together!" "No," he replies, "you are all wrong!" When the people question his optimism, he explains, "My song is a 'song of songs.' It is based on, and created from, two other songs. My song stems from the songs I heard the king and queen sing.[10]"

Similarly, Shlomo HaMelech wrote *Shir HaShirim* based on the songs that he knew *Klal Yisrael* and Hashem were singing about their love for each other. Even though Hashem would eventually send away *Klal Yisrael*, allowing onlookers to make the terrible mistake of thinking that the special relationship was all over between them, Shlomo HaMelech knew otherwise. This is because Shlomo HaMelech could hear the songs of love that *Klal Yisrael* and Hashem were singing. After hearing those songs, Shlomo HaMelech was certain that they would never give up on each other and would eventually reunite. Based on those songs, he was inspired to write another song: a song of those wonderful future times. This, the Ohr HaChaim concludes, is what the "the song of songs" means. It is a song created from other songs.

The approach of the Ohr HaChaim helps us overcome one of the difficulties presented by *Shir HaShirim*. At first glance, this megillah may seem to be a jumble of songs mixed together: a few verses about the greatness of *Klal Yisrael*, followed by a few about the greatness of Hashem, then back to *Klal Yisrael*, and in the middle, another few verses about the nations praising *Klal Yisrael*, etc. According to the Ohr HaChaim's approach, however, this difficulty falls away. *Shir HaShirim* is one song declaring the everlasting bond between *Klal Yisrael* and Hashem, but the one song is based on other songs that Shlomo HaMelech heard and understood. Indeed, we can broaden the parable and suggest that the prince heard many other songs, all of which inspired him to his new song. In addition to the principal songs of the king and queen, he heard other songs. He heard the song of the people highlighting how wonderful the king and queen

---

10 This explanation accords beautifully with the grammar of the phrase *Shir* ("song," in the singular) *HaShirim* ("songs," in the plural).

were together, and the song of the women who had hoped to be chosen queen and who were jealous of the queen in the past, but who now acknowledged that only the queen was worthy of such a wonderful king. Furthermore, the king would sing songs from different periods of time: songs that describe his initial love for the queen as well as songs from much later in their relationship. So, too, in the Nimshal: While the song of *Shir HaShirim* is based primarily on songs between Hashem and *Klal Yisrael*, it also includes the heathen nations' songs of praise for *Klal Yisrael* due to their faithfulness to Hashem, and it even includes praise from the angels. It also includes songs that describe *Klal Yisrael*'s love for Hashem's Torah and their gratitude that Hashem saved them from Egypt — songs from the beginnings of the Jewish People and songs from much later periods. Looked at this way, *Shir HaShirim* can be understood as one song of hope which includes all the small songs that are the basis and foundation for this inspiration.

HASHEM, [THE GOD] OF PEACE

The verse continues, "[dedicated] to Hashem, [the God] of peace." Rashi explains that the name שְׁלֹמֹה (*Shlomo*) in this verse does not refer to Shlomo HaMelech but rather to Hashem. *Shlomo* comes from the word "*shalom*," which means "peace." The verse refers to Hashem as *Shlomo* because Hashem is the God of peace. This name for Hashem is repeated a number of times in *Shir HaShirim*.

Before discussing why Shlomo HaMelech chose this name in particular when there are more conventional names for Hashem, we need to understand what "God of peace" means. Here, "peace" does not simply mean the absence of conflict, but rather a state of true harmony and tranquility. Hashem is called the "God of peace" because true peace and contentment can be found only in serving Him.

When a person is forced to work with someone else who has a different agenda or goal, there is going to be discord. Imagine a group of people working together on a project, but each person in the group has different goals and aspirations. One wishes to make as much money as possible, a second wants to see how to help others, and yet a third person is looking for fame. Even if there is no open conflict, there will be a constant undercurrent of tension between them.

Both our intuition and experience tell us that true harmony depends on a congruence of desires. When people who have different desires are forced to be together, resentment ensues. Since every person has different desires, it is impossible to have complete and true peace in this world until all desires become unified.

Furthermore, when someone finds himself doing something that he is not meant to do, there is going to be discord. Imagine the profound discontent of a person who loves children and enjoys spending time with them being consigned to a biology lab or imagine that a professor of biology is drafted to teach in a kindergarten — or other such scenarios.

The entire world was created to serve Hashem and draw close to Him. The deepest need of every person is to connect to Hashem. Ultimately, we will all realize that our greatest goal and desire is to serve Him. Serving Hashem is the only goal which every human being — and, indeed, every item in the universe — was created for. It encompasses all the true desires and aspirations of every being. Therefore, true peace in the world will only come about when everyone is serving Him and coming closer to Him.[11] Hashem is thus the "God of peace." Only with Hashem, can true peace occur.

The ultimate service of Hashem is to connect with Him and love Him. *Shir HaShirim* describes that ultimate closeness between Hashem and *Klal Yisrael*: the nation that was chosen to become the closest to Hashem. When the entire world is utilized to help *Klal Yisrael* love and draw close to Hashem, then true, absolute peace will come about. In *Shir HaShirim*, even the heathen nations declare *Klal Yisrael*'s faithfulness and love for Hashem. Therefore, in the realm of *Shir HaShirim*, there is true peace in the entire world. That is why Shlomo HaMelech chose to describe Hashem in *Shir HaShirim* as the God of peace.

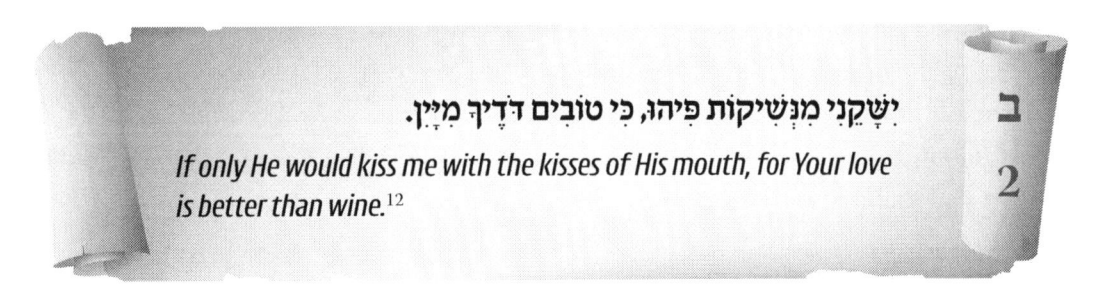

> יִשָּׁקֵנִי מִנְּשִׁיקוֹת פִּיהוּ, כִּי טוֹבִים דֹּדֶיךָ מִיָּיִן. ב
>
> *If only He would kiss me with the kisses of His mouth, for Your love is better than wine.*[12] 2

Allegorical Translation — If only Hashem would once again speak to us face to face as He did at *Matan Torah* because the love He showed us then is more precious and sweeter to us than all forms of delight and pleasure.

Subject of the Verse — *Klal Yisrael* is speaking to Hashem and yearning for His love, asking that their former love be restored.

Mashal — An estranged wife recalls with longing her husband's former love and expresses

---

11 We pray for this fervently on Rosh HaShanah and Yom Kippur, asking Hashem: "May all of mankind form one group to do Your will wholeheartedly."

12 The *Shem MiShmuel* offers a homiletic explanation based on an alternative understanding of the מ in the last word of the verse as meaning "coming from" instead of "better than": "For Your love [i.e., closeness to Hashem] is good when it comes (מ meaning coming from as in ממצרים, from Egypt, (*Bereishis* 13:1)] from wine (i.e., Torah)" (*Lehavos Kodesh*, p. 92). As will be shown, "wine" often alludes to Torah. The *Shem MiShmuel* means that while many try to become close to Hashem in a variety of ways, the outcome is truly good only when it comes from Torah learning and Torah observance. Seeking spirituality in any other way might yield a temporary high but will not truly bring about a bond with Hashem.

Nimshal — her wish that he would relate to her as he did in the past, that he would once again be close and intimate with her and kiss her as a husband kisses his wife — on the mouth[13] — because his love is sweeter to her than wine, the classic symbol of earthly pleasure.[14]

Nimshal *Klal Yisrael* reminisces about and yearns for Hashem's love, declaring how precious Hashem's love is to them. The verse opens with a plea that Hashem shower *Klal Yisrael* with more love and revive their past love. It continues with *Klal Yisrael*'s declaration of how very precious Hashem's love is to them.

IF ONLY HE WOULD KISS ME

Klal Yisrael's plea that Hashem return to them and be as close to them as He was in the past includes a plea and a yearning for Mashiach. They ask for Mashiach not because of a desire for power, wealth, or any superficial benefit but only due to a desire to reconnect to Hashem. It is expressed in terms of a kiss on the mouth, something that is reserved for one's spouse, only, as Rashi tells us, at a time of intimacy.

In the historical relationship between *Klal Yisrael* and Hashem, the verse is referring to *Klal Yisrael* in exile feeling far removed from Hashem.[15] They are asking Hashem to reveal Himself and teach them Torah face to face with a special and intimate closeness, similar to the closeness He showed them at Har Sinai. This will only happen again when Mashiach comes.[16]

The Netziv notes that learning Torah creates the strongest feeling of closeness to Hashem. It is this feeling that *Klal Yisrael* seeks to recapture. Why does learning Torah create such a special closeness to Hashem? To answer this fundamental question, we need a better appreciation of what learning Torah is all about. The *Tanya*'s explanation of why learning Torah is the greatest mitzvah gives us a handle on this question: The closest possible connection one person can have with another is if he knows and feels the other person's mind and heart.[17] Torah is the expression of Hashem's thoughts and

---

13 Rashi.

14 Wine is symbolic of pleasure because drinking wine has always been a foremost type of enjoyment and entertainment. This was especially true in former times when many other kinds of pleasure were not available.

15 Rashi.

16 See the *Gryz on the Torah* (*Shir HaShirim* 8:5), where he discusses the teaching of Torah in the time of Mashiach.

17 Ch. 23. Physical closeness without closeness in thought and feeling does little to bond people together. A passenger in a crowded subway car, for example, feels absolutely no connection or closeness with the individual he is pressed against. In contrast, one can live thousands of miles away from another person, and still be very close — provided their minds and hearts are connected. This is why the Torah describes marriage as "knowing" the spouse (*Bereishis* 4:1). The closest bonding is described as "knowing."

wishes, which are the essence of another being. This is why becoming close to Hashem requires knowing His Torah. Learning Torah is, *ki'veyachol* (so to speak), learning what Hashem Himself thinks. When we learn that a particular act is permitted on Shabbos, we perceive the thoughts of Hashem as well as His wish that this particular act should be permitted on Shabbos. Even though every mitzvah brings a person closer to Hashem, learning Torah brings him closest. At *Matan Torah*, Hashem shared His innermost thoughts with *Klal Yisrael*, and this intimacy is what *Klal Yisrael* is seeking.[18]

IF ONLY HE WOULD KISS ME

Even though *Klal Yisrael* is in exile, they do not ask merely for a slightly closer relationship with Hashem. *Klal Yisrael* wants and needs Hashem's love so much that they will not be satisfied with this. Rather, they beseech Him to relate to them once again with the closest intimacy possible as He did in the past.

Rabbi Ezriel Tauber elucidates this hope through the following analogy. A person born into poverty has very limited aspirations for wealth. His ideas about real wealth are limited by his lack of experience with money. Not so the very wealthy person who has lost all his money. Since he has tasted real wealth, his dreams and aspirations are much greater. Similarly, since we were so wealthy with an abundance of Hashem's love, our aspirations remain very high for a return to our previous "spiritual affluence."[19] Furthermore, since we understand how vital His love is, we are not satisfied with a just a little.

KISS ME

It is noteworthy that the verse uses the first-person singular pronoun: *me*. We can learn from this that even one individual on his own can seek that special closeness with Hashem. Each of us can and should create our own personal relationship with Hashem. We should also feel the yearning expressed in this verse for closeness to Hashem.

HIS MOUTH

The word "mouth" would seem to be superfluous here since all kisses involve the mouth. Therefore, as Rashi indicates, the metaphor is to be understood as the mouth-to-mouth

---

18   The Gemara tell us that the first word of the Ten Commandments, אנכי (I), is an acronym for אנא נפשי כתיבת יהיבת (*Shabbos* 105a). Translated literally, this means: "I wrote Myself, and gave this." Rashi explains that Hashem begins the Ten Commandments by saying that He wrote the entire Torah. The Mekor Baruch, however, suggests homiletically that Hashem is saying: I wrote Myself into the Torah, and gave you the Torah to discover Me (1:421).

19   Mere friendship is not enough of a relationship between marriage partners. We desire more than friendship with Hashem because we know that our relationship is much more than that. It is like marriage.

kissing of a husband and wife.[20]

Rabbi Shimshon Pinkus notes that a kiss on the hand or forehead, for example, is one directional. One can kiss without being kissed back. Here, in contrast, the metaphor of kissing mouth to mouth means that just as one is kissing, one is being kissed at the same time.[21] This teaches us a very fundamental lesson about our relationship with Hashem. When a person connects with Hashem, He always responds in kind. He comes closer to the person and showers him with His Presence. Just as kissing on the mouth is reciprocal, so, too, is "kissing" Hashem by thinking about Him. At that moment, Hashem is connecting to him even though he does not always feel this connection. Furthermore, when Hashem "kisses" us, our natural response should be to turn to Him and connect with Him.

The word *pihu* (פיהו — "His mouth") could have been spelled without the extra letter *hey* (פיו). With the extra letter, the word *pihu* contains the letters of both the words *piv* and *peh*, "His mouth" and "mouth."[22] We are thus asking implicitly that as we attempt to connect to Hashem, we should feel *His* closeness to us, that Hashem should "kiss" us in a way that we feel His connection and respond in kind.[23]

The Rambam elaborates on this concept in his *Moreh Nevuchim*.[24] He writes that when a person is thinking about Hashem, he is connected to Hashem: "The intellect/mind which emanates from God to us is the link that joins us to God. You have it in your power to strengthen that bond, if you choose to do so, or to weaken it gradually until it breaks, if you prefer this. It will only become strong when you employ it in the love of God and seek that love; it will be weakened when you direct your thoughts to other things." This means that a person is free to choose whether to strengthen this connection or to weaken it, depending on what he thinks about. The Rambam continues:

---

20 Ibn Ezra notes that the Torah uses two different grammatical constructions when describing kissing: one with the preposition "ל" and one without, e.g., *yishakeini* (*Bereishis* 27:25). Kissing on the hand, etc., is described in the first way, e.g., *vayishak Yaakov leRachel* (*Bereishis* 29:11). The *lamed* conveys the sense of a kiss that comes "to me." But when describing a kiss from mouth to mouth, the Torah leaves out the *lamed* because then the sense is not that the kiss is coming "to me," but, rather, that I am being kissed — as in our verse. This is another reason why Rashi explains the verse as he does (*Yedei Moshe*).

21 The Kedushas Levi (*Vayikra*) adds that when one kisses the hand, one is symbolically showing love for the actions that the person does for them. When one kisses the mouth, however, one is addressing the feelings expressed by the mouth, and thanking the recipient of the kiss for the love that he or she exhibits. *Klal Yisrael* wish to reach the level where they love Hashem not just for His kindness — symbolized by His hand — but even just for the love that He shows them. Thus, we ask to kiss His mouth.

22 Vilna Gaon. Another way of understanding the extra letter (*hey*) in the word *pihu* ("His mouth") is that it suggests a fullness of kissing (*Yalkut Me'am Lo'ez*).

23 This point is elaborated in connection with our elucidation of 6:3.

24 Vol. 3, ch. 51.

> You must know that even if you were the wisest man in respect to the true knowledge of God, you break the bond between you and God whenever you turn your thoughts entirely to the mundane or to any business. You are then not with God, and He is not with you, for that relation between you and Him is actually interrupted during those moments. The righteous were therefore particular to restrict the time in which they could not meditate upon Hashem, and cautioned others about it: "Let not your minds be vacant from reflections upon God." In this same sense, Dovid said, "I have set Hashem always before me. Because He is at my right hand, I shall not be moved."[25] That is to say, "I do not turn my thoughts away from God. He is like my right hand, which I do not forget even for a moment. Therefore, I shall not be moved, I shall not fail…"

The Rambam's powerful words teach us that it is not enough to think about Hashem once in a while. A person's relationship with Hashem depends on how connected his mind is with Him. Because this is so fundamental to serving Hashem, the concept is hinted at right at the beginning of *Shir HaShirim*.

It is noteworthy that at the very beginning of the *Shulchan Aruch*,[26] the Rema quotes from the continuation of this passage of the Rambam, and enjoins us to think about Hashem constantly:

> "I have set Hashem before me constantly." This is a major principle in the Torah, and one of the virtues of the righteous who walk before Hashem. For a person's way of sitting, his movements, and his dealings while he is alone in his house, are not like his way of sitting, his movements, and his dealings when he is in the presence of a great king. Nor are his speech and uninhibited talk with members of his household and relatives like his speech when in a royal audience. All the more so when one takes to heart that the Great King, the Holy One, blessed is He, whose glory fills the earth, is standing over him and watching his actions, as it is written: "Can a man hide in concealment so that I will not see him? says Hashem."[27] [When he does take this to heart,] he

---

25 *Tehillim* 16:8.
26 *Orach Chaim* 1:1.
27 *Yirmeyahu* 23:24.

immediately acquires awe, subservience, and dread of Hashem, May He be blessed..."

In short, this verse — the first one spoken by *Klal Yisrael* in *Shir HaShirim* — introduces the kind of close relationship we are supposed to desire with Hashem. It is not surprising then, that creating this bond with Hashem is echoed in the very first halachah of the *Shulchan Aruch*.

WITH THE KISSES

The Vilna Gaon also points out that the word "kisses" is plural. He applies the accepted rule that an unspecified plural number refers to two — two kisses, in this case.[28] But what are we to make of *yishakeini* ("He should kiss me"), which seems to indicate a single act of kissing?! The answer lies in the symbolism. These two kisses, the Vilna Gaon tells us, represent the first two of the Ten Commandments which we heard directly from Hashem's mouth. That is why they are referred to as "the kisses of His mouth." And both of these kisses together created that feeling of closeness that we felt at Har Sinai. Since it is the combination of the two commandments which created one feeling of closeness, the verse uses a verb that suggests a single act of kissing.

From the comment of the Vilna Gaon, we learn that closeness to Hashem is based on the combination of these two commandments: 1) To believe in Hashem, and 2) Not to follow other gods.

It is easy for us to connect to the first commandment. We know that we must think about Hashem and believe that He is the Master of the universe, etc. However, the second commandment — not to believe in other gods — seems not to be applicable to us since we have no inclination to believe in other powers. Furthermore, it is difficult to understand how observing this commandment helps create closeness to Hashem.

As we noted earlier, the greatest sense of closeness a person can have with another is through knowing his or her thoughts and feelings. By the same token, when we allow the values and wishes of other cultures free entry into our minds, we destroy our ability to connect to Hashem. The command to believe in Hashem involves more than thinking about His existence once in a lifetime. Rather, it requires us to constantly be aware of Hashem's Presence. Furthermore, the command not to follow other gods requires us to guard ourselves against the influence of any culture that pulls us away from thinking about Hashem. This requirement is applicable today as well. Thus, if we observe the first two of the Ten Commandments by clearing our mind of alien cultures and keeping it

---

28 See *Yoma* 62b.

filled with thoughts about Hashem, we will feel that special closeness to Hashem that we felt at Har Sinai.[29]

FOR YOUR LOVE IS BETTER THAN WINE

Here in the second half of the verse, *Klal Yisrael* speaks of how precious Hashem's love is to them. Wine is symbolic of a grand feast, of which it plays a central role.[30] Therefore, *Klal Yisrael* is saying that even the greatest feast or any other earthly pleasure does not compare to the pleasure of closeness to Hashem.

Wine also rejoices the spirit, as does the love of Hashem. But there is a crucial difference. Wine stimulates the body, thereby awakening the spirit. In contrast, the love of Hashem stimulates the soul, thereby bringing pleasure to the body. The temporary joy caused by wine soon leaves one feeling empty because the spirit was not filled, while the love of Hashem fills the spirit with long-lasting joy. Indeed, "Your love is better than wine."[31]

Rashi notes that the closeness *Klal Yisrael* is talking about is the love they feel through learning Torah. This love — which is the same love we felt at Har Sinai — is more precious that any earthly pleasures.

Rabbi Moshe Shmuel Shapiro, *zt"l*, wrote that without Rashi's clarification, we would have thought that while *Klal Yisrael* felt this closeness to Hashem at Har Sinai, we cannot expect to feel that same love today when we learn Torah. Fortunately, that is not the case. When we learn Torah today as well, it remains more precious to us than all other worldly pleasures. Every time a person learns Torah, he is able to reignite that feeling of closeness to Hashem on a small-scale that we all felt at Har Sinai.[32]

The love that great people have felt for the Torah is illustrated in myriad true stories and accounts. This beautiful verse vividly evokes this love. Full appreciation of this verse — and indeed every verse in *Shir HaShirim* — comes not just by understanding it, but also by feeling the emotions that accompany it.

---

29 Rabbi Moshe Feinstein, *zt"l*, wrote that he was able to reach the truth in Torah because he never soaked up any *goyishe* ideas (*Iggros Moshe, Even Ha'Ezer*, II:11).

30 Rashi.

31 Malbim.

32 *Zehav MiSheva*. Elaborating on the verse "Hashem gives wisdom *from His mouth*" (*Mishlei* 2:6) by way of analogy, the Gemara says that a king may sometimes invite his servants to a meal prepared by his workers, but he will share that which he himself eats with his closest friends (*Niddah* 70b). Similarly, Hashem personally gives the wisdom of Torah to His closest "friends," the Jewish People. This is why the wisdom of Torah reawakens closeness with Hashem. When He gives wisdom, He gives of Himself. That which He "enjoys," *ki'veyachol*, He shares with us. This also explains why good *middos* are essential for the acquisition of Torah (as expounded in the *Pirkei Avos* 6:6). Since learning Torah binds us to Hashem, only someone who is truly righteous is worthy of this union.

FOR YOUR LOVE IS BETTER THAN WINE

When a person receives a gift, there are two elements that give him joy: the value of the gift and the love represented by the gift. The quality of the relationship will determine which is more important. In a very loving relationship, the love behind the gift is far more important than the value of the gift. In this verse, *Klal Yisrael* describes Hashem showering them with pleasures, symbolized by wine, and declare: "Your love," i.e., the love You show us, "is more precious than the pleasures You give us because Your love is the most important thing we aspire to."[33]

FOR YOUR LOVE IS BETTER THAN WINE

The Hebrew word for "Your love" (*dodecha*) can also mean "those who love You." Thus, we find *Chazal*[34] explaining this verse homiletically as follows: "For those who love You[35] [i.e., the words of the Sages who love You] are more precious than wine [i.e., words of Torah, symbolized by wine]. But how can this be?! Surely the words of Torah given by Hashem are greater than the words of the *talmidei chachamim* who add to the Torah from their own understanding? Rabbeinu Yonah explains that the laws of *Chazal* were generally instituted to keep us away from sin. They established fences and safeguards for the laws of the Torah so that we would not come to stumble and sin inadvertently. When we observe their enactments, we demonstrate how careful we are being in our service of Hashem. It shows how concerned we are to avoid sin. We thus demonstrate that we are truly fearful of Hashem in a way that observing the actual laws of the Torah does not. Therefore, with regard to fear of Hashem — which is one of the highest levels of greatness a person can achieve— observing the laws of *Chazal* is greater than observing the laws of the Torah itself.[36]

---

33 *Ohr Yahel, Shevevei Ohr.*

34 In a number of places, e.g., *Avodah Zarah* 35b.

35 The word *dodim* in this verse was translated above simply as "love." But this word (which appears many times in *Shir HaShirim*) actually has several meanings. The Torah Temimah shows that it is used in three distinct ways: as a relative (e.g., *Vayikra* 25:19); as a friend/beloved (e.g., *Shir HaShirim* 5:1); and as a loving act (e.g., *Mishlei* 7:18).
Basing itself on the symbolic meaning of "wine" as Torah, the Midrash on this verse says that "words of Torah are related to each other, similar to each other, and love each other." The Midrash is drawing on all three meanings of the word *dodim* (here, as *dodecha*) to teach us that the words of Torah enhance each other and that learning one subject well increases the understanding and the love for others.

36 *Avos* 1:1 and *Shaarei Teshuvah* 3:7.

לְרֵיחַ שְׁמָנֶיךָ טוֹבִים, שֶׁמֶן תּוּרַק שְׁמֶךָ; עַל כֵּן עֲלָמוֹת אֲהֵבוּךָ. ג 3

Your pleasant fragrance is like the smell of good oils; Your fame is like poured perfume; therefore, young maidens fell in love with You.

Allegorical Translation — When Your good Name spread to the ends of the earth through Your miraculous deeds when You took us out of Egypt, then Your Name was praised by all. People of other nations thus came to convert to be part of Your nation.

Subject of the Verse — *Klal Yisrael* is praising Hashem.

Mashal — The wife praises her husband's pleasant smell, and declares that even his memory (i.e., his fame) was so pleasurable that other maidens fell in love with him and desired him. Not only did she love him, but so did all those who came in contact with him.

Nimshal — *Klal Yisrael* continues speaking, reminiscing about the greatness of Hashem. They liken Hashem's good name to a good fragrance and poured perfume.[37] This means that awareness of Hashem's miraculous deeds spread throughout the world and people everywhere were amazed and drawn to Hashem. *Klal Yisrael* add that not only do they love Hashem, but that even the other nations do as well. The other nations are referred to as "maidens," girls not chosen for marriage. Just as a husband chooses his wife from among all the maidens, so, too, Hashem chose *Klal Yisrael* from among all the nations. On some level, the other nations compete with *Klal Yisrael* for Hashem's love just as the maidens compete with the wife for the husband's attention. This means that not only *Klal Yisrael* love Hashem, as they said in the earlier verse, but other nations do as well.

YOUR PLEASANT FRAGRANCE IS LIKE THE SMELL OF GOOD OILS.

The wife, i.e., *Klal Yisrael*, is saying that Hashem's Name has spread far and wide, like sweet-smelling oil. This resulted in people from the other nations coming to love Hashem. To illustrate this, Rashi brings the examples of Yisro and Rachav who ended up converting to Judaism.

---

37 When perfume is poured from bottle to bottle, it gives off a pleasant smell (Rashi).

Both in the Mashal and in the Nimshal, the focus is not on the other maidens/nations who are attracted to Hashem. That other nations came to serve Him as well is merely an indication of the greatness of the husband/Hashem.

Let us note how the metaphor changes here from wine to perfume. *Klal Yisrael*'s love for Hashem in the previous verse was compared to wine. In this verse, which speaks of the nations' appreciation of Hashem, the verse uses the metaphors of good-smelling oil/perfumes to praise Hashem. There is a fascinating insight behind this switch. Consider the salient difference between enjoying wine and enjoying perfume. Only the person who is drinking the wine gets to enjoy it and knows how good it tastes. In contrast, the fragrance of perfume spreads through the air, and anyone in the vicinity can inhale and enjoy it.[38] Hashem pours love and kindness over *Klal Yisrael* for them to enjoy. They enjoy this goodness because Hashem has given it to them directly. Hashem created the world for *Klal Yisrael*, and all the kindness is given directly to us like a person pouring someone a cup of wine for him to enjoy. To the nations, however, Hashem does not give direct pleasures. This means that the pleasures they receive were not intended directly for them. Rather, they enjoy Hashem's goodness by being "in the vicinity" — being in this world which Hashem created, like a person who enjoys the smell of a good perfume worn by someone else.[39] In the allegory as well, the husband is not going to give good wine to other women even though they may enjoy the pleasant fragrance emanating from him.

In other words, Hashem created the world and all of its goodness for *Klal Yisrael*; the other nations get to enjoy it by also being in this world. The closer they get to *Klal Yisrael*, the more they benefit.

YOUR PLEASANT FRAGRANCE...YOUR FAME IS LIKE POURED PERFUME.

At first glance, the metaphors of this verse may seem repetitive. There is, however, a crucial difference between a good fragrance and a good perfume. Although a fragrance may be very pleasant, it lacks permanence. Perfume, in contrast, has permanence; it is something tangible. The Midrash teaches that the "pleasant fragrance" alludes to the Avos, whose exemplary conduct made the world aware of Hashem's "pleasant fragrance," and the "poured perfume" alludes to *Klal Yisrael*, who spread the name of Hashem like flowing perfume. The Midrash seems to be saying that *Klal Yisrael* is, at

---

38   Incidentally, this is why it is immodest for a woman to put on too much perfume. The result of doing so is that she draws the attention of all those around her.

39   Rashi (*Shemos* 16:21) tells us how when the manna would melt and become a liquid, the deer would drink from it. Gentiles in the area would hunt the deer, and thus get a small taste of what the manna was like. This was a tangible example of how heathen nations would receive secondary benefit from the beautiful smells of *Klal Yisrael*.

least in this aspect of permanence, greater than the Avos. What does this mean?

Although the Avos, and especially Avraham Avinu, spent a lot of time traveling and publicizing the name of Hashem to the world, we do not do this. The Ramban explains that until there was a nation that served Hashem, the way to publicize His name was by circulating among people and teaching them about the existence of God and how wonderful it is to serve Him. But once there is a nation serving Him, the belief in God is publicized through their actual existence and conduct.[40] In a sense, the Avos were the concept of, and the inspiration for, serving Hashem, and we are the practical application.

This is a bit like someone who wishes to market a new product. Since no one has heard of it, he has to publicize it. But once people know about the product and a significant number of people begin using it, the best way to push it further is by showing how users of the product are benefiting from it. If, however, those using the product are disappointed, no amount of explaining the theory behind the product and how good it is will counteract consumer disappointment. The Avos were teaching the world a new way of living, i.e., serving Hashem. Once there was a nation serving Hashem, then the world looked to see what those people were doing. They were able to see for themselves how much better off *Klal Yisrael* was as a result of serving Hashem, how much holier, greater, happier and more successful they were in so many different ways.[41] Through their very essence and existence, *Klal Yisrael* declare the greatness of Hashem to the world. This is a constant obligation. It is our duty to make sure that our conduct reflects what serving Hashem is truly about, and to thereby spread Hashem's "beautiful fragrance."[42]

The verse is telling us how the nations of the world were attracted to Hashem. "Your pleasant fragrance" refers to the Avos who spread the good fragrance of Hashem with their teaching. "Your fame is like poured perfume" refers to *Klal Yisrael*. *Klal Yisrael* actually lives according to Hashem's ways, so they are likened to tangible good perfume that constantly produces a good smell.[43]

---

40 *Bereishis* 12:8, *s.v. vayikra b'shem Hashem*.

41 Because the Avos served Hashem as individuals, they could not model this. Furthermore, a lot of people doing something has a much greater influence than individuals doing it. (See Ramban, ibid.)

42 A good example of this is Shimon ben Shatach's returning a diamond he found on a donkey he had bought from an Arab. His honesty prompted the Arab to exclaim, "Blessed is the God of the Jews!" (Talmud Yerushalmi, *Bava Metzia* 2:5). There was no need to teach the Arab about the existence of Hashem and the importance of serving Him because he could see the greatness of Hashem through those who serve Him.

43 There is another reason why *Klal Yisrael* is likened to good-smelling oil. Oil does not mix with other liquids. Even if one mixes oil with water, the oil will separate and rise to the top. Likewise, we remain apart from, and higher than, the other nations even while we live among them.

1:4 ETERNAL LOVE

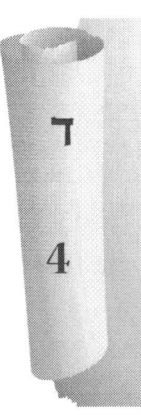

> מָשְׁכֵנִי אַחֲרֶיךָ נָּרוּצָה, הֱבִיאַנִי הַמֶּלֶךְ חֲדָרָיו, נָגִילָה וְנִשְׂמְחָה בָּךְ;
> נַזְכִּירָה דֹדֶיךָ מִיַּיִן, מֵישָׁרִים אֲהֵבוּךָ.
>
> **ד**
> **4.**
>
> *You drew me, and we ran[44] after You.[45] The King brought me into His chambers. We are glad and we rejoice in [our relationship with] You. We recall Your love [and it is more precious to us than] wine. They loved You with a straightforward love.*

Allegorical Translation — When You took us out of Egypt, You merely hinted to us to come and join You, yet we immediately ran after You into the harsh and barren desert without taking time to prepare provisions. There in the desert, You brought us into Your canopy of clouds. Even now, when we are in exile, we still rejoice over our relationship and the love we have with You. We remember that Your love is more precious than any pleasure. And we remember the strong and true love our forefathers displayed to You.

Subject of the Verse — *Klal Yisrael* is describing their own great love and devotion to Hashem.

Mashal — The wife describes the beginning of her relationship with her husband, how loyal and devoted she was to him then. She declares that even after all the events that threatened to compromise their relationship, it is still strong, and their love is still the best thing that ever happened to them.

Nimshal — *Klal Yisrael* is still speaking in this verse. According to Rashi, this verse is describing a number of events. The first event is that *Klal Yisrael* came rushing out of Egypt to follow Hashem even before they had prepared provisions for the journey. This is the beginning of the verse, "You drew me, and we ran after You."

---

44 A question arises from the seeming contradiction in this verse: "You drew me," and "we ran." The first phrase suggests that Hashem was making the effort to draw us to Him while the second phrase suggests that we eagerly ran towards Him without any prompting from Hashem. The many explanations of this verse all resolve this fundamental question, each one in its own way.

45 The *Yalkut Me'am Lo'ez* explains these words differently from Rashi (as presented in our allegorical translation), using the following Mashal of a decent person who fell in with a group of robbers. One day, he met an old friend and said to him wistfully, "If only I would get caught." His friend replied, "That's a strange request for a robber!" Answered the robber, "I made a terrible mistake joining this group, but now I can't leave them because I am so entangled in all of their dealings. If only I would get caught, I would gladly leave them!"
Similarly, *Klal Yisrael* is trapped by the *yetzer ha'ra*. They wish that Hashem would pull them out of its hold even just a little, and then they would come running. The opening of the verse, then, means. "You draw me out, and we will run after You because we are so happy to leave the *yetzer ha'ra* behind." Although this is not the simple meaning of the words, there is a lot of truth in it.

The verse goes on to describe how Hashem brought *Klal Yisrael* "into His chambers." That is an allusion to the heavenly clouds⁴⁶ which Hashem provided to shelter them in the desert. The verse moves on to the period of exile, where *Klal Yisrael* declare that despite being sent away, that "we [still] rejoice in [our relationship with] Him. We recall Your love [and it is more precious to us than] wine." Finally, *Klal Yisrael* declare that their love is sincere, true and straightforward.⁴⁷

YOU DREW ME, AND WE RAN...

Although all the nations are attracted to Hashem, as we learn in the previous verse, Shlomo HaMelech proceeds to point out that the love and devotion we have for Him are of a completely different caliber, being far greater than the superficial love and devotion of any other nation. This verse now mentions the various actions and behaviors that set our love apart from that of the other nations. This verse can also be seen as answering a question that arises from the previous one, which describes how all the nations are drawn to Hashem. In what way are we better than the other nations who are attracted to Hashem, and how is our relationship with Hashem superior to theirs?⁴⁸

The basic question to be asked on this verse is: What is the deeper connection between the events and other elements spotlighted here? But first, let us examine each section of the verse.

The verse begins by describing *Klal Yisrael* leaving Egypt hurriedly. They followed Hashem into the desert, ignoring all the dangers involved. This showed a tremendously high level of trust and love. We have to think a bit about what that means. Imagine taking a whole family into the scorching desert, where there is no water, no food, and no shelter — only snakes and scorpions as well as other enemies of flesh and blood.⁴⁹ *Klal Yisrael* went unquestioningly. Although, later, they did complain a number of times, we

---

46   Rashi.

47   Rashi.

48   One of the challenges of learning *Shir HaShirim* properly is to be able to see how the verses flow and continue from one another. We have tried to address this issue when it arises, as here.

49   To get a better sense of this, think how much money a government must spend to support its troops in a foreign country as the American government did in recent years providing top conditions for their soldiers in Iraq even though they were all young and healthy. But young strong men were not the only ones to leave Egypt. The whole of *Klal Yisrael*, including babies and the elderly, went as well.
Another way to appreciate this is to think about how many preparations we make before going on even a short trip — usually to a place fully stocked with all the necessities. And then contrast this with *Klal Yisrael* travelling into a desolate and barren desert for a very long journey with their entire families as soon as Hashem told them to. They did not even prepare bread! Indeed, we can exploit the occasion of onerous packing for a trip to remind ourselves of the greatness of *Klal Yisrael*.

must see this in perspective. Generally speaking, the vast majority of the nation showed genuine trust in and loyalty to Hashem most of the time.

The next part of the verse describes how Hashem took *Klal Yisrael* into His personal chambers inside the Clouds of Glory (*Ananei HaKavod*). Surrounded by these holy clouds, *Klal Yisrael* felt as if they were inside a king's resplendent private suite.[50] Usually a king only invites his ministers and other VIPs to his main headquarters, but *Klal Yisrael* was invited to His most private quarters. It was like moving into the private rooms of Buckingham Palace or the White House. In fact, it was much more than that. The Yom Tov of Sukkos is based on this wonderful experience. Again, without thinking a little about the loving feeling we felt then, the power of the verse will not be appreciated.

The verse continues, "We are glad and we rejoice in [our relationship with] You." The emphasis here is that we get joy only from the love of Hashem. The side benefits of the relationship, for example, do not interest us.

The verse carries on describing how *Klal Yisrael* feel about Hashem's love, "We recall Your love [and it is more precious to us than] wine." Even though we have been in exile for so many years, and Hashem's love seems to be a distant memory, the memory of His love is more precious than anything else.[51] This is clearly illustrated when we answer the question: When are *Klal Yisrael* truly happy? We find our true joy on Yom Tov, when we reminisce about Hashem's love, when we learn Torah which connects us to

---

[50] In the previous verse, we noted that the other nations get secondary pleasure from the good perfumes. In this verse, we find *Klal Yisrael* entering Hashem's inner chambers and enjoying the good perfumes firsthand.

[51] The *Midrash Rabbah* (on this verse) tells the true story of a couple who had no children for many years. They went to consult Rabbi Shimon bar Yochai, who told them that they had no choice but to get divorced. However, he advised them that since they still loved each other, they should not get divorced out of anger. Rather, they should throw a party to celebrate the good times they had shared, similar to the party they made when they got married.

At the beautiful party they made at Rabbi Shimon's suggestion, the husband generously and lovingly said to his wife, "Choose anything you want to take from my chambers as a departing gift." The wife instructed her servants that when her husband fell asleep, they should move him to where she would now be living.

When he woke up in a strange place, he asked his wife what had happened. She answered, "You said I could choose anything for a farewell gift, so I chose you. I do not want to get divorced!"

They went back to Rabbi Shimon bar Yochai and told him what happened. He was so impressed that he told them that they did not need to get divorced, and that he would daven for them to have children. Sure enough, his *tefillah* was effective, and they had children!

Now, two obvious questions arise from this story: Why did Rabbi Shimon bar Yochai not daven the first time around, and what does this story have to do with this verse? The Kol Yaffe suggests that Rabbi Shimon originally felt that since Hashem did not give them children, they did not deserve them, and thus they should get divorced. But when he saw the wife's devotion, he concluded that the devotion alone would be enough of a merit for them to have children, and thus they did not need to separate. From the story, we see the power of devotion. Similarly, we say to Hashem here that all we want is His love. We hope that our devotion will give us the merit to earn His love. This explanation fits in beautifully with the flow of the verse. "The King brought me into His chambers [where everything is available, and we could take what we want, yet] we are glad and we rejoice in [our relationship with] Him [and all we chose was His love]." Therefore, we ask that [just as seen in the story from the Midrash, in the great merit of this devotion to Hashem,] He will grant us His wonderful love.

Him, and when we celebrate a *simchah*, which is a time for us to contemplate how kind Hashem is to us and how He is still looking after us.[52] Even in exile, we are happy on these occasions that we are Hashem's nation.

The verse concludes that our ancestors and ourselves have had a true and sincere love for Hashem: "They have loved You with a straightforward love."

As we mentioned, this is the third consecutive verse of singing to Hashem by *Klal Yisrael*. After they declare their yearning for Hashem and note that Hashem is loved by all nations, *Klal Yisrael* emphasizes how their love for Hashem is greater and completely different from that of any other nation. Let us try to understand why this is so.

On a very basic level, there are two types of relationships. One is based on mutual gain, like a business partnership. Each partner has his own interests in mind, but they both appreciate that it is to their own benefit to have a relationship with the other side. The second type is based on love, not personal benefit. In a marriage, for example, each spouse genuinely and unselfishly cares about the other one's welfare. This is the type of relationship *Klal Yisrael* has with Hashem. In contrast, the other nations only have a relationship with Hashem based on mutual benefit.

That *Klal Yisrael* has unconditional love for Hashem is seen in a number of sources. For example, when Shlomo HaMelech built the Beis HaMikdash, he davened that the prayers of a Jew should be answered only if he deserves it, but the prayers of a non-Jew should always be answered. He understood that a Jew would continue serving Hashem regardless of whether or not Hashem gives him all that he wants, but a non-Jew would not.[53] Shlomo HaMelech wanted everyone to honor the Beis HaMikdash and realized that unless a non-Jew gets what he asks for, he would snub Hashem and the Beis HaMikdash, but a Jewish person would not. This is hinted at in the previous verse describing the nations attraction to Hashem: "Your fragrance is like *good* oils." The other nations love Hashem when He provides them with good things. But if they feel that He is no longer giving them good things, they stop loving Him. They are only willing to accept good from Hashem.[54] *Klal Yisrael*, however, love Hashem and serve Him regardless of what happens to them.[55]

---

52 There is no shortage of remarkable documentation showing the Jews suffering terrible poverty in the ghettos yet being truly happy on Shabbos and Yom Tov or in shul through feeling Hashem's love.

53 See *Melachim I* 8:43, and Rashi there.

54 See Seforno who points this out in commenting on this verse.

55 The Midrash (*Midrash Rabbah, Bereishis* 89:4) notes that in the dreams Pharaoh wanted Yosef to interpret, he was standing *on* the Nile (*Bereishis* 41:1). Yaakov, however, dreamed that Hashem was standing *over* him (28:13). The Midrash comments on the contrast: The wicked stand on (or over) their gods (the Nile being one of the gods worshipped by the Egyptians), unlike the righteous, whose God stands *over* them. The positioning suggests that the wicked see serving their gods as a way of getting what they want and need. Thus, they stand on them as if their gods are essentially a steppingstone for success, or at least a way of realizing their aspirations. The righteous, however, serve Hashem, and

This unconditional love is the underlying message of the entire verse. The verse starts with *Klal Yisrael* saying that they hurried after Hashem into the desert before He had prepared their needs. This was an act of showing love, regardless of personal gain. When a person enters a business deal, he makes sure that there is a mutual commitment. Otherwise, he may find himself investing and doing the lion's share of the work. In a relationship of love, however, the partners do not constantly check to see who is doing more. Indeed, it often happens that one spouse has to do much more for the other. Yet, if it is a good marriage, this will not diminish the love — it might even enhance it. This would certainly *not* be the case in a business partnership! *Klal Yisrael*'s hurrying into the desert after Hashem was a display of their pure love.[56] Without knowing how much Hashem would do for them, they were happy to follow Him.

The verse goes on to tell us that Hashem brought *Klal Yisrael* into His personal chambers. Again, this is normal behavior for a relationship of love, not a business partnership. When there is no love, one does not reveal personal matters. Personal matters are not part of such a limited relationship, and thus there is no reason to reveal them. On the contrary, partners are often wary about revealing such things to one another lest the information later be used against them. In contrast, Hashem brings *Klal Yisrael* into His personal chambers like a husband does his wife. Since he wants his wife to know him and he trusts her, he shares even the most secret intimate aspects of himself, even things that may make him vulnerable. Similarly, Hashem trusts us, *ki'veyachol*, and wants us to be as close as possible to Him. That is why He brought us into His innermost chambers.

The verse continues: "We are glad and we rejoice in [our relationship to] You." We find joy only in Hashem's love; other things do not interest us. In a business partnership, the main interest of each party is the benefit he gains from the relationship. The relationship

---

are thus willing to "bear His burden," *ki'veyachol*, knowing that their purpose and success are found in serving Him. Thus, the Torah describes Hashem as standing, *ki'veyachol*, over (or on) them.

56 While *Sefer Yirmeyahu* is full of criticism of *Klal Yisrael* and prophecies impending doom if they fail to repent, the prophet Yirmeyahu says clearly right at the outset that *Klal Yisrael* is holy and special to Hashem, and that He will eventually punish harshly those who harm them. Why is *Klal Yisrael* so special to Hashem? This is because Hashem Himself declares that they followed Him into the desert after the Exodus from Egypt:

"...I remember...the affection of your youth, the love [you showed at the time] of your wedding; how you followed Me into the wilderness, into a land that was not sown." *Klal Yisrael* is Hashem's holy portion, His first fruits. All those who consume [them] shall be held culpable; evil shall come upon them, says Hashem. (*Yirmeyahu* 2:2-3)

This is a beautiful and vivid evocation of *Klal Yisrael*'s greatness in following Hashem into the desert – an act of love, like a wife following her husband. It was motivated purely by love, not the expectation of personal gain. *Klal Yisrael* thus demonstrated their selfless devotion to Hashem. For His part, Hashem promised that their love would be reciprocated and that they would never be completely rejected, even when they deserve to be punished. This is *middah k'negged middah* (measure for measure). Since we, *Klal Yisrael*, acted with devotion above and beyond the letter of the law, Hashem will treat us more mercifully than the law dictates.

itself is not important. In a relationship of love, however, the opposite is true. The side benefits — such as a delicious meal a wife might prepare for her husband, or a magnificent gift a husband might buy for his wife — do not compare with the relationship itself. Here we declare that we rejoice in Hashem, not in the benefits we gain from Him.

The verse goes on to describe how *Klal Yisrael* remember Hashem's love. When a business partnership dissolves, it is natural for the partners to move on and start over again. There is no reason to recall the actual relationship since it was based simply on the benefits that would accrue from it. Once the relationship is finished, there is no reason that the memory of the relationship should stir any emotions. In contrast, a loving relationship stirs up many blissful and exciting feelings long after the relationship has concluded. Therefore, even many years after Hashem sent us away, we remember His precious love with longing. It is like the love of a wife who truly loved her husband. Even if the relationship comes to end, for whatever reason, the memory of it is never forgotten.

The verse concludes that our love is true and sincere. It is unlike that of business partners. Even when the partners conduct themselves with absolute honesty, the bond is based on self-interest. Not so a relationship of love. *Klal Yisrael*'s love is sincere, true, and straightforward. There are no hidden agendas. This verse encapsulates the special and unique nature of our relationship with Hashem.

THE KING BROUGHT ME INTO HIS CHAMBERS; WE ARE GLAD AND REJOICE IN [OUR RELATIONSHIP WITH] YOU.

Let us take note of a completely different understanding of these words, according to which Shlomo HaMelech is describing a young woman betrothed to a simple commoner. A king who desires her brings her into his palace and tries to dazzle her with his immense wealth and power. But the young woman holds her own. She declares loyally that she rejoices in her relationship with her groom. All the king's efforts to woo her by lavishing wealth on her fail.

According to this interpretation, the king represents the nations who rule over us, and the commoner is Hashem, whose greatness is hidden while we are in exile. The nations seem to dazzle the world with their power and glory, while Hashem does not display His greatness. We declare that even when the heathen nations try to woo us with their wealth and power, we remain loyal to Hashem. The verse would then read this way: "The king [i.e., the powerful nations] brought us [*Klal Yisrael*] into their chambers [to woo us with their wealth]. [But] we are glad and we rejoice (only) in [our relationship with] You, Hashem."

Indeed, it is remarkable how many great Jewish leaders were brought up in the palaces of the nations, yet remained loyal to Hashem and His people. Let us consider a few examples. Yosef was second only to the Egyptian monarch, Pharaoh, yet he spent his time making sure that *Klal Yisrael* would be able to flourish in Egypt. Moshe Rabbeinu left the comforts and pleasures of Pharaoh's palace to see how he could alleviate the pain of his Jewish brethren. Rus left the palace of Moav to join the Jewish People. Esther, while serving as Achashverosh's queen, risked her life to save her people, and heeded Mordechai HaTzaddik's every word. Daniel was a brilliant and gifted minister in the palace of Darius. He could have had the pick of any beautiful woman and even could have had the run of the palace. But because his heart was always meditating on Hashem and as this was his sole pleasure in life, all those temptations meant nothing to him. In later Jewish history, Don Yitzchak Abarbanel left the Spanish king's court, and led the Jewish People into exile after the Expulsion. They and many others[57] demonstrated that all the gold in the world did not blind them from the truth that only loyalty to Hashem is of value.

In our time, while we may not find ourselves in such a situation, we must still learn from this not to be blinded by all that the world has to offer which only serves to distract us from truly serving Hashem. Wealth and success, homes and possessions, and even friends can all pull us far away from what focusing on what is the most valuable asset in our lives: our relationship with Hashem.[58]

ה	5	שְׁחוֹרָה אֲנִי וְנָאוָה, בְּנוֹת יְרוּשָׁלָ‍ִם; כְּאָהֳלֵי קֵדָר, כִּירִיעוֹת שְׁלֹמֹה.
		I am black and I am beautiful, daughters of Jerusalem. [I am as black] as the tents of Kedar, [but I am easily cleansed to be] like the curtains of the Master of Peace.
ו	6	אַל תִּרְאוּנִי שֶׁאֲנִי שְׁחַרְחֹרֶת, שֶׁשֱּׁזָפַתְנִי הַשָּׁמֶשׁ; בְּנֵי אִמִּי נִחֲרוּ בִי, שָׂמֻנִי נֹטֵרָה אֶת הַכְּרָמִים, כַּרְמִי שֶׁלִּי לֹא נָטָרְתִּי.
		Do not look at me [disparagingly] because I am black,[59] for it is the sun that has tanned me. My mother's sons[60] clashed[61] with me; they made me a keeper of their vineyards. My own vineyard, [however,] I did not guard.

---

57 Nechemyah, Chananyah and his friends, to name just a few.

58 Rabbi Avigdor Miller.

59 Generally, the word *shachor* is used for *black*. Here, however, *sh'charchores* (with the middle letters of *shachor* doubled) is used. This word connotes a deep and strong black color (see Rashi on *Vayikra* 13:49). The message is that even when *Klal Yisrael* seem to be very black and sinful, the truth is that their essence is beautiful.

60 This is a reference to other nations, specifically the *eirev rav*. See the following notes.

61 The word נחרו is understood to mean "quarreled" or "clashed" by the Midrash (and Rashi on *Yeshayahu* 55:44, s.v. *hanechorim*). The *Targum*, however, understands it as "caused to be angry," from the root חרון, meaning *anger*. According to this, the meaning of the phrase is: "My mother's sons caused [Hashem] to be angry with me." Other commentators explain the word נחרו to mean "enticed" (Seforno). The general meaning is that others caused *Klal Yisrael* to stray from Hashem by brute force and through their bad influence.

These two verses are to be read and explained together.

Allegorical Translation

5 You nations of the world should realize that we, the Jewish People, should not be disgraced in your eyes. Do not think that Hashem has rejected us completely because of our sins. Even though we are black with sin, we are beautiful due to the great deeds of our forefathers, and also due to some beautiful mitzvos that even we have fulfilled. Even though now we are sullied by sin, like the dirty tents of the Bedouin Arabs, we are easily cleansed to be like the curtains of Hashem.

6 Do not look at me with disdain since I am now black because of my sins. The dark color is only due to the sun and is easily whitened. The people who joined me — the *eirev rav*[62] — clashed with me and made me serve other gods so that I neglected the service of my true God.

Subject of the Verses

Klal Yisrael is speaking to the nations. They justify their few sins, explaining why they do not reflect badly on them, and assert that, in fact, they are extremely beautiful.

Mashal

The wife is speaking to her detractors who think poorly of her because of her dirtiness. She explains and excuses her blackness by saying that it is not her fault and that her dirtiness will not remain for long since she will be cleansed easily.

Nimshal

Let us notice that in both of these verses, *Klal Yisrael* is speaking to the nations (not to Hashem, as in the earlier verses). The other nations are referred to as the "daughters of Yerushalayim." This is because they will come to see Yerushalayim as the capital of the world when Mashiach comes.[63]

Klal Yisrael justifies their ugly appearance, saying that they are intrinsically

---

62 The *eirev rav* was a large group of people of many nationalities, the majority of whom were Egyptians, who joined the Jewish People when they left Egypt. Even though their belief in Hashem prompted them to join His nation, they soon started sinning and proved to be a detrimental influence on *Klal Yisrael*. Here they are referred to as the "sons of my mother" since they "grew up" together with the Jewish People in Egypt.

63 At first glance, it would seem strange to call the heathen nations "daughters of Yerushalayim" simply because they will eventually come to see Yerushalayim as the capital of the world. Why are nations who have caused us so much harm, enslaved us, and influenced us badly entitled to such a complimentary appellation? The short answer is that even when these nations come to recognize Hashem and have reached their highest spiritual level (in the time of Mashiach), we will still be much greater and far more precious to Hashem. This concept requires further elaboration, but the basic idea is that the highest level the nations will ever reach does not come close (in terms of how much Hashem loves them) to the lowest level to which *Klal Yisrael* will ever fall. That is why we say to the nations: even when you will be on the level of the "daughters of Yerushalayim," we are still far more beautiful than you.

beautiful and that their ugliness is only external.

Rashi helps us understand the apparent self-contradictions in these verses, as we shall now see. "I am black, and I am beautiful." Since black is symbolic of ugliness,[64] where is the beauty? Rashi explains that even though we are ugly in some ways, we are also beautiful in other respects. Therefore, the verse needs to be understood this way: Although I look black [in some ways], I am beautiful [in other respects]. "Although [I am as black] as the tents of Kedar [Bedouin tents that are dirty, torn, and ugly, I am easily cleansed and become like] the curtains of the Master of Peace." The "Master of Peace" is an allusion to Hashem, and these curtains are the beautiful curtains of the Mishkan, the house of Hashem.[65] "Do not look [down] at me [disparagingly] because I am black [because this is not my real appearance], for it is the sun that has tanned me." "My mother's sons" — i.e., all the other nations — hated me and made me look after their vineyards. I was thus unable to take proper care of my own vineyard. The "vineyard" symbolizes a provider.[66] The sense is that we had to serve the other nations' gods — i.e., engage in idol worship — so we were not able to serve Hashem.

I AM BLACK, I AM BEAUTIFUL...

The basic message of these two verses is that *Klal Yisrael* is truly beautiful. In a sense, this is the message of the entire megillah. If we contemplate these inspiring verses, we may well be overcome with emotion about how, even when *Klal Yisrael* seems ugly, they are indeed very beautiful. Indeed, the stories about Jews who seemed to be totally evil but who suddenly displayed a noble characteristic or did something wonderful, derive their inspiration from these verses which teach that there is no such thing as a truly ugly Jewish person. His inner core of goodness remains forever uncontaminated. If there is ugliness, it is no more than skin deep, or it has come from the influence of others. Since it is not an original part of the Jew's soul, the blackness can be removed

---

64 The color black is being used symbolically here and in no way suggests that those who have dark skin are sinful or dirty. As is well known, the color black is often used to convey denigration, as in the expression, "so-and-so *blackened* my name." The beauty of a person's soul, not the color of his skin, is the true measure of his worth.

65 See Alshich. The Midrash and the Ramban, however, consider this an allusion to the beautiful blue skies, Hashem's "curtains" around the world. Either way, the meaning is essentially the same. The tents of the Bedouins, which are never washed and stand in the open deserts together with their animals, are symbolic of ugliness and dirt. In contrast, Hashem's curtains — either the beautiful clear skies or the exquisite and magnificent curtains of the Mishkan — are symbolic of beauty and cleanliness.

66 Just as a vineyard provides wealth and pleasure, so do the pagan gods (in the mistaken view of the pagan) provide for their adherents.

quickly and easily, as the verse teaches.

We find that Yaakov Avinu conveyed the same idea. When rebuking his sons Shimon and Levi for killing the people of Shechem, he said, "Their weapons are stolen."[67] He meant, as Rashi explains, that while Eisav (and his descendants) are people who kill, killing is not a fundamental part of who you are because you are members of *Klal Yisrael*. You must have stolen the concept from Eisav.[68]

Before we look at these verses in detail, let us note how they connect with the previous verse. In the previous verse, *Klal Yisrael* describes their wonderful relationship with Hashem, and how loyal and devoted they are and have always been. This statement evokes an obvious question: Why do they look so bad if they have such a great connection to Hashem? How come *Klal Yisrael*, the devoted nation, has become black? In other words, why are they not more spiritually beautiful? Hashem chose *Klal Yisrael* to be the "chosen nation, a holy nation," yet they seem to commit plenty of *aveiros*. How can that be?

Indeed, this very important question is asked even nowadays by non-Jews. When people doing *kiruv* work praise the wonderful life of Torah, they, too, may be asked why there are corrupt *frum*[69] Jews. Truth be told, observant Jews sometimes ask this question to themselves.

In these verses, *Klal Yisrael* answers this question. Basically, *Klal Yisrael* has an inner beauty; it is only the external, short-lived ugliness that the nations see. The verses are written allegorically of course, as if they were about a beautiful queen who now looks ugly. The queen is explaining to her friends why she, the great queen who was chosen by the great king, now looks ugly. On the metaphorical level, *Klal Yisrael* is explaining why their spiritual appearance is not as beautiful as would be expected.

I AM BLACK, I AM BEAUTIFUL...

A careful look at these verses reveals that there are really four answers here: 1) While it is true that I look ugly in some ways, I am beautiful in other respects; 2) Even though I look dirty, I am very easily cleansed; 3) I am not really black, but only suntanned; 4)

---

67 *Bereishis* 49:5-6, and Rashi there.

68 See our commentary on 6:11 below.

69 Often these questions are asked not out of a desire to understand, but rather as a way of quieting the questioner's own conscience and justifying his own lack of observance. "If a so-called religious person behaves like that, then I do not have to become religious." The accusations may not even be true but are readily publicized by the anti-religious. Sometimes it is not a religious person who commits a crime, but only someone who appears religious in dress or habit. The question, then, is not "Why did he sin?" but "Why does he pretend to be religious?!" Furthermore, the questions are often unfair or loaded. Be that as it may, the underlying question deserves an answer: Why aren't *Klal Yisrael* as a whole, and religious Jews in particular, looking and behaving better than they do? This is the subject of these two verses.

Because other wicked nations enslaved me, I was unable to take proper care of myself. These answers progressively increase in their scope and power, as will be explained.

Klal Yisrael start by acknowledging a degree of ugliness but insist that there is a lot of beauty as well. The Midrash cites a list of illustrations (some of which Rashi cites as well):

> I may be ugly in my actions, but I am beautiful in the actions of my ancestors who served Hashem with tremendous *mesirus nefesh*. I may be ugly in the sin of the *eigel* (the Golden Calf), but I am beautiful in the acceptance of the Torah and in declaring: "*Na'aseh v'nishma*" ["We will do and we will listen" to all that You command]. I may be ugly in the ongoing complaining in the desert, but I am beautiful in the enthusiasm of building the Mishkan. I may be ugly in the Sin of the Spies, but I am beautiful in the allegiance of Yehoshua and Calev to Hashem. I may be ugly in becoming so absorbed in the mundane during the week, but I am beautiful on Shabbos when I devote myself to the spiritual…

This memorable passage contains many other examples of the greatness of *Klal Yisrael* despite their faults and failures. The message is that while *Klal Yisrael sometimes* act inappropriately, their conduct *often* reflects greatness. While there are *those* who sin, *others* are act righteously. This is applicable today, as well. We find remarkable examples of *Klal Yisrael's* dedication to Hashem. There are many good Jews doing many wonderful deeds. It is true that there are also faults, but the verse is saying: Why focus on the faults when there is so much good?! If we see something which we feel is a demonstration of how "black" we are, we must immediately bring to mind something beautiful about our nation.[70]

In their next answer, *Klal Yisrael* say that although they may be dirty, they are easily cleansed. Even when they do *aveiros*, they are quick to repent. This is symbolic of the ease and the speed with which *Klal Yisrael* often do *teshuvah* (repent). The ability to completely turn their lives around with such speed and sincerity is unique to *Klal Yisrael*. *Chazal* point out this phenomenon in many places. Many great Chassidic stories confirm it as well — true stories about Jews who had no connection to *Yiddishkeit* and

---

[70] This teaching is applicable in all aspects of life. When we see another person in a critical light, we will find, that if we look a little bit more closely, that there is also what to compliment and praise them for. A person has the choice to focus either on what is good or what is bad. The *yetzer ha'ra* has the ability to convince us to focus on one tiny aspect which is bad and ignore the many aspects of good in a person. Criticism is, more often than not, a reflection of the one who is criticizing: He has chosen to look at what is bad rather than at what is generally good.

were filthy from sin. But after a small reminder, such as the blowing of a shofar, they suddenly repented and cast off their old ways. This is what the verse is saying: We may do *aveiros* and look as bad as the Bedouin tents, but we easily repent and cleanse our souls until we are as beautiful as the curtains of the Mishkan.[71] This can be seen today in the waves of *ba'alei teshuvah* who come from spiritual wastelands but made the decision to go to a yeshivah to drink from the wellsprings of Torah.

The reason that we are so easily cleansed, the Maharal notes, is because at heart, every Jewish person wants to do the right thing.[72] When we sin, the evil is only skin deep. Because it is not inherently part of who we are, the "blackness" comes off easily.[73] It is the difference between changing the color of an item from black to white, and just removing a black stain. The former task is extremely difficult, while the latter is relatively easy.[74]

Klal Yisrael's third answer is that we are not really black, but we have become dark because of the sun. We were once beautiful, but since we have been cast into exile, and are now further removed from Hashem's protection,[75] the sun has burned us. The sun is symbolic of outside influences. We have been affected by the wickedness of all of the nations who are outside our camp. The fact is that a person is influenced by his surroundings. The nations have influenced *Klal Yisrael* in many ways and left their mark.

---

71   After the Jewish People sinned through the *eigel hazahav* (Golden Calf), they felt rejected. Even after they repented, they were not sure that Hashem completely forgave them. But when Hashem came and "dwelt" in the Mishkan they had built, they saw this as a clear indication that He had completely forgiven them. (See Rashi on *Shemos* 38:21. He explains that the Mishkan was actually called the "Mishkan of Testimony" because it bore witness to the fact that Hashem forgave *Klal Yisrael* and loved them.) When *Klal Yisrael* would see the curtains of the Mishkan (which was all that could be seen of the Mishkan from the outside), they were reminded of the great power of their own repentance. This explains beautifully why, when they speak of cleansing themselves from sin through repentance, they use the image of the curtains of the Mishkan. "It is true that we have sinned," they exclaim, "but we can become as clean and beautiful as the curtains of the Mishkan which stand in testimony and remind us that Hashem forgave our sins. We are now considered as pure and as beautiful as before!"

72   *Gevuros Hashem*, ch. 8.

73   See our commentary on 5:6 where we mention the Rambam's observation that, deep down, every Jew wants to do the right thing, but this desire is sometimes eclipsed by external factors. This is all part of the message of these verses.

74   The Gemara (*Eruvin* 19a) tells us that even the wicked among the Jewish People will not be burnt in Gehinnom, Tosafos (ibid., *s.v. poishei*) notes an apparent contradiction: Elsewhere in the Gemara (*Chagigah* 27a), we learn that Torah scholars will not be burnt in Gehinnom. This seems to imply that the wicked among the rest of the Jewish People might indeed get burnt. Tosafos explains that the scholar's Torah study ensures that he will not even get singed, whereas a Jewish person without Torah will be punished with superficial burns for his sins. As for the wicked nations, the fires of Gehinnom will consume them. As indicated above, this is due to the fact that since the purpose of Gehinnom is to purify and cleanse people of their sins, the Jewish People, whose sins are only skin deep, only require superficial burning to be cleansed. In marked contrast, the evil people of other nations, whose very essence is black, will be burned completely (*Ashirah Uzo*).

75   This is a continuation of the previous verse. Earlier, we said that Hashem brought us into His chambers where we felt protected. Now we have been thrown out into the sun, and it has debilitated us.

Rashi explains further that when one is born black, there is no chance that things will change. In contrast, a suntan fades on its own after a period of time. This means that we are not intrinsically bad but that there is hope for us. We became blackened by succumbing to outside influences, and with time, we will naturally regain our beauty. When does this happen? The Midrash offers a few different time frames: On Yom Kippur, *Klal Yisrael* look like a wonderful nation, everyone joining together in prayer and unity, and striving to be better. On Shabbos, we all behave better and try to be more holy, donning our beautiful and spiritual Shabbos clothes. There are other times during the year as well when our beauty shines out. Finally, when Mashiach comes — may it be speedily in our days — the entire nation will reveal its true beauty. This proves that we are not truly ugly. If we were, we could never become as beautiful as we are on these special occasions. Indeed, if we today would want to show someone how religious Jews look at their spiritual best, their davening on Yom Kippur or even on any Friday night would a good choice.

In their fourth answer, *Klal Yisrael* point the finger at the nations who now wish to disparage us: "Our condition is actually all *your* fault!" The nations have enslaved us and forced us to look after them and their interests. As a result, we have neglected the way we look and our real interests, i.e., the mitzvos. That is why we have become tarnished. In other words, we always wanted to do the mitzvos and lead a spiritual life, but we were derailed by the cruelty and nastiness of the other nations. Sometimes their cruelty was simply so harsh that we were unable to do mitzvos, and other times their cruelty was directed specifically at preventing us from doing mitzvos. Perhaps, some of the best-known examples are the persecution of the Syrian Greeks during the era of the Second Beis HaMikdash, the Inquisition, and more recently, the suppression of Jewish observance under Communism in the former Soviet Union. Of course, these are hardly the only examples. In the long history of *Klal Yisrael*'s suffering, this has happened in many ways.[76]

The following episode, movingly told by Rabbi Hanoch Teller, illustrates this. A certain *ba'al teshuvah* had himself tattooed with a lewd image back before he became religious. Naturally, he was very embarrassed about it, so he never went to *mikveh*. On Erev

---

76 A more subtle example of this dynamic occurred in the world of business and finance. In the past (especially in the Middle Ages) many heathen nations barred Jews from owning land or working in the professions, forcing many into poverty or into money lending. At the same time, they would mock the poverty of *Klal Yisrael* or criticize the reliance of many Jews on usury as a way of making a living. They would thus claim that Jews were not productive citizens. Now, this may be relatively minor in light of the atrocities that we have suffered, but it is illustrative. The heathen nations force a set of circumstances on the Jewish People and then scorn them for the conduct that is a direct result of their oppressive decrees.

Yom Kippur, however, he felt that he must go. He was very careful when undressing at the *mikveh*, wrapping himself with a towel and making sure not to reveal his body until he was in the water. However, he tripped and fell when he was coming out of the water, and everyone saw the vulgar tattoo. He felt terribly ashamed of himself and was unable to look up at anyone else around him. Then a Jew came up to him and showed him the number that was tattooed on his arm by the Nazis at Auschwitz.

"Look," he said, "those accursed people have not only influenced us, but they have also been able to stamp their ugliness onto our bodies. However, the main thing is that we have been able to put it behind us and not let it stop us from living as good Jews." These warm and comforting words put the *ba'al teshuvah* at ease.

This, then, is the meaning of the verse. We have indeed become less beautiful than what we once were because the nations were able to blacken us.

Klal Yisrael defend themselves with answers that get progressively stronger. At first, they acknowledge their sins but point out that they have also performed many mitzvos. Then they note that even their sins are not enduring because they eventually repent and are easily cleansed. Next, they exonerate themselves even for their brief periods of sinning: "Even our sins are not really our fault, but rather a result of our living among the other nations, and we will naturally revert back to our true beautiful selves." They conclude with a biting accusation that not only were the other nations a bad influence on them, but they also coerced them into going against Hashem.

The Midrash sums up the burden of *Klal Yisael*'s defense with a lengthy parable. We are including it here in abbreviated form:

> A certain black[77] maidservant said to her friend, "Now the king will marry me."
>
> Asked the friend, "What makes you say that?"
>
> Answered the maidservant, "I saw the queen today, and she has chapped hands. What king wants a wife with red hands?! Surely, he will divorce her and marry me!"
>
> Her friend laughed and said, "If you think the king will not want to remain married to his beloved queen because her hands are temporarily unsightly, surely he will not want a mere servant whom he never loved — one who is totally and irreparably ugly!"

Similarly, the Midrash says, the heathen nations claim that Hashem will reject *Klal*

---

77   As mentioned earlier, the color black is merely symbolic of ugliness.

Yisrael on account of their sins and choose them instead. *Klal Yisrael* respond: Hashem will never reject us in favor of you. Our ugliness is only partial and temporary. We will eventually recover our beauty. Besides, Hashem has loved us for many years. But you heathen nations are ugly all over and will remain so.

There is much more that could be written about these verses which speak of the true beauty of *Klal Yisrael* and how quick they are to repent. Suffice it to say that we can draw much inspiration from them. We must always remember to see the good in *Klal Yisrael* and realize that since an evildoer can easily turn around and become good, we must not give up on anyone.[78]

THEY MADE ME A KEEPER OF THEIR VINEYARDS; MY OWN VINEYARD, [HOWEVER,] I DID NOT GUARD.

With these words, we declare that instead of focusing on "our vineyard" — our spiritual growth and our relationship with Hashem — we became a keeper for other nations "vineyards" — for *their* beliefs and interests. Throughout our long exile, many Jews have left the life of Torah and invested their minds and energies in foreign enterprises. The very long list of Jewish Nobel prize winners and famous leaders in the realms of science, innovation, and even revolution (including Communism) is a source of wonder to the world. For us, however, it should sometimes be a source of sadness. Many of these misguided souls could have done so much in *our* vineyards instead of wasting their energies, sometimes in the development of destructive inventions that have actually harmed the Jewish People. We must stop wasting our greatest resource — the Jewish intellect, energy, and lives around the world — and focus on using it for building and maintaining what is important for us: bringing ourselves closer to Hashem.

---

78 The following story bears out these verses in a memorable way. The head of a certain Orthodox Jewish family in early twentieth-century America refused to work on Shabbos even though it meant losing his job every Friday. As a result, his family suffered terrible poverty. They eventually became so poor that they were evicted from their home for not paying their bills. They could not find a place to live until someone graciously let them move into his cellar where his coal was stored. One day, an irreligious, wealthy Jew heard children (who appeared to be blacks from the coal) speaking Yiddish. He could not understand how blacks could speak such good Yiddish. He looked into it and heard their story. He was so horrified that he immediately offered money to their mother. She asked him if he observed Shabbos, but he had to admit that he did not. She thus turned down the money, explaining that if they live this way because of their Shabbos observance, they could not possibly accept money earned on that holy day. The wealthy man told his wife what had happened. She was so moved that she begged her husband to stop working on Shabbos. And he agreed! After that, the poor family was happy and grateful to accept his generosity.

This story shows the true beauty of *Klal Yisrael*. It also shows how quick they are to repent (verse 5). To this family, we can apply the verse: "Do not look at me [disparagingly] because I am black." Their blackness was truly as beautiful and clean as "the curtains of the Master of Peace." And to the wealthy person, we can apply the verse: "[I am as black] as the tents of Kedar, [but I am as easily cleaned] as the curtains…"

> הַגִּידָה לִּי שֶׁאָהֲבָה נַפְשִׁי, אֵיכָה תִרְעֶה, אֵיכָה תַּרְבִּיץ בַּצָּהֳרָיִם;
> שַׁלָּמָה אֶהְיֶה כְּעֹטְיָה, עַל עֶדְרֵי חֲבֵרֶיךָ.
>
> Tell me, You whom my soul loves,[79] where will You [let your flock] graze, where will You make Your flock rest in the heat of the day? Why should I be like one who is shrouded [in mourning] alongside the flocks of Your companions[80]?!

Allegorical Translation — Please tell us, our beloved Hashem, where and how You will look after Your precious nation among all the nations that wish to destroy it? And how will You give the Jewish People respite during the painful *galus*? It is surely not fitting for You that Your nation should be in constant mourning while all the other nations who trust in idols should live in peace and tranquility.

Subject of the Verse — The Jewish People turn to Hashem and ask Him how they will endure the terrible exile.

Mashal — The wife asks her husband how he will take care of the sheep (i.e., their children) in the face of burning heat and wild wolves who wish to devour them. Surely, she says, you also love them and do not wish to see them suffer. Furthermore, would it not be a great humiliation to you if your flock is struggling while all the other flocks are thriving?!

Nimshal — *Klal Yisrael* is asking Hashem how they will survive the exile. In this verse, they are likened to sheep, and the question asked allegorically is: Where will they graze and where will they rest? Noon is the hottest time of the day. It is a very uncomfortable time for the sheep, just as the exile is a very difficult time for *Klal Yisrael*. The verse concludes that if *Klal Yisrael* will not have any safe haven, they will become like one who is veiled, i.e., a mourner. (In former times, mourners would cover their faces.) They will become mourners next to the other nations. That would be a major *chillul Hashem*, a disgrace to Hashem.

---

79   When *Klal Yisrael* speak to Hashem, they do so lovingly. To fully appreciate these verses, we have to try to feel the love they are expressing.

80   This refers to the gods and leaders of the heathen nations who see them as their shepherds and therefore seem like companions of Hashem, the True Shepherd of His nation. The Gemara (*Berachos* 58a) tells us that "Hashem modeled earthly royalty on the Heavenly one." Therefore, the term "companions" is appropriate here because there is some resemblance (*Divrei Yedidya*).

TELL ME, YOU WHOM MY SOUL LOVES...

This plea follows *Klal Yisrael*'s explanation (in the previous verse) that they look sullied due to the detrimental influence and persecution of the other nations. Now *Klal Yisrael* turn to Hashem and ask what they are supposed to do so that the nations will not cause them so much spiritual harm. In other words, "How can we survive the very damaging exile?" This is how this verse is a sequel to the previous one.

Until now, *Klal Yisrael* were likened to Hashem's wife/queen. Now the metaphor changes to Hashem's sheep. That is because the focus now is not Hashem's love, which is symbolized by marriage, but Hashem's protection. *Klal Yisrael* is asking how they can be protected from the ravages of exile. This is symbolized by a shepherd caring for his sheep. Two key points lie behind the symbolism:

1. Sheep are very weak and have no natural way to defend themselves because they lack strong claws and teeth, powerful horns, etc. Since they are so vulnerable, they need a lot of looking after.
2. Sheep are very valuable,[81] and are therefore given extra protection.

In the famous Chapter 23 of *Tehillim*, "*Mizmor l'Dovid, Hashem roi...* — A Psalm of Dovid, Hashem is my Shepherd...," Dovid HaMelech touchingly describes how he felt Hashem's protection. It is not surprising, then, that he speaks of himself as a sheep, and Hashem as the kind, loving shepherd.

TELL ME, YOU WHOM MY SOUL LOVES...

There are really two questions posed here in this verse:

1. Where will the sheep, i.e., *Klal Yisrael*, graze? Or as Rashi expresses it: Where can they eat in safety without being attacked by the wolves?
2. Where will they rest? Or as Rashi expresses it: Where can they escape the heat of the midday sun?

Exile among the nations has always caused two main challenges: 1) surviving the actual danger of the cruel nations trying to harm us, and 2) remaining true to Hashem in the face of the negative influences of both hostile and friendly nations.[82] *Klal Yisrael*'s two questions symbolize the exile's two most formidable difficulties. Fear of the wolves is our fear of suffering from the evil nations who want to destroy us. The sun's heat is

---

81 While nowadays a person's wealth is often gauged by his stock holdings, in Biblical times it was gauged in terms of his flocks. (When the Torah wishes to tell us that someone was wealthy, it mentions that he had a great number of sheep).

82 This dual threat is often mentioned in our sources. We find it expressed, for example in Yaakov's prayer before meeting his brother Esav: "Please save me from my brother, from Esav" (*Bereishis* 32:12). The commentators call attention to the seemingly repetitive way in which Yaakov refers to his brother. They explain that this was a prayer regarding twin dangers: Save me from his influence if he acts towards me in brotherly manner and save me from his ruthlessness is he conducts himself as Esav usually does.

symbolic of the nations' bad influence on us. Just as the sun blackens those exposed to it for too long, so do those who remain under the influence of the nations become sullied (as we also saw in the previous verse).

The Vilna Gaon offers a somewhat different interpretation. He notes that every community has two main needs: living space and food/nourishment. When the Jewish People dwelled in Eretz Yisrael, the Beis HaMikdash was a conduit of blessing and brought them an outpouring of sustenance. The beautiful land of Eretz Yisrael was also a very comfortable dwelling space, able to accommodate a larger and larger population — even stretching bigger when necessary. So, they had enough food and they were able to live in comfort. Once the exile began, however, they lost both. According to the Vilna Gaon, then, this is the meaning of the two questions: "Where will they graze," i.e., "Where will their food come from?" and "Where will they rest," i.e., "Where will *Klal Yisrael* thrive without Eretz Yisrael?"

WHY SHOULD I BE LIKE ONE WHO IS SHROUDED?

The verse concludes with the rhetorical question: "Why should I be like one who is shrouded [in mourning] alongside the flocks of Your companions." *Klal Yisrael* is saying to Hashem: Even if we deserve to suffer in exile because of all our sins, You must help us not fall into humiliation because our disgrace is Your disgrace. The suffering of *Klal Yisrael* brings disgrace to Your name. This is because it causes the people of the world to wonder why only Your flock should be suffering and be "like one who is shrouded in mourning," while all the other "flocks [belonging to] Your companions" (i.e., the other nations who serve other gods) seem to be doing fine. It looks like all the other gods are lavishing success on their nations while You seem to be unable to help Your nation. We are asking for Your help to avoid this huge *chillul Hashem*!

Indeed, this is a classic Jewish prayer: Even if we do not deserve Your help, please look after us for the sake of Your Name.[83]

---

83   Perhaps the most prominent one is to be found in *Tehillim* (115:1-2):
     "Not for us, Hashem, not for us, but rather give honor to Your Name so that [people should be aware of] Your kindness and truth. Why should the nations say, 'Where is their God…'"?

> אִם לֹא תֵדְעִי לָךְ הַיָּפָה בַּנָּשִׁים; צְאִי לָךְ בְּעִקְבֵי הַצֹּאן, וּרְעִי אֶת גְּדִיֹּתַיִךְ עַל מִשְׁכְּנוֹת הָרֹעִים.
>
> **ח**
> **8**
>
> *If you, the most beautiful of women, do not know,[84] go out and follow the flock's tracks. Then [you will be able to] nurture your kid goats [even] among the dwellings of the other shepherds.*

Allegorical Translation — If you, My (Jewish) People, who is the most beautiful of all nations, do not know where to go to be safe from all those who would harm you, contemplate the pathways that your forefathers chose (i.e., their observing My Torah and My mitzvos), and follow in their footsteps. As a reward for doing so, you will be able to nurture your children even among the hostile nations.

Subject of the Verse — Hashem is responding to the question asked by *Klal Yisrael*, advising them how to survive unharmed and even develop in exile.

Mashal — The husband replies to his wife's question, lovingly calling her "the most beautiful of women." He advises her that when the flock gets lost, the best way for it to survive is to follow in the footsteps and tracks made by previous flocks who made it to safety.

Nimshal — Hashem answers the question *Klal Yisrael* asked Him in the previous verse about how to survive the exile. He answers that if they do not know how to live in exile, then they should follow in the footsteps of the flock. This means that they should follow the way of their forefathers. Then Hashem assures *Klal Yisrael* that they will be able to survive the exile even near the other shepherds' tents. "The other shepherds" represent the leaders of other nations that *Klal Yisrael* fear. Hashem is telling *Klal Yisrael* to conduct themselves like those earlier generations who accepted the Torah and observed its mitzvos.[85]

---

84 Rabbi Eliyahu Lopian *zt"l* explains this verse homiletically: "If you…do not know [Torah]," then even if you are "the most beautiful of women" — i.e., even if you look sophisticated and cultured, and are well-mannered — you should "go out." Hashem is telling those outwardly impressive people who lack a Torah-true foundation to leave His Presence.
The Pirchei Aharon (*Bereishis* 27:46) offers a homiletic explanation of his own: "If you do not know who is the most beautiful among women — i.e., you do not know which woman is righteous and spiritually beautiful and which woman is not — go out and follow the tracks of the flock [i.e., the little children]." He explains that a mother has the most influence over her children — more than their father, more than their teachers, and more, even, than their Rabbanim. A truly righteous woman can be identified by the love and *chinuch* she invests in her little children.

85 This is Rashi's approach. See *Shaarei Emunah* by Rabbi Shimshon Pinkus for another interpretation.

THE MOST BEAUTIFUL OF WOMEN

Hashem calls *Klal Yisrael* "the most beautiful of women." The Vilna Gaon explains that here Hashem is endorsing the claim of *Klal Yisrael* in verse 5. They had said that they are truly beautiful, and their blackness is only superficial and easily cleansed. Their dirtiness is not their own, but rather from other nations. Here, Hashem is accepting their justification and affirming that *Klal Yisrael* is truly beautiful. Needless to say, an endorsement from Hashem is the highest form of approval. It should fill us with joy!

FOLLOW THE FLOCK'S TRACKS

The basic message of this verse is that the only way *Klal Yisrael* can survive is by observing the mitzvos. By characterizing this as "following in the footsteps of the [previous] flocks," the verse is adding that the tradition of our forefathers should serve as our guiding light whenever we have a question about how to proceed. Indeed, this verse is an important source for upholding *minhagim* and not changing our way of life.[86] *Chazal* call this concept "*minhag avoseinu b'yadeinu*," the custom of our forefathers is what we have in our hands [to observe].[87]

In his *Derech Eitz HaChaim*, the Ramchal writes that this applies not only to how we conduct ourselves but also to how we think about life: "A person should think every day for a substantial amount of time: What did my forefathers do that made Hashem love them so much? What did Moshe Rabbeinu do? What did all the previous generations do? What did they think about that brought them such success?" We should think a lot about how previous generations conducted themselves in order to learn from them.

To do otherwise is to act like the foolish mountain climber in the following scenario. Imagine a person losing his way while climbing a steep and treacherous mountain. He suddenly sees a path which has many footsteps on it, or he encounters someone who advises him that this is the path which many have used in the past to reach the summit. This should surely bring him a huge sense of relief since he now knows how to proceed. But instead of following this path, the person decides that he will make his own way. Is there a greater foolishness than that?! Since he does not know the way — never having been to the summit — how can he rely on his own judgment?! Unfortunately, there are those who consider themselves cleverer than all those who came before them and try

---

86   The Seforno explains the verse slightly differently than Rashi: "When you do not know [a halachah because the exile's bitterness has caused you to forget it], follow the footsteps [i.e., the accepted *minhag*]." We see this approach in a famous episode recorded in the Gemara (*Pesachim* 66a). Once the Torah leaders were unsure of a law regarding how to carry the knife to slaughter the *korban Pesach* on Shabbos. Hillel advised them to wait and see what the people did!

87   *Shabbos* 35b, among many other instances.

following their own way. We see, unfortunately, that unless they return to the original path, they may fall off some high cliff or become lost from the nation.[88]

NURTURE YOUR KID GOATS

The verse continues, "then [you will be able to] nurture your kid goats." It emphasizes that by following the previous generations, we will be able to nurture the *young*. Upholding tradition is important for everyone. However, it is especially important for the sake of the children. If a child hears derogatory remarks about the ways of our elders or about our precious *minhagim* — even if they relate only to certain details — there is a grave danger that he will not follow in those paths at all. Children are easily influenced and see everything as black or white, good or bad. If we want them to follow in the ways of the Torah, they have to see us respect every aspect of the ways of the Torah, even those we may find difficult. It is healthy for a child to hear from his father, "I do this because this is how my father did it, and how his ancestors did it going back many generations," or "This is the same mitzvah that Moshe Rabbeinu taught us when he came down from Har Sinai." When a father speaks this way, he invests his message about upholding tradition with tremendous power. Furthermore, he demonstrates with pride that we are linked to those previous generations that devoted themselves to Hashem. If, however, a father communicates that he knows better than his father, the child is likely to innovate, feeling that he, too, knows better than his father. That is why the verse says: If you make sure to follow in the footsteps of the *mesorah*, "[you will be able to] nurture [even] your *kid goats* among the dwellings of the other shepherds."

AMONG THE DWELLINGS...

In verse 7, *Klal Yisrael* ask how they will survive in exile among the other nations. Hashem answers here in this verse that they should follow in the ways of the generations that preceded them. What is added by the end of this verse: "then [you will be able to] pasture your kid goats [even] among the dwellings of the other shepherds"? These words drive home the point that especially when we are living among the other nations, we must make sure to keep our traditions. Some misguided people believe that when we are among the other nations, we should loosen up, accept what we can of their conduct,

---

88 In the introduction to his *Chayei Olam*, the Steipler discusses this phenomenon. He says one should ask all those who are looking for a new way (thinking that the old way is wrong): "Do you really consider yourself wiser than all the previous generations who certainly knew of your questions but still followed the traditional path of Torah? You can rely on the Rif, the Rambam, and all the other great Torah leaders who were far wiser than you will ever be and who knew this to be the true path." Those who seek a new path are motivated by arrogance, not by a burning desire to seek the truth. Therefore, the best approach is not to explain or try to prove anything to such people. Their only hope is to acquire some humility. Then the truth will become self-evident to them.

and not show our Jewishness too much so as not to antagonize them — that we should let them think we are just like them. But this verse calls on us to do the opposite. When we find ourselves in close proximity to the other shepherds' tents, we must be especially careful to follow our traditions and continue in the pathways of our forefathers because, in this situation, the danger of being negatively influenced is much greater.[89]

The Alshich notes that the word "*al*," translated here as "among," often means "over" and "above." Understood thus, the verse reads: "Nurture your kid goats *above* the dwellings of the other shepherds." In other words, when we follow the direction our forefathers set for us, we will become so triumphant that even our young and weak will rise above all our enemies.

In short, this verse is not simply telling us the right way to behave. It is telling us that this is the *safe* way to behave. As Rashi explains, if we follow in the footsteps of our ancestors, Hashem will look after us. Our safety does not depend on adapting to the ways of the heathen nations. On the contrary, history has proven that this misguided approach brings destruction upon us.

ט	לְסֻסָתִי בְּרִכְבֵי פַרְעֹה, דִּמִּיתִיךְ רַעְיָתִי.
9	Through My horses [battling] Pharaoh's chariots, I have shown [My love] to you, My dear one.[90]
י	נָאווּ לְחָיַיִךְ בַּתֹּרִים, צַוָּארֵךְ בַּחֲרוּזִים.
10	Your cheeks are beautiful with rows [of jewelry], your neck with strings [of precious stones].
יא	תּוֹרֵי זָהָב נַעֲשֶׂה לָּךְ, עִם נְקֻדּוֹת הַכָּסֶף.
11	We will make for you rows of gold [jewelry] besides engraved pieces of silver jewelry.

---

89   This applies to matters relating to Jewish practice. In contrast, there is much to be said for religious Jews trying to keep a low profile. For example, walking in a non-Jewish main thoroughfare while wearing a *talis* is frowned upon by many great Rabbanim.

90   This reference to the Splitting of the Sea connects with two of the Gemara's explanations (*Shabbos* 133b) of the famous words זה קלי ואנוהו (*Shemos* 15:2) which *Klal Yisrael* sang to Hashem upon crossing the Sea: "This is my God, and I will beautify Him [by using beautiful items when serving Him]"; and "This is my God, and I will try to emulate Him [by being merciful, kind, etc.]" That is because the words דמיתיך רעיתי in this verse can be understood as, "I have displayed [Your beauty] my Beloved [i.e., the beauty of Hashem's mitzvos that *Klal Yisrael* display]" and as, "I [Hashem] have made you similar to Me [i.e., emulating Hashem's merciful traits]." The explanations that follow (above) are encapsulated in these two ideas (*Vezos LeYaakov*).

1:11 ETERNAL LOVE

Allegorical Translation

9 When I, Hashem, gathered My horses (angels) to fight against the chariots of Pharaoh, I showed the world My love for you, *Klal Yisrael*.

10 Through the spoils from the Reed Sea, you have become beautified with many adornments.

11 We [I, Hashem, together with My Heavenly entourage] decided to give you a tremendous amount of spoils at the Splitting of the Sea, in addition to the smaller number of spoils you already received when I took you out of Egypt.

Subject of the Verses

Hashem is speaking to *Klal Yisrael*. He tells them how, at the beginning of His relationship with them, He demonstrated His love for them.

Mashal

After the wife attests to her love, the husband goes ahead and describes his love. He speaks to his wife about his devotion to her, and how much kindness and jewelry he bestowed on her when they first met, thereby showing everyone his great love for her.

Nimshal

Shir HaShirim opened with *Klal Yisrael* describing how loyal and devoted they were to Hashem from the very beginning of their relationship, following Him into the desert and showing their true love. The following verses touch on both how this love and purity remain despite being tarnished by the exile and on how to cope with the exile. Here, in these three verses, Hashem replies. In response to *Klal Yisrael*'s declaration of devotion to Him, He expresses His devotion and love for them. Hashem notes that He, too, lavished His love upon them from the very beginning.

Rashi explains that these three verses all refer to the miracle of the Splitting of the Sea. That amazing miracle was a demonstration of Hashem's love for *Klal Yisrael*.

The first verse is fairly explicit: "I [Hashem] showed you [*Klal Yisrael*] My love through My horses battling Pharaoh's chariots." Of course, Hashem did not battle Pharaoh's forces with actual horses. The term is used metaphorically, alluding to Hashem's awesome power.

The next two verses speak of various kinds of jewelry. Hashem says to *Klal Yisrael* that they look beautiful in the jewelry and necklaces He gave them. He wants them to remember just how many gifts He showered them with. Then Hashem says that He wanted to give them rows of gold jewelry at the Splitting of the Sea in addition to the silver jewelry He gave them at the time of the Exodus. As Rashi explains, the wealth that *Klal Yisrael* acquired at the

Splitting of the Sea was much greater than the wealth they acquired when they left Egypt. That is why the verse refers to the jewelry at the Splitting of the Sea as gold, in contrast to the considerably less valuable jewelry they acquired when they left Egypt, which is likened only to silver.

THROUGH MY HORSES [BATTLING] PHARAOH'S CHARIOTS...

From these three verses (9-11), it is clear that even though the Exodus from Egypt was a tremendous event — an event that shaped our *emunah*, our belief in Hashem — the Splitting of the Sea was a greater display of Hashem's love for us. (This explains, in part, why the gifts we received at the Splitting of the Sea were much greater than those we received upon leaving Egypt.) We find this concept in a number of sources.[91] But, indeed, why is this so? Why was the Splitting of the Sea a greater demonstration of Hashem's love?

To answer this question, we will need to think more deeply about the Splitting of the Sea. We know that Ten Plagues preceded it. But it is a mistake to view the Splitting of the Sea as just another plague — a kind of eleventh plague intended to further punish Pharaoh for his misdeeds or to further demonstrate Hashem's greatness. If that were the purpose of the Splitting of the Sea, Hashem could easily have wrought more plagues — greater plagues or harsher plagues.

By the time Pharaoh agreed to send *Klal Yisrael* out of Egypt, he was a broken man, ready to do anything to get *Klal Yisrael* to leave. Hashem had, so to speak, won the argument, and Pharaoh now had to obey Him. Yet, after they departed, Hashem purposely provoked him and encouraged him to chase after his former slaves. Hashem did this by making *Klal Yisrael* appear to be lost in the desert and by hardening Pharaoh's heart. The reason for this was to throw him and his entire army into the sea.[92]

What was the point of this additional blow? *Klal Yisrael* was safe, Pharaoh had essentially surrendered and had been humbled. What was the need for another great miracle?

The answer is that there is a fundamental difference between the Ten Plagues and the Splitting of the Sea. The Ten Plagues were intended to show Pharaoh and the entire world that Hashem is in control of everything, and thus everyone must obey Him completely — including His order to let the Jewish People go free. Once Pharaoh surrendered

---

91 In the prayer *Ezras Avoseinu* recited just before the weekday morning *Shemoneh Esrei*, we describe the Splitting of the Sea. In this prayer, we find a number of different indications of Hashem's love for *Klal Yisrael*. For example, *Klal Yisrael* is called: Your beloved ones (*yedidim*), Your firstborn (*bechorchah*), etc.

92 The Torah clearly states this. See *Shemos* 14:2-4.

and acknowledged that he must obey Hashem, this was accomplished. But Hashem still had two items on His agenda, *ki'veyachol*: Not only did he want to punish Pharaoh for all the harm and suffering he had caused the Jewish People, but He also wanted to give *Klal Yisrael* gifts. Both of these things proved Hashem's love for *Klal Yisrael*.

This can be better understood with a small illustration. Imagine a person who sees one child beating up another child. If he is a stranger to these children, he will go over and try to separate them. Once they have stopped fighting, he has fulfilled his duty. If he is the father of the child who was being pounded, however, he will go on to comfort him and shower him with love. He will also want to punish the bully and avenge[93] his beloved son. So, too, Hashem had shown that He is in charge and "stopped the beating," but that was not enough because His precious nation had been hurt. By making Pharaoh and all the Egyptians suffer for their cruelty to His children and by showering *Klal Yisrael* with gifts, Hashem was demonstrating His great love for them and how He was aiming to "offset" all their suffering. This was the essence of *Kriyas Yam Suf* (the Splitting of the Sea). Even though *Yetzias Mitzrayim* demonstrated Hashem's control and taught us *emunah*, His great love for us was demonstrated by *Kriyas Yam Suf*.[94] Therefore in this verse where Hashem says, in effect, "See how much love I showed you when I first chose you as a nation," He points to the Splitting of the Sea.

WE WILL MAKE FOR YOU ROWS OF GOLD JEWELRY...

At the beginning of a marriage, the gifts given are usually much larger than those given later on. Large gifts given at the outset demonstrate one's love, but one is not expected to keep up those standards. Indeed, this is often not even possible. A bride receives very special gifts from her husband at the first, exciting stage, but she has no expectation that this will continue. In contrast, Hashem first gave *Klal Yisrael* more modest gifts (silver jewelry) and then gave them even more valuable gifts (gold jewelry). This was to show

---

93 We are not expressing an opinion about whether this is the right thing to do but only indicating what the person might be feeling. Indeed, Divine "vengeance" is completely unlike vengeance taken by a human being. The latter is forbidden by the Torah.

94 This fundamental difference helps us understand a number of unique phenomena surrounding *Kriyas Yam Suf*. Foremost among them is *Klal Yisrael*'s being stirred to sing a song of love and appreciation when they crossed the Sea, but not when they came out of Egypt. This difference also explains why the heavenly "Prosecuting Angel" criticized *Klal Yisrael* for their sins just before they were saved with the Splitting of the Sea (see Rashi on *Shemos* 14:19) but not when they were saved through the Ten Plagues. The Angel understood that through *Kriyas Yam Suf*, Hashem was showing that we were His favorite nation, and this is what prompted a protest. This is also why — in contrast to the plagues — there was no warning at *Kriyas Yam Suf*. At this stage, Hashem was not looking for Pharaoh to repent or agree to serve Him.

For our purposes, these illustrations will have to suffice. It should be noted that we are underscoring the principal lesson learned from each of these monumental events. Needless to say, both the Ten Plagues and the Splitting of the Sea demonstrated both Hashem's power and His love for us.

Klal Yisrael that Hashem's love for them keeps growing all the time.[95]

Furthermore, jewelry is a very loving and intimate gift. Generally, one gives jewelry only to one's wife. That Hashem uses the metaphor of jewelry shows that *Klal Yisrael*'s relationship with Him is one of extreme closeness.

I SHOWED THE WORLD MY LOVE...

In the allegorical translation above, Rashi understands the key word דִּמִּיתִיךְ (*dimisich*) to mean, "I showed," from the root דמה, meaning "to liken."[96] Hashem was *likening* and showing His love through the Splitting of the Sea of Reeds. This same root also means "to consider," but can be understood in the same way: I thought and deemed to show the world that you are My beloved.[97]

Rashi offers an alternative translation of the word *dimisich*, stemming from the root of the word *domeim*, "quiet."[98] The meaning of the verse would then be: "I quieted you." *Klal Yisrael* was crying out from utter fear on the shores of the Red Sea. Through the miracle Hashem performed, He quieted and calmed them.

The Midrash offers a novel insight based on this way of reading the verse. It tells the story of a princess who was kidnapped by enemies of her father, the king. Out of fear, she started trying to find favor in their eyes so that they should be kind to her. She told them, "I also do not like the king! He is a nobody, and there is nothing good about him! I have always supported your efforts against him…"

Unbeknownst to her, following her kidnapping the king had immediately gathered a huge army to save her. Indeed, the king and his forces were already in earshot when his daughter was saying all of these disloyal words to her kidnappers. He said to her, "Be quiet, my daughter, I am here to save you!" The daughter was terribly ashamed of her disloyalty and her lack of faith in her father.

Similarly, when *Klal Yisrael* saw the Egyptians chasing them, some of them became frightened and started promising that if they let them live, they would go back to being their slaves. Then Hashem said to *Klal Yisrael*, "Alongside the horses of Pharaoh [i.e., while you were standing near the horses and were terrified and started speaking with lack of faith], I quieted you [by telling you that I was here to save you]." We failed to appreciate how close Hashem was and how easily He could save us at any time.

We can all learn from this Midrash. We sometimes find ourselves in situations where

---

95 Another reason was to show Hashem's greatness. Because He is unlimited, He is able to constantly increase His gifts.

96 See Rashbam on *Yeshayahu* 40:18.

97 Rashi (from the root of the word *dimu* meaning "thought," as it is used in *Shoftim* 20:5).

98 As in וידם אהרן Aharon was quiet (*Vayikra* 10:3).

we say or do things that we would be ashamed to say or do if we really believed Hashem was next to us and ready to save us. For example, we might find ourselves speaking to our boss about a raise in salary with utter reverence, somehow imagining that our boss is the only one in charge of our livelihood. If we would be aware that Hashem, who is our real protector and boss, is right there with us in the boss's office, how ashamed we would be! An even worse scenario would be if the boss asked us to reveal *lashon hara* about a fellow employee. If we only had an inkling of Hashem's awesome power, then we would immediately realize how disgraceful it is to even consider abasing ourselves in front of a puny man while disrespecting our awesome God. The truth is, of course, that Hashem is always next to us, and thus we always need to be careful of what we say and do.

THROUGH MY HORSES...

In keeping with our approach, we have explained these verses according to Rashi. The other *meforashim*[99] agree with Rashi that here Hashem is declaring His love for *Klal Yisrael*, but they see these verses alluding not to the Splitting of the Sea but to the giving of the Torah. This was also a tremendous display of Hashem's love for *Klal Yisrael*. Indeed, the Midrashim on these verses are largely focused on Torah. Since there is much to be learned from this line of interpretation and since it is mentioned by many commentators, we will proceed to discuss it here.

In his *Nefesh HaChaim*, Rabbi Chaim of Volozhin writes that when Hashem created man, He gave him the power to control the destiny of the world through his deeds.[100] Every mitzvah creates new worlds of merit and blessing which, although we cannot see them, ultimately control the future of the world we live in, and every sin destroys these worlds. When Hashem gave *Klal Yisrael* the Torah, He took that power away from the human race as a whole and placed it exclusively in the hands of *Klal Yisrael*. In so doing, He essentially gave them the power to run the entire creation. Thus, every mitzvah creates blessing for this world, and every *aveirah* causes destruction. Rabbi Chaim of Volozhin elaborates on this profound concept.[101] If, *chalilah*, *Klal Yisrael* were

---

99 See *Rinah shel Torah* and *Nefesh HaChaim*, ch.1, as well as the Midrash.

100 Ch. 1. He notes that this is alluded to in the very difficult verse, "God created man in His image..." (*Bereishis* 1:27). The verse is difficult because we know that Hashem has no image. In what sense, then, can man be said to be "created in the image of Hashem"? Rabbi Chaim explains that just as Hashem has the power to create worlds and destroy them, so does man. Through his mitzvos, he creates worlds, and through his *aveiros*, he destroys them. See there for further elaboration.

101 This means that our responsibility is absolutely awesome. Let us recall, for example, that when the evil Romans destroyed the Beis HaMikdash, they were only "grinding ground flour," because the sins of the Jewish People had previously stripped the world of its merits so that the Beis HaMikdash was no longer something we deserved (*Shir HaShirim*

to stop doing mitzvos, the world would be destroyed. It would be as if Hashem were powerless to stop it.[102] This demonstrates Hashem's love for us. One does not hand over to a stranger the keys to his car and certainly not the keys to his destiny. Yet, Hashem gave power over the entire creation, which He made with ultimate care and wisdom, to *Klal Yisrael*. This should fill us not only with a sense of tremendous responsibility, but also with pride and joy that Hashem loves and trusts us.

We can see this power operating in the failure of the Egyptian pursuers to save themselves at the Reed Sea. The Midrash tell us that when the sea started closing over the Egyptian cavalrymen, they wanted to turn around and tried desperately to escape. However, Hashem made a miracle, changing the horses' nature so that they took control and led the riders directly into the water. All the efforts of the Egyptian cavalrymen to lead their horses the other way was to no avail. Instead of the riders having control, the horses controlled their masters.

This, says Rabbi Chaim of Volozhin, mirrors Hashem's conduct toward *Klal Yisrael*. Hashem, who is the Creator and Master of this world, has given control of it to *Klal Yisrael*.

> According to this approach, verse 9 is to be understood as follows: "To the horses of Pharaoh's chariots [who took control of their masters], I [Hashem] have likened you [*Klal Yisrael*, by giving you the power of running My world], My beloved."

The Midrash on verse 9 comments that the less common word *rayasi* is used here for "My beloved" instead of *ahuvasi*. This is because *rayasi* also connotes "my shepherd/feeder."[103] The Midrash explains that *Klal Yisrael* provide Hashem with "food," *ki'veyachol*, through their *korbanos*. Furthermore, this word also connotes "my partner."[104] *Klal Yisrael* is Hashem's partner in the Creation, because had they not accepted the Torah, the world would have ceased to exist. The Midrash is pointing out not just that *Klal Yisrael* is Hashem's beloved but that they now have the responsibility of looking after what Hashem brought into being. *Klal Yisrael* is, *ki'veyachol*, both Hashem's "partner" and His "shepherd"! By offering up the *korbanos*, the Jewish People bring the source of blessing into this world, and by doing mitzvos, they support and maintain Hashem's universe. Today, even though we cannot offer up *korbanos*, our Torah learning keeps

---

Rabbah 3:2). It was as if the Romans did nothing since the sins of *Klal Yisrael* were the *real* cause of the Destruction. In the positive sense, every mitzvah a Jew performs has tremendous ramifications, bringing much blessing to the supernal worlds and to this world as well. (The reward for every deed will be commensurate.)

102 We are discussing how Hashem wants us to feel about doing mitzvos. This is not a theological statement about Hashem, about whom we have no concept whatsoever.

103 From the word "*ro'eh*" (shepherd).

104 From the word "*ray'ah*" (partner).

the world running. Without us, it would cease to exist. That Hashem trusted us with His world shows His profound love for us.[105]

When did Hashem invest us with such vast power — power even over Him, *ki'veyachol*?[106] He did so at *Matan Torah*. According to this approach then, these verses do not refer to *Kriyas Yam Suf*, but to *Matan Torah*. Accordingly, the next two verses are to be understood as follows:[107]

> **10** Your cheeks [i.e., your speech, represented by the cheeks which facilitate all speech] are beautiful with *Torim* [i.e., the words of "Torahs"[108]]; your neck [a reference to the Sanhedrin] with strung beads [precious halachos].
>
> **11** We will make for you gold jewelry in the form of pillars [an allusion to *Kesuvim*] besides engraved pieces of jewelry [made out] of silver [an allusion to Nevi'im].

We will now explain the symbolism here. The "neck" is an allusion to the Sanhedrin because the neck is the connection between head and body, between the intellect that decides what is right, and the rest of the body that follows its instruction.[109] So, too, the Sanhedrin is the connection between the Torah and *Klal Yisrael*, who follow the words of the Torah. *Charuzim* (strung beads) is an allusion to halachah. This is because reaching a correct halachic decision in any situation depends on the ability to extrapolate correctly from earlier sources and apply them correctly to the current question. This can be done only by a Torah scholar who can tie together different contexts, sources, and other relevant *halachos*. This is similar to a necklace made out of beads or pearls

---

105 One does not give control over one's affairs to anyone but those closest to him.

106 We see this in the following episode, recorded in the Gemara (*Bava Metzia* 59b), involving a halachic disagreement between Rabbi Eliezer and his contemporaries. To prove he was right, Rabbi Eliezer declared: "If I am correct, let the nearby carob tree jump to another place…let the stream of water flow uphill…let the walls of the *beis midrash* cave in…" Each of these miraculous things happened one after the other, yet the other sages were unwilling to change their view. Finally, Rabbi Eliezer declared: "Let a heavenly voice declare that I am right!" And, indeed, a heavenly voice rang out, justifying his position. The response of Rabbi Yehoshua was: "The law is decided by us not in Heaven!" The Gemara concludes by relating that Eliyahu HaNavi came and reported that Hashem rejoiced that His beloved sons "were victorious over Him," *ki'veyachol*. This episode shows how Hashem, because of His love for us, gave us His Torah as well as the ability to decide Torah questions on His behalf.

107 As explained in the Midrash.

108 The plural here represents the Written Torah and the Oral Torah, both of which were given to us by Hashem at Mount Sinai.

109 Later in the *megillah* (7:5), when Hashem praises *Klal Yisrael* for their beauty, we see that Rashi too explains the neck to be a reference to the Sanhedrin. (See our commentary.)

that are strung together. Only when properly attached to each other are they beautiful.[110] So, too, the Sanhedrin, the body that determines Jewish Law, is beautiful with the necklaces adorning it because their rulings create firm and correct links between the relevant sources and the final halachic ruling.[111]

The next verse (1:11) goes on to tell us that in addition to the wonderful gift of the Torah, we also received additional magnificent gifts in the form of *Nevi'im* and *Kesuvim*. Both *Kesuvim* and *Nevi'im* are likened to beautiful jewelry, precious, intimate gifts from Hashem. Why is the pillar-shaped gold jewelry connected with *Kesuvim* and the engraved pieces of jewelry with *Nevi'im*? *Kesuvim* is much longer than *Nevi'im*, and generally the meaning of the verses in *Kesuvim* are much clearer. They are thus likened to pillars, which are clearly seen and very conspicuous. In contrast, *Nevi'im* need a discerning eye in order to understand them, much like engraved pieces of silver jewelry need a discerning eye in order to appreciate their magnificence.

יב עַד שֶׁהַמֶּלֶךְ בִּמְסִבּוֹ, נִרְדִּי נָתַן רֵיחוֹ.

12 [Even] while the King was still at His [wedding] feast, my nard [spice] gave forth its fragrance.

יג צְרוֹר הַמֹּר דּוֹדִי לִי, בֵּין שָׁדַי יָלִין.

13 My beloved is to me like a bundle of myrrh that resides between my breasts.

יד אֶשְׁכֹּל הַכֹּפֶר דּוֹדִי לִי, בְּכַרְמֵי עֵין גֶּדִי.

14 My beloved is to me like a cluster of kofer in the vineyards of Ein Gedi.

---

110 The Menorah, which symbolizes the light of Torah, was hammered out of one block of gold into its beautiful design. Contrary to its appearance, it was not formed from many pieces attached together (*Shemos* 25:31 and elsewhere). This aspect of the Menorah is repeated many times in the Torah. The Netziv explains the symbolic significance of this feature of the Menorah: When one learns Torah, one does not "add on" to the Torah. Rather, everything has to be "hammered out" and understood from the Torah itself. This is a deep understanding of how halachic decisions are made. The power of the great *poskim* is not that they come up with their own new ideas and add them to the existing laws of the Torah. Rather, they are able to deduce and draw out from the Torah we received at Sinai the halachos relevant to whatever question arises.

111 There is a well-known episode recorded in the Talmud Yerushalmi (*Chagigah* 77), as well as here in the Midrash, which corroborates this concept. A number of *talmidei chachamim* learned Torah together at the feast made in honor of Elisha ben Abuyah's *bris milah*. This caused a heavenly fire to come down and separate them from the other guests. Seeing the great respect they were accorded in Heaven, the baby's father decided to dedicate his son to Torah. Now, we are told that those *talmidei chachamim* learned Torah on that occasion by starting from the *Chumash*, going on to *Nevi'im*, and then to *Kesuvim*, and then on to *Mishnah*, *Gemara* etc. This is the best way to learn Torah: to start at the source, and then work through the different levels, clarifying the different contexts and then to connect all the sources and material to reach the right conclusion.

1:14 ETERNAL LOVE

Allegorical Translation

12 While the Divine Presence was still at Har Sinai at the wedding feast (i.e., the Giving of the Torah at Mount Sinai when Hashem chose us as His nation and beloved), we sinned and abandoned our pleasant smell.

13 Nevertheless, Hashem gave us the *mitzvah* of building the Mishkan, thus demonstrating His forgiveness and giving us the opportunity to give forth a lovely smell once again. He promised that His Presence would dwell between the carrying poles of the *Aron Kodesh* (Holy Ark).

14 Hashem later forgave us a number of times for our sins (which we committed in the desert).

Subject of the Verses

Klal Yisrael is speaking to Hashem, praising Him for forgiving them even though they betrayed Him in the worst possible manner, having sinned not just once, but a number of times.

Mashal

The wife recalls how she betrayed her husband at their wedding feast but was nevertheless forgiven. She is full of contrition over her own disloyalty and foolishness and is full of love to such a kind husband who constantly forgives her.

Nimshal

According to most *meforashim*, these three verses discuss the same subject. In Rashi's view, they discuss Hashem's greatness and His willingness to forgive *Klal Yisrael* for all of their sins. According to the Midrash, however, they discuss *Klal Yisrael*'s devotion to Hashem. We will look first at Rashi's explanation.

The verses allude to *Klal Yisrael*'s sin of the Golden Calf and the fact that Hashem did not stop loving them as a result. The verse likens this terrible sin to that of a new queen who betrays her husband, the king, at their wedding feast. This is like *Klal Yisrael,* who, at Har Sinai, began their wonderful relationship with Hashem by promising to observe His Torah, only to betray Him soon afterwards through the sin of the Golden Calf while still encamped at Har Sinai, the place where their "wedding" took place. In the end, Hashem did not reject *Klal Yisrael*. Instead, He told them to build a Mishkan where He would dwell among them. Hashem forgave their subsequent sins again and again.

According to this interpretation, the verses are to be understood as follows:

"[Even] while the king [Hashem][112] was still at His [wedding] feast, my nard

---

112 Hashem is referred to here as the King, not as the husband. This is to emphasize Hashem's kindness. For a wife to betray her husband is bad enough, but for a queen to betray her husband, the king, is outright rebellion, punishable by death. Furthermore, a queen is held to a higher standard, and *Klal Yisrael*, Hashem's "Queen," did not live up to this standard.

gave forth its fragrance [i.e., I, *Klal Yisrael*, gave off a bad smell from the sin of the Golden Calf]."

"My beloved [Hashem] is to me like a bundle of myrrh [due to His forgiving us and giving us a new, fragrant spice so that we should smell good again] that resides between my breasts [in His agreeing to dwell alongside us in the Mishkan]."

"My beloved is to me like a cluster of *kofer* [i.e., because I, *Klal Yisrael*, sinned repeatedly, Hashem had to renew my good smell by constantly forgiving me with an entire "cluster of *kofer*"] from the vineyards of Ein Gedi [where spices and flowers bloom a number of times each year – unlike in most places which only bloom once a year.]

The repeated blooming represents Hashem's repeated forgiveness."[113] This verse tells us that Hashem's forgiveness was copious both in quantity (an entire cluster) and in frequency (blooming repeatedly).

WHILE THE KING...

True love pardons all mistakes. A person can gauge his love by seeing how easily he forgives the one he loves. As the verse says, "Love covers over all sins."[114] These verses

---

Even so, Hashem forgave us.

113 The Gemara (*Shabbos* 88b) offers a different interpretation of this verse: "Hashem forgave me for the sin of the 'sheep' (the word *gedi* can mean sheep alluding to the Golden Calf) that I added (*karmei* can meaning 'accumulated')." The expression "that I added" seems strange. Rashi answers that, at the time of the *eigel*, *Klal Yisrael* wanted many idols. Therefore, the verse says this was like an addition.
But since the sin of idolatry in the desert involved a calf, not a sheep, how are we to understand this interpretation? In his *Ta'ama d'Kra*, Rabbi Chaim Kanievsky explains that this terminology stems from *Klal Yisrael's* sin of engaging in idol worship in Egypt. The Egyptians worshipped sheep as idols (Rashi, *Bereishis* 46:34). The Midrash tells us that *Klal Yisrael* did as well. Indeed, the angels asked Hashem at the Splitting of the Sea why such idol worshippers were worthy of being saved. Hashem answered that *Klal Yisrael* had been forced to worship idols while they were under the domination of the Egyptians. However, once *Klal Yisrael* worshipped the Golden Calf in the desert *of their own free will*, this proved that their idol worship in Egypt was also done of their own free will. By sinning with the Golden Calf, they revived the charge against them of the idolatry of sheep in Egypt.
Accordingly, this verse relates that Hashem forgave *Klal Yisrael* for their sin of idol worship in the desert, which they added to their sin of worshipping sheep in Egypt. This explains why the verse uses the word "sheep" when, in fact, a calf was used.
According to this, Hashem forgave *Klal Yisrael* for the sin of the Golden Calf even though, through this action, they seemed to prove that they were not really worthy from the beginning. This is like a wife who betrays her husband during the wedding feast after formerly having been disloyal to during their engagement, having defended herself in the past by saying that at the time she was not yet committed to her husband. Such a disloyalty is far more damaging to the relationship. Despite this flagrant disloyalty, Hashem forgave us and continues to love us. This is why we mention the sin of the "sheep"; it shows a forgiveness for a disloyalty which is much greater than we can possibly imagine.

114 *Mishlei* 10:12.

describing Hashem's constant forgiveness of *Klal Yisrael* demonstrates His love for us. The greater the sin, the greater the display of love if the sin is forgiven. In this verse, *Klal Yisrael* acknowledge that their sin of the Golden Calf was the ultimate betrayal and chutzpah, like a bride being unfaithful to her husband at their wedding. By acknowledging the magnitude of the sin, we underscore Hashem's love for us in granting us forgiveness.

These beautiful verses vividly evoke Hashem's love for us even after we sinned. Verse 12, which speaks of the sin of the *eigel*, uses a strangely positive expression: "My nard gave forth its fragrance." We would have expected it to say that we emitted a bad smell or that we lost our good fragrance.[115] Instead the words themselves seem to communicate that we gave off a good smell. The Gemara takes note of this seeming incongruity and explains that the positive expression is meant to show how Hashem still loves us despite our momentary betrayal.[116]

MY BELOVED IS TO ME LIKE A BUNDLE OF MYRRH...

Here in verse 13, *Klal Yisrael* exclaims: "My beloved [Hashem] is to me like a bundle of myrrh that resides between my breasts." This alludes to the fact that the Divine Presence would dwell between the staves of the *Aron Kodesh*.[117] Usually when a person has been very disloyal to a friend, coldness and distance remain even after forgiveness has been granted. Here, however, we regained our closest intimacy after Hashem forgave us.[118] Rashi explains why the metaphor of "residing between my breasts" is very apt. The long carrying poles of the *Aron Kodesh* would protrude into the curtains separating the *Kodesh HaKodashim* from the rest of the Mishkan, creating a breast-like appearance in the Mishkan. It was here that the Shechinah dwelt.

This vivid portrayal of Hashem's closeness has additional significance. After all, the *Aron Kodesh* represents Torah, the source of all nourishment for *Klal Yisrael*. Therefore, the "breasts" symbolize the concept of Hashem nurturing and nursing *Klal Yisrael* with the teachings of the Torah.[119]

The Vilna Gaon adds that this symbolism shows closeness without any barriers.

---

115 Tosafos (*Shabbos* 88b, s.v. *v'lo kesiv*) notes that the Torah avoids negative language. Therefore, the expression "bad smell" would not have been used in any event. Still, according to Tosafos, we would have expected the verse to say that we emitted a "smell," something that is neither positive nor negative. By using this positive term, the verse highlights Hashem's love. (But see Rashi ibid., s.v. *nassan*.)

116 *Shabbos* 88b.

117 Rashi.

118 In his *Mesillas Yesharim* (ch. 11), the Ramchal emphasizes that when one grants forgiveness, he should do so wholeheartedly so that the original closeness is restored. In doing so, we emulate Hashem.

119 This idea is enlarged upon and further elucidated in our commentary on a later verse (4:5).

Nothing interposes between *Klal Yisrael* and Hashem. The Netziv explains that through Torah, one reaches such closeness to Hashem that it is as if one is intimate with Him.

This verse (13) tells us that not only did Hashem forgive us, but He also gave us the opportunity to build a Mishkan for Him. The Vilna Gaon notes that if not for the sin of the Golden Calf, we would not have had a Mishkan. This shows Hashem's great love for us: Instead of punishing us for our grave sin, He gave us the opportunity to do something special and feel that we were putting right our mistake. Paradoxically, our sin ended up giving us extra merits! Only the tremendous love of Hashem could bring about such a thing!

The Mishkan gave us the exhilarating feeling that Hashem was ready to live with us. It also gave us the feeling that we were doing something special for Hashem by building Him a Mishkan. In truth, of course, it was really Hashem being kind to us in agreeing to have His Presence dwell among us. In the terms of the metaphor, Hashem's kindness also included His providing us with pleasant-smelling myrrh, thereby making us smell good. He did not just take away our bad smell but gave us the ability to produce a pleasant smell. This can be likened to the kindness done by a kind and perceptive individual who gives a person who commits "foul-smelling deeds" a way to make amends by doing the opposite. This is the ultimate kindness — even better than simply ignoring the "smell" or bringing one's own "perfume" — because he thereby restores that person's good feeling about himself.[120][121]

MY BELOVED IS TO ME LIKE A CLUSTER OF KOFER...

This verse (14) says that Hashem kept having to renew the good smell for us. Hashem gave us a "cluster" (a large quantity) of *kofer* (forgiveness)[122] by forgiving us repeatedly. In the very first years after coming out of Egypt, we sinned in a number of ways, among them: complaining about the temporary lack of water and then the lack of food, making

---

120 When we do a kindness for someone and then act as if that person is doing us a favor, we are emulating Hashem's conduct here in asking *Klal Yisrael* to make a Mishkan for Him. Perhaps the most famous example of such noble conduct was Rachel Imeinu's willingness to forfeit to Leah the privilege of marrying Yaakov Avinu. Indeed, it seems that not only did Leah never know about this, but she even felt that Rachel had usurped her place by becoming Yaakov's second wife. (See *Bereishis* 30:15 where Leah criticizes Rachel for taking away her husband!) This great *chessed* led to Hashem's accepting Rachel's *tefillah* when *Klal Yisrael* were driven into exile after the destruction of the First Beis HaMikdash. We can apply this in our daily lives if, for example, we find our seat in shul taken by a stranger who, seeing our perplexity, "kindly" lets us squeeze in beside him into our children's seats, and then thank him without pointing out that he is really occupying our seat. This is how Hashem conducts Himself with us all the time.

121 In a similar vein, Rabbi Yosef Kimchi understands this verse (13) as follows: just as one gives flowers to a bride to enhance her beauty, so Hashem gave *Klal Yisrael* opportunities to do mitzvos and enhance their beauty. The verse would thus read: "My beloved, [Hashem, gave] me a bundle of myrrh [special mitzvos]...."

122 "*Kofer*" also means "atonement."

the Golden Calf, and believing the slander of the spies. Hashem forgave us over and over again and continued to show us His love.

WHILE THE KING...

We have explained these verses (12-14), mainly according to Rashi's approach. Interestingly, the Midrash looks at these three verses in an almost opposite way: as praising *Klal Yisrael* and their devotion to Hashem. Indeed, the Midrash says that *Shir HaShirim* is about *Klal Yisrael's* greatness, not their sins![123] Let us now proceed to examine how the Midrash sees these key verses.

The Midrash explains that even before our "wedding feast" with Hashem had ended, we gave off a pleasant smell. In the allegory, the meaning of the feast not yet being finished is that Hashem had not yet shown Himself to be our complete husband (since we had not yet "gone home" together). The Nimshal is that even before Hashem proved Himself by showing us what was in the Torah, we were ready to accept it. *Klal Yisrael* said to Hashem, "*na'aseh v'nishma* — We will [first] do [the mitzvos], and [only then] understand," even though Hashem had not yet given us the Torah. Thus, *Klal Yisrael* is saying:

> **12** [Even] while the king [Hashem] was still at His [wedding] feast [before the wedding had reached its conclusion], my nard [*Klal Yisrael*] sent forth its [wonderful] fragrance.

This can be likened to a bride recalling her own wedding day. Most grooms, she thinks to herself, see their bride's greatness and beauty only after the wedding — and might actually worry during the wedding feast if they married someone special. But she herself showed her greatness and devotion through her wonderful actions such that her groom realized already then just how wonderful and pleasant she was.

The next verse (13) goes on to say that even though Hashem was, so to speak, tough and unpleasant with *Klal Yisrael*, they still wanted to be close to Him. How was He tough with them? Rashi explains that He punished *Klal Yisrael* for the *eigel*, and even so, they wanted Hashem in the Mishkan.[124] The *Torah Temimah* suggests that it is an allusion to the exile, where *Klal Yisrael* suffer greatly and constantly feel Hashem's wrath,

---

[123] According to Rashi's approach, these verses indirectly illustrate the greatness of *Klal Yisrael* because Hashem loves them so much that He forgives them again and again. Be that as it may, the perspective of the Midrash is that even mentioning the forgiving of the sins of the Jewish People is not appropriate material for *Shir HaShirim*, the *megillah* of love between Hashem and *Klal Yisrael*.

[124] *Shabbos* 88b.

yet they still yearn for His closeness. According to this interpretation, the verse is to be understood this way:

> **13** [Even though] my beloved [Hashem] is [sometimes] harsh and bitter[125] to me, [I long for Him to] reside between my breasts.

The final verse in this three-verse series (14) is explained by the Midrash in a fascinating way. The mention of Ein Gedi here is a reference to the miracle that happened in Ein Gedi in the time of King Yehoshafat.[126] So many different enemies came to attack *Klal Yisrael* that they had no chance of defeating them on their own. The righteous King Yehoshafat, together with a large part of the nation, thus fasted and davened to Hashem. Hashem responded by causing the attacking nations to become confused and mistake their allies for their enemies. They attacked and battled one another until they wiped themselves out![127] *Klal Yisrael* then found the battlefield full of dead soldiers and valuable spoils. This miracle happened in the valley of Ein Gedi. The Midrash explains the next verse accordingly:

> **14** The one who has everything[128] [i.e., Hashem] rejected[129] [the nations] and chose me, the beloved, in the vineyards of Ein Gedi.

Now, we might ask: What does this have to do with the previous two verses? Also: Why is this particular miracle recalled here? After all, Hashem has performed so many miracles for *Klal Yisrael* over the centuries!

The answer to these questions may well be as follows: In these verses, we describe *Klal Yisrael*'s loyalty to Hashem. They always viewed Hashem as their Friend, even before Hashem had proven Himself, and even when things got tough. As a reward for this loyalty and devotion, Hashem made it clear that He was *Klal Yisrael*'s Friend by helping them and saving them, such as He did at Ein Gedi. This last verse, then, is the reward for our loyalty, as highlighted in the previous two verses.

Let us try to understand this more deeply by recalling a point made and developed by the Chovos HaLevavos.[130] He writes that one of the biggest tests in life is being able to

---

125 According to this explanation the root of the word *tzeror* is *tza'ar* (pain), and the root of the word *ha'mor* is *mar* (bitter).

126 This remarkable, but for some reason unfamiliar, episode is described at length in *Divrei HaYamim II* 20. As mentioned earlier, Shlomo HaMelech wrote *Shir HaShirim* with *ruach HaKodesh* and was thus able to foresee future events.

127 The Metzudas (ibid) explains that the nations made alliances in order to attack any nation they believed was threatening them. But then mistrust developed between the allies, and they attacked one other.

128 The Midrash understands the word *eshkol* to be a combination of two words: *ish* — "the Man," as in "Hashem is *the Man* of war (*ish milchamah*)" (*Shemos* 15:3) — and *kol* ("[who has] everything").

129 The Midrash understands the word *hakofer* here as "the one who rejects." In Hebrew, a heretic is called a *kofer*.

130 *Shaar Yichud HaMaaseh*, beginning of ch. 5.

recognize who is a true friend and who is not. Our *yetzer ha'ra* (as well as the enemies of *Klal Yisrael* and even sometimes evil and corrupt friends) often pretends to be our "best friend." They act as though their advice stems from a genuine concern for our welfare. The truth, of course, is that they are our true enemies whose entire aim is to deceive us and destroy us. The Chovos HaLevavos vividly describes how the *yetzer ha'ra* pretends to be our truest friend but is actually our worst enemy — even testifying against us after death in the Heavenly Court.

On the other hand, sometimes when the *yetzer ha'tov* (or our Rabbis and teachers, or even Hashem) tells us to do something, it is not always easy for us to see that this advice comes from true love. Sometimes, the words sound harsh, or the request seems too demanding. A person can mistakenly think that the advice is motivated by self-interest, not deep love and concern for us. To be constantly aware of who is a true friend, and thus whose advice should be heeded, is one of life's tests.

Over the centuries, *Klal Yisrael* has, generally speaking, passed this test, and were able to identify their true friends. They were able to see that listening to Hashem was the best thing for them, even before Hashem fully described what He wanted them to do.[131] Even when things got difficult, *Klal Yisrael* held onto the belief that Hashem is their best friend, and they always desired His closeness. This is what the first two verses in this series are telling us. The last verse describes how Hashem reciprocated, remaining a true friend to *Klal Yisrael*, saving them when the other nations attacked. The other nations became confused about who their allies were and who their enemies were. This is what caused their total destruction — not only in that particular battle, but right through history, the heathen nations never learned to properly distinguish between friend and foe. This particular miracle is cited here because it highlights this particular issue. That battle is a Mashal and a true example of the harm this kind of mistake can cause a nation. We, *Klal Yisrael*, never fail to distinguish between friend and foe, and this has been the source of our survival. Since we have always looked to Hashem as our true Friend, He rewards us by always looking after us as a true friend.

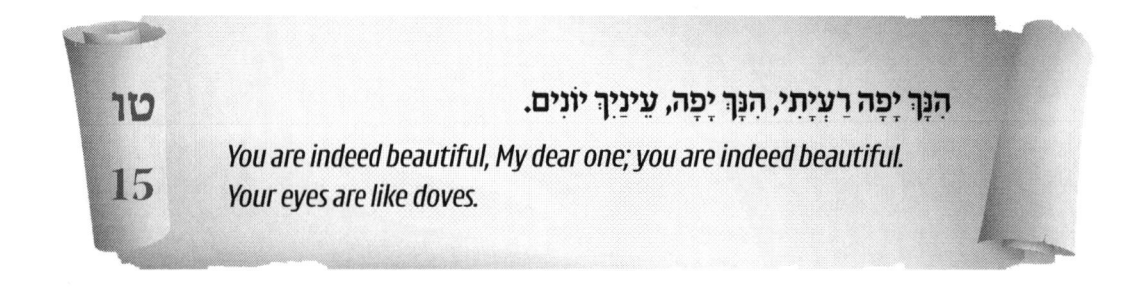

טו / 15

הִנָּךְ יָפָה רַעְיָתִי, הִנָּךְ יָפָה, עֵינַיִךְ יוֹנִים.

You are indeed beautiful, My dear one; you are indeed beautiful. Your eyes are like doves.

---

131 Herein lies the greatness of our proclaiming *na'aseh* before *nishma* at Mount Sinai, promising to do Hashem's will even before knowing what it entailed. In contrast, the other nations refused to accept the Torah because they thought it was not in their best interest. The failed to realize that Hashem acts only out of true kindness.

Allegorical Translation	You, *Klal Yisrael*, are beautiful to Me (Hashem). You are beautiful in every way because the righteous among you were loyal to me as a dove is loyal to its mate.
Subject of the Verse	Hashem is speaking to *Klal Yisrael*, praising them and encouraging them.
Mashal	Earlier, the wife had described her feelings of shame and remorse for her previous misdeeds (1:12-14). Here in this verse, her husband reassures her that he sees her as eternally beautiful and attractive and praises her loyalty.
Nimshal	The last few verses describe[132] how *Klal Yisrael* feels contrition for all their sins, and how wonderful Hashem is to them for forgiving them. In this verse, Hashem encourages *Klal Yisrael* by telling them that not only does He forgive them, but that they are beautiful in His eyes.[133] Hashem repeats these words of endearment twice. The verse concludes by likening their eyes to doves, who have tremendous beauty, as we will show.

YOU ARE INDEED BEAUTIFUL...YOU ARE INDEED BEAUTIFUL

The repetition of "beautiful" in this verse calls out for explanation. And indeed, the Midrash offers quite a few. Rashi conveys two of them: The first is an allusion to *Klal Yisrael's* unqualified embrace of the Torah at Sinai: "You are beautiful" for saying "*Na'aseh*" ("We will do [the mitzvos]"), and "You are beautiful" for saying *Nishma* ("We will [then] listen [and understand them]"). Alternatively, the verse is referring both to the beauty of *Klal Yisrael's* ancestors[134] and to the beauty of *Klal Yisrael* themselves.

The Vilna Gaon suggests that the double expression of beauty in this verse is an allusion to both outer and inner beauty. He notes that when the Torah describes the beauty of our Imahos (Matriarchs), it uses the double expression, "*yefas toar vi'yefas mareh*"[135] (beautiful in form and beautiful in appearance). He says "appearance" refers to one's

---

132   According to Rashi.

133   Rashi's words give us a clear and uplifting picture of the theme of this verse: אני הייתי בושה בקלקולי והוא חזקני בדברי רצויים לומר סלחתי כדבריך והרי את יפה ויפה כי עיניך יונים כלומר כלה שעיניה כעורים כל גופה צריך בדיקה ושעיניה נאים אין גופה צריך בדיקה והדוגמא זו היא מחלתי לך על עונך והרי את יפה בנעשה והנך יפה בנשמע...

"I [*Klal Yisrael*] was ashamed of my corrupt behavior, but He [Hashem] strengthened me with words of conciliation saying: 'I [Hashem] have forgiven you, and you [*Klal Yisrael*] are exceedingly beautiful because your eyes are like doves!'" A bride whose eyes are ugly needs to be checked completely [for blemishes], but if her eyes are pleasant, then she does not need to be checked further. In other words, Hashem is saying: "I have forgiven you for your sins, and you are beautiful in that you said *na'aseh* [at Sinai], and you are beautiful in that you said *nishma*..."

134   The Vilna Gaon explains that Hashem is telling *Klal Yisrael* that in His eyes, they are totally beautiful – in contradiction to the way *Klal Yisrael* spoke about themselves earlier (in verses 5-6). *Klal Yisrael* said earlier that their actions may have been ugly, but their ancestors' actions were beautiful. Hashem is reassuring them their actions are beautiful to Him as well.

135   *Bereishis* 29:17.

deeds, while "form" refers to one's essence, i.e., one's feelings and thoughts. A person may not always be able to perform all the righteous deeds he wishes to due to various constraints that Hashem, for His own reasons, has imposed on him. Therefore his "appearance" may not be overly impressive, but his form is very much so because he wishes to do the right thing. Alternatively, a person may do wonderful things for the wrong reasons, and thus have a good appearance, but a bad form. Our Imahos had both types of beauty: beauty of form and beauty of appearance. The double expression of beauty here in this verse conveys that the whole of the Jewish People possesses this virtue as well.

We would like to suggest that the Vilna Gaon's interpretation above actually dovetails with Rashi's understanding that the double expression of beauty here alludes to *Klal Yisrael*'s double embrace of Torah through their declaration of *"na'aseh v'nishma."* After *Klal Yisrael*'s unqualified agreement to do all that Hashem asked (*na'aseh*), what was the greatness of their subsequent commitment to "listen" and understand the mitzvos (*nishma*)? The answer is that fathoming the *penimius*, the inner understanding of the mitzvos, represents a higher level. We thus develop an inner spirituality by understanding from the mitzvos what Hashem wants us to be focused on in life. In other words, Hashem is declaring the beauty both of *Klal Yisrael*'s outer physical actions and also their inner efforts to learn more. Indeed, Rashi's second explanation, that the double expression refers to our forefather's beauty and as well as our beauty, also connects with the Vilna Gaon's insight about inner and outer beauty. Through their greatness, our Avos and Imahos imbued in our spiritual DNA their greatness and devotion to Hashem.[136] When we act upon this greatness, then our outer beauty reflects our inner beauty.

YOUR EYES ARE LIKE DOVES

Commenting on the provocative comparison between eyes and doves, Rashi tells us that the eyes represent the whole person. He cites *Chazal*'s statement that if the eyes of a prospective bride are beautiful, this indicates that her whole body is beautiful. If they are not, she should be checked carefully for blemishes.[137] Let us pause for a moment to ask ourselves: why should the eyes, which are such a small part of a person, reflect one's entire beauty?

The eyes are windows to a person's feelings and emotions. We can get a good sense of another person's emotions from his or her eyes. Furthermore, the eyes reflect the

---

136 *Ruach Chaim*, Avos 5:1.
137 *Ta'anis* 24a.

person looking into them, thus creating a bond between the two individuals. When we wish to connect and communicate personally, we try to establish eye contact. Rashi means that if one finds the bond created by looking into the eyes pleasant, then even if one has differences regarding minor issues, one can be sure that he will find everything about the relationship good. Similarly, when Hashem looks into our eyes, *ki'veyachol*, and sees how we wish to have a close relationship with Him despite our past sins, He finds us beautiful.

Another way of understanding this is that the eyes represent how a person looks at things. If a person has "good eyes," i.e., a positive outlook, this reflects on the goodness of the entire person. Rabbi Eliezer Silver, *zt"l*, related that shortly after the Holocaust, he met a Jew who told him that he would never pray again. This Jew explained that in the concentration camp where he was incarcerated, there was a person who owned a siddur, but would lend it only to those who gave him their bread rations. He was so upset about seeing someone abuse the mitzvah of prayer in this way that it turned him off to praying altogether. Rabbi Silver asked him: "Why do you focus on the one individual who, under those intolerable circumstances, gave in to his base instincts?! Why don't you focus on the many who, through extreme self-sacrifice, gave away their last bit of food in order to pray?!" A person always has a choice about what to focus on. The eyes of a person who sees good around him reflect an inner goodness that chooses to see good.[138]

Rabbeinu Yonah makes a similar point.[139] He tells us that we can discover how worthy a person is by noticing what he chooses to look at and praise. If a person tends to notice good deeds and righteous people (and praise these people and their deeds), we can be sure he is a truly good person. But if he admires the wicked and praises acts of sin, then even if his own actions are good, we can be sure that he is rotten at the core and that he does not really love Hashem. Applying this to our verse, we understand that the praise of *Klal Yisrael*'s eyes means that they focus on the righteous, and therefore they are truly beautiful.[140]

---

138 In his comments on *lashon hara*, Rabbi Shimshon Pinkus corroborates this concept (*Tiferes Shimshon, Bamidbar*, pp. 145-151). He points out that on the one hand, *lashon hara* is the worst of all sins (see Yerushalmi, *Peah* 1:1). But on the other hand, *Chazal* tell us that everyone is guilty of committing, at least partially, this terrible sin (*Bava Basra* 165a). He explains this paradox by showing that the need to talk about one's experiences is embedded very deep in one's soul. (He also explains this at great length.) Only someone who has completely eradicated the interest in negativity from his viewpoint will be able to make sure not to speak ill of others. The test of *lashon hara* is, therefore, the ultimate litmus test. Whether a person sees good or evil ultimately depends on what he is truly interested in.

139 *Shaarei Teshuvah* 3:148.

140 This is why the Torah commands us "not to stray after our hearts and eyes" (*Bamidbar* 15:29). Let us note that many *meforashim* point out that the order here would seem to be wrong. Doesn't the seeing come first, followed by the desire of the heart? The answer is that one sees that which the heart wants to see. The Mashal is given of several people

Alternatively, a good eye means a kind eye, i.e., a person who is full of generosity and kindness.[141]

Rashi also tells us that the eyes are symbolic of the leaders of the generation. The leaders are called "the eyes of the nation." This is because they see (and teach us) the correct way to live. The Dubno Maggid illustrates this with the following parable. In former times, guards would be stationed in high watchtowers where they could look out into the distance to see if enemies were approaching. If one of these guards would shout out that the enemy was coming but someone below would insist that he did not see any danger, the man below would be considered a fool. Of course, he cannot see; he is not in a position to see. Similarly, the leaders are the ones who "see" for *Klal Yisrael* and warn them of any dangers.

According to this interpretation, then, our leaders are like doves. But what is special about doves? Rashi explains that doves are faithful to their partner for their entire lifetime. So too, even when *Klal Yisrael* sinned, the leaders remained faithful. In other words, the "eyes" (leaders) of *Klal Yisrael* are as faithful as doves. As we know, the tribe of Levi did not sin along with the rest of *Klal Yisrael* in making the Golden Calf. We can take this a step further based on the teaching cited by Rashi that when the eyes are good, the whole body is considered good: When the leaders are faithful, then the whole nation is good. Since the leaders are faithful to Hashem, the whole of *Klal Yisrael* is constantly reminded that they too must serve Hashem, and this is what has saved them over the centuries. Indeed, this has always been the beauty of *Klal Yisrael*: Even when they have strayed, they have always had great and righteous leaders who remained devoted and faithful to Hashem. And their adherence to their leaders' guidance has kept them from straying too far. This reminds us how our success depends on following our righteous leaders, and how grateful we should be for having them.

YOUR EYES ARE LIKE DOVES

Klal Yisrael themselves are likened to the dove several times in *Shir HaShirim*. The Midrash explains the comparison to the dove in the following ways: Just as the dove is modest in its behavior during mating, so *Klal Yisrael* is modest in its behavior. Just as the dove is honest in not taking food that is not its own, so *Klal Yisrael* is honest. Just

---

looking out their living room window to the street below. The driver sees all the new cars, the teenage daughter sees the new clothes people are wearing, while the cleaner notices that the windows are dirty. In other words, the eyes see that which is in a person's heart. They therefore indicate what kind of person he is.

141 We find this concept in *Avos* (2:9). When Rabbi Yochanan ben Zakkai asked his students to identify the path that a person should choose for himself to reach the proper service of Hashem, Rabbi Eliezer replied "A good eye." The Meiri (ibid.) explains that when one is generous, it leads a person to all types of good behavior.

as the dove is distinctive, so *Klal Yisrael* is distinct from all nations in their dress and their practice of *bris milah*. Just as the dove accepts its death without a struggle, not fidgeting when it is slaughtered, so *Klal Yisrael* accept Hashem's decrees. Just as the dove engenders forgiveness (since it is sometimes brought as a *korban*), so *Klal Yisrael* bring forgiveness to the world. Just as the dove carries on flying with one wing even when the other wing is too tired to function, so *Klal Yisrael* never stop serving Hashem even when they are tired…

The following episode in the Gemara[142] ties in with this last trait. The ancient Romans once forbade the wearing of *tefillin* and decreed that anyone caught with them would be killed. Elisha continued wearing them and was spotted by a Roman soldier. The soldier chased Elisha, who quickly took off his tefillin. When the soldier caught up with Elisha, he asked the Jew what he had in his hands. Elisha answered, "the wings of a dove." Sure enough, a miracle happened, and the *tefillin* changed into the wings of a dove!

Rabbi Meir Shapiro, *zt"l*, explains the exchange this way: The soldier's real question was, "What gives you the strength to disobey our laws?" Elisha answered, "I have the wings of a dove." As was mentioned above, doves continue flying with one wing when the other wing is too tired to continue. Similarly, when *Klal Yisrael*'s physical side is weakened, their spiritual side is still strong. In other words, Elisha was telling the Roman soldier: "The more you try to afflict us physically, the more we rely on our spiritual power to defy you. Therefore, you will never stop us from serving Hashem!"

YOUR EYES ARE LIKE DOVES

One of the Midrash's comments on the doubled expression of *Klal Yisrael*'s beauty is: "*Klal Yisrael* is beautiful before sin and beautiful after sin." But what, we may wonder, is the beauty after sin? And how does the next phrase, "Your eyes are like doves," connect with this concept? These questions are answered by a novel interpretation of Rabbi Chaim Berlin, *zt"l*, which grew out of an incident that happened to him. Rabbi Berlin was a *rav* in Moscow when the Communists were in power. As is well known, at one point they forbade the mitzvah of performing *bris milah* and meted out severe punishments to those who disobeyed this law. One day, a high-ranking member of the Communist Party came to him in private and asked him to perform a *bris milah* on his newborn son. Rabbi Berlin, who was also a *mohel*, readily agreed, and asked the official where to meet him. The official provided his address but insisted that Rabbi Berlin perform the *bris* only when he was away from home. He also imposed one condition: that no one

---

142 *Shabbos* 130a.

ever find out about it because it could cost him his life. At the very least, he would lose the position of power that had taken him years to reach. Rabbi Chaim Berlin arranged to perform the *bris* in total privacy. A few days later, the father came to pay him and to tell him that the child was all right. The Rabbi refused the money, but he asked, "Please explain to me what makes you risk everything for such a mitzvah when it is evident that you rejected the Torah long ago?" The father explained, "I know deep down that while Yiddishkeit will last, Communism won't. When that happens, I'd like to have the option to come back. Furthermore, I want my child to have the possibility of returning as well, regardless of how far he strays from the Torah. To make that option possible, he must have a *bris milah*. Without a *bris*, he may forget his identity and may never know how to come back."

In light of this moving incident and in light of the Gemara's teaching that a dove never goes so far from its nest that it cannot see the way back,[143] Rabbi Chaim Berlin was inspired to explain the verse and the Midrash quoted earlier in the following way. "Behold, you are beautiful, my love" — before sinning, you are beautiful and unblemished. "Behold, you are beautiful, your eyes are like doves" — even after you sin, you are beautiful in that your eyes can still see your "nest" (like the dove) because you do not stray too far. No matter how far *Klal Yisrael* stray from Torah, they want to be able to find their way back. This is something that they feel deep inside.[144]

The Midrash offers another explanation of the doubled expression of *Klal Yisrael*'s beauty. The first mention of beauty alludes to *Klal Yisrael* before they sinned, and the second to *Klal Yisrael* after they have repented. Indeed, if we connect this with Rabbi Berlin's interpretation of "eyes like doves" above, this verse also indicates why *Klal Yisrael*'s repentance is beautiful: even when they sin, they make sure that the option of coming back is always open to them. Accordingly, the second half of the verse should be interpreted as follows: "You [*Klal Yisrael*] are indeed beautiful [after you repent]; [and your repentance is effective because] your eyes are like doves [who always look to see how to get back to their nest]."

---

143 *Bava Basra* 24a.

144 Rabbi Chaim Berlin used to recite *Shir HaShirim* every Friday afternoon. When he reached this verse, he would start crying. His *talmid*, Rabbi Aryeh Levin, who used to witness this every week, once mustered the courage to ask him the reason. Rabbi Berlin related the incident involving the high-ranking Communist Party official. He explained that when he gets to this verse, he remembers how far this man went to ensure that he had a way back.

SHIR HASHIRIM 1:17

טז הִנְּךָ יָפֶה דוֹדִי, אַף נָעִים; אַף עַרְשֵׂנוּ רַעֲנָנָה.

16 *Behold, You are beautiful, my Beloved, You are also pleasant; even our bed is fresh.*

יז קֹרוֹת בָּתֵּינוּ אֲרָזִים, רַהִיטֵנוּ (רחיטנו כתיב) בְּרוֹתִים.

17 *The beams of our houses are of cedar, and our panels are of cypress.*

Allegorical Translation

16 *Klal Yisrael* reply: The beauty is not mine; rather, it is Yours. You are also pleasant, and because of Your pleasantness, the Mishkan is fresh with the gathering of our sons and daughters.

17 The Mishkan was built with strong, beautiful, and very valuable beams of wood.

Subject of the Verses

Klal Yisrael is speaking to Hashem and expressing that He is the source of all their beauty; and through His kindness, they were given the magnificent Mishkan.

Mashal

The wife replies to her husband that her beauty is only because of him. Furthermore, she praises her loving husband for his kindness, mentioning that their beds and homes are full of life and pleasantness because of him.

Nimshal

Klal Yisrael is speaking here in these two verses. After Hashem says that He not only forgives them, but that they are also beautiful in His eyes, *Klal Yisrael* respond that it is Hashem who is beautiful, not them. In other words, Your beauty and Your pleasantness led You to forgive us and to dwell among us in the Mishkan.[145] *Klal Yisrael* go on to characterize the Mishkan. This follows naturally since the Mishkan was the place where Hashem's love was evident.

The Mishkan is described here as a "fresh [or flourishing] bed." What is the meaning of this symbolism? Rashi explains that this is a euphemistic allusion to *Klal Yisrael*'s growing children. Freshness symbolizes new growth. The Mishkan is the source of *Klal Yisrael*'s growth. In the merit of the Mishkan, *Klal Yisrael* was fruitful. Therefore, the Mishkan is referred to as the "fresh bed"

---

145 Rashi.

of *Klal Yisrael*.¹⁴⁶

In the next verse (17), *Klal Yisrael* continue to speak of the greatness of the Mishkan.

BEHOLD, YOU ARE BEAUTIFUL

Klal Yisrael seem to be responding to Hashem: "No, it is not the case that we are beautiful and that You forgave us because of our beauty. Rather, it is You, Hashem, who are beautiful and kind, and that is why You forgave us."

Are we to understand, then, that *Klal Yisrael* is just answering back? The answer is that they are saying something much deeper. They are telling Hashem gratefully that their beauty comes from Him. Hashem brings out the good and the beauty of *Klal Yisrael*. Just as there are people who, unfortunately, bring out the worst in the people around them, there are also people who bring out the best in others. Their exceptionally good conduct influences the people around them. *Klal Yisrael* is saying that Hashem is the reason for their good conduct. He is the One who is bringing out the "beauty" in this relationship. While in a bad marriage, each spouse brings out the worst in the other — and then suffers the consequences — in a good marriage, each spouse has the ability to bring out the best in the other. That is the greatest kindness a spouse can bestow, and it obviously brings its own great blessing.

There is another sense in which *Klal Yisrael*'s beauty comes from Hashem: through the commandment to emulate Him. We members of *Klal Yisrael* try to incorporate Hashem's attributes (such as compassion, kindness, and generosity) into our lives. Thus, *Klal Yisrael* is saying in this verse that their beauty comes from Hashem because they emulate His beauty.¹⁴⁷

YOU ARE ALSO PLEASANT

Klal Yisrael continue their praise of Hashem, using a term that is highly relevant to Torah and mitzvos themselves. To illustrate, let us recall that a thorny plant is not used

---

146 "Bed" is often used as a euphemism for marriage. And through marriage, of course, one becomes fruitful.
The connection between *Klal Yisrael*'s fruitfulness and the Mishkan can be seen also from the fact that those who participated in the inauguration of the First Beis HaMikdash (which was essentially the continuation of the Mishkan) had baby boys not long after (*Shabbos* 30a). Elsewhere, the Gemara tells us that in the short time that the *Aron HaKodesh* was in the home of Oved Edom, his wife and eight daughters-in-law all had sextuplets (*Berachos* 63b). See also our commentary below on 3:7.

147 In a similar vein, the *Navi* Yeshayahu declares: "Through Hashem, all the children of Yisrael have become righteous and praiseworthy" (45:25). In his *Shaarei Teshuvah* (2:1), Rabbeinu Yonah explains this to mean that our inspiration and our entire growth result from simply thinking about Hashem. That is to say, contemplating Hashem's kindness and greatness is the method we use to become greater people ourselves.

to fulfill the mitzvah of shaking the Four Species on Sukkos. Why? Because the ways of the Torah are pleasant, and this would be unpleasant.[148] This does not mean that mitzvah observance will always be undemanding. It can sometimes be quite hard, but it always brings satisfaction, and always involves elements of pleasantness. Mitzvos are never cruel.[149]

Picking up on the dual meaning of the word "*af*" (which can mean "also" or "angry"), the Midrash understands *Klal Yisrael* to be saying that even when Hashem is angry, He is also pleasant. After *Klal Yisrael* praise Hashem for His beauty and kindness, they go on to praise Him for His pleasantness, even in times of anger. As we all know, some people are very kind when everything is fine, but when things go wrong, they are unbearable. Hashem, however, is always pleasant, even when it is necessary for Him to show anger and punish us. A good parent will remain pleasant even when they need to punish their children. Indeed, that pleasantness, which is shown when the children are least deserving, teaches volumes not only about what the parent truly feels towards them, but also about how to behave.

This is a continuation of what *Klal Yisrael* said before: Our beauty comes from You, Hashem. It stems from Your constant pleasantness, which causes us to behave in the good way we do. That pleasantness, even during a time when Hashem must show anger for our own good, motivates *Klal Yisrael* to be as good as they are.

EVEN OUR BED IS FRESH

The verse ends by referring to the Mishkan as a "fresh bed." As Rashi explains the Mishkan was the source of all growth and fruitfulness in *Klal Yisrael*. A "fresh" bed also reminds us that our relationship with Hashem should not be old and stale; rather, it should be fresh and full of vigor. Furthermore, *Klal Yisrael* is praising Hashem for revitalizing their relationship with Him after they sinned. The eye-opening discussion of revenge in *Mesillas Yesharim* is relevant here.[150] The author points out that the sin of revenge can also be committed in a mild way. After all, there are many levels to a relationship. And when a person has been hurt, even when he forgives the offender, he will still have to struggle to renew the relationship. Indeed, he will often try to be cooler and more distant vis-à-vis the one who hurt him. The author gives the example of a friend whose revenge is simply not to be as friendly to the offender as he was before. This is also a forbidden form of revenge. In sharp contrast, Hashem forgave *Klal Yisrael*

---

148 *Sukkos* 32b. See also *Yevamos* 15a, where the Gemara decides a halachah based on this principle. The source of this principle is the verse in *Mishlei* (3:17) "Its [the Torah's] ways are pleasant, and all of its pathways [bring] peace."

149 If one feels that the mitzvos are cruel, he is evidently observing them incorrectly.

150 Ch. 11.

for the sin of the Golden Calf and renewed their former closeness. In this verse, *Klal Yisrael* praise Hashem for this and note that their relationship embodied in the "fresh bed," the Mishkan, is vigorous.[151]

THE BEAMS OF OUR HOUSES ARE CEDAR...

This verse (17) further describes the greatness of the Mishkan. It tells us that the Mishkan's beams are cedars and its panels are cypresses. If we overlook the specific wording of the verse, we will understand simply that these are special kinds of wood and mentioning them enhances *Klal Yisrael*'s praise of the Mishkan.

But if we look more closely, we will notice that the verse does not say that the Mishkan was "made from" cedars. Rather, it says that the Mishkan "is" cedars and cypresses. That is, its walls and panels are referred to as trees, not as coming from trees.

To understand this, let us first recall and explain the concept behind the miraculous tree of gold that Shlomo HaMelech planted when he built the Beis HaMikdash.[152] This tree was alive and produced golden leaves and fruit! Its golden fruits and leaves would be plucked on a regular basis to help pay for the upkeep of the Beis HaMikdash. When the Beis HaMikdash was destroyed, this tree shriveled up. What was this miraculous tree all about?

People sometimes make the mistake of thinking that Hashem is "so to speak, alive," as if Hashem is not *truly* alive, but only almost, "as if." The fact is that Hashem is the only life there is; we are the ones who are only, "so to speak, alive." Hashem is called the "God of life" because Hashem is truly alive. He creates all of life and is, in fact, all life. It is actually difficult for us to understand what place in life we have, since all of life is only Hashem. Rabbi Shimshon Pinkus once explained that the reason we train our children from such a young age to kiss the *Sefer Torah* or any *sefer* is to drive home this lesson. We kiss things that are alive, and we want our children to understand that there is real life in these things too. Unfortunately, this is often forgotten.[153]

The tree in the Beis HaMikdash symbolized how Hashem is the source of life. The source of life in the Beis HaMikdash was so strong that even gold could grow from it. But once Hashem, the source of life, left the Beis HaMikdash, this tree shriveled up.

This verse expresses how the Mishkan was so alive that its walls were cedars and cypresses, as if they were still growing and thriving trees. *Klal Yisrael* is praising the

---

151 We emulate Hashem when we keep a close relationship from deteriorating even though we have been hurt by a family member or friend.

152 *Yoma* 21b.

153 Rabbi Shimshon Rafael Hirsch's guidance on viewing Hashem as a reality (even though He is not physical) appears in the Introduction to this *sefer*.

Mishkan as a place of life. It follows that when we attach ourselves to Hashem, we deserve life because we are connected to life. As the Torah says, "You, who are attached to Hashem, your God, are all living today."[154]

As mentioned in the Introduction, the chapter divisions in the standard edition of *Shir HaShirim* may not be significant. Still, for the sake of clarity, we can summarize this first chapter by saying that it shows us the foundations of the deep love between Hashem and *Klal Yisrael*. *Shir HaShirim* goes on to show us the love that was expressed and developed through particular events, such as *Yetzias Mitzrayim* and the building of the Beis HaMikdash.

---

154 *Devarim* 4:4.

פרק ב'
CHAPTER 2

> **א / 1**
> אֲנִי חֲבַצֶּלֶת הַשָּׁרוֹן, שׁוֹשַׁנַּת הָעֲמָקִים.
> *I am the rose of Sharon, the rose of the valleys.*

Allegorical Translation — We, *Klal Yisrael*, are like a rose for Hashem due to our beautiful deeds, like a rose in the valley which is protected, and therefore produces especially nice petals. So, too, we generate wonderful achievements.

Subject of the Verse — *Klal Yisrael* is speaking to Hashem, describing their beauty to Him.

Mashal — Wishing to find favor in the eyes of her husband, the wife speaks of her beauty and her love for him, as if she were his flower.

Nimshal — Wishing to find favor in the eyes of Hashem, *Klal Yisrael* speak of their devotion and beauty in metaphorical terms.

I AM THE ROSE OF SHARON

We have rendered both *chavatzeles* and *shoshanah* as "rose." This approach follows Rashi, who says they are both the same flower.[1] The difference is that one grows on the hills, the other in the valleys.[2] (Although Rashi does not identify this flower, the

---

1. The Seforno (like the Midrash here) understands that a *chavatzeles* is a small *shoshanah*. In contrast, the Ibn Ezra says that they are two totally different species.
2. The Midrash underscores the praise of *Klal Yisrael* implicit in this verse. *Klal Yisrael* is likened here to the very best since the rose is considered the best flower, and the rose that grows in the valley is the best species of rose. This is because the land in the valley is particularly fertile since there is plenty of moisture as well as protection from the

shoshanah is commonly thought to be the rose.³)

I AM THE ROSE OF SHARON

In the first chapter of *Shir HaShirim*, *Klal Yisrael* liken themselves to a devoted wife in order to illustrate how much they love Hashem. They also liken themselves to lost sheep in order to illustrate how much they need Hashem's protection. Here, in this verse, *Klal Yisrael* liken themselves to flowers. What are they communicating through this simile?

Let us think for a moment about the "role" played by flowers. Flowers have no intrinsic worth; we do not value them because of their usefulness. Flowers are essentially objects of beauty. This is both their strength and their weakness. We can barely do anything practical with flowers, but this is exactly what makes them the ultimate symbol of goodwill. When Hashem created other items, He did so because we need them: we need food to eat, water to drink, air to breathe, etc. But when He created flowers, He did so for the sole purpose of giving us pleasure and joy.⁴ That is why a gift of flowers given by one person to another demonstrates affection and love more than a useful item like a pot or a tool.

When we liken ourselves to the flowers of Hashem, we are communicating that we cannot really do anything for, or give anything to, Hashem. He is omnipotent, and everything is His. All we can do — and this we must do and have done throughout history — is to express our love for Him. By doing what Hashem commands and giving Him what He asks of us, even though we know that we are not really giving Him anything since everything is already His, we show that we love Him and want to please Him. Like flowers, we give nothing, but display beauty and love.

The flower symbol used in this verse also alludes to the aspect of nurturing. Unlike many other items, such as furniture, that generally survive as long as they are not damaged, flowers need special care and appropriate conditions. For flowers to bloom nicely, they require a certain amount of water, a certain amount of sunshine, the right humidity, etc.⁵

---

withering heat of the sun. The Midrash concludes that even when parables are employed in connection with the Jewish People, only the best are used!

3   See *Peirush HaRav Temach* on *Shir HaShirim*, who also identifies the *shoshanah* as a rose.

4   We recite a special blessing during the month of Nissan when fruit trees start to blossom, thanking Hashem for making beautiful trees and creations. Unfortunately, there are many who go out to recite the blessing, but don't look at the blossoms again until the following year. This is like a wife who thanks her husband for the flowers he bought her, and then puts them away, never to look at them again! If the husband were to notice this, he would feel terrible that his wife did not enjoy the flowers and would conclude that his gesture was wasted on her. Hashem created the blossoms to beautify our world and convey His love. Of course, we must thank Him and bless Him for this gift, but that is only the first step. We must then take the time to enjoy the beauty and feel His love and graciousness in creating all this for us.

5   Rabbi Simcha Zissel, *zt"l*, commented that we can learn a profound lesson from flowers. Without water, a beautiful

When we compare ourselves to Hashem's flowers, we are also communicating that we only blossom under His tender, loving care, and without Him, we would instantly wither away.

THE ROSE OF THE VALLEYS

In this verse, *Klal Yisrael* is likened both to "a rose of Sharon" and to a "rose of the valleys." The double portrayal alludes to two different stages in their relationship with Hashem.

The Midrash explains that the first half of the verse is a characterization of *Klal Yisrael* before they left Mitzrayim, the second half, after they had been saved. Similarly, the Midrash says that the first half of the verse alludes to *Klal Yisrael* at present in exile, the second half, to *Klal Yisrael* after the Redemption.[6] At first, *Klal Yisrael* say they were like a rose of the Sharon: a dry rose wilting on the mountainside, battered by the winds, rain, and harsh sunshine. With Hashem's help, however, they became like a rose of the valley. As Rashi explains, the rose of the valley is more beautiful because it enjoys more water, shade, and protection.

Klal Yisrael in Mitzrayim were full of love and goodwill towards Hashem, as if they were His flowers. But they were not beautiful flowers because they were battered by all the Egyptian influences, like flowers compromised by the harsh elements. However, once they had been taken out and carefully placed under His protection, they become like the beautiful rose of the valley.

To better appreciate the dramatic change, let us imagine a wise gardener facing a wilting and unattractive plant. Realizing its potential, the gardener is able to bring out its beauty and make sure that it blooms nicely by giving it the extra care and attention it needs. Hashem did likewise when he redeemed us from Egypt. He saw our great potential even though we seemed withered. He will do so again in the future when He redeems us from our current exile, and thus brings forth the beauty of our souls, and makes His flowers blossom once more.[7]

---

flower will wilt and die a few short hours after being picked. Similarly, a Jew who loses his connection with Hashem cannot grow and flourish. Indeed, this lesson is also implicit here in our verse. We, *Klal Yisrael*, are like flowers needing a constant connection with Hashem.

6   According to the Midrash, the verse should be understood this way: "I *was* like a rose of Sharon, [and I have *become* through Hashem's salvation] like the rose of the valleys."

7   Rabbi Shimshon Pinkus points out that just as a newborn baby needs very special care, so did *Klal Yisrael* when they came out of Egypt. On the night preceding the Exodus, *Klal Yisrael* was born and saved. The many stringencies on Seder Night, our commemoration of that auspicious night, reflect the extra care needed by "spiritual newborns." This is reflected here in the metaphor of a flower needing to be tenderly cared for.

> כְּשׁוֹשַׁנָּה בֵּין הַחוֹחִים, כֵּן רַעְיָתִי בֵּין הַבָּנוֹת.
> **ב 2**
> Like a rose amidst the thorns, so is My dear one among the maidens.

Allegorical Translation Hashem replies: You, *Klal Yisrael*, are indeed like a rose which remains beautiful despite the thorns surrounding it. Similarly, you have remained faithful and beautiful despite being among all the nations who have tried to maim you.

Subject of the Verse Hashem is speaking to *Klal Yisrael*, accepting and expanding upon their likening themselves to roses.

Mashal The husband acknowledges his wife's beauty and devotion and adds to her praises by saying that she stands out from among the maidens like a rose from the surrounding thorns.

Nimshal Hashem agrees that *Klal Yisrael* are His flowers and adds that they are like flowers among the thorns, i.e., a chosen nation among the other nations[8] who do not interest Him at all.

LIKE A ROSE AMIDST THE THORNS

Now Hashem is speaking. He agrees that *Klal Yisrael* is like a rose but adds that they are like a rose amidst the thorns. This reaction is similar to that of the loving spouse who hears a compliment about his or her spouse. He or she will not simply agree but will naturally find a way to add to the compliment. Hashem therefore immediately adds that *Klal Yisrael* is like a precious rose among the useless thorns (which refer to the heathen nations). The compliment here lies in the fact that even though the thorns prick and threaten the flower, the rose looks nice. Similarly, even though the nations that surround us have not stopped pricking us, we continue to remain faithful and beautiful to Hashem.[9]

The Midrash tells us that the beautiful smell of the rose is emitted when it is pricked. Until then, it is contained within the rose. The seemingly useless and nasty thorns actually bring out the beautiful smell of the rose. The nations who "prick" us think that by doing so they will destroy us and make less beautiful in the eyes of Hashem. The reality,

---

8 "Maidens" in *Shir HaShirim* refers to the other nations who compete with *Klal Yisrael* for Hashem's attention, like the maidens who vie for the husband's attention (as explained earlier in our commentary on 1:3).

9 Rashi.

however, is just the opposite: the suffering causes us to improve ourselves. And when we remain steadfast in the service of Hashem despite all the suffering other nations inflict on us, the good smell lying dormant within us begins to emanate. We thereby become more precious to Hashem. The "pricked rose," then, is a beautiful metaphor for the way that suffering bring out the best in our nation. Indeed, our history testifies to the fact that every time a nation starts a war against Israel, or a tragedy befalls us, the tremendous sweetness of *Klal Yisrael* becomes demonstratively clear.

This is one of many evocative word pictures in *Shir HaShirim*. Their purpose is to awaken in us feelings of love for Hashem. We are to imagine a beautiful rose in a bush full of thorns, how precious the rose is in contrast to the rest of the bush, and how the whole effort of the gardener is to bring forth this cherished rose.[10] In the same way, *Klal Yisrael* is precious to Hashem, and His entire involvement in this world is for the sake of His rose, the Jewish People.

LIKE A ROSE AMIDST THE THORNS…

Another distinguishing feature of a flower or a plant is that it comes from almost nothing. Most items require components of good quality. For instance, to make a good table, one needs sturdy wood. A plant is totally different. A tiny seed in a bit of dirt yields a beautiful flower! It is something special that comes from the most mundane.

Indeed, the Midrash teaches that the rose in this verse is an allusion to Rivkah Imeinu (as well as to *Klal Yisrael* in Egypt and throughout history). Rivkah Imeinu, a tiny seed, came from a wicked father, a wicked family, and a wicked town. Yet, out of all this, she blossomed into a prominent matriarch of *Klal Yisrael*! *Klal Yisrael* emerged from the slavery and moral abyss of Egypt to become a nation that serves Hashem. In exile, we are a tiny nation planted in pile of earth (i.e., all the many nations), and yet we will blossom into a beautiful, powerful nation!

---

10 This image ties in with the concept that one is judged in relation to his surroundings (see Rashi on *Bereishis* 6:9). For example, when a child gets a grade on his report card, it is often accompanied by the average grade of the class. This helps the parents know how well their child is succeeding. If the average is a lot less than the child's grade, even if the child's grade is not so high, parents know that their child is doing well, and vice versa. Here Hashem declares that not only are *Klal Yisrael* as special as a rose, but that all the other nations are like thorns, this means that not only are *Klal Yisrael* doing well in their own right, but compared to all other nations, they are exceptionally special. Indeed, when one sees lowly conduct on the part of *goyim*, one should remind himself that this highlights, by comparison, the greatness of *Klal Yisrael*.

> כְּתַפּוּחַ בַּעֲצֵי הַיַּעַר, כֵּן דּוֹדִי בֵּין הַבָּנִים; בְּצִלּוֹ חִמַּדְתִּי וְיָשַׁבְתִּי, וּפִרְיוֹ מָתוֹק לְחִכִּי.
>
> Like an apple tree among the trees of the forest, so is my Beloved among the young men.[11] I yearned for His shade, and sat under it, and His fruit is sweet to my palate.

Allegorical Translation — Just as the sweet-smelling apple tree is more treasured than all other trees, so Hashem is preferable to all other gods. Therefore, we chose to take shelter under Him. His words of Torah are sweet in our mouths.

Subject of the Verse — *Klal Yisrael* is speaking to Hashem, explaining that they chose to serve Him instead of all other gods because His patronage is far more special than all other gods. This is why they seek His shelter and His fruit, i.e., His Torah.

Mashal — The wife tells her husband that just as the apple tree is the most beautiful fruit tree, and gives off the nicest fragrance, so he was the finest among the young men, i.e., all other suitors. That is why she chose him as her husband.

Nimshal — *Klal Yisrael* explain why they chose Hashem as their beloved. They underscore Hashem's greatness by comparing Him to a nice-smelling and pleasant-tasting apple tree in a forest full of trees that do not bear fruit. Therefore, they chose His shelter and His fruit, i.e., His protection and His commandments.

LIKE AN APPLE TREE

At first glance, this verse is puzzling. The uniqueness of an apple tree is its fruit. It is thus understandable that *Klal Yisrael* would desire and enjoy its fruit. But why would this cause *Klal Yisrael* to want to sit in its shade?

The Netziv poses this question and offers a lengthy and profound answer based on his understanding that the tree in this verse alludes to the Torah. We will try to summarize his key points here. A tree has many parts: a trunk, roots, branches, blossoms leaves, and most importantly, fruit. Indeed, the fruit is the main purpose of the tree. So, too, the tree of Torah has many parts. But the most important part, the "fruit," is knowing

---

11 We noted earlier (commentary on 1:3) that maidens are symbolic of the heathen nations who compete with *Klal Yisrael* for Hashem's attention just as other maidens compete for the husband's attention. Similarly, the young men mentioned in this verse are symbolic of other gods who try to seduce *Klal Yisrael* away from Hashem, just as other men may try to lure a girl away from her suitor.

the principles of Torah. Besides the fruit of the tree, there are also leaves that protect the fruit, branches that support the fruit, a trunk that provides a base for the tree, etc. So too, to be able to truly understand Torah, one needs many other things which all help support or protect Torah. For example, there is the trunk, which symbolizes all the necessities a person has to have to be able to live.

There is, however, a point of contrast, and that is highlighted by the verse. When it comes to trees, we might choose to eat the fruit of one tree, but use another for shade, and still another for support. But when it comes to the tree of Torah, we should have so much affection for Torah that the tree that produces the fruit of Torah should be the same tree we look to for shade and support. We should look to be constantly in the shade of Torah even when we are not actually eating its fruit, i.e., learning the actual words of Torah. In practical terms, this concept teaches us that if one is looking to get married, he should aim to marry the daughter of a Torah scholar; if one is doing business, he should preferably do it with a Torah scholar.[12] Even how one dresses and how one talks should preferably be learned from Torah scholars.

In light of this explanation of the Netziv, we have an answer to our original question about why *Klal Yisrael* seek the shade of an apple tree. The tree in this verse is the tree of Torah. Because the fruits of Torah are so precious to us, even when we need only shelter (i.e., the necessities of life), we seek these in Torah as well.[13]

The Metzudas Dovid takes a different approach to our verse, one that revolves around the nature of the shade provided by an apple tree. Although the apple tree produces beautiful fruit, it does not provide much shade because it has few leaves. In contrast, there are barren trees like the oak that have lots of leaves, and thus offer plentiful shade. When the heathen nations see the paltry shade of the apple tree, they look elsewhere. But *Klal Yisrael* has learned not to expect things immediately, but wait for gratification. If one is willing to be patient and content with the apple tree's lack of shade, one will eventually enjoy its beautiful fruit. Indeed, *Klal Yisrael* has this attribute of forbearance, while the other nations seek immediate gratification. Being loyal to Hashem often requires that one be willing to wait — whether it is to wait for Mashiach, or for one's reward in the World to Come, or even waiting before eating a fruit until one first recites the blessing. These, of course, are only a few examples of how waiting and patience are

---

12 See *Pesachim* 49a.

13 With this understanding, the Netziv explains the first chapter of *Tehillim* which describes the beauty of the righteous person as a tree growing alongside a river. The righteous person has within him all aspects of Torah – not just the fruit. Every part of him is inspired by the tree of Torah. In this context, the Netziv sharply reproaches those who learn Torah but see it only as a religious rite, not as a way of life. Learning Torah as spiritual exercise and then looking for *other sources* of inspiration about how to conduct oneself is the antithesis of how a Jew should live. A Jew is supposed to see Torah as the source of his conduct and his calling.

part of our service of Hashem. In this verse, *Klal Yisrael* congratulate themselves for having the wisdom and patience which eventually lead them to be able to enjoy the sweet fruit.[14]

LIKE AN APPLE TREE...

Perhaps the main lesson we learn from this verse is that because of Hashem's kindness and greatness, *Klal Yisrael* was drawn to put themselves under His protection. Examples of Hashem's protection abound. For instance, Hashem lit up the way for *Klal Yisrael* in the desert with His Pillar of Fire.[15] He also sent a Pillar of Cloud to protect *Klal Yisrael* from the Egyptians, gave them the manna for bread, and gave them water from a rock. We should feel privileged and happy that we are under the wonderful protection of Hashem!

LIKE AN APPLE TREE...

Up to this point, we have primarily developed Rashi's first explanation that our verse is underscoring Hashem's greatness. But Rashi offers an alternative approach as well — that the verse is describing *Klal Yisrael's* greatness. Here, too, Hashem is likened to an apple tree providing little "shade," but the emphasis is that *Klal Yisrael* chose to find shelter under it nonetheless. Only *Klal Yisrael* was willing to go under Hashem's patronage, while all the other nations saw His tree, His protection, and rejected it because they considered it to be lacking in goodness. This verse, then, is alluding to how

---

14   Our custom is to recite *Shir HaShirim* at the end of the Pesach Seder. In a sense, the Seder itself drives home this point, as we see from the following anecdote about a non-Jewish soldier who was looking around for a good meal on the first night of Pesach. He decided to pretend to be Jewish, and thus get invited to a Seder. Knowing that Jews are very hospitable, he was sure he would get a delicious meal. All went well at the beginning: He enjoyed the cup of wine and bit of a *karpas*. But then he found himself waiting for a very long time (during *Maggid*). When the next course (*maror*) was finally served, it was so bitter that he hightailed out of there, convinced that Jews were not very hospitable after all. The next day, he complained bitterly to his Jewish companions. They informed him that had he remained a little while longer, he would have enjoyed a very tasty Yom Tov meal! By having the necessary perseverance, we have enjoyed — and will enjoy — eternal success.

15   This example of how Hashem protects us was retold by Onkelos the convert, with remarkable results (*Avodah Zarah* 11a). The Roman emperor of the time sent soldiers to drag Onkelos back to Rome in order to put him on trial for observing mitzvos. However, Onkelos spoke to these soldiers so winningly about the authenticity of Judaism that they all converted as well! This happened several times. Eventually, the emperor forbade the soldiers he sent to arrest Onkelos from talking with him about all religious matters. Onkelos then spoke with the next group of soldiers about matters of government. He noted that while society dictates that servants wait on their masters, Hashem, the true Master of the universe, looks after the Jewish People. He pointed to Hashem's use of the Pillar of Fire as just one example of this. But his telling them about this one seemingly small occurrence, how Hashem lit up the way for the Jews in the desert, made these soldiers all want to convert to Judaism as well. Finally, the emperor gave up, and stopped sending soldiers!
Now, if this is the kind of impression the Pillar of Fire made on those lowly Roman soldiers, how much more so should we, the sacred Jewish People and the beneficiaries of the miracle, be impressed! Indeed, we should be thinking about and appreciating everything that the Torah tells us Hashem did for us.

the heathen nations shunned Hashem's Torah and turned their back on His mitzvos. Only *Klal Yisrael* chose to observe His Torah and rely on His protection.

There is a famous description in the Gemara[16] of how Hashem offered the Torah to the nations. First, He offered it to the nation of Esav. They asked what is written in the Torah, and were told, "You shall not murder." Upon hearing this, they declined the offer. Hashem then offered the Torah to the nation of Moav, and they, too, asked what is written in it? When they were told, "You shall not commit adultery," they also declined the offer. This scene repeated itself with the other nations as well. They considered Hashem's demands, as expressed in the Torah, to be too taxing and oppressive, and preferred what they thought would be a better deal and better protection by serving pagan gods. In contrast, and to their everlasting credit, *Klal Yisrael* immediately accepted the Torah even before they knew what would be expected of them. Our verse, then, can be understood in terms of this famous Midrash, as highlighting *Klal Yisrael*'s greatness in being the only nation to accept the Torah.

HIS FRUIT IS SWEET TO MY PALATE

Our verse ends with these words spoken by *Klal Yisrael*: "and His fruit is sweet to my palate." But why do they add the seemingly superfluous words, "to my palate"? The Midrash explains what they meant: *Klal Yisrael* found the fruit of Torah to be sweet, while the other nations found it to be bitter and thus rejected it. Only *Klal Yisrael* appreciated the taste of Torah. Since the sweetness of Torah is an acquired taste, we are to understand that *Klal Yisrael* is mentioning their own greatness in finding Torah sweet to *their* palate, while others chose to find sweetness elsewhere.[17]

A deeper understanding of these words emerges from the following true story. A boy who was finding learning Torah unpleasant came to the Rosh Yeshivah and *Gadol Hador*, Rabbi Aharon Yehudah Leib Steinman, *zt"l*, and asked if the Rosh Yeshivah would be willing to hear him out since he was feeling very upset. When the Rosh Yeshivah agreed, the boy asked him if enjoys thick, juicy steak? Rabbi Aharon Leib, a person who was extremely far removed from materialism and indulgence, replied that he had never tasted such a food and did not even know what it was. The boy started crying and exclaimed: "Everyone enjoys different foods! Just because one person enjoys steak does not mean that others will. Similarly, even if the Rosh Yeshivah would tell him that Torah

---

16 See *Avodah Zarah* 2b, where it is mentioned briefly, and *Sifri* 343, where it is related in detail.

17 A little child licking a lollipop thinks that is the sweetest food in the world. And when he sees an adult eating a healthy meal with fruit and vegetables, he cannot understand how the adult gets pleasure from it. The reality is that as one matures, one learns to train the palate to enjoy truly tasty food — without ruining it with artificial sweeteners. The heathen nations got so caught up in artificial sweetness that they could not appreciate the sweetness of Torah.

is pleasant, that doesn't mean that he enjoys it. How can he be told that Torah is sweet when for him it is bitter?!" Rabbi Aharon Leib answered that if one would taste honey, and insist that it was bitter, everyone around would understand that this person must have wounds or blisters in his mouth and that he is not tasting the honey but rather his own sores. Similarly, Torah is always sweet. If one has no spiritual infections, he will enjoy it. If one does not find Torah sweet, this means that the impurities in the person's soul and mind are ruining the pleasurable experience. If one, heals himself, he will once again enjoy the true sweetness of Torah.

This, then, is the deeper meaning of this verse. When *Klal Yisrael* declare that "His fruit is sweet to my palate," they mean that there is something special about their palate that finds His fruit sweet. While the palates of the other nations have been ruined by their immoral and sordid diet, our palate is still pure and could thus taste the sweetness of Torah!

There is still another dimension here in our verse: The sweetness of Torah is unique in that the more one tastes of it, the sweeter it becomes. A person who has just started learning Torah may not find it so sweet. The longer he continues learning, however, the sweeter it becomes to him. With other foods, it is just the opposite: the more one has, the less sweet they become.[18] Even too much honey makes a person want to throw it up.[19] In contrast, the more one partakes of Torah, the sweeter it becomes to the palate.

LIKE AN APPLE TREE

The Gemara[20] offers a different perspective on our verse. The Gemara says that the apple tree can be understood as a symbol of *Klal Yisrael*[21] (not Hashem, as Rashi indicates). The uniqueness of this tree is that it grows fruit before it grows leaves.[22] This is the opposite of what usually happens with fruit trees, where the leaves normally grow first so that the fruit that follows is immediately protected. Similarly, *Klal Yisrael* said that they would accept the mitzvos even before they heard what the mitzvos would involve. This is, of course, not the normal order: people usually insist on first knowing what they

---

18   This is because the sweetness of other pleasures lies mainly in the desire for them. Once one has indulged, the sweetness diminishes. In contrast, the sweetness of Torah lies in the Torah itself. Thus, the more one partakes of it, the sweeter it is.

19   *Mishlei* 25:16.

20   *Shabbos* 88a.

21   This approach presents a difficulty since the verse seems to be referring to Hashem, not *Klal Yisrael* (Tosafos, *Shabbos* 88a, *s.v. piryah*). The *Nefesh HaChaim* (end of *shaar* 1) resolves this difficulty by noting that Hashem acts toward *Klal Yisrael* according to the way *Klal Yisrael* themselves act. (See our commentary on 1:9.) Therefore, even though this verse is talking about Hashem, it is describing the conduct of *Klal Yisrael*.

22   The Tosafos say that we do not see this phenomenon with an apple tree. They say that the fruit tree mentioned in this verse is not an apple tree, but an *esrog* (citron) tree (*Shabbos* 88a, *s.v. piryah*).

are committing themselves to. This verse then, alludes to the uniqueness and greatness of *Klal Yisrael* in accepting Hashem's offer of Torah straightaway, like the tree whose fruit precedes its leaves.[23]

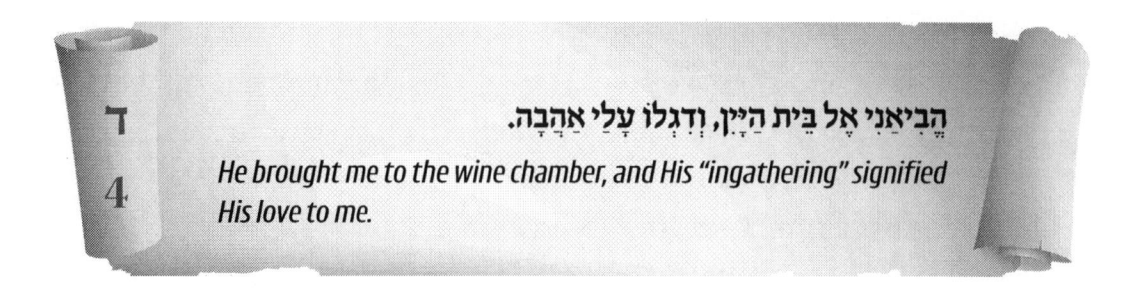

> ד
> 4
> הֱבִיאַנִי אֶל בֵּית הַיָּיִן, וְדִגְלוֹ עָלַי אַהֲבָה.
> He brought me to the wine chamber, and His "ingathering" signified His love to me.

Allegorical Translation Hashem brought me (the Jewish People) into His Mishkan, where He gave

---

23 The Gemara here is pointing to something much deeper than just the simple resemblance between this tree's fruit preceding its leaves and *Klal Yisrael*'s commitment preceding their understanding of what they were committing themselves to.

Let us examine what was so special about *Klal Yisrael*'s declaration of "*na'aseh v'nishma* — We will do, and [then] we will listen [and understand]."). The Gemara (*Shabbos* 88a) reveals that when *Klal Yisrael* said this, Hashem exclaimed, as it were, "Who revealed *this secret* to My children?! This is the language that the angels speak!" What, indeed, is this secret? (See *Madreigas HaAdam* [1:4] for a fuller discussion of the points that follow.)

When a person is asked, "Can you do something for me," he generally inquires about the nature of the favor before agreeing. He does so in order to ascertain whether he will be able to do it or whether it is something that he even wants to do. The request may be too difficult or may even be illegitimate. But if the person trusts the one making the request, he might well forego a request for clarification and reply immediately, "Yes, I will do whatever you ask." In answering *na'aseh v'nishma*, *Klal Yisrael* showed that they trusted Hashem implicitly and were sure that His requests would be doable and desirable. Now, while this demonstrates the trust and love *Klal Yisrael* had for Hashem, we might still wonder: What is the *secret*, and why do only angels speak this way? As we suggested just above, the same type of response might be forthcoming from one friend with full trust in another.

Included in *Klal Yisrael*'s declaration of *na'aseh v'nishma* was the promise to fulfill each of Hashem's commands even if a command were *beyond* their capabilities. In fact, the Gemara here (ibid.) relates an episode in which a heretic was watching Rava learn Torah with such concentration that he was unaware that he was causing himself to bleed. This prompted the heretic to declare that you, the Jewish People, accepted the impossible. In other words, with their statement, *Klal Yisrael* were showing more than just simple trust in Hashem. They were showing innovatively how to commit oneself to doing Hashem's will. They realized that if Hashem commands something, then even if they *cannot* do it at present, they must make the attempt, and Hashem will then provide the means for fulfilling the mitzvah. Instead of *Klal Yisrael* checking first to see if they could do that which Hashem was asking of them and only then agreeing to do it, they committed themselves right away, fully confident that Hashem would provide whatever help they needed to observe all the mitzvos. This is the language of the angels because when angels receive Hashem's command to do something, they immediately receive the power to do it. Before and after the command, they are powerless. In a sense, angels are created for a specific command with all the capabilities needed to fulfill it. Therefore, they can never have any "doubts" about being able to carry out Hashem's commands.

This is the message of the tree in our verse that grows the fruit without its protection, "knowing," as it were, that the leaves will grow later. (Obviously, a tree does not choose to do this; rather Hashem created this tree as a symbol of how we should conduct ourselves). We must agree to do what Hashem asks even before knowing how we will be capable of fulfilling the request because we know that Hashem will provide the means and assistance that we may need to carry it through.

me all the laws of the Torah; and His gathering us around His Mishkan[24] will always remain as a loving memory.

Subject of the Verse — *Klal Yisrael* is reminiscing about how Hashem showed His love by dwelling among them in the Mishkan and teaching them His Torah.

Mashal — The wife reminisces about how, at the beginning of their courtship, her husband took her to the most wonderful wine banquet where they had the most delightful time. She also says that she has this loving memory of his being together with her.

Nimshal — *Klal Yisrael* recall some of their earliest beloved memories: Hashem bringing them to the wine chamber is, according to Rashi, Hashem bringing *Klal Yisrael* to the Mishkan. The Midrash, explaining a bit differently, sees this as Hashem bringing *Klal Yisrael* to Har Sinai. Both agree that the "wine chamber" — understood as wine cellar — symbolizes the Torah. Just as the wine cellar is full of different types of wine, so the Torah has many different explanations. According to Rashi, the verse is alluding to the place where Hashem *taught* the Torah to the Jewish People, the Mishkan. According to the Midrash, the verse is alluding to the place where Hashem *gave* the Torah, Har Sinai.

At the end of the verse, *Klal Yisrael* go on to speak of the loving memory of Hashem gathering *Klal Yisrael* around His Mishkan. When we were in the desert, Hashem divided us into tribes and camps, and each one given its own special place to dwell. Each tribe was given its own unique banner and leader, and all gathered and encamped around the Mishkan. *Klal Yisrael* say that these gatherings and banners were a gesture of love between Hashem and them.

HE BROUGHT ME TO THE WINE CHAMBER

"Wine" symbolizes Torah. Let us mention a few of the many reasons for this symbolism. Just as wine comes in many different flavors, so Torah has many different explanations. Just as people crave wine, and some even become addicted to it, so we should crave, desire, and even become "addicted to" Torah. Just as wine intoxicates a person, making him forget about everything else, so one who is engrossed in Torah should be oblivious to everything else.

Normally, the more one eats of a particular food, the less he desires it because it

---

24 The word דגלו means "His flag." By extension, "flag" connotes a gathering because a flag calls on people to come to gather around it. *Klal Yisrael* gathered around the Mishkan.

becomes boring and sickening. Wine is the exception: as a person drinks, he wants more and more. So it is with Torah: as a person learns it, he wants more and more of it.[25] Just as wine gets ruined if one adds different liquids or foods to it, so Torah is compromised when it is mixed with other streams of knowledge or with foreign thoughts. Unlike most foods, where the quality deteriorates with age, the quality of wine improves with age. Similarly, the Torah of those who have been learning for many years is superior to the Torah of those just starting to learn. In a similar vein, the Torah knowledge of earlier generations is superior to the Torah knowledge of later generations — indeed, the older the better. This contrasts with the realms of science and medicine, where modern-day knowledge surpasses the knowledge of earlier generations.

The numerical value of *yayin* (wine) is, in fact, seventy. This hints at the fact that the Torah can be explained in seventy different ways.[26]

In this verse, the Torah is being likened not just to a bottle of wine, but to an entire room full of different types of wine — a wine chamber, containing dry wine, sweet wine, semi-dry wine, etc. Each type of wine has its own smell and taste. As the Midrash notes, Torah, too, can be "consumed" (i.e., understood) in a variety of ways. There are the simple explanations, the complex ones, the Kabbalistic approach, etc. And the various *meforashim* offer different ideas and explanations.[27]

The concept here is that there are many interpretations to every verse in the Torah — and Hashem loves them all. Newcomers to Torah sometimes find the variety of viewpoints and interpretations very puzzling.[28] Eventually, they come to appreciate

---

25 Many have said that if one finds it hard to love and enjoy Torah learning, the best approach is often to begin learning anyway. "The appetite comes with the eating!"

26 *Bamidbar Rabbah* 13:15.

27 Rabbi Shmuel Rozovsky, *zt"l*, (as quoted in *Migevaos Ashurenu* by Rabbi Chizkiyahu Mishkovsky) offers a different perspective. He points out that one bottle of wine can make a person drunk only once, but a wine cellar can keep a person drunk all the time. Similarly, a *talmid chacham* who learns Torah should always be "drunk" from Torah: filled with happiness and oblivious to the irrelevant things happening around him.
    The Ponevezher Rav once gave an example of such "drunkenness." A certain *talmid chacham* was caught by Lithuanian soldiers during World War I. They accused him of being a spy and took him to be executed. At that moment, he was in the middle of studying a passage from the Rambam, and thus told them that it would be very cruel to kill him before he fully understood it. He asked them to let him finish thinking about this passage before executing him. Despite the strangeness of this request, they agreed to let him finish. Ultimately, the *talmid chacham* was saved because a fresh battle broke out in that town and the soldiers then had to attend to more urgent matters!

28 One of the interesting things about learning Torah is that conclusions are reached through argument and discussion. Indeed, the Gemara teaches that a person should not learn Torah by himself (*Berachos* 63b). For those who have never seen men learning Torah together, it is surprising to see how much arguing it involves. The Gemara itself is full of debates and discussions, questioning and answering, all with the aim of arriving at a correct interpretation. One might have thought that the best way to learn a Torah topic would be through listening and accepting a single explanation. This verse teaches us that Hashem gave us the Torah with its many alternative explanations because true understanding and appreciation of Torah depends on our examining a number of perspectives regarding every point. Without this, we would only be seeing a very small part of what Torah really is.

that far from being a deficiency, this is greatness of Torah, like a multifaceted diamond which has so many different colors shining from it. This should help us understand that even when we encounter explanations and interpretations that seem contradictory, it does not mean that only one of them is the correct one. On the contrary, they could be all correct — and that is the greatness of the Torah! Incidentally, this truth helps us appreciate the different ways of serving Hashem.

HIS "INGATHERING" SIGNIFIED HIS LOVE

The Midrash offers a novel interpretation of this verse by reading the word *vediglo* (translated above as "His ingathering") as "his stumbling."[29] In other words, when a person is learning Torah and stumbles in the reading of it, Hashem still loves him. Since the person means well and is trying to read it properly, even though is unable to, Hashem accepts his effort and loves him for it.[30] The Midrash goes on to provide several examples of how, when a person makes a mistake and innocently comes up with an incorrect explanation, even this is beloved to Hashem. The Midrash goes so far as to say that even if a person makes a slight, but horrible, error in pronunciation, and says "*ve'oyavta eis Hashem*" instead of "*ve'ahavta eis Hashem*" ("You shall hate Hashem" instead of "You shall love Hashem"), Hashem nevertheless loves the person for his efforts.[31][32]

---

29 From the root of the word *dilug*, meaning "a jump."

30 It is told that Rabbi Levi Yitzchak of Berditchev once reprimanded a man who was mispronouncing the words in davening. The man responded that when his baby "talks," all the noises are unintelligible and most people get no pleasure from the babble. As the baby's loving father, however, he is happy to hear even the babbling, and he even "understands" what the baby is trying to say. So too, since Hashem loves us, He will understand and welcome even our incorrect pronunciation of the davening. The Rebbe accepted this man's argument. (In fact, the Rebbe said to him that his whole life had been worthwhile just to hear this line of defense for *Klal Yisrael*.) Actually, the Midrash on this verse reflects this idea. The Midrash says that when a child reads the Torah incorrectly, Hashem responds, "His gurgle is beloved to Me."
Of course, this message has to be understood in the correct perspective: It *is* extremely important to pronounce the words of *tefillah* correctly. Still, for those who tend to be obsessive about this type of thing or worry about saying the words of prayer incorrectly, this Midrash is particularly relevant.

31 The Bnei Yissaschar (Kislev 3:11) makes the following pertinent observation about the halachah that if the Chanukah candles go out after they are lit — even if they go out immediately — one is not obligated to relight them (*Orach Chaim* 673:2). He says that the light of the menorah represents the light of Torah and cites this Midrash from which we learn that all Hashem wants is for us to make the effort. Even if the outcome is pitiable, it is precious to Hashem. To remind us of this, *Chazal* instituted that all one has to do to fulfill the mitzvah is to light the menorah, even if no lasting light is produced.

32 There is a memorable story in *Mishnas Chassidim* that illustrates this concept dramatically. It is told that back in the time of the Arizal, a simpleton once heard his Rav speaking about the mitzvah of *lechem hapanim*. When the Beis HaMikdash was standing, the *Kohanim* would put special loaves of bread on the golden table in the Sanctuary every Erev Shabbos. The simpleton did not realize that this mitzvah only applies in the Beis HaMikdash, and he somehow understood that there is a mitzvah to bake bread for Hashem. So, he asked his wife to bake some very special and tasty bread for him to bring to Hashem every week. After that, every Friday the simpleton brought these special loaves and

The Midrash adds that the word *v'diglo* (which literally means "and His banner") here at the end of our verse, has the numerical value of forty-nine. This hints at the forty-nine methods of applying every halachah to render something forbidden, and forty-nine methods to render it permitted.[33] This also illustrates how Torah is extremely complex and multidimensional.

The Torah Temimah adds that this Midrash also shows us the love *Klal Yisrael* has for Hashem and His Torah. When a person is obliged to obey a law that has many loopholes or more permissible interpretations, one is naturally inclined to take advantage of these. But because *Klal Yisrael* love Hashem, they do not look to do this and "take the easy way out." Even though there are so many ways to render everything permitted, they still adhere to all of the halachos without trying to find ways to make the forbidden permissible or to cutting corners though other shortcuts.

In a similar vein, the Gemara[34] says that when two *talmidei chachamim* learn Torah together, their "gathering"[35] is beloved to Hashem. The Gemara is telling us that when two people discuss Torah, even if one is not making sense, Hashem loves their gathering to debate the issue. The debate itself indicates a desire to understand Torah correctly, and this shows tremendous honor for Torah. This is beloved to Hashem. Furthermore, when two *talmidei chachamim* are debating a point back and forth, each one is showing that he enjoys a different understanding or feature of the Torah, like two people arguing about which part of a lesson they enjoyed more. In Hashem's eyes, both are showing their love and appreciation for Torah. It is actually a tribute and a compliment to Hashem when people argue about what He meant when He articulated a certain law or verse.

We can add that since Hashem loves us, He enjoys even our botched attempts to please Him. This is like parents enjoying a very amateurish picture made especially for

---

    put them in the *aron kodesh*. The *gabbai* of the shul noticed them there and could not figure out who was doing this or why, so he decided to take them home for himself. On Shabbos, when the *aron kodesh* was opened and the bread was not there, the simpleton was delighted and reported to his wife that Hashem had taken their bread.

    This continued for some time until one day the Rav saw the simpleton bringing the bread to the shul. He asked him about it, and the fellow explained it all. The explanation evoked words of mockery from the Rav. He made it clear to the simpleton that somebody must be enjoying his wife's hard work, but it is not Hashem, because today there is no such mitzvah. After a short investigation, the truth came out that the *gabbai* was eating the bread, and the simpleton stopped this practice. When the Arizal learned about this episode, he sent a message to the Rav that he would die shortly because he had stopped a sincere act of love for Hashem that gave Him tremendous pleasure. Sure enough, this is what happened!

33   See *Maseches Sofrim* 16:5 regarding this complex topic.

34   *Shabbos* 63a.

35   From the root of the word *degel*, i.e., a banner that draws people around it.

them by their child. The effort of the child and the love shown by this effort is very precious in their eyes.

This can be seen in yet another Gemara.[36] The Gemara tells us that there was a disagreement between two *talmidei chachamim* (Rabbi Evyasar and Rabbi Yonasan) on a certain point. In this instance, they were able to ask Eliyahu HaNavi who Hashem sided with, i.e., which one of them was correct?

Eliyahu quoted Hashem as saying, "My son Evyasar says as follows, and My other son Yonasan says as follows…" In other words, Hashem accepted both opinions. As we said above, whenever there is a debate about a point in Torah, Hashem loves both explanations. We see from the way Hashem is quoted here that He responds this way because of His love for us. When He says, "My son," He means that He sees every person as His child and therefore accepts even an incorrect idea.[37]

HIS BANNER OVER ME IS LOVE[38]

After saying that Hashem "brought me to the wine chamber," *Klal Yisrael* conclude: "His banner over me is love." What is the connection between the two halves of the verse, i.e., between the wine cellar and the love Hashem has even for our incorrect explanation of Torah?

As explained earlier, the verse likens Torah to a wine cellar because Torah is filled with an exciting variety of possible understandings and explanations. Unlike a simple painting which can be understood and appreciated at a glance, Torah is like an intricate tapestry. Great wisdom is required to see what is being depicted, and even then, one never truly sees everything. If an observer were to claim that this intricate tapestry includes something that is not actually depicted in it, this does not detract from the tapestry as it would from a simple picture. For example, if a normal person mistakes a picture of a ball for a picture of a tree, it is obvious that the painter and painting are faulty. But if one looks at a very complex tapestry, and mistakenly thinks that he sees a tree, this shows how intricate the tapestry is and that he needs to devote more time to studying it. This phenomenon also occurs with fine wine. Each person who tastes it might describe it differently, something that does not happen when tasting basic foods. When one tastes something in the wine which is not actually there, this only shows just how fine and "sophisticated" the wine is.

---

36   *Gittin* 6b.

37   In the previous verse, *Klal Yisrael* mention how they accepted the Torah without questions. This showed great love for Hashem. The present verse can be seen in this context. Since we showed such love and acceptance, Hashem reciprocates by accepting our efforts to serve Him, even if they are not exactly what He was expecting from us.

38   As explained above, this is the way the Midrash translates the first part of the verse.

This, then, is the connection between the first and the second half of the verse. Since Torah is likened to a wine cellar — with so many possibilities and intricacies — even the mistaken explanations of Torah demonstrate the complexity of Torah and thus add to its splendor.

HIS "INGATHERING" SIGNIFIED HIS LOVE

Klal Yisrael felt loved by Hashem when He gathered them around the Mishkan — each tribe with its own flag and its own place.[39] The Torah describes at great length — and more than once — where each tribe was encamped, who each tribe's leader was, and the order in which the tribes traveled.[40] What is to be learned from all this? The basic idea is that every person in *Klal Yisrael* had his own role in serving Hashem.[41] Each of the twelve tribes had a different way of serving Hashem, and each one saw Hashem from its own vantage point and understood Torah from its own perspective. Yet they were all precious in His eyes. Therefore, Hashem placed each tribe in the place that was best for it, and the honor of Hashem was generated by the entirety of *Klal Yisrael*. On a simple level, this can be likened to a team, where each person realizes that he has his own place, and his own role, and nobody is superfluous.

According to this interpretation, the connection to the first half of the verse is quite clear. Hashem gave us the Torah, which has many meanings, and He loves every way that *Klal Yisrael* serve Him, as long as it is within the boundaries of the Torah. Therefore, Hashem gives each tribe its own flag and its own place, and He sets them all around His Mishkan. This made *Klal Yisrael* feel that Hashem loves every single individual and accepts his individuality. This is what they mean when they say, "His ingathering [of all of Israel around Him] signified His love to me."

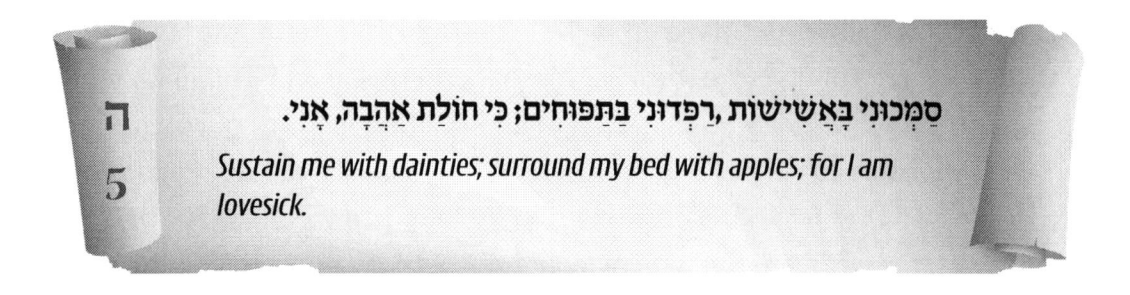

ה

5

סַמְּכוּנִי בָּאֲשִׁישׁוֹת, רַפְּדוּנִי בַּתַּפּוּחִים; כִּי חוֹלַת אַהֲבָה, אָנִי.

Sustain me with dainties; surround my bed with apples; for I am lovesick.

Allegorical Translation I (*Klal Yisrael*) am asking to be sustained and nourished in exile with comforting food such as fine bread and apples because I feel unwell without His love.

---

39   Rashi.
40   The first three *parshiyos* in *Bamidbar* focus on this.
41   See our commentary on 6:1 for further elaboration.

Subject of the Verse	*Klal Yisrael* is expressing their deepest feelings.
Mashal	The wife says: now that I have been left by the husband whom I loved so much, I am feeling very low and require tender, loving care to help me survive.
Nimshal	*Klal Yisrael* in exile feel ill because they are missing Hashem's love. They ask that Hashem provide them with support in the form of special food, which is symbolic of Torah, to comfort them in their sickness.

SUSTAIN ME WITH DAINTIES

The Midrash explains that "dainties" represent the halachos (laws) and "apples" represent the Aggados ("inspirational ideas"). Suffering from the pain of losing Hashem, *Klal Yisrael* in exile are trying to strengthen themselves with halachos and Aggados.

This explanation of our verse dovetails with a Midrashic interpretation of the verse in *Eichah*, "This I bring to mind, and therefore [my] hope [in Hashem] is restored"[42] "This," the Midrash says, refers to Torah, as in the verse, "*This* is the Torah that Moshe placed..."[43] The Midrash offers the following parable to show why *Klal Yisrael* see the Torah as their elixir. A certain newly married king promised his bride that he would give her a wonderful dowry. But before delivering on his promise, he took off and left her alone for many years. Despite this, the wife remained loyal and waited for the king. Her neighbors would mock and taunt her, insisting that she was waiting in vain. She would become despondent, and only by rereading the written promise of her wonderful dowry would she feel a new sense of hope. When the king returned, he asked her how she managed to remain faithful. She replied that she was sustained by reading the promise of the dowry. The king replied: "I will fulfill all that is written in it — and much, much more!"

Similarly, when the heathen nations mock *Klal Yisrael*'s faithfulness to Hashem and cause them to become despondent, they reread the Torah in which Hashem assures them of His love and reward. This restores their faith and love. Our verse in *Shir HaShirim* alludes to this: when we, *Klal Yisrael*, are sick with pining for Hashem, we ask to be supported with words of Torah, which sustain us by reminding us of Hashem's love for us.

Why are halachos described as "dainties," and Aggados as "apples"? The Midrash explains that dainties are a type of tasty, refined bread. Based on this identification, we are to understand that "bread" here represents a staple food. Halachos are likened to bread,

---

42 3:21.
43 *Devarim* 4:44.

something that everyone should incorporate into his daily life.⁴⁴ In contrast, "apples" are a luxury, like Aggados, which a person does not need to have on a daily basis.

Another explanation of the symbolism here is that apples give off a pleasant fragrance and are beautiful to look at while bread is enjoyed only by the person who eats it. So, too, halachos require a person to sit down and consume (i.e., learn) them, while a person can gain inspiration just by casually hearing a bit of inspiration from the realm of Aggadah.⁴⁵

FOR I AM LOVESICK

Klal Yisrael describe themselves as being "lovesick."⁴⁶ According to Rashi, they mean that they are pining for Hashem and missing His love. The Midrash understands their intent somewhat differently. *Klal Yisrael* is saying: even though we are spiritually unwell due to our many sins and faults, Hashem overlooks all this and loves us anyway.

When Hashem took us out of Egypt, we had descended to what *Chazal* call "the forty-ninth level of impurity," the lowest level of spirituality from which we could still be saved. This is quite remarkable if we consider the way most marriages evolve. At first, the young man and the young lady make every effort to dress nicely, behave nicely, and generally make the most favorable impression they can. Only after being married for some time does this facade start slipping away, unfortunately. Indeed, newlyweds may wonder whether their love for one another will diminish when the less attractive aspects of their personality come to light. In marked contrast to this scenario, Hashem chose us when we were at our very worst, and we slowly worked our way up. The awareness that Hashem chose us even after seeing our worst side and that He still showed His love for us, reassures us that Hashem will always love us.⁴⁷

LOVESICK

The Rambam writes that a person should not observe mitzvos only out of fear of Hashem. Rather, one should be motivated by love for Hashem.⁴⁸ The Rambam goes on to explain what kind of love is meant: "…a love so tremendous, boundless, and powerful that a

---

44   The Midrash also notes that the term used to refer to halachos, *ashishos*, can mean "foundations," from the root *she-siyah*, a foundation stone. This is because halachic conclusions have to be built on proper foundations, proven from earlier sources, and established on the basis of similar cases.

45   *Eitz Yosef.*

46   This term appears a number of times in *Shir HaShirim*. See our commentary on 5:8 for further discussion of this term.

47   According to this Midrash, then, the Jewish People is communicating: "I have been chosen and loved despite my illness, but now I wish to recover so that I can display my more appealing attributes. So please, Hashem, give me the nourishment and support necessary to make me well again.

48   *Hilchos Teshuvah* 10:3.

person's spirit is bonded with the love of Hashem, and he is constantly meditating and thinking about this love. Just as one who has become lovesick [over a woman] is unable to think of anything else..."[49] The Rambam concludes that a person should be constantly blundering because he is preoccupied with Hashem's love, as Shlomo HaMelech says in this verse of *Shir HaShirim*, "I am lovesick." The Rambam concludes that the whole of *Shir HaShirim* is a parable to this effect.

We see that the Rambam explains this verse differently from Rashi. According to the Rambam, *Klal Yisrael* is describing their love for Hashem. They are "lovesick" in the sense that they are so totally wrapped up with their love for Hashem that the love makes them sick (i.e., they behave abnormally).[50]

It is noteworthy that out of all the verses in *Shir HaShirim*, the Rambam cites this one to describe the overwhelming love that a person should have for Hashem. The Rambam is conveying that true love for Hashem goes beyond what a person's mind tells him. Once love based on logic switches to love rooted in emotion, then a person has truly begun to love Hashem.

According to the Rambam's approach, then, *Klal Yisrael* wants to learn Torah (symbolized by dainties and apples) because they are lovesick in the sense that they are full of love for Hashem. Through Torah, they can strengthen that love. The Netziv adds that this verse teaches us that the best way to fully enjoy and appreciate the love of Hashem is by learning Torah.

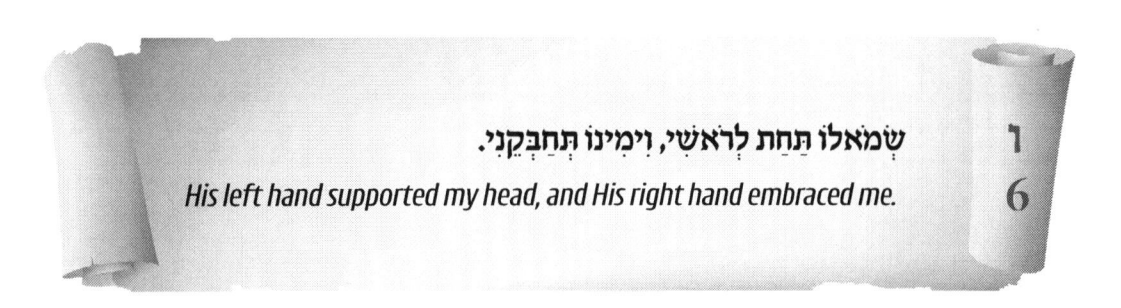

ו
6
שְׂמֹאלוֹ תַּחַת לְרֹאשִׁי, וִימִינוֹ תְּחַבְּקֵנִי.

His left hand supported my head, and His right hand embraced me.

---

49   See the beginning of our Introduction for a fuller citation of this halachah from *Hilchos Teshuvah*.

50   We may wonder why the Rambam suddenly discusses how to love Hashem at the end of his *Hilchos Teshuvah*. The explanation for this starts with the statement in the Talmud Yerushalmi that a person should serve Hashem with both love and fear, because one without the other is not enough (*Sotah* 5:5). The Yerushalmi continues that if one serves with love, he will not hate, and if one serves with fear, he will not "kick." Love and fear are both fundamental emotions and basic motivating forces. If one serves Hashem only out of fear, he will eventually come to hate Him. If one serves Hashem only out of love, however, he will eventually "kick," i.e., become lax and disobey the halachos. Therefore, we must make sure to cultivate both emotions. A person who has committed a sin has already disobeyed Hashem, so he needs to work on his fear of Hashem in order not to disobey again. If he goes too far in this direction, however, there is a danger that he will forget about loving Hashem. For this reason, after focusing on the concept of reward and punishment in order to instill fear, the Rambam concludes that we should not forget to love Hashem as well.

Allegorical Translation	I recall how Hashem would show me His love and support by providing me a pleasant camping site in the desert, and by providing all of my needs, such as the manna bread.[51]
Subject of the Verse	*Klal Yisrael* is reminiscing about how Hashem used to show them His love and support.
Mashal	In the previous verse, the wife lamented how hard it is for her because she is missing her husband's love. Here she goes on to mention just how loving her husband used to be, supporting her and embracing her. Thus, his absence is all the more painful.
Nimshal	In the previous verse, *Klal Yisrael* said that they are lovesick because they are missing Hashem's love. Here, they go on to note just how wonderful that love was — and therefore how great their pain now that it is missing. They describe in metaphorical terms how Hashem openly graced them with His love and protection.[52]

HIS LEFT HAND SUPPORTED MY HEAD

Hashem gave us two hands, one weaker and one stronger. Among the reasons for this is so that we will understand that certain actions should be done with strength (symbolized by the right hand) and others with less enthusiasm (symbolized by the left hand). For example, *Chazal* tell us that even when we need to rebuke or punish someone, we should make sure to use our left hand, but when we draw someone near and give a reward, we should use our right hand.[53] In other words, drawing others near and showing love must be done with much more strength and regularity than punishing.

Another reason that we have two different hands with different levels of strength is so that we should understand that Hashem uses two different approaches when

---

51 Rashi explains that the left hand supporting *Klal Yisrael* mentioned in the verse symbolizes Hashem's care for them in the desert. The right hand embracing them symbolizes Hashem's clearing the way for them as they travelled.

52 There is something important to be learned from the order in which *Klal Yisrael*'s situation is presented here. We are first told about the result (*Klal Yisrael* feeling a strong need for Hashem's love) and only then the cause (*Klal Yisrael* is missing Hashem's "embrace"). Would it not have been more appropriate to present the cause and then the effect: Because *Klal Yisrael* miss His "embrace," they therefore need "the dainties..."? The explanation is that *Shir HaShirim* is intended to awaken us to how much Hashem loves *Klal Yisrael*, and how much they are missing His love. It is more dramatic and more stirring to describe the feelings before the cause. ("I am so excited because such-and-such happened!" is a more emotional outburst than "Such-and-such happened, and it is making me excited.") This is a subtle but important point regarding learning all of *Shir HaShirim* and other parts of *Nach*. We are not merely learning new ideas. Rather, we are supposed to be stirred by them. Therefore, the way the information is conveyed is often one that works more on the heart than the mind.

53 *Sotah* 47a.

running the world — one "weaker," and one "stronger."[54] The Midrash explains that the left hand of Hashem represents His weaker approach. Therefore, it often represents the aspect of Hashem's judgment (justice) and punishment because Hashem engages less in judgment than He does in showing mercy. His right hand represents His stronger, more prevalent behavior. Therefore, it represents Hashem's mercy.[55][56]

As applied to our verse, this means that Hashem's punishments (administered with His "left hand") have always sustained *Klal Yisrael* because they cause us to remain faithful to Hashem. If there would be no judgment, we would become lax, *chas v'shalom*, in serving Hashem and would fall in our level of behavior. His judgment and punishment support us because they keep us from stumbling and falling in sin. But when Hashem is merciful and loving to *Klal Yisrael* (using His "right hand"), it is as if He is embracing us. We then feel all of Hashem's love and warmth.[57] The verse tells us that *Klal Yisrael* need Hashem's judgment (justice) to support them, i.e., to make sure they do not stumble in their service of Hashem. And they need Hashem's mercy to envelop them with love.

---

54 As explained in our Introduction, Hashem created everything in this world so that we should better know and serve Him.

55 Commenting on *Shemos* 15:6, Rashi tells us that "when *Klal Yisrael* fulfills the will of Hashem, His left hand becomes right" (*s.v. yemincha* to explain why the verse uses the term "right hand" twice). According to the explanation above, this means that when *Klal Yisrael* is doing mitzvos, Hashem's Attribute of Strict Justice becomes one of Mercy.

56 The Netziv sees this verse as a continuation of the theme he identified in the previous verse: The best way to come close to Hashem is through learning Torah. He explains that this verse alludes to learning Torah on two different levels. When one learns Torah on a weaker level (with the "left hand"), the Torah gives him support; but when one learns Torah at a higher level (with the right hand), the Torah embraces a person. What are these two levels? According to the Netziv, learning Torah for one's own benefit is the lower level, while learning Torah for its own sake is the higher level. *Chazal* tell us that when a person learns Torah for his own benefit, he merits the wealth and honor that support him. But when a person learns Torah for its own sake, he merits a life of love from Hashem! Understood this way, the verse reads as follows: "His left hand supports my head [when I learn Torah in the weaker fashion], and His right hand embraces me [when I learn Torah in the stronger fashion]."
This explanation accords well with the present tense used in this verse. With Rashi's explanation, we would have expected the past tense to be used.

57 This concept of the right hand representing mercy and the left hand representing judgment (in the sense of strict justice) is found in many sources. The *Mishnah Berurah* (4:10:22) explains the procedure for handwashing in these terms. He writes that we lift up the cup to wash our hands with our right hand, and then pass it to the left hand, and wash our right hand first (always giving precedence to the right) in order that Hashem's mercy should overcome His judgment. The *Shem MiShmuel* uses the symbolism of left and right to explain a fascinating *Gemara* (*Bava Kama* 92b). *Chazal* tell us that Moshe Rabbeinu blessed Yehoshua using both his hands (as recorded in *Devarim* 34:9) even though Hashem instructed him to use one hand. Now, we may wonder what difference it makes whether Moshe Rabbeinu used one hand or two? The *Shem MiShmuel* explains that Yehoshua had two different roles. On the one hand, he had to draw *Klal Yisrael* near to Hashem, but on the other, he had to push away the heathen nations. For that he needed both the traits of mercy and of judgment. Originally, when Moshe Rabbeinu was told that Yehoshua would be the leader, he was disappointed that the leadership would not stay in his family. Hashem reassured him that his nephew Elazar would help Yehoshua, and He would be the one to help *Klal Yisrael* come closer to Hashem. Therefore, Hashem told Moshe to bless Yehoshua using only one hand (i.e., the left hand) to push away the nations. However, Moshe Rabbeinu, in his generosity, blessed him using both hands, thus endowing Yehoshua with both these traits so that he would be a complete leader.

Both "hands" of Hashem are looking after us, and both are "used" for our good.[58]

This fits in with Rashi's explanation as well. Hashem's supporting *Klal Yisrael* in the desert was an expression of His justice: Since He was the one who took them out, He gave them what they needed. However, what Hashem did by clearing the way three days ahead for *Klal Yisrael* showed mercy. Through that kindness, *Klal Yisrael* felt they were being embraced. Rashi also says that by giving them food in such a pleasant way, it was if Hashem was embracing *Klal Yisrael*. Having Hashem support and embrace them made them feel very loved.[59]

In the previous verse, *Klal Yisrael* say that in exile, they are unwell because they do not feel Hashem's love as strongly as they did in the past. They are thus looking for ways to sustain themselves. How do *Klal Yisrael* want to do this? The verse says (according to the Midrash) that they want halachos and Aggados. Halachos represent Hashem's justice. Learning the rules and laws of the Torah reminds a person of what he needs to do to serve Hashem properly and of the punishments he will incur should he fail to do so, *chas v'shalom*. Halachah thus supports us in the sense that it keeps us from stumbling in sin. It fills in for the loss of Hashem's support which we used to feel through His left hand (symbolizing judgment and justice). Learning Aggados inspires a person to appreciate Hashem's love and mercy to *Klal Yisrael*. This fills in for the loss of Hashem's embrace.[60] The two verses, then, read as follows:

> Sustain me with dainties [help me learn halachos to support me in keeping Your laws], surround my bed with apples [inspire me with Your Aggados]; for I am lovesick [for I am sick, because now I am in exile, and I miss Your love].
>
> His left hand supported my head (before I went into exile, Hashem would support me with justice), and His right hand embraced me (and through His mercy, I would feel His embrace).

---

58 The Ratzba offers still another explanation of our verse based on these ideas. He notes that the beginning of the lives of the righteous is full of trials and tribulations, but eventually they reap eternal reward (see Rashi on *Bereishis* 27:29). *Roshi*, "my head," can also mean "my beginning." According to this, *Klal Yisrael* declare, "In the beginning, I felt His left Hand [through suffering], but this eventually enabled me to feel His right Hand, His abundant kindness" (*Likutei Ratzba*, p. 50).

59 The Midrash gives other illustrations of these two types of support from Hashem. It contrasts, for example, the sukkah that we use today (Hashem's left hand supporting us) with the Clouds of Glory we will have when Mashiach comes (Hashem's right hand embracing us). This means that now in exile, we do not feel totally enveloped by Hashem's love, but the mitzvah of sukkah supports us because it reminds us of His love. In the future, we will feel Hashem enveloping us with love through the Clouds of Glory.

60 This is why regarding "dainties" (halachah), the verse speaks of *sustaining* (supporting) us, while regarding "apples" (Aggadah), it speaks of *surrounding* (embracing) us.

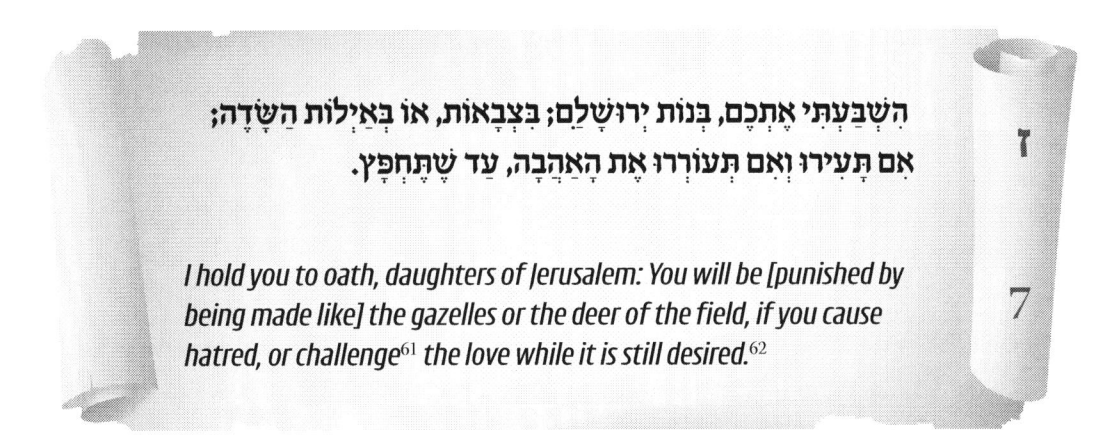

> הִשְׁבַּעְתִּי אֶתְכֶם, בְּנוֹת יְרוּשָׁלָ͏ִם; בִּצְבָאוֹת, אוֹ בְּאַיְלוֹת הַשָּׂדֶה;
> אִם תָּעִירוּ וְאִם תְּעוֹרְרוּ אֶת הָאַהֲבָה, עַד שֶׁתֶּחְפָּץ.
>
> *I hold you to oath, daughters of Jerusalem: You will be [punished by being made like] the gazelles or the deer of the field, if you cause hatred, or challenge*[61] *the love while it is still desired.*[62]
>
> **7**

Allegorical Translation We (*Klal Yisrael*) warn the heathen nations that if they try to cause hatred between us and Hashem, while He still actually loves us, they will be rendered defenseless and free for all to be destroyed just like defenseless deer.[63]

Subject of the Verse *Klal Yisrael* is warning the nations not to cause more trouble.

Mashal The wife warns her associates of the terrible consequences that await them if they try to cause even more of a split between her and her husband.

Nimshal *Klal Yisrael* warn the nations that they should not try to cause conflict between Hashem and *Klal Yisrael*. If they do, they will be vulnerable to terrible punishments like unprotected deer in the wild.

I HOLD YOU TO OATH

Let us clarify the connection between this verse and the preceding ones. *Klal Yisrael*

---

61 Rashi understands תָּעִירוּ as "causing animosity," from the root עָר, meaning "enemy" (as in *Daniel* 4:16), and תְּעוֹרְרוּ as "seeking a challenge," from the root עוֹרֵר, meaning "a challenger" (as in *Kesubos* 109a).

62 This translation follows Rashi.
The Ramban, however, takes a completely different approach. He understands the verse this way: "When you arouse or awaken the love, [keep hold of it] until you have succeeded in putting it into a receptacle." (The word "*techpatz*" comes from the root of the word "*chefetz*," meaning "an object.") This means that a person who feels inspired and closer to Hashem must look to hold onto the feeling by performing an action that will concretize this inspiration. If he does not, the feeling will fade away and soon be forgotten. This is a very important message for us because the *yetzer ha'ra* tries to convince us that our inspiration will remain with us even if we do not act on it. We must make sure never to let an inspiration get lost and must find concrete ways to conserve and cultivate it.
Incidentally, this explains why, at the *Akeidah*, when Avraham Avinu was told not to slaughter Yitzchak, he looked for a sacrifice to bring to Hashem – and even wanted to cut Yitzchak very slightly. He had just reached a very high level in service and subservience to Hashem and wanted to concretize this great emotional event in some way.

63 Most animals have some way of defending themselves, such as their strength or size. Although sheep and cattle do not, they are not defenseless because their owners guard them (due to their value). The exception is the deer (or gazelle) which is not domesticated yet is also not strong enough to protect itself. Therefore, the deer (or gazelle) is the quintessential defenseless animal.

has been expressing how low and rejected they feel in exile. But here they nevertheless warn the heathen nations not to try to undermine the love that remains even further. *Klal Yisrael* is in effect saying to the nations:

> Do not take advantage of the current situation where we are feeling far from Hashem and try to destroy our relationship altogether by enticing us away from Hashem or forcing us to stop serving Him. Even though we feel far from Hashem and miss His support and embrace, you cannot uproot our underlying love altogether. If you try to do this, you will become like the defenseless deer and gazelles. You will be devoured like these animals that are freely attacked by all.[64]

I HOLD YOU TO OATH

The Netziv takes a very different approach here, and identifies the speaker not as *Klal Yisrael*, but as Hashem Himself. He sees this verse as a warning to *Klal Yisrael* not to push for the Redemption too quickly. Since *Klal Yisrael* feel such a strong love from Hashem, which is how the Netziv explains the previous two verses, it is necessary to warn them not to push too hard to conclude the exile.[65]

According to the Netziv, then, the verse is to be understood as follows:

> I (Hashem) hold you to oath, *Klal Yisrael*, not to interfere with the process of exile and redemption. Do not be like the [heavenly] Hosts[66] [i.e., the angels, who exhibit limitless self-sacrifice for the Redemption]. Nor should you be [wicked and unrestricted] like the gazelles or the deer of the field [a situation that would also "force" the Redemption, because, as the Gemara teaches, Hashem will redeem *Klal Yisrael* if they all become righteous or all become wicked]. Furthermore, you should not stir Me up [with too much prayer] or stir yourselves

---

64 It is noteworthy that some of the other religions are based on the belief that *Klal Yisrael* was indeed Hashem's Chosen People at the outset but was superseded due to their sins. This belief became popularized shortly after the Destruction of the Second Beis HaMikdash. While the Beis HaMikdash was standing and all could see the Presence of Hashem in Yerushalayim, such a belief would have been laughable. But once the Destruction occurred and *Klal Yisrael* were exiled and dispersed all over the world, it did seem, superficially, that Hashem was rejecting the Jewish People. In this verse, the fallacy of this belief is being underscored. It is a mistake, say *Klal Yisrael*, to think that just because our love seems weaker, it can be supplanted. Our love remains forever, and terrible calamities will befall those who think otherwise!

65 Why *Klal Yisrael* must not push too hard for the exile to be finished is beyond the scope of this *sefer*. The basic idea is that the exile has to run its course (like a course of medication), and to interfere with it is dangerous.

66 The Netziv understands the word צבאות to mean "legions" or "hosts" — not "gazelles."

[with too much anguish over the exile] to force Me to show My love [and redeem you] until it pleases [Me to do so]."[67]

In a very similar vein, the Gemara teaches that this "oath," which is repeated a number of times in *Shir HaShirim*,[68] is Hashem warning *Klal Yisrael* and the heathen nations how to conduct themselves during the exile.[69] Hashem made *Klal Yisrael* promise that they would not go up en masse to Eretz Yisrael and not rebel against the heathen nations; and He made the heathen nations promise that they would not treat *Klal Yisrael* too harshly. The Gemara cites an opinion that He also made *Klal Yisrael* promise that they would not push off the Redemption by sinning [or force the Redemption by excessive prayer[70]], that they would not seek to reveal when the Redemption will occur and would not reveal the hidden secrets of Torah to the heathen nations.

While this matter is beyond the scope of the present *sefer*, suffice it to say that our exile has a purpose, and for it to fulfill its purpose, certain conduct is required in a number of areas. This can be likened to a husband and wife struggling with serious marital problems who are told that they must have a separation period. The hope is that their separation will cause them to realize how precious their relationship really is and thereby re-ignite their love. A positive outcome could be jeopardized, of course, by certain kinds of behavior. Similarly, Hashem sent us into exile for our good. We must be careful not to jeopardize its ultimate benefit.

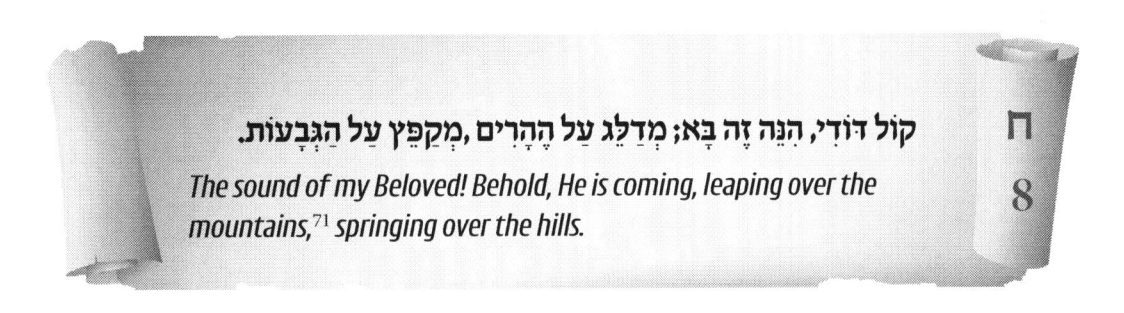

> ח 8 קוֹל דּוֹדִי, הִנֵּה זֶה בָּא; מְדַלֵּג עַל הֶהָרִים, מְקַפֵּץ עַל הַגְּבָעוֹת.
>
> The sound of my Beloved! Behold, He is coming, leaping over the mountains,[71] springing over the hills.

---

67 I have included the Netziv's explanation here and in the previous two verses because many of the Midrashim on these verses fit in well with his approach.

68 3:5, 5:8 (in a different context) and 8:4.

69 *Kesubos* 111a. This is what the Gemara calls "*shalosh shevuos*" ("the three oaths") upon which the Satmar Rebbe, *zt"l*, based his sefer *Va'yoel Moshe*.

70 Rashi.

71 As we go on to explain in the commentary, Rashi understands this verse to be saying that Hashem came quickly to redeem us — so quickly that He seemed to be skipping over mountains. The Gemara, however, takes an entirely different tack by interpreting the "mountains" in this verse to be symbolic of the Avos. Thus, the verse means that in the merit of the Avos — who did good deeds as high as the mountains and were themselves as awesome as the mountains — Hashem redeemed us from Egypt (*Rosh Hashanah* 11a).
Incidentally, the Netziv offers an important insight in explaining why the Avos are likened to mountains. Scaling a mountain seems daunting and can sometimes even seem impossible from down below. But one can reach the top. Of

Allegorical Translation — We (*Klal Yisrael*) heard the voice proclaiming in the name of Hashem that He is coming to save us speedily, as if He is jumping over the mountains and the hills (i.e., overcoming all obstacles that stand in the way of the redemption from Egypt).

Subject of the Verse — *Klal Yisrael* is reminiscing about the events of the redemption from Egypt.

Mashal — The wife calls to mind her loving memories of how, at the very beginning of their relationship, her husband came for her with alacrity, allowing nothing to get in the way.

Nimshal — Having briefly mentioned earlier[72] that Hashem took them out of Egypt, *Klal Yisrael* now speak of those precious memories in some detail. They recall how Hashem took them out of exile without delay, disregarding all the obstacles that could have delayed the redemption.

THE SOUND OF MY BELOVED...

In the previous verse, we learned how Hashem adjures *Klal Yisrael* not to be impatient over the Final Redemption. This verse notes how Hashem hastened the redemption from Egypt and did everything possible to take them out quickly. The connection between these two verses is thought-provoking. When we recall how urgently Hashem saved us from Egypt and how no obstacle stood in His way when He decided it was time to save us, we realize that Hashem's delay in saving us from our current exile is not due to lack of love, ability, or willingness. We understand that it is for our ultimate good. This awareness helps us obey Hashem's directive not to try to force the Final Redemption too quickly, but rather to wait for such time as He sees fit to bring it.[73]

THE SOUND OF MY BELOVED

According to the Malbim, this is the beginning of the second chapter of *Shir HaShirim*.

---

course, it can only be done by taking thousands of smaller steps. Similarly, we should not think that the Avos accomplished everything in one step. Rather, they spent their entire lives constantly doing the right thing until they got to the top. In the merit of their dedication to keep on ascending, we were saved. We, too, must serve Hashem like mountain climbers, taking thousands of little steps one after the next, climbing a little higher with each one.

Another lesson we learn from mountain climbing is that when one reaches the peak, one often finds that he has another peak to climb. Similarly, for every level a person reaches, he should know that there is a still higher level. The Avos kept discovering new heights and reaching new levels.

72 1:4.
73 Rabbi Shlomo Kluger, *Ma'asei Yedei Yotzeir* p. 463.

Rashi explains that this is the start of *Klal Yisrael*'s description of their redemption from Egypt.[74] Even though the redemption was mentioned earlier, here it is recalled in detail. As Rashi notes, this is the way we sometimes talk. We might say, for example, "I mentioned something to you before, but I never really described to you how it all began and just how wonderful it was. Now I want to tell you exactly what happened…"[75]

THE SOUND OF MY BELOVED

Klal Yisrael in Egypt were despondent, having largely given up hope of ever getting out, when suddenly Hashem announced through Moshe Rabbeinu: "I have come to take you out!" The emotion and excitement people felt are reflected in our verse: "The sound of my Beloved, behold, He is coming right now!" We must try to feel them as well. The verse goes on to picture Hashem coming with tremendous speed, jumping over all obstacles, *ki'veyachol*, to redeem us.

The Midrash goes a step beyond Rashi and adds that our verse is not only referring to the redemption from Egyptian slavery, but to all of our redemptions, past and future. This means that when Mashiach comes, we will re-live all of these emotions and experiences. There is no contradiction here since many of the verses in *Shir HaShirim* are understood both in terms of the past and the future. This is appropriate because they are basically referring to a concept or an idea that may already have played out in many ways and at many times — and that will continue to. Our verse, then, is telling us both what happened and what *will* happen. Just as past redemptions were sudden, future ones will be sudden as well.

The Midrash tells us that when Moshe Rabbeinu came to *Klal Yisrael* and announced that the time of their redemption had arrived, they replied that it could not be, as the time was not ripe. Hashem had said they would be in exile for 400 years, but only 210 years had passed. Moshe Rabbeinu answered that since Hashem desired to redeem them already, He was "leaping over the mountains, and springing over the hills." That is to say, He was transcending the original calculation of how long the exile would last because He wanted to redeem them now.[76]

---

74 The Vilna Gaon also writes that this is the beginning of the main narrative of *Shir HaShirim*.

75 This approach accords with the Malbim's opinion that this verse is the start of a new chapter. The Malbim understands that the first chapter tells us the basis of the love between Hashem and *Klal Yisrael*, and the next chapters elaborate on each event mentioned in the first chapter.

76 The Midrash offers two other versions of this interchange: 1) When Moshe Rabbeinu told *Klal Yisrael* that the time of their redemption had arrived, they said that it could not be so because they had not done any good deeds. Moshe countered that Hashem was "leaping over the mountains, springing over the hills," meaning that He was "jumping" on account of the righteous people who did good deeds and would save *Klal Yisrael* in their merit. 2) When Moshe

The Midrash concludes that when Mashiach will come and announce that the time of the Final Redemption has arrived, *Klal Yisrael* will again say that it could not be so. They will point out that Hashem had said they would first have to be enslaved by all of the seventy heathen nations. Mashiach will answer that Hashem is "leaping over the mountains, [and] springing over the hills," meaning that He is jumping over the nations to save them. And the slavery that they endured at the hands of the various people who came from all of the seventy nations will be as if they suffered through seventy exiles.

This beautiful Midrash and this verse teach us that Hashem is willing to save us regardless of the reasons why we might not be deserving.[77] Hashem loves us so much that nothing can impede His bringing us closer to Him. *Klal Yisrael* felt this love then and will feel it again when Mashiach comes.

Rabbi Moshe Mordechai Shulsinger, *zt"l*, observes that even many fine people have the wrong perspective on this matter of the Final Redemption.[78] Because they have heard that all sorts of conditions must be met before Mashiach comes, they think that he cannot come right away. But Rabbi Shulsinger points out that part of the basic belief in the coming of Mashiach is that he *can* come at any time.[79] And when he does, hindsight will enable us to understand how it was possible. It will be very similar to what happened in Egypt, as recorded in the Midrash. When, for example, *Klal Yisrael* told

---

Rabbeinu told *Klal Yisrael* that the time of their redemption had arrived, they said it could not be so because they had engaged in so much idol worship. Moshe countered that Hashem was "leaping over the mountains, springing over the hills," meaning that He was jumping over the *aveiros* they had done and ignoring them. These are only some of the reasons *Klal Yisrael* gave for their lack of optimism. Just as they were redeemed regardless of all the "reasons," so Hashem will redeem us from our present exile regardless of all the "reasons" we may think it cannot happen. Hashem's love overrides everything.

77 Rabbi Moshe of Kobrin notes that this is true not just of the entire nation but of every individual. When a person seeks salvation from a personal trouble or forgiveness for his sins, he may mistakenly think that there are many reasons why Hashem should not help him. He must realize, however, that Hashem loves us more than we love ourselves. Even if we feel that we are underserving, Hashem will save us.

78 In his *sefer*, *Shalmei Sadeh*.

79 In the Thirteen Principles of Faith that we say at the end of davening in the morning, it is written that even though the coming of Mashiach may be delayed, we nevertheless await him every day. Why is this statement added? After all, we do not say regarding the other Principles of Faith that even though we do not see it happening, we still believe... For example, we do not say: Even though Hashem does not always seem to answer our prayers, we will still continue to pray to Him. Rabbi Shulsinger explains that we certainly do *not* mean to say that even though it is hard to believe in the coming of the Mashiach because it is taking so long, we believe, nonetheless. Indeed, it would be disrespectful to say that we believe in such and such even though it stretches the imagination. Rather, we are saying that even though there are reasons why he should not come (e.g., we have not yet repented or Eliyahu HaNavi has not yet arrived), nevertheless, we await him every day because part of the belief in the coming of Mashiach is that he can come at any time regardless of all the calculations.

Moshe that their redemption was impossible because 400 years of exile had not yet elapsed, Moshe countered that since Hashem wished to save them, He would reckon those 400 years from the time of Yitzchak's birth. So, too, Hashem will "find a way" to save us the moment He deems it appropriate, and all other calculations will fall into place. It behooves us to strengthen our belief in and understanding of *bi'as haMashiach* through this inspiring verse.[80]

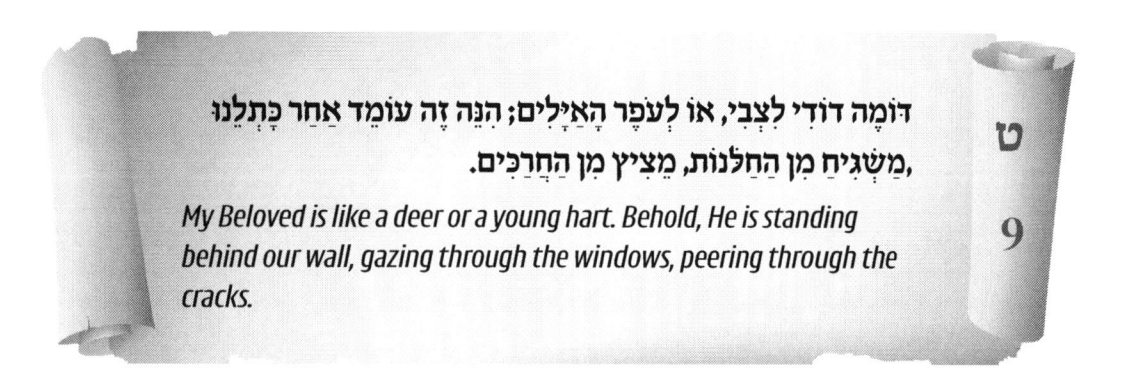

> דּוֹמֶה דוֹדִי לִצְבִי, אוֹ לְעֹפֶר הָאַיָּלִים; הִנֵּה זֶה עוֹמֵד אַחַר כָּתְלֵנוּ מַשְׁגִּיחַ מִן הַחֲלֹנוֹת, מֵצִיץ מִן הַחֲרַכִּים.
>
> My Beloved is like a deer or a young hart. Behold, He is standing behind our wall, gazing through the windows, peering through the cracks.
>
> ט
> 9

Allegorical Translation — In His speed to redeem us, my Beloved (Hashem) was like a fast deer.[81] We also saw how He was always close to us even in exile, standing just behind our wall, watching through the windows and cracks to take care of us.

Subject of the Verse — *Klal Yisrael* continues with their reminiscing about the wonderful events of *Yetzias Mitzrayim*.

Mashal — The wife continues to recall how their relationship began. She describes how she felt her husband coming very fast and enthusiastically for her, how she suddenly realized that he had always been watching out for her, and how happy it made her to realize that long before he actually asked her out, he was already looking out for her and caring for her.

Nimshal — *Klal Yisrael* describes how Hashem speedily saved them and how they suddenly realized that even while they were in exile, Hashem was watching them and taking care of them.

---

80 Rabbi Shulsinger notes that if a person is mistaken in other areas of Jewish thought, he will still be rewarded in the World to Come for his good deeds. But a person who is mistaken about a basic belief (i.e., one of the Thirteen Principles of Faith) can be considered a heretic, *chas v'shalom*, and lose all of his rewards.

81 Deer are renowned for their speed, as we see from the Mishnah that exhorts us be as fast as a deer to serve Hashem (*Avos* 5:20).

MY BELOVED IS LIKE A GAZELLE...

This verse is a continuation of the previous verse, embellishing the theme of the speedy redemption from Egypt.[82] Even though *Klal Yisrael* thought that the redemption was very far away, it was actually very near at hand. (We, too, sometimes make this same mistake in thinking about our Future Redemption.) The verses use three different analogies to convey this idea: Hashem came jumping over the hills; He was like a gazelle; and He was just on the other side of our wall. Each analogy describes another level of surprise that *Klal Yisrael* felt when the redemption arrived – and that we will feel when the Future Redemption finally comes. Firstly, we felt that Hashem was very distant from us, with many impediments between us, but then He came "jumping over the mountains," ignoring all the obstacles. We subsequently felt even more surprised because He came unnaturally fast, like a gazelle. And then we were even more surprised when we realized that He was not really far away at all.

MY BELOVED IS LIKE A GAZELLE... HE IS STANDING BEHIND OUR WALL...

At first glance, this verse seems inconsistent — even self-contradictory. It starts by saying that Hashem was like a gazelle, which gives us a picture of Hashem coming from the distance at high speed. Yet it ends by saying that Hashem is not distant at all: "Behold, He is standing behind our wall." Rashi explains that *Klal Yisrael* originally thought Hashem was very far away and that the exile would end only after a very long time. But then they recognized Hashem's mercy and felt that He was "rushing" to save them. Eventually, as their understanding grew, they realized that Hashem was actually very near them, ready to save them. In other words, as *Klal Yisrael* thought about it more and as their awareness grew, their understanding of Hashem's kindness grew as well.

The *Yalkut Me'am Lo'ez* offers the following parable to help us understand this more deeply. A certain child was living very far away from his father. One day, the child collapsed and was rushed off to the hospital where he remained in a coma. His father came from afar to be with his son and remained glued to the boy's bedside. When the child woke up and saw his father, he was unaware that he had been in a coma for several days. "How did you get here so fast?" he exclaimed. The father answered, "I did not come so fast, but I have been here next to you for a few days already waiting for you to come out of your coma."

---

82   Rashi explains that this verse continues the theme of the speed of the redemption from Egypt. As before, the Midrash explains that it is also referring to the Future Redemption and *bi'as haMashiach*. These different approaches are not mutually exclusive, as explained in our Introduction. Each verse refers to a concept which has many applications.

Similarly, *Klal Yisrael* in exile are blinded and cannot see how close Hashem is. When Mashiach comes, and we wake up spiritually[83] and see Hashem so close to us, we will exclaim, "Look how fast Hashem came!" But Hashem will correct us and let us know that He has been next to us the whole time.

Accordingly, our verse is to be understood this way:

> [I thought that] My Beloved [Hashem] is like a gazelle or a young hart [who came speedily from afar to save us]. Behold, [I suddenly realize that] He [has always been] standing behind our wall [right next to us],[84] gazing through the windows, peering through the cracks.

The underlying lesson of these verses is that we should believe that our redemption is possible at any time and that we should anticipate it all the time. The Gemara tells us that Rabbi Yehoshua met Mashiach and asked him when he was coming to save us. The answer he received was: "Today!" When Mashiach did not come that day, Rabbi Yehoshua turned to Eliyahu HaNavi and asked him why Mashiach had lied. Eliyahu HaNavi explained what was meant by "Today": "I am coming *today*...if you repent.[85] In other words, Mashiach is ready all the time, but it is up to us to facilitate his coming by repenting.[86]

Rabbi Yosef Chaim Sonnenfeld, *zt"l*, had this keen awareness that Mashiach is very close at hand. It is told that he once climbed to the top of his building. When his assistant asked him what he was doing, he answered that he was wondering if Mashiach had already come. Since Rabbi Sonnenfeld lived in a basement, he thought that by climbing high up, he would see farther into the distance, and would then be more likely to spot Mashiach.

In this same spirit, Rabbi Yosef Chaim Sonnenfeld himself told of a woman who

---

83   This is similar to the famous verse in *Tehillim*: "when Hashem brings back the captivity of Tzion, we will have been like dreamers" (126:1). When the dreamer wakes up from his nightmare, all of the fear he felt while asleep suddenly disappears. So too, when Mashiach comes, everything will change suddenly. All the previous fears of exile will seem like a nightmare — not real and of no consequence.

84   Another interpretation of this verse is that Hashem demonstrates His love towards *Klal Yisrael* in two different ways. Sometimes He does so in a way that we feel He is rushing towards us to save us; at other times, He does so in a way that we realize He was right by our side all along, protecting and watching over us. This is not a contradiction. When Mashiach comes, our primary feeling will be that Hashem is coming very fast to save us, as reflected in the beginning of the verse. At other times — especially when we meditate on our past exiles — our primary feeling will be Hashem that looks after us closely and that He was always by our side.

85   *Sanhedrin* 98a. The Gemara also says that Mashiach is always ready to come and therefore does not change more than one of his many bandages at a time so that there will be no real delay when his time to come arrives. Even this very short delay of changing two bandages will be obviated as soon as Hashem wants to redeem us.

86   This is based on the verse, "...[even] today, if you will listen to His voice" (*Tehillim* 95:7).

was asked what she was cooking this week. She answered, "Now, I am cooking lentils. Tomorrow, I hope we will eat from the feast of Mashiach. If he does not come by then, I will have to think of something else to cook. There is no need for me to plan today since it won't be necessary, hopefully because Mashiach will have come."

MY BELOVED IS LIKE A DEER…

The symbols of deer or young harts come up a number of times in *Shir HaShirim*. The Midrash tells us that these animals' many wonderful attributes teach and demonstrate how Hashem looks after us. The following are only a few examples. Even while sleeping, these animals keep one eye open to guard against danger. Similarly, even when it seems to us that Hashem is ignoring us He, has an "eye" watching over us to keep us away from danger. Also, these animals are very hard to spot. One sees a glimpse of a gazelle in the woods, but before one knows it, the gazelle has disappeared from sight since as it moves fast and blends in well with its surroundings. One knows it is there, but it takes effort to find it. Similarly, Hashem runs this world, but not always do we see how He is operating. Sometimes, it looks as if we are left alone, but then suddenly the salvation is in sight. We must make an effort to spot the Hand of Hashem, and His salvation. Furthermore, these animals tend to move around from place to place. Similarly, Hashem goes, *ki'veyachol*, from shul to shul, and from *beis midrash* to *beis midrash*, in order to hear us praying and learning Torah.

HE IS STANDING BEHIND OUR WALL

The verse continues, "He is standing behind our wall." What is this wall? This is the wall of our sins. Because of our sins, Hashem is hidden from us. It is "our wall" because we made it by sinning. Yeshayahu described it this way: "Your sins put a separation between you and your God…"[87] This is the only barrier between Hashem and *Klal Yisrael*.[88] If not for our sins, there would be no division. Hashem wishes to be very close to us, and only because of our sins and the barriers that we create through our foolishness does He, *ki'veyachol*, have to stand behind the wall. Even though we create the wall, Hashem does not say, "If you are not interested in Me, neither am I interested in you." Rather, He stands behind the wall keeping close to us.

Our small feelings of regret and repentance create little cracks in the barrier between us and Hashem. He watches us through these.[89]

---

87 59:2.

88 *Sanhedrin* 65b.

89 *Tzeror HaMor*. The author notes that Hashem exhorts us: "Just make Me an opening the size of an eye of a needle, and I will [respond by] making you an opening the size of a large room" (*Shir HaShirim Rabbah* 5:2). This tells us that Hashem

We can better appreciate the beautiful metaphor in this verse by imagining a parent trying to reach out to a child who is deeply unhappy and lonely yet puts up big barriers blocking any chance of a real relationship. The parent tries to look for small cracks in these barriers, hoping to find a way to get through to show his love and care. He or she tries to find the right time and place to say something kind or give a small gift that will break through the divide. So, too, Hashem wants to shower us with His love, but we block Him in our stupidity. Still, He keeps looking for ways to get through to us to show us that He cares. Understanding the heart of *Shir HaShirim* requires one to open one's own heart and allow Hashem's love to flood in.[90]

GAZING THROUGH THE WINDOWS...

Our verse concludes with two different metaphors: Hashem "gazes through the windows, and peers through the cracks." The Netziv explains that the first represents Hashem's general supervision over the whole of *Klal Yisrael*, while the second represents His special supervision over the tzaddikim. Looking through a window takes no special effort and enables one to see a lot of different people. Looking through a crack, however, takes more effort, and one sees only the person (or persons) he is trying to focus on. Similarly, Hashem looks out generally for the whole of *Klal Yisrael*, but makes more of an effort, *ki'veyachol*, to zoom in on the righteous to take care of their needs.[91]

Rabbi Eliyahu Lopian offers a different explanation.[92] He points out that when a person looks through a window, he can see and be seen, but when a person looks through a crack, he can see, but cannot be seen. Similarly, Hashem looks after *Klal Yisrael* in two different ways. One way is through open, obvious miracles — where not only is Hashem looking after us, but we see Hashem as well. Sometimes, however, Hashem operates through hidden miracles — where Hashem is looking after us, but we cannot see Him. The point is that Hashem is always looking after us, whether we see Him or not. This fundamental concept, anchored here in one verse of *Shir HaShirim*, is really

---

wishes to break through these barriers. If we were to take the initiative and start the process, Hashem would complete it.

90 Rabbi Elisha Galiko takes a somewhat different approach. He sees the verse portraying Hashem watching over us, concealed behind a "wall," i.e., the *Kosel* (the Western Wall remaining from the Har HaBayis). The "windows" (in the continuation of the verse) allude to the "apertures" in Heaven through which our prayers go up to Hashem, and the "cracks" allude to the places of learning which Hashem peers into to reward those who learn His Torah.

91 The Midrash looks at the contrast this way: In the merit of the forefathers, Hashem looks and protects us through the windows, and in the merit of the other tzaddikim, through the cracks. The Midrash concludes that the merit of the forefathers is much greater because one sees much more through a window.

92 *Lev Eliyahu*, vol. I, *Shevivei Ohr*, p. 142.

a subject in itself. We have to understand that Hashem is constantly watching over us. Sometimes we clearly see Him doing this, such as when He took us out of Egypt and split the sea for us.[93] This is symbolized by Hashem gazing through the windows. But sometimes we cannot clearly see Him operating, such as during the events of Purim. This is symbolized by Hashem peering through the cracks. The "miracle of Purim" occurred without any violation of the laws of nature.[94] Let us note that in just a few words of *Shir HaShirim*, we get a profound understanding of the protection Hashem grants us.

GAZING THROUGH THE WINDOWS

In this verse, Hashem is described as watching through the windows. The word used for "watching" is *mashgiach*, the same word commonly used to describe the rabbi in yeshivah whose job it is to supervise, direct, develop, encourage, and help the students reach their highest level. Indeed, the *mashgiach* is always looking out for ways to ensure that each *talmid* realizes his full potential. The present-day application of this word helps us appreciate that Hashem has this "job," *ki'veyachol*, in our lives. There is no greater teacher than Hashem, who, through the millions of things that happen to us during our lives, teaches us humility, patience, and so many other vital qualities. He knows which attributes and qualities we need to improve and makes sure we receive the exact lessons we need. Every person we meet, every comment we hear, every event we experience, and every sight we see, are all being directed by Hashem for our ultimate growth.[95] This is just one aspect of how Hashem is our "*mashgiach*." We

---

[93] Hashem's Presence was so keenly felt then that *Klal Yisrael* exclaimed: "This is my God, and I will praise Him!" (*Shemos* 15:2). In some sense, they were pointing at Hashem while they were singing the Song of the Sea (Rashi, ibid.)

[94] Hashem's Presence was so hidden then that His name does not even appear in *Megillas Esther*.

[95] Here are two of the myriad stories of *hashgachah pratis* which show how Hashem communicates with us "between the lines" if we only pay attention. This first episode, one of the more famous ones, involves the *mussar* giant, Rabbi Yisrael Salanter. He once saw a tailor working late into the night. When he asked the tailor about his late hours, the tailor replied, "While the candle burns, one can still mend." Rabbi Yisrael later said that he understood the message behind the answer to be: "While a person still has the flame of the *neshamah* burning within him, he can still mend his ways." The second story, a more contemporary one, involves a young lady on the fringe of Orthodoxy who was working in a library when she overheard someone *bentching* and saying the words "*velo nikasheil*" ("and we shall not stumble") in the blessing of *Rachem*. These words do not appear in most versions of *Birkas HaMazon*. She told the person that he was mistaken and that they had an argument about whether the words were correct. Months later, the person who had been *bentching* found a printed *bentcher* that included those words. He photocopied the relevant page, circled the words in red, and sent it to the library employee who had corrected him. It turned out that she was going through a religious identity crisis during that period and was actually engaged to a non-Jewish man. Shortly before the wedding, she received this page with the words "we shall not stumble" circled in red. At first, she could not figure out who sent this or why it was sent to her. But then, the argument about these words in the library came back to her. This jolt caused her to break off her relationship with her fiancé and eventually do complete *teshuvah*!

One must learn to listen for the messages of Hashem who, after all, is the greatest *mashgiach* of all.

should be extremely happy and grateful that we have such a wonderful teacher and *mashgiach*. When looking back at their lives, many people see how so many different incidents helped them grow. They may have wanted one thing to happen, but Hashem chose differently, and they later saw how Hashem's choice worked out for the best. Indeed, Hashem is the ultimate *mashgiach*. Our job is only to be receptive to Him and to what He is teaching us.

I was once giving a *talmid chacham* a ride, and we got stuck in very heavy traffic. Seeing my impatience, he said to me, "Imagine that you could receive a free private lesson from a great person on how to be patient. How happy you would be! Now, Hashem is kindly teaching you patience. Be happy and grateful!"

עָנָה דוֹדִי, וְאָמַר לִי; קוּמִי לָךְ רַעְיָתִי יָפָתִי, וּלְכִי לָךְ.

My Beloved called out and said to me,[96] "Arise, My dear one, My beautiful one, and go on your way."

י 10

Allegorical Translation — Hashem called out to me and spoke to me through Moshe: "My beautiful nation, get up because I am going to take you out of Egypt, and then you will be able to go to the place that you desire."

Subject of the Verse — This is a continuation of *Klal Yisrael* describing the delightful events of *Yetzias Mitzrayim*.

Mashal — The wife continues with her recollections, describing how her husband called her in loving terms, making her excited to go out with him.

Nimshal — *Klal Yisrael* is describing how Hashem encouraged them and lovingly spoke to them, in order to get them ready to leave the exile of Egypt.

MY BELOVED CALLED OUT...

This verse and the next few verses all describe *Yetzias Mitzrayim* in some detail. They help us feel the vast love for us that Hashem displayed during that awesome event. Even just hearing how Hashem called us, "My dear one, My beautiful one," should fill us with love and joy.

---

96 This verse can also be understood to mean: "My Beloved called out and said *for my sake*..." That is to say, when Hashem called out to us to leave Egypt, it was for our sake. He redeemed us because of His concern and love for us.

One underlying theme is that Hashem, *ki'veyachol*, cajoles us and almost begs us to come out to Him. This is like a man trying to woo a woman he loves to come out with him so that ultimately, she will become his bride. That Hashem makes such an effort, *ki'veyachol*, to bring us to Him underscores His great love for us.

MY DEAR ONE, MY BEAUTIFUL ONE

Hashem uses two different terms of endearment when He calls *Klal Yisrael* to come out of Egypt: "My dear one" and "My beautiful one." The Midrash tells us that *Klal Yisrael* merited *Yetzias Mitzrayim* because of two mitzvos they performed on the very night they left Egypt: the mitzvah of *korban Pesach* and the mitzvah of *bris milah*. These two mitzvos are hinted at in these words of endearment. The word *rayasi*, "My dear one," can also mean "My shepherd," or "the one who feeds Me."[97] This describes *Klal Yisrael* because they are the ones who bring *korbanos*, which can be considered Hashem's "food," *ki'veyachol*. "My beautiful one" can be read as an allusion to *bris milah* because circumcision makes a person look pleasing and beautiful in Hashem's eyes. An allegorical translation of this verse would thus read this way: "My beloved [Hashem] called out and said to me, 'Arise, My shepherd [you who brought Me the korban Pesach], My beautiful one [you who performed *bris milah*], and go on your way [out of Egypt].'"[98]

---

97   As we explained in our commentary on 1:9.

98   Let us note the spiritually curative power of these two mitzvos by turning for a moment to the first chapter of *Mesillas Yesharim*. The author points out that life is essentially one long test revolving around whether a person will come close to Hashem. Loosely, the test swings back and forth between success and failure in all aspects of life. Success in any area can cause haughtiness and a feeling that one does not need Hashem — and thus one may be less likely to serve Him. In contrast, failure causes a desperate desire for whatever one wishes to achieve and can thus cause one to overlook Hashem's mitzvos in the pursuit of one's desires. The mitzvos of *korban Pesach* and *bris milah* remedy these two underlying errors. The *korban* is the greatest service one can do for Hashem. This is because it communicates the understanding that Hashem owns everything and that one ought to give everything to Him, including his life (see Ramban on *Vayikra* 1:9). This teaches humility and one's awareness that everything belongs to Hashem, including one's life, and certainly all of one's successes. *Bris milah*, which is performed on the organ of desire, serves as a reminder that all desire must be subjugated to Hashem, and therefore the mitzvos of Hashem must trump all of one's desires. When *Klal Yisrael* fulfilled these two mitzvos, they showed that they deserved to be saved because they demonstrated that they would not succumb to either slip-up.

כִּי הִנֵּה הַסְּתָו עָבָר; הַגֶּשֶׁם, חָלַף הָלַךְ לוֹ. **יא**

For, behold, the winter has now passed; the rain has disappeared and gone away. **11**

הַנִּצָּנִים נִרְאוּ בָאָרֶץ, עֵת הַזָּמִיר הִגִּיעַ; וְקוֹל הַתּוֹר, נִשְׁמַע בְּאַרְצֵנוּ. **יב**

The blossoms have appeared in the land;[99] the season of the song[100] has arrived; and the sound of the turtledove is heard in our land. **12**

Allegorical Translation

11 You, the Jewish People, get ready to leave Egypt because the unpleasant exile[101] ("winter") has passed; and even the terribly harsh period of slavery ("rain")[102] has ended.

12 Moshe and Aharon have appeared heralding a happier time to come, just as blossoms herald the advent of new fruit, ready to redeem you. The time for you (*Klal Yisrael*) to sing (at the splitting of the Sea) has arrived. The sound of

---

99 The word נצנים is understood by the Midrash in two different ways: 1) as *blossoms*, for just as a blossom tells us that a fruit will grow, so too did Moshe and Aharon tell us that good things were going to happen; 2) as *victories* (similar to the word נצחונות), as Moshe and Aharon came to be victorious over Pharaoh.

100 There are two words in *lashon hakodesh* that refer to singing: שירה and זמרה. The Vilna Gaon explains (in his commentary on *Tehillim* 27:6) that the first refers to singing without musical instruments and the second to singing accompanied by musical instruments. (With this distinction, the Gaon explains many other verses in which these two terms appear.) Accordingly, the word זמיר in this verse alludes to the song the women sang at *Kriyas Yam Suf*. The Torah tells us that, unlike the men, the women used musical instruments (*Shemos* 15:20). As Rashi (ibid.) explains, the women knew that Hashem would make miracles and therefore took along musical instruments for the express purpose of thanking Him properly. This verse therefore hints that the time of the (women's) musical song has arrived. Their song was more precious because they prepared for it and understood that miracles are intended to evoke praise of Hashem (*Vezos LeYaakov*).

101 The 400 years Hashem said *Klal Yisrael* would be in exile.

102 The eighty-six years during which *Klal Yisrael* suffered particularly badly. In a sense, there were two parts to the exile in Egypt. The entire unpleasant period of 400 years (starting from the birth of Yitzchak, which included the 210 years in Egypt) and the last eighty-six years which were particularly bitter (Midrash). That is why Miriam, who was eighty-six years old when she left Egypt, was given this name. "Miriam" comes from the root *mar*, meaning "bitter," and *yom*, meaning "day," signifying that from the time of her birth, bitter days began. The last part of the exile was especially bitter. The verse alludes to these two parts: "The winter has now passed" to the longer period, which was merely uncomfortable like the winter; "the rain has disappeared" to the last part which was particularly bitter (like rain to the person traveling outside).

Moshe[103] calling out for redemption has been sounded throughout the land.[104]

Subject of the Verses — This is a continuation of *Klal Yisrael* describing the wonderful events of *Yetzias Mitzrayim*. They describe how everything was ready in an ideal manner for the redemption to take place.

Mashal — When a man wishes to take a girl he loves out on a date so that she will want to marry him, he works hard to ensure that the date is a pleasant and exciting experience for her. The *mashal*, then, reads as follows:

11 The wife continues with her recollections, describing how her husband waited until the winter rains ended before calling on her to go with him. He then told her that the difficult times were over and that she could look forward to a happy time together.

12 The wife continues describing how her husband prepared thoroughly so that when she went out with him, everything would be perfect. The husband waited until spring when the blossoms were blooming, the birds were singing, and everything was just perfect for their get-together.

Nimshal — **11** *Klal Yisrael* describes how Hashem told them that the time for their salvation had arrived because they had completed their stint in exile and slavery.

12 *Klal Yisrael* continues to describe how Hashem took them out of Egypt at the optimal time, when everything was ready for a complete salvation.

FOR, BEHOLD, THE WINTER HAS NOW PASSED... THE BLOSSOMS HAVE APPEARED IN THE LAND...

These verses describe how Hashem took *Klal Yisrael* out of Egypt at a pleasant and

---

103 The Hebrew word "*tor*" normally means "turtledove." As such, our verse simply means that spring has arrived, and the turtledoves are singing. However, *tor* can also be understood as "guide" (as in "tour guide"), and it is thus referring to Moshe Rabbeinu. Moshe Rabbeinu was the greatest guide in history. A good guide looks after the people he is guiding and takes them to the places they need to get to. An even better guide takes his group to places they could never get to otherwise, places which change their whole viewpoint. He helps them see things no one has seen before. Moshe Rabbeinu led an entire nation for forty years through many different places and situations, keeping them safe and helping them reach their destination. At the same time, he helped them see miracles and visions no other nation had ever seen or will ever see. Our verse thus announces that "the Guide" has arrived. This is one facet of Moshe Rabbeinu's greatness, and it tells us how *Klal Yisrael* was ready to be saved when history's greatest guide arrived.

104 The Vilna Gaon here cites the Talmud Yerushalmi (*Pesachim* 5:5) which reports that Moshe Rabbeinu's verbal call to the Jewish People to leave Egypt miraculously rang out to a distance of 400 *parsahs* (approximately 1600 kilometers) in all directions. Thus, all of *Klal Yisrael* spread out across the whole of Egypt could hear the proclamation that it was time to leave. Our verse alludes to this miracle.

appropriate time. *Chazal* tell us that Hashem releases prisoners at the correct time.[105] When *Klal Yisrael* came out of Egypt, it was springtime, a pleasant time of year and thus the best time to travel. There is no uncomfortable summer heat or rain and cold of winter. The trees were in blossom, making the journey a pleasant experience. In addition, the birds provided pleasant music for the way, etc. The next verses continue in this vein, mentioning that the figs were blossoming and the vines were giving off their pleasant smell. All of these are signs of the new spring season and indications of why the journey is more pleasant in the spring.[106]

On a deeper level, the verse means that it was the best time spiritually to leave Egypt. Hashem had prepared Moshe Rabbeinu and Aharon HaKohen, the ideal leaders to redeem *Klal Yisrael*, from Egyptian bondage. There were many other reasons as well — some of them beyond our understanding — as to why this was a "spiritually good" time to leave.

The message of these few verses is that *Yetzias Mitzrayim* happened in the best possible way and best possible time both from a spiritual and physical standpoint. Since Hashem loves us, He chose the nicest time for us in all aspects. We are naturally aware of some of these aspects (such as pleasant weather, flowers and birds singing, spiritually great leaders at the helm, etc.). Regarding others, however, we need to put effort into finding and understanding just how much care Hashem took in saving us from Egypt in the best possible way.

On a deeper level, we should understand that the physical changes and pleasures of spring reflect spiritual renewal in our own lives. Spring is a time of warmth and light, a time when people who have not seen each other during the winter come out and renew their relationship. This reflects the warmth and light of Hashem. It hearkens back to how *Klal Yisrael* had gathered together to leave Egypt. The reawakening of the physical world in the spring signals the time of spiritual awakening — when we relive the redemption from Egypt, the miracles at Yam Suf, and the acceptance of the Torah at Har Sinai. Hashem helps us connect to this renewal and joy through the beauty and life of spring.

---

105 *Mechilta, Shemos* 13:4, commenting on the verse, "Hashem releases prisoners *bakosharos*" (*Tehillim* 68:7). According to the *Mechilta*, this word comes from the root of the word *kosher*, which means "good." Thus, the verse is saying that Hashem releases prisoners at the right time.

106 When spring weather finally arrives and we can finally enjoy being outside after a long cold winter of being largely confined to the indoors, we would do well to remind ourselves that Hashem in His kindness arranged to take us out of Egypt in weather like this so that the trek would be as pleasant as possible! Pesach is timed to arrive shortly after the beautiful spring weather begins to enhance this feeling.

THE BLOSSOMS HAVE APPEARED IN THE LAND…

As we noted earlier, these words refer not only to past redemptions of *Klal Yisrael*, but also to the future and Final Redemption accompanied by the coming of Mashiach. Hashem will take us out of exile under ideal physical and spiritual conditions. Indeed, this verse can be read as referring to the coming of Mashiach:

> The blossoms [i.e., Mashiach and Eliyahu HaNavi heralding a happier time to come just as blossoms herald the advent of new fruit] have appeared in the land [to save you]; the season of the song [we will sing when the eventual redemption arrives[107]] has arrived; and the sound of the guide[108] is heard in our land [i.e., the sound of Mashiach's announcement heard throughout the land that the redemption has arrived.][109]

THE BLOSSOMS HAVE APPEARED IN THE LAND…

We have seen that Hashem showed His love for *Klal Yisrael* by taking them out of Egypt in the spring, which is the best time to travel.[110] But we might wonder: wouldn't the Jews in Egypt, like all prisoners and slaves, have cared more about getting out as fast as

---

107 See the *Targum* on 1:1.

108 As noted above, Rashi explains that although the word "*tor*" normally means "turtledove," it can also mean "guide." Here, then, it would refer to Mashiach. Mashiach will be the greatest guide the world will ever know. He will lead an entire nation scattered throughout the world back to its homeland, Eretz Yisrael. He will deal with all the issues that exile has imposed on us, helping us reach our goal, and shielding us from all troubles.

109 The Midrash tells us that the sound of Mashiach calling out for redemption will be heard throughout the world.

110 From these verses, we also learn how we should encourage ourselves to serve Hashem. Rashi tells us that Hashem was coaxing *Klal Yisrael* to leave Egypt and come and serve Him in the desert. (Rashi notes that the verse makes use of an evocative metaphor, echoing the language of a young man who wishes to display his love to his betrothed in order to fully convey the message of the verse.) Hashem told *Klal Yisrael* that the spring is a pleasant time to travel; the weather is good and the flowers are blooming, etc. We might have thought that Hashem would give much more powerful reasons, such as: "You need to leave the impurity of the Egyptians" or "You are going to accept the Torah and start observing the mitzvos." Alternatively, Hashem could have told *Klal Yisrael*: "You must come out with Me! After all, I am your God, you owe it to Me, and I will punish you if you don't!" Instead, Hashem gave them very pleasant and sweet reasons why they should follow Him.

The lesson here is that when we are trying to push ourselves to serve Hashem or trying to teach our children about serving Hashem, we should not approach it as a heavy burden that He has imposed on us. Rather, we should look for ways to make serving Hashem sweet and pleasant. Furthermore, we can inspire ourselves and others with encouraging words, such as: "See how sweet it is to follow Hashem." "The only truly pleasant way of life is one with Torah to guide us, and mitzvos to instruct us." "Those who trust in Hashem live a life of constant joy, while those who do not, suffer anxieties, jealousies, and unhappiness of every kind." As we see in these verses, Hashem is showing us that following Him is pleasant and good for us (*Eved HaMelech* on *Shir HaShirim* by Rabbi Shmuel Hominer). See also *Lev Eliyahu* on *Parashas Vayeitzei* for a similar approach.

A good application of this approach can be seen in Rabbi Moshe Feinstein's practice of putting his son's clothes on a heater to warm them up before awakening him in the winter. He wanted to make more pleasant his son's experience of getting up to go out into the bitter cold to yeshivah to daven and learn.

possible rather than getting ideal travel conditions?!

The answer is that we are being shown a new perspective on the concept of exile. If exile is only a time of suffering and imprisonment, then it is true that the quicker one can get out of it, the better, and it makes little difference whether outdoor conditions are ideal or not. However, if exile is a *process* that *Klal Yisrael* need to go through before they can become spiritually complete, then it is surely in their best interest that redemption come at the right time. In other words, if redemption was only about opening a door and escaping, then the quicker the door opens, the better. But redemption is not simply an escape. It involves the transformation of a person through coming closer to Hashem — a transformation that also includes an escape from suffering.[111]

This can be likened to a complicated operation. The patient wants it to be done at the time that is best in terms of his health and prospects of recuperation. *Klal Yisrael* in Egypt were going through an operation that would heal them spiritually.[112] To use another analogy, let us say that a person's recovery depends on his undergoing a rigorous course of medical treatment. Perhaps he is going through a taxing regimen of physiotherapy in the hospital, and a well-meaning relative takes him out of there before it is completed. Now the person will be limping forever! Not only has the relative not done the patient a favor, but he has done him a tremendous disservice! But if the patient would be told that he is finishing the treatment in time for Yom Tov, he would be thrilled because the treatment is coming to an end at a good time for him. By Hashem arranging the redemption in this way, He was also conveying to *Klal Yisrael* that exile is not just a punishment but a regimen of spiritual healing which they have successfully completed. As Hashem took them out of Egypt, He, in effect, said to them, "See how I have arranged that spring is the best time for your spiritual redemption. I have also arranged for you to have great leaders like Moshe Rabbeinu and Aharon HaKohen." These arrangements and preparations ensured that *Klal Yisrael* would be completely healed spiritually. This holds true regarding our present exile as well: Hashem will arrange for it to end when our spiritual recovery is complete.

---

111 On Seder Night we use four cups of wine to represent the four "expressions of salvation" in the Torah (Talmud Yerushalmi, *Pesachim* 10:1). These four expressions — והוצאתי והצלתי וגאלתי ולקחתי (I will take out; I will save; I will redeem; I will take you [as a nation]) — are not simply four repetitions of the same promise of redemption. Rather, each expression alludes to another aspect or stage of salvation. Indeed, many use a fifth cup to represent the expression והבאתי (I will bring), and name it after Eliyahu HaNavi, who will herald the Final Redemption.

112 In *Shir HaShirim*, we see a number of times that exile is viewed as necessary for the development of *Klal Yisrael* and not simply a punishment for their past *aveiros*. In this *megillah*, which is all about how much Hashem loves *Klal Yisrael*, this is a more appropriate understanding of the exile. In contrast, the aspect of exile as a punishment for *Klal Yisrael's aveiros* is mentioned many times in *Eichah*.

> הַתְּאֵנָה חָנְטָה פַגֶּיהָ, וְהַגְּפָנִים סְמָדַר נָתְנוּ רֵיחַ; קוּמִי לָךְ (לכי כתיב) רַעְיָתִי יָפָתִי, וּלְכִי לָךְ.
>
> **13** *The fig tree has begun to produce[113] its [still] unripe fruit, and the blossoming vines have given off a fragrance. Arise,[114] My dear one, My beautiful one, and go on your way.*

Allegorical Translation

Rashi offers three ways of understanding the first half of the verse.

The time for bringing the *bikkurim* from the figs that have sprouted has arrived, as has the time to pour the wine libations from the blossoming vines on the *Mizbe'ach*.

The righteous (likened to sprouting figs[115]) have blossomed, i.e., they are conducting themselves righteously, and thus give off a pleasant fragrance like the smell of vines in blossom.

The wicked (likened to unripe figs[116]) have died (during the Plague of Darkness) and those remaining have repented and are giving off a good fragrance like a blossoming vine.

The verse concludes: Now that all is ready, you, *Klal Yisrael*, My beautiful one, get up and get ready to come out of Egypt and accept the Torah.

---

113   The Brisker Rav connects these verses with the Torah's statement that Pesach must come out each year in the spring. As the Gemara (*Sanhedrin* 11b) tells us, there are three indications of spring: 1) the post-winter season has arrived; 2) the produce is growing; and 3) the fruit is ripening. In these verses, Hashem is telling *Klal Yisrael* that because the spring has arrived and these three signs have appeared ("the winter has now passed" / "the sprouting has appeared" / "the fig tree has begun to produce"), the time is ripe for *Yetzias Mitzrayim*. The Brisker Rav goes on to explain that it is because the Torah says that Pesach is in the spring that *Yetzias Mitzrayim* had to happen in the spring (*Chiddushei HaGryz U'Beis HaLevi al HaTorah*, sec. 131).

114   The word לך here is written, but not read, with an added י (לכי). The seemingly superfluous letter י — which has a numerical value of ten — alludes to the Ten Commandments. In other words, Hashem is calling out to us: "Arise, My dear one, to receive the Ten Commandments!" This teaches us that Hashem's intent in calling us to leave Mitzrayim was for the purpose of receiving the Torah at Har Sinai (Rashi). That is why we begin counting the forty-nine days of the Omer between Pesach and Shavuos immediately after we celebrate the Exodus from Mitzrayim. We thus express our understanding of the real reason for *Yetzias Mitzrayim* and our great anticipation of the anniversary of *Matan Torah*.

115   Once they mature, figs are very sweet. They are symbolic of the righteous whose behavior is always very sweet.

116   The *Torah Temimah* throws light on the metaphor and the terminology according to this interpretation. He notes that green, unripe figs are bitter, like wicked people, and that the term used for "beginning to produce/yield" is a euphemistic way of saying these people have moved on and died.
    The Eitz Yosef explains that certain figs never ripen properly. These figs thus symbolize the wicked, who never mature enough to understand what is important in life.

Subject of the Verse	This is a continuation of *Klal Yisrael* describing the wonderful events of *Yetzias Mitzrayim*. Here they describe how Hashem made sure the nation was ready and prepared for salvation before telling them to come out of Egypt.
Mashal	The wife continues with her recollections, describing how her husband calls for her to come out with him only when the fruits are blossoming and she is all prepared to go with him.
Nimshal	*Klal Yisrael* continue to describe how Hashem took them out of Egypt at the optimal time, when everything was ready for a perfect salvation. Here they focus on the point that Hashem called for them to leave only when the nation was spiritually ready.

ARISE, MY DEAR ONE, MY BEAUTIFUL ONE…

We should pause for a moment to appreciate the endearing way in which Hashem addresses *Klal Yisrael*: "Arise, *My dear one, My beautiful one*, and go on your way."

THE FIG TREE HAS BEGUN TO PRODUCE…

As we have seen, Rashi tells us that the symbolism of the figs and the vines is multi-faceted. They allude to the mitzvah of *bikkurim*, which *Klal Yisrael* will eventually bring to the Beis HaMikdash, and to the wine libations on the *Mizbe'ach*. They also allude both to the tzaddikim who have ripened and are ready to be redeemed and to the wicked Jews who were eliminated during the Plague of Darkness[117] so that they would not interfere with the redemption. The underlying idea here is that the time of redemption is ripe.

These verses also allude to the Final Redemption. Indeed, the introduction to the *Zohar* discusses these verses, explaining exactly what events need to happen and what processes *Klal Yisrael* need to go through before the time of the Final Redemption will arrive. The Midrash here explains this verse in a similar way. Let us note that although we cannot understand exactly what the *Zohar* and the Midrash are referring to, we do know that certain events will unfold to make the coming of Mashiach ideal. Still, the order of the blessings in the *Shemoneh Esrei* gives us an idea of the process of events. Hashem will first gather in the exiles (*birkas Teka B'Shofar*). Then He will reestablish the Sanhedrin and bring back the righteous judges (*Hashivah Shofteinu*). Then He will eliminate the wicked people and destroy all evil (*V'La'Malshinim*). After that, He will help all the righteous people flourish and succeed (*Al HaTzaddikim*). Only after all of this will Hashem rebuild Yerushalayim and reinstate the throne of Dovid HaMelech (*Bonei Yerushalayim* and *Es Tzemach*).

---

117 See Rashi on *Shemos* 13:18, *s.v. vachamushim*.

The verses above also display these same stages corresponding to the blessings in the *Shemoneh Esrei*:

Shir HaShirim	Mashal	Meaning	Parallel in *Shemoneh Esrei*	Expression of salvation[118]
"The winter has now passed." (v. 11)	The cold which caused people to be uncomfortable has passed	The end of the exile has arrived.	Teka B'Shofar	והוצאתי "I will take you out" of Egypt.
"The blossoms have appeared." (v. 12)	Signs of future fruit are evident.	The leaders are ready.	Hashivah Shofteinu	והצלתי "I will save you" from the nations through the guidance of your righteous leaders.[119]
"The fig tree has begun to produce its [still] unripe fruit."* (v. 13)	The fruit that does not mature becomes moldy in the spring.	The wicked should be eliminated.	V'La'Malshin-im	וגאלתי "I will redeem you" and remove from you all the effects of exile — including the wickedness that you may have picked up.
"The blossoming vines have given off a fragrance." (v. 13)	The good fruits spread their good smell — and everyone appreciates them.	The righteous are successful	Al HaTzaddikim	ולקחתי "I will take you" to the right path by showing you that righteousness succeeds.
"The fig tree has begun to produce its fruit."** (v. 13)	The tastiest fruits are ready to be picked, and thus fulfill their purpose.	The time for the Beis HaMikdash to be rebuilt and the *bikkurim* to be brought to it has arrived.	Bonei Yerushalayim Es Tzemach	והבאתי "I will bring you" to Me (the final stage of redemption and closeness to Hashem).

* The death of the wicked people, according to one of Rashi's explanations

** A reference to the bringing of the *bikkurim*, according to another of Rashi's explanations

---

[118] As mentioned earlier, the four cups of wine and the four "expressions of salvation" in the Torah represent the four stages of redemption.

[119] See Rashi on *Bereishis* 31:16, *s.v. vayatzeil*.

It should be noted that although "פגיה" was translated above as "unripe, bitter fruit." Here, according to this alternative explanation, it connotes figs which are ripening and becoming complete.

The bottom line is that exile is a process of curative treatment that we need in order to reach perfection. When Mashiach comes, it will be at the most appropriate and good time for *Klal Yisrael* — when we are ready to be completely healed and when all the conditions for the redemption will be ideal.

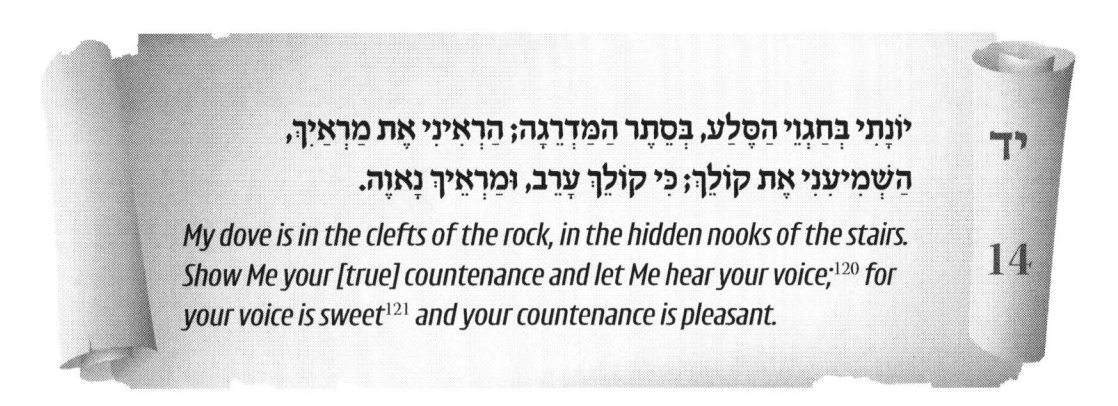

> יד 14
>
> יוֹנָתִי בְּחַגְוֵי הַסֶּלַע, בְּסֵתֶר הַמַּדְרֵגָה; הַרְאִינִי אֶת מַרְאַיִךְ, הַשְׁמִיעִינִי אֶת קוֹלֵךְ; כִּי קוֹלֵךְ עָרֵב, וּמַרְאֵיךְ נָאוֶה.
>
> *My dove is in the clefts of the rock, in the hidden nooks of the stairs. Show Me your [true] countenance and let Me hear your voice;[120] for your voice is sweet[121] and your countenance is pleasant.*

Allegorical Translation — Hashem says: My nation (*Klal Yisrael*), who are as faithful to Me as a dove is to its partner, was trapped in a very dangerous situation. I tell them to show Me your good deeds and let Me hear your prayers because your prayers are sweet and your good deeds pleasant.

Subject of the Verse — Hashem is describing, from His perspective, the events and emotions leading to *Kriyas Yam Suf*.

Mashal — This verse depicts a helpless dove trying to escape the dangers that threaten it. It hides in crevices so that the large vultures cannot attack it but is not safe there either because of the snakes who try to kill it. The owner of the precious

---

120 The Midrash says that "Show me your [true] countenance" alludes to prayer, while "Let Me hear your voice" alludes to learning Torah. Explaining the associations made by the Midrash, the Brisker Rav notes that there are halachos governing how one is to *appear* before Hashem during prayer (e.g., one must be dressed properly, one often needs to stand, one must conduct oneself as he would before a king, etc.). Therefore, "showing one's countenance," alludes to prayer. There are no such halachos, however, regarding Torah study. That is done using one's mouth. Therefore, "letting one's voice be heard" alludes to Torah study.

121 The Midrash takes a different approach, interpreting the "voice" as an allusion to Torah study (which one does with one's mouth), and "[true] countenance" as an allusion to good deeds because kindness is radiated by a kind person, and true beauty is a reflection of good deeds. In the *berachah* of *Ahavah Rabbah* (recited just before the *Shema*), we ask to be able to listen, learn, teach, safeguard, perform, and fulfill all the mitzvos. We see that fulfilling mitzvos comes at the end of the list, communicating that they are the highest level to aspire to. However, the surest way to ensure that a person performs mitzvos and good deeds properly is by his learning about them. Therefore, the verse concludes that first one should make sure that his voice is pleasant with Torah learning, and then his countenance will be pleasant.

Nimshal This verse alludes to the fateful time when *Klal Yisrael* was caught between Pharaoh's army and the Reed Sea. The verse likens *Klal Yisrael* to a dove because a dove is always faithful[123] to its partner just as *Klal Yisrael* is faithful to Hashem. The dove in the cleft and the hidden part of the steps — tight and closed-in places — alludes to *Klal Yisrael* at the edge of the sea, unable to move in any direction. They were surrounded by the murderous Egyptians behind them, the impassable sea in front of them, and the awesome desert in all other directions.

Hashem says to *Klal Yisrael*: "I want to see how you look and how you conduct yourselves at such times. I want to hear you cry out to Me because 'your voice is sweet and your appearance is pleasant.'" This means that Hashem likes to hear *Klal Yisrael*'s prayers and likes to see how they conduct themselves in difficult situations.[124] Indeed, Hashem finds *Klal Yisrael*'s actions and prayers sweet — and He responds by saving them.

---

[122] The Chafetz Chaim uses this allegory to bring home a vital lesson in *bitachon* (trust in Hashem). Sometimes when a person sees how many people in this world rebel against Hashem, his belief in Hashem's ability to provide for and protect those who serve Him becomes weaker. To show that this response is based on a faulty perspective, the Chafetz Chaim offers the following parable of a king who ruled over hundreds of countries and provided all the needs of millions of people. One day, a number of his subjects in one of the far-flung corners of the empire decide to rebel. While deciding how to punish the rebels, the king goes for a walk, and hears a little bird singing. Finding its voice very sweet and its appearance very pleasant, the king instructs a servant to bring it into the palace where it will be given the few grains it needs to eat and where it will bring joy to the king. As he takes the bird into the palace, the servant mutters: "You poor creature, how will you survive now that the king who is taking you in has a rebellion on his hands?!" Another servant scoffs at the stupidity of this doubting servant. He tells him: "You fool! Do you really think that the king, with his seemingly unlimited storehouses of wealth and millions of servants, will not be able to find a few grains for a bird that he loves so much and from whom he gets so much pleasure just because a few weak and foolish people have rebelled?!" Similarly, the Chafetz Chaim comments, Hashem has millions of spiritual worlds filled with millions upon millions of angels, each world greater than ours. And Hashem provides for all their needs. All the needs of the inhabitants of this world are not even like a crumb compared to the other greater worlds. It is only in our small, physical world that anyone attempts to rebel because in all the other worlds, every heavenly being is completely subservient to Hashem. His power and storehouses are unlimited. Can one then doubt that Hashem will be able to provide for *Klal Yisrael* from whom He gets so much pleasure, as we see in this verse that likens the Jewish nation to a bird that He finds beautiful and whose song He enjoys?! When one contemplates the great love that Hashem has for us and the pleasure He gets from us — and His infinite power — one cannot have any doubt as to Hashem's ability to protect and provide for us if we do as He wishes (*Shemiras HaLashon, Shaar HaTevunah*, ch. 10).

[123] See our commentary on 1:15 for other explanations of why *Klal Yisrael* is likened to doves. The loyalty of a dove is actually very shallow. There is no deep or close relationship between doves. In light of this, Hashem is saying to *Klal Yisrael* that even a dove's loyalty is a good thing. We can be close to Hashem even on a very simple level.

[124] The Chasam Sofer had occasion to refer to this verse in a halachic context, as we see from the following episode. In the Chasam Sofer's time, the Haskalah (the so called "Jewish Enlightenment") was spreading through Europe. One day, a *chazzan* who was clean-shaven (indicating his identification with the Haskalah) applied to become a *chazan* in a certain shul. The community asked the Chasam Sofer whether they should hire him. The Chasam Sofer saw that

MY DOVE IS IN THE CLEFTS OF THE ROCK...

Here we have a vivid picture of *Klal Yisrael* trapped and in terrible danger. Hashem tells them: "Show Me your true colors. What do you do in times of danger? To whom do you turn?" When Hashem sees their beautiful character and loyalty to Him, He saves them. This picture gives us a true and deeper understanding of how important prayer is, and why Hashem creates challenging situations for us, as will be explained.

The Midrash tells us that when *Klal Yisrael* was in Egypt, they would cry out to Hashem, but they stopped praying after they were saved. How did Hashem respond? He induced Pharaoh and his forces to pursue them into the desert. When *Klal Yisrael* became terrified at their approach, they cried out to Hashem once again. He said to them: "This is what I desired." The Midrash explains this verse with the following parable: There was once a certain king whose daughter barely talked to him. So, he arranged for everyone around her to go far away, and then he had her kidnapped. Out of fear, she screamed for help. The king saved her, and then revealed that he had orchestrated the entire episode in order to get her to talk to him. So too, Hashem arranged the terrifying threat of Pharaoh's army so that *Klal Yisrael* would daven to Him.[125]

Now, if we think about this parable, we might wonder why the daughter did not want to talk to her father, the king, and how his ploy would solve the problem in the future, after the danger had passed. The answer to both questions is that originally the daughter did not think the king would have any interest in hearing her. But once she knew that the king had arranged the kidnapping, she realized how important she was to him. Similarly, *Klal Yisrael* cried out to Hashem in Egypt, but once they left, they did not see any reason to carry on davening. However, once they realized that Hashem had induced Pharaoh's army to chase them just so that they would daven to Him, they understood the importance of *tefillah* at all times.[126]

This, then, is the meaning of our verse. Hashem deliberately put *Klal Yisrael* in danger

---

this person's conduct was evidently being influenced by the Haskalah, so he advised them not to hire him. When the applicant asked the Chasam Sofer what he had done wrong, the great *posek* answered by pointing to the order of our verse. First Hashem wants to see a person's "countenance," i.e., what kind of conduct he displays, and only then does He want to hear his "voice" in prayer. There is a lesson here that we can learn from even today. A person should be aware that Hashem first wants to see how a person conducts himself. Only if he passes that test does Hashem want to hear his voice.

125 *Shemos Rabbah* 21:5.

126 The Midrash uses the expression "*sichah*" (small talk) in describing what the king wanted to hear from his daughter. This indicates that although the daughter had been speaking to the king about important matters, he wanted to hear her all the time. This explains the conclusion of the verse, when Hashem says, "for your voice is sweet." Hashem wants to hear our voice not because it is necessary, but because it is sweet to Him. He wants us to know that we should be talking to Him all the time — not just about very important matters. A person should feel that Hashem wants to hear from him about everything. He wants to hear even our "small talk."

at edge of the Reed Sea just so He could hear their voices in prayer. The second part of the verse, "let Me hear your voice," is the reason for the first part: "My dove is [trapped] in the clefts of the rock, in the nooks of the stairs." From this Midrash, we learn that davening is not just a solution for troubles and problems. Rather, Hashem presents us with difficulties in order to motivate us to daven to Him. Furthermore, we see that davening is called for not only when one is facing major problems, such as health and financial issues. Hashem wants to hear us daven to Him frequently.[127]

This Midrash goes on to tell us that three of the Imahos, Sarah, Rivkah, and Rachel, were barren initially just so that they would daven. Similarly, Hashem causes many tzaddikim to suffer so that they will daven to Him.[128] All of these examples show us how precious davening is to Hashem. Of course, we should not need unfortunate events in our lives to motivate us to daven.[129]

The Vilna Gaon takes a slightly different approach to our verse. According to him, Hashem caused Pharaoh's army to pursue *Klal Yisrael*, leading to the miracle of the Splitting of the Sea of Reeds, so that *Klal Yisrael* would *sing* to Him. "Let Me hear your voice" does not mean that Hashem wanted to hear *Klal Yisrael* cry out to Him. Rather, it means that Hashem wanted to hear *Klal Yisrael* sing to Him. This was something that had not yet happened in Egypt. The troubles of *Kriyas Yam Suf* and the subsequent miracles created a closeness between *Klal Yisrael* and Hashem evidenced by the spectacular singing of *Shiras HaYam*. Such a thing had not occurred during *Yetzias Mitzrayim*.

Elsewhere in the Midrash, there is a different version of the parable of the king and the princess[130] which fits in nicely with the approach of the Vilna Gaon. In this version, the king saves a princess from danger, and she is very grateful. But after a while, she stops talking to him. The king then reenacts the danger, and she cries out for help. He

---

127 Rabbi Shimshon Pinkus used to point out that Hashem made human beings frail: we need to eat, drink, and relieve ourselves regularly. Why, he asked? Surely it would have been better that a person would not need all of this. That way, he would be able to learn Torah without interruption for much longer periods. Rav Pinkus explained that it is even more important that a person should need to turn to Hashem regularly for all his needs. Otherwise, he could easily neglect his personal relationship with Hashem, and that would be devastating for his spiritual growth.

128 The Midrash notes that Yishmael was born immediately after Hagar married Avraham Avinu, while Yitzchak was born only after Avraham and Sarah davened many years for a child. The Midrash compares this to the difference between growing weeds and growing a vineyard. To grow weeds requires no effort. But to grow a vineyard requires a lot of care and hard work. So, too, to have a Yitzchak required a lot of prayer. When we have a problem and we need to pray, we should remember this. For truly positive growth, one needs to do a lot of praying. If things are going too smoothly, one has to wonder whether he might be growing only weeds. It is only through proper praying that one should expect true success.

129 This idea is discussed at length in *Daas Chochmah U'Mussar*, vol. 2, ch. 72.

130 *Shemos Rabbah* 21:5.

saves her again, and actually marries her this time. The king was not interested in just a repeat of the crying she displayed when he saved her the first time, but rather wanted this new experience of his saving her to cause a closeness that would lead to marriage. As the Gaon explains, Hashem wanted *Klal Yisrael* to go through this experience so that they would become closer to Him, would sing to Him, and would commit themselves to serving Him. Indeed, this is what happened after the Splitting of the Sea, when *Klal Yisrael* sang the *Shiras HaYam* to Hashem. The Vilna Gaon goes on to say that the inspiration caused by *Kriyas Yam Suf* brought *Klal Yisrael* to *Kabbalas HaTorah*. This is reflected in the parable: after the princess cries out and is saved, she marries the king. *Kabbalas HaTorah* was, *ki'veyachol*, the marriage of *Klal Yisrael* to Hashem.

The lesson from all this is that a person should see a time of trouble as an opportunity to get closer to Hashem. It is very possible that Hashem brought on the trouble just to draw the person closer to Him. When problems arise, a person starts davening more, and then when he is saved, he is naturally full of gratitude to Hashem. This creates a new closeness to Hashem. Indeed, one should utilize occasions of difficulty to cultivate the closeness that is created through those events.

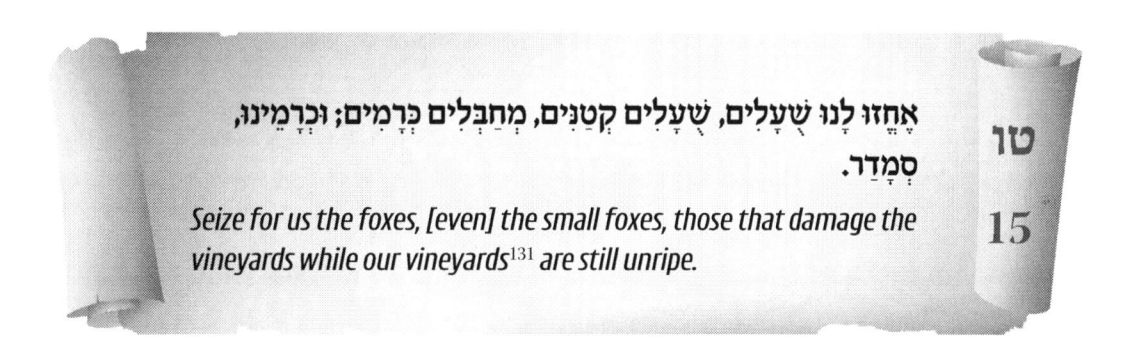

טו 15 אֶחֱזוּ לָנוּ שֻׁעָלִים, שֻׁעָלִים קְטַנִּים, מְחַבְּלִים כְּרָמִים; וּכְרָמֵינוּ, סְמָדַר.

Seize for us the foxes, [even] the small foxes, those that damage the vineyards while our vineyards[131] are still unripe.

Allegorical Translation — May the waters of Yam Suf grab the Egyptians and drown them for My sake. Even the young Egyptians should be killed because they too harmed the children of our nation.

Subject of the Verse — Hashem is commanding the destruction of the Egyptians at the Sea of Reeds.

Mashal — This is a vignette of foxes in the process of ruining a vineyard. The owner and protector of the vineyard wishes to catch all the foxes, even the young ones, because they too cause destruction.

---

131 *Klal Yisrael* is likened to vineyards which produce grapes, a particularly special and valuable fruit. The Midrash adds that vineyards are supported by trellises made out of dead branches. Just as the "dead" support the "living" in the vineyard, so too *Klal Yisrael* is supported by the merit of previous generations who have already passed on.

Nimshal "Foxes" symbolize the cruel and wily Egyptians. The vineyard represents *Klal Yisrael*. This verse speaks of the destruction of the Egyptians at the Sea of Reeds. The small foxes allude to the young Egyptians who also caused harm, and thus also deserve to be eliminated.

SEIZE FOR US THE FOXES...

This verse is the conclusion and outcome of the previous verse (14), where *Klal Yisrael* cries out to Hashem at the Sea to save them. Here in this verse, Hashem decrees that the Egyptian pursuers be destroyed, thereby saving *Klal Yisrael*.

SEIZE FOR US THE FOXES...

This verse alludes to a particular expression of Egyptian cruelty.[132] When Pharaoh decreed that all male Jewish babies be thrown into the Nile, the Jewish mothers hid their babies in secret hiding places and dark cellars. The Egyptians devised a crafty plan to find these babies. They would go into a Jewish home with an Egyptian baby and pinch it hard to make it cry. This would cause the concealed Jewish baby to cry along with the other baby, as babies tend to do. In this way, they were able to locate all the Jewish male babies. This demonic scheme is alluded to here in three different ways. First, the verse calls the Egyptians "foxes." Their crafty, cruel behavior was appropriate for wily foxes, not for human beings.[133] Then the verse calls them "small foxes" because the Egyptians, in their wickedness, hurt their own babies in order to apprehend the Jewish babies. The verse concludes that this was happening "while our vineyards were still unripe." This means that they were murdering the young children of *Klal Yisrael*, the budding fruit of our nation. That they could kill little babies without compunction was another sign of their cruelty.

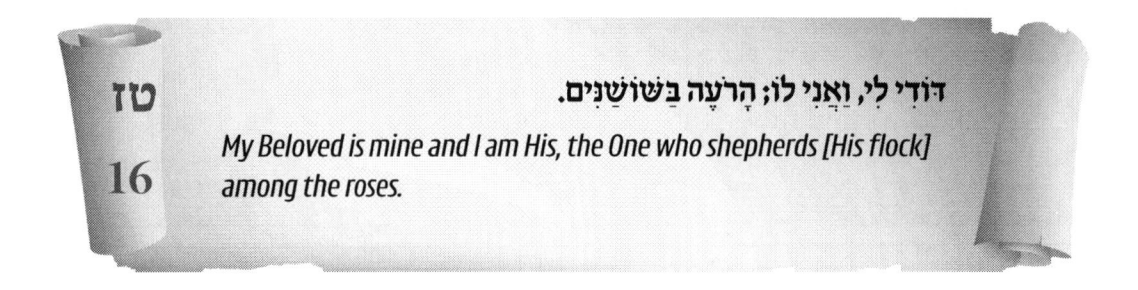

טז דּוֹדִי לִי, וַאֲנִי לוֹ; הָרֹעֶה בַּשּׁוֹשַׁנִּים.

16 My Beloved is mine and I am His, the One who shepherds [His flock] among the roses.

---

132 Rashi.

133 This is the Midrash's explanation. Rashi explains that foxes are always ready to retreat backwards and run away. Similarly, the Egyptians tried to run away from the Sea by retreating.

Allegorical Translation — All that Hashem needs, *ki'veyachol*, He asks only of me, *Klal Yisrael*. And all that I need, I ask only of Him, the One who looks after His flock in the pleasant and good grazing grounds.

Subject of the Verse — *Klal Yisrael* recollects how their relationship with Hashem reached a pinnacle — to the extent where both they and Hashem were, *ki'veyachol*, everything to one another.

Mashal — The wife reflects about how her relationship with her husband was so wonderful that everything they could possibly have needed was provided for by the other.

Nimshal — *Klal Yisrael* sum up their relationship with Hashem in these few beautiful words. Hashem, our beloved, is ours, and we are His. This means that Hashem requests things only of *Klal Yisrael*, and everything that *Klal Yisrael* wish for, they ask only of Hashem. It also means that *Klal Yisrael* get their entire fulfillment from Hashem, and they do not need to look for anything else to satisfy them.[134]

Then *Klal Yisrael* say that the uniqueness of Hashem is that He shepherds His flock, *Klal Yisrael*, among the roses, i.e., on comfortable and pleasant pastureland. This means that Hashem looks after *Klal Yisrael* in a pleasant and comfortable manner.

MY BELOVED IS MINE, AND I AM HIS

After focusing on *Yetzias Mitzrayim* and *Kriyas Yam Suf*, we summarize the pinnacle of the relationship between Hashem and *Klal Yisrael*. The Midrash on our verse is actually the source of the beautiful *piyut* we recite on Yom Kippur just before *viduy*. The *piyut* starts, "Because we are Your nation and You are our God." It goes on to give many metaphors illustrating this unique relationship:

> Hashem is our God, and we are His nation. Hashem is our Beloved, and we are His beloved. Hashem is our Father, and we are His children. Hashem is our Shepherd, and we are His flock. Hashem is our Guardian, and we are His vineyard. Hashem calls us the beautiful nation, and we call Him the beautiful God. Hashem saves us from all our enemies, and we stand up against all His enemies. Hashem declares

---

[134] There is an implicit critique here of those who are devoted to Torah study yet look for other sources to find "fulfillment." Truthfully, all fulfilment should come from our relationship with Hashem.

that we never stop doing good deeds, and we declare that Hashem's kindness never stops. Hashem says we are the sole nation, and we say that Hashem is the sole God...

There are many kinds of relationships in this world. Some are minimal and require very little effort or loyalty, such as the relationship between partners in a sporting event. In contrast, some are all consuming, such as the relationship between a father and child or husband and wife. As explained in the Introduction, each relationship has its own unique beauty, pleasures, and strengths. Our relationship with Hashem includes all the aspects and intensity of all the relationships. Truly, one could spend a lot of time appreciating each aspect of our wonderful, multi-faceted relationship with Hashem. It is all summed up in this verse, "My beloved is mine, and I am His."

Every human relationship has its limitations. For example, when one says, "This is my child," he or she is making a declaration of a very important relationship. At the same time, though, it excludes the intimacy of love one has with a spouse. But, when this verse says, "Hashem is mine, and I am His," without specifying in which way and in what relationship Hashem is ours and we are His, we are including all relationships. We are declaring that in every way, without any limitations, "Hashem is mine, and I am His."

THE ONE WHO SHEPHERDS [HIS FLOCK] AMONG THE ROSES

Rabbi Moshe Soloveichik, *zt"l*, explains the meaning of Hashem "shepherding His flock among the roses" in a unique way. He notes that there are many methods a shepherd can use to ensure that his flock does not wander away from him. He can wield a big stick so that the flock is afraid to stray. He can also shout very loudly to bring them back if they start to wander. There is, however, a much more pleasant way. If the shepherd has a bouquet of roses that gives off a nice smell, the flock will not want to wander off to a place where they cannot smell the roses. This, then, is what the verse is saying: Hashem does not need to shout at us to bring us back to Him. Rather, He uses His roses — i.e., His pleasantness — to ensure that we will not want to wander away too far to a place where we cannot feel His pleasantness.[135]

---

135 *Kovetz Palgei Mayaim*, p. 90.
   Rabbi Soloveichik notes that elsewhere *talmidei chachamim* are also likened to roses because they, too, lead their flock with their good smell — i.e., their pleasantness — which draws people to follow them (*Tehillim* 45:1 and Rashi). *Talmidei chachamim* thus lead *Klal Yisrael* by emulating the way Hashem leads His nation. Another point of analogy: just as the rose produces its good smell when the moisture of the dew is absorbed in it, so the *talmid chacham* is able to spread a sweet and genial atmosphere around him by absorbing Torah, which gives life like dew (*Devarim* 32:2 and Rashi).

שיר השירים 2:17

עַד שֶׁיָּפוּחַ הַיּוֹם, וְנָסוּ הַצְּלָלִים; סֹב דְּמֵה לְךָ דוֹדִי לִצְבִי, אוֹ לְעֹפֶר הָאַיָּלִים, עַל הָרֵי בָתֶר.

Until the day sweltered, and the shadows disappeared. [You then] turned around, My beloved, as if You were like a deer or a young hart upon the distant mountains.[136]

יז
17

Allegorical Translation — This close relationship between us and Hashem continued until we sinned through the Golden Calf and the Spies (which brought us discomfort like the sweltering day). Then the protection we had (due to our merits) disappeared, and we caused the Presence of Hashem to flee like a hart running away to the distant mountains.[137]

Subject of the Verse — *Klal Yisrael* bitterly reflects that they ruined their wonderful relationship with Hashem through their sins.

Mashal — After describing the pinnacle of her relationship with her husband, the wife bemoans the fact that this lasted only *until* a certain point, whereupon the relationship deteriorated rapidly, and her husband left her, disappearing like a hart into the distant mountains.

Nimshal — *Klal Yisrael* acknowledge that their special relationship with Hashem was compromised when they sinned. Once they sinned, it was as if the day became hot and uncomfortable, and the shelter protecting *Klal Yisrael* disappeared. The heat of the day alludes to suffering, and the loss of shelter symbolizes the loss of Hashem's protection. Then Hashem became very distant, like a young hart fleeing to the distant mountains. Both the speed of the hart running away and the distant mountains underscore this sense of detachment.

---

[136] The *Zohar* offers a homiletical reading of this verse based on an understanding of "day" as the day(s) of one's life (*Parashas Vayera* 99b). Everything in life continues only "until the day blows." That is, the days of a person's life fly away as fast as the wind blows. They slip away quickly like a "fleeting shadow." Therefore, "be like a deer…" Do not waste time but hurry up and do your mitzvos as speedily as a deer runs — even going far away to do mitzvos. This is similar to the teaching in *Avos*: "Be as swift as a deer … to fulfill the wishes of your Father in Heaven (5:20)."

[137] The *Targum* here is similar to Rashi but sees the verse ending on a happy note: "This [success and love] lasted a short time — until we sinned through the Golden Calf. Then the Clouds of Glory, which used to protect us, disappeared, and we were left sweltering in the heat of the day. Our "crowns of glory" [acquired through our unqualified acceptance of Torah at Sinai] disappeared, [and we were in grave danger. Hashem, however, chose to focus on the merit of our forefathers Avraham, Yitzchak and Yaakov] who would serve Him loyally, and run quickly to do His bidding like a deer. [And He remembered the special merit of Yitzchak Avinu who was ready to give up his life to Hashem] upon the distant mountains."

UNTIL THE DAY SWELTERED...

This verse concludes the second chapter. As we noted earlier,[138] the division of the *perakim* in *Shir HaShirim* is not based on our traditional commentaries. However, this verse certainly concludes the chapter, even according to Rashi and the Malbim, because it marks the end of a glorious chapter of our history. The next chapter is going to focus on a much less pleasant part of our past, as we will see.

To recapitulate briefly, the last few verses evoke *Yetzias Mitzrayim* and the wonderful closeness *Klal Yisrael* felt toward Hashem, followed by the feeling of distance created by the sins of the Golden Calf and the Spies. Here in this verse, Hashem is described as if He has fled like a hart to the distant mountains. As explained earlier, this conveys His aloofness when we are in exile. But the hart metaphor can be understood on an optimistic note as well. Even though we feel that Hashem is very distant, we know that He can come back at any time. Just as a young hart can run very fast, we know that the moment we repent and Hashem wants to come back to us, He can come back swiftly, no matter how distant we feel that Hashem is. This is one of *Klal Yisrael*'s basic beliefs: that however far away redemption seems, it can come very quickly.

There is a deeper view of this verse which requires "*Shir HaShirim* lenses" to appreciate. Imagine a couple dating, and all is going well. They both enjoy the time they spend together and find each other's company very pleasant. But then, on one particular date, things go very badly. They behave rudely to one another and have a miserable time together. If they want to take away the sting and continue meeting, they can place the blame on the circumstances: "It was too hot/cold," "We were tired/hungry," "The place we went to was too noisy/quiet," etc. By blaming the circumstances and conditions, they establish that their relationship is essentially sound. This paves the way for another, hopefully much better, date.

Klal Yisrael established in the previous verse just how wonderful their relationship with Hashem was. Now, in this verse, they speak of the worst of times — when they sinned through the Golden Calf and the Spies. But let us listen carefully to how they describe this. As Rashi explains, "This verse refers back to the previous verse: 'Hashem is mine and I am His...'" *Klal Yisrael* do not say, "Our relationship was wonderful until Hashem hated us or punished us or even until we sinned." Rather, they say: "Because the day became unbearable, Hashem left us. Clearly, He will return when the situation becomes more bearable. It is true that we sinned, and that caused the split between us. But because the problems are circumstantial, we are convinced that there is nothing wrong with the actual relationship. When conditions improve, our relationship will be reestablished."

---

138 See end of Introduction.

פרק ג'
CHAPTER 3

> **א** עַל מִשְׁכָּבִי בַּלֵּילוֹת, בִּקַּשְׁתִּי אֵת שֶׁאָהֲבָה נַפְשִׁי; בִּקַּשְׁתִּיו, וְלֹא מְצָאתִיו.
>
> **1** Upon my bed at night, I searched for the One whom my soul loves; I searched for Him but did not find Him.[1]

Allegorical Translation — When I was "bedridden" during the thirty-eight years after the Sin of the Spies until Hashem completely forgave us, I searched for the Presence of Hashem in my midst, but Hashem refused to dwell among us.

Subject of the Verse — *Klal Yisrael* is speaking of the time when Hashem was distant from them.

Mashal — Pining for her husband who has left her, the wife describes how she yearns for him when she goes to bed at night. She goes out looking for him but cannot find him.

Nimshal — This verse alludes to the periods when *Klal Yisrael* yearned for Hashem. They searched for Him but were unable to find Him due to their sins. The night is symbolic of exile, a time of darkness and fear. During exile, it is difficult to find Hashem.

---

1 Since night is often symbolic of death, the Chofetz Chaim sees a homiletic lesson in this verse. When a person has died and is lying in his final "resting place," he will seek "that for which my soul loves," i.e., to fulfill still more mitzvos. This is because his soul will then appreciate just how precious every mitzvah is. By then, however, it will be too late, as the verse concludes: "I searched for it but did not find it." Indeed, we must think about this while we are still alive and appreciate the great desire of the soul to grab every mitzvah opportunity before it is too late (*Shem Olam, Shaar HaChefetz*, ch. 7).

UPON MY BED AT NIGHT

This verse conjures up another vivid picture that illustrates the depth of feeling between *Klal Yisrael* and Hashem. It describes a wife lying in bed, unable to sleep because of the pain of missing her husband. She is pining and yearning for her husband, and finally gets up, desperately hoping to find him. Her search ends in disappointment. This vivid illustration ought to awaken within us these same feelings for Hashem. Like the wife yearning for her husband, we too should be seeking Hashem and yearning for Him.[2]

Rashi connects this verse with the period when *Klal Yisrael* was in the desert for forty years as a punishment for the Sin of the Spies. As mentioned in the Introduction, however, every verse alludes to a number of different events. This is because every verse describes an emotion or aspect of our relationship with Hashem that comes to the fore in different ways. *Klal Yisrael*'s yearning for Hashem repeated itself many times in many exiles. Indeed, the Midrash itself explains this verse in a number of ways, each one representing a different exile.

This verse speaks of *Klal Yisrael* pining and searching for Hashem at night. Night is symbolic of the darkness *Klal Yisrael* felt when they were distant from Hashem.[3] *Klal Yisrael* is saying that without Hashem's Presence, it is as if life is constantly dark and sad. They are like an abandoned wife who feels her whole life is dark without her husband.

The Midrash explains that the verse is alluding to the night of exile. The use of the plural, "nights," alludes to the fact that we have been in a number of exiles. Indeed, the suffering of exile is often likened to the long, dark night. Furthermore, we are described as being "in bed" because, in exile, we are like an unwell nation, weak and in pain. The pain of missing Hashem makes us so unwell that it is as if we are confined to our beds.

This verse yields an additional layer of meaning: At night, when a person has stopped attending to all that he needs to do, his mind is not preoccupied and his true feelings start to emerge. That is why night is a highly emotional time. There are those sufferers who are able to distract themselves during the day, but at night, when they are alone with their feelings, start crying over their fate. This is why *Megillas Eichah* describes our nation weeping over the *Churban* at night.[4] In our verse, it is at night that *Klal Yisrael* naturally reveal their innermost feelings of yearning for Hashem's love.[5]

---

2   See *Chovos HaLevavos, Shaar Ahavas Hashem*, ch. 6.
3   Rashi.
4   *Eichah* 1:2. See this author's commentary in, *Tears of Hope, Seeds of Redemption* (ibid.).
5   Indeed, if a person wants to get a better picture of his true desires, he should examine his thoughts in bed at night. If his

This phenomenon can be better appreciated through the famous *mashal* of Rabbi Yisrael Salanter. He tells of a man who has both a very difficult son and a devoted, hard-working student who lives with the family. It appears to onlookers that he likes his student better than his son. But when he is roused from his sleep by a fire in the middle of the night, which boy does he rush to save first? The answer is obvious. He saves his son first because when instinct takes over, a person's true, deep feelings come out. And a father loves his son more than any other person regardless of how good that other person may be. Similarly, when a Jew wakes up at night, his instinctive thoughts should be about his love for Hashem.

There is a very deep yearning in every Jewish person's heart for Hashem, but the *yetzer ha'ra* tries to hide the true nature of this yearning. It may try to convince us that what we really desire is another piece of cake or any of the many other substitutes that the *yetzer ha'ra* comes up with — some of which are much worse. We must know that the yearning we feel is a yearning to become close to Hashem and must not confuse it or quash it with a superficial substitute.[6] At night when a person's deepest instincts come to the fore, this is doubly important.[7] Here in our verse, *Klal Yisrael* declare: "Upon my bed at night, I searched for the One whom my soul loves…"

If one's spouse's extended absence from home would evoke nothing but indifference from the other spouse, we would understand that there is something flawed about the relationship. The intense feeling of loss over the spouse's absence is an indicator of how great the loving relationship is. Similarly, *Klal Yisrael*'s pining for Hashem teaches us about the importance they attribute to their loving relationship with Hashem.

---

thoughts turn to his business, he should understand that his true interests lie in this realm despite the fact that he may spend a good part of his day doing mitzvos. Incidentally, we should make an effort to channel our thoughts at bedtime to Torah and *emunah* because a person is highly affected by the thoughts in his mind as he is going to sleep. Since they can remain in his mind right through the night, they have a greater effect than such thoughts during the day.

6   There is a verse in *Mishlei*, which is explained by the Vilna Gaon, that connects with this idea: "A man who is lacking will be a lover of joy…" (21:17). If one seeks superficial pleasures to find happiness, it is because he is lacking something. At root, he is lacking the connection to Hashem which is at the heart of all pleasure seeking. The constant pursuit of new pleasures actually stems from man's inner need for spirituality. This is why animals that have enough food and basic comforts are satisfied, while human beings in a similar situation always feel lacking. However, those who transfer their yearning for Hashem onto something else will eventually become disillusioned when it does not satisfy them and leaves them feeling the same lack as before.

7   This is why the Mishnah warns us of the grave danger to one who is awake at night of letting his mind wander and think of futile things (*Avos* 3:4).

> ב
>
> 2
>
> אָקוּמָה נָּא וַאֲסוֹבְבָה בָעִיר, בַּשְּׁוָקִים וּבָרְחֹבוֹת, אֲבַקְשָׁה אֵת שֶׁאָהֲבָה נַפְשִׁי; בִּקַּשְׁתִּיו, וְלֹא מְצָאתִיו.
>
> *I will arise now and go around the city, among the streets and plazas, and I will seek the One whom my soul loves! I searched for Him but did not find Him.*

Allegorical Translation — While we were rejected during the thirty-eight years following the Sin of the Spies, we prayed to Hashem constantly that He forgive us for our sins and return His Presence. But He refused.

Subject of the Verse — *Klal Yisrael* continues the theme of the previous verse: the sadness they felt during the time that Hashem rejected them.

Mashal — The wife, feeling despair over the loss of her love, gets up in the middle of the night and looks for her husband everywhere, even searching the city squares and all the streets, but is still unable to find him.

Nimshal — *Klal Yisrael* describing what it was like when Hashem rejected them, how they would make every effort to search for Hashem, and their lack of success in returning to their previous closeness.

I WILL ARISE AND GO AROUND THE CITY

This alludes to the Jewish People's strenuous, although unsuccessful, effort to reestablish their relationship with Hashem. The metaphor of "searching the streets and plazas" communicates that *Klal Yisrael* tried every possible way to get close to Hashem and to obtain His forgiveness.[8] We also see how much Moshe Rabbeinu davened to Hashem that He forgive *Klal Yisrael*.

Let us take a moment to "feel" these verses. Let us picture someone who misses her loved one intensively and is so upset that she is unable to sleep. She lies in bed, grieving her loss. But instead of doing nothing about it, she gets out of bed and goes looking and searching in every possible way to find the one she loves so much. *Klal Yisrael* feel this way when it seems that they do not have Hashem in their lives — and so must we!

Note that the expression "The One whom my soul loves" appears four times in these

---

8 Alshich.

verses (1-4). We do not refer to Hashem by name or title, but by our feelings towards Him. He is the "One we love." We have to try to feel the tremendous love in these words.

I WILL ARISE AND GO AROUND THE CITY

The Netziv points out that our inability to find Hashem does not mean that all our efforts are wasted. Although we are unable to reestablish the same relationship we used to have, we do get much closer to Hashem through these efforts. The Netziv also suggests that the searching in the streets and plazas mentioned in the verse is symbolic of looking out for other people and providing for all their needs. These acts of kindness bring a person much closer to Hashem. Still, because we are in exile, we are unable to get back to our previous level of closeness.

Let us take a moment to elaborate on the Netziv's understanding of this verse. A *ba'alas teshuvah* once described her initial shock at seeing the extremely great difference between the quest for spirituality in the Torah world and in the gentile world. This *ba'alas teshuvah* had been in a convent for many years, where women who eschewed marriage would spend hours not talking or doing anything — just being totally self-absorbed in trying to find themselves and their connection to God (as they perceived Him). Imagine her shock when first introduced to a Rebbetzin who seemed to spend all her time dealing with the mundane: looking after her grandchildren, chatting with the neighbors, helping her sisters and friends, etc. Where was the spirituality in all of this? When did she have time to find herself?

The answer is that true service of Hashem and the search for spirituality are not selfish acts. One finds Hashem by looking out for others. It may seem very "spiritual" to be locked up in a convent on a remote mountain and very mundane to befriend someone or play with a child. But the reality is that there is far greater spirituality in a Jewish home than one would ever find anywhere else. One who searches in total isolation for their own god will find only their own desires, not spirituality. This is hinted at in our verse: "I will arise and go around the city, among the streets and plazas (looking out for others), and I will thus seek the One whom my soul loves..."

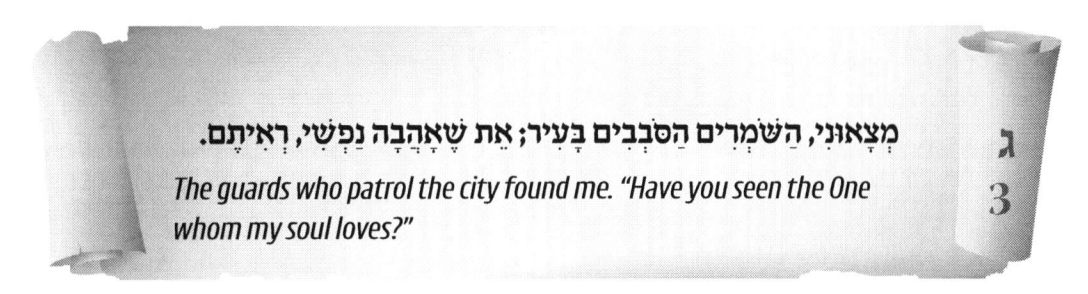

ג
3

מְצָאוּנִי, הַשֹּׁמְרִים הַסֹּבְבִים בָּעִיר; אֵת שֶׁאָהֲבָה נַפְשִׁי, רְאִיתֶם.

The guards who patrol the city found me. "Have you seen the One whom my soul loves?"

Allegorical Translation   My leaders who guard me from sin, Moshe and Aharon, found me, and I asked them, Have you seen Hashem — in the sense that you have been able to bring His Presence back to us as it was before?

Subject of the Verse — *Klal Yisrael* continues their description of their search for Hashem.

Mashal — The wife continues describing her search for her missing husband. She wants him back so much that, in desperation, she even enlists the help of others, and asks the guards roaming the streets if they have seen her husband.

Nimshal — Looking to reconnect to Hashem, *Klal Yisrael* in exile turns to their leaders to be able to reconnect to Hashem.

THE GUARDS WHO PATROL THE CITY FOUND ME

In the process of searching for Hashem, *Klal Yisrael* meets the "watchmen," and asks if they have seen Hashem, the One they love. In keeping with his understanding that the verse alludes to the period of *Klal Yisrael*'s wandering in the desert, Rashi identifies the watchmen as Moshe Rabbeinu and Aharon HaKohen. *Klal Yisrael* turn to Moshe Rabbeinu and Aharon HaKohen for help in getting close to Hashem, knowing that the Torah leaders are best equipped to provide this help. According to the Midrash, however, these verses refer to exile in general, and the watchmen are thus the leaders of every generation.

Metzudas Dovid adds that when someone is in love, he will do things he normally would be embarrassed to do. Out of his desire to be close to the one he loves, he overcomes that embarrassment. It is not surprising, then, that the wife ventures out in the middle of the night to search for her husband and even asks others for help. So too, *Klal Yisrael* is always seeking the One they love, and is willing to ask whomever they think may be able to help them for guidance in this quest.

Let us imagine that we are looking, God forbid, for a lost child on a beach. Would we hesitate to scream out the child's name despite the strange stares of onlookers?! When one really seeks and desires to connect to Hashem, one will ignore what others may think and do everything possible to connect to Hashem.[9]

Midrash Lekach Tov looks at this verse very differently, identifying the watchmen as the wicked nations who exercise control over *Klal Yisrael* in exile, preventing them from going back to Eretz Yisrael. The question *Klal Yisrael* poses to these nations is this: Have you ever seen [anyone as great as] the One who my soul loves?! By this, they mean:

---

9   This applies also when we need to ask a *she'eilah* (halachic question) of a rav. Even if we are embarrassed to do so, we must remind ourselves of the message here that when something is important, one does not pay attention to discomfort. And there is nothing more important than making sure to keep the mitzvos correctly.

"Why do you keep me away from serving Hashem? Is there any God who compares to Him?! By not allowing me to serve Him, you are causing terrible harm to us and to the entire world. Allow me to serve Him because He is the greatest power!

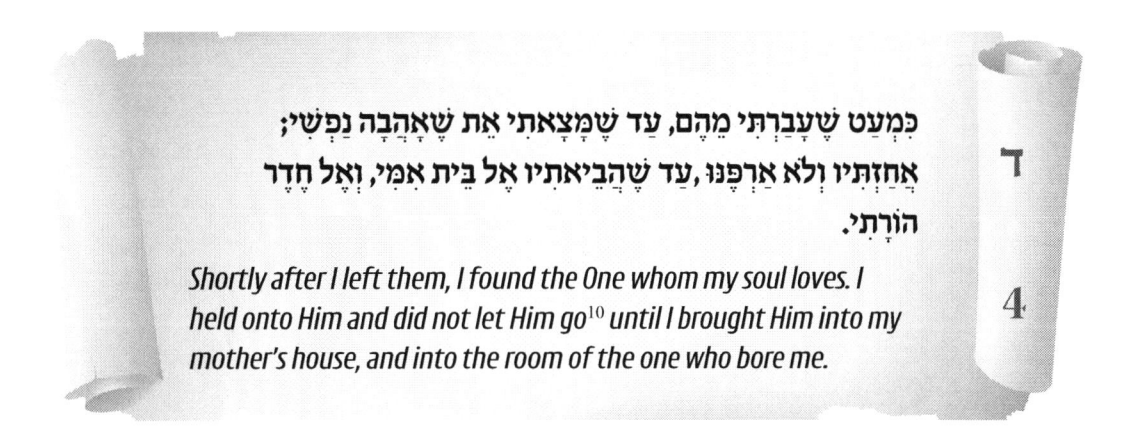

> כִּמְעַט שֶׁעָבַרְתִּי מֵהֶם, עַד שֶׁמָּצָאתִי אֵת שֶׁאָהֲבָה נַפְשִׁי;
> אֲחַזְתִּיו וְלֹא אַרְפֶּנּוּ, עַד שֶׁהֲבֵיאתִיו אֶל בֵּית אִמִּי, וְאֶל חֶדֶר הוֹרָתִי. ד 4
>
> Shortly after I left them, I found the One whom my soul loves. I held onto Him and did not let Him go[10] until I brought Him into my mother's house, and into the room of the one who bore me.

Allegorical Translation — Shortly after Moshe Rabbeinu and Aharon HaKohen left us, the Presence of Hashem returned to us. We held on tightly to Him by being careful not to sin. We were thus able to bring His Presence into the Mishkan of Shiloh.

Subject of the Verse — *Klal Yisrael* continues to describe the events that followed their rejection by Hashem.

Mashal — The wife relates that after she left the guards, she was able to find her beloved husband. After experiencing the terrible pain of separation, she is much more careful, and she holds onto him tightly until she is able to bring him home into her mother's house. She considers this an appropriate place for them because there they could remain together forever without distraction.

Nimshal — *Klal Yisrael* is finally able to reconnect to Hashem. When they do, they make an extra effort not to lose Him because they realize how bad it was when their sins caused separation. Now they are able to bring the Presence of Hashem into an appropriate place where they can remain together.

---

10 After *Klal Yisrael* felt Hashem's closeness once again, they made a special effort not to let go. This approach has widespread applicability in the realm of spiritual growth. Often, one is inspired by a *shiur*, a *sefer*, or a special event, and feels closer to Hashem, but then as time passes, he forgets or allows the closeness to dissipate. From this verse, we learn that there is a special duty to make sure not to let go but to keep up that feeling of inspiration, working hard to stay close to Hashem. Just as it takes effort to elevate oneself and draw close to Hashem, so too does it take effort to remain elevated. People mistakenly think that the enthusiasm they feel one day is so strong that it will last forever, but reality has shown countless times that it can soon fade into a distant memory.

UNTIL I BROUGHT HIM INTO... THE ROOM...

After finding Hashem, *Klal Yisrael* bring Him, *ki'veyachol*, to the special "room."[11] The is an allusion, Rashi tells us, to the Mishkan of Shiloh, which was built shortly after they left the desert.[12] Unlike Rashi, the Midrash sees this verse alluding to the various places where *Klal Yisrael* and Hashem "rendezvoused" during the course of Jewish history.[13] Among these are: the First Beis HaMikdash built by Shlomo HaMelech, which he hoped would be a permanent dwelling place for Hashem's Shechinah, and the Second Beis HaMikdash, which was built after the anguish of the First Destruction and subsequent exile. This verse also adumbrates what we will feel when Mashiach comes. After grieving for so long over the loss of Hashem's Presence in our lives, when He finally returns, we will hold onto Him and bring Him into the special "room," i.e., the Third Beis HaMikdash. At that time, we will no longer sin because of our tremendous desire to remain close to Him.

The basic message of the verse is that after losing Hashem and realizing the devastating magnitude of the loss (as described in the previous verses), and finally getting Him back, *ki'veyachol*, we were much more careful and looked for ways to cement the relationship. The "repairing" of our relationship with Hashem was so successful that it actually enhanced our relationship

Rashi explains that this verse refers to the period when Yehoshua brought *Klal Yisrael* into Eretz Yisrael. This was a time of great closeness between Hashem and the people, who cultivated this closeness until they brought Hashem's Presence into the Mishkan, cementing the relationship.

The Midrash learns from this verse that once Hashem's Shechinah came into the Mishkan, He stopped giving prophecy to the other nations.[14] Because *Klal Yisrael* had repented and were looking for ways to strengthen their relationship with Hashem, He repaid them in kind and found ways to make the relationship even more exclusive. This new relationship with *Klal Yisrael* was so strong that He did not want to connect with the others. Of course, we are not accustomed to prophecy today, and therefore have no real understanding of its importance, and how special it was that only *Klal Yisrael* merited this. When Hashem

---

11   See the next section for our commentary on why these holy places are connected with *Klal Yisrael*'s "mother."

12   This is in keeping with Rashi's understanding that these verses allude to the period of *Klal Yisrael*'s wandering in the desert and entry into Eretz Yisrael.

13   The Midrash identifies "my mother's house" as a reference to Har Sinai and "the room of the one who bore me" as a reference to the Mishkan (*Vayikra Rabbah* 1:10). According to Rashi, who understands that these verses allude to the period following *Klal Yisrael*'s entry into Eretz Yisrael, "my mother's house" refers to the Mishkan in Shilo and "the room of the one who bore me" refers to the Beis HaMikdash.

14   *Vayikrah Rabbah* 1:12. The Midrash explains that the story of Bilaam was a unique occurrence which Hashem orchestrated for the sake of *Klal Yisrael*.

spoke to a nation through one of its people, it showed how precious that nation was, and how close they were to Him. However, once Hashem's Presence dwelt in the Mishkan, He decided that this privilege would now be the exclusive prerogative of the Jewish People. This was one practical expression of how close the relationship became — despite the sin of the Golden Calf — once it was cemented and repaired through the Mishkan.

The implication of this verse for us today is that if we sin, God forbid, we must contemplate the resulting devastation and then find ways to repair and cement our relationship with Hashem. An ideal way to do this is to spend more time learning Torah in the *beis midrash* (a modern-day equivalent of what *Klal Yisrael* did by building a Mishkan). When we do so, we can recall with hope that once our people repented in ancient times, Hashem made sure to cement their relationship further. When we look for ways to repair the relationship, Hashem bestows extra love and closeness upon us.[15]

Midrash Lekach Tov adds that when Mashiach finally comes, we will never go into exile again because, as our verse communicates, after being apart for so long and truly experiencing the bitterness of exile, we will never let go of Hashem, and Hashem will never reject us again.

There is a mundane lesson to be learned from this as well. A husband and wife may occasionally quarrel and even feel distant from one another during the period of disharmony. Even though one hopes this will never happen, if it does, they must try to see the opportunity created by this upsetting situation. Once they see how unpleasant it is to quarrel, they should be motivated to look for ways to cement their relationship so that they do not lose their closeness ever again. In some ways, their relationship can be better than that of a couple who have never squabbled. Aware of how terrible a row is, neither spouse would, for example, make a rude comment to the other, even in jest.[16]

I BROUGHT HIM INTO MY MOTHER'S HOUSE

As we noted earlier, the expression "my mother's house" alludes either to Har Sinai, the Mishkan, or the Beis HaMikdash. How are we to understand the symbolism here? "Mother's house" symbolizes a place from where all good things and happy memories

---

15 In the *mashal*, this would be like one of the spouses — after realizing how harmful their split was — taking it upon himself or herself not to have a warm relationship with anyone who could threaten the marriage.

16 The Gemara tells us that even the completely righteous cannot reach the (high) place where *ba'alei teshuvah* (penitents) stand in the World to Come (*Berachos* 34a). Now, we many wonder why someone who sinned, even though he repented, is considered worthier than someone who never sinned. The answer lies in the dynamic we have been discussing: when one has sinned and then regrets it, the sin itself becomes an impetus to be more vigilant and to put more effort into serving Hashem. The result is that one's service of Hashem rises to a higher level.

emanate. Indeed, a mother's kitchen is often the place where a child feels safest and happiest. A person who is going through a very hard time may be comforted just by remembering his mother's house.[17] These places (i.e., Har Sinai, where the Torah was given, and the Mishkan/Beis HaMikdash, where the Presence of Hashem dwelled) represent the places from which our fondest memories and most comforting spiritual memories emanate. These are our most precious places, and therefore are represented by the most precious and comforting symbol.

I FOUND THE ONE WHOM MY SOUL LOVES. I HELD ONTO HIM AND DID NOT LET HIM GO

These words teach us that just as we must exert ourselves to find Hashem, i.e., to *become* spiritually elevated, we must exert ourselves to stay close to Hashem, i.e., to *remain* spiritually elevated. We have to be aware that when we have a spiritual elevation, we can lose it and fall quickly if we are not careful. We must never be complacent and must keep striving to remain close to Hashem.[18]

UPON MY BED AT NIGHT, I SEARCHED FOR HIM... I WILL ARISE AND GO AROUND THE CITY...

Rabbi Simcha Bunim of Peshischa, *zt"l*, offers a striking homiletical interpretation of these opening verses of Chapter Three. According to his approach, they allude to an individual who wishes to get close to Hashem but is not interested in investing the effort. As the jocular saying goes, "A person wishes to become a *talmid chacham* in just one night, but he also wants to get a good night's sleep." More common is the individual who wishes to earn a nice living and discover the world, all the while hoping naively that he will somehow become close to Hashem. If we ask our Torah leaders how to get closer to Hashem, they tell us that this is possible only by moving away from these desires. This, then, is the way Rabbi Simcha Bunim interprets the first four verses in this chapter:

1. "[While I am still lying] upon my bed at night [being lazy], I searched for the One whom my soul loves [without exerting effort]; I searched for Him but did not find Him [because I was still in bed!]."
2. "I will arise and go around the city, among the streets [looking to earn a lot of money or find the latest gadget or bargain] and plazas [discovering new sights], and I will seek the One whom my soul loves [while I am busy with all these

---

17 This reminds us that one of parents' many obligations is it to make their home a place where their children feel comfortable and safe.

18 Because the *yetzer ha'ra* is constantly pulling a person away from Hashem, one must make sure to hold on tight.

pursuits]. I searched for Him but did not find Him [because I was pursuing my worldly interests]."

3. "[I asked] the guards, [the righteous] who patrol the city [and who] found me, 'Have you seen the One whom my soul loves? [i.e., Can you teach me how I, too, can find Him?]'"

4. "[They replied, 'Keep away from your desires,' and, indeed,] shortly after I left them [these desires mentioned previously], I found the One whom my soul loves. I held onto Him and did not let Him go until I had brought Him into my mother's house, and into the room of the one who bore me [i.e., into the *beis midrash*. If one wants to get close and keep close to Hashem, this is the place to be]."

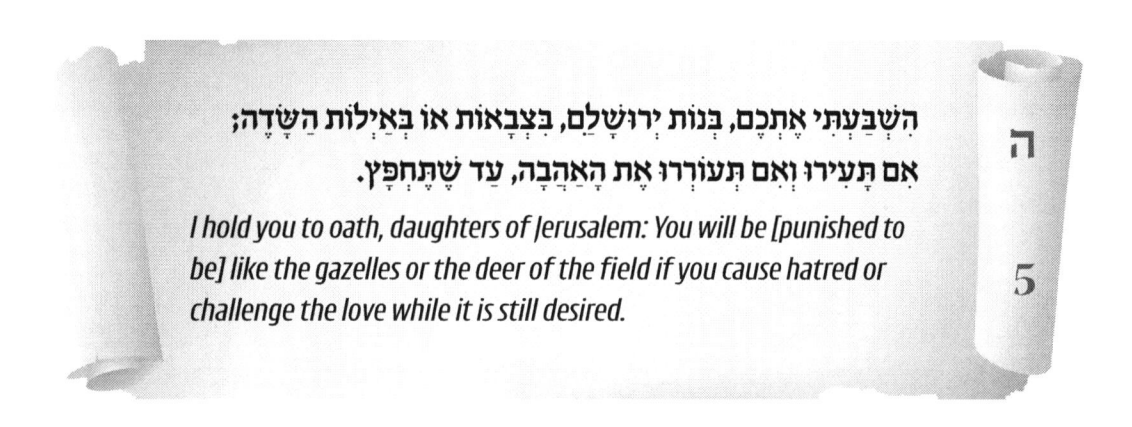

הִשְׁבַּעְתִּי אֶתְכֶם, בְּנוֹת יְרוּשָׁלִַם, בִּצְבָאוֹת אוֹ בְּאַיְלוֹת הַשָּׂדֶה; אִם תָּעִירוּ וְאִם תְּעוֹרְרוּ אֶת הָאַהֲבָה, עַד שֶׁתֶּחְפָּץ.

ה

5

I hold you to oath, daughters of Jerusalem: You will be [punished to be] like the gazelles or the deer of the field if you cause hatred or challenge the love while it is still desired.

Allegorical Translation — We (*Klal Yisrael*) warn the nations that if they try to cause hatred between us and Hashem, while He still actually loves us, they will be made defenseless and free for all, to be destroyed just like deer.

Subject of the Verse — *Klal Yisrael* is warning the nations not to cause (more) trouble.

Mashal — The wife warns her associates of the terrible consequences that await them if they try to cause even more of a split between her and her husband.

Nimshal — *Klal Yisrael* warn the nations not to try to cause friction between them and Hashem; and threaten that if they do, they will be unprotected from terrible punishment just like defenseless deer in the wild.

I HOLD YOU TO OATH

This pivotal verse both brings the theme of the preceding verses to a conclusion, and introduces the next six verses, which take us to the end of the chapter. In this last verse of the previous sequence, *Klal Yisrael* caution the heathen nations against trying to damage their special relationship with Hashem, and warn of severe consequences if they do:

"Don't think that because you saw us sin, and we and Hashem had a big row, *ki'veyachol*, that you can get in the way and destroy the relationship! We will never let that happen again. On the contrary, since we have seen how bad the break-up was, we are now even more careful than before. Our relationship is actually stronger after this episode."[19]

The verses that follow show why and how their relationship became so strong.

I HOLD YOU TO OATH...

Because of its important message, this verse is repeated in almost identical language three times in *Shir HaShirim*.[20] Furthermore, each repetition hints at a different one of the promises described earlier: Hashem had *Klal Yisrael* promise that they would not go up en masse to Eretz Yisrael, and that they would not rebel against the heathen nations; and He had the heathen nations promise that they would not treat *Klal Yisrael* too harshly.[21]

The Metzudas adds that at this point, we have, *ki'veyachol*, moved in with Hashem — into the Beis HaMikdash. Because our relationship has become far stronger, the heathen nations will certainly not be able to cause discord. It is fitting, then, that this verse should be repeated here.[22]

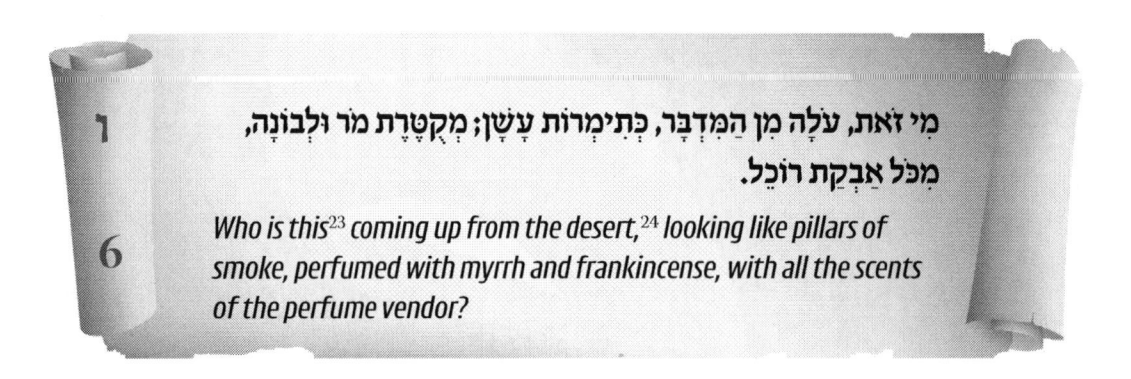

> ו
>
> מִי זֹאת, עֹלָה מִן הַמִּדְבָּר, כְּתִימְרוֹת עָשָׁן; מְקֻטֶּרֶת מֹר וּלְבוֹנָה, מִכֹּל אַבְקַת רוֹכֵל.
>
> 6
>
> Who is this[23] coming up from the desert,[24] looking like pillars of smoke, perfumed with myrrh and frankincense, with all the scents of the perfume vendor?

---

19 By way of analogy, let us consider a married couple who have a terrible row and then make up. Their relationship will be stronger than that of a couple who have never argued. Even a particularly evil "third party" with designs on the wife would never try to bring this couple to divorce. If they had never argued, he might think, "If I could just get them into a big row with each other, then they would lose their love for each other, and I would be able to break them up." But when he sees that even after they broke up, they got back together even more strongly, he realizes that he has no hope. Similarly, in the previous few verses, *Klal Yisrael* show that even when they sin, they repair the relationship until it is better than before. This proves that nothing can destroy the relationship. It gives them the confidence to tell the heathen nations: "Don't imagine that through all your evil efforts you will be able to destroy our relationship with Hashem!"

20 This promise has already been made in 2:7 and is repeated in 8:4.

21 *Kesubos* 111a. See our commentary on 2:7.

22 Now that we have no Beis HaMikdash, we go to the *beis midrash* to stay safe from the influence of all those who wish to compromise our closeness to Hashem. Even today, then, we can echo the declaration here in this verse that when we are with Hashem in our places of learning, no one can destroy the relationship. As the Gemara advises us: If we are accosted by the abominable one (*yetzer ha'ra*), we should pull him into the *beis midrash* (*Sukkah* 52b).

23 This is a rhetorical question, an expression of surprise.

24 The Vilna Gaon sees in this verse not only a question, but also an answer. The nations ask, "How did *Klal Yisrael* reach such great heights?!" The answer is "From the [Torah they received in the] desert!" In other words, by learning the Torah

Allegorical Translation — How great are you, the Jewish People, who are coming out of the desert with pillars of smoke in front of you, destroying all the obstacles in your way. The smell of the incense that you burn on your *Mizbe'ach* (made out of many good-smelling powders) spreads out before you.

Subject of the Verse — The heathen nations are giving voice to their wonderment about the greatness of *Klal Yisrael* in the desert.

Mashal — The wife is reminiscing about how her contemporaries looked on as she went through a long and difficult journey. They assumed that she would suffer because of it, but, instead, she flourishes! She is like a wondrous pillar of cloud, and smells like the most beautiful perfumes.

Nimshal — *Klal Yisrael* is quoting the heathen nations expression of amazement and admiration at seeing *Klal Yisrael* coming out of the desert after their long journey with so much splendor and greatness.[25]

WHO IS THIS COMING UP FROM THE DESERT...?

This verse evokes the glory of *Klal Yisrael* traveling through the desert. Although we cannot imagine how great their glory was as they traveled, we must at least attempt to fulfill the Torah's command to "remember the entire journey on which Hashem, your God, led you through the desert..."[26] They walked through complete wilderness without fear because they enjoyed Hashem's protection. They walked in magnificence because they had the beautiful Mishkan with them. They walked with pride because Hashem's Presence was in their midst. No snake or scorpion ever harmed them. Never did they lack food or water. The sun never scorched them, nor did they ever get cold. Their clothes remained freshly laundered, and never wore out. Streams of water with beautiful plants surrounded their camp... And all this is only a very small part of their truly miraculous journey. This wondrous sight caused the nations to declare, as recorded in this verse "How great you are, you Jewish People, who are coming out of the desert..."

---

that they received in the desert, they have become an exalted nation, reaching ever higher. (Since Hashem specifically chose the desert for the giving of the Torah, "desert" has become synonymous with Torah. See *Bamidbar Rabbah* 1:7.)

25 *Klal Yisrael* use the words of the nations, not because of the nations' greatness, but simply as a way of reminiscing about these great events. This can be likened to a person who says that her wedding was so special that even So-and-so said it was wonderful..."

26 *Devarim* 8:2. Remembering our people's journey through the desert is actually a mitzvah.

Elaborating on this verse, the Midrash[27] notes that when *Klal Yisrael* traveled through the desert, Seven Clouds of Glory surrounded them: four in all four directions, as well as one above them and one below. The seventh Cloud appeared as a pillar and would kill all the snakes and scorpions before them, and all thorns and thistles would be burnt away. Furthermore, the Cloud would smooth out the way in front of them. Miraculously, the mountains would be flattened and the valleys elevated. The actual layout and topography of the desert changed for the sake of *Klal Yisrael*. At night, the Pillar of Fire would rise up before them and lead them. The smoke from the *Mizbe'ach* would rise up in a straight column like a very tall pillar. The heathen nations trembled at this awesome sight, and exclaimed, "Who is this coming up from the desert, looking like pillars of smoke…" They would add this is a nation whose Fiery God does all their work for them.

When the manna bread fell for the Jewish People, it piled up so high that all the kings of the world could see it, and thus realize how much Hashem loves us.[28] Furthermore, once the sun came out, the excess manna would melt into streams, and deer would drink from them. When people of the heathen nations ate the meat of these deer, they would get a very small taste of what manna bread tasted like. Hashem wanted them to appreciate the kind of wonderful food He provides for those He loves.[29] In short, the miraculous way *Klal Yisrael* travelled through the desert was an open display of Hashem's love for His chosen nation.

WHO IS THIS COMING UP FROM THE DESERT…?

There was something else that evoked the amazement and admiration of all who saw *Klal Yisrael* conclude their journey through the desert. Normally, a long journey through the desert leaves a person a lot dirtier, weaker, hungrier, smellier, and poorer than he was at the outset. The desert is a very difficult place in which to survive, not to mention, to flourish. Perhaps we can get a better picture of the tremendous difficulty if we remember how we ourselves feel after a long journey nowadays, and then imagine arduous travel by foot in ancient times through rugged terrain without all the modern conveniences we enjoy. *Klal Yisrael* went into the desert as a group of recently freed slaves, many of them suffering from illness and wounds from years of back-breaking work and terrible neglect. And yet, they came out of the desert all healthy, having been miraculously cured of their ailments and with tremendous wealth (from Egypt and the

---

27 *Midrash Rabbah* on *Shir HaShirim*. See also *Targum*.
28 *Yoma* 76a.
29 Rashi on *Shemos* 16:21.

countries of Midian, Sichon and Og). They came out also with the profound spirituality of the Torah from Har Sinai, the wondrous Mishkan and all the miracles that occurred there daily, with the great Sanhedrin established through Yisro's good counsel, with the chosen *Kohanim* and *Leviyim*, with an established kingdom, and with many other gifts as well (including the manna, the Well of Miriam, and the Clouds of Glory). No wonder that the nations exclaimed "How great you are, you Jewish People, who are coming out of the desert!" Look at how special you are even after coming out of the desert. Not only did you not wither there, but you actually flourished there in so many remarkable ways![30]

On a deeper level, it is more precise to say that *Klal Yisrael* did not flourish in spite of the desert, but *because of* the desert. When everything else has been cut away, and there is nothing left besides serving Hashem, that is the best way to flourish. Indeed, the challenges of living in the desert and being totally reliant on the miracles of Hashem made us the nation we are. *Chazal* point out that Hashem chose to give the Torah specifically in the desert.[31] One reason for this is that to acquire Torah, a person has to be willing to forgo everything else. The lack of all delicacies and comforts in the desert enabled *Klal Yisrael* to flourish spiritually in Torah.[32] Unable to understand this dynamic, the heathen nations looked on in wonder. But their words, as Shlomo HaMelech renders them, actually reflect this truth. Their exclamation, "Who is this coming up *from* the desert," hints at *Klal Yisrael*'s spiritual growth and elevation "because of" the desert. Our nation has the ability to come up and rise because it lived in the desert.[33]

There is a very pertinent lesson here for us. Let us notice how Hashem looked after us, and how we flourished under the most difficult conditions. A person does not need

---

30   When we flourish in the most difficult places, it shows Hashem's protection of us. This concept is illustrated by an episode recorded in the Talmud Yerushalmi (*Berachos* 9:1) about a Jewish child travelling by ship with a large group of idolaters. At one point during the journey, a storm broke out, threatening to drown them all. All the idolaters prayed to their gods, but without results. They then turned to the child, who davened to Hashem. All at once, the storm subsided! When they reached their port, everyone on board went off to attend to their business. Before doing so, however, they asked the child what was he planning to do. He replied that being a poor, lonely child, he has nothing to do but wait for the ship to return home. They responded: "You are poor?! No, we are poor! We travel with our gods, but when we are in a difficult situation, they do not help us at all. But you can travel anywhere, and whenever you need help, you can call out to your God, and He answers you immediately and saves you from the worst places!"

31   *Bamidbar Rabbah* 1:7.

32   Furthermore, overcoming difficulties and challenges strengthens a person, and that strength is invaluable in learning Torah. One who has been always pampered and has never had to toil, will not be able to succeed in Torah.

33   The Gemara tells us that this world is "an upside-down world," meaning that those who we think should be honored here in this world are not honored in the World to Come, and vice versa (*Pesachim* 50a). This applies to our perception of our own achievements as well. There are days we think we accomplished so much and deserve so much honor, and days when everything was a struggle and we feel like failures. But in the World to Come, we will see that the opposite is true: Hashem will honor us for the days of struggle (Rabbi Naftali Kopshitz, *shlita*).

to worry about whether his situation is one in which he can flourish. Rather, he should focus on doing all he can to serve Hashem. If he is doing his maximum, then Hashem can help him flourish in any circumstances — and even in the worst of places. Furthermore, we must learn from this verse that struggles only make us stronger, and that living with fewer luxuries give us space to devote ourselves to Hashem.

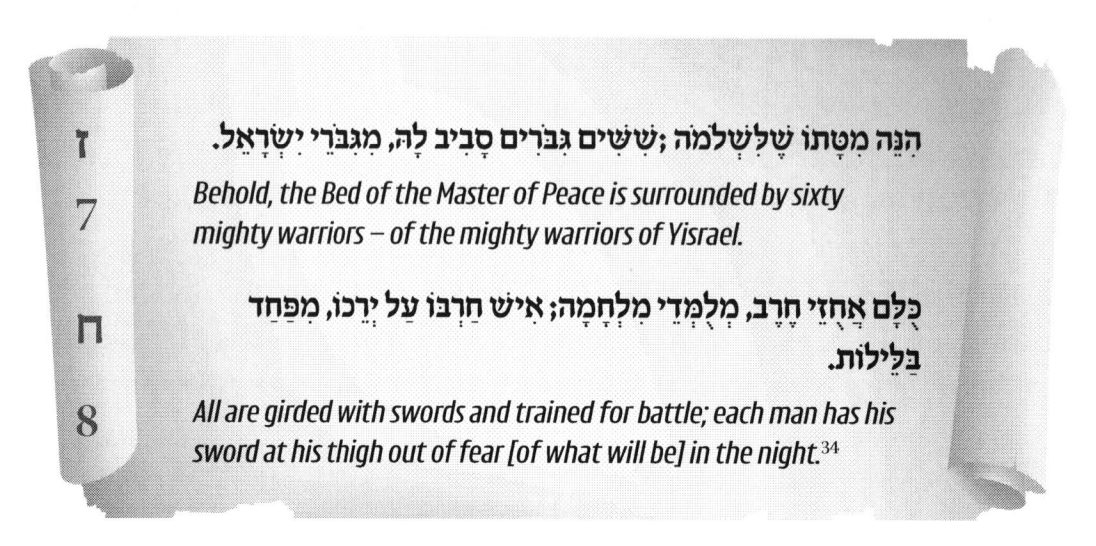

ז

7

הִנֵּה מִטָּתוֹ שֶׁלִּשְׁלֹמֹה; שִׁשִּׁים גִּבֹּרִים סָבִיב לָהּ, מִגִּבֹּרֵי יִשְׂרָאֵל.

Behold, the Bed of the Master of Peace is surrounded by sixty mighty warriors – of the mighty warriors of Yisrael.

ח

8

כֻּלָּם אֲחֻזֵי חֶרֶב, מְלֻמְּדֵי מִלְחָמָה; אִישׁ חַרְבּוֹ עַל יְרֵכוֹ, מִפַּחַד בַּלֵּילוֹת.

All are girded with swords and trained for battle; each man has his sword at his thigh out of fear [of what will be] in the night.[34]

Allegorical Translation

7 Behold it is *Klal Yisrael* who are carrying the *Ohel Moed* and the *Aron Kodesh*, with six hundred thousand strong men capable of doing battle surrounding them, besides the many women and children.

8 All of them are attached to Torah and are trained in learning Torah. Each one has his tools for learning Torah and serving Hashem readily available so that they should not, God forbid, forget [the law], and thus sin, because they are afraid of the terrible tragedies that the dark night of exile might bring along.

Subject of the Verses

These verses are a reply to the question posed in the previous verse: "Who is

---

34 The Midrash takes a homiletic approach to these verses and offers a variety of interpretations. One approach is that these above two verses allude to *Birkas Kohanim*. Accordingly, the verses can be understood as follows: "[*Birkas Kohanim*] is from the tribe [מטה read as '*mateh*' can mean 'a tribe'] of Hashem." (The tribe of Leviyim/Kohanim was always devoted to Hashem.) "It has sixty mighty warriors around it" in the form of the sixty letters making up the three blessings of *Birkas Kohanim*. They give strength to *Klal Yisrael* and help them to be victorious in their battles. "All are girded with swords" in the sense that each of the blessings has the name of Hashem in it. The name of Hashem girds and grasps the blessing, giving it power and efficacy. "Trained for battle" means that these blessings bring fear to the enemies of *Klal Yisrael* and keep them away. Finally, "each man has his sword at his thigh [to keep away] the fear [of what will be] in the night" is an allusion to dealing with nightmares. Even if a person is afraid of the nights in the sense that he is worried about the implications of his nightmare, all he needs to do is to go to shul and daven during *Birkas Kohanim* that his dreams get better, and no harm will befall him. The words of the Midrash should impress upon us the tremendous importance of *Birkas Kohanim*. Incidentally, in the "bedtime *Shema*" these verses are recited immediately before reciting the words of *Birkas Kohanim*.

this coming up from the desert…"

Mashal These verses are a response to the preceding expression of amazement at the sight of a great person coming out of the desert. They explain what this sight is all about. The wife of the king is accompanying the bed of the king, which is surrounded by a mighty army. All the soldiers of this great army are fully armed and ready for battle to guard against all harm and any dangers that can occur during the dangerous nights.

Nimshal *Klal Yisrael* respond to the exclamation in the previous verse, "How great is the one coming up from the desert…" The gist of their response is that *Klal Yisrael* is so great because they have in their midst both the Mishkan (the Presence of Hashem) and those who learn Torah. Let us take a closer look at the stirring, multi-faceted symbolism used here. The "bed" is an allusion to the Mishkan. Just as a bed is one's resting place, so the Mishkan is the place where Hashem rests His Presence. Just as a couple's most intimate moments are those spent in bed, so the greatest intimacy that Hashem had with *Klal Yisrael* took place in the Mishkan. And just as the fruitfulness and reproduction of a person are facilitated by his bed, so the success of *Klal Yisrael* was facilitated by the Mishkan.[35]

The "Master of Peace" is Hashem, the source of all peace.[36] The number "sixty" alludes to the number of Jewish men around the Mishkan (sixty *ribo*, i.e., sixty times ten-thousand[37]).[38] The Gemara interprets "mighty warriors" as an allusion to Torah scholars.[39] "Mighty warriors" alludes to Torah scholars and their ability to be engrossed in the debate of Torah. Engaging deeply with the words and concepts of Torah requires one to utilize all his intellect, employ absolute honesty, and be completely focused on the battle for true clarity. For

---

35 See earlier 1:16. That the Mishkan, with the *Aron*, is a source of fruitfulness can be seen by its impact on the family of Oved Edom. As described in *Shmuel II* 6, Dovid HaMelech decided to put the *Aron* in Oved Edom's home at one point. *Chazal* reveal that Hashem subsequently blessed Oved Edom such that his wife and six daughters-in-law had sextuplets!

36 As explained earlier 1:1.

37 The largest number in the Torah with its own unit name is *ribo* (רבוא), ten thousand.

38 Furthermore, the number sixty alludes to the sixty *masechtot* (tractates) in the Gemara.
The Maharsha explains that "sixty" is sometimes used to signify a large number. Thus, the verse would mean that there are "many" Torah scholars. It is noteworthy that many items are nullified (מבוטל) in a quantity sixty times greater than the item itself. The Ralbag explains that sixty is a comprehensive number and that is why there are sixty seconds in a minute, and sixty minutes in an hour. See also Gur Aryeh (*Bereishis* 26:34) that ten is a whole number and there are six directions so sixty is considered a total large number.

39 See *Chagigah* 14a. We will discuss the Midrash's interpretation of this metaphor momentarily.

these reasons, as well as others, learning Torah has often been likened to a battle.[40] Furthermore, just as an army protects its country and nation, those who learn Torah protect *Klal Yisrael* because without Torah, we would not survive for a moment.[41]

"Warriors girded with swords" symbolize how Torah scholars are deeply attached to Torah and are constantly engaged in Torah thoughts.[42] Just as a soldier, in times of danger, would never dream of leaving his weapon out of reach — knowing that he is defenseless without it — so too do Torah scholars have the words of Torah constantly at their side and on their lips.[43]

Taking a different tack, the Midrash interprets "mighty warriors" as an allusion to the righteous, who are powerful soldiers fighting against their *yetzer ha'ra*. As the Mishnah[44] says: "Who is strong? The one who conquers his evil inclination."[45] "Girded with swords," then, symbolizes how the righteous are

---

40 See our commentary on 2:4. See also *Kiddushin* 30b, where the Gemara says that even fathers and sons learning Torah together "battle" each other for clarity in understanding.

41 The Chafetz Chaim touched on this basic truth through a *mashal* he offered at the start of his speech at the Knessiah Gedolah. A very ill person is hospitalized, and a group of doctors gathers around his bed, each doctor recommending a different course of treatment for the patient's various ailments. Then a senior doctor joins the group and points out that the patient has a weak and ailing heart. "If we can heal that," he says, "then all his other ailments will be cured, but if not, nothing else will help!" So too, said the Chafetz Chaim, *Klal Yisrael* suffer from many different ailments, but the only way to cure them is by healing their heart — and their heart is Torah. If Torah is strengthened, all the rest will work out, but if not, no other solution will help!

42 Rav Shach exemplified this, as we see from the following anecdote. Wishing to help him in his old age, a *talmid* of the Rosh Yeshivah brought him an armchair to sit on so that he would be comfortable. Two years after the armchair was brought to his very small apartment, Rav Shach suddenly noticed it and asked how it got there. The Rosh Yeshivah's preoccupation with Torah kept him from even noticing such things (*Shimushah shel Torah*).

43 One makes sure to remember that which he needs to succeed in his field. A person who knows that the purpose of life is to serve Hashem is always on the lookout for pertinent ideas and methods, just as a tradesman is constantly looking out for ways and means that will help him improve his work.

44 *Avos* 4:1.

45 In keeping with a key theme of *Shir HaShirim* that everything we see here in this world is a reflection of a much greater world of spirituality (as discussed in the Introduction), we must try to appreciate that everything can serve as a steppingstone to come closer to Hashem. How does this apply to the thirst for battle and conquest which reside in the heart of many men? The Chovos HaLevavos vividly shows how the real battle we are supposed to be fighting is the battle against the *yetzer ha'ra* (*Shaar Yichud Hama'aseh*, ch. 5). All wars are minor compared to the ongoing war against the *yetzer ha'ra*, which never stops day and night and never gives up. Because this entire world was created in order that we should battle and conquer the *yetzer ha'ra*, Hashem created in us a deep-seated desire to vanquish opponents or competitors. The thirst for conquest should really be used in fighting the *yetzer ha'ra*.

Those who shirk their duty to "battle" the *yetzer ha'ra*, however, need to have an outlet for the thirst for battle. Over the course of history, this has resulted in many people and nations going to war for illegitimate reasons — simply for the pleasure of conquest. Thankfully, this desire has largely metamorphosed nowadays into the much safer, but no less all-consuming, passion for competitive sports. Of course, those who obsess about sports are substituting the superficial pleasure of victory in a fight that has no real meaning for the genuine feeling of success in a battle that is truly worth engaging in: the

constantly engaged in their battle against the *yetzer ha'ra*, thinking of ways to conquer it.[46] "Trained for battle" alludes to the fact that both Torah scholars and the righteous employ various methods to remember the Torah and to remember to serve Hashem. These include developing mnemonics, regularly reviewing one's Torah learning, and repeating teachings of *Chazal* which urge us to improve. Thus, they are constantly training for battle. Furthermore, "Each man has his sword at his thigh." This means that they constantly keep their Torah and methods of righteousness close at hand so that they are always ready to utilize them, like a soldier with his sword strapped to his thigh.[47] A truly righteous person always has his weapons — his tools to fight the *yetzer ha'ra* — readily available.[48] The verse concludes: "out of fear [of what will be] in the night." As explained earlier, the exile is likened to the night[49] because it is a time of danger, fear, and discomfort. *Talmidei chachamim* and the righteous are keenly aware that forgetting Torah could cause a horrific exile.[50] To save the nation from this danger, they make every effort to remember their

---

battle against the *yetzer ha'ra*. The truly "mighty warriors" of this verse are the ones engaged in this "real" war.

It is noteworthy that the pursuit of war has generally been one that has attracted men more than women. It is beyond the scope of this *sefer* to explain this fully, but part of the reason for this lies in the fundamental difference between the battle against the *yetzer ha'ra* that must be fought by the two different sexes. This is hinted at in the blessing that women recite in the morning שעשני כרצונו, meaning (according to some commentators) that Hashem "created me wishing to do His will." Women, more so than men, naturally tend to want to do the will of Hashem. That is why they do not have the obligation to learn Torah that men have. Men must learn Torah because it is the only antidote to the *yetzer ha'ra* that tries to keep them from serving Hashem (*Kiddushin* 30b). Women do not face the same bitter struggle with the *yetzer ha'ra* that men do. Their main challenge is whether they fully utilize the strengths that Hashem has given them for the good. Since furious battle is not a woman's mission, Hashem did not put into their DNA, *ki'veyachol*, the desire and obsession for war.

46 The Manchester Rosh Yeshivah, Rabbi Yehudah Zev Segal, *zt"l*, was one of those "mighty warriors" who was constantly thinking of ways to win this most important battle. One morning, just after going outside on his way to shul, he came straight back home and got into bed again. When asked about this strange turnabout, he explained that he was not feeling well and decided that he should stay in bed. But he was unsure as to whether he was really so unwell. Perhaps the *yetzer ha'ra* was making his condition appear to be worse than it actually was. He then decided to get dressed again and see how he felt once outside, because by then it would take more effort to go back to bed than to go to shul. That way, he would be able to determine objectively whether or not he really needed to go back to bed.

47 Also helpful are having a Rav nearby whom one consults regularly, having a good friend who makes sure one is doing the right thing, etc.

48 If something is vital to a person's success, he is sure to remember it. We see that a businessman does not forget his business dealings and his bank accounts and is constantly looking for ways to improve his work or business. Similarly, a person who understands that the purpose of life is to serve Hashem never stops looking for ideas and methods to make that happen. This is why there are many stories of great *tzaddikim* who knew huge amounts of Torah and knowledge of Hashem at their fingertips.

49 3:1.

50 Earlier (3:1-4), the verses describe the loneliness and fears of exile, as well as the new-found determination to avoid a repetition of that terrible fate. This verse indicates the concrete steps taken to that end.

learning and to remain righteous.⁵¹ Accordingly, the end of the verse should be understood this way: "Each man has his sword at his thigh [i.e., dedicated to Torah and mitzvos] out of fear [of what would be] in the night [of exile, should it come]."

BEHOLD, THE BED OF THE MASTER OF PEACE...

These verses give us a glimpse at the source of *Klal Yisrael's* beauty and power in the desert: the Presence of Hashem and dedicated Torah scholars. They should also give us a feeling of tremendous pride about who we are as a nation. We are the one and only nation that travelled with Hashem, the Creator of the entire universe, the Power that controls all powers, before whom even the heavenly hosts tremble,⁵² and whose greatness we would be unable to grasp, even if we spent billions of years contemplating it. No other nation can boast of anything remotely similar. Knowing how much He truly loves us and is close to us should add to our feeling of pride. Furthermore, we should be extremely proud of our Torah scholars who are completely dedicated to Torah, and through whom we are saved from so much harm. They are our greatest protectors. It is in their merit, and the merit of Hashem's closeness, that we were able to flourish in the difficult desert. This is the reply to astonishment of the nations, "Who is this rising from the desert?!"

---

51   An alternative explanation follows: Generally, when a person is frightened or unhappy, he is unable to focus on his goals and values. But these righteous *talmidei chachamim* remain ready for battle (i.e., focused on their true goals and their service of Hashem) even during "the fear of the night" (while they are suffering the fears and travails of exile).
   This virtue was very much in evidence when Rabbi Ovadiah Yosef sat *shivah* for a son. When the prime minister came to pay a *shivah call*, Rabbi Yosef immediately told him of his pain that the government was considering forcing yeshivah students into the army. The prime minister tried to change the subject and suggested that "now is a time to focus on your own personal loss." Rabbi Yosef replied that his pain over the loss of Torah — because *bachurim* will be unable to learn Torah — is foremost in his mind, even at the terrible time of mourning his son. Even in the "night," his "sword" was at his side.

52   The Gemara tells us that the Dinor River flows from the perspiration of the angels who constantly tremble with awe at the Presence of Hashem (*Chagigah* 13b).

ט 9

אַפִּרְיוֹן, עָשָׂה לוֹ הַמֶּלֶךְ שְׁלֹמֹה ;מֵעֲצֵי הַלְּבָנוֹן.

The King, Master of peace, made for Himself a canopy out of the wood of Lebanon.[53]

י 10

עַמּוּדָיו עָשָׂה כֶסֶף, רְפִידָתוֹ זָהָב, מֶרְכָּבוֹ אַרְגָּמָן;[54] תּוֹכוֹ רָצוּף אַהֲבָה, מִבְּנוֹת יְרוּשָׁלָיִם.

Its pillars He made of silver, His couch of gold, and its hanging of purple wool. Its interior was furnished with love, from the daughters of Jerusalem.

יא 11

צְאֶינָה וּרְאֶינָה בְּנוֹת צִיּוֹן, בַּמֶּלֶךְ שְׁלֹמֹה ;בָּעֲטָרָה שֶׁעִטְּרָה לּוֹ אִמּוֹ, בְּיוֹם חֲתֻנָּתוֹ וּבְיוֹם שִׂמְחַת לִבּוֹ.

People of distinction, go out and observe the King, master of peace, [wearing] the crown with which His mother adorned Him on the day of His wedding and on the day His heart rejoiced.

Allegorical Translation

9 Hashem arranged for Himself a canopy of honor, the Mishkan, made of the finest wood.

10 The pillars of the Mishkan were adorned with silver;[55] the *Kapores*,[56] upon which Hashem's Presence rested, was like a couch made out of gold; the *Paroches*,[57] which rode on hooks[58] and hung like a curtain around the *Aron*, was made out of purple wool; its innermost sanctuary, the *Kodesh HaKodashim*,

---

53   We see in many sources that the wood of Lebanon was considered beautiful and extremely valuable.

54   A beautiful homiletic explanation of this word is found in the Midrash: The carriage of Hashem in which He places his beloved *Klal Yisrael* is made out of "ארגמן." This word can be read as a mnemonic for the five angels surrounding every Jew (See *Zohar, Parashas Bo* 42a). They are אוריאל, רפאל, גבריאל, מיכאל, נוריאל (*Otzar HaMidrashim*).

55   The literal translation is "the pillars were silver." In fact, the pillars of the Mishkan were actually made of wood and adorned with silver. This, the Midrash tells us, gave them the appearance of being silver. The Gemara notes that besides the *Luchos* (the two tablets upon which the *Asseres HaDibros* were etched) that were stored in the *Aron*, there was also a *Sefer Torah* whose staves were made of silver. It is to these staves upholding the Torah that this verse also alludes (*Bava Basra* 14a).

56   This is the lid of the *Aron Kodesh*. It is likened to a couch, a place where a couple may sit together and bond. The *Kapores* is the place where the *Shechinah* rested and bonded, *ki'veyachol*, with *Klal Yisrael* as symbolized by the *Keruvim*.

57   This was a curtain hanging between the *Kodesh HaKodashim* and the rest of the Mishkan.

58   The verse refers to the *Paroches* as a chariot (מרכבתו). That is because the *Paroches* rode on its hooks like a chariot rides on its wheels.

was decked with items portraying His love[59] — all made by *Klal Yisrael*, His precious nation who will live in Yerushalayim.[60]

11 You who are distinctive through *bris milah*, *tzitzis* and all other Jewish marks of distinctions,[61] go out and gaze upon Hashem now that He is adorned with the crown.[62] [This is the crown] that *Klal Yisrael* [whom He loves so much that He refers to them as His mother] made for Him on the day of *Matan Torah*[63] — which was as special to Hashem as a wedding day — and which they made for Him on the day when the Mishkan was inaugurated,[64] a day which brought Hashem much joy.[65]

---

59. Inside the *Kodesh HaKodashim* were items that displayed Hashem's love for His nation. These included the *Luchos* (inside the *Aron*), a "personal gift" upon which Hashem wrote His commandments to *Klal Yisrael*. The *Luchos* were a constant reminder of the wonderful events of the Giving of the Torah at Har Sinai. The *Aron* itself symbolized Hashem's closeness to us. The *Keruvim* on its lid, facing each other with love, symbolically represented Hashem facing us. Indeed, the interior of the Mishkan was "furnished with items portraying His love."

60. Rashi adds that "Yerushalayim" is a combination of two words: *yirah* (fear) and *shalem* (complete). In this verse, it is as if Hashem says that *Klal Yisrael* is deserving of the title "Yerushalayim" because "they *fear* Me and are *completely* devoted to Me."

    It is noteworthy that elsewhere (1:5, 2:7, 3:5, 5:8, 8:4), Rashi interprets this phrase "daughters of Yerushalayim" as referring to the heathen nations. This discrepancy is addressed by many commentators, including the Shiras Dovid. One explanation is that this verse refers to the Heavenly Yerushalayim. Another explanation is that in this verse, the diminutive prefix "מ" (meaning "of," i.e., "a portion of") precedes the term "daughters of Yerushalayim." Thus, Rashi explains that specifically here it is referring to *Klal Yisrael* (*Ohel Dovid*).

61. We, *Klal Yisrael*, are highly distinguishable from the other nations in many ways: through our clothes, our conduct, and even through our bodies. Therefore, we are fittingly called "people of distinction" here in this verse. The word *metzuyan* (from which the word "*tzion*" in this verse is derived) connotes excelling to such an extent that one is now distinguished above all others. This expression בנות ציון ("people of distinction" or "those who are distinguishable") is a special attribute of *Klal Yisrael*. If we think about the praise implicit in this phrase, we will take special pride in being part of such a wonderful nation.

    Furthermore, part of the ethos of *Klal Yisrael* is to be distinguishable and not to intermingle. Even in Egypt, *Klal Yisrael* kept apart in their language, names, and mode of dress. These words, then, also obligate us to make sure that we are indeed distinguished in all that we do and in how we conduct ourselves. We must demonstrate in every way our uniqueness and our dedication to Hashem.

62. The crown here is actually alluding to two crowns: the Mishkan and *Matan Torah*, as will be explained.

63. What is the crown that *Klal Yisrael* made for Hashem at *Matan Torah*? By accepting Hashem as their King at *Matan Torah*, *Klal Yisrael* essentially "crowned Him." It is as if they gave Hashem a crown.

    Tellingly, the numerical value of "חתונתו" ("His wedding day") is 870, which is equal to that of "הלוחות השניים" ("the Second Tablets") which were given at Har Sinai. This dovetails with the Midrash's explanation that the "wedding day" mentioned in the verse was the day of the Giving of the Torah (*Birchas Peretz*).

64. This part of the verse connects with the urging at the beginning of the verse, as follows: "Go out and gaze upon Hashem now that He is adorned with the crown that *Klal Yisrael*...made for Him on the day when the Mishkan was inaugurated, which brought Hashem much joy." The Mishkan is called a "crown" here because just as a crown is an adornment for the one who wears it, so the Mishkan was an "adornment" for Hashem. By building the Mishkan, *Klal Yisrael*, *ki'veyachol*, gave Hashem a crown.

65. The numerical value of the phrase "וביום שמחת לבו" ("on the day His heart rejoiced") is 862 (with the letters added). This is equal to the numerical value of "בית המקדש." Here we have a hint that Hashem rejoiced with the inauguration of the Beis HaMikdash, just as the Midrash interprets the phrase (*Birchas Peretz*).

Subject of the Verses — The mention of the Mishkan, which accompanied *Klal Yisrael* in their travels through the desert, prompts an elaboration on the greatness of the Mishkan. We must remember that the beauty of the Mishkan reflected the beauty and greatness of *Klal Yisrael*. They were the ones who travelled with it, and they were the ones who built it and consecrated it. All three of these verses describe in a variety of ways the greatness of the Mishkan.

Mashal — Having mentioned the bed of the king, the queen now elaborates on its beauty:

9 The peaceful king, made for Himself a canopy out of the wood of Lebanon.

10 Its pillars, he made of silver, his couch of gold, and its hanging of purple wool. Its interior was furnished with love, from the daughters of Jerusalem.

11 The queen urges all those around her to go and admire the king in his new canopied dwelling: "People of distinction, go out and observe the king, master of peace, [wearing] the crown with which his mother adorned him on the day of his wedding and on the day his heart rejoiced."

Nimshal — As seen in the allegorical translation of Rashi (above), these verses describe the beauty of the Mishkan and the greatness of Hashem whose Presence dwelt there.

MADE FOR HIMSELF A CANOPY OUT OF THE WOOD OF LEBANON...

As discussed earlier, the concept of the Mishkan — that Hashem chose to "dwell" among us — was a dramatic expression of His closeness to us and His love for us. Furthermore, within the Mishkan itself was an array of items which further displayed Hashem's great love. Some of these are alluded to in the verses we are discussing. While it is beyond the scope of this work to fully explore the many symbols, details, and hints connected with the Mishkan, we will at least try to scratch the surface.[66]

ITS INTERIOR WAS FURNISHED/DECKED[67] WITH LOVE...

The Dubno Maggid points out that Hashem could have chosen to make a far more

---

66   Both in his book *Jewish Symbolism* and in his commentary on the Chumash, Rabbi Shimshon Rafael Hirsch elaborates at length regarding all the details of the Mishkan. These are excellent sources for someone interested in learning more about this subject.

67   The word רצוף often means a deck or a flooring (*Esther* 1:8). The Metzudas Dovid, however, sees this word coming from the word *ritzapas* (burning coal). According to this approach, the verse is saying, "Inside [the Mishkan] was a burning coal of love." Just as a home is warmed by burning coals (at least in former times), the Mishkan was warmed by a feeling of burning love between Hashem and *Klal Yisrael* that gave the entire dwelling a warm, welcoming ambience.

beautiful Mishkan. After all, *Klal Yisrael* had accumulated a great deal of precious metal and other resources by this point. Instead of using copper and goat's hair, for example, they could have used gold and diamonds for many items. Indeed, the floor of the Mishkan was just plain desert earth. Why, asks the Maggid, did Hashem not make the Mishkan even more grand?

Characteristically, he explains with a *mashal*. A king wanted to leave his palace and stay with a dear friend who lived in a much simpler home. The palace servants wanted to go ahead and make the house fit for a king. The king told them not to bother. "Why" asked his servants? The king answered, "The simpler the home, the clearer it is how much I love my friend. I desire his company so much that I choose to stay with him regardless of how plain his home is." Similarly, Hashem wanted *Klal Yisrael* to feel that He wanted to be with them because He loved them so much. Therefore, He purposely left the flooring simple to show that however plain their homes are, Hashem wishes to dwell with them. As the verse puts it, "Its interior was decked with love" — not grandeur. It was through the plain flooring that Hashem displayed His great love. Of course, the plain interior had to be counterbalanced by external beauty and grandeur so that we should understand that we ought to serve Hashem only with the best. And that is why some of the accoutrements located inside the Mishkan were indeed made out of gold.

Rabbi Meir Shapiro, *zt"l*, sees another dimension in this phrase, "Its interior was furnished/decked with love."[68] By way of background, he notes that everything in the Mishkan became sanctified when *Klal Yisrael* designated the item, and decided to "give" it to Hashem.[69] However, this could only apply to the actual walls and furnishings of the Mishkan. How did the airspace inside — the area within the Mishkan — become holy?

The answers lie in the fact that when *Klal Yisrael* donated to the Mishkan, they did so with tremendous enthusiasm, so much so that they very quickly gave more than was needed.[70] An announcement had to be made that no more donations be accepted for the Mishkan. People had a great desire to give more, but it was simply not necessary and could not be used. We must imagine the disappointment of many who were in the process of giving or were planning to give. This once-in-history opportunity to donate to the Mishkan had eluded them. Now, we might have thought that their strong desire to give was lost forever, but that was not the case. This unfulfilled desire, which had no item to connect with, remained, *ki'veyachol*, up in the air. Hashem utilized this precious feeling for the purpose of imbuing the entire Mishkan — even the airspace

---

68 *Imrei Da'as* on *Parashas Vayakhel*.
69 See Rashi on *Shemos* 25:2.
70 *Shemos* 36:5-8.

and the interior — with holiness. *Klal Yisrael's* outpouring of love imbued the inside of the Mishkan with holiness. According to this approach, the verse reads: "Its interior was furnished/decked [with holiness] through the love [that *Klal Yisrael* displayed to Hashem]."

We can learn from this that when we wish to do a mitzvah, or when we have any spiritual feeling or feeling of holiness, it is not lost even if we are unable to act on it. In fact, on some level, the yearning to fulfill a mitzvah can be greater than the actual fulfilling of a mitzvah. Why is this? When one is unable to do a mitzvah, he does not have the satisfaction and the proud feeling of having succeeded in doing the mitzvah. Therefore, his desire is "undiluted" by any other feelings.[71] Hashem treasures every spiritual thought and feeling and will eventually utilize them in a concrete manner for a person's spiritual success. We will eventually see how every positive emotion, however fleeting, has brought us so much success and brought us so much closer to Hashem.

WITH WHICH HIS MOTHER ADORNED HIM…

The Midrash elaborates on this, offering a *mashal* of a king who had only one daughter whom he loved very much. Out of his great love for her, he used to call her "my daughter." As his love increased, he called her "my sister," and when his love became even greater, he called her "my mother." So, too, Hashem calls *Klal Yisrael* "His daughter,"[72] and, as His love increases, He calls them "His sister,"[73] and eventually "His mother."[74]

At first glance, the gradation in this *mashal* is puzzling because one generally loves one's daughter more than one's mother — and certainly more than one's sister?[75] The Vilna Gaon explains that "love" here relates to what one receives in the relationship, and the *nimshal* is about the different stages of learning Torah. When a person begins to learn Torah, he is likened to a daughter in that he does not teach or provide any wisdom, but just keeps on receiving. As he learns more, he eventually becomes one who benefits others with his learning, and is thus likened to a sister — more of a peer, where each one helps the other. Eventually, when he becomes a great Torah scholar, he becomes

---

71 There is a deeper concept here as well: Thought and feeling are more spiritual than actions. And when a feeling is not expressed in a physical act, it remains on a higher plane, and has much more spiritual power.

72 *Tehillim* 45:11.

73 *Shir HaShirim* 5:2.

74 In this verse and in *Yeshayahu* 41:4.

75 As much as a person loves his daughter, he enjoys a level of comfort in his mother's home that he does not have in his daughter's home. The reason is that he is more accustomed to his mother's home and also because he is happier to receive benefit from his mother than from his daughter. This is also true regarding one's sister, albeit to a lesser extent. Although love has many facets, there is a unique, comforting love that one gets from one's mother. It is to this love that the Midrash refers (HaRav Mordechai Nachum Steinberg, *shlit'a*, my father).

like a mother who provides for others. He does this through teaching and dispensing wisdom. In fact, *Chazal* tell us that Hashem repeats, so to speak, the words of great *talmidei chachamim* and follows their rulings — almost as if He is learning from them.[76] In that sense, they can be called "His mother."[77]

The Shiras Dovid offers a similar explanation. He notes that at the dawn of human history, Hashem provided for this world despite the fact that no mitzvos were being done.[78] This is similar to parents' relationship to a daughter (or son) inasmuch as they provide for their offspring without receiving anything in return. Later, once Avraham Avinu taught the world to serve Hashem, the relationship became more reciprocal, so to speak — Hashem provided life and sustenance, and people served Him in return. This is more like one's relationship with one's sister, where responsibility is shared. Eventually, Hashem gave control of the destiny of this world to *Klal Yisrael*.[79] *Klal Yisrael* then became, in a sense, Hashem's "mother" in that they provided "strength" to Him, *ki'veyachol*, through their mitzvos. Therefore, the ultimate love that Hashem has for *Klal Yisrael* is likened to that of a child for a mother — as if they provide for Him, and as if He needs them. This even includes the concept that a tzaddik is able to nullify a divine decree because Hashem treats *Klal Yisrael* as if they are as important as His mother.[80]

GO OUT AND OBSERVE KING SHLOMO [WEARING] THE CROWN WITH WHICH HIS MOTHER ADORNED HIM ON THE DAY OF HIS WEDDING

On the literal level, the verse seems to say that Shlomo HaMelech received a crown from his mother on his wedding day, and that people should go out and see this crown. The Midrash asks: Which crown is this? We do not find that Shlomo's mother,

---

76 See, for example, *Bava Metzia* 86a.

77 The Shiras Dovid points out how apt this explanation is in light of the continuation of the verse, which refers to *Matan Torah*. At *Matan Torah*, Hashem transferred to *Klal Yisrael* the power to apply the laws of the Torah. From then on, laws cannot be decided in Heaven (*Bava Metzia* 59b). In that sense, *Klal Yisrael* became the "mother" in the relationship.

78 *Sanhedrin* 99b.

79 As explained in our commentary on 1:9 and in the opening chapters of the first section of *Nefesh HaChaim*, and in *Ashira Uzo*.
These terms (daughter, sister, and mother) also hint at the three festivals and the corresponding relationship between *Klal Yisrael* and Hashem. On Pesach, Hashem saved *Klal Yisrael* even though there were unworthy, having descended to the "forty-ninth level of impurity" — just as a parent does not hesitate to save a wayward daughter. On Shavuos, Hashem gave *Klal Yisrael* His Torah which was a kind of marriage meaning that the relationship came, so to speak, to an equal footing, like a brother to a sister. Later in the relationship, on Sukkos, *Klal Yisrael* is commanded to provide a "meal" for Hashem in the form of the sacrifices (*Sukkah* 55b), like a child providing for a mother (*Otzar HaMidrashim*).

80 *Yefei Kol* on the Midrash. See also *Kol Tzofiach* which explains at length that a person has to reach the level of being a giver and a source of life rather than just a taker or consumer.

Batsheva, made him a crown? *Chazal*[81] tell us that on the day the First Beis HaMikdash was completed by Shlomo, he married the daughter of Pharaoh. She brought in a thousand musicians and used witchcraft to make the ceiling look like a dark, starry sky, thereby causing Shlomo to oversleep the next morning because he thought that it was still night. Since Shlomo had the keys to the Beis HaMikdash under his pillow, this caused a delay in the morning service of the Beis HaMikdash. His mother, Batsheva, came to wake him up, and rebuked him severely. She told him off for drinking so much wine and for other faults. *Chazal* say that she even tied him to a tree, whipped him with a belt, and hit him with her shoe. She complained: "Your father, Dovid HaMelech, had many wives, and they all prayed that the child born from him would be the future king. But when I married him, I prayed only that my son should learn Torah and fear Hashem.[82] Yet, here you are, oversleeping and forgetting your role and your obligations to Hashem!" Shlomo accepted her rebuke and thanked her for it. In fact, he subsequently wrote a song praising her which we know as *Eishes Chayil*,[83] sung by many on Friday night before Kiddush. The wisdom and fear of Hashem that Shlomo acquired from his mother is truly the greatest crown he could get.[84] This, then, is the meaning of the verse: "Go out and observe [i.e., contemplate] King Shlomo with the crown [of knowledge of how much greater fear of Hashem is than any other success], the one with which His mother adorned him on the day of His wedding."[85]

---

81 *Sanhedrin* 70b, *Bamidbar Rabbah* 10, and *Vayikra Rabbah* 12.

82 This shows Batsheva's tremendous greatness. After all, she knew that the king who succeeded Dovid HaMelech would be the one to build the Beis HaMikdash and would be the ancestor of all the future kings, including Mashiach. Nonetheless, she preferred that her son be a commoner and a great tzaddik rather than a king with a lower level of *yiras Shamayim*.

83 This is actually the last chapter of *Mishlei*.

84 We echo this in *Dror Yikra*, sung at the Shabbos table during the second meal: "Acquire knowledge for yourself, and it shall be a crown on your head..." Wisdom and fear of Hashem are a person's crowning glory.

85 Alshich, *Kol Mevaser*, p. 164, and other commentators.

פרק ד'
CHAPTER 4

INTRODUCTION

The whole of this fourth chapter, as well as the first verse of the next chapter, portrays Hashem singing the praises of the Jewish People. These verses are an outpouring of approval, love, and praise from Hashem. They describe *Klal Yisrael*'s wonderful traits and recall their wonderful deeds. The underlying message is that *Klal Yisrael* is a wonderful, unique, and great nation in so many ways. These "non-stop" verses of praise, for more than an entire chapter, together with the many other verses of praise for *Klal Yisrael* elsewhere in *Shir HaShirim*, help us appreciate the magnitude of Hashem's love for us, and the high caliber of our People. This is a topic which one should often speak about.[1]

MASHAL AND NIMSHAL OF THIS CHAPTER

In the *mashal* (allegory) here, the husband is praising his wife and describing her immense beauty as it is reflected in every part of her body. In each verse, he praises his wife for another dimension of her beauty. Rashi explains that since *Shir HaShirim* is an allegory about *Klal Yisrael* being like the beloved wife of Hashem, the compliments that Hashem gives are cast in the form a husband's praise of his beautiful wife. Unlike other chapters of *Shir HaShirim*, where the speaker and the topic change any number of times, here the speaker and the topic remain constant.

It is, of course, still necessary to explain the nature of the praise in each verse since some of it seems mystifying at first glance. For example, if a husband would come home and tell his wife that her hair is like a flock of goats, it is doubtful whether she would appreciate it! It is also necessary to understand the *nimshal* since, when Hashem praises

---

1. Talking about the greatness of the Jewish People and praising tzaddikim are considered precious forms of speech (Rambam, *Shemoneh Perakim*, ch. 5).

the "hair" of *Klal Yisrael*, for example, it is obviously meant symbolically. The symbolism in each verse calls out for explanation.

When reading the commentaries on this chapter, and indeed all of *Shir HaShirim*, we may at first be puzzled by explanations that seem to clash. Rashi and the Midrash often give different interpretations of these verses praising *Klal Yisrael*, focusing on different periods of time or different great deeds or individuals. But since *Shir HaShirim* describes the whole of the Eternal People, *Klal Yisrael*, allusions are not limited to just one period or just one individual. Furthermore, because every verse has many layers of depth, the scope of any verse cannot be limited to a single explanation. Rather, each verse describes *Klal Yisrael*'s eternal greatness using a specific wonderful event, great individual, or inspiring conduct only as an example and illustration. Each verse touches on another facet of *Klal Yisrael*'s distinction and is not limited to the specific person or time period to which it may be alluding.

This key point can be better understood with a mundane analogy drawn from the physical realm. Let's say that a sports fan was complimenting a world-class runner who won a gold medal at the Olympics. He would not just be praising the runner's fast legs for those few minutes of the race. Rather, his compliment would implicitly include the runner's health and strength, his years of determined training, his self-discipline, etc. When one knows that someone has achieved something so special, he has a window into understanding part of the greatness of the individual.

Similarly, but on a much, much greater scale, each of the verses here provides a new insight into, and view of, the greatness of *Klal Yisrael*. For example, a description of *Klal Yisrael*'s great leaders illustrates not only the greatness of some individuals, but the spiritual health and distinction of *Klal Yisrael* as a whole. These leaders bespeak, among other things, the greatness of a people capable of producing such individuals,[2] the success of *Klal Yisrael* in sanctifying the world with such people, their spiritual enrichment by having such great people in their midst, their strength in adhering to their leaders, and their virtue in choosing and revering holy leaders who serve God and not merely individuals who are wealthy or physically strong. Indeed, a verse that focuses on our great leaders should engender feelings of pride and joy in the entire nation!

Let us consider one more analogy to drive the point home. This one from the world of values. When we compliment someone for a significant act of kindness, for example,

---

2 A leader is born out of his surroundings, both for the good and the bad. Just as it is to the eternal glory of *Klal Yisrael* that a person like the Chofetz Chaim came from their midst, it is to the eternal shame of the Austrians that Hitler, ימ"ש, was a product of their society.

we do not intend to limit our praise to a single action. Rather, we are saying that this action illustrates a virtue that the doer possesses. Even though we may be pointing to a particular instance, we are usually aware of many other similar instances.[3] So too, when Hashem praises *Klal Yisrael* for one specific action, as He does repeatedly in the upcoming verses, it is to be understood as just an illustration of the virtue that lies behind it. Each verse, then, is illuminating another facet of the spiritual beauty of *Klal Yisrael*.

Metzudas Dovid points out that Hashem has praised *Klal Yisrael* earlier in *Shir HaShirim*, but these praises are in response to the devotion *Klal Yisrael* displayed in the previous chapter. When *Klal Yisrael* praise Hashem and show their loyalty to Him, they become even more beautiful in His eyes. This explains the additional outpouring of love and praise from Hashem here in this chapter.

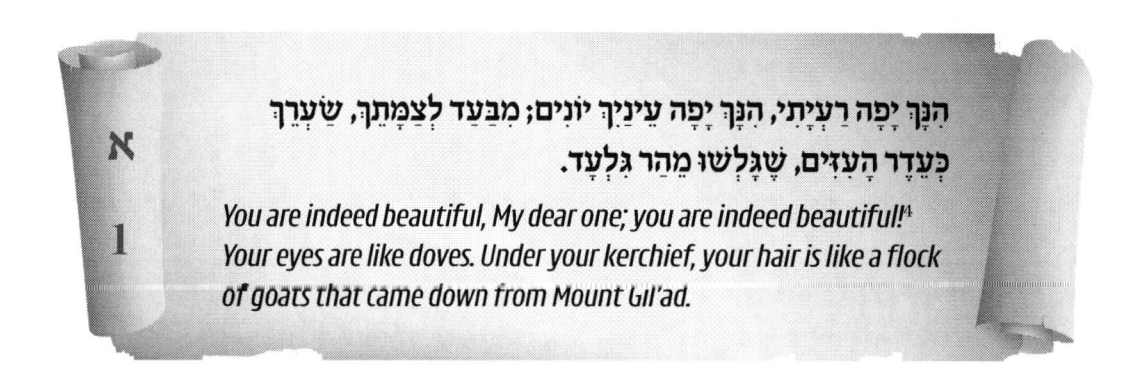

> **א**
> **1**
>
> הִנָּךְ יָפָה רַעְיָתִי, הִנָּךְ יָפָה עֵינַיִךְ יוֹנִים; מִבַּעַד לְצַמָּתֵךְ, שַׂעְרֵךְ כְּעֵדֶר הָעִזִּים, שֶׁגָּלְשׁוּ מֵהַר גִּלְעָד.
>
> *You are indeed beautiful, My dear one; you are indeed beautiful!*[1] *Your eyes are like doves. Under your kerchief, your hair is like a flock of goats that came down from Mount Gil'ad.*

Allegorical Translation — You, *Klal Yisrael*, are indeed beautiful to Me. You are as faithful as doves. Even the empty ones among your camps are precious to Me like the sons of Yaakov Avinu when they came down from Mount Gil'ad (leaving Lavan and his influence behind).

Subject of the Verse — Hashem is singing the praises of *Klal Yisrael*.

Mashal — The husband first praises his wife's beauty twice in a general way. He goes on to praise her beauty in detail: "You are as faithful as a dove. Your hair, which is

---

3 When Rabbi Yaakov Kamenetzky, *zt"l*, received a silver Kiddush cup as a gift from his community, he went to have it appraised. When asked why, he explained that he saw it as an addition to his salary, and wanted to know how much tax he owes. Obviously, this illustrates an entire way of life founded on truthfulness. When one tells this story, one is not just admiring Rabbi Kamenetzky for that single act but for his lifelong commitment to absolute honesty. Rabbi Yaakov Yosef Herman once served a bowl of cholent to a mentally unstable guest. The fellow proceeded to throw it back at him because he did not like it, and then he ran out of the house. Instead of getting annoyed, Rabbi Herman chased after him, placated him, and served him a fresh bowl of food. This one act gives us an indication of an entire life of *chessed*.

4 The doubled expression, "You are indeed beautiful," underscores how beautiful *Klal Yisrael* is in the eyes of Hashem. The Gemara tells us that a doubled expression is often used in the context of a vow (*Shavuos* 36a). Applied here, this would mean that Hashem is promising and guaranteeing that He finds *Klal Yisrael* beautiful.

Nimshal covered by a kerchief, is as shiny as the goats that gleam in the distance as they come down the mountains."

Nimshal While the first part of this verse describes the entirety of *Klal Yisrael* as being very beautiful, the second part, as well as all the succeeding verses, touch on different aspects of that beauty. The first part of this verse, then, is a kind of introduction to the entire chapter. Hashem begins by saying that *Klal Yisrael* is very beautiful, and then elaborates on each aspect of that beauty.

The beauty is first likened to doves. Just as doves are faithful to each other, so *Klal Yisrael* is faithful to Hashem.[5] The second part of the verse touches on the beauty of *Klal Yisrael*'s "hair." The various interpretations of this image will be discussed below.

YOU ARE INDEED BEAUTIFUL...

The word *hinach* (הִנָּךְ) used here and in many other places in *Shir HaShirim* to address *Klal Yisrael* in the second person — "you [are beautiful]" — is spelled *hey-nun-chaf sofi* ("final *chaf*"). When these letters are considered in the framework of one form of *gematria* (numerical valuations of the letters of the Hebrew alphabet) known as "*at-bach*,"[6] they yield an important insight. In the *at-bach* system of *gematria*, all the letters are seen as pairs with the numerical equivalent of either tens, hundreds, or thousands. Thus, *aleph* (one) is paired with *tes* (nine) to make a value of ten. Similarly, *beis* (two) is paired with *ches* (eight) to make a "complete" number of ten. In the same way, *yud* (ten) is paired with *tzadi* (ninety), equaling one hundred. Furthermore, and this aspect of the *at-bach* system is less known, the final letters *chaf sofi, mem sofi*, etc. equal five hundred, six hundred, etc. respectively. (Since the last letter of the alphabet, *tav* has a numerical value of four hundred, the final letters continue from there.) Therefore, *kuf* and the *tzadi sofi* equal a thousand.

It turns out that only three letters do not have any pair because they equal five, fifty, and five hundred: *hey, nun*, and final *chaf*: the letters of *hinach* (הִנָּךְ)! When speaking of *Klal Yisrael*'s beauty, Hashem uses these letters specifically to hint that *Klal Yisrael* is absolutely unique among all other people in their beauty and are unparalleled in being beloved to Him.[7]

It is important to note that while English does not distinguish between the plural "you"

---

5   This phrase first appears in 1:15. See our commentary for further elaboration.
6   See *Sukkah* 52b.
7   Vilna Gaon.

and the singular "you," *lashon hakodesh* does. The word *hinach* is singular. (*Hinchem* is the plural form.) Hashem is actually speaking to every individual in *Klal Yisrael* saying that each and every one is truly beautiful. Alternatively, *Klal Yisrael* is all one unit and therefore is addressed in the singular. This teaches us the importance of realizing we are all one, and how negatively Hashem views conflict and disunity.

YOUR HAIR IS LIKE A FLOCK OF GOATS...

Rashi explains that hair is symbolic of the weaker elements in *Klal Yisrael*. It differs from most of the body in that it does not contain any nerves or muscles; it is flimsy and weak and cannot move itself or do anything on its own. It is just like something attached to the body. Also, hair provides no essential need for the body. Therefore, hair is symbolic of the "empty people" in the nation, as Rashi calls them, who are pulled along by the rest.[8] Yet the greatness of the Jewish People can even be found in its hair, i.e., in the "empty people."

The verse emphasizes that they are beautiful when their hair is held back by their kerchief. Rashi explains this to mean that when they are within the camp (i.e., tied to the community), they are beautiful. The verse continues that their hair is like the goats going down the mountain of Gil'ad. Gil'ad was famous for its pastures,[9] which attracted many flocks of beautiful goats with clean white wool. As they descended the mountain, their bright wool could be seen from the distance, creating a beautiful sight. In metaphorical terms, this means that the beauty of even the weaker ones in the community could be seen and appreciated.

A person might think that he would do better and shine more if he left the fold or pursued his own individual greatness without being part of a community. Our verse teaches us that this is not so. If a person stays with his "flock," his beauty will shine more. As Rashi explains, this is especially true regarding the weakest elements of *Klal Yisrael* (the hair). They, too, add beauty, but only if and when they are "under the kerchief," as part of the community. When they leave the community, their beauty — and the beauty of the entire nation — is diminished. This, too, is implicit in the comparison to the goats. A single goat on the mountain does not create a beautiful sight, but when the flocks of goats gather together and come down the mountain, the beauty can be seen from even a great distance.

This is an important lesson. A person often thinks that he/she can attain greatness

---

[8] Nowadays, the term "on the fringe" is sometimes used to describe those struggling to connect to their Judaism. It is noteworthy that the term "fringe" relates closely to hair.

[9] See *Bamidbar* 32:1.

only by being outstanding and doing something different from everyone else. The reality is that by being part of a community — being part of something larger than oneself — one can reach a much higher level of greatness than one can on one's own.

The *Midrash Lekach Tov* explains this concept as it relates specifically to hair. It notes that a single hair on its own does not create beauty. Indeed, loose hair can actually detract from beauty. Furthermore, when hair is loose and scattered about, it does not add to a woman's beauty. A woman's hair looks nicer when it is gathered together neatly.[10] Similarly, *Klal Yisrael* is beautiful only when they are gathered as one, not when they are in conflict. An individual's attempt to glorify himself will only backfire.[11]

YOUR HAIR IS LIKE A FLOCK OF GOATS

The Vilna Gaon see this entire chapter as being about the greatness of Torah scholars. According to his interpretation, "hair" alludes to the Torah scholars who are able to deduce many laws from every hair-like line in the hand-written Torah scroll. These are the thin lines coming out from the tops of many of the letters. The very great Torah scholars were able to deduce many laws from these almost inconspicuous lines.[12] To explain the connection between the "hair" (Torah scholars) and the flock of goats, the Gaon reminds us that the very first people to set up a yeshivah to learn Torah were Yaakov and his sons,[13] who fled from Lavan to the mountain of Gil'ad.[14] This verse, then, is communicating that the great Torah scholars who study every tiny aspect of Torah are similar to the very first Torah scholars — Yaakov and his sons — who came down from Mount Gil'ad.

To understand this a bit more deeply, it is important to note that there were many who learned Torah before Yaakov Avinu, but he was the first to set up a yeshivah for *Klal Yisrael*. A yeshivah is not just a technical arrangement for a group of people to learn together. It is one of the oldest, if not the oldest, and most important institutions in *Klal Yisrael*, providing a place dedicated exclusively to understanding and clarifying Torah. The Gemara tells us that the yeshivah institution has never lapsed in the Jewish

---

10 The Gemara tells us that Hashem braided Chava's hair in plaits to make her attractive to Adam HaRishon (*Berachos* 61a).

11 The Midrash interprets the word *tzamoseich* in this verse not as "kerchief," but as "constrained," related to the word *tzimtum* ("limiting"). It notes that *Klal Yisrael* shine best when they constrain themselves in shul. We might mistakenly think that when we are neatly packed into shul in tight rows, we are limiting ourselves. The opposite is true, as the Midrash here is teaching us. A shul filled with people davening with devotion is a truly wondrous sight!

12 See *Eruvin* 21b and *Menachos* 29b.

13 See Rambam, *Hilchos Avodah Zarah* 1:3.

14 *Bereishis* 31:23-54.

world,[15] not even in the worst of times. As the first Rosh Yeshivah, Yaakov is the one all *talmidei chachamim* aspire to emulate. Likening Torah scholars, who study every tiny "particle" of Torah, to Yaakov is the greatest praise possible.

Furthermore, it is no accident that this verse alludes to Yaakov and his sons as they were escaping from Lavan to Mount Gil'ad. Let us recall that Lavan pursued Yaakov when he and his family left without notice. Lavan did not chase him because he loved him. On the contrary, Lavan HaRasha hated Yaakov. He had always hoped to influence Yaakov and his family to embrace his immoral and idolatrous ways.[16] While Yaakov lived with him, he was sure that Yaakov or his sons had become connected to him and part of his world. When Lavan saw that Yaakov had gone and that he had been unsuccessful in destroying Yaakov's spirituality, he chased after him to try to leave some small mark, if not on Yaakov, then at least on one of his children. But he was unsuccessful in this as well. As Yaakov left him on the mountain of Mount Gil'ad, taking all his children with him to Eretz Yisrael to serve Hashem, Lavan realized that he had failed. The yeshivah of Yaakov was uncontaminated and was going to be forever the greatest source of spirituality in this world. Once there was an established yeshivah, there was no chance that Torah would be forgotten. The verse evokes this scene because it shows the planting of the seed of *Klal Yisrael*'s spiritual future.

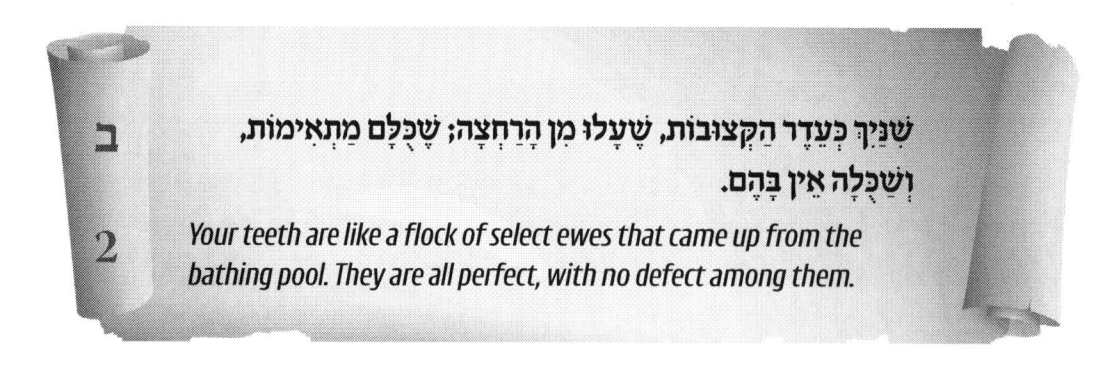

ב

שִׁנַּיִךְ כְּעֵדֶר הַקְּצוּבוֹת, שֶׁעָלוּ מִן הָרַחְצָה; שֶׁכֻּלָּם מַתְאִימוֹת, וְשַׁכֻּלָה אֵין בָּהֶם.

2 Your teeth are like a flock of select ewes that came up from the bathing pool. They are all perfect, with no defect among them.

Allegorical Translation — Hashem continues heaping praise on *Klal Yisrael*: "Your warriors are select righteous soldiers, free of sin like clean ewes who have just been washed; your soldiers are perfect, not having become blemished through the sin of immorality or theft."

Subject of the Verse — Hashem is singing the praises of *Klal Yisrael*.

Mashal — The husband continues praising the beauty of his wife, this time with the

---

15 *Yoma* 28b.
16 See full discussion in *Hagaddah Ma'aseh Nissim* by Rabbi Yaakov of Lisa, *s.v. tzei u'lemad*.

emphasis on the beauty of her teeth. He says: "Your teeth are all in perfect symmetry, and clean like ewes that have just been washed. All of your teeth are whole, without any defects."

Nimshal By way of background, Rashi tells us that shepherds would carefully select and set aside a designated number of their best sheep immediately upon birth. They would transfer them to a special shepherd whose job it was to watch over them so that they would not get dirty, and to wash them regularly to ensure that they remained perfectly clean. In this way, the sheep's wool would be especially valuable and would sell for a higher price. Teeth, in this verse, are therefore compared in cleanliness and perfection to these sheep.

"Teeth" in this verse are symbolic of the warriors of the Jewish People. Just as teeth are the hardest part of the body, so soldiers are the strongest part of the nation. Just as teeth consume and crush food, so soldiers are able to consume and annihilate their enemies. Unfortunately, soldiers in battle often become sullied by sin. Any accurate history of warfare is full of the lowliness into which soldiers very quickly descend, even soldiers from the best backgrounds. Since battle arouses the worst and basest emotions in a man, it often leads him to commit sins. One of the most common is stealing. When an army is overwhelming the enemy, it is almost inevitable that its soldiers will want to take something for themselves. This is symbolized by teeth which, because they are constantly used for chewing and consuming food, easily get dirty and often have food particles stuck between them. The teeth are sullied by the food they are consuming. In sharp contrast — and to the eternal credit of *Klal Yisrael* — their warriors ("teeth") remain perfectly clean.[17] In all the battles they fought, from the time they traveled in the desert until they completed the conquest of Eretz Yisrael — vanquishing thirty-one armies in Eretz Yisrael alone — only *once* did a soldier steal.[18] All the others remained clean like the sheep which are continually being washed.

---

17 Rashi connects this specifically to the victory over Moav in which twelve thousand Jewish soldiers participated. None of them stole anything or did anything immoral (*Bamidbar* 31:11-12,49). This was an especially impressive moral achievement in view of the fact that the people of Moav tried to use their daughters to cause *Klal Yisrael* to commit immoral acts and thus dressed them in particularly immodest ways. *Chazal* tell us that even during the heat of battle, the soldiers made sure to avert their eyes from these women regardless of the dangers and difficulties involved.

18 Rashi and Seforno. Rashi also mentions refraining from immorality. We realize from the fact that an *eshes yefas toar* is permitted to a soldier just how difficult it is to remain morally pure in battle (see *Devarim* 21:10-14, with Rashi). Battle awakens the worst instincts in a person, yet the virtuous Jewish soldiers remained pure and moral, as this verse attests.

If this is how great and pure the soldiers, who are prone to sin, were, how much more so was the greatness of the rest of the nation!

THEY ARE ALL PERFECT, WITH NO DEFECT AMONG THEM

The Midrash explains that the absence of "defects" was the soldiers' reward. Because all but one soldier maintained his moral cleanliness, they suffered no casualties.[19] The end of the verse, then, is to be understood as follows: "Because the soldiers are all perfectly sinless, no death or injury befell them."

That the verse likens the virtue of not stealing to the cleanliness of sheep teaches us another lesson. This is because, as the *Mesillas Yesharim*[20] explains, constant vigilance is required to avoid all forms of stealing. Even though very few people actually go out and steal, they may end up with other people's money in their hands if they are not careful. A worker who does not put in the full number of hours for which he is being paid, a salesperson who exaggerates the quality of his goods, and one who takes or borrows a small item without permission, all have what the *Mesillas Yesharim* calls "sticky and dirty hands." (Just as hands get sticky and dirty unless one is careful with them, so too a person will find money that is not rightfully his "sticking" to him unless he is careful.) Unfortunately, the majority of people fail in this area.[21] It is not enough for a person just to stop himself from going out and stealing. If he wishes to be morally clean, he must be very careful, and constantly "wash away" (back to the rightful owner) any resources that might be "stuck in his hands." This is why a righteous person is given the title "the one with *clean hands*."[22] The soldiers who did not steal took a lesson from shepherds who keep their sheep clean. Because wool soils easily, and many things can get trapped in it, shepherds who wish to have clean wool must constantly watch and clean their sheep. So, too, only with constant vigilance and an uncompromising commitment to return others' resources that "got stuck" to one's hands, can a person keep his hands clean.

This also explains the comparison of soldiers to teeth. Generally speaking, as long as one avoids dirt, one remains clean. The exception is teeth. They require constant cleaning because they naturally become dirty due to the food which gets caught in them. The soldiers, the "teeth" of the Jewish People, remained clean not only because they did not actively sin, but also because they made an effort to keep morally clean.

---

19   The one exception was the battle of Ai. Achan's theft resulted in losses for the Jewish People. See *Yehoshua*, ch. 7.
20   Ch. 11.
21   *Bava Basra* 165b.
22   *Tehillim* 24:4.

YOUR TEETH ARE LIKE A FLOCK OF SELECTED EWES

Pointing to a number of similarities, the Midrash interprets "teeth" here as being symbolic of Torah scholars.[23] Just as teeth are the hardest part of the body, so Torah scholars are the firmest part of the nation. Just as the power of clenched teeth is needed to chew, so strength is required to work through Torah. Just as teeth cut through food, so *talmidei chachamim* "cut" and distinguish between right and wrong, and cut through the intricacies of complicated Talmudic questions. The Midrash goes on to point to another facet of teeth: for teeth to bite and chew properly, they must be opposite one another. (On its own, one tooth cannot bite effectively; and even a number of teeth will not be able to chew if they are not opposite one another.) Similarly, Torah scholars succeed only when they are sharpened against each other, i.e., when they study with a partner who challenges and corrects any mistake in their learning.[24] Indeed, the Gemara tells us that the Torah learning of those scholars who learn entirely on their own becomes blemished.[25] According to this interpretation, the verse is to be understood in the following way:

> "Your Torah scholars are perfect and clean, like a flock of select ewes, that came up from the bathing pool; they all correspond to one another[26] [by learning and working together; and therefore] they are perfect, with no defects [in the form of mistaken rulings or conclusions] among them."

YOUR TEETH ARE LIKE A FLOCK OF SELECTED EWES

Tzror HaMor identifies a completely different layer of meaning in this verse:

> "Your [teeth-like] enemies, who wish to bite and consume you, are like a flock of selected [counted] ewes [in the sense that the suffering they inflict on *Klal Yisrael* is carefully calculated and counted by Hashem to ensure that the suffering yields positive results. And

---

23 The Vilna Gaon adopts this approach.

24 The Gemara notes that just as a knife is sharpened best when it is stroked against another knife, so *talmidei chachamim* are best "sharpened" by being "stroked" or brushed against one another (*Ta'anis* 7a).
Rabbeinu Yohanson comments (on *Bereishis* 38:20) that this is true of all people. Everyone should have a trusted friend who is truthful, courageous, and righteous enough to point out where one is mistaken in his life. This, he says, was the role of Chirah HaAdulami whom Yehudah took as a friend once he separated from the rest of the Shevatim (*Bereishis*, ch. 38). He adds that, unfortunately, most people talk to their friends about trivial matters and not about how their personal life should be lived.

25 *Makkos* 10a.

26 Alluded to by the word *ma'asimos*.

Hashem makes certain that there is enough "space" between the instances of suffering so that *Klal Yisrael* has time to recover — just as space is left between flocks.[27] As a result of the suffering, Klal Yisrael] come up [closer to Hashem] from the bathing pool [cleansed of their sins like sheep emerging clean from a bathing pool]. They are [now] all perfect, with no defect among them."

What follows is an elaboration of the Tzror HaMor's interpretation:

It may seem that our enemies consume us or cause us to lose out. In reality, however, Hashem makes sure that they are unable to do so. Anything they have taken, Hashem will replace — and more.[28] So, there is "no defect or anything missing among them." Furthermore, once they have suffered to the full extent that Hashem ordained, *Klal Yisrael* will never suffer again because their sins will have been atoned for. On the contrary, they will all then merit their full reward in the World to Come. No member of the Jewish People will miss out on this reward. So, there will be "no Jewish person missing" when the reward is distributed.

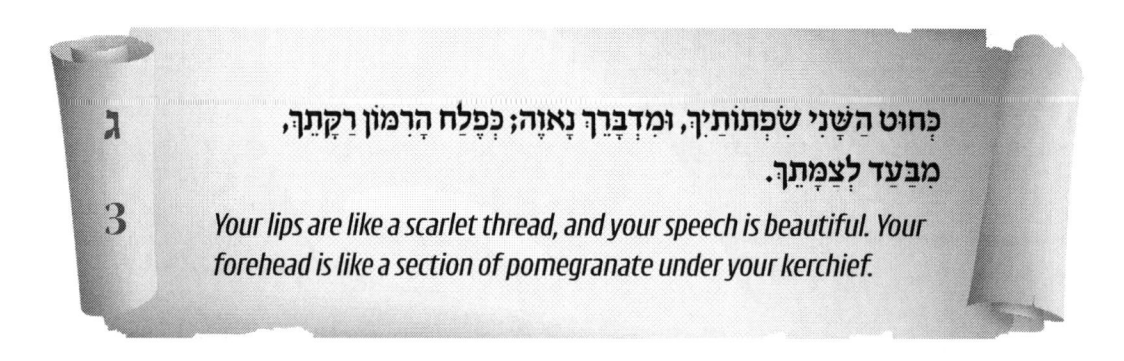

ג

כְּחוּט הַשָּׁנִי שִׂפְתוֹתַיִךְ, וּמִדְבָּרֵךְ נָאוֶה; כְּפֶלַח הָרִמּוֹן רַקָּתֵךְ, מִבַּעַד לְצַמָּתֵךְ.

3 *Your lips are like a scarlet thread, and your speech is beautiful. Your forehead is like a section of pomegranate under your kerchief.*

Allegorical Translation   Hashem continues His praise to *Klal Yisrael*: "Your speech is trustworthy and pleasant. Even those who are empty among you are as full of mitzvos as a pomegranate [is full of seeds]."[29]

---

27 As Yaakov did when he sent his flocks to Esav, his brother. See Ramban on *Bereishis* 32:17 who comments that these essentially forced gifts to Esav symbolized the Jewish People's future suffering. Through his actions of separating the flocks and putting distance between them, Yaakov was praying to Hashem that there should always be space between the suffering of the Jewish People.

28 We see this in Yaakov's life. After being in Lavan's spiritually contaminated home for twenty years, and being injured by the angel of Esav, and suffering the financial loss from the gifts he felt compelled to give Esav, Yaakov arrived in Eretz Yisrael complete and whole: *shalem* (*Bereishis* 33:18). As Rashi explains, Yaakov returned home whole in Torah, whole in health, and whole in finances. He ultimately lost nothing from all of those setbacks.

29 In our commentary on the previous verse, we cited the explanation of the Tzror HaMor (which is completely different from Rashi and the Midrash). Following his previous line of explanation that the verses are referring to the suffering of *Klal Yisrael*, he explains this verse as follows:

"Your lips are like scarlet thread" — Even when suffering, Klal Yisrael do not change their manner of speech (by starting

SHIR HASHIRIM 4:3

Subject of the Verse Hashem is singing the praises of *Klal Yisrael*.

Mashal Continuing to praise his wife, the husband says to her: "Your lips are as red as scarlet thread. Your speech is beautiful. Your forehead, which peeks out from under your kerchief, is as red[30] and rounded as a piece of pomegranate."

Nimshal Continuing to extol *Klal Yisrael*, Hashem praises the beauty of their lips and speech, likening *both* to distinctive scarlet (red) thread. As we know from our own experience, red is a particularly distinct color.[31] And scarlet thread retains its strong red color for a very long time, even after many washings. The allusion here is to the utter reliability of the promises that the Jewish People make. Just as scarlet thread does not quickly change color and is clearly visible and distinct, so too the word of the Jewish People does not suddenly change and is "illuminating" in its reliability.[32] The Midrash lists a variety of promises and pledges that the Jewish People made and fulfilled. For example, they promised to accept the Torah, saying *"Na'aseh v'nishma* — We will do, and [then] we will listen," and for thousands of years, millions of Jewish people have kept this promise despite innumerable hardships and struggles. Indeed, we have given up our comforts, our money, our homes, and even our lives in fulfillment of this promise. We gave our word, and we have generally kept to it. Our fulfillment of the mitzvos of *tefillin*, matzah, and so many other mitzvos is meticulously done in the same fashion Moshe Rabbeinu commanded us thousands of years ago — and to which we committed ourselves. What other nation has kept a promise so long and so diligently?!

An example of another sort is the promise made to Rachav that the Jewish

---

to curse or speaking badly) and accept their sharply felt suffering without complaining, just as scarlet thread does not change color even when washed with strong detergents.

"And your speech is beautiful" — Just as you thank Hashem with beautiful language for the good, you thank Him for the bad.

"Your empty ones are like a piece of pomegranate under your kerchief" — Even when the empty ones of Klal Yisrael suffer and are broken into pieces like a sliced pomegranate, they remain within the fold, and do not leave the Jewish People.

There are many examples of this remarkable phenomenon wherein even the lowest of the Jewish people — even in the face of terrible torture (such as during the Spanish Inquisition) and even when they have been split up and scattered around the globe — have nevertheless refused to give up their Jewish identity and have remained faithful to their people.

30 Being ruddy was considered beautiful in ancient times.

31 This is why the color red is commonly used for posting vitally important instructions or for printed signs indicating danger.

32 Metzudas Dovid. See *Midrash Rabbah, Rus* 3:18, that reliability is one of the key characteristics of a righteous person.

People would not harm her and her family when they conquered Yericho. Although the promise was given under enormous duress and had to be kept during a fierce battle in a cramped walled city, it was kept! The beautiful red lips in the verse are the lips used for articulating words that have reliability and value — and not empty promises.[33]

The second half of the verse describes the beauty of *Klal Yisrael*'s "forehead." The Gemara teaches that this is an allusion to the "empty" people, i.e., the wicked.[34] The word for "empty" (רק) and word for "forehead" (רקתך) mentioned here share the same root letters.[35] This verse, then, is praising the Jewish People for the fact that even their wicked are like pomegranates. The Gemara explains that just as pomegranates are filled with seeds, so the wicked are filled with mitzvos and merits.[36]

As discussed in the Introduction, when we learn *Shir HaShirim*, we see the world through a different lens — one of pure love between us and Hashem. From this vantage point, we do not see wicked people as evil. Rather, we focus on the good deeds they have done. When we hear amazing stories about how much kindness and goodness certain non-religious Jewish people have done, we are reminded of this verse. Indeed, one of most beautiful and inspiring aspects of our nation is that even the "emptiest" of Jews are full of merits.

The verse concludes "under the kerchief." This means that the "empty people" are part of the nation and have not left it.[37] Once they leave the community, even if they have good deeds, they make themselves into outcasts.

SECTION OF POMEGRANATE...

We might wonder: How can someone full of merits like a pomegranate be called "wicked"?[38] Here is one of the memorable answers to this question. There is a

---

33 That Hashem praises *Klal Yisrael* for reliability teaches us how important this trait is. Indeed, an unreliable person is lacking a basic Jewish trait.

34 *Berachos* 57a.

35 The word "forehead" stems from the word "empty" also because it is "empty" of hair (Vilna Gaon).

36 Commenting on this verse, the Malbim tells us that because a pomegranate has 613 seeds, it is used as a symbol of observing the 613 mitzvos. Rav Chaim Kanievsky was asked how it could be that many have counted and found that there are far less than 613 seeds. He answered that the Malbim means that even the largest pomegranate does not have more than 613 seeds (*Siach HaPesach*).

37 See our commentary on 4:1.

38 The Kli Yakar understands that Hashem is praising the wicked people *after* they have repented. All of their sins then

basic difference between a pomegranate and most other fruits. The edible part of a pomegranate, the seeds, are separate from the part of the fruit that we eat — unlike other fruits, such as apples and plums, where the edible, fleshy part of the fruit is the fruit itself. There is no distinction between "an apple" and "the fruit of the apple." But the seeds of a pomegranate can be said to be completely separate from the pomegranate since we actually remove the seeds from the pomegranate to eat them. The wicked do some good deeds, but the good deeds are separate from their essence. The wicked are mostly focused on fulfilling their desires, and their good deeds never really become part of them. In contrast the good deeds of a righteous person become part of his essence.

What are a person's real interests and desires? If they are mostly evil, the fact that he may do some good deeds does not take him out of the category of being "wicked." Therefore, it is possible to be empty, i.e., without a true connection to Hashem, and still be full of merits "like a pomegranate." To be righteous, it is not enough to do good things; the desire for good must penetrate the person's very being and become an integral part of his essence. Goodness must become integrated into the doer of kindness. This is particularly important in *chinuch* (education). Children must see that when a righteous person performs good deeds, it is because he is internally motivated and that goodness is an integral part of the doer. If they sense that a person is mainly interested in his desires — only doing good deeds to assuage a guilty conscience or for some other ulterior motive — they will not be inspired to be good.

The Midrash teaches that the wicked are full of merits due to all the sins they *refrained* from committing. When one has the desire and opportunity to sin but refrains, he is rewarded as if he actually did a mitzvah.[39] This is a very important and uplifting message for us today. We may sometimes sin and act wickedly, but when we pass over an opportunity to sin, this makes us precious in the eyes of Hashem — like the righteous, who are full of merits. We are painfully aware that our generation has so many opportunities to sin, perhaps as never before. But if we resist all the temptations, we actually accumulate merits in greater quantities than ever before. This point was made forcefully by a certain person of stature: "I was on a trip and had no time to learn Torah. Finally, in my hotel room, I took out a Gemara, but unfortunately, fell asleep in front of it. When I awoke, I felt terribly guilty, thinking my grandfather would certainly

---

become merits (*Yoma* 86b). This is how the "empty" people are filled with merits. Accordingly, the verse is extolling *Klal Yisrael* for the fact that even the wicked among them often repent and are quick to repent — and thus they are usually full of merits. This is a common theme both in *Shir HaShirim* and in our long and rich history. There have been any number of wicked Jews who completely repented and changed their lives for the good as a result of a minor incident or small comment.

39 *Kiddushin* 39b.

not have fallen asleep like this. Then, looking around, I saw the television, and thought, 'Well, my grandfather did not have to stop himself from turning on this contraption!'"[40] Our reward for self-control in a generation of indulgence and extravagance will be immeasurable.

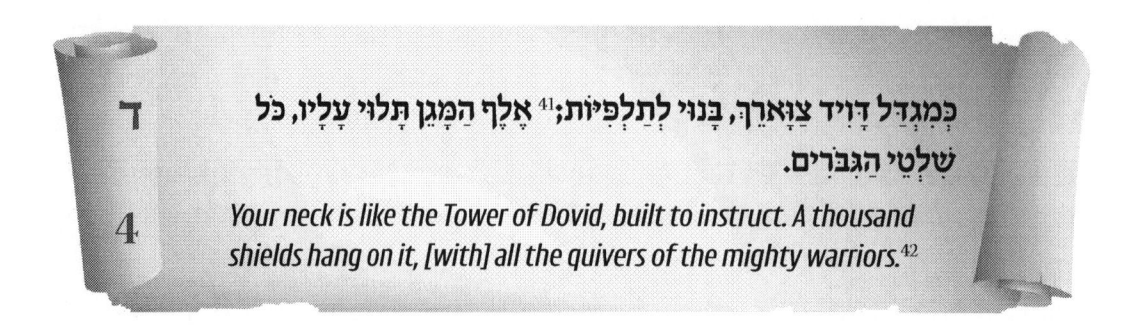

> ד
>
> 4
>
> כְּמִגְדַּל דָּוִיד צַוָּארֵךְ, בָּנוּי לְתַלְפִּיּוֹת;[41] אֶלֶף הַמָּגֵן תָּלוּי עָלָיו, כֹּל שִׁלְטֵי הַגִּבֹּרִים.
>
> *Your neck is like the Tower of Dovid, built to instruct. A thousand shields hang on it, [with] all the quivers of the mighty warriors.*[42]

Allegorical Translation Your Sanhedrin is as strong and powerful as a tower from which Torah emanates. Like the tower on which soldiers hang their shields and quivers to demonstrate that the tower is a source of protection, so the Sanhedrin and the Torah they taught are the source of protection for the nation.[43]

---

40   Although this anecdote is dated since the advent of the Internet — with all of its temptations and horrific potential for misuse — the message holds true. In fact, since the Internet has come on the scene, our reward has greatly increased when we control ourselves.

41   On the simple level, the word תלפיות stems from the word "instruction" and "teaching," from the root א-ל-ף (as in *Iyov* 35:11). It is an appropriate way of describing the Beis HaMikdash since the Beis HaMikdash was a was landmark building, teaching humanity how to behave. The Gemara (*Berachos* 30a) offers an alternative way of connecting תלפיות with the Beis HaMikdash. It sees תלפיות as a combination of two words, תל (elevation) and פיות (mouths), an elevated place that all mouths turn to (תל שכל פיות פונים לו). Wherever in the world a person is when he prays, he turns towards the Beis HaMikdash. Thus, those further west, like most of Western society, face east when they pray, while those further east, face west. This means that not only was the Beis HaMikdash a place through which all prayers were channeled, but it also had a tremendous unifying effect, causing all of *Klal Yisrael* to turn to the same place. This unifying effect is applicable even today since we continue to daven towards the place of the Beis HaMikdash. Furthermore, Jews from all backgrounds and walks of life daven together to the One God at the *Kosel*.

42   The shields and quivers that had been used in great battles were commonly hung on the walls of towers. Visitors to old castles can still see this today.

43   Rashi sees this verse as alluding to the greatness of the Sanhedrin. Unfortunately, the tremendous greatness of the Sanhedrin is not so well known today. To be a member of the Sanhedrin, one had to be eminently knowledgeable in Torah (as well as many other disciplines), and one had to have tremendous piety and dedication to the truth. Members of the Sanhedrin also had to have a commanding presence and be tall and handsome. They had to be able to annul all witchcraft and know all the languages of the world (*Sanhedrin* 17a). The greatness of each person on the Sanhedrin is beyond our grasp. *Klal Yisrael* had a Sanhedrin for hundreds of years, filled with the greatest scholars who ever lived. No question or uncertainty was ever left unresolved in this greatest place of learning. We should try to envision the greatest scholars in the world learning and discussing Torah together in holiness and purity. Nothing could compare to this! One of the major facets of *Klal Yisrael*'s beauty was its Sanhedrin. And here Hashem praises them for it. See our commentary on 7:3 for further discussion of the Sanhedrin.

Subject of the Verse — Hashem is singing the praises of *Klal Yisrael*.

Mashal — Continuing to praise his wife, the husband says to her: "Your neck is tall and beautiful. Like a tall tower adorned with many shields and quivers, so is your neck high and adorned with much jewelry."

Nimshal — The "neck" of the Jewish People is the Beis HaMikdash.[44] Just as all of one's nerves, life, and energy traverse the neck, so all spirituality flowed through the Beis HaMikdash.[45] Just as a cut to the neck is life-threatening because of all that flows through it, so the cutting loss of the Beis HaMikdash was like a death blow to the Jewish People.[46] Furthermore, just as the neck is high up on the body, so the Beis HaMikdash was high up on a mountain. Just as most jewelry hangs around the neck area, so most of the "beauty" of the nation was found in the Beis HaMikdash. The service of the *Kohanim*, the singing of the *Leviyim*, the sacrificial service, and the teaching of the Sanhedrin — all the "jewelry" of *Klal Yisrael* — were to be found in the Beis HaMikdash.

In likening the Beis HaMikdash to the Tower of Dovid, this verse is alluding to another aspect of its beauty: It served as a fountainhead of knowledge and taught humanity how to behave. A tall tower is a landmark, indicating to people where they are and where they should be going — in the language of the verse, "built to instruct." The Beis HaMikdash was a "landmark" because it reminded everyone of where they were and what they should be doing because it showed the world that Hashem was there. It was a building where Hashem's Presence could be felt by everyone and where miracles occurred on a daily basis — a powerful reminder of Hashem's existence and the importance of serving Him. The actual building was a source of instruction. Unfortunately, since we lost it so many years ago, it is hard to imagine the powerful effect the Beis HaMikdash had on the people. It was a place where one could say, "Here dwells the Shechinah; here miracles happen all the time." As a very mundane illustration, let us recall how someone zipping along on a fast road reacts when

---

44 Midrash. Rashi sees the neck as symbolizing the Sanhedrin. There may be no contradiction here since the Sanhedrin was located in the Beis HaMikdash and was one its greatest attributes.

45 The neck also alludes to the Sanhedrin (located in the Beis HaMikdash) and the Torah they taught because Torah is our lives, and the neck "transmits" life-giving air to the body. A further point of analogy: just as the mind sends signals through the neck to the rest of the body, directing its operation, so did the Sanhedrin (symbolized by the neck) convey the laws of Hashem Above (the "Head") to *Klal Yisrael* below (the rest of the body).

46 The *Segulas Yisrael* quotes the *Shem MiShmuel* which says that just as the neck connects the body to the head, the righteous connect *Klal Yisrael* to their Father in Heaven.

he sees a police car by the side of the road. He quickly checks to see that his speed and his driving are appropriate. The Beis HaMikdash was an infinitely greater reminder of how a person should be checking himself to make sure that he is behaving correctly.

Furthermore, in the Beis HaMikdash, there was a chamber known as the *Lishkas HaGazis,* the seat of the Sanhedrin. From there, Torah was taught to the nation. All of the most difficult questions from the entire nation were sent to the Sanhedrin and were resolved in this chamber by the many great Torah scholars who learned and taught Torah there. These halachic triumphs are symbolized by the quivers and shields that adorned the towers of the heathen nations. In ancient times, soldiers would hang the shields and quivers that they had used in victorious battles on the walls of their towers. The idea was to decorate the walls with depictions of their power and prowess. This would be their way of showing off their greatest triumphs. The great scholars who would wrestle with profound and complicated Torah questions in the Beis HaMikdash are likened to great warriors and great weapons. Just as other nations are proud of their great warriors, *Klal Yisrael* is proud of their Torah scholars. The Torah laws which they clarified and resolved would "adorn" the Beis HaMikdash because they are our greatest triumphs and our greatest display of prowess. As the verse concludes, "a thousand shields hang on it [i.e., the Beis HaMikdash] with all the quivers of the mighty warriors [i.e., the Torah scholars]."

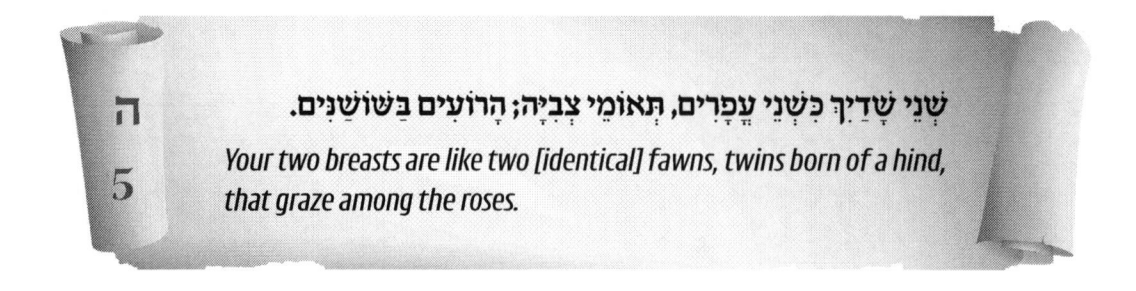

ה 5

שְׁנֵי שָׁדַיִךְ כִּשְׁנֵי עֳפָרִים, תְּאוֹמֵי צְבִיָּה; הָרוֹעִים בַּשּׁוֹשַׁנִּים.

Your two breasts are like two [identical] fawns, twins born of a hind, that graze among the roses.

Allegorical Translation — Continuing His praises to *Klal Yisrael,* Hashem says to them: "Your two leaders, Moshe and Aharon, were equal in beauty and greatness, like identical twin fawns born of a hind. They led you in the straight and pleasant path (of serving Hashem)."

Subject of the Verse — Hashem is singing the praises of *Klal Yisrael.*

Mashal — The husband continues to praise his wife: "Your two breasts are beautiful and identical. They look like two identical twin fawns, born of a hind, while they are eating from the roses. When they eat from the beautiful roses, they create a very striking view."[47]

Nimshal This verse describes the beauty of *Klal Yisrael*. Rashi tells us that it is common for hinds to have identical twin baby fawns, and that is why they are used as an example. Metzudas Dovid adds that fawns are particularly beautiful. The analogy to fawns, then, has three aspects: identical in appearance, born as twins, beautiful to behold. The verse emphasizes these three points: "Your two breasts are like two [*identical*] fawns, *twins* born of [a particularly beautiful creature], a *hind*..."[48]

The breasts highlighted in the verse represent Moshe Rabbeinu and Aharon HaKohen, the leaders of *Klal Yisrael*. Just as a woman's two breasts are similar, so Moshe and Aharon were equally great.[49] Just as the breasts are the beauty of a woman, the leaders of our nation bring out our beauty. Just as a mother's breasts nurture her baby, so these two leaders nurtured the Jewish People and took care of them like a mother feeding her young. Just as breasts are full of nourishing milk, so Moshe and Aharon were full of nourishing Torah.[50] Just as a baby would die if not for the milk that the mother provides (or a suitable replacement), so *Klal Yisrael* could not have survived without the Torah of Moshe and Aharon.[51] Just as a mother's breasts provide nourishment for her

---

47 Metzudas Dovid.

48 All these three aspects apply well to breasts. There are always two breasts and they are more appealing when they look the same and are a beautiful part of the body.

49 Rashi on *Shemos* 6:26, based on the Midrash. Since Moshe was certainly the greater prophet, the commentators address this puzzling assertion that they were equal in stature. *Maskil L'Dovid* (on *Shemos* 6:26) explains that they were equal in deeds. Alternatively, they both realized their full potential in serving Hashem. The Shiras HaLevi suggests that they were equal in helping the Jewish People. Rabbi Avraham, the brother of the Vilna Gaon, explained that Moshe was the greatest regarding the mitzvos "between man and God" (בין אדם למקום), while Aharon was the greatest regarding the interpersonal mitzvos (בין אדם לחברו). Aharon's greatness in this realm is borne out by the Mishnah that tells us that Aharon was the epitome of one who seeks peace and kindness (*Avos* 1:12). In short, they were equal in that they were both the greatest in their individual service.

50 The Meshech Chochmah (on *Vayikra* 10:3) adds that just as the breasts do not retain anything, serving only as a conduit to provide for the baby, so too the true leaders of the nation do not act in order to benefit themselves. They do not look to add to their wealth and honor, but just wish to provide for the nation.

51 The Gemara notes that just as a baby always finds pleasure and food in its mother's breasts, which do not dry up as long as it suckles, so too a person who endeavors to learn and understand Torah will always discover more pleasure (in the form of ideas and lessons) in what he is learning (*Eruvin* 54b). Unlike all other types of wisdom, Torah is not a finite source of knowledge. The more effort one expends on Torah study, the more wisdom he will absorb. This is why the verse likens Moshe and Aharon teaching Torah to a mother nursing her baby, and thus providing it with a ceaseless supply of pleasure and nutrition.

child from that which she ate herself, so our leaders nourish us with Torah from what they themselves have learned. Given all of these points of similarity, it is no wonder that the twin leadership of Moshe and Aharon is symbolized by a woman's breasts.

For much of our subsequent history, our nation also benefited from twin leadership. We had either a king or *Nasi* ("prince") who was in charge of the material affairs of the nation, and the *Kohen Gadol*, *Navi* or head of the Sanhedrin, who was in charge of the nation's spiritual affairs.[52] These leaders would work together to help the Jewish People in every way.

The verse concludes that "they graze[53] [their sheep] among the roses." This means that the leaders of the nation take good care of their people, like a shepherd who finds his flock pleasant places to graze. The Tzror HaMor adds that it is because they take good care of their people that they merit to become leaders. This verse, then, is not just teaching us what the great leaders do, but how they merit to become great leaders.

The symbolism of the breasts in this verse may also be understood in terms of the two stone tablets upon which the Ten Commandments, the basis of our Torah, were written.[54] Just as the two breasts are similar and complement one another, so the two stone tablets were similar and complemented one another. From a quick glance, one may come to the mistaken conclusion that they contained two separate and different sets of laws. The first tablet contained the laws governing how a person should conduct himself towards God (to believe in God, observe the Shabbos, etc.), and the second tablet contained the laws governing how a person should conduct himself toward his fellow man (not to murder, not to testify falsely, etc.). However, the truth is otherwise. All of these laws have things in common, and they enhance each other. One who serves Hashem properly will be kind to his fellow man, and vice versa.[55] Furthermore, the two tablets of the Ten Commandments correspond to each other, as Rashi explains in great

---

52 Vilna Gaon. Moshe Rabbeinu had the status of a king, while Aharon HaKohen was, of course, the *Kohen Gadol*. As explained earlier, twin leadership roles were continued throughout the generations.

53 This verb can connote both the sheep grazing as well as the shepherd giving the sheep the opportunity to graze.

54 Rashi.

55 This concept accords with the explanation above that the two breasts allude to Moshe and Aharon, the former distinguishing himself particularly in the realm of mitzvos "between man and God" (בין אדם למקום), the latter in the realm of "interpersonal mitzvos" (בין אדם לחברו). The two leaders complemented one another much in the way that the *luchos* complement one another.

detail. Believing in God (first on the right-hand side of the *luchos*) prevents one from committing murder (first on the left-hand side of the *luchos*) because killing a human being who is created in God's image shows a lack of respect and lack of belief in God Himself. Not serving other gods (second on the right side), i.e., not betraying one's true relationship with the One God, is also the essence of not committing adultery (second on the left side) which is an act of betrayal. Not swearing falsely (third on the right side) also prevents one from stealing (third on the left side), as those who steal eventually come to swear falsely. Failure to observe Shabbos (fourth on the right) is a form of false testimony (fourth on the left) because it is almost as if one is bearing witness that Hashem did not create the world (while refraining from creative labor on Shabbos is a testimony that Hashem, who created the world, desisted from creating on that day). Honoring one's parents properly (fifth on the right) is only possible when one does not covet another person's wife (fifth on the left), thereby avoiding adulterous relationships which yield children who cannot identify their true parents.

To teach this message that the two *luchos* were equal and complemented one another, Hashem made a special miracle enabling the many more words on the first *luach* to fit on a stone table the size of the second *luach*.[56]

YOUR TWO BREASTS ARE LIKE TWO [IDENTICAL] FAWNS

The metaphor of the two breasts teaches us a fundamental lesson. As Rashi points out, beauty is to be found here only if there is symmetry. If one breast is bigger than the other, or different in shape, etc., it detracts from the beauty. Furthermore, the beauty of each one is enhanced by the beauty of the other. In allegorical terms, *Klal Yisrael* is being praised for their amazing beauty of symmetry and how each component part of the nation complements the other.

This verse is praising the symmetry that exists within *Klal Yisrael* and the Torah. One of the most striking aspects of Torah is how all the wide-ranging laws are intertwined and reflect on each other. When one learns any area of Torah, one gains a better appreciation of all the laws of the Torah. Only someone who actually learns Torah can appreciate this. Unlike other legal systems, in which every law has its own rules and parameters — and the different laws often infringe on one another — the laws of the Torah have within them a deep harmony. This is so because they were all given by Hashem for our good (expressed here as Hashem shepherding His flock among the beautiful roses) to bring us closer to Him.

Let us look at this symmetry another way. If one is working on two different projects,

---

56 *Midrash Rabbah, Ki Sisa*, 41:6.

his devotion to one will cause the other to suffer. Or, to use Rashi's illustration cited earlier: being completely subservient to one's leader usually limits the devotion one has to one's friends and family, and vice versa, the efforts one devotes to one's fellow man usually detract from the devotion to one's king. But this is not the case in the Torah system. As Rashi explains, honoring Hashem properly causes one to be kinder to one's fellow man, who is created in His image. And one who is kind to others recognizes the Divine greatness within each person. And because Hashem commanded us to be kind, doing so will bring us closer to serving Hashem. In the symbolism of the verse, one breast enhances the beauty of the other.

There is a deeper lesson here: As a person increases his dedication in one area, e.g., serving Hashem, he must also increase his dedication in the second area, e.g., being kind to others. If one fails to do so, this can actually be detrimental even in the area that one is concentrating on. We occasionally see an individual who does not have this balance and thus sometimes causes a *chillul Hashem, chas v'shalom*. Rabbi Yisrael Salanter would give the example of a person who, in his devotion and fervor in serving Hashem, wraps himself in a *tallis* with great gusto, and thereby hits someone in the face with the *tallis* strings. This is not service of Hashem, but serving oneself, serving one's inner desire to feel special.[57] Another example would be getting up early for prayer or Torah study and carelessly waking up others in one's religious zeal. Similarly, if one bestows much kindness but does not serve Hashem, the kindness itself is flawed.[58] This unappealing lack of balance is symbolized in our verse by the breasts, which must be uniform to be attractive. Having just one breast — whether it is big or small — is not like having half the beauty. On the contrary, it is inappropriate and off-putting.[59]

This verse also implicitly redounds to the credit of Moshe and Aharon in another way. Normally, having two leaders ensures constant bickering as each leader tries to outdo and diminish the other. This ultimately causes a lack of unity and is thus extremely impractical.[60] In sharp contrast, Moshe and Aharon were two leaders who enhanced

---

57   The Chazon Ish discusses this point in his *sefer, Emunah and Bitachon* (ch. 3). He says that when a person "excels" only in one area, and completely neglects another area, this is an indication that he is not actually serving Hashem at all, but rather doing what suits him.

58   History has shown how individuals dedicated to kindness, but without regard for Hashem, end up committing major acts of cruelty. One example is those who would ban *shechitah* in the name of kindness to animals and thereby deprive many of the ability to eat meat and fulfil the true *tachlis* of the animals.

59   When Rivkah Imeinu displayed a very high level of kindness to Eliezer, prompting him to choose her as a wife for Yitzchak, he immediately gave her two bracelets weighing ten gold coins. These represented the two Tablets and the Ten Commandments written on them (*Bereishis* 24:22, with Rashi). Eliezer wished to drive home this point that as wonderful as kindness is, there is another, corresponding element to being a good person: serving Hashem. Indeed, the very word for "bracelets," *tzemidim*, also means "joined," to teach that it has to be a combined effort.

60   There are countries with constantly changing governments. We frequently see a new minister try to diminish the suc-

and supported one another.⁶¹ They were not looking out for their own honor, but only what was good for the nation. Therefore, they always worked in harmony to provide the nation with all its needs and help *Klal Yisrael* become closer to Hashem. They spoke as one; their voices merged together, thereby enriching and empowering their message such that those who heard them felt inspired because of the unity they displayed in conveying Hashem's words.⁶² This arrangement was employed during the many generations that we had both a king and a *Kohen Gadol*. The king was the nation's material leader, and the *Kohen Gadol* was the spiritual leader. When there was no Beis HaMikdash, the *Nasi* and *av beis din* served as the nation's two leaders. Instead of causing friction, this system worked well, and helped the nation reach great heights. Again, this positive outcome resulted from our leaders' singular interest in serving Hashem. Not only did it prove practical to have two leaders, but it actually enhanced the nation's service of Hashem. The two leaders, the "breasts" of *Klal Yisrael*, brought their different talents together.⁶³ Just as breasts enhance each other, so the leaders of *Klal Yisrael* (who "nurse" the nation) complement and add glory to one another.⁶⁴

Taking another tack altogether, *Shevach V'Yakar* interprets the breasts in this verse as alluding to the "twin Torahs," i.e., the Written Torah and the Oral Torah. They complement and enhance each other. Indeed, we cannot even understand one without the other, and together they sustain the Jewish People. The verse continues by likening the two breasts to two fawns, "born of a hind." This means that they emanate from the exact same source, Hashem. One dare not make the mistake of thinking that the Oral Torah has a different source from the Written Torah. Those sects who erred in this way faded out of Jewish history.

---

cesses of his predecessor and create a new program, thereby putting his stamp on society. Unfortunately, such people are often driven by vanity and a desire for honor. The usual result is constant upheaval and very little success.

61   For examples of how honorably they treated one another, see Rashi on *Shemos* 17:9, *Vayikra* 10:16, and *Bamidbar* 17:5.
62   Rashi on *Shemos* 12:3.
63   This is one of the fundamental reasons why the division of the Jewish People into twelve different tribes does not detract from, but actually enhances, our service of Hashem. Of course, this applies only as long as there is unity and an understanding that all the ways of serving Hashem are equally good, as long as they bespeak a genuine effort to serve Him correctly.
64   It is noteworthy that while we do not know what Har Sinai or Har Navo (where Moshe was buried) looked like, we do know that the mountain upon which Aharon HaKohen was buried, Hor HaHar, was shaped like a small mountain on top of a bigger one (Rashi on *Bamidbar* 20:22). This is significant because Aharon was the leader of the Jewish People before he was replaced by Moshe, his younger brother (Rashi on *Shemos* 4:10, *s.v. gam*). Only due to his tremendous greatness did he not only accept Moshe as his replacement, but he even helped him and greatly honored him. In so doing, he and *Klal Yisrael* reached greater spiritual heights than had Moshe or Aharon been the leader the whole time. Therefore, he was honored by being buried on a mountain that symbolized his greatness. He may have been a smaller mountain, but it was on top of a greater one. This composite mountain towered much higher as a result.

THAT GRAZE AMONG THE ROSES

The conclusion of the verse is that these two tablets, i.e., the laws of the Torah "graze and shepherd [us] *among the roses.*" This means that the laws of the Torah not only provide nourishment but do so in a pleasant and exciting manner. Roses, here, are symbolic of nourishment in pleasant surroundings.[65] Alternatively, this image is alluding to the leaders' devotion, and to how they would lead the people in a pleasant manner. Let us note that earlier (2:16), this same phrase, "among the roses," is used to describe Hashem's love for, and devotion to, the Jewish People.[66] Indeed, the inspiration and motivation of Jewish leaders to care for Hashem's nation with so much love and kindness comes from seeing how Hashem Himself does this.[67] Therefore, it is appropriate that this same phrase is used here. The leaders seek to emulate Hashem.

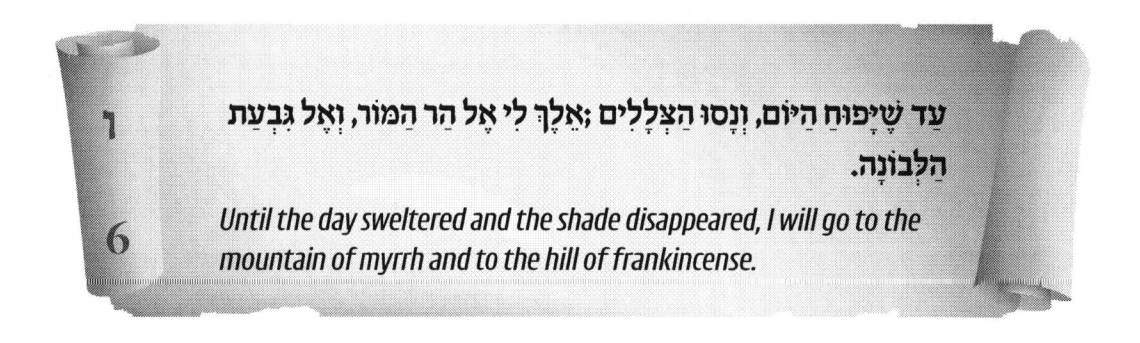

> **6** עַד שֶׁיָּפוּחַ הַיּוֹם, וְנָסוּ הַצְּלָלִים; אֵלֶךְ לִי אֶל הַר הַמּוֹר, וְאֶל גִּבְעַת הַלְּבוֹנָה.
>
> Until the day sweltered and the shade disappeared, I will go to the mountain of myrrh and to the hill of frankincense.

Allegorical Translation — Continuing to speak to *Klal Yisrael*, Hashem says: "You had all this greatness until you sinned in the Mishkan in Shilo. I thus decided to leave Shilo and chose to dwell with you in the Beis HaMikdash where I could regenerate our loving relationship."

Subject of the Verse — Hashem is declaring His desire to save His loving relationship with *Klal Yisrael*.

Mashal — Continuing to display his love to his wife, the husband says: "Your beauty lasted until the sweltering heat of the day when the cooling shades disappeared. I will therefore go with you to a more pleasant place filled with sweet-smelling plants. There we can continue to enjoy each other's company in a more pleasant

---

65 To use a contemporary analogy, let us imagine setting up an elegant banquet. All the plates and food one sets out are all for the sake of nourishment, but the flowers put on the table are there to enhance the pleasant atmosphere. In a loosely similar way, this verse, alluding to our leaders' nursing "breasts," adds the detail of the roses. This teaches that not only must a leader nourish his flock, but he must do so in a pleasant manner. A leader who feels that it is enough to tell off his erring flock, and just "tell it as it is," is unwisely not "grazing [them] among the roses."

66 This phrase is explained in more detail there. The explanation is equally applicable here.

67 *Chazal* teach us that we should emulate Hashem. Just as Hashem is merciful, so we should be merciful, just as He visits the sick, so we should visit the sick, etc. (*Sotah* 14a).

environment and renew our love."

In this verse, the husband is actually recalling the time he found his wife to be unpleasant because she behaved badly toward him. Out of love for her, however, he does not blame her for the unpleasantness, but rather blames the heat and lack of shade. The husband wants to be comfortable with his wife whom he loves, so he goes to look for a more congenial environment so that there he will find her pleasant.

Nimshal In this verse, Hashem alludes to a time that *Klal Yisrael* sinned, thus becoming less beautiful in His eyes.[68] In Shilo, Chofni and Pinchas, the two sons of the nation's leader Eli, treated the *korbanos* with a certain lack of respect. This caused the entire nation to become indifferent to the Divine service in the Mishkan.[69] But because of Hashem's love for them, their sins are not viewed as the nation's fault, but rather more indirectly as a changing circumstance which brought about the necessity for changing the relationship. Heat, in this context, is symbolic of discomfort. Thus, when the nation sins, Hashem is not "comfortable" with us. Shade is symbolic of protection. Thus, when the nation sins, Hashem no longer protects them, resulting in a lack of shade. When this happens, Hashem chooses to find a different place where it will be more pleasant to be with *Klal Yisrael*. Hashem goes to "the mountain," where it is cooler and where the beautiful smells of nature fill the air. The mountain here is an allusion to Mount Moriah, the Temple Mount, upon which the Beis HaMikdash was built.[70] It is the place where our forefathers served Hashem. It is the place where Avraham brought up his son Yitzchak to be a sacrifice, at Hashem's command, before Hashem revealed that this was only a test of Avraham's devotion. It is the place where Yaakov prayed to Hashem and offered *korbanos*. Since it is a place saturated with such great merit for the Jewish People as a result of the dedication of our forefathers, the lovely fragrance of their good deeds makes it a pleasure for Hashem to be there with us once again. Furthermore, because it is a place with such holiness and such wonderfully uplifting memories, *Klal Yisrael* will be influenced to behave better and stop sinning. Then, indeed, it will be more pleasurable for Hashem to be with us.

On a very mundane level, this would be like a couple struggling with their

---

68   The first half of this verse is a repetition of an earlier verse 2:17. See our commentary there.
69   See *Yoma* 9a, with the Netziv.
70   Alternatively, the allusion here is to Har Sinai (See Tosafos, *Ta'anis* 16a, *s.v. har*).

marriage going to a place where they once had very good times together, or where they made promises of love to each other. Going there and recalling their wonderful past will stimulate them to rebuild their relationship.

UNTIL THE DAY SWELTERED...

In this verse, which very delicately refers to the times when we sin, we see Hashem's overwhelming love. Hashem does not criticize us or say that He finds us unpleasant to be with. Rather, He says that the day got hot (blaming the discomfort on an outside influence) and made things unpleasant. Instead of Hashem rejecting us because it is now unpleasant to be with us, He seeks a change of venue, where memories of our merits are aroused and where we will be more pleasing to Him.[71]

UNTIL THE DAY SWELTERED...

The *Zohar* provides us a very different understanding of this verse: "[I, Hashem, am waiting] until the day blows away [all the merits of the nations], and their protective shade disappears. [Then] I will go to the mountain of the Beis HaMikdash which is full] of myrrh and frankincense [because the *ketores* is burned there]."

In other words, the heathen nations who enslave us have some merits and therefore cannot be eliminated. But as they continue to sin and receive the reward coming to them for the few merits they have earned, the time will eventually come when all their merits will have been rewarded, leaving only empty chaff. This will be easily blown away, like stalks of wheat without the inner kernels of grain. Then their protection ("shade") will be gone. Only then will the Final Redemption arrive, and Hashem will be free, *ki'veyachol*, to return with the Jewish People to the mountain of myrrh (Beis HaMikdash) where the sweet smells of *ketores* will be everywhere. The *Zohar* concludes that this is like a husband who says to his wife: wait for me to finish dealing with all the strangers, and then I will be able to devote myself exclusively to you. So, too, Hashem says to *Klal Yisrael*: wait until the right time when I will be able to seclude Myself with you in the Beis HaMikdash — to the exclusion of all others.

---

71   We must learn from this and try to emulate Hashem in how we conduct ourselves in this situation. If we find it unpleasant to be with someone, we should blame the circumstances and not the person. We should look for places so pleasant that they will help make all meetings there enjoyable, regardless of whom we are with. This approach is equally applicable in a marital context as well. If a husband comes home and finds his wife very irritable, instead of becoming upset and critical, he should say something like: "You appear to be unwell (or overworked). Let us go on a holiday (or walk) together."

SHIR HASHIRIM 4:7

> כֻּלָּךְ יָפָה רַעְיָתִי, וּמוּם אֵין בָּךְ.
>
> You are perfectly beautiful, My beloved one; and there is no blemish in you.
>
> **7**

Allegorical Translation — Hashem says to *Klal Yisrael*: "There [in the Beis HaMikdash], where I will go with you, I will find you perfect in all your deeds,[72] free of all sin."

Subject of the Verse — Hashem is praising the beauty of *Klal Yisrael*.

Mashal — Continuing to praise his wife, the husband says: "You are perfectly beautiful, my beloved one — without a blemish."

Nimshal — In this verse, Hashem declares how beautiful he finds *Klal Yisrael*. Once all the unpleasant distractions have been taken care of (as mentioned in the previous verse), and after going to a place where *Klal Yisrael* is more pleasing, Hashem declares without any reservations that He finds *Klal Yisrael* beautiful and without fault. Let us imagine how we would feel if we heard these words directly from Hashem! What a warm feeling and pleasant glow would suffuse us, hearing that Hashem finds His people absolutely perfect. Metzudas Dovid points out that in order to declare something as perfect, one has to see the whole thing and also check every aspect of it. If so, this means that Hashem checked us out thoroughly, inside and out, and found us to be perfect.

Imagine if a husband would tell his wife that she is perfect in every way — externally, internally, spiritually, intellectually, emotionally, in her conduct,

---

72. Rashi explains that *kuleich* ("all of you") refers to *all* of your (*Klal Yisrael*'s) sacrifices and deeds. Alternatively, it means that "*all* of you" is beautiful. That is to say, "beautiful in every way" — perfectly beautiful.

The Rinas Dodim understands that *kuleich* ("all of you") refers to all of *Klal Yisrael* together, i.e., when they are all together. The beauty of *Klal Yisrael* is that they are all together in unity. He draws on the Midrash (*Bereishis Rabbah* 38:6) which expounds on the verse in *Hoshea*: "Efraim is attached to idols. Leave him alone" (4:17). On the simple level, this means that *Klal Yisrael* was so attached to idol worship at that time that there was no point in rebuking them. The Midrash, however, explains that when *Klal Yisrael* is as one, i.e., the people (of Efraim) are attached to one another — even when they serve idols — Hashem does not punish them. This, then, is the way to read our verse, says the Rinas Dodim: "Because you are all together in unity, you are beautiful, My beloved one; and there is no blemish in you." Hashem is saying: "When you have the beauty of being all together in unity, then even when you sin, I [Hashem] ignore your blemishes and consider you beautiful." This is a very powerful source for the importance of unity in *Klal Yisrael*.

Still another way to understand our verse is this: "All of you together (*kuleich*) in one combination are beautiful." The Jewish People is like a puzzle. Each piece on its own is not very special, but when they are all combined together, they are beautiful.

past actions, and *middos*, etc. — and would actually feel that way about her! How complimented and loved his wife would feel!

Since the verse is cast in the singular, we are to understand that every single Jewish person is beloved by Hashem. To each one individually, Hashem declares: "You are perfectly beautiful, My beloved one; and there is no blemish in you."

YOU ARE PERFECTLY BEAUTIFUL...

These loving words should stimulate us to feel tremendous joy and love. Any further explication, however insightful, runs the risk of diminishing the wonderful feeling this verse should evoke in us.[73] Let us suffice with an analogy from the *Zohar*.

The *Zohar* tells us that the *esrog* symbolizes the Jewish People.[74] Now, when we select an *esrog* for Sukkos, we examine it extremely carefully. We invest a great deal of time, money, and effort to make sure that our esrog is absolutely clean and prefect, preferably, without even the smallest black dot. As we search for a beautiful *esrog*, we should also be thinking about how this symbolizes Hashem viewing us as clean and without blemish. What a wonderful thought to keep in mind when we check an *esrog*, or see others searching for a nice *esrog*, or lovingly carrying their precious *esrogim* to shul. We are Hashem's perfect and beautiful *esrog*!

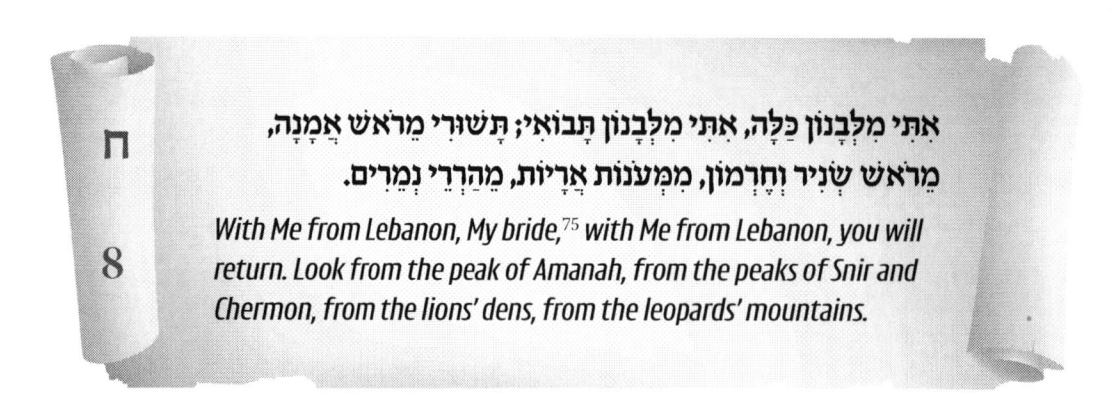

ח
8

אִתִּי מִלְּבָנוֹן כַּלָּה, אִתִּי מִלְּבָנוֹן תָּבוֹאִי; תָּשׁוּרִי מֵרֹאשׁ אֲמָנָה, מֵרֹאשׁ שְׂנִיר וְחֶרְמוֹן, מִמְּעֹנוֹת אֲרָיוֹת, מֵהַרְרֵי נְמֵרִים.

With Me from Lebanon, My bride,[75] with Me from Lebanon, you will return. Look from the peak of Amanah, from the peaks of Snir and Chermon, from the lions' dens, from the leopards' mountains.

---

73 In general, one must be careful not to get so caught up in analyzing a verse that its main message and emotion are lost in the process.

74 *Parashas Emor*. An *esrog* is shaped something like a heart. *Klal Yisrael* is the heart of the entire world, pumping life into it.

75 We have translated the word *kallah* in the conventional way as "bride." It is noteworthy, however, that the Metzudas Dovid understands the word as "all-encompassing" (i.e., having all the good qualities) related to the word *kellulah*. Hashem endearingly describes *Klal Yisrael* as the nation that is "all-encompassing" because they have within them all forms of beauty, greatness, and perfection. This is a very beautiful endearment.

Allegorical Translation Hashem tells *Klal Yisrael*: "Even when you go into exile, I will go with you, and I will remain with you until you come back to Eretz Yisrael. When I gather you in from exile, you will see and understand the great reward that you are receiving for the faith you placed in Me right at the outset: by following Me into the desert after leaving Egypt,[76] and then to a place of harsh mountains controlled by powerful kings. The latter are likened to lions in their dens and leopards on their mountains."[77]

Alternative Allegorical Translation Hashem tells *Klal Yisrael*: "Even when you go into exile, I will accompany you and I will remain with you until you come back to Eretz Yisrael. On your way back to Eretz Yisrael, you will begin singing from the tops of the mountains of Amanah, Snir, and Chermon. This is because you will already be able to see the beautiful land of Eretz Yisrael from there, having escaped terrible exiles under powerful rulers, which are likened to lions' dens and leopards' mountains."

Subject of the Verse Hashem is praising and reassuring *Klal Yisrael*.

Mashal Although the husband has taken his wife to a beautiful place and found her pleasing (as described in the previous two verses), he is aware that they will not remain there forever. He thus reassures his wife regarding what will happen afterwards: even when you will have to leave this beautiful place, I will always accompany you and protect you — even when you are in dangerous places such as high mountains or lions' dens — until we reach safety.

Nimshal To understand how this verse connects with the preceding ones, let us recall the context. In the previous verses, Hashem speaks of His love for *Klal Yisrael*; He speaks of how, when they sinned, He took them to a better place (the Beis HaMikdash) where He could, as it were, enjoy their company fully. Then, in the next verse, Hashem describes how beautiful they are in this new place. Here in this verse (v. 8), Hashem is addressing His beloved *Klal Yisrael* whom He has brought to the Beis HaMikdash. He foresees that *Klal Yisrael* will sin and be driven into exile — and the Beis HaMikdash destroyed. He now reassures them that even when this happens, all will not be lost. Hashem says: "With Me from Levanon, My bride, with Me from Levanon you will come." Levanon (from the root meaning "white") is an appellation for the Beis HaMikdash. It was called thus

---

76 See our discussion of this great act in connection with 1:4.

77 This means that the reward for our great act of faith in following Hashem into the desert will not be fully given until the Final Redemption. At that time, we will see and understand just how great Hashem's reward is for those who put their faith in Him.

because the Beis HaMikdash would whiten and clean all the sins of *Klal Yisrael*.[78] If we understand how terrible a sin is and how damaging its outcome, we will appreciate what a tremendous joy it is when a sin is forgiven. There is no greater praise for the Beis HaMikdash than that it "whitens the sins" of *Klal Yisrael*.[79]

Alternatively, "Levanon" is a reference to a famous, huge, beautiful, and majestic forest which dominated the landscape. It is used here as a symbol for the Beis HaMikdash, which was a renowned, majestic, and beautiful structure that could be seen from the distance.[80] According to both interpretations, Hashem is promising that when we have to leave the Beis HaMikdash ("Levanon") and go into exile, He will be with us.[81]

This verse, then, is to be understood as follows: "Together with Me [i.e., *Klal Yisrael* together with Hashem, will go into exile] from Levanon [Beis HaMikdash], My bride, together with Me, [we will go into exile] from Levanon.[82] You will return [back to the Beis HaMikdash when it is rebuilt]."[83] In other words, Hashem will remain with us right through the exile, and not leave us until we are safely back.

The second part of the verse alludes either to the reason why Hashem will

---

78 *Yoma* 39b.

79 If this does not fully register with us, we must invest some serious thought regarding the gravity of sin and regarding the great kindness Hashem does when He grants forgiveness for sin. After all, a sin is worse than any illness. If there were a hospital in which all illnesses could be completely cured, its great reputation would be known around the world. In a loosely similar way — but on a much greater scale — the Beis HaMikdash was renowned for atoning for sins.
It is noteworthy that in the Haggadah, following *Dayeinu*, when we list all of the great kindnesses that Hashem has done for us, from taking us out of Egypt all the way to building the Beis HaMikdash, we conclude: "to atone for all our sins." Giving us a way to have our sins forgiven is the pinnacle of Hashem's kindness. (See *Tehillim* 48:3 with commentaries, and *Midrash Rabbah, Shemos* 36:1.)

80 *Sifri, Devarim* 6.

81 *Chazal* tell us that when the Babylonians counted their Jewish captives to make sure that none had escaped, they were always puzzled to find the number one more than they expected. *Klal Yisrael*, however, understood this to be a sign from Hashem that He was with them. This was a very tangible way of Hashem displaying His love and concern for them. This phenomenon is reflected in "*Baruch Hashem Yom Yom*," one of *zemiros* that we sing Shabbos morning: "להוריד בריחים נמנה בינימו" — when the Jewish captives went down in ships (to Babylonia), He was counted among them (*Ma'agal HaShanah*, pp. 236-237).

82 A repetition of the previous statement to emphasize that this will indeed be the case. Divrei Yedidyah adds that the repetition hints that Hashem will go into exile with us twice: after the destruction of the First and the Second Beis HaMikdash.

83 Divrei Yedidyah points out that the words, "אתי מלבנון — with Me [you will go into exile] from Levanon," are repeated twice, but the word "תבואי" ("you will return") is not repeated. He sees this as a hint that while Hashem accompanied us into exile twice, He did not return with us twice. Because part of the nation did not return to the Second Beis HaMikdash, Hashem, *ki'veyachol*, chose to remain in exile as well. He will, however, "return" at the time of the Final Redemption. (See similar approach in Maharsha on *Megillah* 29a.)

protect us — the merit of the faith *Klal Yisrael* placed in Hashem when they followed Him into the desert after the Exodus[84] — or to the song that will burst from the lips of those returning from exile upon seeing Eretz Yisrael from atop the mountains of Amanah,[85] Snir, and Chermon.[86]

MY BRIDE

Even though *Klal Yisrael* has been likened to a wife numerous times in this megillah, now they are called a "bride." This term brings to mind the extra, special kind of love felt by a new couple just after their wedding. It is a time when the relationship is exciting, both bride and groom are still completely enthralled with one another, (presumably) no disagreements have yet occurred, etc. In this verse, we are taught that Hashem always harbors this special love, and these feelings, for the Jewish People.

The Netziv points out that there are special laws governing how a husband has to relate to his wife during the week of *sheva berachos*. First of all, he is not allowed to leave her to go to work, etc.[87] Second of all, he must hold parties to celebrate. (Nowadays, family members usually arrange this, but the strict halachah is that the obligation falls on the husband, and he cannot say to his wife: "Let us not bother celebrating our wedding.")[88] Finally, even though a wife is obligated to perform certain tasks for her husband,[89] she is exempt from these obligations during the week of *sheva berachos*. When Shlomo HaMelech describes how Hashem refers to *Klal Yisrael* as His bride, he is hoping and praying that these arrangements will be in place. That is to say, we hope that Hashem will not leave us even for a moment despite His other "commitments," *ki'veyachol*. We hope that He celebrates His marriage to us with joy. And we hope that even if we do not fulfill all of our obligations to Him, Hashem will love us nonetheless, and that we will not have to suffer any hardships as a result – like a bride who is taken care off by her *chassan* without having to work hard. Indeed, the *Navi* teaches us that

---

84 According to Rashi's first explanation.

85 Rabbi Chaim Kanievsky offers a beautiful explanation of why they will begin singing from that particular mountain top. The Gemara tells us that when great rabbis from abroad would come to Eretz Yisrael or leave Eretz Yisrael, the rabbis of Eretz Yisrael would greet them or take their leave of them in the border city of Akko. They wanted to avoid leaving leave Eretz Yisrael unnecessarily (*Gittin* 76b). In a similar way, when Mashiach will gather all the exiles from around the world, all those in Eretz Yisrael will come to greet them at the mountain of Amanah, also located at the border. When everyone meets at the border, the singing will begin so that everyone can join in. Furthermore, this is when the true joy will be felt because we will finally all be together. Hence, the singing will take place on top of this mountain.

86 According to Rashi's second explanation.

87 *Shulchan Aruch, Even Ha'ezer* 64:1.

88 Ibid 64:4.

89 As enumerated in the Gemara (*Kesubos* 59b).

when Mashiach comes, Hashem will rejoice over us like a *chassan* with his *kallah*[90] — in the special manner described above. May it happen very soon…in our lifetime!

LOOK FROM THE TOP OF AMANAH

As we saw above, Rashi offers two different ways of understanding the words, "*tashuri mei'rosh amanah*" in our verse. Here is the first way, word by word: *tashuri* (you will see);[91] *mei'rosh* (from the first, as in *rosh* means head/first); *amanah* (faith as in *emunah*). This means: You will see and understand the reward for that first act of faith. As the verse goes on to describe, that first act of faith was *Klal Yisrael*'s willingness to follow Hashem into the harsh desert after they left Egypt.

Rashi's second way of understanding these words is as follows: *tashuri* (you will sing — *shirah* is a song), *mei'rosh* (from the top), *amanah* (Amanah Mountain). This means: You will sing (at the Final Redemption) from the mountaintop of Amanah. As the rest of the verse indicates, this will be a song of joy and relief for having been redeemed from the harshness and horror of exile.

The Vilna Gaon combines parts of these two explanations. Understanding "*tashuri*" as "singing" and "*mei'rosh amanah*" as "head [beginning] of faith," he explains that a person who has true faith is constantly singing to Hashem. This is what happened at the splitting of the Reed Sea. The Torah tells us that *Klal Yisrael* had faith in Hashem and then immediately goes on to say that they all sang to Him.[92] The verse teaches us that the acquisition of faith engenders "song" from the very beginning. This gives us a glimpse of the life of true joy lived by those who believe in Hashem.[93]

Our verse can also be understood another way: You will sing (*tashuri*) for that which you had only faith at the outset (*mei'rosh amanah*). These words point to the fact that throughout our bitter exile, many events occur which we do not understand. All we have is faith that Hashem is in charge and that everything He does is for the good. When Mashiach comes and we understand all events and how good they were, we will sing about them. Even the events which seemed bad — and which we endured only through our faith[94] — will then be seen as good. They will be a cause for such joy that they will prompt us to sing.

---

90 *Yeshayahu* 62:5.

91 Similar to *ashurenu* ("I see him") in *Bamidbar* 24:17.

92 *Shemos* 14:31 - 15:1.

93 The *Shelah HaKodosh* (*Parashas Beshalach*) translates "*tashuri mei'rosh*" as "singing before (i.e., before the miraculous redemption)" and "*amanah*" as "faith." He explains that those who have faith are able to sing and praise Hashem before miracles happen because of their confidence in Hashem's salvation.

94 *Shiras Dovid*.

> לִבַּבְתִּנִי, אֲחֹתִי כַלָּה; לִבַּבְתִּנִי בְּאַחַת (באחד כתיב) מֵעֵינַיִךְ, בְּאַחַד עֲנָק מִצַּוְּרֹנָיִךְ. **ט**
>
> *You have captured My heart, My sister, [My] bride; you have captured My heart with [just] one of your eyes,[95] with [just] one bead of your necklace!* **9**

Allegorical Translation — Hashem says to *Klal Yisrael*: "You have drawn My heart to you whom I love, as to My sister and to My bride.[96] "You have drawn Me to you with even just one of your good features or good aspects of your conduct.

Subject of the Verse — Hashem is praising *Klal Yisrael*.

Mashal — Praising his wife, the husband says to her: "You are the one who I love like my sister and like a new bride. You made me fall in love with you and captured my heart, with just one of your eyes, with one part of your necklace." The husband declares that even one eye or one bead of her necklace would be enough to make her beloved in his eyes. The one eye or one bead is symbolic of one aspect of her beauty or greatness. This means that not only is she perfect as a whole, as he said earlier,[97] but each individual feature is so wonderful that it would capture his heart even if it would be her only good point. And all the more so is he smitten when she possesses so many worthy attributes.

Nimshal — Adding to His lavish praise of *Klal Yisrael* taken as a whole (in v. 7), Hashem now says that each individual feature of *Klal Yisrael* is so wonderful that it

---

95 This verse communicates how Hashem loves *Klal Yisrael* for even just one of their eyes. (See our commentary on this.) Understanding the verse literally, the Talmud Yerushalmi comments that modest women would cover themselves completely when going outside and would reveal only one eye (*Shabbos* 8:3). This very high level of modesty was very attractive to Hashem, and that is what prompts His exclamation: "You have captured my heart (when you reveal only) one of your eyes." It should be noted, as Rashi points out (*Shabbos* 80a, *s.v. be'ironios*), that in many places this was not the accepted norm, and a woman should conduct herself according to the standard of modesty in her locale.
We see how much Hashem loves modesty. Based on this verse, we would add that every individual has a choice either one can try to attract the attention of someone of the opposite gender through immodesty, *chas v'shalom*, or to attract Hashem's love and attention through modesty. Only a fool would choose fleeting and superficial attention over the boundless and limitless love of Hashem.

96 The Avodas Gershuni explains that a person feels a closeness to his wife due to the relationship they have developed, and a closeness to his sister simply because of their family connection, without any personal effort. Hashem loves *Klal Yisrael* so much because they enjoy both a relationship based on "kinship" as well as a relationship that they have built together.

97 Verse 7.

causes Him to love them and be completely drawn to them. And how much more so when they possess so many different types of virtue! This is very high praise. One needs to imagine a husband saying this to his wife — and how special she would feel. This is how Hashem "feels" about us.

Hashem's use of the word *libavtini* ("You have captured My heart!") communicates that Hashem is, *ki'veyachol* "overwhelmed" by the love He feels for *Klal Yisrael*. It as if we have somehow captivated Him with our virtues, and He is completely enamored with us. These powerful words of praise should touch us deeply.

WITH ONE OF YOUR EYES

In the Midrash, we find many examples of this concept that Hashem loves us for even one of our virtues, and all the more so for our complete array of virtues. For instance, Hashem says to *Klal Yisrael*: "I would have loved you just for having a forefather named Avraham; I would have loved you just for having a forefather named Yitzchak; and I would have loved you just for having a forefather named Yaakov. How much more so do I love you because you had all three!" Addressing us in another context, Hashem says: "I loved you on account of just one of your righteous *shevatim* (tribes) or righteous kings. How much more so because you had so many!" Addressing us in still another context, Hashem says: "I loved you for saying '*na'aseh*' ('We will do [the mitzvos]'), and even more for saying '*v'nishma*' ('And [only afterwards] we will hear [the explanations]')."

WITH ONE OF YOUR EYES, WITH ONE BEAD OF YOUR NECKLACE

The verse continues: "You have captured My heart with one of your eyes, with one bead of your necklace." Let us consider the most obvious difference between an eye and a bead of a necklace: the former is an actual part of a person, while the latter is just an ornament on the person. Similarly, *Klal Yisrael* is blessed with many unique virtues of their own, e.g., they are merciful, modest, and kind.[98] In addition, they have also been blessed with many wonderful "adornments" throughout history, such as wonderful leaders and peerless forefathers. The verse therefore tells us that *Klal Yisrael*'s specialness lies in one unique virtue of their own or in one of the great assets they have been given.

Chazal teach: "Because Hashem wished to bring merit to the Jewish People, He gave them an abundance of Torah and mitzvos."[99] In commenting on this Mishnah, the Rambam explains that when one performs a mitzvah perfectly — exactly according

---

98 *Yevamos* 79a.
99 *Makkos* 3:16.

to the law and without any ulterior motives — for this act alone, he merits the right to enjoy the World to Come, with all the rewards that go along with it.[100] Different people in different circumstances may find it difficult to perform certain mitzvos correctly. For example, those who are very introverted may find interpersonal mitzvos especially difficult, and those who are poor may find mitzvos requiring a financial outlay to be difficult. Hashem thus gave many different mitzvos so that every Jewish person, in whatever circumstances he finds himself, should be able to observe at least one of the mitzvos properly and thereby merit the World to Come. This, then, is the meaning of the Mishnah: because Hashem wanted to bring merit to the Jewish People, He made many different kinds of mitzvos so that every person will be able to fulfill at least one of them correctly.[101] Hashem does not love only those who are perfect. It is enough that one small aspect of our life is good for Hashem to love us.

By ensuring that there are many different ways in which a Jew can be found pleasing to Him, Hashem makes it easy for us to please Him.[102] This is also an important lesson about how we should behave and feel towards others. There are people who find only those who are kind to be pleasing, or those who are wise, or those who study a lot, etc. But that approach greatly limits one's appreciation of how wonderful all people are. By giving us a wide variety of mitzvos, Hashem was also teaching us that there are many ways for a person to achieve distinction, and thus there are many reasons for us to love and appreciate other people.[103]

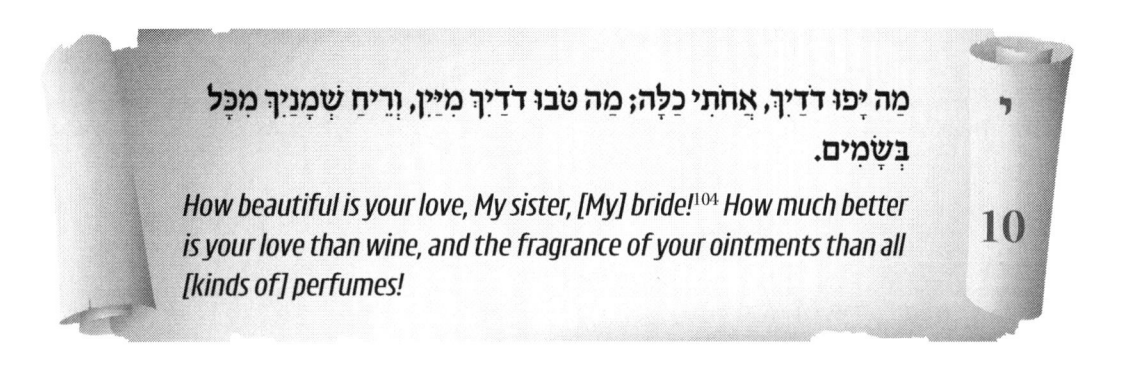

> מַה יָּפוּ דֹדַיִךְ, אֲחֹתִי כַלָּה; מַה טֹּבוּ דֹדַיִךְ מִיַּיִן, וְרֵיחַ שְׁמָנַיִךְ מִכָּל בְּשָׂמִים.
>
> *How beautiful is your love, My sister, [My] bride!*[104] *How much better is your love than wine, and the fragrance of your ointments than all [kinds of] perfumes!*
>
> **10**

---

100 *Peirush HaMishnayos*.

101 We find that there are people who choose to spend their lives concentrating on a specific mitzvah, feeling that this mitzvah is their *tafkid* (unique role), and that they were, so to speak, made for that mitzvah. This approach is based on the concept in this verse that Hashem loves a person for just one aspect (*Ashirah Uzo*). Of course, one needs to be very careful with this approach. Only a great person can decide such a thing, and it obviously does not mean that one can scant all the other mitzvos.

102 *Shiras Dovid*.

103 We see this in Rabbi Chiya's approach to his very difficult wife. He was very kind to her and told his son how grateful he was to her that she looked after their children and saved him from sin (*Yevamos* 63a). Rabbi Chiya managed to find the good aspects of a person who was, superficially, very unpleasant.

104 This expression is used in the previous verse. See our commentary there.

Allegorical Translation — Hashem continues to praise *Klal Yisrael*: "How beautiful is your love! Wherever you display it, I find it pleasurable. How much better[105] is your love than all pleasures[106] and your good name than all other nations."

Subject of the Verse — Hashem is praising *Klal Yisrael*.

Mashal — The husband praises his wife by telling her that the pleasure of her love is more precious to him than all other pleasures: "How beautiful is your love, how much better is your love than wine! The scent of your perfume is more attractive than all other kinds of perfumes."

Nimshal — Hashem praises *Klal Yisrael* by telling them that their love is beautiful, and that it surpasses all other pleasures; and that their good name is nobler than that of all other nations.

HOW BEAUTIFUL IS YOUR LOVE

As we saw above, Rashi interprets the first half of the verse this way: "How beautiful is your love! Wherever you display it, I find it pleasurable." Rashi adds that Hashem is referring to the fact that *Klal Yisrael* displayed their love in many places: in the desert after the Exodus, in the Mishkan in Gilgal, in the Mishkan in Shiloh, and in its subsequent locales, Nov, Givon, etc. In all these places, Hashem found their display of love pleasurable.[107] Indeed, *Klal Yisrael* showed their love for Hashem in many ways, all of which Hashem found pleasing and exciting.

Let us translate this concept into the mundane realm of the *Shir HaShirim* "*mashal*" for a moment. A wife can show her husband how much she loves him in many areas and in many ways. These would include: the way she prepares his food, the way she talks to him, the gifts she gives him, the way she greets him, the way she treats his family, the way she conducts herself on the intimate level, etc. There are many languages of love. Sometimes she will find one language of love in which she is very skilled — and the husband really appreciates — while in others, she struggles. It is unusual that she

---

105 The Netziv notes the two different expressions used in this verse to describe *Klal Yisrael*'s love: "How *beautiful* is your love" and "How much *better* is your love." He explains that something that is beautiful is not necessarily valuable or useful. Many beautiful and attractive things are actually harmful. Conversely, many valuable or useful items are neither beautiful nor attractive. Here, Hashem praises the love of *Klal Yisrael* as being both beautiful and good, i.e., both appealing and valuable.

106 Wine is symbolic of all pleasures (see Rashi on 1:2). Thus, the phrase, "Your love is better than wine," means that *Klal Yisrael*'s love is greater than all physical pleasures.

107 This interpretation is reinforced by the fact that the word for "love" in this verse is in the plural (*dodai'ich*), i.e., multiple displays of loves.

will be able to show her love well in every way. In contrast, Hashem finds every way *Klal Yisrael* show their love to be beautiful, precious, and exciting, so much so that He refers to them all as love from "My sister, My bride." Similarly, every attempt we make to show our love to Hashem is precious to Him.[108] Whether it is through our *Shacharis*, *Minchah*, or *Ma'ariv* prayers; whether it is through our *Pesach*, *Shavuos*, or *Sukkos* observance; whether it is through our *kashrus* or our *tzitzis* and *tefillin*; whether it is through our kindness or Torah study, etc. — Hashem loves all of our efforts to show our love for Him.

HOW BEAUTIFUL IS YOUR LOVE...

In light of the fact that the *gematria* of יין (wine) is seventy, the Rokeiach[109] suggests that wine here in this verse represents the seventy nations of the world. Furthermore, the word *besamim* (בשמים), meaning "perfumes or spices," can also be read *ba'shamayim*, meaning "in the Heavens."[110] Accordingly, the second half of the verse can be understood as follows: "How much better is your love than the love of all seventy nations, and the fragrance of your ointments than (the love of the angels) in the Heavens!" Hashem is thus declaring that His love for *Klal Yisrael* is greater than all the love He has for all the nations or all the angels. In other words, the mitzvos *Klal Yisrael* fulfill are more valuable and precious to Hashem than anything the other nations do and even anything the angels accomplish. At first glance, this explanation may seem forced. But a closer look shows how this fits into the main understanding of the verse.

Wine is a symbol of all earthly pleasures.[111] This is because drinking wine, in ancient times, was people's main entertainment and highest pleasure. By extension, wine is also symbolic of the non-Jewish peoples because one of their main preoccupations is finding ways to indulge themselves. In contrast to wine, nice-smelling spices offer a more spiritual pleasure. Indeed, the Gemara teaches that smelling fragrant spices is the one pleasure in this world that only the soul enjoys, not the body.[112] On Motza'ei Shabbos, we smell spices since the soul is saddened that the additional soul we are endowed with on Shabbos has departed for the week.[113] Furthermore, the only one of the five senses

---

108 In a marriage as well, husband and wife should try to see as appealing every effort by their spouse to display love even if the effort falls short or is not in the language of love that they prefer.

109 In his *Yayin HaRokeiach*.

110 Since the written megillah does not have vowels, a word is sometimes explained as if it has vowels different from the ones dictated by tradition for reading.

111 See Rashi on 1:2.

112 *Berachos* 43b.

113 *Shulchan Aruch, Orach Chaim* 297:1 and *Mishnah Berurah*, from *Beitzah* 16a.

that did not "participate" in the primordial sin of the eating from the fruit of the Tree of Knowledge was the sense of smell.[114] This is why the burning of the *ketores* (special mixture of spices) was the most effective way to stop the Angel of Death,[115] whose powers stemmed from that first sin.[116]

Hashem is thus communicating that He gets more pleasure from *Klal Yisrael* than any earthly pleasures that can be offered by anyone else in this world (symbolized by wine) — more even than all spiritual pleasures which the angels in the next world can offer (symbolized by spices). Now we see how the interpretation of the Rokeiach actually fits into the words of the verse.

Nothing in the upper or lower worlds is as precious as what we, *Klal Yisrael*, "give" to Hashem. This concept is echoed in the special *piyut*, *Asher Tehilasecha*, that we recite on the *Yamim Nora'im*. The *piyut* describes how the angels praise Hashem with such holiness and grandeur, yet Hashem much prefers and desires our praises even though they are puny by comparison. One who meditates on the message of this verse can easily find himself overwhelmed with love for Hashem and joy in Hashem.

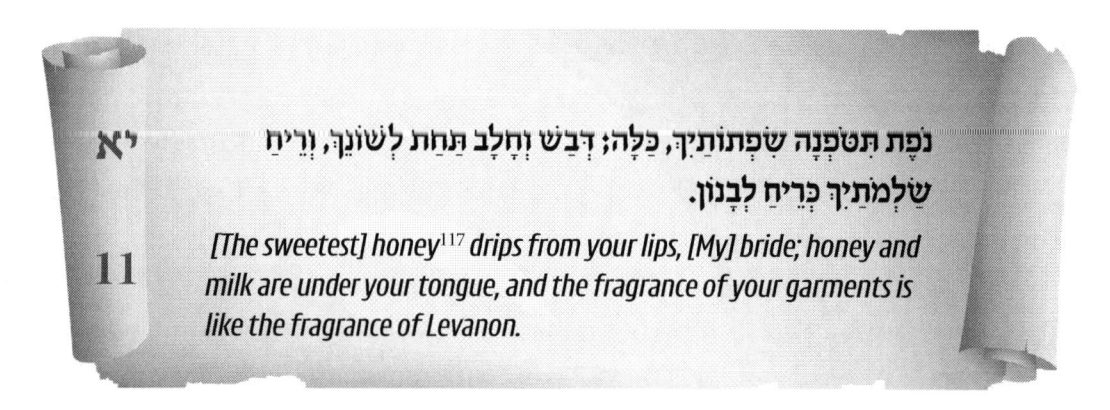

> **יא**
> נֹפֶת תִּטֹּפְנָה שִׂפְתוֹתַיִךְ, כַּלָּה; דְּבַשׁ וְחָלָב תַּחַת לְשׁוֹנֵךְ, וְרֵיחַ שַׂלְמֹתַיִךְ כְּרֵיחַ לְבָנוֹן.
>
> **11** [The sweetest] honey[117] drips from your lips, [My] bride; honey and milk are under your tongue, and the fragrance of your garments is like the fragrance of Levanon.

Allegorical Translation   Hashem praises *Klal Yisrael* by saying to them: "Sweet explanations of Torah

---

114   See *Bereishis* 3:6 with Rashi: Chavah enjoyed *hearing* the words of the snake; the fruit was pleasing to *look* at, and *tasty* to the palate; and the snake caused Chavah to *touch* the tree. But *smell* was not part of the sin.
     Indeed, it is called ריח because it is a spiritual (רוחני) type of pleasure (Aruch Hashulchan Orach Chaim 216:1). Furthermore, Hashem blew a soul into Adam HaRishon through his nostrils (*Bereishis* 2:7), the same orifice used for sensing smell.
     See *Bnei Yissachar* (*Nissan*, *Ma'amar* 4) which adds that the Torah emphasizes "a pleasing smell" in connection with the bringing of sacrifices (*Vayikra* 1:9) because a smell is a spiritual pleasure. The Gemara goes so far as to say that Mashiach will be able to decide a law with his powerful sense of smell (*Sanhedrin* 93b).
     Interestingly on Yom Kippur the most spiritual day of the year - a day free from sin - the minhag is to smell *besamim* (*Mishnah Berurah* 612:18).

115   *Bamidbar* 17:13, with Rashi.

116   *Chazal* speak of the "smell" of Gan Eden (see Rashi on *Bereishis* 27:27).

117   *Nofes*, honey dripping from the honeycomb, is particularly sweet.

drip from your lips, and secrets of Torah are hidden in your mouth. The mitzvos you do with your clothes are precious to Me like the sacrifices in the Beis HaMikdash."[118]

Subject of the Verse — Hashem is praising the beauty of *Klal Yisrael*.

Mashal — The husband praises his wife further: "Even the dribble that drops from your lips is as sweet to me as honey dripping from the honeycomb; and the saliva under your tongue is as dear to me as honey and milk; and the fragrance of your garments (which for others may be smelly or sweaty) is to me like the fragrance of a beautiful forest."

Perhaps we can better understand this perspective by thinking of a mother's response to her baby spitting up. Even if others may be put off by this, the mother still finds her baby to be sweet. So, too, when a person loves another intensely, everything about the loved one is attractive. Indeed, this is the basic idea of this verse.

Nimshal — Hashem loves *Klal Yisrael* with such intensity that everything about them is attractive to Him. This includes everything they say, their deep Torah thoughts, and even the superficial aspects of their beauty. The verse describes how Hashem loves all of *Klal Yisrael* from its most innermost aspect, "under the tongue," to its most external aspect, "clothes."

DRIPS FROM YOUR LIPS

Speech is referred to here as that which drips from the lips. The specific reference is to speech without thought, casual speech which "falls out of" one's mouth.[119] Even that is sweet to Hashem. Normally saliva is off-putting, but from a person whom one loves

---

118 Clothes sometimes symbolize good *middos*. Just as clothes must fit properly, so must a person's *middos* be "made to measure," i.e., fit according to personality and circumstances (*Hilchos Deios* 1:4). The word "*middah*" actually means "measure" (Rashi on *Vayikra* 6:3). Many things can be bought without measuring to see if they fit the person for whom they are being bought (such as food, furniture, books, and crockery). In contrast, clothes need to be bought to measure — similar to *middos* that need to fit the individual.

The Gemara tells us that if a person forgives others for their bad behavior towards them, Hashem will forgive his own bad behavior (*Rosh Hashanah* 17a). Furthermore, if one acts with charity and kindness, Hashem forgives all his sins (*Berachos* 5b). When the Beis HaMikdash stood, it was the place where one could earn forgiveness. But now that we have lost it, how can we be forgiven? Hashem reassures us: "Your clothes" (good *middos*) are precious to Me like the sacrifices in the Beis HaMikdash." Just as the Beis HaMikdash once brought forgiveness, so do good *middos* bring forgiveness to a person (*Divrei Yedidyah*).

119 The expression "lip service," connoting empty promises or meaningless talk, reflects this same idea of words coming from the lips without thought. The Netziv adds that just as spit and dribble that leak out of the mouth are particularly unpleasant, so is speech without thought.

intensely, everything is pleasant. For this reason, Hashem treasures, *ki'veyachol*, the saliva that comes from *Klal Yisrael* who learn His Torah.

In the *nimshal* (the meaning of the parable), the speech being referred to is the words of Torah said casually. Even the casual speech that "drips from the lips" of a real *talmid chacham* teaches a great deal of sweet Torah.[120]

As mentioned in the Introduction, the *mashal* (parable) of *Shir HaShirim* has tremendous depth and importance regarding how to behave in daily life, especially with one's spouse. There is, then, an inherent message here that in a loving relationship, even casual speech must be pleasurable, and the constant communication between spouses must be sweet like honey. Some people make the mistake of thinking that exciting moments and expensive gifts make the relationship, but the reality is that the consistently sweet words and the continuous connection are more important. A child will sometimes remember a casual comment from a parent for years and years. Let us make sure they are all healthy and nourishing.

The verse continues: "Honey and milk are under your tongue." This alludes to words of Torah, speech which comes from a much deeper place, from the hidden recesses of the mouth. This is likened to milk and honey. From a certain standpoint, milk is the most nourishing and beneficial of all foods. Every person is completely dependent on it at the first stage of his/her life. Honey, of course, is a symbol for the ultimate sweetness. Torah which is taught with thought is the most nourishing and the sweetest of all foods for the soul. This verse underscores just how sweet and beneficial Torah is.[121]

The verse closes with praise of "the fragrance of your garments…" Clothes are the most external and superficial aspect of a person's beauty. On the symbolic level, this means that even the most external part of Torah — the simplest meaning, without any depth — is precious to Hashem. That is why the verse emphasizes the "fragrance" of the garments. Fragrance is something which spreads around, and which others can appreciate. Even those not in close contact with a person can smell the nice fragrance from his clothes. Symbolically, this means that even those who are not closely bonded with Torah can appreciate its simple meaning and learn a lot from it. Furthermore, a *talmid*

---

120 As the Gemara says, even the most casual speech of a *talmid chacham* should be studied because it is edifying (*Sukkah* 21b). Many biographies of *gedolim* contain anecdotes showing how a seemingly casual comment from a great Torah leader had tremendous depth and a great impact.

121 There is a *minhag* to eat milk and honey on Shavuos (the day we received the Torah) to remind us of how nourishing and sweet Torah is (*Mishnah Berurah* 494:13). In this vein, the Ohr HaChaim comments: "If people would taste the sweetness and pleasure of Torah, they would be so enthralled with its pleasure that they would pursue it with such fervor that all the gold and silver in the world would be worthless in their eyes…." (*Devarim* 26:8). Indeed, this is what we should be striving for.

chacham should create a good and pleasant atmosphere just as scented clothes spread a nice fragrance around.

HONEY AND MILK ARE UNDER YOUR TONGUE

As noted above, dribble from the lips and saliva "under the tongue" are particularly off-putting. Indeed, the Midrash comments there is no liquid as repellent as liquid one produces while coughing up saliva and mucus from under the tongue. Yet here in our verse, it is likened to the sweetest of foods. This, the Midrash says, teaches us that all Torah, even that which may seem to be distasteful, is truly sweet and pleasurable.[122] Even though certain laws may at first seem off-putting, and certain narratives may at first seem unimportant, the reality is that everything in Torah is both sweet and nourishing.

In light of the fact that the tongue symbolizes speech and teaching, the Midrash also sees in the verse the axiom that when one teaches Torah, one must make sure that the listeners find the Torah sweet and nourishing like honey and milk. This is a tremendous responsibility.[123] As the Midrash concludes, if one is unable to convey the sweetness of Torah, it is better that one does not teach.[124]

HONEY AND MILK ARE UNDER YOUR TONGUE

We are all familiar with the Biblical expression "milk and honey" to describe something sweet or pleasant.[125] But why are milk and honey so often the symbols of sweetness? Let us think for a moment about the origin of these two foods. Honey comes from bees, which sting and which are forbidden to be eaten. Milk comes from parts of the blood.[126] In short, although both milk and honey come from sources that are unappealing (and actually forbidden to be consumed), they are transformed into the most pleasing of

---

122 Rabbi Shimshon Pinkus tells the story of a boy who fell asleep over his (volume of) Gemara while learning Torah on Friday night. When he woke up, he was very upset that he had fallen asleep and that he had slightly damaged his Gemara with saliva that dribbled from his mouth. His mother told him reassuringly: Hashem finds that saliva more precious than any other liquid because it came from the mouth of one who exerted himself to learn Torah. Hashem treasures that saliva and will use it (in some sense) to help revive the dead!" Our verse hints at this outlook of those who truly love Torah.

123 To appreciate the sweetness of Torah, one must have clarity. When one is confused, the true sweetness of the Torah will be lacking. The Vilna Gaon notes in his commentary on *Mishlei* that clarity has been achieved when one is able to properly articulate an idea (*Mishlei* 2:3). When an idea is just floating around one's head, and one is unable to explain it, then it is obviously not very clear. But when one elucidates it for others, or is at least able to do so, he has achieved clarity. According to the Shiras Dovid, our verse hints at this truth: "Sweet explanations of Torah drip from your lips." He understands "drip[ping] from the lips" to mean that the Torah insight has been articulated (with the lips) and explained. It is sweet because it is clear. Clarity brings out the sweetness.

124 This is also learned from the words of the verse "under your tongue." It is best to keep the knowledge hidden under the tongue when one is unable to convey the sweetness and greatness of the Torah.

125 See *Shemos* 3:8, one of many instances.

126 *Bechoros* 6b.

foods. This teaches us that much good can come from that which seems bad to us. Learning Torah can be difficult and can sometimes seem like a major struggle, but so much good comes from it — like honey from bees and milk from blood. The same is true regarding everything that happens to us in life. It all comes from Hashem. Even those occurrences which seem unpleasant and harsh can be transformed into milk and honey if one utilizes them to serve Hashem better. When Hashem praises *Klal Yisrael's* sweetness, He uses metaphors of sweet things which come from unpleasant things to teach us that a lot of good can come from that which we think is bad.[127]

Eretz Yisrael, praised by the Torah as a "land flowing with milk and honey,"[128] also has this unique power to bring forth good from evil. When a terrible war or tragedy occurs, there is suddenly so much unity and kindness in evidence, until the land is flowing with sweetness. Indeed, it is a land in which the harmful and unpleasant give rise to milk and honey.

The Gemara explains the phrase "honey and milk are under your tongue" to mean that sweet, profound Torah ideas are hidden under *Klal Yisrael's* tongue.[129] This is an allusion to certain occult or mystical parts of Torah, such as the knowledge of Hashem's throne and Kabbalah. Even though they are particularly sweet, they are to be kept hidden and not revealed to those who are unworthy of learning them. This is actually more praise of *Klal Yisrael*. Although they know many precious secrets of Torah, they do not flaunt this knowledge. Because of their respect for the Torah, they keep it hidden. For example, the unique name of Hashem was known only to a select few for many, many years. Out of respect for Hashem, it was a closely guarded secret.

THE FRAGRANCE OF YOUR GARMENTS

This verse concludes with praise of *Klal Yisrael's* clothes. Rashi understands this as an allusion to mitzvos connected with clothes, such as *tzitzis*, the special garments of the *Kohanim*, the prohibition against wearing *sha'atnez*, etc. Clothes are connected with our external service of Hashem, but this is no less important than our inner service. Indeed, in some ways it is more important.

This point was driven home by Rabbi Amnon Yitzchak, *shlita*, in response to the following question: "Why should I wear *tzitzis*?! Hashem know what is in my heart, and in

---

[127] This dovetails with the concept that even when *Klal Yisrael* has sinned, they are actually very close to repentance — an act which can turn sins into merits. This is like transforming forbidden blood into permitted milk.

[128] *Shemos* 3:8.

[129] *Chagigah* 13a.

my heart, I love Him!" Now, obviously, this question is based on a number of erroneous assumptions, e.g., that we do mitzvos when we understand them or that we do mitzvos for Hashem's sake. Nonetheless, an answer was needed that spoke to the questioner on his level. And Rabbi Yitzchak provided it. He proceeded to ask the questioner what he does for a living. The person replied that he imports and sells sportswear. "Does the manufacturer's logo appear on all the items?" asked the Rabbi? "Of course! The logos are displayed in every place possible, and we spend huge sums of money branding our products!" he replied. "But surely it is enough to tell people that it is better quality and provide documentation that identifies the manufacturer?!" countered the Rabbi. "People want to display what they are wearing, and be proud of it," answered the importer. "We too," said Rabbi Yitzchak, "should wear our *tzitzis* out to show that we are proud of who we are!" We must display our "logos" in every way we can and in every way possible. We must wish to express our joy and pride in our identity and this is part of the preciousness of the mitzvos we do with our clothes.

THE SWEETEST HONEY DRIPS FROM YOUR LIPS

The Netziv interprets the entire verse as being about prayer. Unfortunately, sometimes prayer is said without *kavanah* (thought and concentration). Although words spoken without thought are generally off-putting, Hashem still considers our rote prayer to be "particularly sweet honey drip[ping] from [our] lips." Even prayer that drips mindlessly from a person's lips (as explained earlier the symbol of that which "drips from the lips" refers to speech without thought which "falls out of" one's mouth) is sweet to Hashem because the person at least wanted to pray. The verse continues, "Honey and milk are under your tongue." This alludes to prayer *with* proper intent — with *kavanah*. "Under the tongue" is the deeper place within a person from which genuine, heartfelt prayer emanates. That is likened to milk and honey. It is not just sweet, but it also nourishes and sustains a person like milk.

The verse concludes: "The fragrance of your garments is like the fragrance of Levanon [the Beis HaMikdash]." The Netziv points out that the word for "garments" used here, *salmosai'ich*, denotes clothes that cover the entire body like a cloak.[130] This alludes to our shuls, which envelop the entire congregation. Just as a cloak wraps around the entire body, so a shul encompasses the entire community. When everyone in the community goes to the same shul to serve Hashem, Hashem finds the "fragrance" as

---

130 The more common word for "clothes" is *begadim*.

pleasing as the smell that emanated from the Beis HaMikdash. As Hashem puts it, "The fragrance of your garments is like the fragrance of Levanon [the Beis HaMikdash]."[131]

Hashem finds our shuls very pleasing, and likens them to the Beis HaMikdash, as long as they are places that truly encompass the entire community and are not places of conflict. Therefore, we should relate to our shuls with tremendous reverence and respect, as we would the Beis HaMikdash. If we do, we will surely be privileged to serve Hashem in the Beis HaMikdash as well.

THE SWEETEST HONEY DRIPS FROM YOUR LIPS

The Vilna Gaon explains that the four substances mentioned in this verse (the sweetest honey, honey, milk and clothes) allude to the four basic levels of understanding Torah: *sod* (the secrets), *remez* (the hints), *derash* (the analysis), and *peshat* (the simple meaning). "The sweetest honey"[132] alludes to *sod*, the secrets of the Torah, which are particularly sweet. "Honey" alludes to *remez*, the hints of the Torah, which are sweet like honey. "Milk" alludes to *derash*, the analysis, which is the most nourishing part of Torah. "Clothes" alludes to *peshat*, the Torah's simple meaning, which is its external cover. The seemingly simple symbolism identified by the Vilna Gaon actually reveals a great deal about the four ways of learning Torah. A careful review of the various interpretations of the verse cited above will reveal how the explanation of the Vilna Gaon encapsulates many of these messages of this verse.

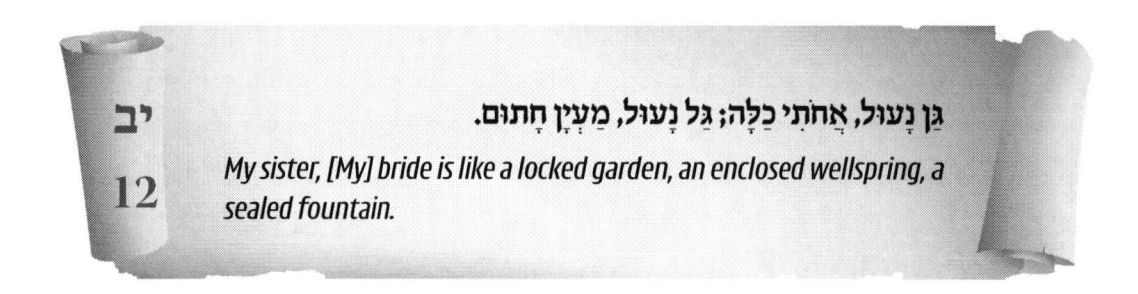

יב
12
גַּן נָעוּל, אֲחֹתִי כַלָּה; גַּל נָעוּל, מַעְיָן חָתוּם.
My sister, [My] bride is like a locked garden, an enclosed wellspring, a sealed fountain.

Allegorical Translation — Hashem praises the modesty of *Klal Yisrael*: "Jewish girls are modest and keep themselves secluded like a locked garden, an enclosed spring,[133] and a sealed fountain."

Subject of the Verse — Hashem is praising the modesty of *Klal Yisrael*.

Mashal — The husband praises his wife for her modesty in keeping herself closed off from

---

131 As explained earlier, in connection with verse 8.
132 See note on the honey (*nofes*) that "drips from [the] lips" on the translation of the verse above.
133 Rashi offers an alternative translation: a locked gate.

other men like a locked garden, an enclosed spring and a sealed fountain.

The "locked garden" image prompts us to imagine an extremely beautiful garden filled with the most precious roses and other flowers; and how the owner secures it so that no strangers or animals trample on it. Similarly, a marital relationship is to be kept safe and modestly hidden, a private affair between husband and wife.

Nimshal As is clear from the allegorical translation above, this verse alludes to the outstanding modesty of *Klal Yisrael*. As such, this verse will be explained in a guarded manner due to the sensitivity of the topic. The three metaphors used here — locked garden, enclosed spring, and sealed fountain — relate, in order of appearance, to the modesty of married women, unmarried girls, and men. The order follows the level of stringency required by the laws of modesty, from highest to lowest. The fact that these laws cover all three groups points to the greatness of *Klal Yisrael*. Not only are married women expected to be modest, but so are unmarried women, who have less of a reason to be modest since they need to find a husband. And even men, whose responsibility for modesty is less, are expected to safeguard their modesty.

A "locked garden" is closed to all except the owner. This symbolizes a married woman, who keeps herself very beautiful, like a garden, but is inaccessible to all except her husband. A spring is usually ownerless and accessible to all, but when it is enclosed, no one can get pleasure from it. Similarly, an unmarried girl is potentially available to any man, but until she is actually married, a Jewish girl makes sure that no man takes his pleasure from her.[134] A fountain is a public display of liquid spouting forth. This symbolizes a man for two reasons. Firstly, a man is permitted to be — and sometimes must be — in the public eye. Secondly, both from a physical and spiritual standpoint, a man is external like a fountain. He contributes to the continuity of the world by propagating in an outward manner. In contrast, a woman exerts her influence by developing and building an inner sanctuary — in her body, in her life, and in her home. A "sealed fountain" is not blocked off, but rather guarded and locked. This means that a man must make sure to guard himself from going forth into areas and places which should be sealed off from him.

---

134 According to Rashi's alternative translation, "locked gate," the allusion is to the *besulim* (hymen) which is like a gate. Jewish girls are being praised for utilizing the natural gate which Hashem created to maintain their modesty before marriage.

An alternate approach to these metaphors is that they allude to the three aspects of the great modesty in Jewish married life: 1) Husband and wife do not display their physical love publicly; 2) Others are out of bounds; 3) Even the husband and wife themselves stay apart during certain times of the month. A "locked garden" is a beautiful place, but totally private. Similarly, when a couple wish to show affection for one another and enjoy their garden of love, they should do so only in private. An "enclosed spring" communicates that for everyone else, they are "enclosed" and out of bounds.[135] A "sealed fountain" can be opened and closed. A seal is a kind of lock that can be opened and closed. Similarly, there are certain times of the month when husband and wife must be "closed" to one another (due to menstruation), and certain times when they are open and available to one another. According to this approach, the fountain is symbolic of the flow of menstrual blood.[136]

So much for an understanding of the metaphors in this verse. The bottom line is *Klal Yisrael*'s greatness is in their unrivalled modesty, in observing family purity and not straying into other relationships. Indeed, *Klal Yisrael* has always been renowned for their tremendous modesty. It is one of trademarks of being a Jew[137] and one of the areas in which the difference between Jews and other nations is so pronounced. Even Bilaam noticed this and praised *Klal Yisrael* for it.[138] For being so modest and for observing all these laws, *Klal Yisrael* is praised in this verse.

A LOCKED GARDEN

There is a very important message from this verse. Modesty actually applies in two distinct areas. We have been discussing modesty in the relationship between men and women, both before marriage and during marriage. But modesty is also necessary in the bathroom: when relieving oneself, etc. These two areas of modesty should not be conflated. Even though laws of modesty apply in both, they are completely different in essence. Modesty in the bathroom derives from a feeling of shame that one has such

---

135 Still, they are like a spring from which flows water that is beneficial to all. Similarly, they benefit the world with the kindness that flows from them. Only at its source is this "spring" enclosed, i.e., strangers cannot become too close to their inner world. When a marriage is secure, the entire world benefits. But when a marriage is too open, no one benefits. Furthermore, the marriage itself is ruined like a spring contaminated at its source.

136 Indeed, it is the because of the "fountain" that they are sealed. The phrase should thus be understood: "sealed because of the fountain." The Midrash hints at these explanations. See there and *Torah Temimah* on this verse for further elucidation.

137 *Shir HaShirim Rabbah* 1:10.

138 *Bamidbar* 24:5.

lowly needs. In fact, in ancient times, Jews would ask the angels who escorted them not to accompany them into the bathroom because they were embarrassed to have the angels see that they have these bodily needs.[139] The Gemara tells us that one of the reasons Hashem created these needs is to make human beings humble.[140]

The modesty and chastity in the relationship between male and female, however, is not due to this shame. Rather, it has to with the precious nature of the relationship. Indeed, in this verse, the modesty of *Klal Yisrael* is likened to three places of beauty and sources of joy. But because of their beauty and their precious nature, they need to be protected and sealed. In the *Kodesh HaKodashim* (Holy of Holies), the most secluded and holy place in all of *Klal Yisrael*, there were two golden *keruvim* (angel likenesses) in the form of a boy and girl embracing[141] placed on top of the *Aron* (Holy Ark). Now, it would be totally unthinkable that there should be a miniature golden bathroom there because that would be disgrace.[142] But the likeness of a male and female was there in a most pronounced way. This shows us how completely different these two areas of modesty are. These two distinct realms of modesty are sometimes confused and conflated, unfortunately, because some of the relevant laws are similar. Indeed, by using intimacy as a *mashal*, the whole of *Shir HaShirim* teaches us how different this area of modesty is from others.

יג 13	שְׁלָחַיִךְ פַּרְדֵּס רִמּוֹנִים, עִם פְּרִי מְגָדִים; כְּפָרִים, עִם נְרָדִים. *Your arid fields are a pomegranate orchard, with luscious fruits; koffers with spikenard plants.*
יד 14	נֵרְדְּ וְכַרְכֹּם, קָנֶה וְקִנָּמוֹן, עִם כָּל עֲצֵי לְבוֹנָה; מֹר וַאֲהָלוֹת, עִם כָּל רָאשֵׁי בְשָׂמִים. *Spikenard and saffron, spice cane, and cinnamon, with all [kinds of] frankincense trees; myrrh and aloes, with all the choicest spices.*[143]

---

139 See *Berachos* 60b and *Orach Chaim* 3:1. *Chazal* comment that a human being is similar to an angel in three ways, and similar to an animal in three ways. The human being's need to relieve himself is an example of the latter (*Chagigah* 16a).

140 In his arrogant effort to pretend he was a god, Pharaoh tried to deny that he needed to relieve himself. To put him in his place, Hashem arranged that Moshe Rabbeinu would meet him when he went to the Nile secretly to do so (Rashi on *Shemos* 7:15, *s.v. hinei*). See also *Bava Basra* 75a on how Hashem humbled King Chiram, another self-declared god, in a similar way.

141 *Yoma* 54a.

142 See *Yechezkel* 8:16 with Rashi.

143 It is beyond the scope of this *sefer* — and the grasp of the author — to properly identify all of these plants and spices and to elucidate their deeper meaning.

Allegorical Translation **13** Hashem continues His praise of *Klal Yisrael*: "Your little ones are fresh and vigorous, producing good deeds as numerous as the fruit of an orchard. Their good behavior is pleasing and is as desirable as fruit that both tastes and smells good."

14 Hashem finds the good deeds that *Klal Yisrael* do as attractive and pleasing as all the wonderful scents enumerated here.

Subject of the Verses Hashem is praising *Klal Yisrael*.

Mashal After likening his wife to a garden, spring, and fountain (in the previous verse), the husband elaborates: Her garden, spring, and fountain give rise to beautiful plants and fruit from which emanate all the wonderful scents in the world. These plants and fruit are her good deeds, all of which are pleasing and special to him.

Nimshal *Klal Yisrael*'s "garden," "spring," and "fountain" (described in the previous verse) give rise to so many good descendants and so many good deeds — all of which are pleasing to Hashem.

YOUR ARID FIELDS

"Arid fields" at the beginning of the verse alludes to the young of *Klal Yisrael*.[144] Just as an arid field usually does not produce much fruit, so the young are usually unable to fulfill many mitzvos. But Hashem is saying here that *Klal Yisrael*'s "arid fields" are unique in that they produce much "fruit." Despite their youth, they fulfill many precious mitzvos.

The Rinas Dodim and many other commentators understand "arid fields" as an allusion not to the youth but to the simple people in *Klal Yisrael*[145] who are "dried out" in the sense that they seem to lack enthusiasm for Torah and mitzvos. Yet, they too produce much abundant "fruit" in the form of good deeds.

The author of *Ashirah Uzo* points out the depth of the "arid fields" metaphor as it pertains to the youth or the simple. There is nothing intrinsically wrong with an arid field. It has the potential to grow wonderful produce. All it needs is to be properly irrigated. Similarly, the youth or the simple people in *Klal Yisrael* have tremendous potential. If they are carefully cultivated, they will produce all good things.[146] Just as there is no way

---

144 Rashi.

145 In actuality, there is no such thing as a "simple Jew," as this verse and many others demonstrate.

146 *Midrash Rabbah* (*Tzav* 8) tells of an occasion on which Rabbi Yanai disparaged a certain ignoramus. Later, Rabbi Yannai discovered the many merits of this simple Jew, and was overcome with remorse for not appreciating the greatness of every Jew.

to fully grasp how much a field — especially an arid field — is capable of producing, so there is no way to grasp the full potential of a Jew. This verse reminds us that when we see little children or "dried out" Jews, we should not view them only as they are now or belittle their capabilities. No, we should picture their potential and make sure to cultivate them correctly!

YOUR ARID FIELDS...

These verses evoke the beauty of even the simple or the young people of *Klal Yisrael* through the metaphor of fruit. The verses actually allude to three qualities. We are told that they produce many fruits ("pomegranate orchard"[147]), that they are also sweet ("luscious fruits"), and that they are also sweet-smelling ("all the choicest spices").[148] These three qualities allude to three aspects of a Jewish person regardless of how "simple" they may seem. They are filled with a great many good deeds,[149] their conduct is pleasant and "sweet,"[150] and they attract people with their "nice smelling" conduct. Indeed, over the centuries, many non-Jews decided to join our nation after having seen the behavior of "simple" *Yidden*.

WITH ALL THE CHOICEST SPICES

This verse teaches us the insidiousness of the accusation that our laws of modesty limit the acts of kindness done by *Klal Yisrael*. It is based on the misapprehension that because there are barriers to interaction between the genders, there is less friendliness and helpfulness. The distance kept between people of different genders can seem like aloofness to those who are not used to it. But this verse links the "locked garden" and "sealed fountain" (of the previous verse) to the wonderful "fruit" of kindness mentioned here. This plentiful fruit is produced specifically in this very secluded place. Modesty protects the source and keeps the garden safe and the fountains pure, enabling them to produce so much goodness. If the garden is ransacked or the spring compromised by people coming and taking whatever they want, it may seem that more kindness is being spread. But, in the big picture, there is no longer a source of continued goodness. Similarly, if the fortifications of marriage are trampled on and strangers allowed into a couple's private life, the basis of the Jewish home will be destroyed, and there will then

---

147 The pomegranate is always a symbol of the many since it has many seeds; and an orchard, of course, has many, many fruits.

148 *Devash V'Chalav* adds that usually when there is an over-abundance of fruit growing in one place, the sweetness of the fruit is compromised. Here the verse emphasizes that despite the abundance of fruit, they are all luscious and sweet smelling. The symbolism is clear: *Klal Yisrael* produce many good deeds – and they are all precious.

149 See our commentary on 4:3.

150 As the Gemara says, Jews are merciful, bashful, and kind (*Yevamos* 79a).

be no source of kindness. The Jewish home, protected as it is by the walls of modesty, produces and provides unparalleled amounts of kindness. It can do so only because of the strength of the "seals" around it. This connection is reinforced by the continuation of the symbolism from the previous verse.

SPIKENARD AND SAFFRON, SPICE CANE, AND CINNAMON...

Rabbi Elisha Galiko counts twelve different good-smelling fruits and spices in these two verses: 1) pomegranate; 2) luscious fruits; 3) *koffer* 4) spikenard plants; 5) spikenard; 6) saffron; 7) spice cane; 8) cinnamon; 9) frankincense trees; 10) myrrh; 11) aloes; 12) the choicest spices.[151] They symbolize the Twelve Tribes, with each one exuding a different fragrance. Hashem finds them all pleasing, and He treasures them all. Furthermore, when combined together, they produce the most wonderful fragrance that is our nation.

There is a very potent lesson here for all of us. We all have our unique *tafkid*, our unique mission and role in life. Each of us produces his or her own unique and wonderful fragrance. Hashem combines them all together to make the sweetest of perfumes. Just as we appreciate that smelling the same scent all the time is not as pleasant as smelling a variety of different scents, we should appreciate that Hashem wanted there to be many forms of beautiful fruit and many assorted scents. That is to say, He wanted many different kinds of people producing different kinds of *avodas Hashem*. To a significant extent, Hashem put into their heart to choose their way in life, and each one is special to Hashem. We should not expect, or even want, everyone to think or behave just like us. Therefore, when we encounter someone producing a "scent" that is different from ours, we must appreciate that it does not diminish or detract from ours. Clearly, we should not seek to belittle or cheapen it.

It is noteworthy that the verses do not simply list these fragrances but repeat the conjunctions "and" and "[together] with." We find "pomegranate *with* luscious fruits; *koffer with* spikenard...*and* saffron, spice cane, *and* cinnamon, *with* frankincense trees; myrrh *and* aloes, *with* all the choicest perfumes." This tells us that the combination of the fragrances creates a new and far greater fragrance than any individual one.[152] The point is that by combining our talents with those of others, we achieve so much more.

---

151 The Ibn Ezra makes the same calculation. The Rinas Dodim objects, however, because he understands that spikenard plants and spikenard (numbers 4 and 5) are essentially the same — one being the plant and the other being the fruit. He explains that the verse is enumerating the fruits and scents made by the "arid fields" i.e., the simple part of the nation (as explained previously). Even they yield such wonderful products. The tribe of Levi, however, was never "arid." Therefore, the verse lists only eleven different scents produced by the other eleven tribes who were sometimes weak and "arid."

152 *Metzudas Dovid.*

These verses thus drive home the importance, beauty, and power of *achdus* (unity) in our community.

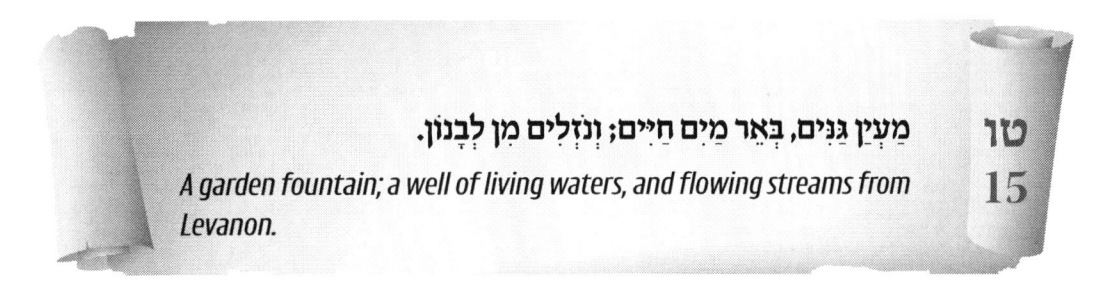

> טו מַעְיַן גַּנִּים, בְּאֵר מַיִם חַיִּים; וְנֹזְלִים מִן לְבָנוֹן.
>
> 15 A garden fountain; a well of living waters, and flowing streams from Levanon.

Allegorical Translation — Hashem praises the dedication of *Klal Yisrael* to family purity and reiterates the theme of the previous verses: "The origin of these gardens of beautiful fruit (i.e., the basis of these families which produce so many acts of kindness) is the care they take to immerse in fresh, clean spring water (i.e., a kosher mikveh)."[153]

Subject of the Verse — Hashem is praising *Klal Yisrael*.

Mashal — The husband develops the metaphor of his wife as a source of water: Her waters are fresh, like those of a well of fresh waters, and flowing streams from beautiful forests. In other words, she is as pure and as unsoiled as fresh water.

Nimshal — As indicated in the allegorical translation above, Hashem praises *Klal Yisrael* for their dedication to family purity and praises the freshness of the waters they use for immersion. These include "flowing streams from Levanon." Levanon here refers to a beautiful, pure forest from which pure streams flow. When water flows through muddy and dirty places, the water itself gets dirty. In a forest, the water remains clean.[154]

A GARDEN FOUNTAIN...

The verse teaches us that *Klal Yisrael* produce the outstanding fruits and fragrances mentioned earlier — wonderful children who do wonderful deeds — because they have a very clean water source. That is, they are careful with the mitzvah of family purity, and go to the *mikveh*.[155]

---

153 Despite all of the many difficulties and challenges, *Klal Yisrael* has observed this mitzvah over the millennia with tremendous commitment and devotion.

154 Rashi.

155 *Segulas Yisrael.*

A GARDEN FOUNTAIN...

This verse alludes to three special qualities of water. It is a beautiful sight, it provides life, and it cleans. A "garden fountain" calls to mind the beauty of water since a fountain is often used to enhance the beauty of a garden. A "well of *living* waters" alludes to the life-giving quality of water. The very term "*living* waters" reminds us that water gives life. Furthermore, a well was usually used by everyone to get their drinking water. "Flowing streams from Levanon" alludes to water's connection to cleanliness. Streams are clean because they are not stagnating water, and since these waters flow from a forest, they do not become muddy.

These are words of praise for the Jewish wife and mother who brings the Jewish family into being. Like water, she is a source of beauty, life, and cleanliness. A mother brings to the family her sense of beauty and is the one who makes Torah and mitzvos beautiful, attractive, and appealing for the family. She is the one who brings life into the world by having children and looking after them. In addition, she keeps the home clean from sin by protecting her husband and her home from all evil influences.

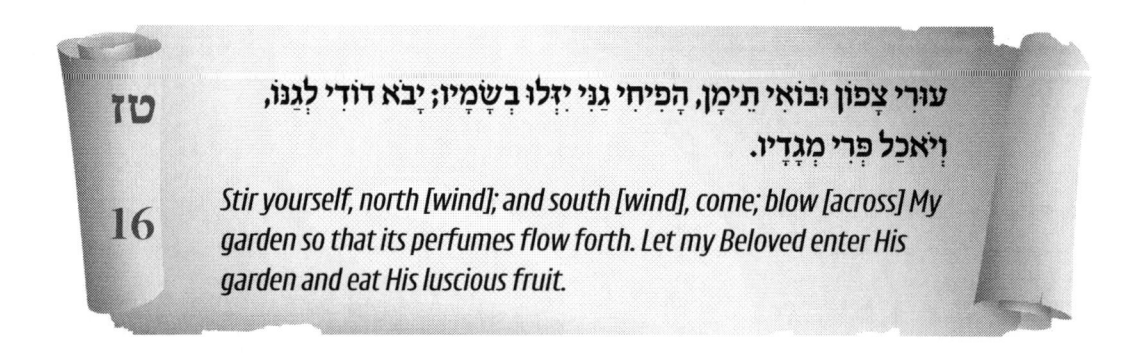

טז

עוּרִי צָפוֹן וּבוֹאִי תֵימָן, הָפִיחִי גַנִּי יִזְּלוּ בְשָׂמָיו; יָבֹא דוֹדִי לְגַנּוֹ, וְיֹאכַל פְּרִי מְגָדָיו.

16 Stir yourself, north [wind]; and south [wind], come; blow [across] My garden so that its perfumes flow forth. Let my Beloved enter His garden and eat His luscious fruit.

Allegorical Translation

Hashem says: "Since your (*Klal Yisrael's*) scent is so lovely and so pleasant to Me (as mentioned in verses 13-14), I will command all the nations to bring you to My city, Yerushalayim. There, your potential can blossom into reality, and I can enjoy your company. And from there, your beautiful scent will spread across the world, and everyone will recognize your greatness."

Klal Yisrael replies: "You, Hashem, should come to Yerushalayim and the Beis HaMikdash. Once *You* are there, it will indeed be beautiful.[156] And once You

---

156 Hillel used to sing the following words in the Beis HaMikdash at the *Simchas Beis Ha'shoei'vah*: "If I am here, all is here; but if I am not here, then who is here?!" (*Sukkah* 53a). Rashi (ibid.) clarifies that Hillel was speaking on behalf of Hashem. (Hillel himself was very humble and would not make such a statement about himself.) This was a reminder to everyone not to sin, and was meant this way: "If I, Hashem, am here in the Beis HaMikdash, then all is here, and it is indeed a wonderful place. But if you all sin, causing Me to leave, then nothing is here, and the Beis HaMikdash will be

are in Yerushalayim, You will be able to eat from the sacrifices that we will bring You."

Subject of the Verse — Hashem and *Klal Yisrael* are engaging in a loving dialogue about returning to Yerushalayim.

Mashal — Continuing the comparison of his wife to a beautiful garden with nice-smelling fruit, the husband says: "I wish the wind would blow, and your beautiful scent would thus spread." He thus communicates to her: "I would like your potential to blossom into actuality so that I can experience even more of the beauty and the joys of your company." To this, the wife replies: "Come into your garden, and enjoy its fruit." In other words, "I too look forward to the time when you can come and spend time with me (whom you likened to a garden) and enjoy my deeds.

Nimshal — As can be understood from the allegorical translation above, this verse reflects Hashem's "longing" for the Final Redemption, when *Klal Yisrael* will all be brought to Yerushalayim, and *Klal Yisrael*'s yearning for Hashem to come there, too. The "blowing of the winds" symbolizes all the nations bringing *Klal Yisrael* together. Just as the wind quickly pushes items in one direction, so the nations will one day gather *Klal Yisrael* to bring them to Yerushalayim.

The spreading of the fragrance by the wind represents the awareness that all will have of *Klal Yisrael*'s good deeds and good name when the Final Redemption comes. The greatness of *Klal Yisrael* will be renowned throughout the world. As the beautiful fragrances of a garden are spread by the wind.

The verse concludes with *Klal Yisrael* begging Hashem to come into the "garden" — an allusion to the Beis HaMikdash that was as beautiful and special as a garden — to enjoy the fruit (i.e., the *korbanos*).

STIR YOURSELF, NORTH [WIND]; AND SOUTH [WIND], COME...

There is a beautiful portrayal in the Midrash of how the heathen nations — represented

---

desolate." This idea is taught here in our verse, as Rashi explains it. *Klal Yisrael* responds to Hashem: "You come into the 'garden,' and then it will truly be beautiful."

On a deeper level, *Klal Yisrael* and Hashem are having a loving disagreement regarding what will make the Beis HaMikdash beautiful. Hashem says: "Let the heathen nations bring you like the wind to the Beis HaMikdash, and then your reputation will spread..." To this, *Klal Yisrael* reply: "Unless You, Hashem, come, it will not be of any value!" *Klal Yisrael* tell Hashem that they want Him there.

by winds here in this verse — will respond to the coming of Mashiach.[157] The Midrash says that they too will wish to come to the Beis HaMikdash. On the way, they will ask themselves what gift they can bring Hashem. They will say: "Gold and silver belong to Him anyway, and diamonds, too. So, what can we bring?" They will decide that the best gift is a Jewish person. They will look for a Jewish child and will lovingly gather him up. Indeed, kings will be given the great honor of carrying him. They will hug the child, feed him, bathe him, and give him every possible honor and then lovingly bring the Jewish child to the Beis HaMikdash as a gift to Hashem.[158] Our verse hints at that great occurrence: *Klal Yisrael* being gently "blown home" by the heathen nations.

The *Pesikta*[159] says that when Mashiach comes, Yerushalayim will expand and encompass Eretz Yisrael, and Eretz Yisrael will expand and encompass the entire world. If so, asks the *Pesikta*, how will *Klal Yisrael* be able to come every week and every month to the Beis HaMikdash?[160] The *Pesikta* answers that the winds and the clouds will miraculously lift us up, and carry us back and forth. Accordingly, this verse is to be understood not just metaphorically, but also literally.

LET MY BELOVED ENTER

Klal Yisrael had been likened to a "locked garden" several verses earlier (v. 12). The beautiful garden is enclosed to protect it so that it will not be trampled on and ruined. Now *Klal Yisrael* declare: "Let my Beloved enter His garden and eat His luscious fruit." For Hashem, the garden is open and accessible. The Metzudas Dovid elaborates: *Klal Yisrael* here are rejecting all other gods and saying that they are open only to believe in Hashem and to serve Him.

As explained earlier, a "locked garden" is not totally inaccessible. Rather, it is reserved exclusively for the owner to come and enjoy. In the *mashal*, the wife is saying that she is available exclusively for her husband, and completely closed to strangers. In the *nimshal*, it is *Klal Yisrael* saying that they are always available for Hashem, as they affirm in this verse.

STIR YOURSELF, NORTH [WIND]; AND SOUTH [WIND], COME…

The Gemara explains this verse in a different way.[161] To understand the Gemara's

---

157 *Tanna D'bei Eliyahu* 16.

158 See *Yeshayahu* 43:5-6 and 66:20, with Metzudas Dovid, for a vivid description of these events.

159 1:3.

160 See the *Pesikta* (ibid.) for how we know that we will indeed have to come to the Beis HaMikdash every week and every month.

161 *Zevachim* 116a.

explanation, a short introduction is required. A non-Jew is allowed to bring a *korban* as a gift to the Beis HaMikdash, but only an *olah* (burnt offering). The *olah* was slaughtered in the northern half of the courtyard of the Beis HaMikdash and was completely consumed by the fires of the *Mizbe'ach*. None of it was eaten. On the other hand, a Jew may also bring other *korbanos* as a gift, including a *shelamim* ("peace" offering). The latter could also be slaughtered in the southern half of the courtyard. Unlike the *olah*, part of this offering was eaten by the owners, part by the *Kohanim*, and part of it was burnt on the *Mizbe'ach*.

Now, in light of where the *korbanos* of Jews and gentiles are slaughtered, the Gemara interprets our verse as follows. In the time of Mashiach, Hashem will say to the "North," the heathen nations whose *olah* may be sacrificed only in the northern part of the Temple courtyard, "Stir yourself!" The Gemara understands this in the negative sense: "Move aside." But to the "South," *Klal Yisrael* who also bring a *shelamim* offering which may be slaughtered in the southern part of the Temple courtyard as well, Hashem says, "Come!" "Come forth and succeed!"

But, at first glance, there is something very puzzling about this interpretation. Why is the superiority of *Klal Yisrael* underscored by the seemingly minor point that they can also bring *shelamim*? Furthermore, the *olah* is more holy than the *shelamim* in a number of ways. It is completely burnt on the *Mizbe'ach*, and as the Gemara itself points out, it is only sacrificed in the north.

The Shem Mi'Shmuel[162] makes everything clear by explaining at great length the difference between the righteous non-Jews — such as Noach, Shem, and Ever — and the righteous Jewish people. One of the fundamental differences is that when the non-Jews serve Hashem, they do so by separating themselves from the mundane world. They are unable to infuse it with holiness and therefore can only be spiritual to the extent that they are able to withdraw from this world.

In contrast, the righteous Jewish people see this world as a means to come even closer to Hashem. They are thus able to be holy while sanctifying this world. This is symbolized by their ability to bring a *shelamim*. Although this is a sacrifice to Hashem, part of it is *eaten* by its owner. Righteous non-Jews, however, wonder how eating meat can possibly be part of a sacrifice, a spiritual service. Therefore, the only sacrifice they can bring is the *olah*, which is given away completely to Hashem.

Klal Yisrael is able to bring a *shelamim*. They are able to instill holiness into that which seems mundane because they realize that, in actuality, nothing is mundane. Everything can be used to become closer to Hashem. For them, even eating is an act of holy service

---

162 *Parashas Pekudei*, 672.

to Hashem. The *avodah* of a Jew is not to disengage from this world or to ignore it, but to utilize it to serve Hashem.

In light of this exposition of the Shem MiShmuel, the Gemara's interpretation of our verse can now be seen as inspiring. When the Final Redemption arrives and the purpose of Creation — to fill this mundane world with spirituality — is in the process of being realized, the heathen nations will be cast away. Even the righteous among the non-Jews who serve Hashem are unable to sanctify the mundane world. All they can do is ignore it. They are unable to contribute to this highest ideal. In contrast, *Klal Yisrael*, who have always brought spirituality into all earthly matters, will be asked to come forth because they are the ones who will fulfill the true destiny of the entire world. Incidentally, we see from the Gemara's understanding of this verse that even the greatest among the non-Jews, who serve Hashem and bring Him *korbanos*, are marginal compared to the Jewish People.

This concept clearly requires much more clarification, but that is beyond the scope of this *sefer*. We should note, though, that the Gemara's interpretation of this verse as explained by the Shem Mi'Shmuel is closely connected to the core of *Shir HaShirim*. *Shir HaShirim*'s use of a mundane parable to portray Hashem's love for *Klal Yisrael* is a prime example of *Klal Yisrael*'s ability to infuse holiness into the physical world. While others may see a garden and enjoy its beauty, *Shir HaShirim* sees it as a metaphor for how Hashem views us. While others may see sheep and wonder about their vulnerability, *Shir HaShirim* sees them as a reminder of Hashem's protection of us. While others may see a marriage and think of how it is simply a civil way to fulfill their desires, *Shir HaShirim* sees it as a symbol of our relationship with Hashem... In this way, we can elevate everything in this world to be a means to come closer to Hashem.

פרק ה'
CHAPTER 5

> בָּאתִי לְגַנִּי, אֲחֹתִי כַלָּה; אָרִיתִי מוֹרִי עִם בְּשָׂמִי, אָכַלְתִּי יַעְרִי עִם דִּבְשִׁי, שָׁתִיתִי יֵינִי עִם חֲלָבִי; אִכְלוּ רֵעִים, שְׁתוּ וְשִׁכְרוּ דּוֹדִים.
>
> I entered My garden, My sister [My] bride. I gathered My myrrh with My perfume; I [even] ate My honeycomb with My honey. I drank My wine with My milk. Eat, friends; drink, and become intoxicated, [My] loved ones.
>
> **א / 1**

Allegorical Translation — Responding to *Klal Yisrael*'s plea (in the previous verse) that He come to the Beis HaMikdash, Hashem says: "I (Hashem) have already been in the Mishkan with you in the past. I partook of your sacrifices there — even those that were unusual. Out of love for you, I ate from those as well. Your wine libations were as pleasurable to Me as milk. I commanded Aharon and his sons to eat with Me, and *Klal Yisrael* to join in the celebrations."

Subject of the Verse — Hashem is reminiscing about how He showered *Klal Yisrael* with love in the past.

Mashal — The husband replies to his wife's plea (in the previous verse) that he join her. He points out that in the past he did spend time in her garden, i.e., enjoying her presence. He then reminisces about that period, and says, in effect: "I was so excited by you that I ended up eating things which you made for me even though they were unusual." That is to say, he conducted himself like one crazed with love. He also invited everyone to celebrate with him.

Nimshal — The garden here in this verse is an allusion to the Mishkan, Hashem's beautiful dwelling place. This verse evokes the events of the *Chanukas HaMishkan* (the inauguration of the Tabernacle). "I entered My garden" means that Hashem came into the Mishkan in the past. "I gathered My myrrh with My perfume" means that Hashem, *ki'veyachol*, enjoyed the *korbanos* offered in the Mishkan like one enjoys the nice plants in the garden. "I [even] ate My honeycomb with My honey. Since one normally eats the honey from the honeycomb, but not the actual honeycomb itself (which is usually discarded), this means that Hashem was, *ki'veyachol*, overcome with excitement to the point that He "ate" even that which is not normally eaten, like a person who is in love does strange things. This alludes to Hashem accepting the *korbanos* brought by the *Nesi'im* (the princes of the tribes) during the days of the Mishkan's inauguration, even though some of these *korbanos* — e.g., the *chatas* (sin offering) — may not normally be brought as a gift. Furthermore, the *ketores* is normally never brought as gift, nor is it offered on the outer *Mizbe'ach*, as it was then. But on this special occasion, Hashem lovingly accepted them all. Hashem, *ki'veyachol*, dispensed with the usual limitations because of His great "excitement" in dwelling among *Klal Yisrael*. "I drank My wine with My milk" communicates that Hashem appreciated the wine libations brought then as if they were nourishing, like milk. "Eat, friends; drink, and become intoxicated, My loved ones" is how Hashem invited everyone to join in the celebration of the inauguration of the Mishkan.

I ENTERED MY GARDEN

This verse is a direct continuation of the previous chapter, and actually closes the topic. The fact that a new chapter starts at this verse is misleading, as will be explained later.

The main thrust of this verse is that while *Klal Yisrael* yearn for Hashem's return to the Beis HaMikdash — and may be tempted to despair due to the exceedingly long wait — Hashem reminds them that He was actually there once. This is a great comfort because it is very difficult to hope for an event that never happened, but much easier to hope for the recurrence of an event.[1] Indeed, we are supposed to contemplate Hashem dwelling in the Mishkan and see it as so real that we are confident it will happen again. Furthermore, in this verse, Hashem implies that it is up to us: "I am ready to rejoin you

---

1   See Sar Shalom on this verse. This is like a newly married couple who are struggling with their marriage. If they have had even just one truly wonderful experience together, they can use this as reminder that they are capable of being happy together again. Similarly, Hashem says that His reminder of the wonderful experiences of the *Chanukas HaMishkan* should make us hopeful about how close our relationship with Hashem will be in the future.

as I have done in the past. The delay is due to you. I am waiting for you to repent. As soon as that happens, I will come back."

This verse also underscores the excitement and love that held sway at the inauguration of the Mishkan. *Chazal* tell us that love breaks down normal modes of behavior: אהבה מקלקלת את השורה.² One way of gauging love, then, is to see how much it is affecting normal conduct. By telling us, in metaphorical terms, how unusual the conduct was during the inauguration of the Mishkan, the verse gives us a glimpse of Hashem's great love for *Klal Yisrael*. Indeed, the love and excitement were so great that extraordinary things happened there.³ These included the bringing of special *korbanos* as well as the eating of *korbanos* by *Kohanim* in a state of *aninus*.⁴

Furthermore, Hashem, in His great joy, invited His beloved *Klal Yisrael* to join the celebrations "Eat, friends; drink, and become intoxicated, My loved ones." "Friends" refers specifically to the *Kohanim*. They were allowed to eat from the *korbanos*,⁵ but were forbidden to drink wine since an intoxicated *Kohen* is not allowed to serve. Therefore, they were invited to eat, but not to drink. The rest of *Klal Yisrael*, who were not quite as close to Hashem as the *Kohanim*, are referred to only as "loved ones," but they are even allowed to drink wine.⁶ These invitations to eat part of the *korbanos* are invitations to be a part of Hashem's joy, *ki'veyachol*.

It is noteworthy that when the First Beis HaMikdash was inaugurated, *Klal Yisrael* ate even on Yom Kippur as they were celebrating this momentous occasion. This, too, reflects the concept in our verse that due to Hashem's joy about being able to "dwell" among *Klal Yisrael*, He abrogated the regular rules. In light of these two inaugurations, how can we not be eager to witness the inauguration of the third Beis HaMikdash?! When Hashem displays His love and excitement to us on that occasion, the event will surely outshine any previous one!

---

2   *Bereishis Rabbah* 55:8 and, similarly, *Maseches Sanhedrin* 105b.

3   In a similar vein, the Ohr HaChaim (on *Shemos* 19:2) writes with tremendous emotion that when the Torah was given on Har Sinai, there was such excitement that the Torah itself was, *ki'veyachol*, overcome with emotion. Thus, when describing the events, it recorded them in a manner that does not seem fully coherent, with some of the verses written in a peculiar order in order to reflect this excitement.

4   Aharon had just lost his sons Nadav and Avihu. Generally, in such a state, both Aharon and his remaining sons would have been forbidden to eat from the *korbanos*. Here, however, they were told to partake of them. See *Vayikra* 10:12. The *Devash V'Chalav* adds that when both the first Beis HaMikdash and the Second Beis HaMikdash were inaugurated, many lines were crossed, *ki'veyachol*, and sacrifices were offered in ways that were normally forbidden. The Rambam says that this will happen once again when the third Beis HaMikdash is inaugurated (*Ma'asei Hakorbanos* 2:14-15). In an ecstatic display of love, Hashem will once again abrogate many laws governing the sacrificial service to show how much He loves us.

5   The commentators discuss exactly which sacrifices they ate, and how they are symbolized in this verse. See *Ashirah Uzo* and *Devash V'Chalav*.

6   *Divrei Yedidyah*.

INTRODUCTION

As we noted in our general introduction to *Shir HaShirim*, the Malbim and many other commentators see the next verse as the beginning of a new chapter. The printers erred when they chose to begin this chapter with the previous verse. Their perspective is borne out by the fact that a new subject is introduced at this point.

In these next few verses of *Shir HaShirim* lie a wealth of *Klal Yisrael*'s emotions[7] as well as profound insight into much of Jewish history. Because of the beauty and importance of these verses, a special introduction has been included below to explain their theme and message.

MASHAL OF THE CHAPTER

In these verses, Shlomo HaMelech describes a would-be encounter between a husband and an apathetic wife, symbolically representing Hashem and the Jewish People. The husband tries very hard to reunite with his wife, but she ignores him. He keeps trying, even knocking on her door and begging to be let in, but she finds flimsy excuses not to oblige. Only when he has left her does she suddenly realize her utter stupidity and loss. She tries to return to her husband, but by then it is too late. She is forced to wander, searching for him while she describes to her friends, who cannot understand why she still desires him after being separated for so long, how wonderful he was and why she will never give up her search for him, and that she will always be loyal to him.

NIMSHAL OF THE CHAPTER

To a large extent, this is the story of Jewish history. Hashem tries hard to reach out to *Klal Yisrael* — to wake them up from their slumber and bring them close to Him — but *Klal Yisrael* ignores Him and refuses to repent. Hashem then leaves them and sends them into exile. When this happens, *Klal Yisrael* realize their stupidity, but by then it is too late. Getting out of exile is much harder than avoiding exile in the first place.[8] *Klal Yisrael* is then forced to search for Hashem through a long and bitter exile. They promise to remain loyal to Hashem, and they describe His greatness to all the heathen nations. The latter respond by challenging them constantly as to why they remain loyal when they have been separated and in exile for so long.

---

7   *Kol Dodi Dofek*, a collection of Rabbi Shalom Schwadron's writings and lectures, takes its name from the words of the coming verse, a verse that reflects Hashem's profound love for *Klal Yisrael* as well as where *Klal Yisrael* went astray. An entire section of that *sefer* is devoted to these few verses. Some of what follows is adapted from there.

8   As will be explained in the following verses.

This chapter should be understood on a number of different levels. When understood on a national level, this story represents the many times in history that we ignored Hashem's attempts to bring us closer to Him, only to bitterly regret our foolishness. But it also can be understood on an individual level. As will be pointed out, all the verses are written in the singular. Throughout a person's life, he or she has opportunities to become closer to Hashem. Hashem is constantly "knocking on our door," asking us to come closer to Him. While we do not necessarily hear the knocking, we can notice it if we are alert through the different opportunities Hashem sends. These opportunities may come in many different guises — a special event, a unique encounter, an inspiring *shiur*, etc.[9] This may also include a moment of inner yearning to become closer to Hashem. This, too, is a Heaven-sent message of awakening.[10] These opportunities are not haphazard. Rather, they are purposely orchestrated by Hashem to bring the person closer to Him. If he does not utilize these opportunities, he will have rejected the love that Hashem is trying to show him. If he comes to see this in such a light, he will realize that there can be no greater loss than the loss of pushing away the One who loves him most.

THEME OF THE CHAPTER

It should be clear by now that this chapter contains many of the fundamental beliefs and emotions that have accompanied us through this long exile. These verses describe Hashem's love for us, His desire to bring us closer to Him, and our love and faithfulness to Him. Therefore, they need to be studied and understood on an especially deep level.

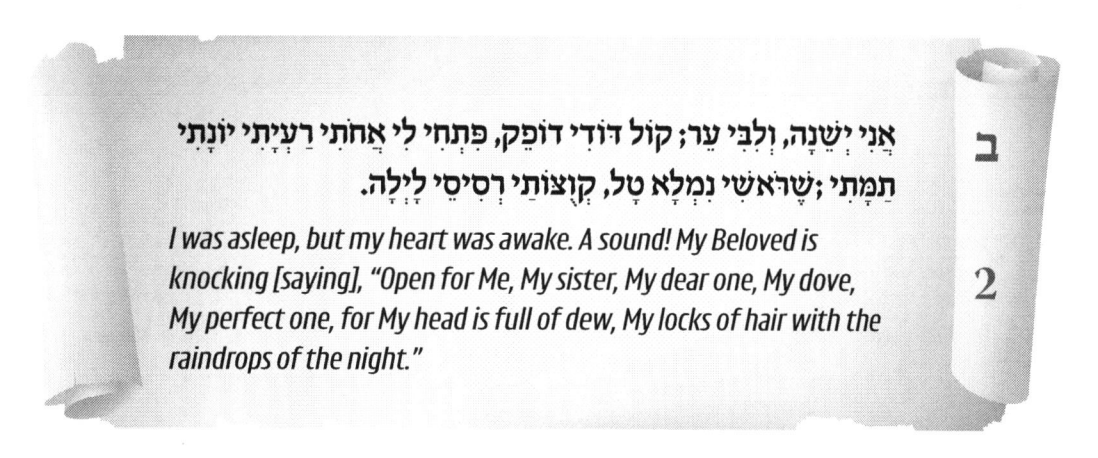

אֲנִי יְשֵׁנָה, וְלִבִּי עֵר; קוֹל דּוֹדִי דוֹפֵק, פִּתְחִי לִי אֲחֹתִי רַעְיָתִי יוֹנָתִי תַמָּתִי ;שֶׁרֹאשִׁי נִמְלָא טָל, קְוֻצּוֹתַי רְסִיסֵי לָיְלָה.

I was asleep, but my heart was awake. A sound! My Beloved is knocking [saying], "Open for Me, My sister, My dear one, My dove, My perfect one, for My head is full of dew, My locks of hair with the raindrops of the night."

ב

2

---

9   Rabbi Avigdor Miller observes, in his *sefer*, *Most Beautiful Nation*, that the burning bush that caught Moshe Rabbeinu's attention (*Shemos* 3:2) and Moshe's calling out, "Who is for Hashem should come to me (*Shemos* 32:26)," after the sin of the golden calf was a small message from Hashem which those who live mindless lives might not have noticed. Similarly, when Sarah Shneirer saw girls who were spiritually lost and needed direction and education, she heard the message from Hashem calling her to become the educator who would save their lives spiritually. One needs to be "awake" to hear these messages.

10 See *Marginta Tava* #12 cited at the end of *Ahavas Chessed* who exhorts one to write down and uphold his/her spiritual yearnings and commitments explaining that these are subliminal messages from Hashem.

Allegorical Translation — *Klal Yisrael* recall that when everything was going well, they became complacent and lazy about serving Hashem, as if they were asleep. Hashem, who is like our Heart, was awake and taking care of us. He warned us constantly through His prophets: "Do not cause Me to leave you, My beloved nation whom I love in so many ways [as a sister, dear one, dove, and perfect one]. I come bearing gifts and rewards for those who observe the mitzvos, and punishments for those who disobey Me."

Subject of the Verse — *Klal Yisrael* is reminiscing with regret about their foolish behavior in the past.

Mashal — The verse vividly describes how the loving husband tries to make his aloof wife aware of his presence and tries to arouse within her a desire to allow him into her life. This is depicted as the husband knocking on his sleeping wife's door, trying to awaken her. The husband then calls to his wife from outside her door: "Open for me, My sister," and continues with other words of endearment to communicate how much he loves her, and thereby convince her in the most loving manner to open the door for him. He tells her that he is standing outside in the rain and dew waiting for her. In other words, he is willing to put up with much discomfort in order to persuade her to open the door because he loves her so much.

Nimshal — This is a compact parable about Hashem reaching out to *Klal Yisrael*. The various metaphors will all be elucidated in the Commentary. The general idea here is that Hashem tries hard to wake us up so that we do not lose our connection with Him.

I WAS ASLEEP, BUT MY HEART WAS AWAKE

The Dubno Maggid offers the following parable that encapsulates the emotions of these verses.

A loving and devoted father had an only son who lived far away. He looked after him unfailingly, sending him money, gifts, and everything that he needed. The father had not seen his son for a long time. At one point, he wrote his son, asking him to please come and pay his father a visit. The child replied that he could not oblige: the journey was too long, and he was too tired, etc. Out of love for his child, the father decided to make the long journey himself. This was a very long and difficult journey, involving a long boat and train ride, and then a wagon ride from the station to the son's house. But he resolved to undertake it for the sake of his beloved son. He thus sent a letter to his son, informing him that on a certain day he would arrive at a certain port.

When the father finally reached the port, he looked around for his son, but, to his great disappointment, his son was not there to meet him. The father decided to give his son the benefit of the doubt…maybe he could not get there, etc. But he was sure that he would find him at the train station waiting and ready for him. So the father sent a message saying that he would be arriving by train to the son's town on a certain date. But when he arrived at local train station, the son was nowhere to be found. The father forgave his son for this as well. When he finally arrived at his son's house, he found the door locked. He wondered if his son was so busy preparing for his arrival that he did not have time to come and meet him. But when he looked through the window, he saw that his son had made no preparations for him whatsoever. Since he was already there, he decided to swallow this slight as well, and knock on the door. His son responded to the knocking this way: "Father, now is not a good time to come in. I am sleeping, and I cannot be bothered to get out of bed."

The father realized that his son was totally apathetic to him, and that there was actually no valid reason for his not coming out to greet him. So, he retraced his steps, and began his long journey back. At this point, his son suddenly realized how badly he had behaved and rushed to open the door, but his father had already left. Now for the son to see his father again, he would have to make the long and arduous journey to his father's house.[11]

The father is Hashem, who tried many times to reach out to His sons, *Klal Yisrael*. *Klal Yisrael*, however, were never willing to do that small and simple action of opening the door for Hashem. They said they were too busy, too tired, etc., to invite Hashem into their lives. When they finally woke up and realized the mistake they had made, Hashem had already left. Since then, it has been very difficult for *Klal Yisrael* to find Him. Our overwhelming feeling of frustration and outrage over the son's behavior in the parable should be directed at ourselves — at our own failure to open the door for Hashem when He comes to us.

---

11 In verse 5, we will see that the efforts *Klal Yisrael* expend to reconnect with Hashem are insufficient, and Hashem rejects them. The question arises: if Hashem was ready to make so much of an effort to come towards us at the outset, why did He rebuff our response — albeit belated — in the end? This question will be discussed in greater detail in our commentary on verse 5. But there is another insight that emerges from this parable. Upon seeing his son's conduct, the father realizes just how much his son takes him for granted. He concludes that in order for there to be a real relationship, his son must truly understand how badly he has behaved and must make a genuine commitment to his father. The son will not learn anything from this experience if his father returns as soon as the son calls him back. That is why he goes back home. He wants his son to invest a lot of effort in restoring the relationship. Similarly, Hashem kept trying, *ki'veyachol*, to connect with us. But when we displayed a complete lack of interest, Hashem wanted us to fully appreciate our stupidity in not opening up for Him when He asked us to and the great loss of His rejection. The effort we exert in coming back to Hashem builds within us an increasingly greater understanding of how important it is to be close to Hashem, as well as feelings of regret for leaving Him.

This is the general picture. To fully appreciate these verses, however, we have to try to see their depth and feel the emotion behind them.

I WAS ASLEEP, BUT MY HEART WAS AWAKE...

Rashi says that these verses could be alluding to a number of different times in Jewish history.[12] However, he favors the interpretation that they are alluding to the later years of the First Beis HaMikdash.[13] This was a time when Hashem sent many prophets to encourage *Klal Yisrael* to repent. Indeed, the Midrash informs us that Hashem sent two new prophets every morning and two new prophets every evening![14] Unfortunately, *Klal Yisrael* ignored them. We have to appreciate how much Hashem invested in this effort to get *Klal Yisrael* to repent. But the many different words of admonishment and inspiration fell on deaf ears.

I WAS ASLEEP, BUT MY HEART WAS AWAKE...

Rashi explains that the heart alludes to Hashem. He is the heart of *Klal Yisrael* in the sense that He keeps life going in *Klal Yisrael* just as the heart keeps life going in the body. And just as the heart is the most important organ, Hashem is the most important aspect of *Klal Yisrael*. Hashem was "awake," i.e., aware of our needs and looking after us, while we were "asleep" i.e., not serving Him. The Midrash also identifies the heart as Hashem, but the intent is a bit different. Even when we, *Klal Yisrael*, are "asleep," i.e., neglecting our relationship with Hashem, Hashem is "awake," i.e., trying to awaken us to repent. Hashem is constantly trying to stir up our hearts to serve Him. This is like a couple where one spouse is conscious of keeping the relationship healthy, while the other is not.

The Midrash offers an alternative interpretation that identifies both the one asleep and the one awake as *Klal Yisrael*. According to this interpretation, the verse is saying that although *Klal Yisrael* was sleepily neglectful of their duties in some ways, they were awake and aware of their duties in other ways. The Midrash gives many examples which show this contrast in *Klal Yisrael*'s conduct. For example, they may sleep vis-à-vis the mitzvos (either not doing them at all or doing them without any interest, as if in a daydream), but are awake doing *chessed*. The heart is symbolic for *Klal Yisrael*'s kind heart.[15]

---

12 Commenting on 5:8, *s.v. hishbaati eschem*.
13 Commenting on this verse, *s.v. ani*.
14 *Eichah Rabbah* 2:13.
15 This is especially noticeable in our time. We see Jews who unfortunately have no connection to Torah and mitzvos, but still have a very kind heart.

Alternatively, they may sleep vis-à-vis the sacrifices, but are awake in prayer.[16] The common denominator of all these explanations is that even when *Klal Yisrael* is "sleeping," i.e., not behaving correctly, they have a heart that is "awake" and still beating, ready to serve Hashem. However badly *Klal Yisrael* behave, they still have a good heart. It might not be good enough to get them to behave correctly, but it is good enough to show that there is still hope that they will eventually return to Hashem.[17]

Here are two additional ways of interpreting this rich verse: 1) "I may seem to be in a coma, but I am actually half-awake — the proof being that I hear the sound of my Beloved knocking, and sense His call to repent;[18] 2) "I may seem to be asleep, but deep down in the depths of my heart, I am awake to Hashem [because of the inner, hidden spark possessed by every Jewish person that burns with love for Hashem]."[19]

OPEN FOR ME...

The verse continues, "Open for Me..." The Midrash teaches that Hashem is telling *Klal Yisrael*: "Make Me even a small opening — even as tiny as the eye of a needle — and I will make you an opening as big as the entrance to the Beis HaMikdash." In other words, if we make a genuine effort to open up and connect to Hashem, He will open up to us and help us become truly bonded to Him. The eye of a needle is a tiny hole, but it is a real hole, one that does not close by itself like a hole dug in sand. This means that although our effort need only be small, it has to be *genuine*. Rabbi Leib Chasman, *zt"l*, adds that this is a promise directly from Hashem, whose guarantee is absolutely reliable.

---

16 Among the other explanations is one based on *gematria* which is included in *Yalkut Me'am Lo'ez*. The word ישנה ("asleep") has a numerical value of 365. The words ולבי ער ("my heart is awake") have the numerical value of 248, excluding the letter ע from the word ער; the letter ע stands for the word עשה ("a positive mitzvah"). As we know, there are 365 prohibitory mitzvos and 248 "positive" mitzvos that we are obliged to perform. The verse is therefore hinting that even when we are sleeping and not properly observing the 365 prohibitory mitzvos, we are still awake with regard to observing the 248 positive mitzvos. This is an interesting phenomenon: that *Klal Yisrael* keep and are more stringent and awake concerning the mitzvos *asseh* than they are concerning the mitzvos *lo saaseh*.

17 The Ramban takes a similar approach, noting that sleep may be deep or light. The difference is gauged in terms of how much effort is needed to wake the person up. *Klal Yisrael* may be sleeping, but their heart — their senses and consciousness — is still awake, and therefore they are easily stirred. Indeed, we observe this phenomenon today in Jews who seem to be deep in their slumber (apathetic to Torah and mitzvos) who are easily awoken and stirred to do *teshuvah*.

18 *Toras MaHaritz, Vayikra*, p. 81. The author points out that if a person loses consciousness, the doctors may prod him to see if there is a reaction. If the individual does not respond, this is a sign that he is in an alarmingly deep coma. But if he responds to prodding or other stimuli, this is a positive sign. Similarly, when *Klal Yisrael* react to the prodding of Hashem, this shows their "health." Applying this idea, the author points out that when trouble arises, we should at least be aware that it is Hashem prodding us to wake up and turn to Him. This would demonstrate that we are not, God forbid, sunk in such a deep stupor.

19 *Leket Reshimos, Beis HaMikdash*, p. 26. This interpretation also explains why the Heavenly "Gates of Tears are always open" (*Bava Metzia* 59a). Tears come from the depths of the heart, and since the heart is awake to Hashem, Hashem is open to the tears. The innermost part of Jew is pure and close to Hashem.

If we make an effort, Hashem will help us beyond our greatest expectations. This comforting promise has within it an implied rebuke because it means that if we do not feel that Hashem is "opening up to us," this is a sign that we have not made that initial effort because Hashem always keeps His word.

OPEN FOR ME, MY SISTER, MY DEAR ONE, MY DOVE, MY PERFECT ONE

Hashem knocks on the door, and calls to *Klal Yisrael* to wake up and serve Him properly. He calls out to them using multiple expressions of love: "Open for Me, My sister, My dear one, My dove, My perfect one." Rabbi Shalom Schwadron points out that the verb "open" is in the singular.[20] Hashem is addressing this loving message to every individual Jew: "Open up to Me, you whom I love." Let us try to appreciate the endearment and loving words that Hashem showers on *Klal Yisrael* even when they are sleeping (i.e., being wicked).[21]

Wanting us to notice just how much love there is in these words, the Midrash points out that Hashem loves *Klal Yisrael* so much that He refers to them as "My sister." But that is not enough for Hashem, so He calls them "My dear one." But that is also not enough for Hashem, so He calls them "My dove." But even that is not enough for Hashem, so He calls them "My perfect one." Each one of these expressions has many layers of meaning, and each speaks volumes about the love that Hashem has for *Klal Yisrael*.

The Midrash offers a number of additional insights regarding these four expressions of love. It explains the expression "My sister" as "the one with whom I have a bond."[22] This is more than just a relationship; this is a connection based on a deep bond they have together. As the Midrash explains, this alludes to the blood of the *bris milah* and the *korban Pesach* in Mitzrayim, which created a bond between *Klal Yisrael* and Hashem. It is as if *Klal Yisrael* and Hashem are, *ki'veyachol*, "blood brothers." They have a connection that goes beyond the feelings of love; there is a feeling of union and bonding.

Then Hashem calls *Klal Yisrael* "My dear one." This is a straightforward expression of love between Hashem and *Klal Yisrael*. The term "My dove" is a term expressing

---

20   This cannot be conveyed in the translation. Unlike *lashon hakodesh*, English does not differentiate between the singular *you* and the plural *you*. Had the verb "open" been in the plural, *pischu* would have been used, not *pischi*.

21   We see that it is better to use words of love than words of harsh criticism when trying to influence someone to repent.

22   The word *achosi* is being understood here as stemming from the root of the word *lachos*, which means "to sew together," as in *Moed Katan* 26a and *Sanhedrin* 56a, where the word is used for repairing a tear in an item of clothing. It would seem that the Midrash does not remain with the simple meaning of the word "sister," because "sister" is not a common expression of love. The Midrash understands that Hashem is pointing out that there is more than just love between *Klal Yisrael* and Himself. There is an actual bond.

faithfulness. We explained earlier[23] that the dove is a symbol of faithfulness because it does not betray its partner.

Finally, Hashem calls *Klal Yisrael* "תמתי," translated here as "My perfect one." The compliments here go in ascending order, and this is the highest compliment one can pay another. The Midrash points out that "תמתי" can also be understood as "My twin"[24] in the sense of "My equal." Being called an "equal" by a great person is a special compliment. Being called an "equal" by Hashem, the most powerful of all beings, is the greatest compliment. The Midrash also points out that just as a twin more readily feels the pain of the other twin, so Hashem feels our pain. Of course, these expressions are all metaphorical and are not to be understood superficially. The words of this verse and the explanations of the Midrash are intended to wake us up to just how much *Klal Yisrael* is loved by Hashem, and how precious they are in His eyes.

MY SISTER, MY DEAR ONE, MY DOVE, MY PERFECT ONE

The Vilna Gaon points to four basic reasons why a person may come to develop a loving relationship with someone else:

1. The other person helps him with all his needs. This, the Vilna Gaon says, is the love one generally has for his parents and relatives since they usually step in to help him with all his needs.
2. The other person is pleasant to be with. This is usually the love between a husband and wife, who enjoy each other's company.
3. The other person has good qualities and exemplary behavior. This is why we come to love the righteous; we recognize and appreciate their greatness.
4. The other person loves him very much. Under these circumstances, he will reflect these emotions, and eventually — even if none of the above reasons are present — reciprocate the love of the other without any effort.

The Vilna Gaon concludes that because Hashem wishes to arouse love for Him in the Jewish People, he touches on all four reasons in the words of this verse:

> "Open for Me, My sister" — Love Me as you love a relative since I, like a relative, help you with all your needs.

> "My dear one" — Love Me as a wife loves her husband, both enjoying one another's company, since being with Me is wonderful and pleasant.

---

23 1:15.

24 From the word "תאומים" meaning twins. (See *Bereishis* 25:24 where this word is spelled without an *aleph*, as here.)

"My dove" — Love Me as you love the righteous since I, like a dove, am kind and faithful to those who serve Me.

"My twin/mirror image" — Love Me since I love you, and that alone should arouse within you a love for Me.

We owe it to ourselves to pause for a few moments to contemplate the beauty and warmth in these loving words that Hashem uses to help us come to love Him. May we be privileged to use the ideas behind them to cultivate this love!

FOR MY HEAD IS FULL OF DEW...

The verse ends with one last attempt on Hashem's part to cajole *Klal Yisrael* into opening up for Him: "...for my head is full of dew, my locks of hair with the raindrops of the night." In the allegory, this is the husband standing outside, wet from the rain. His willingness to go out and stand in the rain to speak with his wife shows his devotion. But what does this mean in terms of the *nimshal*?

Rashi explains that dew is a symbol of blessing and reward. This is because dew comes to people without any hardship, and it brings much blessing to the world. Rain, on the other hand, can cause hardship for those traveling outside or those who have produce in the open fields. Here, it is symbolic of difficulty. Hashem says to *Klal Yisrael* that He has a great deal of dew (blessing/reward) for those who serve Him.[25] But He also has much rain (difficulty/punishment) for those who fail to serve Him.[26] Thus, Hashem is saying: "Open up for Me because it is well worth it for you!"

If we listen carefully to these words, we can almost hear a tone of pleading. Hashem is saying: if you open the door, I have wonderful presents for you. We see how Hashem loves us more than any father loves his son. Because Hashem wants us to return to Him so much, He will even try to "bribe" us.

THE VOICE OF MY BELOVED IS KNOCKING...

Sefer Shiras Dovid explains that there are three methods that can bring a person to repent: 1) admonition, 2) love and encouragement, and 3) the promise of reward.[27] This verse describes how Hashem uses all three. The verse says, "The voice of my Beloved is knocking." Knocking is symbolic of exhorting and admonishing the Jewish People.

---

25 In addition, Hashem is saying that He is drenched with pleasure, *ki'veyachol*, because of Avraham Avinu's good deeds, which were as pleasing to Him as dew, and He is ready to shower *Klal Yisrael* with blessings if they will return to Him.

26 Rashi offers another interpretation of these symbols: Hashem rewards a person both for fulfilling the easy mitzvos, symbolized by dew, and for the difficult mitzvos, symbolized by rain. The rewards differ depending on the amount of effort invested in fulfilling the mitzvah. Here, Hashem tells us that He has all the different rewards ready for us.

27 As elaborated in *Gryz al HaTorah, Eichah*.

"Open for Me, My sister, My dear one, My dove, My faithful one." Through these words of love, Hashem tries to wake up the Jewish People and encourage them. "My head is full of dew, My locks of hair with the raindrops of the night." As Rashi explains, this is the promise of great reward if we repent.

FOR MY HEAD IS FULL OF DEW

In elucidating this verse, the Midrash offers a remarkable parable told by Hashem Himself.[28] The Midrash says that when Hashem will bring Mashiach (may it happen soon, in our lifetime), He will come and comfort the Jewish People. However, they will tell Hashem that after He has rejected them for so long and left them out in the exile, they feel so betrayed that they cannot be comforted.

Hashem will then reply with a parable:

"A certain man married his sister's daughter — his niece.[29] One day, he became extremely annoyed with her, and sent her away. Much later, he came to make up with her. She flatly refused: 'After you sent me out of your house, you come and comfort me?!' The husband replied, 'Do you think that after I sent you out, I went back into my palace and forgot about you? Of course not! You should know that from the day you left my home, I too left it. I have been wandering around in the rain and the difficult nights missing you.'"

So says Hashem to the Jewish People: Do not think that after I sent you away, I went back to my palace and forgot about you. On the contrary, while you were in exile, I was in exile. And if you do not believe Me, feel the hair on My head — how it is wet from years of rain and dew falling on it while I have been out of My palace, as the verse says, "My head is full of dew, my locks of hair with raindrops." With this, the Jewish People is comforted.

This verse and Hashem's parable vividly describe how Hashem shares the pain of the Jewish People. Obviously, this is not to be understood literally because Hashem is not a physical being. But if we would contemplate this parable, how Hashem is, *ki'veyachol*, not going into His "house" while we are unable to go home to our land, we would get a whole new appreciation of Hashem's tremendous love for us.

---

28 *Eliyahu Zuta* 21.

29 The Gemara says that marrying one's niece (specifically a sister's daughter) is an extremely righteous act (*Yevamos* 62b). Rashi explains that since a person loves his sister, marrying her daughter will result in a marriage filled with love and care for his wife, which is a wonderful thing. Therefore, in the story, Hashem describes the ultimate marriage as a parable to His relationship with the Jewish People.

THE VOICE OF MY BELOVED IS KNOCKING

The *sefer Massok Ha'Or* tells of an episode that took place before World War II in Novardok. A fire broke out in a wooden house and quickly spread. The mother of the family, who had escaped, started screaming frantically to her son, "Wake up, Moishy! Wake up, Moishy!" Her son was a bit of a sleepyhead, and called back, "Mommy, you are always waking me up. Let me sleep a bit longer." She shouted, "But the house is on fire! The house is on fire!"

Unmoved, the boy called back that he wanted to sleep, and tragically, was consumed by the fire.

One can imagine the urgency with which the mother called out, the effort she made to wake her son up, and the tremendous pain she felt when her son did not listen. The mother would have tried every possible method to wake up her child. Commenting on this tragedy, Rabbi Bentzion Brook said: "Hashem is also calling out to us urgently: Wake yourselves out of your stupor! Repent, and thereby you will be saved from this terrible exile! Hashem tries everything to wake us up. How painful it is for Him when we do not listen, and instead choose to carry on sleeping away our lives and remain in the stupor that brought on our bitter exile."

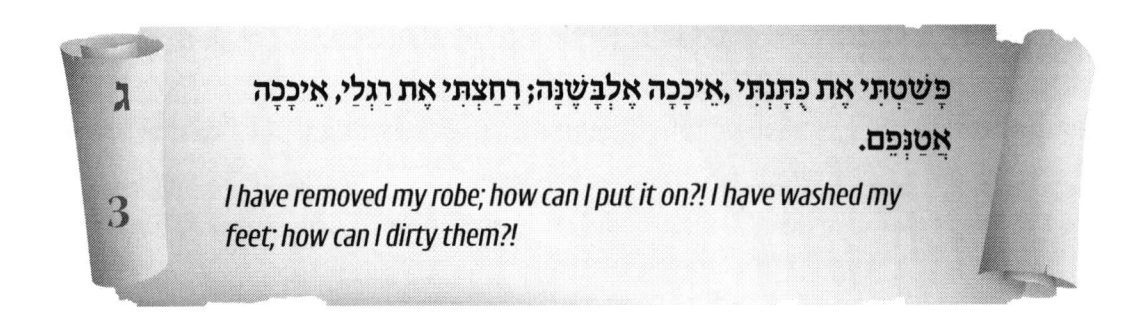

> ג
>
> פָּשַׁטְתִּי אֶת כֻּתָּנְתִּי, אֵיכָכָה אֶלְבָּשֶׁנָּה; רָחַצְתִּי אֶת רַגְלַי, אֵיכָכָה אֲטַנְּפֵם.
>
> 3
>
> I have removed my robe; how can I put it on?! I have washed my feet; how can I dirty them?!

Allegorical Translation — Replying to Hashem's urgent appeals to open up to Him, *Klal Yisrael* say: "We are accustomed to our wicked ways, and we will not return to You. Our current behavior seems correct[30] and easy. We cannot be bothered to change."

Subject of the Verse — *Klal Yisrael* is reminiscing regretfully about their foolish behavior in the past.

Mashal — After the previous verse describes how the husband tries so hard to get his wife to open the door, this verse tells of the wife's refusal. To her husband's knocking

---

30 One of *Klal Yisrael*'s terrible blunders was actually starting to believe that serving idols was righteousness and serving Hashem a sin. Indeed, they told Yirmeyahu that they were being punished for not serving idols better (*Yirmeyahu* 44:18). This was a consequence of their sinning for so long they became blind to the truth. The excuses of the "wife" here in this verse hint at their tragic misapprehension.

and entreaties, the wife answers that she has already gotten undressed and cannot be bothered to put her clothes back on. She has already washed her feet and does not wish to dirty them by coming to the door. The verse vividly portrays the wife's laziness and apathy towards her husband, and how she is unmoved by all of his entreaties.

Nimshal This verse portrays *Klal Yisrael*'s refusal to listen to Hashem's entreaties that they repent and come closer to Him so that He will not need to leave them and send them into exile. The excuses of not wanting to "get dressed" again and "wash" again, Rashi explains, are to be understood this way: we are set in our ways; we are so used to committing sins that we cannot be bothered to change our behavior. Rashi adds that the verse uses these metaphors because it is continuing in the similar vein from the previous verse describing such a scenario of a person going to bed and the husband knocking from outside etc.

I HAVE WASHED MY FEET...

Metzudas Dovid explains that going on the long journey to Yerushalayim to the Beis HaMikdash necessitated putting on additional clothes and getting one's feet dirty. As shocking as it may seem to us, *Klal Yisrael* was objecting to making *aliyah la'regel* because of this.

We are, of course, very disturbed by the behavior *Klal Yisrael* displayed — their apathy and laziness, their unwillingness to trouble themselves for the sake of Hashem. But we must ask ourselves if we do not do likewise. A man who comes late to davening is essentially saying that speaking to Hashem is not very important to him. A woman who cannot be bothered to be dressed nicely when her husband comes home or to greet him nicely is also saying "I have removed my robe; how can I put it on?! I have washed my feet..." We must remember that the Shechinah, Hashem's Presence, dwells in the home of every Jewish couple. By showing apathy towards one's spouse, one is actually driving away the Shechinah itself.[31] Just as we are shocked by the thought that someone would not want to make *aliyah la'regel* on the festivals, we should be shocked with ourselves. These verses paint a vivid picture of the wickedness and foolishness of those who reject the call of Hashem. They should arouse within us a determination never to conduct ourselves in such a manner.

---

31 The Ramban tells us that the *Shechinah* that dwelled in the tents of our Avos and Imahos moved from their home to the Mishkan, and eventually to the Beis HaMikdash (Introduction to *Shemos*). Rabbi Avigdor Miller adds that the presence of the *Shechinah* in every Jewish home is founded upon that original Divine Presence, and we must treat it with the due respect and awe it deserves (*Most Beautiful Nation*).

I HAVE REMOVED MY ROBE…

The Vilna Gaon understands removing the "robe" as abandoning good *middos* (character traits or virtues), and getting accustomed to bad ones. *Middos*[32] are like clothes — they're made to measure. When it comes to a piece of bread, it is not important what shape or size it is, but clothing of the wrong size cannot be worn. So too, *middos* have to be the right measure for every person.[33] "I have washed my feet…" alludes to having changed one's habits. Habit is called "*hergel*" in *lashon hakodesh*, stemming from the same root as the word for foot (*regel*). Habit is very powerful and has a powerful effect on where a person ends up in life. Just as we do not need to think about how to move our legs while walking, we do not think about other actions when they become habitual or second nature. And just as we stand on and rely on our legs, so do we stand on and rely on our habits.[34] Thus, *Klal Yisrael* is saying that not only have they abandoned their good *middos* ("removed their robe"), but they have taken on bad habits by washing away their good habits ("washed their feet") and therefore cannot repent.

I HAVE REMOVED MY ROBE…

Rabbi Shalom Schwadron offers an original interpretation of this verse through a parable: A certain individual has been traveling in the same clothes for an entire year. (We have to imagine just how full of dirt and filth he would be and how smelly he and his clothes would be.) Finally, he gets to a place where he can take a bath. As he cleans himself and is enjoying the wonderful feeling of being clean for the first time in a year, he suddenly realizes that he doesn't have a clean change of clothes. The thought of getting back into the same filthy and smelly clothes sickens him. He starts to feel that there is no hope for him to become clean, and he decides he may as well wallow in the mud.

Similarly, we sometimes repent, and then we feel cleansed. We emerge from Yom Kippur, for example, feeling that we are going to be better people. But then we start to think about the necessity of returning to our grubby habits and day-to-day routine. We fear that the lifestyle we are trying to leave will surely draw us back in, and therefore we give up hope. This, then, is what the verse is saying: "I have removed my [dirty] robe; how can I put it back on?!" In other words, "I will still need to put on the 'clothes' that I

---

32 It is no accident that the word literally means "measurements."

33 Just as when buying clothes, we check most carefully to be sure that they are the right measure and size, so we should constantly check our *middos* to make sure that they appropriate. See our commentary on 4:11.

34 Someone whose legs have been badly hurt in a car crash or other accident, God forbid, may need to put tremendous effort into learning how to walk again. When we see this, we are reminded of Hashem's kindness in enabling us to walk without effort. Indeed, one of Hashem's many kindnesses to us is that when we get into the habit of doing something, it becomes easy. This saves us from having to exert ourselves in most of our actions. But this gift can be potentially harmful if it used to develop bad habits.

removed. The lifestyle that I am trying to leave will surely draw me back in, and therefore I have no hope." Thus, *Klal Yisrael* does not repent because they have given up on themselves.

Of course, the truth is that Hashem helps us. He cleans us and our clothes.[35] We should never give up working on ourselves because when we do what we can, Hashem helps clean us up and finds a way to take us out of the mess we put ourselves into.

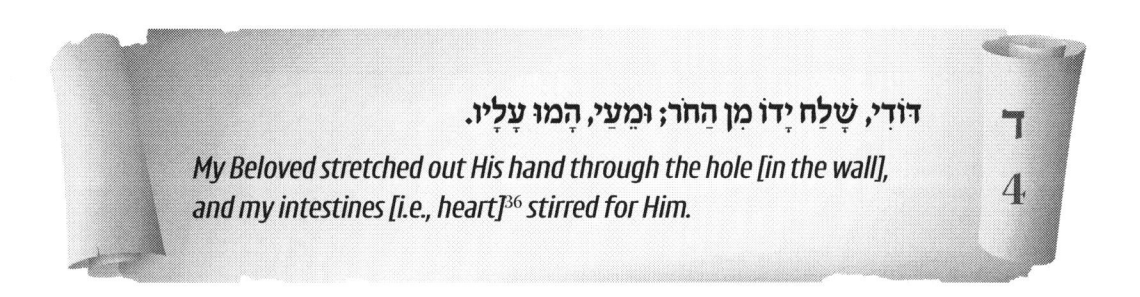

> דּוֹדִי, שָׁלַח יָדוֹ מִן הַחֹר; וּמֵעַי, הָמוּ עָלָיו.
>
> My Beloved stretched out His hand through the hole [in the wall], and my intestines [i.e., heart][36] stirred for Him.
>
> ד
> 4

Allegorical Translation   *Klal Yisrael* continue describing the events connected with their stubborn refusal to repent. Hashem responded by sticking His "hand" threateningly through a hole in the wall and gave them a small punishment. This caused *Klal Yisrael* to be stirred somewhat to repent.

Subject of the Verse   *Klal Yisrael* is reminiscing regretfully about their foolish behavior in the past.

Mashal   Seeing his wife's stubbornness, the husband makes a threatening gesture to her. She is stirred to realize how badly she has behaved.

Nimshal   Hashem makes one more attempt to convince *Klal Yisrael* to repent. He succeeds in getting *Klal Yisrael* to realize their mistake. Even though they do not do much, and do not fully repent, their heart is stirred.

MY BELOVED STRETCHES OUT HIS HAND…

According to Rashi, this verse alludes to the period during the First Beis HaMikdash when *Klal Yisrael* was sinning. Out of love and concern for them, Hashem sent prophets time after time to convince them to repent. Unfortunately, *Klal Yisrael* ignored them. Yet, Hashem still wished to save the nation and bring them to do *teshuvah*. What did Hashem do to force *Klal Yisrael* to repent? The verse alludes to it this way: "My Beloved stretches out His hand, (threatening) through the hole (in the wall)." Hashem sent the

---

35   As it is written: "If your sins are red, they will become as white as snow" (*Yeshayahu* 1:18).

36   That is, the seat of the emotions. See *Eichah* 1:20.

king of Aram to fight against *Klal Yisrael*. His army killed many Jews. This was Hashem's warning shot during the reign of King Achaz. His son, King Chizkiyahu, repented and managed to get the whole of *Klal Yisrael* to return to the Torah. This is what the verse means when it says, "and my heart was moved for Him." *Klal Yisrael* was stirred up enough to start serving Hashem again. The story of Kings Achaz and Chizkiyahu is encapsulated in this verse.

Rashi notes that this verse also alludes to what happened in the time of the kings Menashe and Yoshiyahu. Because Menashe was evil, Hashem punished him by sending an army against him. His righteous grandson Yoshiyahu, however, stirred the people to repent.

This verse can also be seen as an allusion to what happened in the time of Mordechai HaTzaddik.[37] When *Klal Yisrael* sinned, Hashem made a warning gesture through Haman, and the people were stirred to repent.

The common denominator here is that during all of these periods, *Klal Yisrael* was doing *aveiros*, and Hashem wanted to wake them up. Nothing moved them until Hashem took drastic measures, such as bringing on a devastating war or having the wicked Haman target the Jews. These threats of annihilation prompted *Klal Yisrael* to repent their sins, if only partially (as we will explain). Indeed, this verse could be applied to many other times in Jewish history as well.[38] And it is also applicable in one's personal life. When a person is sleeping spiritually and ignores the messages from Above, Hashem sometimes finds it necessary to wake him up in a jarring manner.

We should be feeling the love inherent in this verse. It shows Hashem threatening to punish us for one reason only: to wake us up from a dangerous slumber. Whereas a person might decide to give up on a faltering friendship, Hashem never wants to let go of us, just as a parent never wants to abandon his child. We see that Hashem so much wants us to repent and come closer to Him that He will do anything to make that happen — including sometimes punishing us in order to stir us. If a mother trying to wake up her son in a burning house (see our commentary on v. 2) would throw a stone at him in desperation, would that be an act of cruelty? Of course not! It would be an act of love to save the child. All of Hashem's punishments are "last-ditch" acts of love to save us.[39]

---

37 Rashi says (in his commentary on v. 8) that the later verses also allude to the period of Mordechai HaTzaddik. Thus, this entire episode should be viewed as one scenario that repeated itself at various times in Jewish history (Rabbi Yehuda Leib Wittler, *shlita*).

38 While we are obviously not able to offer any authoritative explanations of Hashem's actions, the last hundred years or so seem to resemble this pattern. *Klal Yisrael* appeared to be falling lower in their commitment to Torah, and thus Hashem brought on an unthinkably terrible Holocaust to wake us up.

39 This is how we should view the suffering that Hashem sends our way.

MY BELOVED STRETCHED OUT HIS HAND...

The Midrash offers a very different — and daring — way of understanding the meaning of Hashem putting His hand through a hole in the wall: Hashem was, *ki'veyachol*, stretching out His Hand like a beggar, begging us to come back to Him. The Midrash likens this to a poor man knocking on the door, asking for food. When no one obliges, he puts his hand out, begging for help. The Midrash points out that putting one's hand through a hole is not a respectful thing to do. This action showed that Hashem was so "desperate," *ki'veyachol*, for *Klal Yisrael* to open up that He was willing to "humiliate" Himself, *ki'veyachol*, in order to awaken us. Although, unfortunately, *Klal Yisrael* did not repent completely, their heart was stirred (as the verse describes).

In the *mashal*, this would be like a husband making yet another attempt to convince his stubborn and apathetic wife to get up and open the door for him. He stretches his hand through a hole in the wall so that his wife will see him, and he continues pleading with her to open up. Even though she does nothing immediately to oblige him, her heart is finally moved for him. Her love for her husband is stirred, and her desire to re-connect is awakened.

The Tzror HaMor adds that up to this point, there was no mention of a hole in the wall. He explains that the wall is a symbol of the barrier between *Klal Yisrael* and Hashem created by *Klal Yisrael*'s sins.[40] When they experience a small feeling of regret, this creates a hole in the wall. According to this interpretation, the verse is saying: "My Beloved (i.e., Hashem) stretched out His hand through the hole in the wall (created when) my heart was moved for Him." Every feeling of repentance and yearning to become closer to Hashem — even if imperfect and incomplete — chips away at the barrier between us and Hashem, and eventually creates a hole in the barrier that helps us unite with Hashem.

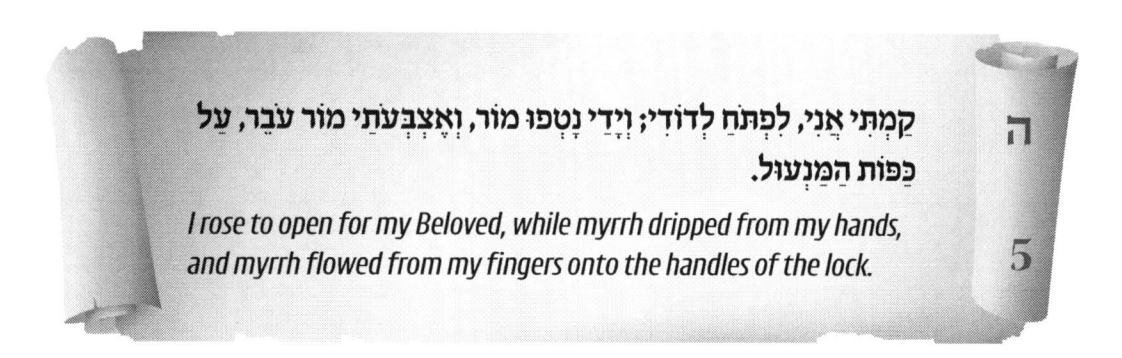

> ה קַמְתִּי אֲנִי, לִפְתֹּחַ לְדוֹדִי; וְיָדַי נָטְפוּ מוֹר, וְאֶצְבְּעֹתַי מוֹר עֹבֵר, עַל כַּפּוֹת הַמַּנְעוּל.
>
> 5 I rose to open for my Beloved, while myrrh dripped from my hands, and myrrh flowed from my fingers onto the handles of the lock.

Allegorical Translation   We, *Klal Yisrael*, finally got up to return to Hashem. Just as a wife perfumes

---

40   See *Sanhedrin* 65b and our commentary on 2:9 where this point is explained at greater length.

	herself to make herself more attractive to her husband, so we adorned ourselves with Torah and good deeds to be more attractive to Hashem.
Subject of the Verse	*Klal Yisrael* continues to reminisce.
Mashal	Finally, the wife takes action and gets up for her husband. Moreover, she tries to please her husband by opening the door with her fingers full of nice-smelling spices in order to show her love for him.
Nimshal	*Klal Yisrael* start doing something for Hashem. They finally get up to open the door for Him. As Rashi explains, *Klal Yisrael* come lovingly towards Hashem with hands full of Torah and mitzvos in order to show Hashem how much they want to please Him.[41]

I ROSE TO OPEN FOR MY BELOVED...

As we will see in the next verse, Hashem is not satisfied with this belated response to His overtures. In fact, by the time *Klal Yisrael* open up, Hashem has, *ki'veyachol*, gone away, and *Klal Yisrael* cannot find Him. Why? What is wrong with *Klal Yisrael's* repentance? In this verse, it seems that *Klal Yisrael* is repenting completely. Why, then, is Hashem not there for them? The simple answer (also implied by Rashi) is that it is too late. There is a limit to how many sins *Klal Yisrael* can commit with impunity. Under these circumstances, Hashem refuses to accept their repentance. Something similar happened before the Babylonian exile. Even though King Chizkiyahu and his generation repented, Hashem was not prompted to annul the decree that *Klal Yisrael* should go into exile.

Getting out of exile is much harder that making sure not to go into exile in the first place.[42] Had we opened up to Hashem in the beginning, we would never have been rejected and sent into exile.

---

41 Rashi says that this alludes to the generation of Chizkiyahu which was devoted to Torah (*Sanhedrin* 94b). The Seforno adds that Chizkiyahu urged *Klal Yisrael* to repent. He wrote letters to the entire nation, delivered by special messengers who went from place to place to remind people to serve Hashem. This is hinted at here by the expression "Myrrh [repentance, which smells nice to Hashem] flowed [streamed across the nation] from my fingers [that wrote the letters]" (*Divrei Yedidyah*).

42 The Midrash (*Yalkut Shimoni, Yeshayahu* 65) drives home this truth with a parable. A certain traveler was still on the road when it started to get dark. A farmer called to him and said, "Come stay in the hut over here. It is dangerous to be out at night!" For his own reasons, the traveler declined the farmer's offer. Once it got dark, however, thieves and wild animals attacked him. Realizing his mistake, he ran to the farmer to open his door and let him in. The farmer answered, "Now it is too late. I am no longer willing to open my door for you." Similarly, Hashem offered *Klal Yisrael* His protection. They rejected it. They did not want to live in what they felt was an uncomfortable situation. Afterward, when they were cast into exile, it was too late. Hashem was no longer willing to open up for them. (See notes to 5:2 FN #11 – explaining why feeble repentance shows a lack of understanding of how one has sinned.)

Rabbi Shalom Schwadron gives two other answers to the question of what was wrong with *Klal Yisrael*'s repentance. His first answer is that *Klal Yisrael*'s repentance was too slow. He sees this in the fact that *Klal Yisrael*'s fingers were full of perfume. (Unlike Rashi, he considers this to be uncomplimentary to *Klal Yisrael*.) This tells us that the wife first concerns herself with cosmetics and only then deigns to open the door to her husband. Similarly, *Klal Yisrael* took their time to repent and did not do so with alacrity. Why delay and waste time putting on perfume? If they realized they made a mistake and that they should open up to Hashem, they should have pulled open the door immediately. Their lack of urgency showed that they were not truly repentant. That is why Hashem refused to accept their efforts.[43]

Another explanation, according to Rabbi Schwadron, is that *Klal Yisrael* was too proud of their repentance. They say, "*I* rose... *my* hands... *my* fingers..." The fact that *Klal Yisrael* emphasize their importance — that they are being "good" and opening the door — is the reason Hashem rejects their repentance. A person has to realize that serving Hashem is a privilege. If he thinks he is doing Hashem a favor, Hashem rejects that kind of service.

The essence of all these answers is that *Klal Yisrael* had gone wrong for hundreds of years in not appreciating how fortunate they were to be serving Hashem. Had Hashem accepted a small effort of repentance, *Klal Yisrael* would not have realized how badly they had erred. The misconception that serving Hashem is a burden could only be undone through years of realizing that it is an honor and joy — and that one needs to be worthy to be allowed to serve Hashem. To undo all the damage their sins had caused through years of apathy, they needed to exert themselves for Hashem. When Mashiach comes, we will be all the more grateful for the privilege of serving Hashem in the Beis HaMikdash, having yearned for this for so long.

I ROSE TO OPEN FOR MY BELOVED...

The Midrash applies this verse to still another time: the beginning of the period of the Second Beis HaMikdash. It recounts that the good Persian King Koresh granted permission for Jews to return to Eretz Yisrael and rebuild the Beis HaMikdash. He even offered help and support for those who chose to do so. A short time later, King Koresh was traveling through his kingdom and was distressed to discover that one of his towns was desolate. He asked his soldiers where everyone had gone. They answered

---

43 One should flee from sin by repenting as one would escape from prison — at the first possible moment and with great alacrity. One who fails to do so obviously does not see sin as terrible (*Shaarei Teshuvah* 1:2).

that the former residents were Jewish, and they had accepted his offer to go to Eretz Yisrael. Koresh replied that he had not realized how his policy would negatively affect the country and was therefore retracting his permission. He thus sent out an edict that henceforth no Jew could leave to go to Eretz Yisrael. He did say, however, that those who had already left and crossed the Euphrates did not have to come back. This created a strange situation. The Jews who had left immediately went to Eretz Yisrael with the backing and support of the king. The ones who still wished to go, but had taken their time in leaving, were now stuck in exile. Only much later did King Darius permit them to leave.

The Midrash, then, understands our verse this way: "I rose up to open to my Beloved, and my hands dripped with bitterness…onto the handles of the lock [i.e., the ban that forbade Jews from returning to Eretz Yisrael]." While Rashi notes that *mor* (myrrh) is a pleasant spice, the Midrash focuses on the meaning of the word's root letters, מ-ר, meaning "bitter." The Midrash paraphrases the verse this way: "I, *Klal Yisrael*, opened up to Hashem, but there was a feeling of bitterness that so many Jewish people were left behind."

Aside from the other lessons one can learn from this interpretation, the fundamental one is that if a person delays in doing a mitzvah, he might lose the mitzvah opportunity completely. The Jews who delayed in taking Koresh's offer saw nothing terrible in reaching Eretz Yisrael and the Beis HaMikdash a little later.[44] But the truth is that by delaying, they ended up getting stopped from going altogether. Our verse implicitly warns us that lack of alacrity in performing any mitzvah can also lead to an indefinite delay.

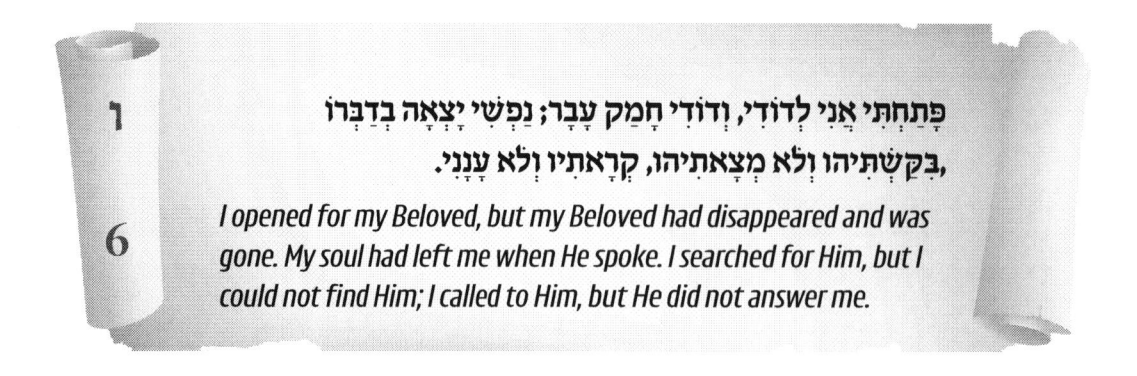

> **6** פָּתַחְתִּי אֲנִי לְדוֹדִי, וְדוֹדִי חָמַק עָבָר; נַפְשִׁי יָצְאָה בְדַבְּרוֹ, בִּקַּשְׁתִּיהוּ וְלֹא מְצָאתִיהוּ, קְרָאתִיו וְלֹא עָנָנִי.
>
> *I opened for my Beloved, but my Beloved had disappeared and was gone. My soul had left me when He spoke. I searched for Him, but I could not find Him; I called to Him, but He did not answer me.*

Allegorical Translation I (*Klal Yisrael*) opened up for Hashem, who is My Beloved, but My Beloved had disappeared and was gone. My soul left me when He had spoken the words that He was now leaving me. I searched for Him, but I could not find Him; I called Him, but He did not answer me.

---

44 This interpretation dovetails with the first interpretation of Rabbi Shalom Schwadron above.

Subject of the Verse	*Klal Yisrael* reminisces regretfully.
Mashal	The wife finally comes to the door with perfumed hands to open up for her husband, but her husband had already left. She tries desperately to find him, but to no avail. When she realizes what she has lost, she is devastated beyond words. She calls out to him, but he ignores her because he is so hurt by her treatment of him.
Nimshal	This verse pinpoints the cause and essence of exile. When *Klal Yisrael* do not repent properly, Hashem leaves them. Furthermore, this verse portrays the feelings of *Klal Yisrael* in exile, especially the dreadful feeling of loss. The terrible loss of Hashem's closeness makes us feel faint, as if our soul has departed. We yearn to find Hashem but are unable to do so. That is the true suffering of the exile: not being able to feel close to Hashem.

Again, let us pause for a moment to contemplate the power of these words. "My soul left me" means that we were so upset and devastated that Hashem had left us that we felt as if we had died. The loss of Hashem in our lives devastated us beyond all measure.

MY BELOVED HAD DISAPPEARED AND WAS GONE

The Divrei Yedidyah explains the seeming repetition in the phrase "had disappeared and was gone" this way: At first, *Klal Yisrael* thought that Hashem had hidden Himself, and thus they searched for Him. Eventually in exile, they felt so rejected that they actually thought He was no longer hiding but had left them: "He was gone."

In line with Rashi's understanding that this verse alludes to the destruction of the First Beis HaMikdash, the Vilna Gaon finds hints here to the five things missing from the Second Beis HaMikdash that were present in First Beis HaMikdash:[45]

1. "I opened for My Beloved" (i.e., I rebuilt the Second Beis HaMikdash, opening a home for my Beloved), "[but] My Beloved was concealed." The *Aron Kodesh* was hidden away and concealed.
2. "Was gone." The Shechinah, the Divine Presence, was missing. (The *Aron* was only hidden away, but the Shechinah actually left.)
3. "My soul left me when [I contemplated the loss of] 'He spoke.'" *Ruach HaKodesh* — Hashem speaking to us — was no more.
4. "I searched for Him, but I could not find Him." Fire stopped coming down from

---

45 *Yoma* 21b.

Heaven. ("I would search" for the sight of the Heavenly fire, which symbolized His Presence, but "could not see it" because it was not clearly visible.)

5. "I called to Him, but He did not answer." The *Urim V'Tumim* were lost. In earlier times, Hashem would respond to all of *Klal Yisrael's* questions through them.

MY SOUL LEFT ME WHEN [IT] SPOKE

The words "when He spoke" can also be understood to mean "when it spoke." When a person wastes words in idle chatter, his life ebbs away, since every person is allotted only a limited number of words that he can speak during his lifetime. This is hinted at by the words of this verse, "My soul left me when it spoke."[46] The lifetime allotment of words, however, only applies to frivolous speech. When a person speaks words of Torah, not only do they not detract from his life, but they restore it, as it is written: "The words of Torah are perfect; they restore the soul."[47] The greatest asset a person has is his power of speech. We see this from the fact that Adam HaRishon was called a *"nefesh chayah"* at the time when he was created. The *Targum* translates this as a "talking being." When a person fritters away his speech, he is showing a lack of regard for this most important aspect of his life. He therefore does not deserve an abundance of it.[48] Furthermore, when a person chatters, he is extremely likely to sin, as Shlomo HaMelech tells us: "In a profusion of words, sin will not be absent" (*Mishlei* 10:19). We must, then, never forget the words of this verse: "My soul left me when it spoke [too much]."[49]

I SEARCHED FOR HIM, BUT I COULD NOT FIND HIM...

There is still another dimension to this verse — this one bearing on every person's relationship with Hashem. As a person gets closer to Hashem, he develops a greater appreciation of Hashem's greatness and thus realizes how much further he needs to go. He also realizes that he can never really find Him. Those who do not seek Hashem's closeness may mistakenly think that they are actually very close to Him and will not feel a yearning for Him. Only those who seek Hashem and realize His greatness feel an unfulfilled yearning. Therefore, the yearning itself is a sign of greatness. While unfulfilled yearning regarding mundane matters is painful and upsetting, yearning for Hashem is valuable and precious in its own right. In addition to being a sign that

---

46 *Shomer Emunim*, I:124.

47 *Tehillim* 19:8.

48 The Beis Yisrael explains (*Vayikra*, p. 170) that we customarily say, "*lchaim*" ("to life") when drinking alcohol because getting intoxicated makes one overly talkative, something that diminishes life. Thus, we pray for life.

49 Of course, a person sometimes needs to talk in order to feel better. Then, obviously, speech is recommended (*Orchos Yosher*, ch. 2).

closeness to Hashem is important, this yearning also creates the "vessel" for closeness to Hashem. The hole in the heart created by the yearning to become close to Hashem is the place one can fill with love for Hashem. Without hunger, food will not be appealing. Similarly, without desire to become closer to Hashem, one cannot find the space to bring Hashem into one's life. Even in marriage, an important ingredient is the desire of both husband and wife to become closer and know one another better. Without this, the marriage grows stale.

The aspiration to become closer to Hashem is one of the most precious feelings that a person can have, even when it seems to be unrealized. On a deeper level, the more a person searches for Hashem, and the greater the aspiration, the closer he gets to Hashem. This, in turn, causes him to realize how much more he should seek to become closer to Hashem. Indeed, life should always be accompanied by the feeling, "I searched for Him, but I could not find Him…because even when I do find Him, I realize how much I still have not found Him, and therefore I continue to search for Him…"[50]

I OPENED FOR MY BELOVED

Sefer Shiras Dovid comments on the persistent repetition of the word "I" or "me" in the last two verses.[51] He explains it in terms of the famous ruling of the Rambam that a *beis din* is allowed to administer *makkos* (lashes) to a husband who refuses to give his wife a divorce even when they order him to do so.[52] They beat him until he "willingly" grants the divorce. Even though a divorce is invalid if not given willingly, this is considered a willing divorce because, as the Rambam explains, every Jewish person genuinely wishes to do the right thing — in this case, heeding the *beis din* and granting the divorce. If a Jew fails to do the right thing, it is because he is overcome by his evil inclination. Once he is beaten, causing the evil inclination to lose its grip on him, the only desire remaining is his true desire: to do the right thing. Therefore, it is a willing divorce. Similarly, the previous verses show the Jewish People's reluctance to be awakened by Hashem, and only in these last two verses are they finally doing the right thing. Therefore, these verses repeat that now the true and real "I" is functioning. Finally, the true "I" has risen up and wants to serve Hashem as it always wanted to do. Indeed, this is one of the main messages of *Shir HaShirim*: that the truest desire of a Jew is to serve and love Hashem.

---

50   Rabbi Meir Chadash in *Ha'Meir*, I:304.

51   *I* rose to open for *my* Beloved …dripped from *my* hands…flowed from *my* fingers… *I* opened for *my* Beloved, but *my* Beloved… *My* soul left *me* when He spoke. *I* searched for Him, but *I* could not find Him; *I* called Him, but He did not answer *me*.

52   *Hilchos Geirushin* 2:20.

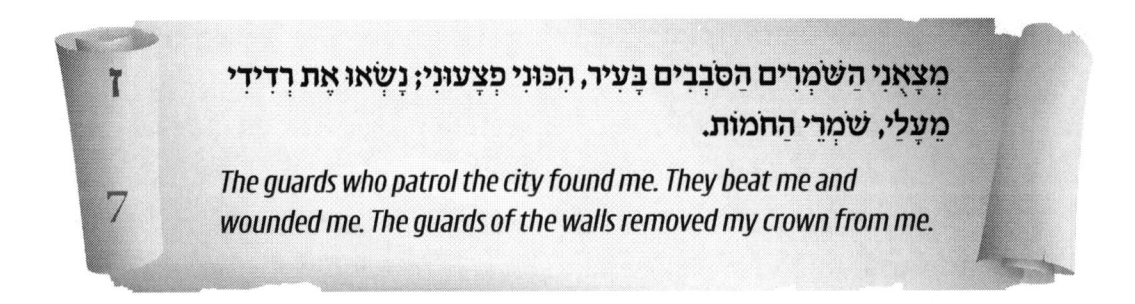

> מְצָאֻנִי הַשֹּׁמְרִים הַסֹּבְבִים בָּעִיר, הִכּוּנִי פְצָעוּנִי; נָשְׂאוּ אֶת רְדִידִי מֵעָלַי, שֹׁמְרֵי הַחֹמוֹת.
>
> **ז**
>
> *The guards who patrol the city found me. They beat me and wounded me. The guards of the walls removed my crown from me.*

Allegorical Translation — *Klal Yisrael* describe the events of the *Churban*: "Our foes found us. They killed many of us and captured many others. Even the angels who had been my guards until then helped my foes by destroying and burning the Beis HaMikdash."

Subject of the Verse — *Klal Yisrael* is reminiscing regretfully.

Mashal — This sequel follows the queen's account of her stubbornness and misbehavior which resulted in her husband, the king, leaving her. She was forced to try to find her husband to seek his protection. But the situation just kept getting worse. She describes how much she suffered this way: "The guards who patrol the city found me. They beat me and wounded me. The guards of the walls removed my crown from me."

Nimshal — This verse is a continuation of the previous verses. Now that Hashem has rejected *Klal Yisrael* and the spiritual connection has been broken, Hashem's protection is gone, and the physical suffering of the exile begins. The guards are the wicked nations, like Nevuchadnetzar and his henchmen. They find *Klal Yisrael*; they hit and wound them, and eventually take away their crown, i.e., the Beis HaMikdash.

THE GUARDS…

This verse describes the suffering that is the natural consequence of *Klal Yisrael*'s rejection of Hashem described in the previous verses. These verses encapsulate much of Jewish history. Time and time again, this pattern has been repeated. When *Klal Yisrael* sin, Hashem leaves them, and they lose His special protection. Soon afterwards, they are harshly assaulted by the wicked heathen nations. Indeed, this is the central theme of *Parashas Ha'azinu*,[53] and was clearly manifested in the times of the Judges, as recorded in *Sefer Shoftim*. Even though it may not be as apparent nowadays on either a national or individual level, this cycle is the reality. The more we serve Hashem, the greater His protection. If we choose to find other

---

53   See Ramban on *Devarim* 32:40.

means of finding success, *chas v'shalom*, then we eventually lose out and end up suffering.

THE GUARDS...

The "guards" symbolize the enemies and wicked nations. Why are the wicked nations and our foes represented as our guards? The theme of *Shir HaShirim* is that Hashem always loves *Klal Yisrael* and wants their success and their healing. In that sense, the ultimate purpose of the evil nations is to stop us from sinning by making sure that whenever we stray, Hashem hits us with them. These punishing "guards" are Hashem's way of keeping us in line. As mentioned in our Introduction, when we see things through the *Shir HaShirim* "lens of love," we understand that even the worst nations, from our standpoint, are intended for our good — to guard us.[54] Like a doctor who cuts a patient to heal him, so Hashem arranges that the nations beat us so that we should repent.

REMOVED MY CROWN FROM ME

Rashi sees the crown is an allusion to the Beis HaMikdash. The Beis HaMikdash is our crown of glory, which the nations took away from us. In contrast, the Midrash connects this verse with another era: the aftermath of the Sin of the Golden Calf. It says that the "crown" here alludes to the special crowns we received when we committed ourselves to observe the Torah at Mount Sinai with the words *na'aseh v'nishma*. These crowns were removed when we sinned through the Golden Calf.

As explained earlier, this is not a contradiction since each verse in *Shir HaShirim* alludes to a number of periods in Jewish history. Unfortunately, this verse and scenario have been played out many times. Each time, the loss of the crown represents a different type of destruction. In the Holocaust, the loss of the crown was the annihilation of the many great communities and Torah scholars in Europe.

THE GUARDS OF THE WALLS...

While the guards on patrol are the heathen nations, the "guards of the wall" are the angels.[55] They, who had always protected the walls of the Beis HaMikdash, now took part in its destruction. The Midrash says that they burned the walls of the Beis HaMikdash.[56] This, too, was intended to jolt *Klal Yisrael* into repentance. By Hashem arranging that the loving angels should be the ones who helped burn down the Beis HaMikdash, He

---

54 It is noteworthy that on Tishah B'Av, when we focus on our troubles and how Hashem has seemingly left us and is hurting us, we use derogatory terminology (in *Megillas Eichah*) to describe these same nations such as "foes," "adversaries," and "enemies."

55 Rashi.

56 *Eichah Zutta* 1:7.

caused *Klal Yisrael* to realize that He — and not the wicked nations — was the one who was doing this because He was so displeased by their behavior. He wanted them to understand that He was seeking their ultimate good: their return to Him.

THEY BEAT ME AND WOUNDED ME

Rabbi Yechezkel Sarna, *zt"l*, comments that this verse would seemingly be more appropriate in *Eichah*, which describes the destruction of the Beis HaMikdash, than in *Shir HaShirim*, which describes the loving relationship between *Klal Yisrael* and Hashem. He explains that even in this verse, there is a message of love from Hashem. When a relationship is not especially important to a person, if it goes a bit wrong, he may not hesitate to give up on it. However, when a relationship is very important to a person, he will exert himself to keep that relationship going.[57] A teacher may throw a student out of his class if he misbehaves and may even have the student expelled if his gross misconduct continues. But a father does not have that option and will not reject his son. If the son strays, the father labors to find a way to get the son back on track. This may include shouting at him and punishing him if he thinks it will be helpful.

Now, Hashem is the epitome of kindness. It goes against His nature, *ki'veyachol*, to hurt *Klal Yisrael*. But because He loves *Klal Yisrael*, He will not just write them off if they do not behave properly. He will ensure that we come back to Him, even taking "uncharacteristic" measures such as punishing us. Hashem does not make this effort for other nations. Indeed, they do not suffer as much as the Jewish People here in this world because Hashem lets them go, *ki'veyachol*, like a teacher expelling a very problematic student. This verse illustrates the effort Hashem makes to ensure we do not leave Him. It thus illustrates the depth of love between Hashem and *Klal Yisrael*.

Rabbi Shalom Schwadron illustrates this further with a parable. If a person faints, we first try to wake him up gently. However, if that does not work, we are forced to start slapping and shaking him until he regains consciousness. Similarly, Hashem tries to wake us up gently at first. However, if that does not work, Hashem will start hitting us until we wake up spiritually. Hashem never gives up on us. He will do whatever is necessary to make sure that we do not leave Him.[58]

---

[57] One of the mistakes non-Jewish society has cultivated in recent decades is the conviction that marriage is not vitally important. If it does not go well, breaking up the marriage is seen as an obvious solution. Those who realize the importance of marriage, however, will work hard to make it succeed. These few verses, which portray the relationship between Hashem and *Klal Yisrael* as a marriage going through struggles — and the serious attempts to make it work — teach us that a couple must try everything to make their marriage succeed.

[58] This concept is vividly described by the prophet Yechezkel (20:32-38). Hashem tells *Klal Yisrael*: I will not give up on you; and even if you wish to end the relationship, I will not allow it. I will even force you to come back to Me. See *Rosh Hashanah* 32b.

THEY BEAT ME AND WOUNDED ME

The Maharam MiRotenberg writes that if a person is forced to give up his life to sanctify Hashem's Name (dying *al kiddush Hashem*), Hashem will make sure that the martyr feels no pain if he is truly sacrificing himself for Hashem's sake.[59] He proves this through a remarkable linguistic linkage between the word *hikkuni* in our verse and the same word in verse in *Mishlei* (23:35). These are the only two verses in which this word appears (spelled this way). Our verse says: "They [the heathen nations] *strike me*," and the verse in *Mishlei* says: "*They struck me [down]*, but I did not feel any pain [*hikkuni bal chalisi*]." This unique linkage of the word "*hikkuni*" is a hint that there is no pain when one is being killed for Hashem's sake.

The Maharam cites the testimony of many who had watched Jews being killed, yet the victims never cried out. Unfortunately, in the Middle Ages, there were many such horrors to witness. He concludes that it is not humanly possible to refrain from crying out in such unbearable circumstances unless there is indeed no pain.

We learn from this that someone who is ready to bear the pain that Hashem metes out to him (because he believes this to be the will of Hashem and that it is all for the best) is protected from this pain on some level. The more one accepts Hashem's decrees with love, the more one will receive Hashem's protection and blessing.[60]

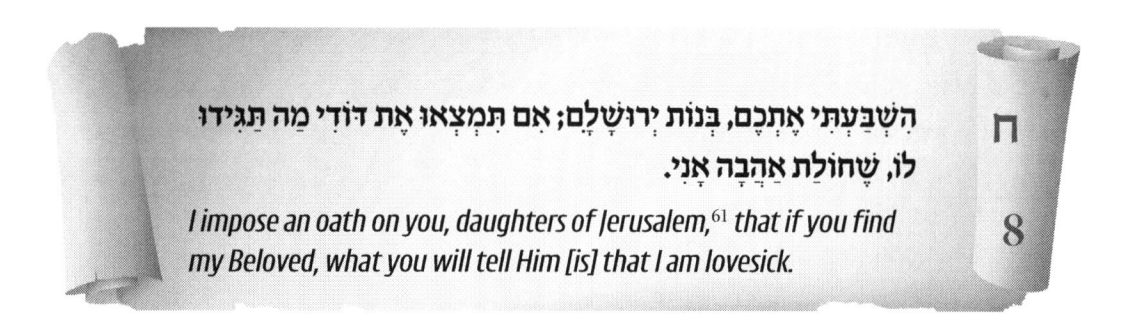

> הִשְׁבַּעְתִּי אֶתְכֶם, בְּנוֹת יְרוּשָׁלָםִ; אִם תִּמְצְאוּ אֶת דּוֹדִי מַה תַּגִּידוּ
> לוֹ, שֶׁחוֹלַת אַהֲבָה אָנִי.
>
> ח 8
>
> I impose an oath on you, daughters of Jerusalem,[61] that if you find my Beloved, what you will tell Him [is] that I am lovesick.

Allegorical Translation We, *Klal Yisrael*, adjure you, the heathen nations, to promise that when the day of Judgment arrives and Hashem asks you about us, you will testify that we suffered mightily for His love.

---

59 *Sheilos U'Teshuvos*, IV:517.

60 In his extended discussion of the subject, the Megillas Amrafel cites many instances of this phenomenon. In this vein, Rabbi Yosef Engel writes that Rabbi Akiva suffered pain when he was tortured and executed by the Romans only because he wished to display his great love and devotion to Hashem and therefore asked that the pain not be removed (*Gilyoinei HaShas, Berachos* 61b).

61 See our commentary on 1:5 for an explanation of this phrase.

Subject of the Verse	*Klal Yisrael* is speaking to the nations.
Mashal	The wife turns to the guards who have been causing her pain, as she described in the previous verse, and says to them: When you eventually find my husband, I want you to promise that you will tell him how much I suffered for his love.
Nimshal	*Klal Yisrael* tell the heathen nations: When you meet Hashem, our Beloved, tell Him that we are lovesick for Him.

I IMPOSE AN OATH ON YOU...

This is one of the most dramatic verses in *Shir HaShirim*. Let us take a moment to put it in perspective and appreciate the powerful scene unfolding in these verses. The King, i.e., Hashem, came to *Klal Yisrael* (His "wife"), and begged them to "open up for Him" by repenting and returning to Him. They refused, but after much cajoling, reluctantly opened up a bit. Hashem was displeased and left them. Once this happened, *Klal Yisrael* realized their mistake and went out to search for Him in desperation. Since they had lost His protection, however, they have to suffer the indignities of exile. The previous verse evokes their terrible suffering and the loss of the Beis HaMikdash. This verse continues the saga. The oppressing nations are now being called upon by *Klal Yisrael*. They are made to promise that if they find Hashem ("my Beloved"), they will speak well of *Klal Yisrael*.

An oath is more than just a declaration. One does not take an oath or insist that someone else do so unless the matter at hand is very important and arouses deep passions. That is precisely the situation here.

IF YOU FIND MY BELOVED

Now, we might well wonder, how should the heathen nations be able to find Hashem if *Klal Yisrael* cannot? Rashi explains that *Klal Yisrael* is referring to the End of Days, when Hashem will judge the entire world. On that day of reckoning, Hashem will call on all the nations to explain their own conduct and to testify about *Klal Yisrael*'s conduct.[62] Obviously, Hashem does not need any nation's testimony. However, Hashem will want the nations to see for themselves that *Klal Yisrael* deserve the great reward that will be coming to them and that the other nations deserve the great punishment they will be getting. Furthermore, praise given by an enemy is more credible and impressive because it comes from those who would have preferred to find fault. Thus, we see from this verse that the praise of *Klal Yisrael* is so well deserved that the nations who have tormented us will be forced to acknowledge it. What will they acknowledge? That *Klal Yisrael* is lovesick!

---

62 See *Avodah Zarah* 2b-3a which describes this day of reckoning.

I AM LOVESICK

The commentators offer a number of interpretations of this powerful statement. What does it mean to be lovesick? On the simple level, *Klal Yisrael* is saying that Hashem's lack of love for them is making them very ill. This is like children who get homesick when they are away from home for an extended period. They miss their parents so much that they truly feel sick.

The Vilna Gaon comments that despite all the suffering we have gone through in exile, as previously described, our true pain stems from one cause: the absence of Hashem's love. Therefore, when we call upon the nations to testify about what happened to us, we do not recount to them any of the other afflictions. This is an eloquent expression of our love for Hashem that nothing upsets us like the loss of love from Hashem.[63]

The Metzudas Dovid takes a similar approach. His inspirational words follow:

> When she finishes relating her story (of suffering), she (the wife) says to the maidens: "I make you promise that if you meet my husband, you will tell him that I am ill because I yearn for his love." In other words: "I am not sick because of all the beatings and wounds that the guards meted out to me. *That pain is nothing compared with the pain of his leaving me.* Only this causes me illness."
>
> In the *nimshal*, it is as if *Klal Yisrael* call on the nations who serve idols to swear that in the future they will testify in front of Hashem that *Klal Yisrael* accepted all of the suffering they endured in exile with love. All that ailed them and all their worry were due only to the lack of Hashem's Presence. *All they ever yearned for and all they ever wished for was the return of Hashem.*

We have endured two thousand years of exile — including the Crusades, the Inquisition, pogroms, massacres, and the Holocaust, among many other forms of sufferings. But all of that is nothing compared with our real loss: the loss of Hashem's Presence in our lives. How wonderful that this is what lies within the heart of *Klal Yisrael*![64]

---

63 It is an uplifting experience to read the precious words of the Vilna Gaon in the original Hebrew.

64 In this vein, the Chovos HaLevavos relates that a Chassid once declared "Hashem, You have made me hungry and taken away all my possessions and left me in darkness. Yet I swear by Your great and holy Name that even if You would burn me, I would only increase my love for You and my joy through which I can serve You!" (*Shaar Ahavas Hashem*, ch. 1). In his *Shaarei Teshuvah* (1:42), Rabbeinu Yonah echoes this thought: "The desire of the righteous, and their pursuit, is to fulfill the will of Hashem. They feel successful when they feel His love…"

Now, there are those who might question this claim. Is it true that our greatest pain is missing Hashem? Most of the time, we seem to be worrying about more mundane matters — not overly concerned with closeness to Hashem. The explanation for this is that sometimes one does not really know or understand what one is feeling. A little child might be crying for a toy for a long time when they are hungry or tired. The wise parent understands that it is not that the child wants the toy but that he or she needs to eat or sleep. Even an adult who is upset might not realize what is truly bothering him, especially if he is not in touch with his feelings. Sometimes it takes an astute therapist or friend to help him discover what is really troubling him.

This verse identifies the deepest feelings of *Klal Yisrael*. It tells us that even if we think that we are upset because of our financial struggles or illnesses, that is an incorrect assessment. The real reason we are upset is because we lack a closeness with Hashem. It might be that we do not notice this, but that is only because we have been distracted by the diversions of the world around us. They have blocked us from connecting with our spiritual desires. If we do not try to connect with Hashem when we feel upset, we are like the person who eats ice-cream to feel better after being hurt emotionally. Using a very superficial and ineffective method to ignore what is really upsetting. This verse, then, helps us know what our focus should be in order to feel happier and more content.[65]

The more we internalize the message of this verse, the easier it will be to notice our deep-seated need to connect with Hashem in our lives. We will then be able to focus on what we truly need: to connect with Hashem.

Let us turn now to Rashi's interpretation of this verse. He understands *Klal Yisrael* to be saying: "You [the heathen nations] will testify that the reason we are not well is because we serve Hashem." That is to say, *Klal Yisrael*'s love for Hashem prompted the heathen nations to make them "sick." Throughout our bitter exile, we have been punished, attacked, and hurt by the heathen nations because we have remained faithful to Hashem. Why was Daniel thrown into the lion's den?! Why were Chananyah, Mishael, and Azaryah thrown into the fire?! Why did Haman wish to murder Mordechai and all the Jews? Because they were loyal to Hashem. Who saw this and can testify about it? The people who threw them in, the people who made them suffer, like Nevuchadnetzar and his cronies. There are literally millions upon millions of examples of how, right through our exile, the heathen nations have harmed us because of our loyalty to Hashem. One day, they will be forced to testify about this.

---

65 We should be very grateful for this marvelous insight that the yearning for Hashem is at the heart of all of our unhappiness because it reveals to us what we truly need.

According to both of these interpretations, by demanding that the nations take this oath, *Klal Yisrael* is showing just how much they value their love for Hashem, and His love for them. For them, the worst thing about the exile is the absence of Hashem's love or the suffering they endure at the hands of the heathen nations in order to remain faithful to Hashem.[66]

The Rambam takes still another approach to this verse. It dovetails with his famous characterization of the love one should have for Hashem: "One should love Hashem with a tremendous, boundless, and powerful love, until his spirit is bonded with the love of Hashem, and he is constantly meditating and thinking about this love. Just as one who has become lovesick [for a woman] is unable to think of anything else…" The Rambam concludes that a person should be constantly preoccupied because his mind is caught up with Hashem's love, as Shlomo HaMelech says in this verse of *Shir HaShirim*, "I am lovesick," meaning, "I behave strangely because of the love." The Rambam concludes that the whole of *Shir HaShirim* is a parable to this effect.[67]

We see that the Rambam explains this verse differently from Rashi. According to the Rambam, this verse tells us that *Klal Yisrael* is describing their love for Hashem. They are lovesick in the sense that they are totally wrapped up with their love for Hashem, like a person who is so obsessed with love that he does not act normally.[68]

---

66 *Klal Yisrael*'s orientation contrasts sharply with that of the other nations. They are willing to praise Hashem only if everything is going well. The Gemara (*Sanhedrin* 92b) tells us that when Nevuchadnetzar saw Chananyah, Mishael, and Azaryah being saved from the fire he had consigned them to for not bowing down to his statue, and when he then saw Yechezkel reviving the dead, he was so impressed that he began praising Hashem with praises never heard before. But because the angels did not want the praises of this wicked king to overshadow the praises of Dovid HaMelech, one of them gave him a slap, and thus got him to stop.
 The Kotzker Rebbe asks about the justice of the angel's actions: Why should Nevuchadnetzar not be allowed to utter praises to Hashem greater than those of Dovid HaMelech should he choose to?! He answers that the angels wanted to demonstrate his fickleness in breaking off his praise of Hashem after only one slap. In contrast, Dovid was "slapped" again and again and suffered in many different ways, yet he never stopped singing to Hashem. Indeed, the greatness of *Klal Yisrael* is the depth of their devotion to Hashem, and they stick to it through thick and thin. Therefore, we call upon the nations to testify to Hashem that this is how we feel and behave, and thus they must admit that they are not deserving of Hashem's love in the way that we are (*Amud HaEmes*, p. 157).

67 *Hilchos Teshuvah* 10:3.

68 A Chassid who was very devoted to the mitzvah of tefillin was involved in an accident and lost his arm. This meant that he could no longer do the mitzvah fully. Devastated, he went to the Lubavitcher Rebbe of his time, the MaHaritz, and asked what he was supposed to do. The Rebbe quoted our verse and explained that what Hashem really wants from us is the *desire* to serve Him. Even if we do not manage to perform the mitzvah in practice, the desire to do it is all that is required of us. The Rebbe elucidated the phrase "I am lovesick" this way: "I desire to fulfill His command and show Him that I love Him, and when I am unable to display my love, I feel ill." Indeed, *Klal Yisrael* pride themselves on growing ill when their love is unfulfilled, when they desire to carry out His commands but are unable to do so. In the next verse, as we will see, the nations are puzzled by this declaration of *Klal Yisrael*. That, the Rebbe explained, is because the heathen nations do not appreciate this concept. They think that the main thing is to actually succeed in doing mitzvos. They cannot understand the point of desiring to do a mitzvah if you are unable to. The truth, however, is that wanting to serve Hashem is the most precious feeling a person can have, even if he is unable to actually serve Him because

> ט
>
> מַה דּוֹדֵךְ מִדּוֹד, הַיָּפָה בַּנָּשִׁים; מַה דּוֹדֵךְ מִדּוֹד, שֶׁכָּכָה הִשְׁבַּעְתָּנוּ.
>
> 9
>
> *Most beautiful of women, how is your Beloved different from any other friend? How is your Beloved different from any other friend such that you hold us to an oath like this?*

Allegorical Translation — Replying to *Klal Yisrael*, the heathen nations ask in wonder: "In what way is your God greater than all other gods that you are so devoted to Him that you made me swear so?!"

Subject of the Verse — The nations reply to *Klal Yisrael*.

Mashal — The guards acknowledge that the wife asked them to testify that she is devoted to her husband but cannot understand why she is so devoted to him that she has become lovesick. They thus ask: What is so special about your husband that makes you so devoted?

Nimshal — The heathen nations' reply to *Klal Yisrael*'s request is that they swear to testify regarding *Klal Yisrael*'s devotion to Hashem. They are amazed by the devotion of *Klal Yisrael* and acknowledge that the declaration of *Klal Yisrael* is indeed true. So, they ask in wonder, "What is so special about Hashem, compared with any other god, that you make us promise this?!"

MOST BEAUTIFUL OF WOMEN, HOW...

In light of *Klal Yisrael*'s devotion to Hashem (displayed in the previous verse), the heathen nations ask: What is so special about Hashem that makes you so devoted?

The nations call *Klal Yisrael* "most beautiful of women," an expression used by

---

Hashem does not actually need anything at all.

The Chiddushei Ha'Rim explains that this is the fundamental difference between the way a Jew and a gentile serve Hashem. He is commenting on the verse that tells us that the princes of the tribes donated to the Mishkan only at the very end, thinking that they would supply whatever was lacking. For this they were punished, as Rashi explains (*Shemos* 35:27). The Chiddushei Ha'Rim comments that their action showed a lack of this understanding that all Hashem wants is our desire to serve Him. Had they felt that true desire, they would have donated immediately. Instead, they showed a non-Jewish attitude in focusing on giving what was actually needed, thinking that their job was to complete the building of the Mishkan. That is why, quips the Chiddushei Ha'Rim, they were punished by having their title spelled without a *yud* (הנשאם). The letter *yud* is pronounced in a way that is almost identical to the way one pronounces the word "Jew" in Yiddish. The hint here is that they lacked the correct Jewish attitude.

Hashem earlier to describe *Klal Yisrael*.[69] It is understandable that Hashem should describe us as such due to His great love for us, but why would the heathen nations do so, and why specifically now?!

The simple explanation is that the heathen nations are forced to acknowledge that the Jewish People is the greatest and most beautiful nation. On a deeper level, they use this highly complementary phrase to imply that if *Klal Yisrael* would abandon its devotion to Hashem, they would treat them most civilly and give them the honor and success that *Klal Yisrael* deserves because they are truly the most beautiful "woman" in the world. (In the *mashal*, this would be like a person telling a beautiful woman who is in a difficult relationship: Why do you remain in this relationship when you are so beautiful and could easily find other love?!) Wishing to undermine our devotion to Hashem, the heathen nations say, in effect: You could enjoy the greatest success because you are so beautiful, but you hamper yourself because of this strange loyalty.[70] Their compliment underscores the question that puzzles the heathen nations; "What makes you, who has such great potential, so devoted to your relationship with Hashem, even at such a high cost?"[71]

Another explanation for their compliment is particularly resonant in our era. Some Jews make the great mistake of thinking that to impress the heathen nations and to get them to like the Jewish People, it is necessary to compromise and hide our religious convictions. Here we see that, on the contrary: when they see and hear our great declaration of faith (as in the previous verse), they are so amazed that they start to view *Klal Yisrael* as "the most beautiful of women." Only when we are completely devoted to Hashem will the gentiles come to honor us and praise our beauty. The more we stray from Hashem, however, the less respect we will evoke.

HOW IS YOUR BELOVED DIFFERENT?

Why do the heathen nations repeat this question twice? The simple explanation is that they are emphasizing their amazement that *Klal Yisrael* is so devoted to Hashem. Furthermore, one must never forget that *Shir HaShirim* is a song, and a song is an expression of deep emotions which necessarily require some repetition for effect.

The Vilna Gaon adds that the repetition corresponds to two implied questions. When

---

69 1:8.

70 It is noteworthy that in the *Akdamus* prayer, when we describe how the nations try to sway *Klal Yisrael* away from Hashem, we mention how they begin by saying: "Why do you, who are so beautiful and could be so well looked after, devote yourself to Hashem at such great cost?!"

71 The Netziv writes in a similar vein that a beautiful woman who naturally thinks she has many options will not be as devoted to her husband as an ugly woman who fears she will never find anyone else. Therefore, the heathen nations say to *Klal Yisrael*: we cannot understand your devotion since you are so beautiful, and thus have other options.

we see a wife extremely devoted to her husband, a woman who sacrifices everything to be with him — as *Klal Yisrael* do for Hashem — two explanations present themselves: either the husband is very special or the relationship is very special. For example, a woman married to a major *talmid chacham* or an extremely kind person would surely be devoted to him because of how special he is.[72] But even a woman married to a simple man would be devoted if the relationship is very fulfilling because of how much she enjoys the relationship. Here the heathen nations query *Klal Yisrael* on both counts: What is special about Hashem, and what is special about the relationship that you, *Klal Yisrael*, are so devoted to Him? Eventually (as will be explained), *Klal Yisrael* reply that indeed, Hashem is truly special and the relationship with Him is special.

INTRODUCTION TO VERSES 10-16

To better understand the following verses, let us take a few moments to summarize where matters stand. Hashem (the king) came to *Klal Yisrael* (his wife) and begged them to open up for Him by repenting and returning to Him. They refused, and only after much cajoling, did they reluctantly open up a bit. Hashem was displeased and left them. Once this happened, *Klal Yisrael* realized their mistake and began searching for Him in desperation. Since they lost His protection, they had to suffer the indignities of exile. *Klal Yisrael* declare their great love for Hashem by asking the nations to promise that if they find Hashem ("my Beloved"), that they should testify to their loyalty and devotion. *Klal Yisrael* (the wife in the *mashal*) is asked by the gentile nations (the maidens) to explain their undying love and great devotion.

In the *mashal*, the wife goes on (in verses 10-16) to answer this question by praising her husband at great length. She describes what a wonderful and handsome man her husband is, how kind and great he is. In the *nimshal*, *Klal Yisrael* is being asked by the nations what is so special about Hashem that their love for Him is so great. *Klal Yisrael* gives their answer in these verses that describe the tremendous greatness of Hashem and thereby explain why *Klal Yisrael* is so devoted to Him. Since *Shir HaShirim* uses the *mashal* of husband and wife to describe the relationship between Hashem and *Klal Yisrael*, their answer resembles the language in which a wife praises her husband. Just as when Hashem praised *Klal Yisrael* earlier on, using the metaphor of a beautiful

---

72 In the Artscroll biography of Rabbi Ovadia Yosef by Yehuda Heimowitz, the author beautifully describes how young R' Yosef would sometimes neglect to give his future wife, Margalit, his undivided attention due to his great dedication to Torah. But because Margalit recognized his greatness, she chose to marry him nevertheless (pp. 114-117).

woman, here in praising Hashem, *Klal Yisrael* uses the metaphor of a handsome and kind husband.

It is noteworthy that when *Klal Yisrael* speak of Hashem's beauty in these verses, they begin with His "head" and conclude with His "legs," working their way down, *ki'veyachol*. But when Hashem praises *Klal Yisrael*, He does so in the opposite direction, from the "feet" to the "head" (7:2-7). The reason for this is that Hashem's main Presence is in the Heavens above, so we wish to bring Him down, *ki'veyachol*, to be closer to us. Therefore, the direction is downwards. In contrast, we are here on this lowly earth and Hashem wants to draw us up. Therefore, the relevant direction for His praise is upwards, drawing us up to Him.

All of this, like the whole of *Shir HaShirim*, is metaphorical and not meant to be taken literally. Indeed, this should be self-evident since none of these verses make any sense according to the literal meaning of the words. After all, they are describing Hashem, and He is not corporeal in any way. To think otherwise is *apikorsus* (heresy).

Each of the following verses describes a different aspect of Hashem's greatness. It is beyond the scope of this *sefer* to elucidate the exact meaning of each metaphor. The greatness of Hashem is beyond anything we could ever understand.[73] Indeed, we have no inkling of His greatness.[74] Our main focus here is what we can appreciate and learn from these verses.

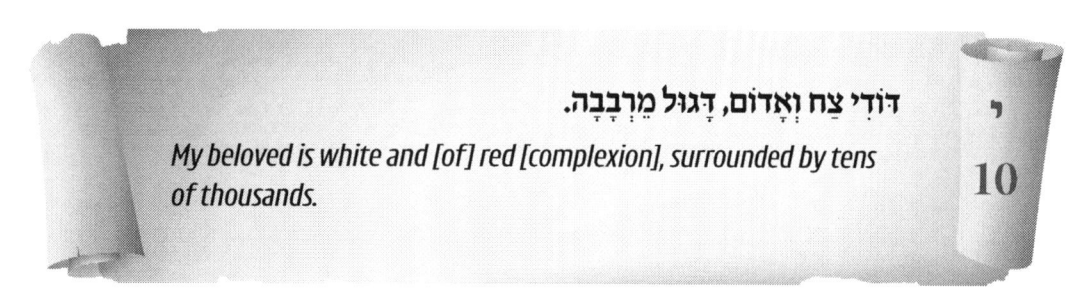

> **י** דּוֹדִי צַח וְאָדוֹם, דָּגוּל מֵרְבָבָה.
>
> **10** My beloved is white and [of] red [complexion], surrounded by tens of thousands.

Allegorical Translation   *Klal Yisrael* praise Hashem: "Hashem forgives our sins and makes them white;[75]

---

73 Perhaps this is the reason that there are many more verses describing the greatness of *Klal Yisrael* than the greatness of Hashem in *Shir HaShirim*. Since the greatness of Hashem is beyond our grasp and thus our praise of Him is limited to that which we can appreciate, these few verses are sufficient for that purpose.

74 The feeling of describing a God whom we love dearly, but whose greatness we cannot fathom at all, is beautifully encapsulated in *Anim Zemiros*: "אספרה כבודך ולא ראיתיך אדמך אכנך ולא ידעתיך" — I shall relate Your glory although I have not seen You; I shall allegorize You, I shall describe You, although I do not know You!"

75 This metaphor appears in a verse from *Yeshayahu* (1:18) that we recite many times in our prayers during the year: "אם יהיו חטאיכם כשנים כשלג ילבינו אם יאדימו כתולע כצמר יהיו" — If your sins will be red like scarlet [I (Hashem) will clean them and then] they will be as white as snow; if they are red like red dye, they will be as white as wool."

and He punishes the sinners.[76] He is surrounded by myriads of angels."

Subject of the Verse — *Klal Yisrael* is praising Hashem and thereby explaining why they are so loyal to Him.

Mashal — Through her praise, the wife explains why she is so loyal to her husband. She notes his complexion, which is a beautiful mix of white and red, and the fact that he is surrounded by many loyal friends.

Nimshal — As explained in the allegorical translation, this verse is about Hashem forgiving those who deserve forgiveness and punishing the wicked. It also mentions that He is surrounded by angels. All these magnificent attributes evoke loyalty from *Klal Yisrael*.

WHITE AND RED

At first glance, this description is puzzling since usually something cannot be both white and red. Rashi explains that "white" is symbolic of peace and forgiveness (in the sense of cleaning the slate). "Red/Ruddy" is symbolic of anger and revenge (in the sense of bloody vengeance). Hashem is both very forgiving of the Jews who seek His forgiveness, and very vengeful towards the wicked nations who remain sinners. Contrary to human beings, who normally are inclined towards one of these modes or the other, Hashem encompasses both. Indeed, Hashem encompasses all modes of conduct and can execute opposite modes of conduct with equal power at the very same time. The Midrash gives many examples of this.[77] One instance occurred at the Splitting of the Sea. While *Klal Yisrael* was feeling Hashem's tremendous love as they walked across the sea bed as if on dry land and enjoyed many other miracles as well (such as having food and drink available through the "miraculous walls" of the sea on either side of them), the Egyptians were feeling Hashem's full wrath as the sea closed over them, and each of them suffered "tailor-made" kinds of death.[78]

---

76   The color red symbolizes blood and retribution.

77   Here are just a few other examples from the Midrash:
Hashem is white (forgiving) to *Klal Yisrael*, but red (vengeful) to the wicked nations.
Hashem is white (forgiving) on Yom Kippur, but red (vengeful) during the rest of the year.
Hashem is white (forgiving) on Shabbos, but red (vengeful) during the rest of the week.
Hashem is white (forgiving) towards *Klal Yisrael* in the World to Come, but red (vengeful) here in this world.
(Some people have the custom to wear white on Shabbos and Yom Kippur because of this Midrash – a reminder of Hashem's gentleness on those precious days).

78   In the *Shiras HaYam*, *Klal Yisrael* said, "Hashem is a man of war; Hashem is His name" (*Shemos* 15:3). Rashi explains that the Name "Hashem" as it is spelled there denotes mercy. Normally, when a king is at war, he cannot involve himself with acts of kindness. When Hashem is at war, however, His Name remains "Hashem," meaning that He is still acting

This awareness motivates *Klal Yisrael* to feel a very strong loyalty toward Hashem. They understand that being a servant of Hashem ensures a tremendous amount of love and forgiveness from Him, while going against Him ensures an astonishing amount of punishment. If a person knows someone who is always very gentle and merciful, he does not need to make an effort with him, knowing that whatever happens will be fine. Alternatively, if a person knows someone who is always nasty and difficult, he will try to avoid that individual altogether, convinced that there is no way to get through to him. But Hashem is extremely kind to those who serve Him, while He is extremely vengeful to those who disobey Him. This ensures that we will always want to do our best to serve Him.

The Tzror HaMor explains that Hashem's "vengeance" is only for our sake: to purify us from sin. In line with this explanation, the verse should be understood as follows: "My Beloved 'whitens us' [cleanses us] through 'red' [i.e., punishment]." This verse, then, reminds us that everything Hashem does is for our own good, even the suffering and punishment. This, too, evokes loyalty. A servant who realizes that his master does only kindness for him, and even actions that seem harsh are truly acts of love, will be very loyal.

The Metzudas Dovid understands *Klal Yisrael*'s words very differently. According to him, they are declaring the simple truth that Hashem is the Master of all powers, and that all the other gods are worthless. That is their answer to the question: What is special about your God? *Klal Yisrael* reply that He cannot be compared to all other gods since He is the only one who has power. They express this by saying "[Only from] my Beloved comes all good [white] and all suffering [red], and all powers in this world [symbolized by myriads of angels]," so why should we serve any other power?!⁷⁹

SURROUNDED BY TENS OF THOUSANDS

The second part of this verse alludes to the many angels who serve Hashem and carry out His will. Every angel serving Hashem is another soldier, *ki'veyachol*, in His army, each one capable of performing a different kind of function. This is a simple way of saying that Hashem has an inconceivably huge, powerful, and varied arsenal of power ready to do His bidding.

As we saw in connection with the "white and red" in the first part of this verse, Hashem is capable of operating in two opposite ways simultaneously. This theme is

---

with kindness to the world.

79 The more a person drives home this simple message to himself, the more he will serve Hashem alone. A person who mistakenly feels that other human beings have power over him will not be able to focus all his energies on serving only Hashem.

developed here. The "tens of thousands" that "surround" Hashem are His myriad powers and modes of conduct, all of which are under His control. People can excel in a very small number of different skills or areas of expertise, but Hashem in every single way transcends all powers.

> **יא 11** רֹאשׁוֹ כֶּתֶם פָּז; קְוֻצּוֹתָיו תַּלְתַּלִּים, שְׁחֹרוֹת כָּעוֹרֵב.
>
> *His head is [like] an ornament made of the finest gold;[80] His locks of hair are curled, and black as a raven.*

Allegorical Translation — From the first of His words, His message was illuminating like gold. From every hair-like protrusion, from every letter in the Torah, many laws are learned.[81] His Torah is written with black fire.

Subject of the Verse — *Klal Yisrael* is praising Hashem.

Mashal — Praising her husband, the wife says his head is bright and shiny, like the finest gold; his locks of hair are curled and as black as a raven.

Nimshal — The first half of the verse alludes to the first words Hashem spoke at Sinai. They were as clear and brilliant as fine gold. The head is symbolic of the beginning of the Ten Commandments. The comparison to gold communicates that His opening message was bright and clear from the outset. As Rashi explains, the very first words Hashem spoke – *Anochi Hashem Elokecha* (I am Hashem, your God) – made clear His mastery and our obligation to obey Him. Hashem did not just present us with a long list of instructions without explanation. Rather, He first established why we have to obey Him. Once we became illuminated with understanding, He taught us the Torah.

The hair represents the *tagim*, the little crowns on many of the letters that look like hairlines coming from the letters. Even these small nuances in the letters

---

80   In our morning prayers, we begin the praises of Hashem, the *Pesukei D'Zimrah*, with the blessing "*Baruch She'Amar.*" The Anshei Knesses HaGedolah (Men of the Great Assembly from the beginning of the Second Beis HaMikdash) received a script from Heaven with this lofty blessing consisting of eighty-seven words. This blessing is alluded to in the opening words of praise here in our verse: ראשו כתם פז, meaning "His head [i.e., the beginning of His praises] is [like] an ornament made of the finest gold [פז]." The word "פז" has a numerical value of 87 (*Mishnah Berurah* 51:1).

81   The word "תלתלים" (curled) can also mean "heaps upon heaps" (a תל is a great heap). In other words, many great heaps of laws are learned from the smallest details in the Torah.

teach us many important laws. From the fact that every minuscule part of Torah teaches us so much wisdom, we see the amazing depth of Torah. As the Gemara[82] tells us, Rabbi Akiva was able to learn many mountains of laws from these hair-like "crowns."

The raven-like black color alludes to the actual letters of the Torah, normally written in black ink. When Hashem originally gave the Torah, however, it was written in "black fire on white fire." This represents its utter spirituality and holiness.

HIS HEAD IS [LIKE] AN ORNAMENT MADE FROM THE FINEST GOLD

The Vilna Gaon notes that the word "כתם" (ornament) is also an acronym for כהונה, תורה מלכות: the priesthood, Torah, and kingship. These are the three crowns that a Jew may be privileged to acquire.[83] Hashem has them all, *ki'veyachol*.

Significantly, the verse does not say that there is an ornament of gold "*on* His head," but rather, "His head *is* [like] an ornament made from the finest gold." This reminds us that those who wear golden crowns are of two types. Some wear a crown to show that they are deserving of royalty. When they take off their crown, however, no one can possibly know of their greatness. They are dependent on external adornments to define their greatness. In contrast, there are others so great that they actually embody royalty. It is as if their head itself is a golden crown. This is the meaning of the praise here in our verse: "His head *is* [like] an ornament made from the finest gold." Hashem Himself embodies greatness. Hashem's greatness is such that our praise does not exalt Him, nor would our lack of praise diminish Him in any way. He is supreme royalty. He does not need a golden crown to be recognized as such.[84]

HIS LOCKS OF HAIR ARE CURLED AND BLACK…

The Metzudas Dovid sees the curled locks as an allusion to Hashem's actions. Although Hashem has a reason for everything He does, we are not always able to see and understand all the twists and turns, and how all the different events are ultimately connected. This is like curly hair that one cannot track from one end to the other. The locks of hair (i.e., actions) are dark in the sense that they are hard for human beings to perceive clearly. The verse praises the actions of Hashem as coming from His very deep thought (mind), like hair coming out of the head, but tells us that we cannot follow

---

82 *Menachos* 29b.
83 *Avos* 4:13.
84 *Metzudas Dovid*.

them, just as we cannot follow dark, curly hair.

The Vilna Gaon sees the hair here as symbolizing Torah. He comments that hair seems to be the most superfluous part of the body. If a person had to have a part of his body removed, he would certainly choose his hair. It has no muscles and cannot do anything. This verse likens Torah to hair in order to teach us that even the most superfluous parts of the Torah — such as the verses whose purpose we do not understand[85] — are praised because they can actually teach us so much and have so much importance.

Looking at the verse as a whole, we see that it begins by praising the most important part of the body (the head) and concludes by praising the least important part (the hair). In terms of the Vilna Gaon's interpretation, the verse begins by praising the First Commandment (*Anochi Hashem Elokecha*), ostensibly the most important part of the Torah, and concludes by praising the ostensibly least important part. This is intended to teach us that actually all parts of Torah are equally precious and significant.

Indeed, the Torah is different from all books of instruction, which more or less fall into one of two categories. On the one hand, we have study books written to be as clear as possible. While they are easy to understand, we cannot deduce anything from seemingly superfluous words or sentences. (Many of the wonderful study aides published in recent years to help people understand Gemara and Mishnah, etc., fall into this category.) On the other hand, we find profound academic books written for great scholars. They are difficult to understand, but tremendous depth often lies behind the words and nuances. (The *sefarim* of the Vilna Gaon are good examples of this.)

Torah is the exception. It is written in the most clear and systematic way, as Rashi explains. At the same time, every single letter and nuance has tremendous depth. This verse begins by praising Torah for its clarity and light: "From the first of His words, His message was illuminating like gold." It goes on to praise it for its intricacies: "From every hair-like protrusion, from every letter in the Torah, many laws are learned." The verse thus highlights the uniqueness of Torah, which features both aspects.[86]

BLACK AS A RAVEN

The Gemara teaches that this phrase alludes to how a person merits the acquisition of Torah. It derives three different methods from the terminology used here, "black as a raven."[87]

---

85   See, for example, *Bereishis* 36:12 with Rashi, and *Sanhedrin* 99b.

86   The same Torah that every child learns today was learned by the greatest Torah scholars of previous generations. This demonstrates how Torah is both clear and extremely deep.

87   *Eruvin* 22a.

The first method is that one must be completely dedicated to Torah, getting up early to study and studying late into the night.[88]

The second is that one needs to be black (i.e., ugly) as a raven. One who spends his time primping himself cannot truly acquire Torah. Only if one ignores all the temptations of superficial beauty of this world will one find the inner beauty of Torah.

The third method is derived from the cruelty of the raven in not feeding its offspring. To truly acquire Torah, one must not be overly sensitive to every worry that might befall his family. He must realize that Hashem will help take care of his family if he dedicates himself to Torah learning. Only by this single-minded devotion to learning Torah will one acquire it.[89]

HIS HEAD IS [LIKE] THE FINEST GOLD...

The Netziv raises the following question here: *Klal Yisrael* is ostensibly explaining their loyalty to Hashem by praising Him, yet most of the praise focuses on the greatness of Torah. Indeed, according to many *meforashim*, this is also true of many of the later verses comprising *Klal Yisrael's* response to the heathen nations. The Netziv explains that there are only two ways to know Hashem. One is through His actions. This includes the entire created world as well as all the events that occurred from the time of Creation. The second is through the Torah. The second way, says the Netziv, is greater than the first.[90] Knowing His true essence, of course, is impossible.

To elaborate, if someone says, "I know that person," but all he knows is the person's profession or bank balance, he knows only a small part of that person. In contrast, if one

---

88 This understanding derives from the close similarity between the word "שחורות" (black) and "שחרית" (early morning), and the close similarity between "עורב" (raven) and "ערב" (evening).

89 This needs to be understood properly. The Gemara is not saying that one should not do kindness in his pursuit of learning Torah. The point is that sometimes one gets great pleasure from indulging his children, and in pursuit of this pleasure, irresponsibly ignores his true duty, which is to serve Hashem. The Gemara teaches us that one who does so will not truly merit the acquisition of Torah.

90 We see this in the order of the two blessings we recite just before *Kriyas Shema* in the morning prayers: *Yotzer Ohr*, which speaks about Creation, and *Ahavah Rabbah*, which speaks about Torah. These blessings help us understand His greatness. As we get closer to the *Shema*, where we declare our belief in Hashem, we wish to get a truer appreciation of Hashem. The blessing focusing on Torah is second because it is on a higher level. Its placement just before the *Shema* communicates that it is through Torah that one gets a clearer understanding of Hashem.

This concept is hinted at in a verse from *Tehillim* (93:4-5) that we recite in the *Kabbalas Shabbos* prayers: מקולת מים רבים אדירים משברי ים אדיר במרום ה', עדתיך נאמנו מאד. This verse can be rendered: "From the roar of the mighty waters...[of Creation], Your Name, Hashem, is exalted; [however,] Your testimony [i.e., the Torah] is more faithful [to truly convey Your essence and greatness]."

When Rabbi Aharon Leib Steinman was flying to Canada to give *chizuk* to Jews in that country, the pilot announced that they would be crossing Niagara Falls. Everyone rushed to look through the windows except for the Rosh Yeshivah, who continued his Gemara learning. Someone asked him: Even though Torah is special, isn't there a concept of מה רבו מעשיך ה', that one should admire Hashem's beautiful creation?! He replied: Torah is also Hashem's beautiful creation!

knows the person's thoughts, desires, and feelings, then he does indeed know the person. Because the Torah, *ki'veyachol*, represents Hashem's thoughts, desires, and feelings, it is actually the truest way of knowing Hashem. Therefore, praising Torah is actually praising Hashem as we know Him. That is why most of the praise of Hashem here is in the form of praise of the Torah.

This is better understood when one appreciates that Hashem and Torah are intertwined. As discussed earlier,[91] Torah is the embodiment of Hashem's will. When it comes to human beings, we can distinguish between the person who knows something and his knowledge, between the knowing and the known. Hashem, however, is One in the absolute sense, and is completely indivisible. Therefore, the Torah He knows is the essence of the One who knows it.[92] Therefore, when *Klal Yisrael* wish to portray Hashem's greatness in order to explain why they are so devoted to Him, they thus focus on His Torah. That is the truest way of "knowing Him."

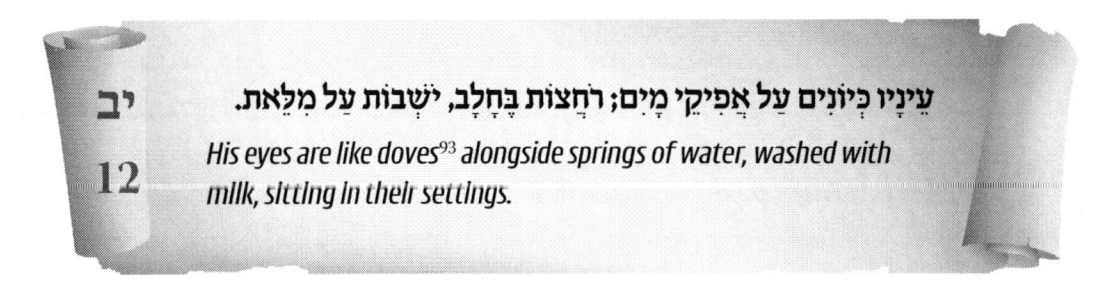

יב

12

עֵינָיו כְּיוֹנִים עַל אֲפִיקֵי מָיִם; רֹחֲצוֹת בֶּחָלָב, יֹשְׁבוֹת עַל מִלֵּאת.

His eyes are like doves[93] alongside springs of water, washed with milk, sitting in their settings.

Allegorical Translation

Klal Yisrael continue to praise Hashem. Rashi offers three interpretations of this verse depending on whether it is alluding to Hashem, to those who learn the Torah of Hashem, or to Torah itself. Even though, as we explained earlier, *Klal Yisrael* is praising Hashem here, since Hashem and His Torah are intertwined, praising one is like praising the other. What follows are three renderings of the verse according to each of these three interpretations:

1) Hashem's eyes focus and look (as a dove looks with devotion to its nest) towards the shuls and *batei midrash* which bring forth Torah which is likened

---

91   See our commentary on 1:2.

92   *Tanya* (ch. 4), explaining the statement in the *Zohar* (I:24a) that Torah and Hashem are one. In light of this caution, let us emphasize that the Oneness of Hashem precludes any division whatsoever. The portrayal of Hashem as both "white" and "red," as having many different powers, etc., is only how we perceive Him. In reality, Hashem is completely One in every aspect, with no changes in His conduct (*Derech Hashem*, 1:1:5).

93   See our commentary on 1:15 for a fuller discussion of the metaphor of doves.

to water.⁹⁴ Hashem has an absolutely clean and clear perspective⁹⁵ as He looks at this world — as if His eyes (i.e., viewpoint) are as clean as milk — and administers pure justice. Hashem sees and tracks all actions and keeps the entire world in its setting and positioning (like a carefully set diamond) with His justice.⁹⁶

2) Hashem created *talmidei chachamim* to be the eyes of the world,⁹⁷ seeing what needs to be done and lighting up the world with their knowledge. They move from place to place to learn Torah just as doves move from one nest to another.⁹⁸ They teach Torah, which is likened to springs of water. They elucidate and clarify Torah as if they were washing it with clean milk. They explain Torah clearly in a way that all the subjects and issues are established in their settings and fit into their context (like a carefully set diamond).

3) Torah topics⁹⁹ are organized as beautifully as a dove (which does not flit around but walks sedately).¹⁰⁰ In the places of learning which produce Torah — which is likened to spring water — the Torah is made clear like milk. The words of Torah are organized and structured in a perfect system, like a diamond beautifully positioned in its setting.¹⁰¹

Subject of the Verse   *Klal Yisrael* continues to praise Hashem.

Mashal   Continuing to praise her husband, the wife says that when he looks at springs

---

94   In a loosely similar way to human beings who constantly look at things that are important to them or give them pleasure, Hashem constantly looks at the shuls because they are so important and because He derives great pleasure from them.

95   Only Hashem sees with absolute clarity. As He told Shmuel, "While a person sees only with his eyes, Hashem can see into the heart" (*Shmuel I* 16:7). Furthermore, human beings are biased, and have their own prejudices and preferences. Although absolute clarity is impossible for a human being, we obviously must try to emulate Hashem, and have a *pure and clean perspective* when deciding how to conduct ourselves, how to discipline a child, etc.

96   Although we do not know Hashem's calculations, we know that He is constantly monitoring and administrating this world, making sure that it stays on its intended course.

97   This is explained earlier in connection with 1:15.

98   The Mishnah tells us that for the sake of learning Torah, a person should even go into exile (*Avos* 4:14). Throughout the history of *Klal Yisrael*, countless *talmidei chachamim* have travelled far and wide to enhance their learning. Even today, there are tens of thousands of young men who leave their home to go to learn Torah. This verse extolls this virtuous sacrifice.

99   According to this explanation the word "עיניו" does not mean "eyes," but rather "topics," like the word "עינייניו" (his topics), and refers to Torah, which is Hashem's favorite topic.

100   Maharzu on the Midrash to explain Rashi.

101   Torah is extremely well organized, so much so that many *halachos* are learned simply from the order in which they are written.

of water, his eyes are as beautiful as doves. (Rashi explains that because bodies of water are beautiful to look at, it was common for young men to stand and look at springs. Seeing them in that pose was a vision of beauty). His eyes are clean as if they have been washed with milk. They are beautifully set in their place, meaning that they neither protrude nor are not sunk in.

Nimshal *Klal Yisrael* praise Hashem. As we saw, there are number of ways of interpreting this verse. The *nimshal* for each one is made clear in the allegorical translations of Rashi above. Here we will show how the *mashal* corresponds to the *nimshal*.

Water is symbolic of Torah. Of the many reasons given for this metaphor, we find the following: just as water gives life, so does Torah; just as water flows down to the lowest point, so does Torah (in the sense that it is absorbed by the humble, and rolls off the arrogant); just as water is free even though it is the most vital thing for survival, so Torah is free for all who wish to learn it even though it is essential for a person's spiritual survival.

In light of the fact that dirty items are often referred to as being black, milk is symbolic of cleanliness because of its very white color. This symbolic meaning is used here in connection with clarifying Torah or administering "clean" justice, as explained above.

Settings evoke the idea of a perfect fit. A diamond setter, for example, is very careful to put each precious jewel in its exact setting.[102] The phrase "eyes... sitting in their settings," then, alludes to the precision of the Torah's language and its laws. Alternatively, it alludes to the absolutely precise nature of Hashem's justice. A person is never punished even one iota more than he deserves. This is something no human judge can possibly do.[103]

---

102 Setting a diamond in its exact setting was a special art (Rashi on *Shemos* 31:5).

103 *Tzror HaMor*. There are many examples in the Torah of the most intricate and minute calculations made by Hashem to give everyone exactly what he deserves, e.g., Yosef being carted down to slavery in Egypt in a wagon full of nice-smelling spices and his being separated from his father for exactly twenty-two years.

> יג לְחָיָו כַּעֲרוּגַת הַבֹּשֶׂם, מִגְדְּלוֹת מֶרְקָחִים; שִׂפְתוֹתָיו שׁוֹשַׁנִּים, נֹטְפוֹת מוֹר עֹבֵר.
>
> **13** His cheeks are like a bed of perfume spices, where sweet herbs grow. His lips are like roses; they drip flowing myrrh.

Allegorical Translation His words (emanating from His cheeks) at Har Sinai were as sweet and joyful as a bed of perfume spices. His words (emanating from His lips) at the *Ohel Moed* flowed with forgiveness, like flowing myrrh that alleviates bad smells (so His forgiveness alleviated the bad smell caused by our sins).

Subject of the Verse *Klal Yisrael* is praising Hashem.

Mashal Continuing to praise her husband, the wife says that his cheeks resemble a bed of perfume spices and important plants which are constantly cultivated and embellished; his lips are beautiful, like roses, and produce a good smell, like flowing myrrh.

Nimshal *Klal Yisrael* praise the words of Hashem and exclaim how much pleasure and delight His words bring. They refer both to the Torah He taught, which brings delight, and His words of forgiveness, which take away all the damage caused by our sins.

HIS CHEEKS ARE LIKE A BED OF PERFUME SPICES

The Gemara tells us that every word Hashem spoke at Har Sinai caused the entire world to be filled with perfume. He had to send out a wind to blow the perfume away into the storehouses of the World to Come to clear the way for the new perfume of the next word He would say.[104] This is hinted at in our verse.[105] The message is that every word of Hashem has so much goodness within it that it is possible for the entire world to be enhanced from it. We are supposed to emulate Hashem, and thus we should make sure

---

104 *Shabbos* 88b.

105 The Hebrew word for "his cheeks" ("לְחָיָו") hints at the similarly spelled word "לוּחוֹת" (the tablets of stone on which the Ten Commandments were inscribed), and "flowing myrrh" here hints at the perfumes which flowed to make room for the next wave of perfume. According to this, our verse should be understood as follows: "His [words that come from the] tablets are perfume spices; [and to clear the way for the perfumes that would come from the words of] His lips, the myrrh flowed."

that our words always leave behind a pleasant atmosphere.

The Metzudas Dovid differentiates between the "innermost" speech emanating from the "cheeks" and the more "external" speech emanating from the "lips." From the "cheeks" come Hashem's own words of Torah, while from the "lips" come the words of His emissaries and spokesmen, the prophets. The words of Hashem are a "bed of perfume spices" in the sense that they have the ability to grow and produce wonders and greatness. The words of the prophets are like flowing myrrh because they spread the word of Hashem far and wide.

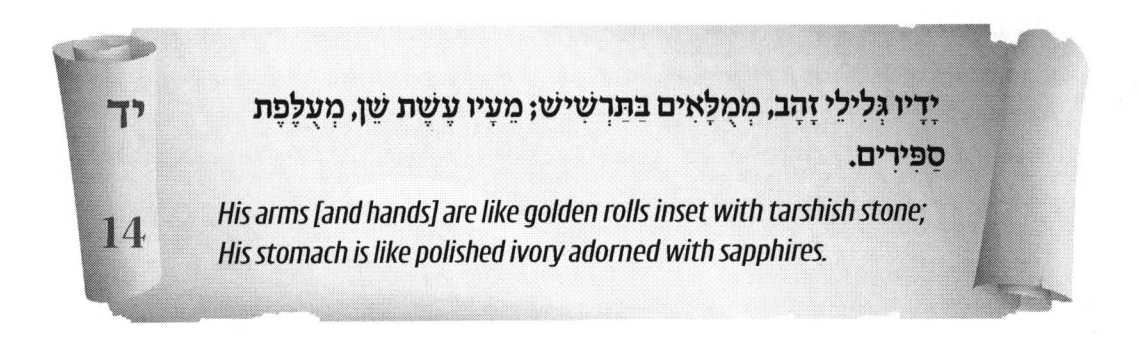

> יָדָיו גְּלִילֵי זָהָב, מְמֻלָּאִים בַּתַּרְשִׁישׁ; מֵעָיו עֶשֶׁת שֵׁן, מְעֻלֶּפֶת סַפִּירִים.
>
> **14** *His arms [and hands] are like golden rolls inset with tarshish stone; His stomach is like polished ivory adorned with sapphires.*

Allegorical Translation — The *Luchos* (the tablets of stone given and inscribed by "His hands") were miraculously rolled up (even though they were hewn from sapphire) and had written on them words more precious than gold. They were filled with all 613 mitzvos. *Vayikra*, also known as *Toras Kohanim*, the middle book of the Torah (like the stomach in the middle of the body), appears to be as smooth as ivory. In reality, though, it has many intricate and complex laws, more like smooth ivory intricately overlaid with precious stones and sapphires.

Subject of the Verse — *Klal Yisrael* is praising Hashem.

Mashal — Continuing to praise her husband, the wife says that his arms look like golden columns studded with stones of *tarshish*. His stomach is clean and shiny, like polished ivory adorned with sapphires.

Nimshal — The *nimshal* is as explained in the allegorical translation above, based on Rashi. Let us just zero in on how the words of the verse convey the *nimshal*.

The hands (literally, "arms") represent the *Luchos* given and created by Hashem's "hands," *ki'veyachol*. Obviously, everything in the world was created by Hashem, but the *Luchos* were special in that they were crafted directly by Him through His intense focus, and they were given personally by Him.[106]

As used here, "gold" communicates just how precious the words of the *Luchos* were that they were valuable like gold.

"Rolls" teach us that the *Luchos* were able to be rolled up miraculously even though they were made of hard sapphire. Hashem made this great miracle to teach us about the greatness of the *Luchos*. Just as something that is rolled up has many hidden layers, so each word of Hashem has many different layers of meaning. And just as something which is rolled up and circular moves around easily, so the *Luchos* readily roll goodness throughout the world. Furthermore, just as a rolled object which is unrolled spreads out and covers a much larger surface, so the words of Torah spread goodness and reward over much greater areas than people can ever imagine.

"Inset with *tarshish* stone" communicates that just as a fine piece of jewelry often contains many special stones, so each word of Torah contains hidden treasures. As Rashi notes, all 613 mitzvos are contained within the words of the *Luchos*.[107]

The praise of the stomach, located in the middle of the body, is meant as praise for *Sefer Vayikra*, the middle book of the Torah. Furthermore, the stomach area (literally, "innards") is not known for its beauty. Indeed, the innards seem to be filled with waste and unappealing organs. Similarly, the laws of *korbanos, tumah,* and *taharah* (sacrifices, impurity, and purity) do not seem appealing. Yet, just as we cannot live without the stomach and all its inner organs, so the entire world

---

106 "The *Luchos* were the handiwork of Hashem" (*Shemos* 32:16). "Handiwork" connotes an accomplishment, not just something that a person happened to make. "From his right Hand, laws of fire were given to them" (*Devarim* 33:2). These were the *Luchos*.

107 Rashi on *Shemos* 24:12, *s.v. vaetnah*. See the *Azharos* (liturgical poem) of Rabbi Saadyah Gaon, mentioned by Rashi, for an elucidation. The word "*tarshish*" (תרשיש) has the *gematria* of כל המצוות תריג, meaning "all mitzvos are 613." Both add up to 1210 (Chida in *Chomas Anach*). The Melo HaOmer sees "תרשיש" as a compound word hinting at both the 613 Mitzvos and the six orders of the Mishnah, which were also contained in the *Luchos*. The numerical value of תרי (together with its three letters) is the equivalent of 613; and שש (six) is the number of orders of the Mishnah.

cannot exist without the merit of the *korbanos* (and nowadays, by our learning about them).[108]

"Ivory" communicates that the laws of *Vayikra* first seem smooth like ivory, and easy to execute. Yet they are "adorned with sapphires." This means that only when one examines these laws carefully is one able to see all the intricate nuances and minute details connected with them.

HIS [HANDS] ARE LIKE GOLDEN ROLLS…

According to the Netziv, this entire verse alludes to the way Hashem runs the world. "His [hands] are like golden rolls" communicates that Hashem's deeds are pure, like pure gold untainted by alloys. They are all done with absolute fairness, untainted by any bias, etc. And just as gold does not decay even after a long time, so Hashem's deeds last forever. Still, we often do not understand them. They are "rolled up" in the sense that they are mostly hidden. Yet, they are "inset with *tarshish* stone," meaning that just as we see this precious stone catching the light every so often, so we see sometimes perceive something which gives us an understanding of why Hashem is operating in a certain way. So Hashem's actions are like golden rolls, which have a hidden purity but also have revealed precious stones, small bright lights of understanding.

"His stomach [i.e., innards] is like polished ivory." Ivory is very hard. A great many people have sensitive stomachs such that they get a pain in the stomach if they eat something a bit spoiled. Even if they are just agitated or excited, they are unable to eat well, and get a churning inside.[109] Hashem, however, has a "stomach" like ivory: hard and strong enough to "stomach" many evil people.[110] Indeed, one of the astounding aspects of Hashem's greatness is that despite the fact that He created the world and looks after all its inhabitants, He "stomachs" the disrespect that He is often shown without impatience or discomfort. It is a great strength not to be affected by the terrible behavior of others towards us. Hashem is able to do this on the grandest scale imaginable: He stomachs all the terrible behavior of the world without it affecting His kind conduct and His profound and wise plans.

Yet His conduct is "adorned with sapphires." The Netziv explains that sapphire

---

108 Let us recall that we admire gastroenterologists who heal people with serious stomach problems. Nobody in their right mind would say that these specialists should be ashamed of themselves for getting involved in these distasteful matters. Indeed, they often saves lives. Similarly, we should admire Rabbanim who delve into the laws of purity, or those who learn the laws of sacrifices, since our spiritual lives depend on this.

109 This is how Yirmeyahu describes the anguish of the terrible destruction of the Beis HaMikdash: "My stomach has churned" (*Eichah* 1:20 and 2:11).

110 Those who never suffer indigestion are often said to have an "iron stomach."

reflects all images, and any small change is immediately seen on the surface of the sapphire. This means that Hashem deals with the righteous, His precious sapphires, in a "reflective" manner: As soon as they sin, He immediately shows His displeasure.[111] Because He wants to keep them close to Him, He sets any small deviation right. The righteous are similar to sapphires in another sense. Since they look very carefully at what is happening, they perceive how Hashem administers justice, punishing the wicked and rewarding the righteous. Like the sapphire, they see and reflect the changing light.

We know from experience that when we care deeply about a relationship, we frequently check to how the other person feels towards us, keeping a finger on the pulse of the relationship. Since the righteous care about their relationship with Hashem, they watch closely to see how Hashem "feels" about them. They ask themselves if they are pleasing in His eyes and whether or not they are becoming closer to Him. Therefore, they actually sense His love or displeasure. But the wicked do not care about their relationship with Hashem. They are oblivious to Hashem, and Hashem responds in kind, acting as if He does not care about them either.

In summary, our verse helps us understand what at first seem to be contradictions in Hashem's ways. They are just, but their reasoning is not clear to us due to our limitations. His ways are hidden, but sometimes we are afforded a glimpse of light.[112] Hashem "stomachs" the worst kind of behavior but reacts quickly to the righteous.

> טו שׁוֹקָיו עַמּוּדֵי שֵׁשׁ, מְיֻסָּדִים עַל אַדְנֵי פָז; מַרְאֵהוּ כַּלְּבָנוֹן, בָּחוּר כָּאֲרָזִים.
>
> 15 His thighs are like marble pillars supported on sockets of fine gold. His appearance is like Levanon; He is distinguished like a cedar tree.

Allegorical Translation Like a pillar or a column firmly set in a pedestal at the bottom and a crowning crest at the top, each section of the Torah is well connected to the subject in the previous and succeeding section.[113] The more one examines Torah, the more ideas one sees. It is like a forest in the sense that the more one looks at it, the more trees and leaves he sees growing there. He (Hashem) is distinguished

---

111 The Netziv cites many examples of this. Perhaps the most striking is Hashem eliminating Nadav and Avihu immediately because of a small sin. (See *Eruvin* 63a for a discussion of exactly what sin this was.)
112 As in the story of Purim.
113 Rashi cites examples of how one topic in the Torah is closely connected to the next.

from among all beings like a cedar is distinguished from among all trees.

Subject of the Verse *Klal Yisrael* is praising Hashem.

Mashal Continuing to praise her husband, the wife says that his thighs are as strong and firm as marble pillars and as beautiful as if they rest on sockets of fine gold. His general appearance is wondrous like the Levanon forest (one of the biggest forests of the time), and he is majestic like the striking cedar tree.

Nimshal Again, the *nimshal* is as explained in the allegorical translation above, based on Rashi. So, we need only focus on how the words of the verse convey the *nimshal*.

The image of "thighs like marble pillars supported on sockets of fine gold" represents how Torah is well established in the sense that all the topics are organized one after the other just as a pillar stands firmly between the pedestal below and the crown above. This interlocking organization has a number of ramifications. For one, it made it possible for *Chazal* to learn laws and Divine lessons simply from the order of the topics. The appropriate fit of the pedestal and crown reflect the fact that the laws of the Torah are all organized in the correct and most appropriate manner, with each topic being connected to the topic before and after. And just as pillars are finely balanced, so the words and expressions of the Torah are carefully balanced. Each utterance of rebuke or praise is finely tuned.

"Sockets of fine gold" hints at the way that even the lowest parts of Torah (sockets), which are symbolic of the simplest explanations, bring light to the surroundings just as gold shines and brightens the surroundings.

"His appearance is like Levanon." As mentioned above, Levanon was a huge forest. And just as a huge forest harbors millions upon millions of leaves and buds and endless things to see and discover, so the Torah features myriad explanations and meanings. Just as one can never fully absorb all that there is in a forest, so one can never fully absorb all the lessons in the Torah.

"He is distinguished like a cedar." A cedar tree is very tall and imposing, hinting at the awesomeness and magnificence of Hashem. All other things pale in comparison to the majesty of Hashem.

HIS THIGHS ARE LIKE MARBLE PILLARS...

According to the Netziv, who interprets the previous verse in terms of how Hashem runs the world, the symbolism here is to be understood differently. The thighs, situated in lower part of the body, allude to our lowly world.[114] "Pillars of marble (שש) can also be understood as "pillars of six," the six days of Creation during which Hashem made this lowly world.[115] Just as thighs keep a person standing and moving, so this lowly world, through Torah and the mitzvos we do in it, supports the Heavenly Spheres. Indeed, even if all the angels in the higher realms would continue to serve Hashem, the entire spiritual universe would cease to exist in the absence of our lowly world. Furthermore, the mitzvos we do create changes and movement in the Heavenly Spheres, like thighs that move a person from place to place. The fine gold of the "sockets" represents good deeds which, like gold, never become dim or rusty. The reward for our good deeds lasts forever.

How is Hashem both like a forest and a cedar tree? From a distance, a forest looks like one big mass. It is almost impossible to distinguish one leaf or plant from another. Yet the cedar tree is highly distinguishable. In a loosely similar way, from a distance, we do not perceive how Hashem treats every person individually, according to his deeds. But the reality is that just as a cedar tree is distinct and clearly seen, so Hashem watches over every person and every deed carefully. He makes sure that everything that happens to a person accords with His distinct plan. Hashem does not run the world through sweeping "forest-like" actions, taking into consideration only big issues. Rather, He has a careful, personalized plan for every individual.

According to the Netziv, then, our verse should be understood this way: Our lower world, created in six days, supports the Heavenly Spheres through the mitzvos and good deeds done here which are as bright as gold, and garner a reward that, like gold, lasts forever. Although it sometimes seems to us that Hashem runs our world in a general way, He actually employs individualized Divine Providence.[116]

The message here is one of the fundamentals of *emunah*. Hashem takes every little detail of every human being into consideration. The King of Kings is not like a king of flesh and blood who might punish an entire city because some of its people deserve punishment. In His actions, He is also not like an artist painting a forest, where only the general view is in focus, but the details are obscure. Rather, He is like an artist painting an individual item, with careful attention to each detail.

---

114 As Yeshayahu HaNavi exclaims: "The heavens are Hashem's throne, and the earth His footstool…" (66:1).

115 The angels and the Heavenly worlds, notes the Netziv, were all created in one day: the second day of Creation.

116 The Netziv explains the conclusion of the verse this way: "His appearance (i.e., the *appearance* of how He runs the world is) like Levanon (a forest without clear distinctions, between different people and deeds, but *really*) He is distinguished (in the sense that He distinguishes between all deeds) like a cedar (is distinct)."

HIS APPEARANCE IS LIKE LEVANON

The Midrash sees this verse alluding not to Hashem's actions, but to Hashem Himself. According to this approach, His "appearance" is like Levanon, an enormous forest, in the sense that things are continuously growing and changing there. Every time one looks, there is another leaf or fruit growing. It is impossible to see all that there is to be seen in a forest. Similarly, every time one tries to see Hashem, he sees another aspect of His greatness, another wonderful quality, etc. It is impossible to see all of Hashem's greatness. The Ibn Ezra adds that the deeper one goes into a forest, the greater and more impressive the trees that come into view. Similarly, the more deeply one contemplates the greatness of Hashem, the greater the attributes that he sees.

Our verse can also be seen contrasting a forest and cedar tree in another way. A forest is beautiful because it combines many different trees, while a cedar is unique because it is tall and majestic. When one wishes to present beautiful flowers, one can choose to combine many beautiful flowers to make a bouquet, or one can take one especially precious flower and present it on its own. Hashem combines within Him both aspects. In this verse, He is likened both to a forest and a cedar tree. A forest has a huge number and variety of plants symbolizing Hashem's huge variety and number of wonderful attributes. In contrast, a cedar tree is grand and majestic on its own. Each of Hashem's attributes is grand and majestic in its own right, even without the enhancement of other attributes.

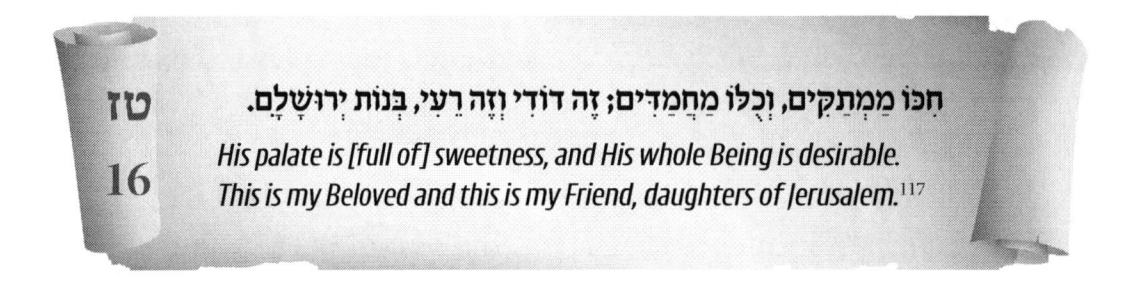

טז / 16

חִכּוֹ מַמְתַקִּים, וְכֻלּוֹ מַחֲמַדִּים; זֶה דוֹדִי וְזֶה רֵעִי, בְּנוֹת יְרוּשָׁלָם.

His palate is [full of] sweetness, and His whole Being is desirable. This is my Beloved and this is my Friend, daughters of Jerusalem.[117]

Allegorical Translation

Klal Yisrael conclude their praise of Hashem this way: "Hashem's words are sweet to us, and He is completely desirable and pleasurable." Turning to the heathen nations, *Klal Yisrael* respond to their question about what motivates their own loyalty to Hashem: "This [all of the aforementioned praises of Hashem] is a portrayal of My Beloved and Friend." In other words, "We have described to you who our Beloved really is and how special He is. Now you can appreciate why we love Him so and why we are wholeheartedly devoted

---

117 See our commentary on 1:5 for an elucidation of the expression "daughters of Jerusalem."

to Him."

Subject of the Verse — *Klal Yisrael* explains their devotion to Hashem to all the nations by praising Him and communicating the greatness of the One they love, with whom they share a precious relationship.

Mashal — The wife, who had been challenged by her guards regarding her boundless devotion to her husband, enumerates all of his wonderful attributes, and concludes by saying: "His palate is full of sweetness and his whole being is desirable." She comments: Now that you have had a glimpse of my beloved and my friend, you understand why I am so devoted to him.

Nimshal — This verse concludes the section which began in verse 2. To summarize briefly, Hashem tried to convince *Klal Yisrael* to repent, but they refused. As a result, He sent them into exile, where they suffer because of their devotion to Him. The heathen nations mockingly question the rationale behind their loyalty. *Klal Yisrael* respond by highlighting the greatness of Hashem, concluding that they remain loyal to Him because of this greatness (verses 10-16). This verse is the glorious conclusion and the proud summary statement about the uniqueness of Hashem and *Klal Yisrael's* relationship with Him.

The *nimshal* is as explained in the allegorical translation above, based on Rashi. So, we need only focus on how the words of the verse correspond to the *nimshal*.

The "palate" here alludes to Hashem's speech, which emanates from the palate.

The "sweetness" communicates how sweet Hashem's words are both in the sense that learning Torah is very pleasurable and in the sense that His words convey kindness and love. To illustrate, Hashem commands us not to mutilate ourselves in grief over the dead and adds that He will reward us for refraining.[118] Hashem is willing to reward us for not causing ourselves harm! Normally, a person is paid and rewarded for doing things that are difficult or dangerous. But here we are rewarded for *not* harming ourselves! To illustrate further, Hashem commands us not to eat worms and blood,[119] items which a person naturally finds revolting. Yet He promises a great reward for observing these effortless commandments. Furthermore, Hashem tells us that if we repent, our sins will be turned into merits.[120] Let us try to appreciate how remarkable this is. Someone sins

---

118 *Vayikra* 19:28.
119 *Vayikra* 3:17, 11:43.
120 *Yechezkel* 33:19, *Yoma* 86b.

against Hashem, the mightiest and kindest King, who has dutifully looked after this person and given him everything he ever needed. Not only is the person not punished when he repents, but his sins are turned into merits! Is there a kinder or sweeter thing to say?![121]

"His whole Being is desirable" communicates that everything about Hashem is delightful.

"This is my Beloved and this is my Friend…" *Klal Yisrael* conclude their response to the heathen nations by saying that Hashem, whom they love and to whom they remain loyal, is everything they have just described.

HIS PALATE IS [FULL OF] SWEETNESS, AND HIS WHOLE BEING IS DESIRABLE

Rabbi Simcha Zissel of Kelm explains that from the little we do know and understand about Hashem, and from our glimpses at His kindness and sweetness, we infer that everything else about Him is delightful.[122] Therefore, the verse should be translated "[Since we see that] His palate is [full of] sweetness,[123] [we realize that] His whole Being is desirable." Although we do not really grasp Hashem at all, we can infer from the little that we do know how wonderful and kind He is. This is true regarding the mitzvos as well as that which happens in our lives and in the world. We do not know why Hashem gave us each and every mitzvah, or the reasons for all that happens. But from the little we do know, we see how sweet and kind Hashem is. We need only think of His rewarding us for effortless mitzvos and His willingness to turn our sins into merits when we repent, as explained above, to appreciate that all His commandments and all His actions are expressions of kindness.

Let us delve a bit deeper and point out that there is a difference between sweetness and desirability. Many things are desirable, but not sweet. That is to say, they are good for a person, and a person wants them even though they are not actually sweet. For example, medication can sometimes be bitter, but still be desirable. The verse begins by describing Hashem's sweetness and concludes by describing how all of Him is desirable. The Melo HaOmer explains that since we see Hashem's sweetness, we understand that even the things which we do not find sweet are actually desirable. Consider a very sweet and loving father punishing his child. If we see how truly sweet the father usually

---

121 *Midrash Yelamdeinu*, p. 6, and Rashi.

122 *Chochmah U'Mussar*, vol. I, ch. 208.

123 Hashem's words are symbolized by the singular noun "palate" (חכו), yet the modifier, "sweet," is in the plural (ממתקים). The Netziv (on 2:3) explains the seeming inconsistency this way: The words of Hashem are always sweet, but each person only tastes the sweetness of Hashem according to his own level of devotion and closeness to Him. It turns out that Hashem's "palate" has many levels of sweetness, according to the person tasting it.

is, then we can appreciate that even the punishment is actually desirable and good for the child. Indeed, "His palate is sweetness, and His *whole* Being is desirable." From the sweetness of His palate, we know that His *whole* being is desirable. Even if we do not see His whole being as sweet — i.e., not everything Hashem does do we find sweet — we know that everything He does is desirable.

THIS IS MY BELOVED AND THIS IS MY FRIEND

Klal Yisrael was challenged by the heathen nations as to why are they so devoted to Hashem. As explained earlier,[124] there are two inherent questions here: 1) In what way is Hashem special? and 2) In what way is the relationship between you and Hashem special? Behind these questions lies the assumption that devotion is caused either by seeing how great a person is or by having a wonderful relationship. *Klal Yisrael* conclude here that they have both. "This is my Beloved" communicates that the praises I have just been singing describe the greatness of Hashem, who is my Beloved. "And this is my Friend" communicates that Hashem is my best friend, meaning that the relationship is unique and special.[125]

---

124 Verse 9.

125 It is true, as the expression goes, "One ingredient of happiness is being married to one's best friend." The phrase, "This is my Beloved and this is my Friend," teaches us that *Klal Yisrael* is privileged to enjoy that special happiness.
As mentioned in the Introduction, we need to learn not only from the *nimshal* of *Shir HaShirim*, but also from the parable itself. This statement teaches us that we should endeavor to develop our marital relationship such that our spouse is also our best friend, thereby ensuring a very happy marriage.

פרק ו׳
CHAPTER 6

> **א / 1** אָנָה הָלַךְ דּוֹדֵךְ, הַיָּפָה בַּנָּשִׁים; אָנָה פָּנָה דוֹדֵךְ, וּנְבַקְשֶׁנּוּ עִמָּךְ.
> *Where has your Beloved gone, most beautiful of women? To where has your Beloved turned, that we may search for Him with you?*

Allegorical Translation — The heathen nations say to *Klal Yisrael*: "You, who are the most beautiful nation, where has Hashem gone and left you, and where has He turned to? We want to join you in your search for Him so that we can be part of the relationship and also impair your unique relationship with Him."

Subject of the Verse — The nations taunt and mock *Klal Yisrael* that their Beloved, Hashem, has left them.

Mashal — The young women, who are jealous of the wonderful relationship between the wife and her husband, and who have just heard the wife praise him to the utmost extent (verses 5:11-16), decide to mock her by asking, "So where is he?!"

Nimshal — The *nimshal* is self-evident. Having heard *Klal Yisrael*'s profuse praise of Hashem, the heathen nations try to make them give up on Him, pointing out that He has abandoned them.

WHERE HAS YOUR BELOVED GONE

These verses are a continuation of the last chapter where we saw that Hashem left *Klal Yisrael* because of their sins. They were sent into exile and suffer there from the heathen nations. When *Klal Yisrael* declare their undying devotion to Hashem to the nations, the latter ask: "Why do you maintain this devotion?" *Klal Yisrael* give a beautiful description of Hashem, and they explain that they will never leave Him because there is no God like Him. Now, in the exile, the nations mock *Klal Yisrael*. They pretend that they are speaking out of concern but are actually taunting *Klal Yisrael*. They ask, "Where has your beloved gone?" They mean to communicate that however wonderful Hashem is, He has abandoned them.

The nations say, "To where has your Beloved turned, that we may search for Him with you?" It sounds as if they want to help, but they really just want to hinder. Rashi tells us that this refers to the time of the building of the Second Beis HaMikdash, during Koresh's reign, when the enemies wishing to subvert the rebuilding offered to help with it. By being part of the project, they were hoping to cause trouble and conflict and interfere with the rebuilding to halt the progress. But *Klal Yisrael*, realizing their true intentions, declined the offer. Indeed, many times in Jewish history, when the heathen nations seem to wish to "help" us, we have had to be careful and investigate their true motivation.[1]

The repetition in this verse – "Where has your Beloved gone?" and "To where has your Beloved turned?" accomplishes two things. From a literary standpoint, as we have mentioned previously, repetition and near-repetition in songs and poems are often intended to awaken the emotions. From a substantive standpoint, the repetition here reflects the two ways the nations wish to mock us. Their first "jab" is that Hashem has gone. Their second "jab" is this: "Now that He has turned away from you, let us join in, and we will be equal to you in our relationship with Him." By using the word "turned," they communicate that Hashem has turned away from *Klal Yisrael*, thus giving them a way into this relationship.[2]

The heathen nations interpret *Klal Yisrael*'s exile as Hashem turning away from them, and opening up, *ki'veyachol*, to new "relationships." They seek to taunt *Klal Yisrael* with this insinuation, to make them feel lowly and to weaken their resolve to serve Hashem. They also hope to replace *Klal Yisrael* as the new "Chosen People."[3]

---

[1] Unfortunately, we have to be wary of offers of help also from our own people who reject the importance of observing Torah and mitzvos. When Chaim Weitzman offered to help Rabbi Yosef Chaim Sonnenfeld, *zt"l*, with the running of yeshivos, Rabbi Sonnenfeld rejected his offer outright, knowing that Weitzman's main intention was to decimate the bastions of Torah. He even quoted the famous verse from *Ezra* (4:3): "It is not for you to join us in our rebuilding of the House of our God." This statement encapsulates the message and theme of the verses we are discussing (*Guardian of Jerusalem*, p. 375).

[2] In our commentary on 5:9, we cited the Vilna Gaon's interpretation that the heathen nations wonder about the greatness of Hashem and the uniqueness of our relationship with Him. He adds that here they play on both points: Regardless of how great He is, He will not help you because He has abandoned you; your special relationship has been ruined because He has turned away from you.

[3] The supposed rejection of the Jewish People by Hashem is one of the main pillars of classical Catholic theology.

WHERE HAS YOUR BELOVED TURNED, THAT WE MAY SEARCH FOR HIM WITH YOU?

Unlike Rashi and the Midrash, who interpret these words as a sarcastic taunt, the Metzudas Dovid sees them as sincere. He understands that when the heathen nations hear the praises of Hashem (in the previous chapter) and *Klal Yisrael*'s devotion to Hashem, they are stirred and convinced, and now genuinely want to help *Klal Yisrael* reconnect to Hashem. He explains that just as a woman seeking her beloved might be scared to go out on her own to search in places of darkness and danger and would welcome the assistance of others, so *Klal Yisrael* has occasionally been supported by the heathen nations in serving Hashem. Even though the heathen nations have generally impeded *Klal Yisrael*'s service of Hashem, there have been exceptions inspired by *Klal Yisrael*'s exceptional behavior. When a *kiddush Hashem* occurs, they sometimes begin to appreciate how wonderful it is to serve Hashem and decide to help us do so. In his autobiography, Rabbi Yitzchak Zilber describes how one time during the winter, the Ribnitzer Rebbe found that the local river had frozen over, and he was unable to immerse himself on Shabbos (due to the prohibition against crushing ice) as he was used to doing every day. As the Rebbe was standing there helplessly wanting to immerse, a KGB officer noticed, and broke the ice for him![4] Even someone high up in an organization that had the eradication of Torah and mitzvos as one of its goals, was inspired to help a tzaddik fulfill his desire to serve Hashem.

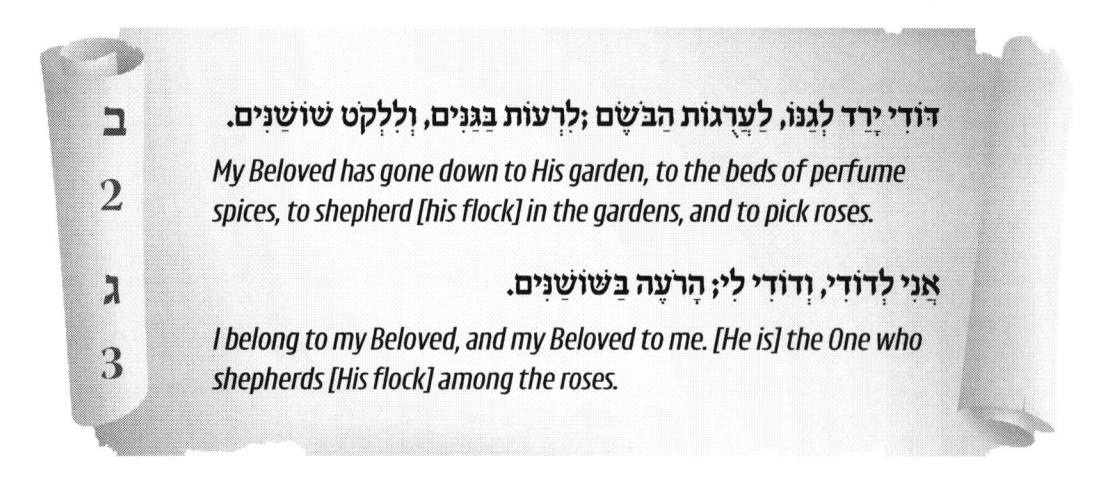

ב 2 דּוֹדִי יָרַד לְגַנּוֹ, לַעֲרֻגוֹת הַבֹּשֶׂם; לִרְעוֹת בַּגַּנִּים, וְלִלְקֹט שׁוֹשַׁנִּים.

My Beloved has gone down to His garden, to the beds of perfume spices, to shepherd [his flock] in the gardens, and to pick roses.

ג 3 אֲנִי לְדוֹדִי, וְדוֹדִי לִי; הָרֹעֶה בַּשּׁוֹשַׁנִּים.

I belong to my Beloved, and my Beloved to me. [He is] the One who shepherds [His flock] among the roses.

Allegorical Translation

2 *Klal Yisrael* reply: Hashem has gone into the shuls and places of learning to listen to our Torah and prayers and record our merits.

3 Hashem is with us alone, and we are alone with Him, the One who looks

---

4 *To Remain A Jew* (p. 466).

Subject of the Verses: *Klal Yisrael* rejects the taunts of the heathen nations.

Mashal **2** Undaunted by all the taunts, the wife answers confidently that her husband still loves her, and he has actually not gone far away. He has only gone to the garden, and only for her sake — to collect flowers for her. (In other words, he is just busy doing things that demonstrate his love for her.)

3 The wife continues rejecting her competitors' approach. She says that her relationship with her husband is exclusive and that no one else is allowed into it. She also insists that her husband is still very kind and loving to her.

Nimshal **2** *Klal Yisrael* refuse to allow the nations to weaken their resolve. They reply that Hashem has not gone far. He is still with us, and still comes to listen to our prayers and our Torah learning. He does so to "stockpile" our good deeds in order to reward us eventually.

3 Furthermore, our relationship with Hashem is exclusive, and no one else can join it. Hashem continues to look after us in a pleasant way.

MY BELOVED HAS GONE…

The nations challenge *Klal Yisrael* in two ways: 1) Hashem has abandoned you, and 2) Let us join the relationship. Each one of these verses rejects one claim. The first verse declares that Hashem has not left us and gone far away but is still with us. The second verse declares that our relationship is exclusive and will not tolerate strangers getting involved.

Essentially, the message of these verses is that *Klal Yisrael* remain confident in Hashem's eternal love even through exile. They appreciate that He is still showing His devotion in various ways, even those that are difficult to understand.

The heathen nations claim that Hashem has turned away from *Klal Yisrael*, but they reply that He has simply gone to look for flowers for them. Imagine a wife being taunted that her husband has gone away and responding confidently and proudly: "No, he has not! He has just gone to get me flowers!" It is with this kind of feeling and sentiment that *Klal Yisrael* reply to the nations. They caution the nations against thinking that Hashem has completely forsaken them, and that they can now feel free to disturb and hinder their relationship with Him. Even in their exile, they still have a personal relationship with Hashem, one that does not include the heathen nations. It may not be as good as it used to be and it may not be as large as it used to be, but Hashem is still watching over

Klal Yisrael. Although Hashem is not with them openly, He is still busy looking after their interests and doing things to show His love.

In verse 2, *Klal Yisrael* say, "My Beloved has gone down to His garden…to pick roses." Gardens are symbolic of shuls and places of learning.[5] The heathen nations say that Hashem has left us, but we reply that He has only gone to the garden. While he is temporarily not in our "home" — i.e, the Beis HaMikdash — He is only in the adjoining garden. In other words, we feel that even in exile, Hashem is not far from us. Furthermore, a garden is a place of beauty. It is an ideal place for a couple to spend pleasant times together. So too, Hashem has gone into the "garden" because it is a pleasant place where we can easily bond with Him. As mentioned, the garden is to be understood as the shul, the place of learning, or the *Yiddishe heim* where one can easily and pleasantly bond with Hashem. The roses being picked are the special mitzvos that a select few righteous people perform. Hashem collects and treasures them. The basic message of the verse is that even in exile, there are places where we can feel the Presence of Hashem. And even in exile, Hashem treasures the mitzvos that we fulfill.

Klal Yisrael conclude their rebuttal with the words "I belong to my Beloved." In his commentary, Rashi encapsulates the essence of *Klal Yisrael*'s response by quoting from *Ezra* and *Nechemiah*, where *Klal Yisrael* say to the heathen nations: "It is not for you to join us in our rebuilding of the House of our God," and "You will have no portion, merit, or mention in [our city] of Yerushalayim!"[6]

The expression "I belong to my Beloved, and my Beloved to me" reminds us of *Klal Yisrael*'s earlier declaration, "My Beloved is mine, and I am His" (2:16). Only the order is reversed. The idea, of course, as we explained there, is that *Klal Yisrael* and Hashem have a unique relationship. Hashem chose only *Klal Yisrael*, and *Klal Yisrael* chose only Hashem. Just as *Klal Yisrael* has never rejected Hashem, He has never rejected them.

HIS GARDEN...

Let us take a few moments to understand why Rashi says that the garden alludes to the shul, and why "picking roses" alludes to Hashem's "stockpiling" the mitzvos of the tzaddikim? Normally, a shepherd lets his flocks graze in wide, open fields not in a small, cramped garden. This verse, however, has Hashem shepherding His flock in a garden. Why? The idea is that when a flock needs extra care, either because there is more danger or because the sheep are ill, the shepherd will sometimes bring his flock to an enclosed place, where he can watch over them more carefully. Similarly, when

---

5 Rashi.

6 *Ezra* 4:3 and *Nechemia* 2:20.

the Beis HaMikdash was standing, *Klal Yisrael* was safely under Hashem's protection wherever they were. Even out in the open, they could feel Hashem's Presence and sense His protection. They were like sheep in a field. But once the Beis HaMikdash was destroyed, it was necessary to be much closer to Hashem in order to be under His protection. Therefore, in exile, Hashem has to shepherd His flock only in the confines of the "gardens." Only there is *Klal Yisrael* safe. This means that during the exile, we cannot truly become close to Hashem and feel His protection everywhere. We have to go to a place of Torah or a place of prayer or live in a *Yiddishe heim*, where Torah and mitzvos are being scrupulously observed. When we are in shul, we are safely in the Presence of Hashem. But out in the open, we are not. Hashem has taken us into the "spiritual gardens — the shuls, *batei midrash*, and Jewish homes — to carefully protect us during the exile.

This verse teaches us never to forget that Hashem does not forsake us completely in exile. His Presence is indeed to be found there, but in more confined and exclusive spaces.

Verse 2 continues with Hashem "pick[ing] roses." In an ideal situation, a person goes out to the garden and enjoys the sight of many rose bushes. But when plant diseases are rampant in the garden, one picks the few flowers that still look healthy, and takes them inside. Because there are no rose bushes flourishing out in the open, one is concerned that the remaining roses will similarly become blighted and ruined.[7] When the Beis HaMikdash was standing, there was a whole nation fulfilling mitzvos. In the exile, however, there is no abundance of people doing loads of mitzvos. Rather, there are some individuals doing some great mitzvos. Hashem carefully picks out those beautiful deeds and treasures them, just as a person whose rose garden is full of blight, plucks out the few roses that are still good to take home and admire. These few roses are very precious now because they survived the disease and are all that is left of the once-thriving garden. Every mitzvah done in exile is especially precious to Hashem because of the many challenges and extra effort required in this difficult situation. And since there is a tremendous scarcity of mitzvos during exile, each mitzvah is especially precious.

---

7   The Midrash tells us that when a great tzaddik passed away (particularly if he died young), they would eulogize him with this verse: Hashem has gone down to His garden (i.e., this world) to collect His roses (i.e., His precious souls), which He treasures (*Shir HaShirim Rabbah* 6:4). In line with the interpretation of our verse being discussed here, the message is that when Hashem sees a world full of sin (and thus needing punishment), He quickly plucks the righteous so that they should not sin or become harmed with the rest of the generation. This means that when a righteous person passes away, we must be concerned that Hashem is taking them away from a wicked generation for their protection. This should prompt us to daven that no harm befalls us because it is a sign of potential great danger.

The knowledge that Hashem lovingly and admiringly collects all the good deeds we are doing ought to give us great joy and satisfaction.

I BELONG TO MY BELOVED...

Klal Yisrael conclude their rebuttal here (in verse 3) by declaring that even in exile, "I belong to my Beloved...and my Beloved to me." This verse parallels a similar verse in Chapter 2 (v.16), but the order of the two phrases is reversed. Let us see why.

The words of the earlier verse emanate from a time in which Hashem was performing a lot of miracles for us. It follows the description of Hashem saving us from Egyptian slavery. After all the miracles He did for us, we declare that Hashem is devoted to us, and we reciprocate by serving Him, becoming attached to Him, and being devoted to Him. Here, however, we are describing the exile. In exile, we do not plainly see Hashem's love and devotion. But those who remained devoted to Hashem through the *Churban*, Crusades, massacres, and the Holocaust, felt Hashem reciprocating their love and devotion. During these dark periods, our devotion came first. Hence, "I belong to my Beloved...and [then] my Beloved to me."

Klal Yisrael is unique in their service to Hashem both during the good periods and the dark periods. The earlier verse teaches us that no other nation would be as good as *Klal Yisrael* if Hashem performed as many miracles for it. No, even when Hashem performs many miracles for *Klal Yisrael*, they are unique in their dedication to Him. Other nations would take it all in stride and neglect to thank and serve Him.[8] But when Hashem is "for us," by doing kindness for our nation, it causes us to become even more devoted to Him. Our verse completes the picture by showing the uniqueness of *Klal Yisrael* when they are suffering. It teaches us that even in exile, when we are suffering and do not plainly see that Hashem is "for us," we are still "for Him," knowing that He is really for us. When other nations suffer, they reject their gods since they see that their gods are not helping them.[9] But *Klal Yisrael* is unique. Even though it may not appear that Hashem is "for us," we are for Him.

I BELONG TO MY BELOVED, AND MY BELOVED BELONGS TO ME

This expression teaches us another concept: Hashem is "for me" — an alternative translation to "belongs to me" — to the extent that I am "for Him." Hashem relates to a person according to the way that person relates to Him.

In his *Moreh Nevuchim*,[10] the Rambam elaborates on this concept. He explains that

---

8   See Rashi on *Devarim* 7:7, *s.v. ki*.
9   See Rashi on *Melachim I* 8:43, *s.v. kechol*.
10 *Moreh Nevuchim* III:51.

when a person is thinking about Hashem, he is connected to Hashem. But even the wisest of men, those who know all about Hashem, will find that their link with Hashem is broken when their mind is focused on their earthly desires because then they have disconnected from Him. The Rambam's powerful words teaches us that it is not enough to think about Hashem once in a while. A person's relationship with Hashem depends on how connected his mind is with Him.[11]

I BELONG TO MY BELOVED, AND MY BELOVED TO ME...

The Kedushas Levi[12] explains that Hashem directs all His love and praise to *Klal Yisrael*, and *Klal Yisrael* invest their time and energy praising Hashem. We see this in the Gemara's teaching that while our tefillin contain praises of Hashem, Hashem's "tefillin" contain praises of *Klal Yisrael*.[13] Nowadays, we do not wear tefillin all day. One of the reasons for this is that we are unable to fulfill the halachic requirement to think about the tefillin all the time that we are wearing them. Hashem, however, is certainly capable of this and therefore wears tefillin, *ki'veyachol*, all the time. If, *chas v'shalom*, a person says negative things about *Klal Yisrael*, it is as if he is telling Hashem that the tefillin He is wearing and thinking about are *pasul* (invalid). That would be the greatest impertinence![14]

This verse tells us that Hashem is "for us" in the sense of focusing His praises and kind thoughts on us, and we are "for Hashem." We feel that Hashem is on our side, caring for us, and He is *there* for us. In a good, healthy marriage, this is how it should be. Both husband and wife feel that the other spouse will always be there for them in every way.

I AM FOR MY BELOVED, AND MY BELOVED IS FOR ME

The acronym of these words, אני לדודי ודודי לי, is אלול, the Hebrew month of Elul.[15] This is a hint that these words epitomize the goals of Elul. Elul is, of course, a special month during which we strive to become ever closer to Hashem. As Rabbi Shimshon Pinkus points out, the days of Elul followed by the High Holidays are like a ladder reaching higher and higher. We start with the advent of Elul, move on to the days of Selichos

---

11 See earlier 1:2.

12 *Shemos* 12:27.

13 *Berachos* 6a.

14 The Kedushas Levi uses this concept of mutual appreciation to explain why we call the Yom Tov in which we celebrate the redemption from Egypt "Pesach," while the Torah calls it "Chag HaMatzos." The word "*pesach*," meaning "He passed over," recalls the kindness of Hashem in passing over our houses and killing only the first-born of the Egyptians, but not of the Jews. In contrast, "Chag HaMatzos" hints at the greatness of *Klal Yisrael* who followed Hashem into the desert with only matzos to eat. We wish to recall Hashem's kindness, while He emphasizes our greatness.

15 *Mishnah Berurah* 581:1.

followed by Rosh HaShanah. Then comes the Asseres Yemei Teshuvah capped by Yom Kippur; then Sukkos with Hoshana Rabbah, and finally Shemini Atzeres with Simchas Torah. On Simchas Torah, we reach the highest level. We rejoice in our bond with Hashem,[16] as there are no other mitzvos that day (unlike Pesach or Sukkos, when we have the mitzvos of matzah, lulav, etc.). Yet, right from the very beginning of the month, we are taught that "Elul" is an acronym for "I am for my Beloved, and my Beloved is for me." We might wonder: Isn't this the theme of Simchas Torah, the top of the ladder?

Rav Pinkus explains that when we begin a journey, we must be very clear about our ultimate destination. Otherwise, we may never get there. Therefore, we begin Elul remembering that our destination is our joyous bond with Hashem: "I am for my Beloved, and my Beloved is for me." That is what we aspire to from the very beginning of our journey, and all that we do during this period is to be able to reach that goal.[17] This perspective helps us understand just how special these words are. They are nothing less than the motto of all the days starting from the beginning of Elul all the way through to the end of Sukkos. Some of the explanations given so far help us understand the true greatness of what it means to feel "I am for my Beloved and my Beloved is for me."

I BELONG TO MY BELOVED...

The Chasam Sofer explains that when a person carries out the will of Hashem, Hashem responds by carrying out his will, as it is written, "He will fulfill the desire of those who fear Him."[18] This, says the Chasam Sofer, is the meaning of our verse, "I am for my Beloved, and my Beloved is for me." I do His will, and He does mine.[19]

TO PICK ROSES

Rashi sees this phrase as an allusion to gathering the merits of those who speak *divrei Torah*.[20] He writes: "Hashem listens and heeds those who speak the words of His Torah, to gather their merits and record them in the 'Book of Remembrance' before Him." Rashi cites *Malachi* 3:16 as a source for this concept. There, the Prophet describes how

---

16   *Pesikta D'Rav Kahana* 28.

17   *Chazal*'s choice of the words "I am for my Beloved, and my Beloved is for me," a phrase that encapsulates the message of love of *Shir HaShirim*, to characterize the feelings of these days is illuminating. It underscores the fact that the month of Elul and the holidays that follow are actually days of feeling Hashem's tremendous love for us. Though they are called "Days of Awe," they are actually also "Days of Love."

18   *Tehillim* 145:19. See *Avos* 2:4, on which the Bartenura comments that Hashem nullifies the will of every would-be menace (and even His own decrees) to protect a person who subjugates his own will to that of Hashem.

19   *Zichron LeMoshe* 36b.

20   The reward for engaging in *divrei Torah* is so much greater when done under duress in exile. *Klal Yisrael* point this out here to demonstrate to the heathen nations that while they mistakenly see Jewish exile as the rejection of *Klal Yisrael*, it is actually an opportunity for greater reward.

Hashem listens to the words of *yiras Shamayim* which we speak while we are in exile and has them carefully inscribed in a "Book of Remembrance."

Rabbi Simcha Zissel Ziv of Kelm, *zt"l*, often talked about the greatness of every word of *yiras Shamayim* that a person speaks. He writes that we see from *Malachi* 3:16 how much importance Hashem attaches to these words.[21] The verse says, "Then those who feared Hashem spoke with one another, and Hashem listened, and heeded [them], and a Book of Remembrance was written before Him for those who fear Hashem and honor His name." Each word of praise in the Torah is worth a tremendous amount. Rabbi Simcha Zissel Ziv points out that the Midrash[22] tells us that it would have been better for Shlomo HaMelech to have been a cleaner of gutters than to have a verse in *Tanach*[23] say that he was influenced negatively by his wives (even though, as the Gemara clarifies, he never actually sinned[24]). Indeed, this minor criticism was devastating to him. From here we learn the importance of every bit of criticism (or praise) found in the verses of *Tanach*.[25]

Malachi 3:16 contains a full list of strong praises for people who speak words of *yiras Shamayim*. Indeed, eight separate terms highlight the importance of such people. The verse says that when those who (1) "feared" Hashem spoke, (2) Hashem "listened" (3) and He "heeded [them]", (4) and it was "written" (5) in a "Book of Remembrance" (6) that was put "before Hashem" (7) for those who "fear Hashem" (8) and "honor His name". Each one of these terms is elaborated on by Rabbi Simcha Zissel Ziv.

Even though Hashem knows everything, He makes a point of "listening" in order to demonstratively hear these special words. Then there is listening and taking note. Hashem is not satisfied, *ki'veyachol*, with just listening. He is so happy with these words that He "heeds" them. But that, too, is not enough. Words of *yiras Shamayim* are so special that Hashem has them "written" down to show how precious they are to Him. Although things can be written down on just any piece of paper or even in a document,

---

21 *Chochmah U'Mussar*, vol. 1, pp. 388-394.

22 *Shemos* 6:1.

23 *Melachim I* 11:4.

24 *Shabbos* 56b.

25 This is because the power of a verse in the *Tanach* is infinite. This can be better understood by appreciating how the giver of the compliment or criticism influences its impact. A note from a kindergarten teacher saying that a child was good that day will only garner the child a small reward from his parents — perhaps a sweet or a cookie. A note from a school principal is much more important, of course, and a critical note may mean that the child will be expelled, causing months of aggravation. A graduation certificate can have a much greater impact. A ticket from a policeman or a sentence from a judge has even greater impact. A badge of honor from the king or president can be a cause for national celebration. A verse from *Tanach* is essentially a note from the King of all kings, an infinite source of praise or criticism, and thus an endless source of joy or anguish. This is why the verse containing minor criticism of Shlomo HaMelech was so devastating to him.

Hashem is not "satisfied" with this. He makes a "book" out of these words. We must appreciate what this means. Every time a person speaks words of *yiras Shamayim* with a friend, another "book" is "published" in Heaven — with all that publishing a book represents. And let us keep in mind that there are different kinds of books. Some books are looked at only occasionally, but others, like diaries, are used every day. The verse says that the book Hashem makes out of these words is a "book of remembrance," i.e., a special book to be constantly looked at that is placed "before Hashem." The verse continues to praise those who speak words of *yiras Shamayim* by calling them those who "fear Hashem" and "honor His name."

Why is this so great in Hashem's eyes? Rabbi Simcha Zissel Ziv explains that the verse is talking about a time when *Klal Yisrael* is in exile and there are no public expressions of fear of Hashem. On the contrary, there is open rebellion against Him. As the previous verses describe, people at the time were saying that there is no gain in serving Hashem and that being wicked would bring success. At such a time, going against the tide and speaking words of *yiras Shamayim* shows true devotion. Therefore, words of such *yiras Shamayim* are infinitely precious to Hashem, and that is why the verse attaches such significance to them. The historical context is hinted at in the word "then" that begins the verse: "Then those who feared Hashem spoke with one another..."[26] Then — when everyone else rejects the service of Hashem — those who continue to serve Him are especially treasured. This is the metaphor of "picking roses." Hashem picks and chooses those special roses to treasure and guard. This is the lesson that we learn from our verse.[27] It should inspire us to feel that especially in exile, every mitzvah is precious to Hashem. Our mitzvos in exile have a certain unique quality and preciousness in the eyes of Hashem. Although they are certainly not done with the spiritual power of our predecessors, they are extremely precious to Hashem because we do them at a time when it is so difficult.

TO PICK ROSES

According to the Yerushalmi,[28] this verse tells us that Hashem collects all the beautiful souls from all the nations and brings them into the fold of *Klal Yisrael*. The Yerushalmi presents a parable of a king who has a young son he loves dearly. Whenever the son would see a rose he fancied, the king would pick it for him — even from someone else's field (as a king is permitted to do). Similarly, Hashem loves *Klal Yisrael* and thus gathers

---

26 See Radak on *Malachi* 3:16.
27 According to Rashi.
28 *Berachos* 20a.

beautiful souls from all the other nations and brings them to *Klal Yisrael* to enhance the beauty of our People. Indeed, we have been blessed throughout the generations with converts who have greatly enhanced the Jewish People through their inspiration and inner greatness.

The Gemara tells us that Hashem sent the Jewish People into exile in order to increase them, like one who plants grain so that he should have a much greater crop.[29] When *Klal Yisrael* is in exile and the gentiles see them, some are inspired to convert and thereby increase our numbers.[30] Of course, exile is a punishment, but in some of our sources — especially *Shir HaShirim* — it is viewed as Hashem looking after *Klal Yisrael* in a different manner that even has certain benefits. In the previous verse (verse 1), the heathen nations mock the Jewish People by saying that Hashem has left them and turned away from them. *Klal Yisrael* respond that Hashem is still watching them and taking care of them, albeit in a different manner, as explained previously.

In these few words about how Hashem "picks roses," we get an entirely new perspective on our exile. It can also be an opportunity for us because it gives us exposure to the world, and thereby increases converts — something that adds beauty to our nation. This interpretation of the Yerushalmi fits the context perfectly because it strengthens *Klal Yisrael*'s argument that Hashem has not left us at all, but, in fact, even the exile is for our greater benefit.

Of the many lessons that can be gleaned from these verses, let us summarize two of the main ones. One is the importance of the places of Torah and *tefillah* in the exile. These are the only places where Hashem's Presence is clearly evident. It is only there that a person is shepherded and looked after by Hashem. When the Beis HaMikdash was standing, Hashem's Presence was evident everywhere, and thus a person who was "outside" would not be influenced negatively. Nowadays, only in the confines of the shuls and places of Torah learning can one feel Hashem's Presence. A person who leaves these places is in spiritual danger.

The second lesson is that even in the exile, where there are a lot of bad influences, one should not minimize the importance of every mitzvah. On the contrary, in the exile, Hashem takes note of every mitzvah and beautiful deed that we do. As Rashi says,

---

29 *Pesachim* 87b.

30 The Gemara (ibid) is expounding on a verse in *Hoshea* (2:25) that describes how Hashem, *ki'veyachol*, "sows *Klal Yisrael* in the land." The simple meaning is that just as seeds are scattered when sown, so we have been scattered in the world. But the Gemara sees the positive aspect as well — that Hashem is "planting us" in order to gather a greater harvest.

Hashem carefully plucks the beautiful roses to cherish and treasure. These are all that is left from the great fields of roses that once existed.

INTRODUCTION TO VERSES 4-10

In the *mashal* (allegory), these next few verses (4-10) show the husband praising his wife's wonderful character traits as well as her physical beauty, and declaring how much he loves her. In the *nimshal*, they show Hashem praising *Klal Yisrael*, and their many virtues, and declaring how much He loves them. Since it is obvious that these verses are not intended to describe *Klal Yisrael*'s physical beauty, we will be focusing on their symbolic meaning. As we have been doing all along, we will point to some of the many lessons that can be learned from these verses.

It will be remembered that we encountered a very similar theme and similar verses in Chapter Four. Why the repetition? The answer is that when Hashem witnesses the devotion of *Klal Yisrael* expressed in these last few verses, He is, *ki'veyachol*, "aroused" to begin praising them once again.

The praises in this chapter are much more limited than the praises in Chapter Four because these verses are describing *Klal Yisrael* when they are not at their peak (either in exile or during the period of the Second Beis HaMikdash).[31] Even when their conduct is not what it should be, however, they are still deserving of praise. In this way, these verses powerfully underscore the greatness of *Klal Yisrael*. Even when Hashem does not bring them back to Him completely because they are not worthy of this, they are still very special.

There are two ways to describe the strength of a relationship. One is by describing how wonderful the relationship was at its peak, when everything was perfect. The second is by describing how kind and pleasant the two parties are to each other even when their relationship is rocked by many challenges. Each one shows a different facet of how good the relationship is: idyllic when things are going well, and still healthy even in the face of challenges.

The earlier verses were describing *Klal Yisrael* and Hashem during the "honeymoon" period, while these verses describe the relationship in, or after, *Klal Yisrael*'s exile. While they are more limited in praise, they add another dimension to the portrayal of our wonderful relationship with Hashem.

---

31 See Rashi and Midrash.

> יָפָה אַתְּ רַעְיָתִי כְּתִרְצָה, נָאוָה כִּירוּשָׁלָיִם; אֲיֻמָּה כַּנִּדְגָּלוֹת.
>
> You are beautiful, My dear one, [through] your pleasing [deeds], lovely as Jerusalem, awesome as [an army grouped around] banners.

Allegorical Translation — Hashem praises *Klal Yisrael*: "You are beautiful when you are trying to be pleasing to Me, you are lovely as you were in Yerushalayim; you are as awesome as angels."

Subject of the Verse — Hashem is praising *Klal Yisrael*.

Mashal — Praising his wife, the husband says that she is beautiful in the way she chooses to please him. She is as lovely as the city of Yerushalayim (before its destruction). And she is awe-inspiring, like an entire army around its banners.

Nimshal — The first part of the verse, "You are beautiful, My dear one, through your pleasing deeds," communicates that *Klal Yisrael* knows how to please Hashem. This is no small praise. Often a person tries to do something pleasing for a friend or spouse, but even though the gesture is appreciated, does not really hit the mark. This may be because he did not think seriously about what would be nicest for the recipient or because he does not know what the other person really likes. In contrast, *Klal Yisrael* succeeds in pleasing Hashem when they attempt to do so. This is because *Klal Yisrael* really knows what pleases Hashem. Furthermore, Hashem appreciates the effort that we put in. The actual outcome is not critical, as will be explained.

The phrase "lovely as Jerusalem" connotes incomparable beauty since Yerushalayim was a most beautiful place. Unfortunately, as a result of our long and terrible exile, we can no longer fathom how truly beautiful it was. It is the highest praise to say that *Klal Yisrael was* as beautiful as Yerushalayim.[32]

The image of an "army grouped around banners" portrays the awe that *Klal Yisrael* evokes when they are unified. When one sees a large group, all devoted wholeheartedly to one cause, this inspires awe. A modern-day example might be a military parade. When *Klal Yisrael* works in unity, it brings forth awe.

---

32 See *Eichah* 2:15 and *Tears of Hope, Seeds of Redemption*, pp. 154-157, for a better understanding of Yerushalayim's beauty.

The unidentified group gathered around their banners here could, in principle, be any group of individuals who join together for a common cause. But Rashi tells us that it is an allusion to the angels.[33] The reason is as follows: a banner is a rallying symbol for a group of people devoted to the cause represented by the banner. A banner can thus be considered a tool by which to unify people to a cause. The more important and more central to a person's life the cause is, the more compelling the banner. The greatest of all causes is that of serving Hashem. It is the only true, ultimate goal, and it encompasses all of one's life and efforts. Other causes, such as a political party or business, also unite people, but usually only for a limited time, and not on a deep level. Now, the angels are called *Tzeva'os*, the army of Hashem[34] because they are wholeheartedly devoted to Hashem.[35] When we describe those who rally to the banner, we mean the angels because they are the ones who rally completely to the banner.

The verse therefore tells us that *Klal Yisrael* is as awesome as angels who rally to one banner. Two types of awe are present here: awe caused by angels[36] and awe caused by a group rallying together. In the future, when the true greatness of *Klal Yisrael* will be clear to all, the people of the world will tremble in front of every single Jew, just as one would tremble at the sight of an angel. And since a group completely devoted to one cause inspires awe and fear, *Klal Yisrael* will inspire that awe and fear because of their united devotion to Hashem.

YOU ARE BEAUTIFUL…

This verse contains three praises of *Klal Yisrael*. They are described as beautiful, lovely, and awesome.[37] Rashi explains that this verse is essentially a continuation of the previous verses: Hashem is reacting here to *Klal Yisrael*'s rebuff of the heathen nations. Hashem was delighted, *ki'veyachol*, when *Klal Yisrael* was not swayed by the nations who came

---

33 As earlier, 5:10.

34 *Tehillim* 68:13, *Shabbos* 88b.

35 This is mentioned in the blessing before the morning *Shema* recitation, *Yotzer Ohr*, and is described by the Ramchal in ch. 11 of *Mesillas Yesharim*.

36 We find many instances in *Tanach* of awe inspired by the sight of an angel. When Bilaam saw an angel, he felt compelled to dismount and bow down to it (*Bamidbar* 22:31); Manoach thought that he would die from seeing an angel (*Shoftim* 13:22, and Rashi on *Bereishis* 16:13).

37 The Rinas Dodim adds that, generally speaking, an awesome, angry face is not lovely or beautiful. In the case of *Klal Yisrael*, however, there is no self-contradiction. Their greatness is that while maintaining an awesomeness that reflects their serving Hashem diligently and conscientiously, they are still "beautiful" because of their dedication to love and kindness. Each aspect enhances the other. It is inspiring to see this, as one can, for example, when one observes an awe-inspiring Gadol who radiates love and compassion.

to disturb their building of the Second Beis HaMikdash, and when they defiantly told them that their relationship with Hashem was still going strong. Hashem praises *Klal Yisrael*'s declaration of loyalty this way:

> "You are beautiful, My dear one, when you are being pleasing [by being loyal to Me]; lovely as Jerusalem [now, in light of your dedication to rebuilding the Beis HaMikdash, you are as lovely as Jerusalem i.e., as if it were already built[38] [39]]; awesome as an army with banners [i.e., the angels, and thus you need not be afraid of the nations coming to hinder you]."[40]

Indeed, the Beis HaMikdash was rebuilt even though many tried to prevent this.[41] It was successful because of the dedication of the builders. This is a lesson for all times. When we show our dedication and are not swayed or intimidated by our enemies, Hashem finds us even more pleasing and helps us succeed.[42]

YOU ARE BEAUTIFUL....THROUGH YOUR PLEASING [DEEDS]

The Midrash understands the words, "You are beautiful...through your pleasing [deeds]" more literally: "You are beautiful, My dear one, when you wish [to be]."[43] When we desire to serve Hashem, we become pleasing and desirable in Hashem's eyes. Indeed, *Klal*

---

38   The underlying concept here is that when one commits to doing a mitzvah, Hashem considers it as if it has already been done. This extraordinary idea deserves a full discussion, but it is not within the scope of this *sefer*. See Rabbeinu Yonah's *Shaarei Teshuvah* (2:10) for an elaboration.

39   *Devash V'Chalav* adds that even though they were rebuilding the Beis HaMikdash, which was on a lower spiritual level than the first Beis HaMikdash, Hashem was pleased by their efforts. He says here that for Him, it is as pleasing as the Yerushalayim of old, i.e., the First Beis HaMikdash.

40   This "awesomeness of angels" that *Klal Yisrael* displayed is well illustrated by an episode that occurred at the beginning of the period of the Second Beis HaMikdash (as described in *Yoma* 69a). A group of wicked Kuthites went to Alexander the Great and slandered the Jewish People. They told him that in the Beis HaMikdash, the Jewish People plot to rebel against him. Without investigating the matter, Alexander decreed that the Beis HaMikdash should be destroyed, and he travelled to Yerushalayim personally to ensure its destruction. Shimon HaTzaddik came to greet him wearing the clothes of the *Kohen Gadol*. To the great astonishment of all those around him, when Alexander the Great, who was accompanied by his many ministers and great army, saw him, he got off his great horse and bowed down to him. His bewildered ministers asked him: "Do you realize that you who are the greatest king just bowed down to a Jew?!" He replied that a vision of Shimon HaTzaddik goes before him in battle and helps him win. He then gave instructions that the Beis HaMikdash be protected, and that the wicked Kuthites be handed over to the Jewish People for elimination, together with their place of worship.

41   *Sefer Nechemiah* (chs. 3-5) gives us a glimpse at the great difficulties and struggles *Klal Yisrael* faced in rebuilding the Beis HaMikdash. (See also *Ezra*, ch. 4.) In this verse, Hashem reassures *Klal Yisrael* that they will manage if they persevere and remain dedicated. And that is what happened. Eventually, our enemies were struck by dread, and abandoned their efforts to stop the rebuilding.

42   *To Remain a Jew*, the autobiography of Rabbi Yitzchak Zilber, *zt"l*, is a truly remarkable account of this way of living.

43   The word "כתרצה" is understood as "כשאת רוצה".

Yisrael always desire to serve Hashem. Unfortunately, however, this innermost desire is sometimes overcome by the evil inclination and its wiles. It pulls us away from Hashem by enticing us to follow our superficial desires. The Gemara captures this struggle beautifully with the well-known prayer:

> Master of the world, You know full well that our will is to fulfill Your wishes, but what prevents us is the evil inclination ["the yeast in the dough" that causes fermentation in the heart] and the subjugation of the nations. Save us from these so that we can truly follow our wishes to serve You.[44]

In this verse, as explained by the Midrash, Hashem sees our true desire and finds us beautiful indeed.

We see from here the paramount importance of our desire to serve Hashem. Our success or failure — how much we are loved by Hashem — depends on the extent of our desire to serve Him[45] and not necessarily on how successful we actually are in His service. That is not in our hands.[46]

YOU ARE BEAUTIFUL…

The Vilna Gaon sees Hashem praising *Klal Yisrael* here for their kindness. He explains that *Klal Yisrael* once had an abundance of all three of the virtues upon which the world stands: kindness, service of Hashem, and Torah.[47] Although the destruction of the Beis HaMikdash greatly weakened both our service of Hashem and our Torah learning,[48] kindness is something that we can still do. And when we act with kindness, Hashem reckons it as if we are fully engaging in all three of these areas which "hold up" the world. Since we are doing the little that we are still able to do, Hashem considers this to be everything we should really be doing. It is apparently no accident that the kings of Israel,

---

44 *Berachos* 17a.

45 The Gemara (*Chagigah* 5b) tells us about an *Amora* who lived very far from his *beis midrash*. He would set out from home after Pesach, and by the time he arrived, he could stay only one day before having to head back home in order to be with his wife for Sukkos. This scenario repeated itself between Sukkos and Pesach, such that the sage was in the *beis midrash* only two days a year. Yet he is greatly praised because he showed a tremendous desire to learn Torah.

46 See Rabbi Meir Aramah on this verse.

47 *Avos* 1:2.

48 Serving Hashem properly without a Beis HaMikdash is obviously very difficult, but even Torah study has been greatly weakened, as the verse in *Eichah* (2:9) testifies: "Her kings and princes are in exile; there is no Torah."

who were known for their kindness,⁴⁹ had their capital in the city of Tirtzah.⁵⁰ The Vilna Gaon sees an allusion to this in our verse. Accordingly, Hashem says,

> "You are beautiful, My dear one, as in Tirzah [through the kindness demonstrated by your kings who ruled in Tirzah]. [Thereby, you are as] lovely as Yerushalayim [i.e., it is considered as if you are serving Hashem in Yerushalayim, the center of *Klal Yisrael*'s Divine service]; as awesome as an army with banners [i.e., it is considered as if you are learning Torah, similar to the way the Jewish People travelled from Egypt with their banners, and stood around Har Sinai in groups to accept the Torah]."

In other words, "You, *Klal Yisrael*, are beautiful because through your kindness, it is as if you uphold all the values I hold dear, and upon which I set up the world: kindness, Divine service, and Torah." We see the tremendous importance of doing kindness because by upholding this "pillar," we are upholding all the "pillars" of the world. That love of kindness still beats strong within the heart of *Klal Yisrael*.

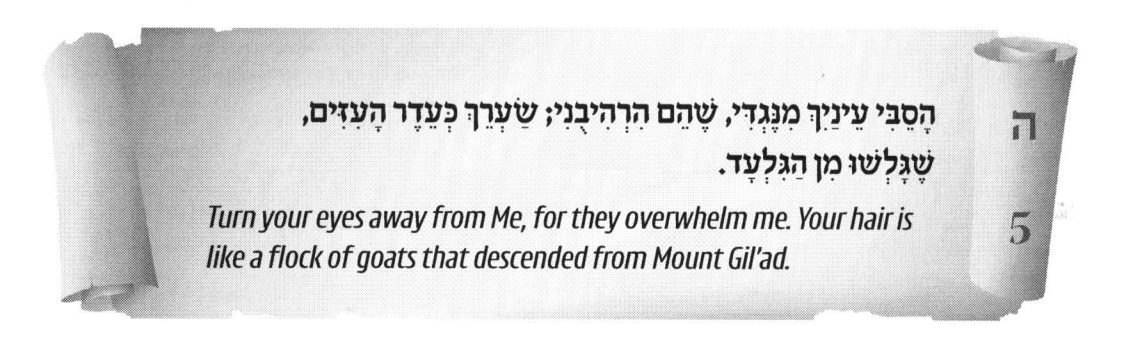

> הָסֵבִּי עֵינַיִךְ מִנֶּגְדִּי, שֶׁהֵם הִרְהִיבֻנִי; שַׂעְרֵךְ כְּעֵדֶר הָעִזִּים, שֶׁגָּלְשׁוּ מִן הַגִּלְעָד.
>
> Turn your eyes away from Me, for they overwhelm me. Your hair is like a flock of goats that descended from Mount Gil'ad.
>
> ה
>
> 5

Allegorical Translation I (Hashem) cannot return to you, *Klal Yisrael*, all the precious items of the First Beis HaMikdash (such as the *Aron* and the *Urim V'Tumim*) for you to use in the Second Beis HaMikdash because they produced such a great love that you became negligent in serving Me. Even the weak ones among you are full of beauty.

---

49 See *Melachim I* 20:31. This should make us stop and think. We are told that even kings like Achav, who worshipped idols, were very kind. The Vilna Gaon points out that the evil Queen Izevel would go to all the weddings and dance in a most enthusiastic manner in front of the brides to make them happy. The fact that she was a powerful queen did not stop her from taking the time and trouble to do what some might have considered belittling herself. We have no real understanding of these people. But evidently, even though they were trapped by the desire for idol worship — something we cannot imagine — they were nevertheless devoted to kindness. How much more should we be devoted since we do not have to contend with the pull of idolatry.

50 *Melachim I* 16:24.

6:5 ETERNAL LOVE

Subject of the Verse — Hashem is explaining His "mixed feelings," *ki'veyachol*, at the time of the Second Beis HaMikdash or during *Klal Yisrael*'s exile.

Mashal — This is a particularly fascinating verse. It starts with the husband telling his wife to turn her eyes away from him. As Rashi explains it, the husband is so overcome by his love for his wife that even her looking at him overwhelms his good sense to the point that he ends up doing things which are inappropriate.[51] The verse closes with the husband praising the beauty of his beloved's hair, how clean and pure it is, like the goats on Mount Gil'ad.

Nimshal — The verse seems to say that Hashem can become overwhelmed by His love for *Klal Yisrael*. What does that mean? The Midrash offers a number of explanations, but they all have one theme.

The Midrash begins with a parable. A king was once betrayed by his queen, and he thus needed to send her away. As she was being sent away, she gave one pleading look to her husband, the king, which rendered him unable to follow through. He thus invited her back. Similarly, *Klal Yisrael* often deserve to be punished, yet Hashem's love for us is so great that when we turn our "eyes" to Him, He cannot "control Himself" and thus forgives us. The "eyes," says the Midrash, refer either to our leaders or our innocent children.[52] When they turn to Hashem, He immediately grants forgiveness.

Our verse, then, is to be understood as Hashem saying to *Klal Yisrael*: "I love you so much that if you turn your eyes to me, I am overwhelmed by My love for you, and I change all of My plans."

The Vilna Gaon offers a similar explanation: Before *Klal Yisrael* is ready for the final salvation, Hashem says to them: "Turn your eyes away from Me, because if you don't, I will be overwhelmed by My love for you and bring Mashiach, even though it is premature. And this will ultimately not be good for you."

---

51 I would like to quote some of Rashi's striking elaboration of the *mashal*: "כבחור שארוסתו חביבה וערייבה עליו ועיניה נאות ואומר לה הסבי עיניך מנגדי כי בראותי אותך לבי משתחץ ומתגאה עלי ורוחי גסה כי איני יכול להתאפק" — This is like a young man whose bride is beloved and sweet to him, and her eyes are beautiful. He says to her: 'Turn your eyes away from me because when I see you, my heart becomes excited and overconfident, and my spirit feels proud, so much so that I am unable to control myself.'" We must remember these words reflect Hashem's feelings for *Klal Yisrael*. His love for us is so great that He is, *ki'veyachol*, unable to control Himself.

52 Leaders may be likened to eyes in the sense that they "see" the approaching dangers and the correct way forward (as discussed in our commentary 1:15). Children may be likened to eyes in the sense that eyes have to be very clean, just as children are completely clean and innocent from sin. (If there is one drop of dirt in an eye, it immediately affects the vision and causes so much discomfort that it has to be washed away.)

The verse ends with praise of *Klal Yisrael*'s "hair."[53] Their hair is likened to the goats going down the Mount Gil'ad. Gil'ad was famous for its pastures, which attracted many flocks of beautiful goats with clean, white wool. As they descended the mountain, their bright wool could be seen from the distance; it was a beautiful sight. Hair, which is the weakest and flimsiest part of the body, represents the weakest elements of *Klal Yisrael*. Yet even they are pure and clean. The verse is telling us that the beauty of even the weaker ones in the community could be seen and appreciated.

Rashi offers yet another interpretation. Hashem is saying, "I gave you so much closeness in the First Beis HaMikdash that you became too comfortable with Me and rebelled against Me. Therefore, I will relate to you with a certain aloofness in the Second Beis HaMikdash. [This aloofness could be felt most keenly in that certain items which were present in the First Beis HaMikdash were absent from the Second Beis HaMikdash.[54]] Please turn away from Me [now at the building of the Second Beis HaMikdash], and don't ask for this degree of love to return. If you do, and I end up giving it to you, eventually you will sin again, and will come to even more harm. Even the weak ones among you are full of beauty [, and I do not want them to be harmed]."

It should be noted that according to Rashi, the verse is speaking about both the greatest segment of *Klal Yisrael* — the "eyes" that "overwhelm" Hashem, *ki'veyachol* — and the weakest segment, the "hair." They are all precious to Hashem. Furthermore, even though Hashem declares that He cannot now bestow on them the earlier degree of intense love, this does not diminish His love for even the weakest of them (as represented by the hair); it is simply because they are not ready for it yet. As mentioned, these verses describe *Klal Yisrael* when they are not at their peak. Still, *Klal Yisrael* is unique in that even under these circumstances, even then the weakest elements among them continue to shine and are loved by Hashem.

TURN YOUR EYES AWAY...

The main message of this very inspiring verse is that *Klal Yisrael* has the ability to sway Hashem with just one plea. We must never forget the awesome power of this one small action, and we must never give it up.

---

53 This is explained at greater length earlier in connection with 4:1, where the identical expression is found.
54 See *Yoma* 21b and our commentary on 5:6.

Perhaps we can appreciate this better by thinking of the adorable baby who pleads with his eyes for something his parents, under normal circumstances, would think is wrong to give him. But swayed by those eyes, they give in. Regardless of whether acquiescence is appropriate from an educational standpoint, their act represents a tremendous expression of love. It is certainly very healthy for the child to know and feel that his parents love him so much.

Up to this point, *Shir HaShirim* has portrayed Hashem's tremendous love for *Klal Yisrael*. Here we see an additional element: *Klal Yisrael* is also, *ki'veyachol*, irresistible to Hashem.

We must try to feel the very powerful love that Hashem has for us. In a sense, we are like the child whom the parent finds impossible to refuse. We need not worry that asking for a certain thing will bring us harm because Hashem will ultimately grant us only that which is good for us as an expression of His love. Therefore, we can, and should, turn our eyes to Him at all times. This verse gives us some understanding of the tremendous power of our prayers, which are truly more powerful than we can ever imagine. We must not forget to use this awesome power to turn our eyes to Hashem.

TURN YOUR EYES AWAY...

Let us conclude our discussion of this remarkable verse with a novel interpretation developed at great length by the Netziv. He begins with a parable about a man who is married to a wife who loves him very dearly — actually, too dearly. She loves him so much that she is barely able to focus on anything else. He comes home in the evening to find that no food has been cooked, that the children have not been looked after, etc., because she is so busy thinking about her love for him. The husband realizes that she is totally obsessed with him and that this is no good for her or for him. He thus tries to dampen the love by being very cold to her. The plan fails, however. The wife feels so hurt and rejected by his coldness that she completely stops doing anything he wants. This leads to the marriage falling apart, and the husband sending her away. All is not lost, however, since the wife comes to realize that her foolish disobedience caused her so much harm. She repents and comes back to her husband, promising to listen to him. But he is concerned that the whole cycle will now repeat itself: she will become obsessed with him and forget about her duties. So, he tells her: "Do not gaze at me. This way you will not be completely obsessed with me, and our love will simmer at the right level."

The *nimshal* is that sometimes *Klal Yisrael* get so caught up with loving Hashem that they forget there are mitzvos to be done — and they must be done according to halachah, without the smallest deviation. The Netziv's parable, then, represents different stages in Jewish history. When the First Beis HaMikdash was standing, we became "overwhelmed" with love, prompting Hashem to try to create a more balanced relationship by being "cold." Instead of responding appropriately, we ended up rebelling and being sent into exile. It is there that Hashem tells us, when we are trying to come back to Him and restart the relationship in a better way, that we must be careful that our love does not take away our focus on the mitzvos.

According to the Netziv, then, the verse reads this way: "Turn your eyes away from Me [and stop concentrating exclusively on loving Me], for they make Me [seem too] elevated." In other words: "When you become caught up in love, you elevate Me and say that I [Hashem] do not need any mitzvos." But the truth is that for *Klal Yisrael*'s own sake and survival, it is necessary to actually fulfill the mitzvos.[55]

The Netziv develops this concept at great length.[56] What emerges is a very sharp warning to those who minimize the importance of doing what Hashem actually asks of us due to their feeling that the main thing is that they love Hashem and Hashem loves them. This approach is totally wrong. The fact is that if we do not fulfill Hashem's commands, we are actually damaging ourselves.[57] When it comes to serving Hashem, love is not enough!

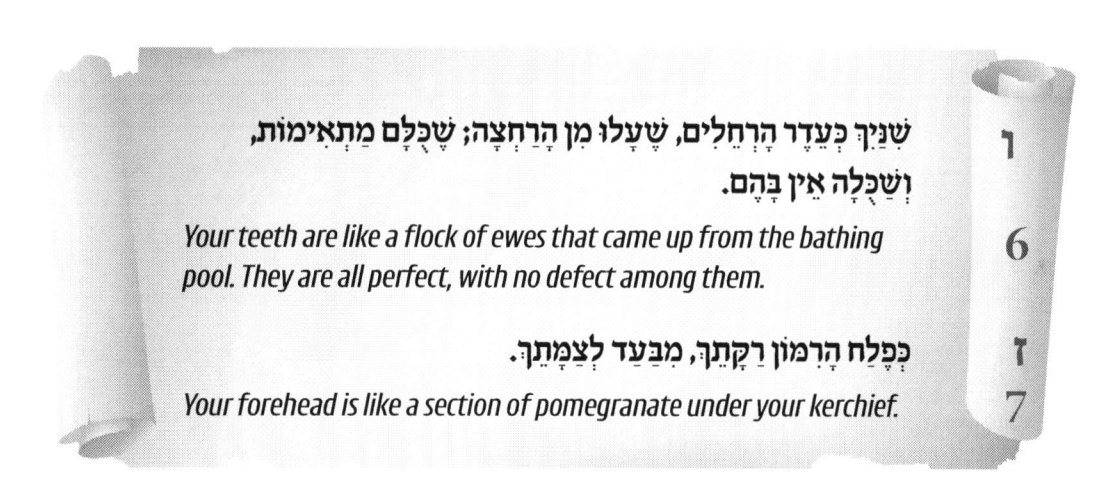

ו שִׁנַּיִךְ כְּעֵדֶר הָרְחֵלִים, שֶׁעָלוּ מִן הָרַחְצָה; שֶׁכֻּלָּם מַתְאִימוֹת, וְשַׁכֻּלָה אֵין בָּהֶם.

6 *Your teeth are like a flock of ewes that came up from the bathing pool. They are all perfect, with no defect among them.*

ז כְּפֶלַח הָרִמּוֹן רַקָּתֵךְ, מִבַּעַד לְצַמָּתֵךְ.

7 *Your forehead is like a section of pomegranate under your kerchief.*

---

55 In a similar vein, the *Nefesh HaChaim* (ch. 4) compares two people who eat matzah on Leil HaSeder. One eats at the right time, but without all the lofty thoughts of loving Hashem, etc. The other gets so caught up in cultivating his feelings of love for Hashem that he does not get around to eating matzah until the correct time has passed. Even though it may appear that the second person is closer to Hashem, he has, in fact, committed a terrible sin. He will not only be punished for it but will actually become more distant from Hashem as a result. In contrast, the first one will not only receive a great reward but will actually be closer to Hashem because he has fulfilled a mitzvah even though it was not with all the lofty intentions.

56 The Netziv uses this concept to explain many teachings of *Chazal*.

57 In this connection, the Netziv mentions the claim of Ravsheiko, a wicked Jew living in the time of King Chizkiyahu, that Chizkiyahu sinned by getting rid of all the *bamos* (private altars), which were totally forbidden at the time (*Melachim II*, ch. 18). Their elimination was, in fact, a great mitzvah. Ravsheiko felt that bringing a sacrifice on a private altar would bring love between a person and Hashem (see Introduction), but Chizkiyahu knew that it was totally forbidden. This episode illustrates just how dangerous it is for one to concentrate completely on loving Hashem while disregarding the mitzvos. Only in the merit of Chizkiyahu's steadfastness was the nation eventually saved from Sancheirev because Hashem was so pleased with the elimination of the *bamos* (as described in *Melachim* ibid).

Allegorical Translation **6** Continuing His praise of *Klal Yisrael*, Hashem says to them: "Your warriors are righteous soldiers, clean from sin like clean ewes that have just been washed. They are perfect because they have not become blemished through the sin of immorality or stealing.

7 Hashem praises the Jewish People further: "Even the wicked in your camp have numerous merits, like pomegranates [have seeds]."

Subject of the Verse Hashem is singing the praises of *Klal Yisrael*.

Mashal **6** The husband continues praising the beauty of his wife, this time with the emphasis on the beauty of her teeth. He says: "Your teeth are all in perfect symmetry and are clean like ewes that have just been washed. All of your teeth are whole, without any defects."

7 The husband continues praising the beauty of his wife: "Your forehead, which peeps out from under your kerchief, is as red[58] and rounded as a section of pomegranate."

Nimshal **6** Hashem praises *Klal Yisrael* for their beautiful teeth, comparing them to unblemished, selected ewes that have just been washed.[59]

By way of background, Rashi tells us that shepherds would carefully select and set aside a designated number of their best sheep immediately upon birth. They would transfer them to a special shepherd whose job it was to watch over them so that they would not get dirty, and would wash them regularly to ensure that they remained perfectly clean. In this way, the sheep's wool would be especially valuable and would sell for a higher price. Teeth, in this verse, are therefore compared in cleanliness and perfection to these sheep.

"Teeth" in this verse are symbolic of the warriors of the Jewish People. Just as teeth are the hardest part of the body, so soldiers are the strongest part of the nation. Just as teeth consume and crush food, so soldiers are able to consume and annihilate their enemies. Unfortunately, soldiers in battle often become sullied by sin. Any accurate history of warfare is full of the lowliness into which soldiers very quickly descend — even soldiers from the best backgrounds.

---

58 Having a very ruddy countenance was an aspect of great beauty in the olden days.

59 In ch. 4 (v. 2), this praise appears almost exactly as it does here. It is noteworthy, however, that the earlier verse mentions how the sheep were counted (קצובות), while this point is omitted here. Since this verse refers to the time when *Klal Yisrael* were on a lower level, it teaches us that even those who are not important enough to be counted individually are still precious in the eyes of Hashem.

Since battle arouses the worst and basest emotions in a man, it often leads him to commit sins. One of the most common is stealing. When an army is overwhelming the enemy, it is almost inevitable that its soldiers will want to take something for themselves. This is symbolized by teeth which, because they are constantly used for chewing and consuming food, easily get dirty and often have food particles stuck between them. The teeth are sullied by the food they are consuming. In sharp contrast — and to the eternal credit of *Klal Yisrael* — their warriors ("teeth") remain perfectly clean. In all the battles they fought, from the time they traveled in the wilderness until they completed the conquest of Eretz Yisrael — vanquishing thirty-one armies in Eretz Yisrael alone — only once did a soldier steal. All the others remained clean like the sheep which are continually being washed.[60]

This should amaze us! If this is how great and pure the soldiers — who are prone to sin – were, how much more so was the greatness of the rest of the nation!

7 The verse describes the beauty of *Klal Yisrael*'s "forehead." The Gemara teaches that this is an allusion to the "empty" people, i.e., the wicked.[61] (The word for "empty" [רק] and word for "forehead" [רקה] mentioned here [in a possessive form] share the same root letters.[62]) This verse, then, is praising the Jewish People for the fact that even their wicked are like pomegranates. The Gemara explains that just as pomegranates are filled with seeds, so the wicked are filled with mitzvos and merits.

YOUR TEETH ARE LIKE...

These two verses are almost an exact repetition of two earlier verses in Chapter 4 (v. 2-3). Our commentary on those verses will apply here as well. These praises are repeated because here Hashem is "singing the praises" of *Klal Yisrael* even in exile. Earlier, Hashem was highlighting their greatness when the Beis HaMikdash was standing. These verses allude to the seemingly lowest elements of *Klal Yisrael,* and tell us that even in exile, they are still special in the eyes of Hashem.

---

60 As explained earlier in our commentary on 4:2, this also communicates that the soldiers did not commit acts of immorality, another sin that is often unleashed by the heat of battle.

61 *Berachos* 57a.

62 The word "forehead" stems from the word "empty" also because it is "empty" of hair (Vilna Gaon).

YOUR TEETH ARE LIKE...

The *Zohar* understands these verses (and the parallel verses in Chapter 4) in a unique manner:

> **6** "Your eating [symbolized by the teeth] is [in the right quantity in the sense that you assess how much you need to eat and do not just indulge yourselves] like a flock of ewes [carefully counted and tracked by the owner], [like a flock of ewes] that came up from the bathing pool [in the sense that your food is completely kosher, like the sheep coming up from the bathing pools are clean of all foreign elements]. They [the various foods] are all perfect, with no defect among them [in the sense that they have no connection with any form of stealing or falsehood].
>
> **7** Your forehead [i.e., your mind, is constantly assessing how to observe more mitzvos, as many as the seeds] of a pomegranate. [This is all done with humility, hidden] under your veil."

FLOCK OF EWES

Rashi reminds us that ewes can be used completely for holy purposes. Its wool can be used for *techeiles* (the blue thread of *tzitzis*), its flesh for a *korban*, and its horns for a shofar. Furthermore, other body parts can be used for the musical instruments that the Leviyim played in the Beis HaMikdash: its leg bones for flutes, its sinews for harp strings, and its skin for drums. In contrast, the wicked are likened to dogs, which cannot be used in any holy capacity. Besides the simple message that Hashem treasures *Klal Yisrael* like people treasure ewes, Rashi is hinting at another important point: a Jewish person serves Hashem with every single part of his life. We must never say about any aspect or area of our life that we cannot connect to Hashem here. On the contrary, we should utilize every one of our traits and actions in the service of Hashem just as every part of the sheep is used to serve Hashem. Even in the way we eat and sleep, we can, and should, connect to Hashem.

> שִׁשִּׁים הֵמָּה מְלָכוֹת, וּשְׁמֹנִים פִּילַגְשִׁים; וַעֲלָמוֹת, אֵין מִסְפָּר.
>
> **ח / 8** There are sixty queens, eighty concubines, and a countless number of maidens.
>
> אַחַת הִיא, יוֹנָתִי תַמָּתִי, אַחַת הִיא לְאִמָּהּ, בָּרָה הִיא לְיוֹלַדְתָּהּ; רָאוּהָ בָנוֹת וַיְאַשְּׁרוּהָ, מְלָכוֹת וּפִילַגְשִׁים וַיְהַלְלוּהָ.
>
> **ט / 9** [But only] one is My dove, My perfect one; she is [as united as] one for her mother, and pure to the one who bore her. The daughters saw her and extolled her, the queens and the concubines [saw her] as well, [and] praised her.

These two verses are making one point and are meant to be interpreted together.

Allegorical Translation **8** There are many nations, some more important because they are descended from Avraham Avinu, and some less important because they are descended from Noach. And from them, there are even more groups and families.

9 But out of all these nations, I, Hashem, chose only you, *Klal Yisrael*, because you are faithful and pure. [Even though you sometimes argue among yourselves regarding the correct interpretation of Torah,] you all desire to get to the truth of Torah. In that way, you are all as one. When Yaakov, your forefather, saw that his entire family was untainted, he rejoiced. All other nations praise your greatness and steadfastness in serving Hashem.

Subject of the Verses Hashem is extolling *Klal Yisrael* by saying that out of all the nations, they are the only one He chose.

Mashal **8** The husband says to his wife: "There are superior women I could choose to marry, and eighty lower-level of relationships I could choose from, and countless young girls who wish to be with me (but…)

9 You, my wife, are the only one I wish to marry since you are the only one who is as beautiful as a dove, perfect in every way. Your mother loves you so much and appreciates your great purity, as if you are her only child. And all the other women are compelled to praise and acknowledge your greatness."

In short, the husband is telling his beloved that even though it may seem that there are many different women of greater or lesser importance that he could have married, as far as he is concerned, there is only one. She is the only one there is for him. Others, too, see her virtues and praise her.[63]

Nimshal Hashem continues with His praises and declares that even though there are many kinds of nations, He is not interested in having a special relationship with them at all. For Him, there is only one: His beloved *Klal Yisrael*. He concludes with the praise that even the other nations extoll her.

That is the basic message of these two verses. Let us proceed to elucidate the specific symbols and images used here.

According to Rashi, the sixty queens allude to Avraham's family, including his descendants through Yishmael and Eisav.[64] Since they come from such an illustrious patriarch, they are spoken about as royalty. They can also be considered royalty because Avraham was declared a king by the heathen nations.[65] The eighty concubines allude to Noach's descendants, who are less important.[66] Finally, the myriad maidens are all the other nations of the world.

Of all these "women," representing all the nations, only *Klal Yisrael* is especially important to Hashem. Indeed, in any healthy marriage, the husband understands and actually feels that there is only one woman for him and that all other women are not even an option.[67] This is the wonderful feeling that Hashem conveys to us poetically in this verse.

Klal Yisrael is then praised as the "one and only" in a number of ways. They are

---

63 As explained above, this sentiment is conveyed to us by Hashem. To fully appreciate this, it might be worthwhile to think of the opposite way of speaking. Imagine if a husband were to say to his wife: "I really wanted to marry someone whom I loved more than you, or who had better *yichus*, or was more beautiful, or had more money, but I simply could not find anyone, so I had to settle for you." This would this make his wife feel horrible. Hashem never speaks like that to us but tells us. He chose us because He loved us, and even though He could have had anyone, He preferred us. Thinking about this should remind us of how special we are in His eyes.

64 The calculation is as follows. Avraham and his fifteen descendants from Keturah, his second wife, make a total sixteen. Yitzchak and his two children are three. Yishmael and his twelve children make thirteen. The sons of Yaakov (himself already counted with Yitzchak's children) are twelve. The sons of Eisav (himself also already counted) are sixteen. This adds up to sixty. The Vilna Gaon's calculation is different from Rashi's. He excludes Yitzchak, Yaakov, and Yaakov's children, but includes Nachor's twelve children as well as Ammon and Moav.

65 *Bereishis* 14:17, with Rashi. Rashi adds here that both Hagar and Timnah, the concubines of Avraham and Esav respectively, were descended from royalty. Recognizing the superiority of Avraham's family, however, they both preferred to join his family, even in a limited way (as a concubine), rather than be a queen in another family.

66 All the descendants of Noach mentioned in the Torah (up to Avraham) number eighty.

67 In the blessings of the *sheva berachos*, we ask that Hashem cause the couple to rejoice like Adam and Chavah. It has often been said that Adam's and Chavah's rejoicing was partly due to the fact that they had no niggling doubts about whether they should be married to one another. They knew for certain that they were meant for each other since there was no one else alive when they married. We thus bless the newlyweds that they should feel certain that they are the only ones for each other.

the "one" who is Hashem's dove in the sense that they are as faithful as a dove.[68] Furthermore, just as a dove is gentle, without sharp claws or a powerful beak able to cut and injure others, so *Klal Yisrael* is a gentle nation and does not look for ways to hurt or wound others.

They are Hashem's "perfect one" in the sense that they are without blemish, flaw, or defilement.[69] Alternatively, they are the one nation who accepts suffering without complaint.[70] According to the Alshich, "תמתי" alludes to the fact that they were the one nation who followed Hashem without question (into the desert, where there is no food or water). He connects it with the word "תמימות" in the sense of "unquestioning faithfulness." Each beautiful term of endearment here calls for contemplation and reflection.

Klal Yisrael is also praised as being "[as united as] one for her 'mother.'"[71] Rashi, based on the Midrash, comments that some may wonder whether she is indeed only one. With all of the many halachic disputes and disagreements, it may appear that *Klal Yisrael* is divided into more than one nation, each serving Hashem in a different manner. The verse thus emphasizes that indeed, she is only one. She is united for her nation,[72] i.e., *Knesses Yisrael*, the "Congregation of Israel."[73] They may seem like many, but because they are all united as one to serve Hashem, they all seek to explain and understand the one Torah, and thus they are all considered one group.[74] This can be compared to a human being.

---

68 See our commentary on 2:14. The Netziv adds that the loyalty of the dove is built into its nature. So, too, loyalty to Hashem is effectively built into *Klal Yisrael*'s spiritual genes. Of course, they had to work to attain this, but once they did, this trait became part of their very essence.

69 See 5:2 and *Metzudas Tzion* there.

70 "תמתי" is understood by the Tzror HaMor to be related to the word "תמימות" in the sense of "accepting wholeheartedly."

71 *Shir Chadash* understands this to mean "she is the only one for her mother." Hashem loves *Klal Yisrael* as deeply as a mother loves her only child, a child she spends her whole life caring for, and nurturing. Her great and deep love for her child is paralleled by Hashem's love for us.

72 Literally, "her mother."

73 See our remarks on the concept of *Knesses Yisrael* in the Introduction.
    Rashi points out that Yaakov's family of seventy people is referred to in the verse there in the singular, while Esav's family of six is referred to in the plural (*Bereishis* 46:26). This is because Yaakov's family worked as one unit to serve Hashem with all family members having a single goal. In contrast, Esav's smaller family was split by beliefs and desires. Therefore, they are considered many. From this textual nuance, we can strengthen our appreciation of unity. If we display disunity in our conduct, we are emulating Esav's family, God forbid.

74 These verses allude to the time of the Second Beis HaMikdash (Rashi). During that period, disputes began in the realm of halachah. Until then, the tradition from earlier generations going back to Moshe Rabbeinu was very strong, and thus there were hardly any doubts. The few questions that did arise were resolved by the Sanhedrin. This means that for approximately the first thousand years after the Torah was given at Mount Sinai, there were no halachic arguments in *Klal Yisrael*. But because of all the terrible travails that occurred during the turbulent times of the *Churban* of the First

Despite having many limbs, muscles, etc., he is one entity. So *Klal Yisrael* is made up of many components, but in essence, is one.

The expression אחת היא לאמה can also be understood to mean, "She is one for her Mother." The "Mother" here is Hashem, the One who brought the world into existence and looks after it. *Klal Yisrael* is the only one who deserves to have Hashem's Presence dwell among them (*hashra'as ha'Shechinah*). So, she (*Klal Yisrael*) is the only one for her Mother (Hashem) to be with.[75] This is a great source of pride and joy for us. If a parent with many children would indicate that he is only happy to stay with one particular child,[76] that would engender a huge feeling of pride and joy in the child, knowing that he or she is deeply loved by the parent. Similarly, Hashem tells *Klal Yisrael* that He has many nations, but He wishes to dwell only among them. We should stop for a moment, let that feeling flow through us and appreciate what this says about us and about how much Hashem loves us.

The verse continues: "She is pure to the one who bore her." When grandparents and great-grandparents see their descendants, they are very proud of them. They see their purity and are grateful to Hashem for this, as Yaakov Avinu was when he bowed to Hashem on his deathbed for having only pure descendants.[77] We should be aware that our ancestors are watching us, full of pride that they have such descendants. Let's not disappoint them.

The verse concludes, "The daughters [i.e., all the other nations] saw her and extolled her; the queens and the concubines [i.e., the great nations and the less great saw her] too, [and] praised her." Praise from one's competitor is praise

---

Beis HaMikdash and the exile in Babylonia, followed by persecution under the Greeks and Romans, many halachic matters were forgotten, and many doubts arose which no one was able to resolve to everyone's satisfaction. As a result, quite a number of disputes developed during the period of the Second Beis HaMikdash. This caused shock and disappointment to a people who was not used to such a thing. Relatively suddenly, there was so much confusion that the nation seemed to be splitting apart through these halachic disputes. This is why the verse here describing those times emphasizes that we are all still one nation devoted to understanding one Torah. All the disputes do not detract from this. Hashem is reassuring and comforting *Klal Yisrael*. As long as everyone seeks the truth and tries his best to understand the Torah, Hashem treasures every opinion. The differences of opinion do not take away from the "oneness" of the nation (*Shiras Dovid*). See Rashi on *Temurah* 16a, *s.v. dofi shel semichah*.

75   *Tzror HaMor*.

76   Obviously, a parent should never articulate this feeling since it would cause friction in the family.

77   *Bereishis* 47:31, with Rashi.
It may be noted that the sight of a group of Jewish children sometimes causes the onlooker to be overcome by the purity that shines through. This is especially true in communities that have been able to protect their children from outside influences. Such a sight should cause us to feel very grateful to Hashem for keeping us pure, and we should feel proud to be part of a nation with such wonderful children.

indeed. A friend or relative may give praise even when its undeserved, but a competitor will only do so if it is crystal clear that praise is deserved. Then he feels compelled to give it. The greatness of the "one and only" is such that all the rest are compelled to admit how special she is, and they praise her for it. This is in keeping with the heathen nations' *raison d'etre*: to help *Klal Yisrael*.[78] One of the ways they do this is by acknowledging their greatness and praising them.[79]

ONLY ONE IS...MY PERFECT ONE

The main theme of these verses is the superiority of *Klal Yisrael* over all the other nations. The wisdom, conduct, accomplishments, etc., of the Jewish People are far superior to those of any other nation. We must be very careful not to be blinded by the superficial brilliance of the other nations and conclude that we should try to emulate their culture and values. In this connection, let us mention the tragic story of Elisha ben Avuya, a great Torah sage in the period of the *Tanna'im*. Unfortunately, he strayed from Torah and became very wicked. He went so far as to betray yeshivah boys to the Romans, thus endangering their lives. The Gemara identifies the root cause of his straying as his love for Greek songs.[80] This is not even a sin, yet it caused a downfall perhaps unmatched in history. The other sages did not bother with gentile songs because they looked down on the nations of the world. Anyone who considers himself superior does not imitate someone inferior. But Elisha failed to appreciate this verse that "Only one is [*Klal Yisrael*]...My perfect one." Once he was stricken with admiration for the Greeks, he was headed for ruin. We must never let our minds be

---

78 In light of the fact that Hashem considers *Klal Yisrael* to be the only "one," as we see here, the purpose of the nations is to support this relationship. They are never an alternative. (See Commentary on 8:11-12.)

79 The *Avodas Gershuni* suggests that these verses allude to Queen Esther of the Purim story. (We must remember that these verses refer to the time of the beginning of the Second Beis HaMikdash, and the great heroine of that era was Esther). This is how the *Avodas Gershuni* reads these verses:
"There are sixty queens, eighty concubines, and a countless number of maidens [i.e., there were many women for Achashverosh to choose from after he assembled all the beautiful women in the world— "wives" and "concubines" reflect the fact that he also took some married women, but only] one is My dove, My perfect one [i.e, only Esther was chosen because of the virtues and righteousness implied by these terms. Furthermore, a dove is loyal to its mate (see earlier 1:15) just as Esther was loyal to Mordechai, her true spouse, even though circumstances beyond her control forced her to be with Achashverosh.] She is united as one for her mother [i.e., through her efforts, she united *Klal Yisrael*, and she united (combined) all her efforts for the sake of Hashem, her protector], and she is pure for the one who bore her [i.e., She remained unsullied despite the influence of Achashverosh, and faithful to her Jewish People from whom she came. (All of the royal wealth and honor did not cause her to sway one iota from her loyalty to Klal Yisrael)]. The daughters saw her and extolled her; the queens and the concubines [saw her] as well, [and] praised her [i.e., all the heathen nations and people everywhere appreciated how beautiful she was. All praised her — even her competitors — as it is written: "Esther found favor in the eyes of all those who saw her" (Esther 2:15)].

80 *Chagigah* 16b.

tainted with admiration for the philosophy of the nations because it can bring total ruin.[81]

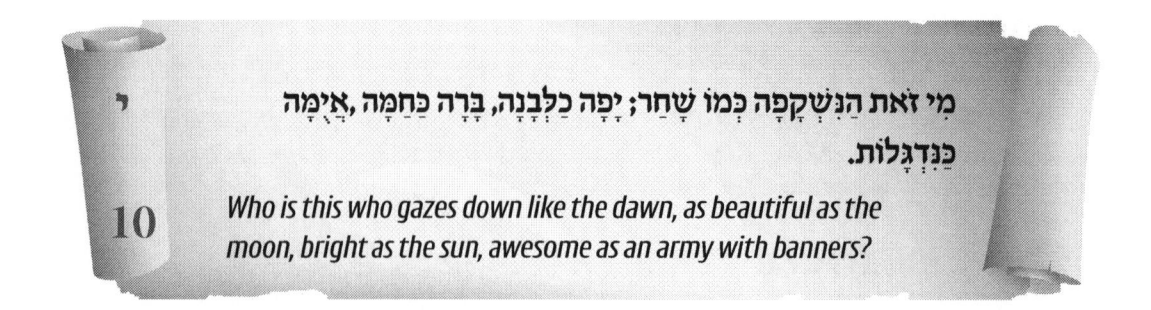

> מִי זֹאת הַנִּשְׁקָפָה כְּמוֹ שָׁחַר; יָפָה כַלְּבָנָה, בָּרָה כַּחַמָּה, אֲיֻמָּה כַּנִּדְגָּלוֹת.
>
> **10** Who is this who gazes down like the dawn, as beautiful as the moon, bright as the sun, awesome as an army with banners?

Allegorical Translation — How great is the Jewish People looking down from the great heights of the Beis HaMikdash. They gradually, but steadily, increase in power. They are as beautiful as the moon, bright as the sun, awesome as the angels.

Subject of the Verse — Hashem conveys the heathen nations' praises of *Klal Yisrael*.

Mashal — The husband repeats to his wife the praises (he alluded to in the previous verse) that she is getting from all the maidens around her: "How great is she who gazes down like the brightness of the dawn, as beautiful as the moon, bright as the sun, awesome as an army with banners."

Nimshal — The previous verse expressed that all the nations are compelled to praise *Klal Yisrael*. Here, Hashem praises *Klal Yisrael* by conveying their praise.[82]

"Who is this?" is a rhetorical question, a cry of astonishment. "Wow! See this great and awesome nation!" This is how the heathen nations express their surprise at the greatness of *Klal Yisrael*.

Klal Yisrael "gazes *down*" from the Beis HaMikdash because, from a spiritual standpoint, that is the highest place in the world. Furthermore, since the world is a globe, it can be viewed from many different angles. Depending on how one looks at it, parts of the world are up and other parts are down. By telling us that Eretz Yisrael is the highest land and the Beis HaMikdash is the highest place, the Torah is teaching us how to view the world: focus on Eretz Yisrael

---

81 See Rabbi Avigdor Miller's *Most Beautiful Nation*.

82 Hashem chooses to convey the praises of the nations instead of His own greater praises because the praises of an enemy indicate how richly deserved they are. An enemy only praises his adversary when the praise is completely deserved, as mentioned previously.

and realize that it is the pinnacle of the world. Viewed in this way, everything else is lower and less important.

The dawn begins with a tiny sliver of light and continually becomes brighter. Similarly, *Klal Yisrael*'s salvation becomes greater and greater with time. This happened a number of times in our history. Preceding the period of the Second Beis HaMikdash, our nation was subjugated to the kings of Persia. The Beis HaMikdash was built only with their permission. But eventually we had our own princes and finally our own kings, the Chashmonaim. This pattern can be identified in Persia itself in the time of Mordechai and Esther. At first, Mordechai was just an advisor sitting at the gates of the king, then he was led around Shushan with the praises of Haman, and finally he became King Achashverosh's deputy. Our awareness of this pattern gives us confidence that even if our light is only shining dimly now, like the early light of dawn, it will eventually shine brightly, just as the dawn eventually brings the full light of day.

As mentioned earlier, these verses describe *Klal Yisrael* not at their pinnacle, but during exile or during the period of the Second Beis HaMikdash, when they had not returned to their full greatness. Fittingly then, *Klal Yisrael* is not likened to the sun at midday but rather to the dawn. The "dawn" symbolizes a dim light which one knows is only going to get brighter. When a person knows that his future is going to get better and better, then even his problematic present situation can be bearable. But when he knows that his future is bleak, he tends to view all that he has now as worthless. *Klal Yisrael* know that their future is becoming brighter and brighter, steadily gaining strength and awesomeness. Therefore, even now when it is dark, they feel happy knowing what the future has in store for them.

The verse concludes the praise of *Klal Yisrael* with "as beautiful as the moon, bright as the sun, awesome as an army with banners." On a simple level, we understand that the praise is getting progressively greater: the weak light of the moon gives way to the strong light of the sun, and then to the light of the angels, whose light is even greater than that of the sun. Furthermore, this progression hints at the Jewish People gradually becoming more and more powerful with the coming of Mashiach: from "as beautiful as the moon," to "as bright as the sun," and finally they become as "awesome as an army with banners," i.e., the angels, who always gather under the banner of Hashem.[83]

In a similar vein, this verse also alludes to the Jewish People coming out of Egypt. At first, they were a nation rising from slavery like the pale light of dawn. Then, they became as bright as the moon in the sense that they reflected the glory of Hashem. And then, when they accepted the Torah at Sinai, they had the fire and strength of the sun. Finally, they dwelt around the Mishkan, just as the angels dwell around Hashem, becoming awesome like the angels.[84]

LIKE THE DAWN

If one has been through a very long, dark night, seeing the dawn brings a great sense of relief. Even though it is not bright at the moment, dawn is the harbinger of the daylight soon to come. Watching *Klal Yisrael*, and especially the righteous, teaches the world that even if things seem dark and evil now, the light of Hashem will eventually spread throughout the world. In this way *Klal Yisrael* is likened to the dawn. *Klal Yisrael* give hope to the world just as the dawn gives comfort to those in the dark.[85]

AS BEAUTIFUL AS THE MOON, BRIGHT AS THE SUN, AWESOME...

The Midrash explains that the moon, sun, and angels each possess their own special greatness, and the verse tells us that *Klal Yisrael* has them all. The moon is beautiful. Even though the moon is much less bright than the sun, it has a beauty that the sun lacks. It also has the virtue of shining even at night. The sun, of course, gives us bright daylight and warmth. The greatness of the angels is awe-inspiring, and they dwell in unity under one banner. *Klal Yisrael* incorporate all of these attributes. They are beautiful like the moon and shine even in the darkest night of exile. And like the sun, they provide brightness and warmth in the sense that their illumination enables the world to distinguish between right and wrong, and to trust in Hashem, thereby gaining the warm comfort of security. And, like the angels, they are also awe-inspiring, and they work together to serve Hashem.

---

83 See our commentary on verse 4 above for a further explanation of this metaphor.
84 See Alshich.
85 Netziv.

> אֶל גִּנַּת אֱגוֹז יָרַדְתִּי, לִרְאוֹת בְּאִבֵּי הַנָּחַל; לִרְאוֹת הֲפָרְחָה הַגֶּפֶן, הֵנֵצוּ הָרִמֹּנִים.
>
> **11** I went down to the nut garden to observe the first ripening plants of the streams, to see if the vine has blossomed, and if the pomegranate trees have budded.

Allegorical Translation — I, Hashem, came to *Klal Yisrael*'s dwelling place to admire their good deeds and to watch the flourishing of the *talmidei chachamim* and the development of those who do good deeds.

Subject of the Verse — Hashem is praising *Klal Yisrael*.

Mashal — The husband says that when he left his wife (as mentioned earlier in verse 1), he did not forget her. Instead, he went to her garden to admire all the beautiful plants that she cultivated in order to remember her and feel connected to her.

Nimshal — This is the concluding verse of Hashem's praises in this chapter. Here, the Jewish People is likened to a beautiful, flowering, and fruitful garden that Hashem comes to see, examine, and enjoy. Hashem says that He has come to *Klal Yisrael* to see "firsthand" how beautiful and wonderful they are.

I WENT DOWN TO THE GARDEN OF NUTS

Let us take a moment to see how this verse connects with the previous verses in this chapter. Earlier (verse 1), the nations mock *Klal Yisrael*, whose beloved God, they claim, had "disappeared." They argue that Hashem had left them and forgotten them — the proof being that He sent them into exile. *Klal Yisrael* responds (in verse 2) with great faith that He has not left them completely or forgotten them, but rather has just gone into the "garden." As explained earlier, this represents a different way of relating to us. This is like someone telling a wife that her husband has left her, to which she replies that he has just gone to the nearby garden; he is still close by and, in fact, he has gone there to collect flowers for her — meaning that he still cares about her. So, too, *Klal Yisrael* say that Hashem is close by them in the "garden." *Klal Yisrael* then declare how their relationship with Hashem is strong and exclusive (verse 3). This devotion brings forth a torrent of praise from Hashem which fills the next few verses.

Here in this verse, Hashem refers back to what *Klal Yisrael* said in verse 2 and acknowledges that He has indeed gone into the garden. There He admires the wonderful deeds of *Klal Yisrael*, as will be explained. The underlying message here is that exile is not as the nations view it — a complete rejection of *Klal Yisrael*. Rather as *Klal Yisrael* insist, even in exile, Hashem does not forget them. He admires the righteousness they produce and the good deeds they do.

Let us proceed to zero in on the various images and symbols in this verse.

I WENT DOWN TO THE NUT GARDEN

In order to fully appreciate what the nut represents here, we would do well to contemplate this remarkable creation of Hashem. A nut is a special kind of fruit, substantially different from all others. It has a very hard shell, making it impervious to dirt. A nut can be used both for eating and for playing. In the absence of all the toys we have nowadays, nuts were often used for play. Hashem created nuts for the same reason He created all things: so that we should serve Him better.

In the creation of nuts, Hashem also gave us a multi-faceted symbol. Rashi says that "nuts" allude to the righteous of *Klal Yisrael*. From the outside, nuts appear to be completely inedible. Indeed, if one would bite a nut while still in its shell, that assumption would be confirmed. But on the inside, of course, nuts are filled to the brim with tasty and nutritious food. So it is with the righteous. They are modest and not pretentious or conspicuous. Their righteousness cannot easily be discerned. Yet, upon further examination, one can see that they are filled with good deeds and wisdom.

"Nuts" also allude to *Klal Yisrael* in exile. Due to their hard and complete shell, they are hermetically sealed. Even if they are thrown in the mud, they are still edible. So, too, even when *Klal Yisrael* is sent into exile among the unclean nations, they remain clean and pure inside because they are sealed off from non-Jewish influences.[86] The Midrash adds that on Yom Kippur, Hashem wipes away all the sins that *Klal Yisrael* has accumulated during the year, and since they are like nuts that are easily wiped and cleaned, Yom Kippur cleanses them properly. Accordingly, when Hashem speaks of having gone down to check the nut garden, this means that He came to look carefully at *Klal Yisrael* and admire how they are like nuts in the sense that their wonderful deeds are concealed — not flaunted — and they are clean from all outside dirt.

Already in Chapter One, we learned that *Klal Yisrael* is intrinsically beautiful, and that any ugliness is only skin deep and not part of their core.[87] This too is symbolized by the nut since its shell and fruit are two separate entities: one cracks the shell, and

---

86 See *Chagigah* 15b. Ibn Yichiyah adds that just as it is sometimes necessary to hit a nut with a hammer in order to get the best part out, so it is sometimes only through blows that the best part of *Klal Yisrael* comes out. How unfortunate it is that in times of peace, there is often discord and other ugliness among *Klal Yisrael*, but in times of trouble, suddenly people are on their best behavior. The hammer blows bring out our best.

87 1:5-6.

out comes a separate nut. When we see ugliness in a Jewish person, we must realize we are seeing only the shell. The inner kernel of every Jewish person is good, like a tasty nut. Furthermore, the peel of most fruits is closely attached to its flesh. Indeed, they are bonded together to the extent that when peeling them, part of the inner fruit will remain attached to the peel. In contrast, the shell of the nut and the fruit inside are completely separate. The "nut" thus symbolizes how the external sins of *Klal Yisrael* is separate from their inner selves. If a Jew is wearing "dirty clothes," they are obviously not part of his essence.[88]

The Midrash adds that just as a stone (or something as hard as stone) is needed to crack open a nut and get out its goodness, similarly Torah, which is as hard as a stone,[89] is needed to break our evil inclination and bring out our goodness. For a Jewish person to bring out his full potential, he must use Torah. Only then will he be able to get rid of the *yetzer ha'ra* which, like an empty shell, has no sweetness.[90]

Furthermore, just as the edible part of the nut embodies the purpose of the entire nut, so those who learn Torah embody the purpose of this world. Therefore, *talmidei chachamim* are likened to the inner kernel of the nut. Those who help and protect *talmidei chachamim* are comparable to the shell which protects the nut. Just as shells are important because they protect the nuts, so those who do not devote themselves to learning Torah, but help and protect those who do, are important and will be greatly rewarded.

There is, however, a condition implicit in the analogy. The shell of an unshelled nut is vital (and adds to the price of nuts, which are bought by weight), but it is discarded when detached. Similarly, those who help Torah and protect it are valuable only while attached to it. The important message here is that only when one is attached to a person learning Torah does he have value.[91]

The Midrash points to additional ways in which Jews and *Klal Yisrael*, as a whole, are similar to nuts. For instance, when one nut is removed from within a pile of nuts, the entire pile shifts and shakes. So, too, when one Jew dies, the entire community is shaken. His passing affects the entire community, and they all mourn the loss. This reminds us of the strong connection between Jews, and how they are all affected by one another.[92]

---

88 Netziv.
89 *Yirmeyahu* 23:29.
90 *Kiddushin* 30b.
91 Midrash.
92 Midrash. This concept also applies, albeit differently, to mitzvos. If a single mitzvah is moved or manipulated, the entire pile — the entire structure — shifts. One may think he is just "adjusting" one, but eventually it can cause a breakdown of the entire edifice of Torah observance. This is also applicable to what some people consider worthless *minhagim*.

Just as eating a nut makes a lot of noise, so *Klal Yisrael* pray to Hashem noisily.

A further point of similarity lies in the fact that nuts are enjoyed by children as toys, but also enjoyed by kings as a tasty food. So too, *Klal Yisrael* is toyed with by the child-like heathen nations (due to their lacking the wisdom to appreciate the greatness of *Klal Yisrael*), but eventually will be respected and honored by kings.

All of these symbols deserve contemplation and have many layers of meaning.[93]

TO OBSERVE THE FIRST RIPENING PLANTS…

Hashem goes down to the nut garden "to observe the first ripening plants of the streams, to see if the vine has blossomed, and if the pomegranate trees have budded." The various types of vegetation mentioned here allude to various groups in *Klal Yisrael*. The "first ripening plants" represent the youthful scholars or the righteous youth who are beginning to ripen. They are "of the streams," in the sense that they are full of full of vigor to serve Hashem, like a plant which grows next to a stream is full of moisture. Hashem rejoices when He sees the young boys and girls who are full of enthusiasm to serve Him. They are at the stage of "first ripening," i.e., starting to serve Hashem, and full of "moisture." "Moisture" symbolizes freshness, while "dryness" characterizes those who have lost vitality.[94] The "vine" alludes to the Torah scholars who sit in the *beis midrash* in neat rows like vines.[95] The "pomegranates" allude to those who are full of mitzvos, like a pomegranate is full of seeds.[96]

In short, Hashem is saying that He has not forgotten about us in exile. On the contrary, He constantly watches to see how every part of the nation is flourishing with good deeds. Because He wants to see this "firsthand," He goes into the garden of exile to admire and praise *Klal Yisrael*. If we would truly appreciate how Hashem is watching and getting pleasure from our good deeds, we would do mitzvos with a very high level of pride, joy, and enthusiasm. Let us resolve to conduct ourselves in a way that gives Him *nachas*.

By altering family customs, even if they do not seem important, one may inadvertently cause the entire pile to shift and fall. This is a very important message that one must very careful not to tamper with even what he may think is an unimportant *minhag* because as he starts making an "adjustment," the entire pile of nuts (mitzvos) shifts.

93 There is a *minhag* to eat nuts on Pesach while one is busy opening them one can think about these symbols!

94 See earlier 4:13 and *Sanhedrin* 92b regarding the "dry bones."

95 In ancient times, the yeshivos where the sages studied were characterized by a very careful seating arrangement. They sat in rows shaped like semi-circles according to their level of scholarship, with the greater sages sitting closer to the front. This was a highly developed system in which all would be able to listen to those greater than themselves and teach those who needed help. This seating arrangement maximized everyone's potential for growth. From a visual standpoint, it looked similar to the rows of a vineyard. In fact, the Yeshivah of the sages in Yavneh was known as *Kerem B'Yavneh*, meaning "the vineyard of Yavneh" (*Berachos* 62b).

96 See earlier 4:3.

SHIR HASHIRIM 6:12

יב לֹא יָדַעְתִּי, נַפְשִׁי שָׂמַתְנִי מַרְכְּבוֹת עַמִּי נָדִיב.

12 I did not know [how to behave, and thus] caused myself to become chariots for a nation of nobility.

Allegorical Translation — We, *Klal Yisrael*, were not careful to avoid sin, and we got caught up in baseless hatred and disputes. Through our own actions, we caused ourselves to be enslaved by the ministers of other nations.

Subject of the Verse — *Klal Yisrael* is reminiscing regretfully.

Mashal — Reminiscing regretfully, the wife speaks of how, through her foolish behavior, she caused herself to be rejected by her husband, the king, and ended up being enslaved by other people. She thereby not only lost the love and protection of her husband, but she also brought upon herself terrible suffering in enslavement.

Nimshal — Upon hearing Hashem's praises, *Klal Yisrael* reflect on their past and express their feelings about it.

According to Rashi, *Klal Yisrael* is expressing regret here for their foolishness during the period of the Second Beis HaMikdash which caused their own exile and suffering. That period is the subject of the previous couple of chapters, and this verse continues describing the events of that period. What actually happened towards the end of that period was most unfortunate. A civil war broke out between the followers of two descendants of the Chashmonaim, Hyrkenos and Aristobulos. Hyrkenos eventually brought in the kingdom of Rome to help him win. But once Rome got involved, they became a powerful force in Eretz Yisrael. They eventually conquered *Klal Yisrael*, destroyed the Beis HaMikdash, and sent *Klal Yisrael* into exile. The followers of both Hyrkenos and the Aristobulos became their slaves.[97]

Our verse, then, is to be understood this way: "Because I did not know how to guard against sin,[98] I caused myself to become a slave and a chariot for the

---

97 *Sotah* 49b, with Maharsha.

98 Alternatively, the verse can be understood to mean, "I did not realize [how terrible sin is]" (*Divrei Yedidyah*). Indeed, we cannot truly fathom just how terrible a sin really is. This applies to sin in general and, in this case, the vileness of *machlokes*, discord and conflict. Those who engage in *machlokes* never truly realize how terrible the damage is going to be and how they themselves will only lose in the end because of it.

ministers of Rome." It is a candid expression of regret and repentance.[99]

I DID NOT KNOW [HOW TO BEHAVE, AND THUS] CAUSED MYSELF…

Many lessons can be learned from this verse. According to Rashi, this verse is telling us how much damage and harm we inflict on ourselves when we fight each other. *Machlokes* (feuding) causes untold suffering and grief. Inviting other nations or other people to get involved in our *machlokes* makes the situation a hundred times worse. This verse is an example. Rome succeeded in enslaving us and destroying our Beis HaMikdash because of our infighting and our invitation to them to get involved. As Rashi emphasizes, we brought this harm upon ourselves. If only we had remained unified and separate from the other nations, we would have been a lot stronger and a lot safer.

The regret expressed by *Klal Yisrael* in this verse is understood differently by the Seforno and Metzudas Dovid. The Metzudas Dovid says they are expressing regret that they did not open the door to their Beloved, as explained earlier in great detail.[100] Hashem pleaded with *Klal Yisrael*, but *Klal Yisrael* showed indifference. This led to their exile and enslavement, as encapsulated in this verse.

The sin of *sinas chinam* (baseless hatred) during the period of the Second Beis HaMikdash was a hidden one. Outwardly, the Jewish People seemed good, but their hearts were filled with hatred. The Gemara (*Yoma* 9b) tells us that because it was a deep-rooted sin, one not easily perceived, the long exile it brought on was hidden in the sense that we do not know when the salvation will ultimately come. (This is in marked contrast to the Babylonian exile which we knew would last only seventy years.) A sin that is external can easily be rectified — not so, a hidden sin, where effort is required to uproot it and heal it. According to this interpretation, our verse is saying, "I did not know *and identify* the hidden sin of *sinas chinam* and therefore became enslaved in this very long exile (*Devash V'Chalav*).

99   There is a famous fable which aptly describes this outcome. Two mice discover a large piece of cheese together. They are thrilled with this very valuable find and split it between them. But then they start fighting to see who gets the bigger piece. Then a sly, evil fox comes by and sees what is going on. He says that he does not wish to see them fighting and offers to help. He explains that he will take a bite from the bigger piece, and then both mice will have an equal portion. They both agree. The fox takes a very big bite from the bigger piece, and says, "Oh no! The bigger piece is now smaller than the original smaller piece. I don't want you to fight about it so will take a bite from the other to make them equal." He takes a bite from the other, and now that one is smaller. This pattern continues until there only crumbs left. The fox leaves them with these words of consolation. "Well, now there is nothing for you to fight about. Enjoy the crumbs." This is what actually happens in every conflict.

Another danger of conflict is that the feuding parties will often do anything to make sure the other side does not win, including damaging their own interests. Hyrkenos must have realized that inviting the Romans in would cause him harm as well, but he preferred that to his brother winning! Bar Kamtza, too, caused great harm to himself by slandering the Jewish People in front of the emperor in his desire to avenge his having been put to shame (*Gittin* 55b-56a). It is noteworthy that the Gemara introduces its retelling of this episode by quoting the verse, "Praiseworthy is the one who is constantly afraid [of sin]" (*Mishlei* 28:14). Indeed, this is the message of our verse: *Klal Yisrael* regret that they were not wary of sin, thus allowing themselves to fall into the sin of internecine conflict.

See *Birkas Peretz, Parashas Va'eira*, who discusses how one inevitably brings harm upon himself in a fight and how this is vividly illustrated by the Egyptian reaction to the Plague of the Frogs. Their relentless hitting of the initial frog only caused more to emerge.

100   See v. 5:2.

Looked at from this standpoint, our verse provides a powerful motivation to serve Hashem. Essentially, here *Klal Yisrael* recognize that by not serving Hashem, they became slaves to others. The undeniable fact is that a person in this world will always have burdens and challenges. A righteous person chooses to utilize his life to serve Hashem, thereby finding true happiness and lasting reward. But if one chooses to throw off the yoke of serving Hashem, one will have other burdens placed upon him for which he will find no lasting happiness and no future reward. *Klal Yisrael* did not open to Hashem, and thus became slaves to other nations. Furthermore, this reminds us that when opportunities from Hashem come knocking at our door, we dare not ignore them.

The Seforno says that here *Klal Yisrael* express regret that they chose to remain in exile even after the Second Beis HaMikdash was rebuilt, and thus caused themselves to become slaves to other nations. Had there been more enthusiasm for the Second Beis HaMikdash, it would have had a greater history. When Hashem gave the Jewish People a chance to return to Eretz Yisrael in the time of the righteous King Koresh, most of the Jewish People chose to remain in exile. They thus brought upon themselves the suffering of the future exile, when the Second Beis HaMikdash was destroyed. They were not dedicated and excited enough to return to Eretz Yisrael to try to build a nation that would not sin again. We, too, must be certain that when opportunities for greatness arise, we dare not let them slip away through laziness or stupidity. Indeed, we must be certain that when Mashiach comes, no thoughts of comfort and the like will deter us from quickly moving to Eretz Yisrael.

Despite their differences, all of the approaches above concur that this verse concludes the story that began earlier: Hashem trying to draw *Klal Yisrael* close to Him, their refusal, and the exile and suffering this caused. Here in our verse, they recall all this with regret and repentance.

I DID NOT KNOW...

The Midrash explains this seemingly ambiguous verse in a completely different way: The noble nation is *Klal Yisrael*, not the Romans! The Midrash begins with a parable. There was once a princess who did not know her true identity. She went around in rags with the beggars to collect grain that had fallen by the way and was free to be taken by all. On one occasion, the king passed by while she was picking up grain and realized that this was his daughter! He took her, dressed her in royal garments, and had her ride in his royal chariot alongside him.

The old friends of the princess said to her: "We are amazed that yesterday you were with us as a beggar collecting food, and today you are an important princess!"

The princess responded: "I am as amazed as you are, for I also never imagined this happening to me!"

Similarly, says the Midrash, *Klal Yisrael* were slaves in Egypt, and suddenly Hashem took them out, and they became a nation of princes. The heathen nations were amazed to see this transformation. "How can it be," they exclaimed, "that you have become so great so quickly?!"

Klal Yisrael answered, "We are equally amazed!" By this, they meant that it is all because of the kindness and love that Hashem has for us; and we are grateful to Him.

According to the Midrash, then, the verse is to be understood this way: "I did not know myself [in the sense of recognizing my own true greatness, and therefore did not imagine that] I would become a noble nation riding on chariots." Accordingly, this verse is one of amazement and gratitude to Hashem.[101]

The Midrash concludes that the same thing happened to Yosef HaTzaddik when he came out of prison, to Dovid HaMelech when he became king, and to Mordechai HaTzaddik when he was saved from Haman. After a period of terrible persecution, they were suddenly saved and put into a position of tremendous greatness.

According to the interpretation of the Midrash, this verse is a great source of comfort. If we occasionally fall into the trap of thinking that our people's situation is so bad or that we will never become a great nation again, we should remember our history — especially the history of those great men, Yosef HaTzaddik, Dovid HaMelech, and Mordechai HaTzaddik. We were a lowly and enslaved nation in Egypt, and Hashem suddenly took us out and made us His chosen people. It happened in such a wondrous manner that we ourselves were amazed. As it says in this verse, we did not imagine that such a thing could happen.

Yosef HaTzaddik was a slave for many years. Then he was falsely accused of a terrible crime and thrown into prison. He was rejected by his own brothers and forgotten by those in Egypt whom he had helped. Suddenly, in the course of one day, he became one of the most powerful men in the entire world. Eventually he helped *Klal Yisrael* settle in Egypt and ensured that they would survive the exile of Egypt. Yosef could never have imagined this amazing chain of events.

We see the same pattern in Dovid HaMelech's life as well. He started out as a shepherd

---

[101] The Rokeiach and the Rinas Dodim prefer to see this verse portraying *Klal Yisrael* not as the rider, but as the chariot. The world, they comment, "rides" on the deeds of the righteous in the sense that the destiny and success of the world depend on the good deeds performed by the righteous. Their reading is in accord with the expression, "Everything *rides on* it," meaning "Everything depends on it." The people of *Klal Yisrael* are the "chariots" of Hashem, the vehicles Hashem uses to move everything forward. This means that the destiny of the world and the honor of Hashem ride on us and our deeds. Everything — including the angels — depends on our mitzvos in order to flourish and survive. This awesome greatness is hard to fully appreciate. According to this interpretation, our verse is to be understood this way: "I did not know myself [i.e., my true greatness, as evidenced by Hashem] making me the one [upon] whose chariots [i.e., deeds] all futures and existences [even of the angels who are] nobles ride."

rejected by his family, was later hunted by his father-in-law, Shaul HaMelech, and eventually became the ultimate king of *Klal Yisrael*. Mordechai HaTzaddik experienced something similar. One day he was wearing sackcloth in mourning, and the next day he was honored by being taken around Shushan wearing the royal garments and riding the royal horse. Leading him around was none other than the king's most important minister, the anti-Semitic Haman, who had to sing his praises.

This should give us hope, no matter what our situation is like at the moment. Just as these figures could not have imagined how great their salvation would be, neither can we imagine how great ours will be as well.

The Midrash concludes that when Mashiach comes, the heathen nations will be very surprised, and exclaim: "Yesterday, you were slaves, rejected by all. But today you are like nobles and kings of the world!" We will reply that we too are equally amazed.

There is a deeper message here. Our lack of appreciation for who we are makes us so surprised when suddenly we become a noble nation. Let us go back for a moment to the Midrash's *mashal* of the princess who did not know that she was a princess. Had she known who she really was, she would not have been at all surprised by the king's actions. On the contrary, she would have expected it. She would not have wasted her life collecting fallen grain but would have gone directly to the king and said: "I am your daughter!" Similarly, if we would appreciate our own greatness as the beloved children of Hashem, we would not be surprised by the thought of salvation. On the contrary, we would be expecting it! We would be coming to Hashem and saying: "We are your children. Please save us!"

We would also conduct ourselves in a way that is fitting for children of a king. And even if we think we are great, we are actually far greater since we are the beloved children of Hashem. There is nothing greater than that. *Shir HaShirim* teaches us to appreciate who we are, and it shows us how much Hashem loves us and helps us prepare for the moment when that love will be crystal clear to all.

פרק ז׳
CHAPTER 7

> **א / 1**
> שׁוּבִי שׁוּבִי הַשּׁוּלַמִּית, שׁוּבִי שׁוּבִי וְנֶחֱזֶה בָּךְ; מַה תֶּחֱזוּ בַּשּׁוּלַמִּית, כִּמְחֹלַת הַמַּחֲנָיִם.
>
> *Turn away, turn away, perfect one; turn away, turn away, and we will appoint you to high positions. What high positions can you offer the perfect one that compare to the encircling camps?!*

Allegorical Translation   The heathen nations say to *Klal Yisrael*: Turn away from Hashem, and we will appoint you to high positions and offer you greatness.

   Klal Yisrael reply: What can you offer to compete with the wonderful honor Hashem gave us by having us dwell around Him in the Mishkan.

Subject of the Verse   The heathen nations try to persuade *Klal Yisrael* to turn away from Hashem by promising them power and positions if they leave Hashem, but *Klal Yisrael* refuse.

Mashal   Jealous of the relationship between the wife and her husband, competing maidens try to lure the wife away from her husband. They promise that they will give her anything she wants if she leaves him. The wife replies: There is nothing you can offer to match what I get from my relationship with my husband.

Nimshal   The heathen nations cajole *Klal Yisrael*, "the perfect nation," to turn away from Hashem. They promise *Klal Yisrael* much love and respect if they will just do this.

   Klal Yisrael answer that the best the nations can give them does not compare to what Hashem gave them with "the encircling camps" — an allusion, according to Rashi, to the various camps of *Klal Yisrael* dwelling around the Mishkan. According to the Midrash, "the encircling camps" is an allusion to *Klal Yisrael* dwelling in camps around Har Sinai at the time of *Matan Torah*. The Midrash identifies the camps as the camp of *Klal Yisrael* and the camp of the angels. Together they witnessed Hashem giving the Torah to *Klal Yisrael*. Nothing the nations are capable of giving *Klal Yisrael* can compare with that awesome event.

TURN AWAY, TURN AWAY...

This verse encapsulates, in general terms, the great test *Klal Yisrael* has faced throughout their *galus*. The heathen nations have often been ready to offer *Klal Yisrael* wealth, comfort, and respect if they give up their relationship with Hashem. But *Klal Yisrael* have, on the whole, stood firm and refused all their enticing offers.

There were periods when a Jew was barred from entering many professions or even from owning property. Keeping one's faith was thus a tremendous test since it involved sacrificing a potential career. Nowadays, we generally do not have a situation where a Jew has to reject his faith in order to advance in his career. But even today, although the gentiles do not directly approach us like this as they did in the past, a Jew understands on some level that he can often find a better job, or have a better chance of being promoted, if he would only give up his faith. On a more subtle level, a person could mistakenly imagine that if he spends less time on prayer or Torah study and more time in the office, he will be wealthier and more powerful; or if he focuses less on *chessed* and mitzvos, he will have a more beautiful home and be generally more successful; or if he becomes very friendly with non-Jewish co-workers and shares more of their lifestyle and pleasures, he could live a better life. These are the lures of the *yetzer ha'ra* and bad friends. Rejecting all this and affirming that serving Hashem is the most valuable pursuit is the theme of this verse. This verse, then, is about one of the key tests the Jewish People has faced in the past and will continue to face again and again.

THE PERFECT ONE

In this verse, *Klal Yisrael* is called "*shulamis*." We translate this above as "perfect one,"[1] since the word "*shulamis*" shares a root with the word "*shalem*" (meaning "whole" or "perfect"). The Midrash offers other possibilities which are not mutually exclusive. One is the "peaceful nation," from the word "*shalom*." The Midrash explains that *Klal Yisrael*

---

1   *Klal Yisrael* is perfect in its faith (Rashi) or perfect in its conduct (Midrash).

is the source of peace in this world.² Furthermore, Hashem will eventually bring *Klal Yisrael* to a peaceful place, i.e., Yerushalayim.³ "*Shulamis*" can also signify the "complete nation" because *Klal Yisrael* bring the world to its completion, or because the world is completely reliant on *Klal Yisrael*. Since we observe the Torah, without which the world would cease to exist, this makes us the nation that is upholding the world and bringing it to completion. Through our merits, Mashiach will come when the world finally realizes its destiny. Since *Shir HaShirim* describes the love Hashem has for *Klal Yisrael*, the Midrash naturally offers quite a few flattering terms to explain the word "*shulamis*." Each one of these terms hints at a number of aspects of our nation's greatness. To delve into each one is beyond the scope of this *sefer*. In short, however, the title "*shulamis*" is one that the Jewish People have earned due to their many wonderful attributes. When we are referred to as *shulamis*, "the perfect, complete, peaceful one," we should feel both joy and pride.

TURN AWAY, TURN AWAY...

The verse repeats the phrase "turn away" four times. The Midrash tells us that this is an allusion to the four exiles *Klal Yisrael* has been through. During our history, we have been enticed to leave Hashem by four different nations. Each one called to us to turn away from Hashem with their own particular method, and each one brought us a different set of challenges. But we have withstood all their challenges and rejected all their approaches.

Now, we have translated the word "*shuvi*" as "turn away," in accordance with Rashi. Yet the literal translation of "*shuvi*" is "return." But this is perplexing. Since the heathen nations try to persuade *Klal Yisrael* to sin and to join them, should they not have used a word meaning "come" (e.g., *bo'iy*)?!

The Shiras Dovid explains that the context here is *Klal Yisrael* in exile (as in the previous chapter) who are now in the process of repenting. But the nations are cajoling them to "return" to their wicked ways. They use the word "return" to emphasize that *Klal Yisrael* has sinned for so long that returning to their "normal" conduct and way of life is to return to their sins, as if to say being wicked is their natural state. There is an

---

2   The Midrash elaborates: The Jewish People's quintessential blessing is for peace (as reflected in the concluding blessing of *birkas Kohanim* וישם לך שלום); the Peaceful One (i.e., Hashem, whose name is Peace [שלום],) dwells among the peaceful Jewish People; when Mashiach comes, he will bring peace; Hashem will make certain that Eretz Yisrael will be a peaceful place; and finally, Hashem always blesses the Jewish People with peace.

3   The city of Yerushalayim was originally called Shalem, meaning "peace." Avraham Avinu called it the "Mount of Yira'eh." Hashem combined the two names and called it "Yerushalayim" (Radak and Midrash Shochar Tov on *Tehillim* 76:3). That the capital of the Jewish People was originally called "Peace," and had the name "peace" incorporated in its eternal name, demonstrates how much Yerushalayim is intrinsically bound up with peace.

important message here for us. Sometimes a person caught up in bad behavior decides to try to change and elevate himself, but the *yetzer ha'ra* or bad friends tell him: "Return to your previous state because that is your true state! You are not a spiritual kind of person!" One has to learn to ignore such debilitating messages. Our real true selves are infinitely great, as we see in this verse, and *sinning* is actually turning away from who we truly are. Even if we have sinned often and for long periods of time, this is not who we really are — it's just an aberration. We must try to return to our true normal state as soon as possible.

The Vilna Gaon understands "*shuvi*" to mean "relax and slow down."[4] The heathen nations tell *Klal Yisrael*: "Even if you wish to repent, proceed at a leisurely pace and without enthusiasm. *Klal Yisrael* reject even this milder form of enticement. They insist that serving Hashem is so valuable and so exciting — as they saw at Har Sinai — that one should do it with all of one's energy and enthusiasm.

WE WILL APPOINT YOU TO HIGH POSITIONS

According to Rashi's first explanation, the nations go on to promise, "We will appoint you to high positions." In other words, "If you turn away from Hashem, we will appoint you to positions of nobility and importance." Rashi offers a slightly different explanation as well, based on an understanding of the key word "*nechezeh*" that is closer to its usual meaning of "seeing." The nations are thus saying: "We will look [out] for you and try to find the best possible type of greatness to give to you."[5]

---

4 In *Yeshayahu* 30:15, the word "*shuvah*" clearly has this connotation.

5 Another way of understanding this verse is "We will prophesize for you" (see *Targum* and Seforno quoted later). The heathen nations try to convince *Klal Yisrael* to turn away from Hashem by serving idols, etc., by claiming that they too can produce prophetic proofs and Heavenly messages that validate their way of life. Indeed, this has been one of the challenges *Klal Yisrael* has faced throughout their history. Besides the pogroms and enticements that the nations use to draw *Klal Yisrael* away from Hashem, they also offer "proofs" of Heavenly revelations that, they claim, confirm their nonsense. But *Klal Yisrael* reply: "What [false] prophecy can you offer that compares with [the true traditions and beliefs we absorbed at] the encircling camps?!" Here the allusion is to *Ma'amad Har Sinai*, as will be explained later. *Klal Yisrael* reject all other religions as being false for many reasons, but perhaps the most significant reason lies in a comparison of what they have to offer with the Torah's account of the revelation at *Ma'amad Har Sinai*. At *Ma'amad Har Sinai*, Hashem spoke publicly to millions of people and clearly broadcast the Torah and mitzvos in broad daylight in a public place. The world knew immediately exactly when and where it happened. It would have been impossible to make this up due to the precise nature of the details, the transparency of the event, and the enormous number of people involved, among many other reasons. In contrast, all other belief systems are based on ambiguous events that were reported only years later, that supposedly took place clandestinely in front of a small number of people. These could easily have been fabricated or conceived in the wild imagination of an unhinged individual. Accordingly, in our verse, *Klal Yisrael* brush off all false beliefs by saying they cannot compare to our traditions based on the unique revelation at *Ma'amad Har Sinai*. See the *Kuzari* (1:87) and the *Sefer HaChinuch* (Introduction) for further discussion of the unique foundation of Jewish faith.

WHAT HIGH POSITIONS CAN YOU OFFER...THAT COMPARE TO THE ENCIRCLING CAMPS?!

Klal Yisrael answer: "Nothing you can give me compares with what Hashem already gave me!" At first glance, this answer is surprising. In the exile, *Klal Yisrael*'s answer could well have been, "I am ready to sacrifice for my beliefs..." or "This would be a terrible sin!" The surprising nature of their answer can be seen more clearly in the *mashal*. The maidens try to entice the wife away from her husband with promises of success if she leaves him. The wife might have been expected to reply: "It would be wrong to betray my husband" or "I must sacrifice for my husband" — a more martyr-type answer. Instead, she replies: "Nothing you can offer me compares with the wonderful joy and goodness I get from my marriage!"

The key to understanding *Klal Yisrael*'s answer is that *Shir HaShirim* is describing the greatness of the relationship between *Klal Yisrael* and Hashem. Thus, the focus is on how nothing can lure *Klal Yisrael* away from that relationship because it is so wonderful — not on the sacrifice involved. Elsewhere in *Nach*, *Klal Yisrael* declare that they are willing to sacrifice for Hashem, but that is not the message of *Shir HaShirim*. And that is why *Klal Yisrael* turn down their would-be seducers by stressing that their relationship with Hashem is so fulfilling. It is not one based only on obligations but rather on feelings of privilege.

It is revealing to compare this reply to the one given in *Akdamus*, the special *piyut* we recite on the first day of Shavuos just before the Torah reading. In *Akdamus*, we describe how the nations mock us for our limitless devotion to Hashem, even if it involves giving up our lives. They promise wealth and honor if we join them in serving their gods. We reply that nothing they can offer has any value compared with what is in store for us when Mashiach comes, when we will all dance around the Shechinah[6] and participate in the special feast for the righteous which Hashem will prepare for us.

This reply can also be seen in our verse since the words *mecholas hamachanayim*, hitherto translated as "encircling camps," can also be translated "the circular dance of the camps."[7] This would then be an allusion to the special dance that will take place when Mashiach comes. The excitement we have when we contemplate this wonderful event makes all the offers of the nations pale in comparison.[8]

---

6 The Gemara tells us that when Mashiach comes, all the righteous will join together in a circular dance before the Presence of Hashem (*Ta'anis* 31a).

7 Rashi, *Eruvin* 3b.

8 See the comment of the *Devash V'Chalav* on Rashi's interpretation of our verse. Rashi says that *Klal Yisrael* reply to the nations that nothing you give me can compare *even* to the encirclement of the Mishkan. The word "even" seems inappropriate since the encampment around the Mishkan was a great thing. He explains that the events of Mashiach

THE ENCIRCLING CAMPS

Klal Yisrael answer that whatever you offer me, it does not compare with what Hashem gave me through "the encircling camps." As we explained above, this is an allusion either to the encampments around the Mishkan (Rashi)[9] or the encampments around Har Sinai (Midrash). But let us add one more thought here. If one would have had the privilege of hosting Rabbi Chaim Kanievsky, *zt"l*, for even one night, he would never forget this wonderful privilege, and he would be justifiably proud of it. How much more so if one had the merit to host the Chafetz Chaim or the Chasam Sofer, etc.?! Well, for forty years in the wilderness, we were privileged to have Hashem in our midst — in the Mishkan we built for Him. Nothing can compare with that feeling of pride and joy!

THE ENCIRCLING CAMPS

To comprehend the greatness of the camps around Har Sinai, we have to appreciate just how awesome the Giving of the Torah was.[10] Although this is not the place to elaborate, it is well worth taking a few moments to see how the Rambam speaks about this event quoting our verse. In his letter known as "*Iggeres Teiman*," the Rambam writes wonderful words of encouragement to the Jews of Yemen who were suffering greatly from the threat of a fanatical ruler's violent religious persecution in the year 4932 (1172) if they did not convert to Islam. In the middle of this letter, he writes that the way to fortify their belief in Hashem and his Torah is to remember the event of Har Sinai:

> Remember the event at Har Sinai which Hashem commanded us to remember constantly. Hashem warned us not to forget this event, but rather to grow up with this knowledge... And it is fitting that you, my brothers, should bring up your children with this great vision [of *Ma'amad Har Sinai*] and that you should talk about its greatness at every gathering... You should make this a very great event in your lives — greater and grander than anything that ever happened to you... This event never happened before and will not repeat itself. No other nation has heard the words of Hashem, the Creator of the world and the One single power, and seen His light with their eyes as you

---

will be far greater, but "even" the smaller "encircling of the Mishkan" was far greater than anything the nations can offer.

9 See our commentary on 2:4.

10 The Tur (*Orach Chaim*, Sec. 47) points out that even though we usually recite just one blessing before doing a mitzvah, we recite two blessings before learning Torah. He explains that the second blessing ("*asher bachar...*") is to thank Hashem for *Ma'amad Har Sinai*, i.e., the momentous manner in which the Torah was given. This means that every single day we actually recite a blessing to thank Hashem for this history-changing event.

have. This happened only so that you should have the strength to cope with the troubles ahead...

Shlomo HaMelech has already compared our nation to a beautiful woman who has no blemishes [*shulamis*]... The other nations that try to entice her away are likened to harlots who seek adultery... But this beautiful woman answers the harlots, with great wisdom: "You are foolish. Why do you try to influence me? Can you give me the joy of the camps?... When you create for me an event as great as Har Sinai, only then I will consider your offers..." At Har Sinai, the camp of our nation and the camp of the holy angels were parallel to each other...[11]

The Rambam cites our verse and explains it according to the Midrash above, that *Klal Yisrael* answer: "What can you give me that compares with this great event at Har Sinai?!"[12]

---

11   It is very worthwhile to read the entire letter of the Rambam, not just an abridged translation.

12   The Rambam goes on to elucidate a challenging verse from the Torah that follows the description of *Ma'amad Har Sinai*. As we shall see, it connects directly with the verse we are discussing here in *Shir HaShirim*. The background is this: When Hashem gave the Torah, displaying His glory and breathtaking power, the people were terrified. They quickly approached Moshe and told him that they were too frightened to have Hashem speak to them directly. Moshe replied that they should not be frightened because Hashem revealed Himself in this way for their sake: "*Ba'avur nasos eschem*" (*Shemos* 20:17). Although the simple meaning of these words is "in order to test you," the intent is not clear since the verse does not tell us what the test is.
Perhaps for this reason, Rashi understands the key word "*nasos*" as coming from the root *neis*, which means "banner." Thus, the intent would be "in order to place you on a high banner." Moshe told them that Hashem revealed Himself in this manner in order to place them — the Jewish People — high up on a banner so that the entire world would become aware of their greatness as the only nation that merited to see the awesome glory of Hashem in such a revealed manner. The Ramban interprets "*nasos*" to mean "to be accustomed to." Hashem made the revelation this way so that we should become accustomed to hearing His voice and be able to listen to Him. Alternatively, the Ramban notes that "*nasos*" can mean "to test." This was a test to see if after such a tremendous revelation, *Klal Yisrael* would be sufficiently grateful and respond to Hashem's profound expression of love for them by loving Him.
The Rambam, however, prefers the simple translation of the word "*nasos*" as "test." He explains that because Hashem would be testing the Jewish People many times over a long period of history, He provided the answer before the test — out of kindness. This can be understood with the following example: If a teacher came into the classroom and said, "Now we are going to have a test on a topic I have never taught you anything about, and you will be punished greatly if you fail." The students would naturally feel unprepared and anxious. The approach of the kind and responsible teacher would be to tell his or her students: "I am going to test you soon on this subject, but before I do, I will teach you all the information that you will need for the test."
Similarly, Hashem has tested us many times, but when did we learn the answers? From where did we get the conviction not to believe in false religions? Where did we get the courage not to forsake Him despite threats and actual persecution? And where did we get our love for Him that is sweeter to us than all the temptations in the world?
The answer, says the Rambam, is that the revelation at Har Sinai, in all its glory, showed us His love, His power, and the clarity of His existence. Now we have the answers. Now Hashem can test us. This is what Moshe was telling us: Do not be afraid. This is for your sake because Hashem is going to test you. Make sure to have the answers.
The Rambam connects this with the main focus of the letter: the Jews of Teiman being severely challenged by a cruel leader. This was a test, and they could look to what happened at Har Sinai for the answer. According to the Midrash,

When *Klal Yisrael* explain why they refuse to be drawn away from Hashem, they tell the heathen nations that there is nothing they can offer that would make it worthwhile for them to leave Hashem. It is noteworthy that they do not reply that Hashem does not let them or that it is the wrong thing to do. There is a lesson here for all time: When one is tested or tempted in this way, he must think about the personal gains he has by serving Hashem — besides thinking about the ultimate reward and the fact that he is doing the right thing. Rabbi Eliyahu Lopian, *zt"l*, discusses this at length.[13] He explains that it is a great mistake to believe that not serving Hashem provides one with a happy and carefree life, and that one has to sacrifice all of this in order to gain a reward in the World to Come. On the contrary, only those serving Hashem are truly happy — even here in this world. This is why Shlomo HaMelech writes at such great length in *Koheles* about the futility of the life of a sinner and only afterward declares that true success for a person is to serve Hashem.

Rabbi Yechiel Yacobson, a well-known educator in Eretz Yisrael, points out that this approach is especially relevant in educating the children of today, who almost unavoidably see the glitter of the outside world. It is imperative that educators make clear to them that serving Hashem does not mean living an unhappy life and that all the glitter outside is not real happiness. On the contrary, real happiness is to be found only in a life of Torah.

Studying this verse and absorbing its message can help a person pass the many tests that he goes through in life and give him the strength to reject the call of the *yetzer ha'ra* who tries to pull us down. Remembering our past glory and anticipating our future triumph can enable a person to tell himself: "I am far too important to involve myself in lowly sin. I am too strong to be weakened by temptation. My pride comes from being a servant of Hashem, and nothing else is worthwhile in comparison."

TURN AWAY, TURN AWAY...

With slight differences in nuance, the *Targum* and the Seforno explain this verse in a completely different way. According to their approach, it is not the evil nations trying to lure *Klal Yisrael* away. Rather, it is Hashem (*Targum*) or the great prophets (Seforno) calling upon them to return to Hashem. The verse thus reads as follows: "Return to Me, please return,[14] perfect one! Return to Hashem's service, and you will be appointed to

---

this is exactly what the Jewish People reply here in our verse to the other nations attempting to seduce them away from Hashem: "Do not bother because after my experiences at Har Sinai, nothing you can say will sway me!"
(All these explanations help us appreciate the importance of learning about the Revelation at Har Sinai.)

13 *Lev Eliyahu*, vol. I, pp. 112-119.

14 This accords with the more common understanding of the word "שובי" as "return" or "repent."

high positions" or "Return to Hashem's service, and we, the prophets, will once again be able to prophesize."[15] In other words, *Klal Yisrael* is being told that if they repent, they will regain their previous lofty position in the world and facilitate the return of prophecy. The verse continues (according to this interpretation) with the true prophets adjuring the evil false prophets: "What good is it to you that you mislead the people of Yerushalayim [by telling them to sin] and defile[16] the holy Jewish camps?!"[17]

INTRODUCTION TO VERSES 2 - 10

These next few verses all describe the beauty of a beautiful woman. Allegorically, they depict the beauty of *Klal Yisrael*. The heathen nations who tried to entice *Klal Yisrael* (in verse one) are forced to concede that their beauty is so great when they serve Hashem that there is nothing that they, the heathen nations, can offer to compete with it. It is only jealousy of *Klal Yisrael*'s elevated position that makes the other nations want to pull them down to their level. Each verse touches on a different dimension of the beauty of *Klal Yisrael*.

Hashem is the speaker in these verses. He is conveying the heathen nations' realization of *Klal Yisrael*'s greatness. This is the third time we have had a set of verses which describe the beauty of *Klal Yisrael*. What is the main difference between them?

In the first set (in Chapter Four), Hashem describes the beauty of *Klal Yisrael* from His perspective at the time of their zenith: when they were all serving Hashem and the First Beis HaMikdash was standing. In the second set (in Chapter Six), Hashem

---

The four-fold repetition of the word "return" hints at the four phases of repentance. These are enumerated in *Shaarei Teshuvah* (4:6), based on the Gemara (*Yoma* 86a.)

15 The phrase "נחזה בך" thus means, "We will prophesize *through* you (in the sense of *because of you*)." Only because of the love that Hashem has for *Klal Yisrael* does He reveal Himself to the prophets (see Rashi on *Vayikra* 1:1).

16 The word "מחולת" is understood to come from the root חלל, meaning "to defile" or "to desecrate," as in the term חילול ה׳.

17 *Targum*.
Unlike the *Targum*, the Seforno understands the last part of the verse to be *Klal Yisrael*'s rejection of the overture to repent: "What can you offer me?! I have had it all before." The verse would then translate this way: "What high positions can you offer the perfect one (*Klal Yisrael*) that compare to [that which we have already had, i.e.,] the encircling camps?" *Klal Yisrael* rejects the call for repentance because, they claim, there is nothing new here. They feel a lack of excitement in serving Hashem because they have done it all already. Unfortunately, this is a feeling that may sometimes afflict even those who have always been used to living a life of Torah. They have become so used to it that they cannot appreciate what is so special about it. In the next few verses, the prophets continue to adjure *Klal Yisrael* by depicting their pilgrimages to the Beis HaMikdash and other aspects of *Klal Yisrael*'s greatness. They hope that invoking these memories and future dreams will encourage repentance. By drawing a picture of the great future that is in store for *Klal Yisrael* when they repent, and Mashiach comes, the prophets hope to encourage them to go ahead and repent. We must also use these depictions in the next few verses to get ourselves excited about what life will be like when the Beis HaMikdash is rebuilt, and thereby create a desire to come back to Hashem and serve Him with enthusiasm.

describes the beauty of *Klal Yisrael* from His perspective at their low point: when they were in exile or during the Second Beis HaMikdash when only a portion of the nation lived in Eretz Yisrael and there was no prophecy, etc. In the third set (here in the upcoming verses), Hashem describes what the nations grasp about the importance of *Klal Yisrael*.[18] This highlights *Klal Yisrael*'s specialness since even their detractors can appreciate them.

Each aspect of physical beauty depicted here alludes to a different aspect of spiritual beauty found among the Jewish People. The commentators offer a variety of interpretations of each aspect. In the following pages, the reader will find an inspiring selection.

Rashi notes that in these verses, the depiction moves from the lower half of the body through the upper half. First the beauty of the legs is described, then the thighs, stomach, neck, etc. When *Klal Yisrael* praised Hashem earlier,[19] their "focus," *ki'veyachol*, was just the opposite: from top to bottom. Rashi explains that *Klal Yisrael* want to bring Hashem "down" to them, so they begin with the top and end with the lowest point. But since Hashem wants to bring *Klal Yisrael* "up" to Him, He begins with the lower half and ends with the top.

The Divrei Yedidyah takes a very different approach to these verses. He understands that the speakers here are the prophets as well as the righteous gentiles. Let us recall, as mentioned earlier,[20] that *Shir HaShirim* is a combination of many songs articulated by a number of different "characters." Together, they show the tremendous love that connects Hashem and *Klal Yisrael*. Now, it is well known that in a marriage that has temporarily gone sour, help can often arrive through a third party, such as a wise Rav or an insightful therapist. As an outsider, he is well positioned to encourage the couple to rebuild their relationship and rediscover their love for each other. He may try to do so by praising each spouse individually and recalling how much love they had for each other. When heard by the couple, this praise is capable of reigniting the love they once had for one another. The words of this outsider provide an additional perspective on just how wonderful and how loving this couple were. In a loosely similar way, when *Klal Yisrael* disobeyed Hashem and were sent away, *ki'veyachol*, there were those who wished to find a way to bring them back together. Among them were the great prophets and leaders of *Klal Yisrael*.[21] The Divrei Yedidyah says that even the gentiles, when they

---

18 The Rinas Dodim (on verse 2) points out that Rashi seems to contradict himself, sometimes explaining that the next few verses record Hashem speaking, and sometimes, apparently, the heathen nations speaking. The Sifsei Chachamim clarifies that Hashem is conveying the praises of the nations, so there is no contradiction.

19 5:10-16.

20 1:1.

21 They are like a third party because they never sinned against Hashem and never wished to leave Him, while *Klal Yisrael*

saw the damage our exile caused to the world, yearned for the separation to be over and for *Klal Yisrael* and Hashem to be reunited.

Shir HaShirim provides a number of perspectives on how much love Hashem has for *Klal Yisrael* and vice versa. But up to this point, it has generally been either Hashem or *Klal Yisrael* speaking. Now our understanding of this great love is enhanced through the voice of the outsider. This entire chapter, including the opening verse, is spoken by those who wish to see Hashem and *Klal Yisrael* reunited. They describe their greatness and love in order to re-ignite the feelings they initially had so that they will want to return to each other. Accordingly, the Divrei Yedidyah understands "*Shuvi, shuvi*" in the chapter's opening verse not as, "Turn away, turn away," but as "Return, return."[22]

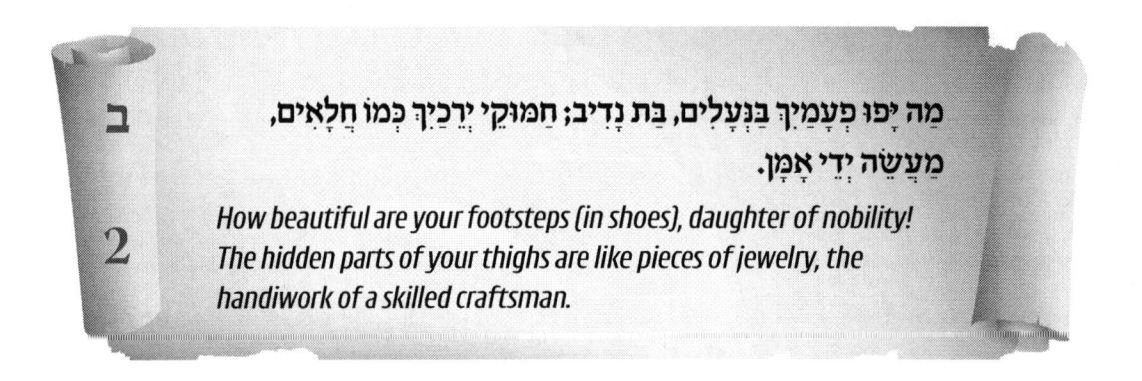

> ב
>
> מַה יָּפוּ פְעָמַיִךְ בַּנְּעָלִים, בַּת נָדִיב; חַמּוּקֵי יְרֵכַיִךְ כְּמוֹ חֲלָאִים, מַעֲשֵׂה יְדֵי אָמָּן.
>
> 2
>
> *How beautiful are your footsteps (in shoes), daughter of nobility! The hidden parts of your thighs are like pieces of jewelry, the handiwork of a skilled craftsman.*

Allegorical Translation — How beautiful were your feet *Klal Yisrael*, when you went up three times a year to the Beis HaMikdash, you who are the daughters of nobility (Avraham, Yitzchak, and Yaakov). The entrenched *shittin* (pipes and underground tunnels running down from the *Mizbe'ach*, into which the wine libations were poured), hidden under the *Mizbe'ach* that reach down to the greatest depths, are as beautiful as ornaments[23] made by the Master Craftsman (i.e., Hashem).

Subject of the Verse — These are praises of *Klal Yisrael*.

Mashal — The husband praises his wife as "a daughter of nobility." He describes the beauty of the lower part of her body: "How beautiful are your feet in shoes! The hidden parts of your thighs are as beautiful as pieces of jewelry — not just any jewelry, but jewelry made by a skilled craftsman."

---

as a whole did turn away from Hashem and were turned away by Him.

22   This is a more literal rendering, as explained in our commentary on verse 1.

23   The word "חלאים" can be understood as "ornament" (Metzudas Zion) and as "entrenchment" or "excavation" (Rashi, *Sukkah* 49a). Rashi here invokes both meanings, as reflected in our allegorical translation above.

Nimshal Hashem praises *Klal Yisrael*'s pilgrimages on foot to the Beis HaMikdash and the *shittin* running down from the *Mizbe'ach* which looked like rounded thighs.

HOW BEAUTIFUL ARE YOUR FOOTSTEPS IN SHOES

The verse alludes to the beauty of *Klal Yisrael*'s footsteps as they made their way up to Yerushalayim three times every year.[24] These pilgrimages were a most amazing sight and event. As much as we can try to describe the magnitude of this event, we cannot truly grasp it. Let us imagine an entire nation — millions of people, young and old, men, women, and children of all shapes and sizes and personalities — walking together in purity, holiness, beauty, excitement, happiness, joy, love, and unity to go and serve Hashem.[25] The Netziv adds that even though there were many very wealthy Jews who could have traveled in style by horse and wagon, they all went to Yerushalayim by foot, as the verse says, "How beautiful are *your footsteps in shoes.*" There were three reasons for this. First of all, this ensured complete unity. If the wealthy would travel on horses, etc., while everyone else walked, this would create both a physical and emotional barrier between the people. The wealthy could start feeling superior and the poor inferior. Furthermore, let us keep in mind that the pilgrimage to the Beis HaMikdash was partly for the purpose of gaining wisdom and fear of Heaven through seeing the daily miracles that occurred there and the dedication of the *Kohanim* serving Hashem and listening to the members of the Sanhedrin and other great tzaddikim based around the Beis HaMikdash.[26] Therefore, they felt that going in a humble way — by foot — would make them more receptive to the *Kohanim*'s words or the rebuke of the Torah leaders. A haughty person does not absorb words of rebuke. Finally, they wished to receive a reward for every footstep and did not wish to detract from this by traveling some other way.[27] We must try to appreciate this. Although walking hundreds of miles

---

24 The word "פעמיך," translated here as "footsteps," can also mean "occasions" (*Shemos* 23:17), yielding the meaning: "How beautiful are your occasions (i.e., the three pilgrimages, *Klal Yisrael*'s greatest annual occasions)!"

25 We sometimes see a huge group of people gathering together for an event. Although this sight arouses wonder or excitement, we must bear in mind that generally there is no true unity or love in these gatherings, nor is there purity, holiness, or true joy. These mass events are nothing compared to what took place three times every year when *Klal Yisrael* streamed to the Beis HaMikdash.

26 As the Gemara tells us, going to Yerushalayim would help a person absorb words of Torah (*Bava Basra* 21a). Tosafos (ibid., *s.v. ki*) explains this was because one would see the holy service of the Beis HaMikdash and the dedication of the *Kohanim*.

27 Although this concept is too deep for a mere footnote, let us at least mention several references and pointers. The Gemara (*Sotah* 22a) tells us that a certain woman would walk to the furthest shul for davening in order to get rewarded for every step she would take. Rabbi Yochanan praised her for this. The Maharal (*Nesiv Ha'Avodah*, ch. 5) clarifies that this is unique to prayer. For other mitzvos, however, there is no reason to go further if the mitzvah can be fulfilled nearby. For example, there is no advantage to walking to a sukkah far away if there is one nearby. The Pachad Yitzchak (*Rosh*

by foot is not easy, the excitement of this precious mitzvah (as well as the other reasons mentioned above), inspired millions to do this three times a year — every single year — even though they could have done so in an easier and more comfortable fashion.

The *Targum* adds that they walked to Yerushalayim in shoes of many different colors. Rabbi Yitzchak Zilberstein explains that they did this out of love for the mitzvah of walking to the Beis HaMikdash. Since that mitzvah is performed with one's feet, they adorned their feet with colorful shoes just as one adorns any mitzvah item![28]

DAUGHTER OF NOBILITY

This expression tells us that when they walked to Yerushalayim, they did so with feelings of nobility. Indeed, this verse teaches us a fundamental point about true humility. The verse emphasizes that even though everyone walked humbly together to Yerushalayim, as explained above, they did not feel unimportant. On the contrary, they walked with a feeling of pride, like a "daughter of nobility."[29] They understood that since they were descendants of Avraham Avinu,[30] who was loved by Hashem, that they too were loved and important. This was not a contradiction to humility. Humility is not a feeling of worthlessness. Rather, it is a belief that a person's importance is not self-created but is due to Hashem's favor and the gifts He has bestowed on the individual.[31]

HaShanah) explains that prayer is essentially coming to Hashem. And the further one travels to greet or visit someone, the more importance he shows that person. Similarly, going to the Beis HaMikdash was a form of "visiting" Hashem, and the more effort exerted, the greater the reward.

28 With this in mind, Rabbi Yitzchak Zilberstein once blessed the owner of a shoe store that he should soon merit to start selling colorful shoes!

29 The Netziv suggests that "daughter of nobility" teaches us that while everyone felt humble, they treated others with respect, as though they were all noble. They did not apply their own feelings of humility to others by treating them as if they were lowly.

30 The Gemara (*Chagigah* 3a) explains that *nadiv*, translated here as "nobility," also connotes "generosity," as we see in the word "*nedavah*," meaning "donation." In view of the fact that Avraham Avinu treated everyone generously and kindly, his descendants — referred to here as *bas nadiv* — are also the "daughter of [Avraham,] the one who was generous." The word *nadiv* also means "nobleman" because the true measure of a noble person is the way he treats others and how kind and generous he is. Avraham Avinu was both noble and generous in every sense of the word.

Why is Avraham alluded to in this context? Let us keep in mind that the verse is talking about *Klal Yisrael* traveling from their homes to the Beis HaMikdash. This was no simple act. It meant leaving behind all of one's property and wealth — three times a year! — which could be ruined or stolen in one's absence. It also meant leaving behind the comforts of home for a long and sometimes difficult journey. The willingness to leave one's home for the sake of Hashem was implanted in us through the precedent set by Avraham Avinu (see *Derech HaChaim* on *Avos* 5:3-4). When Hashem tested him by telling him to leave his father's home to go to Eretz Yisrael, he did so without question. This verse here in *Shir HaShirim* that speaks of our ability to leave home to travel to the Beis HaMikdash alludes to the source of this ability: Avraham Avinu. Furthermore, Avraham Avinu was the first Jew to go to the site of the Beis HaMikdash with a *korban* to perform the *Akeidah*. Thus, all those who make the pilgrimage to the Beis HaMikdash are essentially following in his footsteps (Maharsha, *Sukkah* 49a).

31 Since our verse touches on the difference between healthy humility and an unhealthy sense of inferiority or worthlessness, let us take this opportunity to flesh out this important distinction. First of all, it must be clear that humility does

THE HIDDEN PARTS OF YOUR THIGHS...

This is an allusion, Rashi tells us, to the pipes and underground tunnels running down from the *Mizbe'ach*, through which the wine and water libations were poured. They were "hidden" because they were under the *Mizbe'ach*. These pipes were rounded, like thighs, and were the handiwork Hashem, the "skilled Craftsman," because they were actually created and laid in place during the Six Days of Creation. We see that the Divine service performed on the *Mizbe'ach* was so important that, immediately upon Creation, Hashem established the foundations so that everything would be ready.

Although these pipes through which the daily libations (usually wine, but water on

---

not stand in the way of realizing one's full potential. Moshe Rabbeinu, the humblest of all men (*Bamidbar* 12:3), knew that he was the greatest of all prophets and that no prophet would ever surpass him. Indeed, this is one of the Thirteen Principles of Jewish Faith. (Failure to believe this renders one a heretic.) Moshe's understanding of his own greatness was beyond anything we can imagine. After all, he understood the words of the Torah which describes his greatness (*Bamidbar* 12:7-8 and *Devarim* 34:10-12) on a much higher level than we can understand or appreciate. Yet he was supremely humble. The key to this paradox lies in the fact that humility primarily involves recognizing that everything one has was given to him by Hashem because of His tremendous kindness and love. When one truly appreciates this, he becomes more and more grateful to Hashem for all of the gifts He has bestowed on him. Furthermore, this awareness keeps him from belittling or feeling superior to even the seemingly lowliest person because he recognizes that all are loved by Hashem. And a truly humble person is not jealous of those who have more than him because he recognizes that everything is a gift from Hashem and that He gives every individual what is best for him. He understands that material success is not due to one's own efforts. Having less does not indicate that something is wrong with a person. Rather, Hashem bestows His gifts on the basis of His profound understanding and knowledge of what is good for a person. So, humility brings us closer to Hashem and makes us kinder to others.

In contrast, a sense of inferiority or worthlessness leads one to believe that one has no good qualities. (Incidentally, this is disrespectful to Hashem, the Creator of all beings, as it suggests that He created something useless.) This feeling leads one to anger and resentment towards Hashem for not giving him more. Furthermore, it causes one to need others' approval constantly to convince himself that he has worth.

The continuation of this verse speaks of *Klal Yisrael*'s modesty in not needing to show off when they perform acts of greatness. This is because they attained a true feeling of humility. A feeling of lowliness (a lack of healthy self-esteem), on the other hand, only causes one to want to show off as much as possible. It also causes one to be jealous of those who have more, to feel threatened by them, and to treat others with the same feelings of rejection one has about oneself. A feeling of lowliness distances one from Hashem and from others. In his commentary on *Pirkei Avos*, the Rambam tells us that a feeling of lowliness (depression) also causes many sins. Since such a person feels that he is useless anyway, he does not have the usual compunctions about debasing himself further with sin (*Avos* 2:13). Ironically, such feelings of lowliness are actually caused by false haughtiness. If a person measures his own worth simply by his superiority over others or by all that he owns, when he encounters someone with more than him or suffers a loss, he can easily fall into the trap of feeling down and depressed.

This verse teaches how one should be able to care greatly about other people's honor while being humble and not caring about one's own honor. This comes only from true humility. When one realizes that humility and self-esteem are not self-contradictory — that one should feel humility regarding one's accomplishments, but self-esteem regarding one's true worth — then he will treat others properly. Even those who might seem very unaccomplished will have his respect because everyone is a beloved creation of Hashem.

This is another valuable lesson one gains by learning and internalizing the whole of *Shir HaShirim*. The more one appreciates how Hashem loves every Jew, the more he feels that every Jew, including himself, is truly valued, and the less he will fall into the trap of lowliness. And he will thus not need to try to feel important by highlighting his accomplishments or by showing a lack of respect to others. Rather, he will feel grateful for Hashem's kindness and love for him. All this is incorporated in our verse that tells us: everyone walked by foot in humility, but they walked with a sense that they were noble.

Sukkos) were poured seem to be a minor aspect of the *Mizbe'ach*, they are praised greatly here. Furthermore, the tremendously joyous *Simchas Beis HaShoeivah* on Sukkos, described at length in the Gemara,[32] revolved around the mitzvah of libations. Why?

The answer to this question goes all the way back to Creation. When Hashem created the universe, He divided the waters into upper waters and lower waters. The lower waters complained, *ki'veyachol*, that they too wanted to be close to Hashem. To compensate them, Hashem said that salt from the sea would be used on the *Mizbe'ach* and that there would be water libations. It was an opportunity for the waters that yearned to be close to Hashem to realize their aspiration. Indeed, this should be a model for us. Just as the waters rejoiced when they were offered on the *Mizbe'ach*, so we should rejoice when we become close to Hashem. The yearning and rejoicing of the waters encapsulate what we should yearn for and rejoice about. We thus use this mitzvah to remind ourselves what true happiness is. And because it was so important for these waters to be able, *ki'veyachol*, to reconnect to Hashem, these pipes were arranged immediately upon Creation. It is fitting that here in *Shir HaShirim*, which is all about *Klal Yisrael's* desire for closeness to Hashem, these conduits for closeness to Hashem are praised.[33]

THE HIDDEN PARTS OF YOUR THIGHS...

We learn from this verse, the Gemara teaches, that serving Hashem should be done privately, like the thigh, which is kept hidden.[34] The Gemara understands this section of the verse as follows: "[Just as one keeps out of view] the hidden parts of one's thighs [so, too, one should observe all the mitzvos in private. These mitzvos were inscribed on the *Luchos* which] are as beautiful as pieces of jewelry, the handiwork of a skilled Craftsman [i.e., Hashem]." The Gemara then quotes the verse in *Michah*[35] where the prophet tells *Klal Yisrael* that Hashem wants them to strive for justice, love, and kindness, and to be modest in their ways of serving Hashem.

At times, of course, there is great value in serving Hashem publicly. For example, by publicly declaring one's belief in Hashem, a person strengthens his own belief and that of others, and he establishes the importance of serving Him. However, true service of Hashem is also done privately. Indeed, if there is no reason to publicize one's good deeds, one should refrain. This shows that he was doing them for Hashem and not to

---

32 *Sukkah* 51 and 53.

33 A full treatment of this large topic is beyond the scope of this *sefer*. See further *Tears of Hope*, p. 288, regarding the crying of the water when the Beis HaMikdash was destroyed.

34 *Sukkah* 49b.

35 6:8.

garner recognition. Furthermore, the test of whether or not a person is serving Hashem properly is how he behaves in private.

Chazal tell us[36] that a person who is kind in public must also make sure to be kind in private to his wife and children. Only then will Hashem reward him. It is noteworthy that our verse begins by mentioning the shoes — an external extension of a person, symbolizing the very public mitzvah of *aliyah l'regel* — and concludes with the concealed thighs, symbolizing serving Hashem in private. Mention of both in the same verse communicates that they both should be done — and done sincerely.

Rabbi Shimshon Pinkus used to comment that in order to gauge one's closeness to Hashem, he should check his private thoughts during *Shemoneh Esrei*, and to gauge one's trait of kindness, he should check how he treats his wife in private. On a deeper level, this means that one should develop his own private relationship with Hashem, a relationship that is not affected by other people's opinions and beliefs.

HOW BEAUTIFUL...

The Vilna Gaon sees this verse referring to the beauty of *Klal Yisrael* that results from their remaining apart and not becoming sullied by other nations. He translates, "How beautiful are your occasions when you seal yourself away, (especially during prayers, something you learned from) your noble ancestry..." His interpretation stems from his understands "בַּנְּעָלִים" not as "in shoes," but as "in locks," from the root of the word "מנעול" (lock). *Klal Yisrael* lock themselves, *ki'veyachol*, in their places of worship.[37] This accords with the continuation of the verse: "The hidden parts of your thighs are like pieces of jewelry..." *Klal Yisrael*'s beauty is that they are like a concealed thigh, closed off and hidden away. The verse extolls *Klal Yisrael*'s isolating themselves from all nations to avoid all negative outside influences.

There is another subtle, but fundamental, message in these words. They reflect a certain feeling one should have when serving Hashem. One must "lock" himself into his service and see it as an absolute obligation. One dare not feel that it is a temporary or trivial job that he can take or leave.[38] Obviously, serving Hashem is an endeavor of joy, but a person has to realize it is not a service that can be done without putting all of one's mind and heart into it to the exclusion of all other matters.[39]

---

36 *Eliyahu Rabbah* 17.

37 He explains that the nobility (in the phrase "daughters of nobility") are our Patriarchs who established the prayers.

38 The Talmud Yerushalmi relates us that if one learns Torah without commitment, it is as if he has nullified his covenant with Hashem (*Berachos* 94b).

39 One of the exciting facets of Yom Kippur is that we know we are in shul all day, and there is nowhere else to go, nothing else to do, and nothing else to think about the entire day other than Hashem. That total commitment greatly enhances

> שָׁרְרֵךְ אַגַּן הַסַּהַר, אַל יֶחְסַר הַמָּזֶג; בִּטְנֵךְ עֲרֵמַת חִטִּים, סוּגָה בַּשּׁוֹשַׁנִּים.
>
> **ג**
> **3**
>
> Your navel is like a moon-shaped[40] basin that never lacks prepared drink; your stomach is like a pile of wheat fenced off by roses.

Allegorical Translation — Hashem praises *Klal Yisrael*: "Your Sanhedrin is located in the middle of the world, where the scholars sit in a semi-circle and protect the world[41] with the merit of their Torah study. They never lack satisfactory answers to all questions. Nothing was ever hidden from them (the members of the Sanhedrin) because they were so filled with Torah knowledge. They thus provided the world with all the knowledge it needs."

Klal Yisrael is fenced in by the weakest boundaries and yet they abide by them.

Subject of the Verse — These are praises of *Klal Yisrael*.

Mashal — The husband praises his wife's perfectly rounded navel, and her stomach, which he finds as beautiful as an impressive pile of wheat. She is surrounded by roses, and he comments that she looks beautiful adorned by the roses.

Nimshal — The verse mentions the beauty of the stomach, an allusion to the Sanhedrin. The Sanhedrin was located in the center of the world in Yerushalayim,[42] just as the stomach is situated in the center of the body. The members of the Sanhedrin are likened to a beautiful basin (or pool) of water from which people used to drink and refresh themselves.[43] The Torah they taught rejuvenated and nurtured the nation. "They never lacked drink" in the sense that they never

---

one's ability to daven well, etc. One should try to replicate this feeling every time one davens or learns, clearing everything else from one's mind and focusing completely on the task in hand.

40 The word "סהר" means "moon."

41 The word "אגן" in this verse has two meanings. One is "bowl," as in *Shemos* 24:6: "וישם באגנות" — "[Moshe] put it into bowls." Accordingly, the verse likens the Sanhedrin to a bowl containing a life-sustaining drink because the members of the Sanhedrin contained spiritually nourishing knowledge. Alternatively, the word means "to protect," as the Gemara explains in *Sanhedrin* 37a, from the related word "מגן" (shield). The Sanhedrin protected the world from doing wrong by teaching Torah and instituting special decrees and regulations.

42 The entire world pivots around and is regulated by Yerushalayim. Hence, Yerushalayim is considered the center of the world.

43 Rashi.

lacked knowledge and could answer any question posed to them.⁴⁴ They contained all the Torah the nation needed and would convey Torah rulings to all those who needed them — loosely similar to the way the stomach takes in all the nourishment that is ingested and supplies nutrients to the rest of the body. The "navel" also symbolizes the Sanhedrin in its role as provider of all the spiritual nourishment needed by the nation. Just as the navel is the lifeline of the fetus, so the Torah taught by the Sanhedrin was the lifeline of the nation. And just as detachment from the mother would be deadly to the fetus, so detachment from the Sanhedrin posed a deadly threat to the spiritual life of the nation.⁴⁵ The Sanhedrin is also likened to wheat, the most necessary and basic human food because *Klal Yisrael* needed the Sanhedrin's rulings and its Torah sustained the nation.⁴⁶

YOUR NAVEL IS LIKE A MOON-SHAPED BASIN...

The true beauty and greatness of the Sanhedrin is impossible for us to appreciate. We would have to imagine a world in which our every question was quickly resolved. And not just questions of law. Even questions relating to whether to go to battle or how to explain certain verses in the Torah were all quickly resolved by this dedicated group of Torah scholars whose greatness is beyond our grasp.⁴⁷ Their search for, and commitment to, the truth and service of Hashem was unsurpassed.

We can see this, for example, in the conduct of the leaders of the Sanhedrin known as Bnei Beseira in the period just before Hillel.⁴⁸ They were asked a question they could

---

44 The Midrash (*Pesikta Rabbasi* 10) explains that in the olden days, wine was prepared for drinking by diluting it by two-thirds. That is, one-third wine to two-thirds water. This was called *mezigah*, from the root of the word "מזג" which appears in our verse. Now, the Sanhedrin consisted of seventy-one great scholars. Obviously, they could not all be available all the time. They thus used a system in which at least twenty-three of the judges would remain at their posts when others went to eat, sleep, or take care of personal matters. Since a complement of twenty-three judges (approximately one-third of the Sanhedrin) is sufficient to rule on all questions, including questions of life and death (*Sanhedrin* 2a), any question could be resolved at any time. Thus, when the verse praises *Klal Yisrael* for never lacking the מזג (wine diluted by two-thirds, and thus ready to drink), it is saying that the Sanhedrin was always prepared and available to answer all questions.

45 Although we do not have a Sanhedrin nowadays, the Torah leaders of every generation perform a loosely similar function. We must be very careful not to detach ourselves from them. That would be as deadly as the detachment of a fetus from its only source of nourishment.

46 The Midrash on this verse continues to describe the beauty of the Sanhedrin and how its greatness is alluded to in this verse. The Midrash notes that while other vegetables may look more impressive than wheat, wheat is the most essential part of the human diet (see Rashi on *Bereishis* 18:5). That is why the verse likens the Sanhedrin to wheat. The verse likens the Sanhedrin to water as well (in mentioning the round basin from which people would drink) because water and wheat are mankind's two most essential sources of sustenance.

47 See our commentary on 4:4.

48 *Pesachim* 66a.

not answer. When Hillel, a newcomer, told them the answer, they immediately resigned and appointed him as the head of the Sanhedrin! Can we imagine anyone nowadays resigning from the most prestigious position simply because he could not answer a single question?!

The judges of the Sanhedrin sat in a semi-circle, like the crescent moon. This was in order that they should be in the best position to learn and disseminate Torah knowledge. If they had sat in a row, they would have found it difficult to learn from one other since a person at one end would not be facing a person further down the row. If they had sat in a circle, they would sometimes have their backs to those who would come to listen to their teaching. Therefore, they sat in a formation which optimized their learning, discussions, and teaching.

As noted above, they were always available to answer any question. There were no weekend breaks or summer holidays. This meant that whenever a person needed an answer, he could receive it without delay.

Because we do not have a Sanhedrin today, unfortunately, we very often have halachos which are unresolved or disputed. We thus face the choice of being stringent just in case the stringent opinion is authoritative, being lenient if a Rav rules that there are compelling reasons to do so, or following the ruling of one's Rav while knowing that there are opposing opinions which perhaps should also be followed. When there was a Sanhedrin, however, it was completely different. No question was too difficult, and an answer was always forthcoming. Similarly, there was never an unresolved argument. If a difference of opinion arose, there would be a discussion followed by a vote. Because majority rule was absolute, we always had unequivocal knowledge of Torah. This meant that we were absolutely certain about how to conduct ourselves.

In summary, this verse tells us how much the Sanhedrin is needed; it literally sustained the world. How unfortunate it is that we have lost it; how proud we should be that we once had it, and how wonderful is the thought that one day we will have it restored in all its glory!

FENCED OFF BY ROSES

The verse concludes by saying that *Klal Yisrael* is safeguarded by roses. In other words, *Klal Yisrael* do not need thick, high walls to keep them from sinning. Even a hedge of delicate roses is sufficient. The Gemara connects this metaphor specifically with the laws of marital purity.[49] As Rashi vividly describes, there are no actual barriers to

---

49 *Sanhedrin* 37a. The Gemara relates that a certain heretic said he did not believe that Jews actually observe the laws of family purity. He claimed that there is nothing to stand in the way of strong desire. The Gemara comments that this heretic obviously never heard of this verse which testifies that *Klal Yisrael* has the requisite inner strength such that

keep husband and wife apart during a time when they are forbidden to have relations. Even though the desire may be particularly strong, *Klal Yisrael* guard themselves. The Midrash puts it this way:

> It is the way of the world that when a man marries his wife, he yearns greatly for her. If, after the wedding feast, she says to him, "I have seen what looks like a rose [i.e., a bit of menstrual blood]," he will draw away from her. What causes the man not to come near her? What wall is there between them?! What serpent bit him?! What is it that restrains him? The words of the Torah that are as delicate as roses! ...
>
> Similarly, a hungry traveler sees a cluster of dates on a tree, and reaches out to partake of it, but if others point out to him that it is private property, he instantly draws his hand away to avoid stealing. What causes the hungry man not to eat? ... It is the hedge of roses. Similarly, if a dish of meat is brought to a hungry man, but he is told, "A piece of forbidden fat has fallen into the dish," he will instantly draw his hand away so as not to eat of it. What caused this hungry man not to eat of the dish? ... The hedge of roses!

This verse is praising *Klal Yisrael* who accede to even a flimsy fence to keep them from sinning. To bring out the true beauty of this message, let us ask ourselves why a hedge of roses is used as a symbol of a flimsy fence? Why not something flimsier, such as reeds?! The answer is that this symbol contains another lesson. "A hedge of roses" is hardly an imposing barrier. Despite its thorns, it can be trampled easily by anyone disposed to do so. Yet for someone who truly appreciates roses, it can be the most effective barrier because he would not want to damage them in any way — unlike a strong stone wall that one can just climb over it, knock down, or drill through. The effectiveness of a hedge of roses is its actual beauty, but it only works for those who appreciate its beauty. For a callous person who would trample roses, it is no barrier at all. Similarly, the sanctions of the Torah and the Sages are effective only for those who appreciate and

---

they are safeguarded from sin by the flimsiest of barriers.

It is told that Rabbi Levi Yitzchak of Berditchev once asked his attendant to try to obtain a product which the government of the time had made illegal. Within a short time, the attendant was able to get hold of it. Then the Rabbi asked him to get some *chametz* from a Jew on Pesach. But this he was unable to obtain. Rabbi Levi Yitzchak lifted his hands to Hashem, and said "Look, our dear Father! With all the police, judges, courts, and prisons, they cannot stop illegal activity completely. But You told Your children not to have *chametz* on Pesach, and without a police force, etc., imposing Your will, they are still obeying You wholeheartedly thousands of years later. Please have mercy on such a wonderful nation!"

understand the greatness and majesty of Torah. One who appreciates the beauty and splendor of every mitzvah and every decree of the Sages would never trample them.

Every barrier which the Torah makes is a wonderful gift given to us for our sake. Seen in this light, one would never trespass against it. This is why the verse uses the symbol of a hedge of roses and not a hedge of reeds or the like. This demonstrates the greatness of *Klal Yisrael* — that they allow themselves to be restrained by such weak barriers. The verse hints at how the barrier works. From an objective standpoint, a hedge of roses is really no barrier at all, but it is a formidable barrier for those who respect roses. In a similar way, because the elevated Jewish People loves the words of the Torah and the decrees of the Rabbis, these barriers are effective ones. This is the symbolism of the "hedge of roses." The words of Torah are a gentle reminder to refrain from trespassing against the human soul, the handiwork of Hashem."[50]

This verse begins with an allusion to the Sanhedrin and concludes with an allusion to halachic fences that keep us from sinning because one of the most important responsibilities of the Sanhedrin was to make such fences. They would issue tailor-made decrees and restrictions for each generation with tremendous wisdom and knowledge, depending on what each generation needed. And when the nation would obey, they would be aptly praised for being protected by a hedge of roses. In the absence of the Sanhedrin, each generation's leaders continued to demarcate boundaries. Even though they have no power to enforce these decrees, this does not decrease our obligation to obey. On the contrary, the whole concept of a "hedge of roses" is that even though the barrier is easily overcome, it is enough to keep *Klal Yisrael* from violating it. We must make sure never to disobey the instructions of our leaders, and thereby never lose the laudatory title "a nation constrained by a hedge of roses."

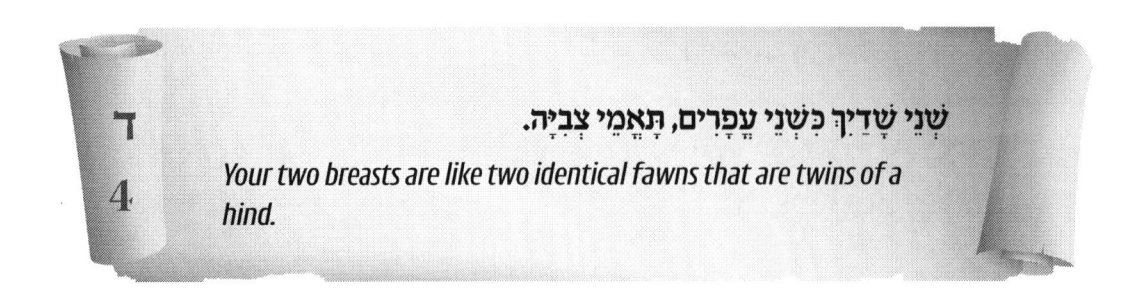

ד
4

שְׁנֵי שָׁדַיִךְ כִּשְׁנֵי עֳפָרִים, תְּאֳמֵי צְבִיָּה.

Your two breasts are like two identical fawns that are twins of a hind.

Allegorical Translation   Hashem praises *Klal Yisrael*: "Your two leaders, Moshe and Aharon, were equal in beauty and greatness, like identical twin fawns born from a hind."

Subject of the Verse   These are praises of *Klal Yisrael*.

---

50   Rabbi Mordechai Gifter, as quoted in the Artscroll edition of *Shir HaShirim* (Brooklyn: Artscroll Publishers, 1976).

Mashal   The beauty of the wife is praised by likening her breasts to beautiful, identical twin fawns.

Nimshal   Rashi tells us that it is common for hinds to have identical twin baby fawns, and that is why this image is used. Metzudas Dovid adds that fawns are appropriate as an exemplar of beauty because they are particularly beautiful. This image of fawns, therefore, has three aspects. They look identical, they are (commonly) twinned, and they are beautiful. All three aspects apply well to breasts.

The Midrash offers many reasons why the breasts here are symbolic of Moshe Rabbeinu and Aharon HaKohen, the leaders of *Klal Yisrael*. Here are a few: Just as breasts nurture a baby, so these two leaders nurtured and cared for the Jewish People like a mother feeding her young. Just as a woman's two breasts are similar, so Moshe and Aharon were equally great. Just as breasts are full of nourishing milk, so were Moshe and Aharon full of nourishing Torah. Just as a baby would die if not for the milk that the mother provides (or a suitable replacement), so *Klal Yisrael* would cease to exist without the Torah of Moshe and Aharon. Just as the breasts are an essential part of the beauty of a woman, the leaders of our nation are the chief beauty of *Klal Yisrael*. And just as a woman nurses her child from that which she ate herself, so our leaders nourish us with the Torah they have learned.

Later generations also enjoyed twin leadership, something that is also alluded to in this verse. We always had a king or *Nasi* ("prince") who was in charge of all the material affairs of the nation, and a *Kohen Gadol*, *Navi*, or head of the Sanhedrin, who was in charge of the nation's spiritual affairs. These leaders would work together to help the Jewish People in every way.

Rashi offers another interpretation of the symbol of the breasts in our verse: the two stone tablets (*luchos*) upon which were inscribed the Ten Commandments, the basis of our Torah. Just as the two breasts are similar and complement one another, so the two stone tablets were similar and interconnected. To drive home this point, Hashem made a special miracle: even though the first *luach* contained many more words than the second one, they both had the exact same dimensions![51]

---

51   *Midrash Rabbah, Ki Sisa* 41:6.

7:5 ETERNAL LOVE

This verse is an exact repetition of an earlier verse[52] in which Hashem describes *Klal Yisrael*'s beauty.[53] That the heathen nations describe *Klal Yisrael*'s beauty in a similar way shows that *Klal Yisrael*'s beauty is obvious and indisputable.

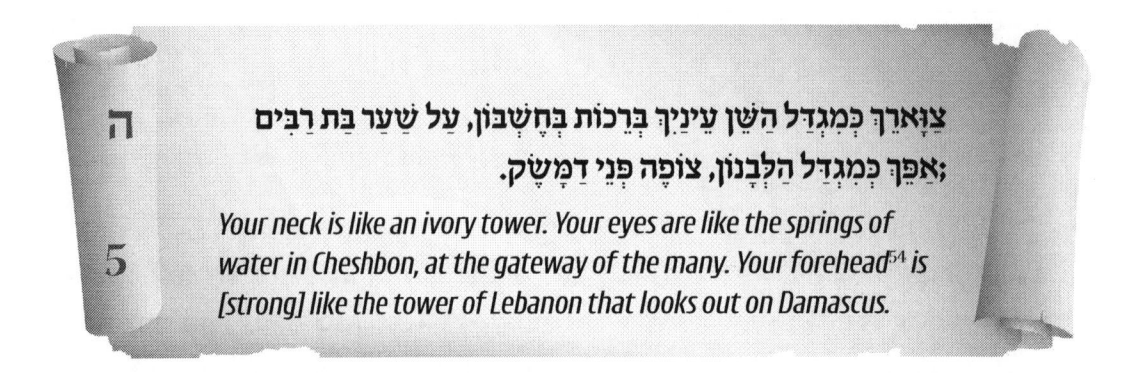

> ### ה
> ### 5
> צַוָּארֵךְ כְּמִגְדַּל הַשֵּׁן עֵינַיִךְ בְּרֵכוֹת בְּחֶשְׁבּוֹן, עַל שַׁעַר בַּת רַבִּים; אַפֵּךְ כְּמִגְדַּל הַלְּבָנוֹן, צוֹפֶה פְּנֵי דַמָּשֶׂק.
>
> *Your neck is like an ivory tower. Your eyes are like the springs of water in Cheshbon, at the gateway of the many. Your forehead[54] is [strong] like the tower of Lebanon that looks out on Damascus.*

Allegorical Translation: Your (*Klal Yisrael*'s) *Mizbe'ach* is prominent and protects the people just like a strong tower. Your Torah scholars irrigate the nation with the knowledge of Torah as they make the yearly calendar calculations in the city of Yerushalayim, which all the nations come to visit. Your strength, not swayed by temptation, is

---

52 4:5.

53 See our more detailed commentary there.

54 Rashi explains at great length that even though the word "אַף" generally means "nose" (as in *Shemos* 15:8), here it cannot mean "nose" — literally or figuratively — and must mean "forehead." The proof is that the verse praises the אַף as being like the tower of Lebanon. Now, what possible praise can there be in saying that the wife has a big and prominent nose?! Furthermore, as noted earlier, the praises here begin from the feet (v. 2), and go steadily up the body, concluding with the hair (v. 6). And since the eyes have just been praised, the nose, which is situated below the eyes, should have been mentioned earlier. Thus, according to Rashi, "אַף" here means "forehead," which is indeed situated above the eyes. Having a prominent forehead is seen as a sign of greatness.

In contrast to Rashi, the Rashbam and Ibn Ezra understand "אַף" in its usual sense as "nose." When the verse praises the nose as being like the tower of Lebanon, it thus means that it is shaped in a fitting manner. Saying that someone has a well-proportioned nose is a compliment. The message is that just as a nose breathes air into the body, *Klal Yisrael* breathe air and life into the world.

Further support for this interpretation can be drawn from the episode in the Gemara (*Ta'anis* 29a) in which Rabban Gamliel was being hunted down during the time of the *Churban*. He was alerted to the danger by a nobleman who called out: "The master of the nose is sought." Understanding the hint, Rabban Gamliel fled. The leader of the generation was referred to as the one with the nose because just as the nose is a lofty organ and brings life-giving air to the body, so the lofty leader brings air and energy to the generation (Maharsha). Alternatively, just as a prominent nose is very conspicuous and helps determine the identity of a person (see *Yevamos* 120a), so too the leaders are very visible and determine the identity of the generation. Furthermore, a great leader may be referred to as a "nose" because he is able to smell quickly if there is something wrong with the way people are behaving (*Sanhedrin* 93b).

The Migdal Dovid explains that anger is symbolized by the nose since one's nose flares up when one is angry. A long nose is a metaphor for one who is slow to anger and that is indeed a great praise! See Rashi on *Shemos* 15:8, *s.v. u'veru-ach*.

On a macrocosmic level, *Klal Yisrael* embody these traits for the entire world. They are the notable leaders of the world. They bring air and life to the world. They are very conspicuous and determine the direction of the world. They are able to quickly sense whether something is good or bad. Hence, they are praised as having a "strong nose."

as strong as a mighty fortification.

Subject of the Verse — These are praises of *Klal Yisrael*.

Mashal — This verse further praises the beauty of the wife. Her neck is straight, clean, strong, and tall like an ivory tower. Her eyes are clear and sparkling like the springs of water in Cheshbon (a famous popular spring). Her forehead is prominent and strong like a powerful tower.

Nimshal — In a sense, the neck is the most important part of the anatomy because it connects between the head, the repository of a person's wisdom, and the body, which performs all the actions. The neck is a connector and transmitter, a conduit between a higher being/head and a lower being/body.

The "neck" here symbolizes either the Sanhedrin,[55] or the *Mizbe'ach*.[56] The Sanhedrin was like the neck in this sense: just as the neck is a pipeline communicating the knowledge and wisdom of the mind to the rest of the body, so the Sanhedrin would transmit all the wisdom of Torah to the nation through their rulings and teachings. The verse continues that the Sanhedrin was like an ivory tower: just as a tower is a symbol of strength and provides protection, so the Sanhedrin was a pillar of strength and provider of protection for the nation against all attacks on Jewish law and tradition.

If the neck symbolizes the *Mizbe'ach*, the analogy can be explained as follows: just as all air, food, and drink that a person needs flow through the neck, so do all blessing and success flow down to the world through the *Mizbe'ach*. Hashem delivers all blessings, sustenance, and life to this world in the merit of the *korbanos* which were brought on the *Mizbe'ach*. The *Mizbe'ach* was thus a conduit of life and blessing to the world.

Furthermore, just as the neck is situated close to the top of the body, so the Sanhedrin and the *Mizbe'ach* were situated at almost the highest part of Eretz Yisrael, next to the Beis HaMikdash, showing their importance.

Our verse then moves up to the eyes: "Your eyes are like the springs of water in Cheshbon, at the gateway of the many." The "eyes" symbolize the nation's leaders because they see developments from afar. In this verse, the eyes are likened to the pools and springs of water in Cheshbon. Cheshbon originally belonged

---

55 See 4:4.
56 Rashi.

to the land of Moav. Sichon, one of the most powerful kings at the time, went to war with Moav to capture this important city.[57] The springs of water of this important place were renowned for their quality. Water, of course, provides life. Where there is no water source, life cannot flourish. Similarly, the leaders provide life to the people. Just as these springs provided life-giving water to the people, so did the leaders provide life-giving Torah (which is likened to water[58]) to the nation. Furthermore, clean "springs of water" symbolize beauty and purity that draw people to them.[59] The leaders of *Klal Yisrael* are clean and pure both in their conduct and in their motivation. This verse teaches us that the leaders are the beauty and sustenance of the Jewish People.

It is also possible to understand "Cheshbon" not as a place name, but simply in terms of its root meaning, "calculation" (חשבון).[60] According to this approach, the verse is praising the nation's leaders for being able to work out the incredibly complex calculations needed to produce a yearly calendar system. This complicated calculation took into account all the movements of the constellations and fit in with all the solar and lunar cycles. As the Gemara[61] tells us, this required particularly advanced knowledge, and thus the entire world admired the greatness of *Klal Yisrael* for having it. Indeed, the knowledge and wisdom involved were so great that everyone realized they were Divinely inspired. And this is true always: the wisdom of our leaders is beyond what we can understand because Hashem helps them and gives them special insight.

The Sanhedrin and the nation's leaders sat "at the gateway of the many" because they were based in Yerushalayim, the main artery of the entire world. People would come from all over the world to visit Yerushalayim. There they would see the greatness of *Klal Yisrael* and the Beis HaMikdash.[62] The Sanhedrin in Yerushalayim was seen and admired by everyone. Its greatness was appreciated like a magnificent monument placed in the gateway of the public square.

Our verse moves on to highlight one of *Klal Yisrael*'s great virtues: "Your forehead is [strong] like the tower of Lebanon that looks out on Damascus."

---

57 See *Bamidbar* 21:26.
58 *Bava Kama* 17a, based on *Yeshayahu* 55:1.
59 The verse uses the metaphor of a spring, not a river, because a spring is purer and cleaner than a river.
60 Rashi.
61 *Shabbos* 75a.
62 See Rashi on *Devarim* 33:19.

When one is being pressured to do something wrong, one needs significant strength of mind to withstand the arguments and persuasion. Here we are praised for having a "strong forehead," i.e., mental perseverance as strong as the mighty "tower of Lebanon." This was actually a tower in Yerushalayim,[63] a well-known symbol of strength from which one could see all the way to Damascus!

Indeed, *Klal Yisrael* can be justifiably proud of its trait of perseverance. For thousands of years, the nation as a whole, and countless individual Jews, have been put under relentless pressure to stop serving Hashem. Yet we have remained steadfast.[64]

A very different interpretation understands the forehead in the verse to symbolize thoughts. As Rashi tells us, the verse then means: the thoughts of the people of Yerushalayim anticipate[65] the day when Yerushalayim will reach Damascus. This interpretation ties in with the fact that when Mashiach comes, Yerushalayim will expand and reach all the way to Damascus. The whole of Eretz Yisrael and Yerushalayim will expand so much that Yerushalayim alone will reach the city of Damascus — hundreds of miles away. One can barely imagine how big the whole of Eretz Yisrael will be! Like the people of Yerushalayim being praised here, we too must constantly picture and eagerly await the wondrous events that will accompany the coming of Mashiach.

YOUR NECK IS LIKE AN IVORY TOWER

Despite its extreme importance, the neck is a weak and vulnerable part of the body and therefore can be harmed easily.[66] It is no wonder that throughout history, killers went first for the neck — so vital to life, but yet so vulnerable. *Klal Yisrael*'s neck is different. It is not just hard, but it is as hard as ivory, one of the hardest substances in nature.

This verse teaches us something very basic about *Klal Yisrael*, whose paramount importance to the world parallels the neck's importance to the body. Like the neck, they are a conduit for spiritual life to this world. And like the neck, *Klal Yisrael* also

---

63   "Levanon" can mean "white." Yerushalayim is thus known as "Levanon" because all the sins of *Klal Yisrael* would be cleansed and whitened there through repentance and the sacrifices offered in the Beis HaMikdash.

64   An inspiring example of this heroic steadfastness is described in *Subbota*, the true story of Eliezer Nanes's twenty years in Russian prison camps. During this long period, the authorities used every tactic possible to get him to stop observing Shabbos, including torture and threats of never being allowed to return to his family. Yet Nanes, a veritable "tower of Levanon," withstood them all and observed Shabbos unfailingly!

65   "*Tzofeh*" can also be understood as "waiting" and "anticipating."

66   The heart is important, but it is protected by ribs; the fingers have no protection, but one can live without them. Only the neck is both essential and vulnerable.

seem vulnerable and weak. They are a nation not known for their large numbers or brute strength, but they are really as strong as ivory. They possess unparalleled spiritual strength, and their devotion is as strong as the hardest substance in the world. Over the course of history, many have thought that they could destroy *Klal Yisrael* or at least sway them away from Hashem due to their weakness. But they have been amazed time and time again by the sheer strength of the nation.

It is said that Dovid Ben-Gurion, the first prime minister of Israel, was often asked why, considering that he and his political party wished to make Eretz Yisrael a secular country, he allowed the religious people to freely continue studying Torah, and why he was not tougher on them when they set up the State. He explained that considering how weak they were — with fewer than five hundred religious men pursuing full-time learning here at the time, and the numbers only going down after the decimation of nearly all the major European Torah learning centers during the Holocaust — he was sure they would disappear. He felt it unnecessary to battle them. Yet, *baruch Hashem*, today there are tens of thousands learning Torah, and many, many more observing mitzvos, while those who thought they would eradicate Torah are dwindling in number and power.

In his *B'Mechitzasam*, Rabbi Shlomo Lorincz, *zt"l*, provides a recent example of the seemingly vulnerable and weak "neck" that was actually a conduit for life and as strong as ivory. The Chazon Ish, the paramount Torah scholar and leader during the early years of the State, was physically weak, often unwell, financially poor, and did not have an official position. Furthermore, relatively few people recognized his greatness. Yet he revolutionized Eretz Yisrael with awesome and unparalleled strength, with commitment and dedication. He set up many new places of Torah learning and helped build religious communities that were totally devoted to serving Hashem. Just by speaking to an individual or writing him a letter, the Chazon Ish was able to influence him positively. Indeed, his spiritual strength was such that his importance is still felt today, many years after his passing. There are hundreds of thousands of people following his directions and learning from his ways! This is a demonstration of the seemingly vulnerable and weak neck, i.e., a lofty leader, high like the neck and providing spiritual life just like the neck is a conduit for life, that is as strong as ivory.

It is noteworthy that Yaakov Avinu and Moshe Rabbeinu were both attacked on the neck. Yaakov was bitten there by his brother, Eisav HaRasha, and Pharaoh tried to have Moshe Rabbeinu beheaded. In both cases, their necks turned to marble, an extremely hard material, causing Eisav's teeth to crack and Pharaoh's sword to break.[67] This miracle exemplifies the concept we are discussing. Eisav and Pharaoh assumed they were

---

67   See the Midrash here regarding Yaakov, and Yerushalmi, *Berachos* 9:1, regarding Moshe.

attacking weak, vulnerable men,⁶⁸ yet Hashem showed them that their would-be victims' spiritual strength was as strong as the hardest substance. This is the symbol of the "neck like an ivory tower."

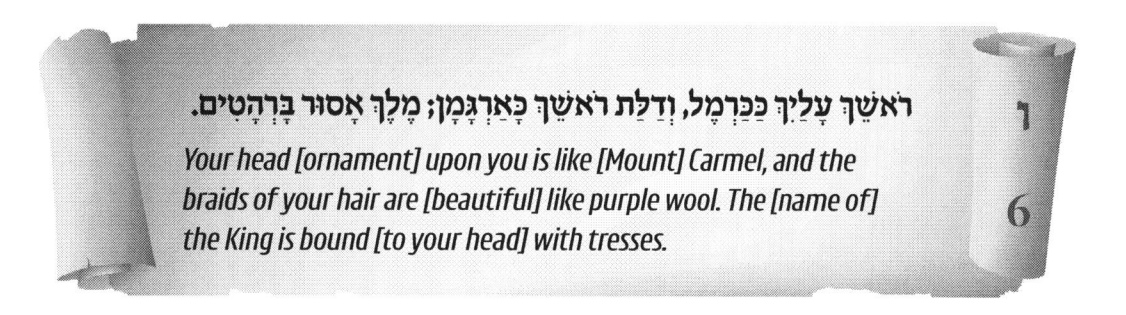

> רֹאשֵׁךְ עָלַיִךְ כַּכַּרְמֶל, וְדַלַּת רֹאשֵׁךְ כָּאַרְגָּמָן; מֶלֶךְ אָסוּר בָּרְהָטִים.
>
> Your head [ornament] upon you is like [Mount] Carmel, and the braids of your hair are [beautiful] like purple wool. The [name of] the King is bound [to your head] with tresses.
>
> **ו 6**

Allegorical Translation — The tefillin on the heads of *Klal Yisrael* is awe-inspiring, like Mount Carmel. The braids of hair of the *nazirim* are as beautiful as purple wool. The name of Hashem is bound to that hair.

Subject of the Verse — These are praises of *Klal Yisrael*.

Mashal — The verse continues to praise the beauty of the wife. Her head is majestic like Mount Carmel, and the braids of her hair are beautiful like purple wool. Even a king is drawn to her tresses.

Nimshal — Rashi explains that "the head" is an allusion to tefillin worn on the head, which is as impressive as Mount Carmel in northern Israel. The sight of tefillin on the head of a Jew inspires tremendous awe,⁶⁹ like the awe inspired by the sight of mountains.

The hair and the tresses in this verse allude to the hair of a *nazir*. Hashem (the King) is associated with this hair because the *nazir* promises not to cut his hair for Hashem's sake. Furthermore, the Torah tells us that the *nazir* wears the crown of Hashem.⁷⁰ Because he dedicates his hair for holiness, it is considered a holy crown. The symbol of purple is the symbol of royalty since

---

68 We can imagine Eisav seeing his brother bow down to him and shower him with gifts and Pharaoh seeing Moshe Rabbeinu, a single man who was forced to run away from him. They both seemed so vulnerable, yet they were actually far more powerful than their enemies could ever imagine, and they eventually overcame them.

69 The Gemara (*Berachos* 6a) explains that the verse, "וראו כל עמי הארץ כי שם ה' נקרא עליך ויראו ממך — When the nations see the name of Hashem called upon you, they will fear you" (*Devarim* 28:10) is referring specifically to the tefillin, which contain the awesome name of Hashem.

70 *Bamidbar* 6:7.

in the olden days all royalty wore purple.[71] The verse teaches us that the *nazir* is considered a royal servant of Hashem. This latter part of our verse, then, is to be understood as follows: "The braids of your [*nazir's*] hair are [beautiful and royal], like purple wool. The [name of] the King is bound with the tresses [of the *nazir*]." The entire verse highlights the greatness of *Klal Yisrael* in that their tefillin inspire awe and their nazirim tes are so holy that the name of Hashem becomes intertwined with their hair. Because *Klal Yisrael* is so special, their mitzvos are able to catapult them to great heights. With just a small decision, a Jew is able to elevate himself and his hair to great holiness. This is because Hashem is bonded with every single Jewish person.[72]

The word "רהטים," translated above as "tresses," can also mean "running."[73] According to this meaning, Rashi explains the second part of the verse this way: "The King (Hashem) is bound up with love to the mitzvos and the running that we do for Him." Every little exertion we make for Hashem is very beloved by Him.

YOUR HEAD [ORNAMENT] UPON YOU IS LIKE [MOUNT] CARMEL…

Rabbi Elisha Galiko interprets the mention of Mount Carmel in this verse as an allusion to the tremendous miracle that Hashem performed there for Eliyahu HaNavi. This miracle prompted the Jewish People to declare wholeheartedly that Hashem is the only true God.

To better appreciate this interpretation, let us briefly summarize this inspiring episode — one that truly requires in-depth study in its own right. The evil Jewish King Achav saw to the murder of nearly all the prophets and drove almost the entire nation into idol worship. He was assisted in his evildoing by almost a thousand false prophets. When Achav ridiculed Eliyahu HaNavi's warnings that there would be no rain if the country served idols, Eliyahu HaNavi brought on a drought which caused a terrible famine. When he finally caught up with Eliyahu, Achav told him that he had destroyed the nation through the drought. Eliyahu replied that Achav was to blame for it by encouraging idol worship. Eliyahu then proposed to Achav the following contest between himself and the numerous false prophets: Whoever offers a *korban* that is consumed by fire from Above has proven his God to be the true one. Achav accepted.

---

71 See *Daniel* 5:6 and *Midrash Bamidbar Rabbah* 12 for the fact that royalty wore purple.

72 This is similar to the idea that if a monarch would make a small gesture, such as giving someone a hug, it would be considered a great act of love or respect. The smallest action of a great person is very special.

73 As in *Targum* to *Bereishis* 18:2.

The entire nation assembled at Mount Carmel, and Eliyahu HaNavi rebuked them for not being fully committed to serving Hashem and for continually being pulled by conflicting emotions between Hashem and idol worship. He made it clear to them that this must end. The people agreed and came to watch the contest. The false prophets, despite using many different tricks and deceit, were unable to generate the fire. Eliyahu then slaughtered an animal and placed it on a *mizbe'ach*. After pouring a huge quantity of water all over it, he prayed to Hashem, and a fire miraculously descended from Heaven and consumed the *korban* as well as the *mizbe'ach*. The nation promptly responded to this miracle by calling out twice, with tremendous enthusiasm and fervor, "Hashem is the true God!" Then Eliyahu killed all the false prophets. He proceeded to pray for rain, bringing an end to the drought. This is one of the most dramatic and inspiring episodes in our very rich history. It is well worth contemplating.

In light of the above, Rabbi Elisha Galiko explains that this verse in *Shir HaShirim* is telling us that the Jewish People's head — that is, the thoughts in our head — will be as pure with faith in the time of Mashiach as they were on Mount Carmel after this tremendous miracle. We must endeavor that even today, despite the fact that the ultimate redemption has not yet arrived, that our "head" should be like the heads of those who witnessed the miracle on Mount Carmel: completely steadfast in our beliefs. Our belief in Hashem and our grasp of the ultimate truth that everything is from Hashem must be as clear as it was then.

The Avodas Gershuni also sees the mention of Mount Carmel as an allusion to the miracle wrought there in the time of Eliyahu, but he stays with Rashi's explanation that the "head" in this verse is an allusion to the mitzvah of tefillin. He thus understands the verse this way: *Klal Yisrael*'s wearing tefillin and thus declaring their belief in Hashem (since *Shema Yisrael*, our declaration of faith, is inscribed on parchment inside the tefillin) is as precious to Hashem as the moment when the nation publicly proclaimed their belief in Him on Mount Carmel.

There is a lesson here for us. We must realize that every time we put on tefillin or recite the *Shema*, we are essentially declaring that Hashem is the only true God, just as the people did at Mount Carmel. We can increase our enthusiasm in performing daily mitzvos by recalling the remarkable events in our nation's history that uplift and inspire us and try to recapture those feelings by appreciating that our "ordinary" daily mitzvos are just as precious to Hashem.

YOUR HEAD [ORNAMENT] UPON YOU IS LIKE [MOUNT] CARMEL...

The Midrash interprets this verse in a completely different way. It understands the word "*rosheich*" not as "your head," but as "your poor ones," from the root word "*rash*," meaning "a poor person."[74] It understands the word "*dalas*" in a similar manner, as "the weak and deprived,"[75] from the root word *dal*, meaning "a pauper."[76] According to the Midrash, Hashem is thus declaring: "The poor [in good deeds] are [as precious to me] as [Eliyahu on Mount] Carmel,[77] and the paupers [in Torah knowledge] are [as precious to me] as [Dovid and Daniel], who wore purple wool [of royalty]."[78] This verse, then, illustrates the love that Hashem has for every Jewish person regardless of his stature.

Rabbi Galiko explains the conclusion of this verse in keeping with the Midrash's approach: "The king [Hashem] is bound [with love] to the hair [i.e., the weakest and flimsiest part of the body]." Hashem is bound with love to the entire Jewish People, even those who can be likened to hair.[79] Since they are part of the "body" of the Jewish People, they are loved even though they are not particularly accomplished.

We can see this idea reflected in the halachah that a Jew must give up his life rather than comply with a demand to kill a fellow Jew.[80] The rationale: "Who knows which life is more precious to Hashem?!" Now, let us consider how far this halachah goes. It means that if the greatest Jewish leader — who is teaching Torah to thousands and rules on all the difficult questions, never wasting a moment — is commanded to kill a simple Jew — who never learned Torah because he cannot read and never helped anyone due to illness and poverty — he must give up his life rather than comply![81] This message is implicit in our verse: just as a parent loves each of his children, and would never agree to spare one at the expense of the other, so Hashem loves each and every Jew.

---

74 As in *Mishlei* 30:8.

75 Not as "braids" [of hair].

76 As in *Vayikra* 19:15.

77 The Torah Temimah poses the question: How does this event connect with the thrust of the verse? He bases his answer on the Midrash that teaches that Hashem accepted Eliyahu HaNavi's prayers there on Mount Carmel in the merit of his having a *bris milah*. Since every Jewish male is circumcised, it can be understood that Hashem accepts all of us, just as he accepted Eliyahu HaNavi and his prayers.
Furthermore, at one point, Eliyahu HaNavi protested to Hashem that *Klal Yisrael* was worthless. Hashem rebuked him for this, and from then on, he became the one who defended *Klal Yisrael* and bore witness to all their good deeds. Thus, the allusion to Eliyahu here reminds us that Hashem only wishes to see good in every Jew, even those whom others might write off as useless.

78 See *Zecharyah* 12:8 with regard to Dovid. See *Daniel*, ch. 5, for more on Daniel's connection with royalty. When Daniel explained the mysterious writing on the wall, Balshetzar appointed him as ruler, and gave him a golden chain and *purple* royal garments to wear.
The Torah Temimah explains what lies behind these allusions. Dovid had a very lowly beginning, and Daniel had a very lowly end, yet Hashem loved them. In the same way, He loves everyone, even the ones who seem lowly.

79 See our commentary on 4:1 indicating that hair always represents the weakest among *Klal Yisrael*.

80 *Yoma* 82b.

81 Rashi (ibid.) emphasizes that this is a logical argument and not derived from the verse.

The Alshich explains each of the previous verses (2-7) as referring to a different component of the Jewish People. Verse 2, which touches on the beauty of the feet, alludes to those who go walking from place to place to teach Torah. They are referred to (in v. 2) as "*bas nadiv*," meaning the descendants of Avraham Avinu,[82] because they followed the example he set by going from place to place in order to teach the world *emunah* in Hashem. The mention of the beauty of the thighs later in that verse is an allusion to *talmidei chachamim* who learn Torah in private, like the hidden thighs. Verse 3, which touches on the beauty of the stomach, is symbolically praising the charitable people who provide food to the poor, and thus fill their stomachs. This verse also likens them to the moon because the moon seems to shrink and become duller, but that is only how we perceive it. In reality, it is not diminished in any way. Similarly, those who give away their money to charity seem to be losing it, but in reality, they are not diminished at all. The continuation of that verse praising the navel alludes to women who lovingly and devotedly carry their babies and then nurture them. And then, after all that effort, they willingly bear more children. The "breasts" in the following verse (v. 4) symbolize the leaders who nurture the nation. The beautiful neck in verse 5 alludes to the unrecognized righteous people who carry the sins and burden of the generation around their neck.[83] The eyes in the following verse (v. 6) are the judges who see what is right and what is wrong. The head (v. 7) refers to the king who is like the head of the nation.

If we compare the Alshich's approach to Rashi's, we find that both explain these verses as evoking the beauty of *Klal Yisrael*. The difference is that while the Alshich sees each verse alluding to a different component part of the nation, Rashi sees each verse alluding to a different attribute or aspect of the nation.

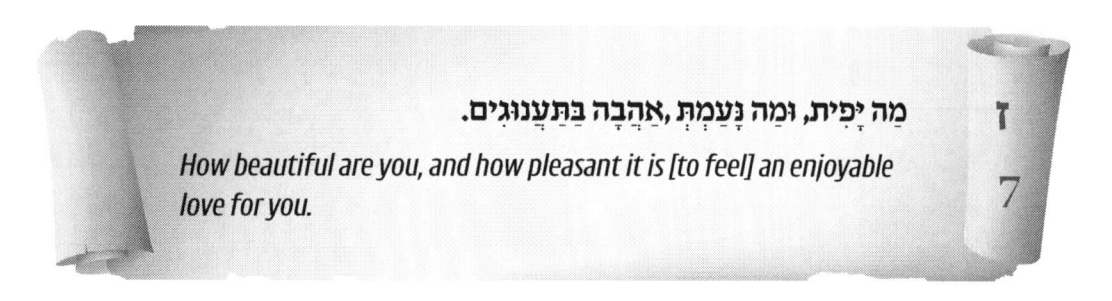

מַה יָּפִית, וּמַה נָּעַמְתְּ, אַהֲבָה בַּתַּעֲנוּגִים. ז

How beautiful are you, and how pleasant it is [to feel] an enjoyable love for you.

7

Allegorical Translation After various aspects of *Klal Yisrael*'s beauty have been highlighted, this verse declares that all of *Klal Yisrael* is beautiful; and it is very pleasant, *ki'veyachol*,

---

82 See our commentary there.

83 In *Derech Hashem* (II:3), the Ramchal discusses in depth the concept of the righteous carrying the burden of the sins of others — how it works, and why it is fair and just.

for Hashem to have an enjoyable loving relationship with *Klal Yisrael*.

Subject of the Verse — These are praises of *Klal Yisrael*.

Mashal — This verse evokes the astonishing beauty of the wife and how pleasant and enjoyable it is to feel love for her.

Nimshal — The message of the verse is that *Klal Yisrael* is beautiful in every regard. "How beautiful!" is an expression of wonder. How astonishingly beautiful you are, *Klal Yisrael*!

Rashi explains that after the verses touching on the beauty of every individual facet of *Klal Yisrael*, this verse offers a summary statement: *Klal Yisrael* as a whole is entirely pleasant and delightful. It is a pleasure to be attached to them and to love them.

The beauty of the words of this verse cannot be fully appreciated on the intellectual level alone. We must try to respond to them on the emotional level as well.

AN ENJOYABLE LOVE

Rabbi Yosef Albo understands this verse to be about loving Hashem, not loving Yisrael.[84] With this assumption, he explains that all love and desire is intertwined with pain, frustration, and worry. Let us start with the realm of desire. For a person to truly enjoy a meal, he must first be hungry. Without the discomfort of hunger, the food is not as enjoyable. To truly enjoy sleep, one must first endure the discomfort of being tired. A person wants money, but the more he acquires, the more he desires. If he has a hundred, he desires two hundred. If he has two hundred, he desires four hundred. The one who has two hundred is actually missing more than the one who has a hundred. It turns out that the more pleasures one gets, the more discomfort he has because he is actually missing more.

Although the dynamics are different, the same basic equation applies in the realm of love. Before a person obtains the object of his love, he suffers while waiting for it. When he obtains a small amount of love, he wishes to obtain more — and is still in pain. The efforts to attain the love often require exertion and difficulty. When a person eventually obtains the love he has sought in its entirety, he often starts to worry that he may become bored. Alternatively, he may become fearful that he will lose the love. As

---

84 *Sefer HaIkkarim* 3:36.

we all know, everyone we love eventually dies; and sometimes people fall out of love. Furthermore, as soon as one obtains his love, his desire subsides, causing him to fear that the love has weakened.

The bottom line is that both desire and love are actually intertwined with worry and pain. The only exception to this rule is the love of Hashem. Man takes delight in Hashem's love, and also in the challenges he encounters to obtain it because he knows that the efforts invested are themselves valuable. This love can never be considered to be complete and boring because God cannot be entirely obtained. As a person attains more, his love and delight increase.[85] God never withdraws from the one who loves Him. And since God is eternal, His love will never be extinguished. There is thus no worry that the love will be lost. It turns out that the love of Hashem is the only completely enjoyable and pleasant love without any pain, as this verse declares, "How *pleasant* it is [to feel] an *enjoyable* love for You."

HOW BEAUTIFUL ARE YOU...

The *Targum* renders this verse in terms of Hashem praising the Jewish People for accepting their suffering with love: "How beautiful are you [when you bear My yoke], [when I chastise you with afflictions, you accept them] lovingly for they [appear] to you as delights." These words remind us of the famous statement of Rabbeinu Yonah[86] that when a person accepts Hashem's punishments and repents, he should rejoice over the suffering and thank Hashem for it. As Dovid HaMelech put it: "I shall raise a cup of salvation and praise the name of Hashem... I shall find pain and suffering, and yet praise the name of Hashem."[87] Accepting suffering as a Divine signal to repent brings so much reward and blessing to a person that he should be as grateful for it as he is for pleasurable things. As the *Targum* understands this verse: "[...you accept them] lovingly for they [appear] to you as delights."

The Alshich sees this verse as *Klal Yisrael*'s response to Hashem who tells them (in the previous verses) how much He loves them. The Alshich reads the verse this way: "How wonderful and how pleasant was Hashem's love when I experienced it in delight, i.e., in a delightful place, meaning the delight of my own land, Eretz Yisrael." Of course, Hashem's love is always wonderful, but we yearn to enjoy it fully. That can only be when

---

85   It is true that the closer one gets to Hashem, the more one yearns to become even closer. But that yearning is a feeling of fulfillment and joy, not sadness or pain. In contrast, the yearning for the pleasures of this world, such as food or money, engenders a feeling of emptiness and causes sadness and unhappiness. See the Chazon Ish's *Kovetz Iggros* (vol. II, letter 173) for more on these two different types of yearning.

86   *Shaarei Teshuvah* 2:4.

87   *Tehillim* 116:4,13.

we are at home, in the place of true delight, Eretz Yisrael. A husband might feel tremendous joy to see his wife anywhere, yet still yearn to be able to go to a place where they can properly enjoy each other's company. So, too, *Klal Yisrael* say: "How beautiful are You [Hashem], and how [much more] pleasant it would be [to experience] an enjoyable love for you [in Eretz Yisrael, the ideal place to experience this love]."

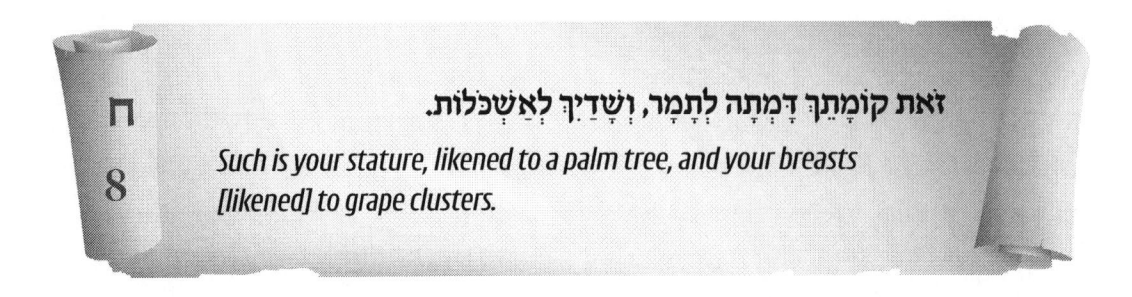

> **ח**
> **8**
> זֹאת קוֹמָתֵךְ דָּמְתָה לְתָמָר, וְשָׁדַיִךְ לְאַשְׁכֹּלוֹת.
> *Such is your stature, likened to a palm tree, and your breasts [likened] to grape clusters.*

Allegorical Translation — You, *Klal Yisrael*, stand upright and steadfast against all pressure like a palm tree. Chananyah, Mishael, and Azaryah taught the world that there is no one like Hashem, and thereby provided the world great inspiration. (Just as grapes give stimulating and nourishing drink, these tzaddikim provided spiritual nourishment.)

Subject of the Verse — These are praises of *Klal Yisrael*.

Mashal — The wife is praised as tall and imposing like a palm tree, with beautiful breasts, like grape clusters.

Nimshal — This is the last verse in this series focusing on the beauty and greatness of *Klal Yisrael*. It introduces the image of the palm tree, a symbol of *Klal Yisrael*'s loyalty to Hashem during their exile. They did not bow to the pressure of the nations. On the contrary, they stood firm and tall like a palm tree, and did not sway even under the pressure of strong "winds."[88] Rashi interprets this as an allusion to the decree of Nevuchadnetzar that everyone must bow down to his idol. All the nations complied — except the righteous among the Jewish People. They stood tall and unflinching, like a tall palm tree which does not bend even in a very strong wind, refusing to bow down.

---

88   Metzudas Dovid understands this image differently. He explains that *Klal Yisrael* is straight and upright — in the ethical sense — like a palm tree. A palm tree stands very straight and erect, so too Klal Yisrael is not crooked or deceitful. This is a very important image we must maintain. Indeed, the essence of the Jewish People must always be its honesty, as it is written: "The remnant of *Klal Yisrael* shall do no wrong, speak no falsehood, and no deceitful language will be found in their mouths" (*Tzefanyah* 3:13). Even the "remnant of *Klal Yisrael*," i.e., the lowly among our people, do not cheat. (See the Netziv's *Emek Berachah*, in his introduction to *Sefer Bereishis*.)

The breasts, likened here to grape clusters, represent clusters of tzaddikim, including Chananyah, Mishael, and Azaryah, who remained faithful and did not bow down. They were a source of spiritual support to all of mankind, teaching them that one must bow down only to Hashem. Just as breasts provide nourishment to a baby, so the righteous provide spiritual nourishment to the world.[89]

These tzaddikim are further compared to clusters of grapes that provide nourishing and invigorating wine. Their faith and conduct gave elevating spiritual nourishment to the entire world by teaching them that Hashem is the only God one must fear.

GRAPE CLUSTERS

The episode of Chananyah, Mishael, and Azaryah, who chose to be thrown into the fiery furnace rather than bow down to Nevuchadnetzar's gigantic statue, is well-known. It is noteworthy, however, that they could have saved themselves without sinning. As the Midrash tells us, once they heard the decree that many of them would have to gather in front of the idol and bow down to it when the signal was given, they went to the Prophet Yechezkel to ask his advice. He told them to hide until the time of the gathering passed. This way, they would not have to bow down, and they would also not be killed. They expressed their reservation that people might not know that they had hidden and might mistakenly assume that they had bowed down. Therefore, they decided not to hide, but rather to go to the gathering and publicly announce to one and all that they would not bow down because one only bows to Hashem. They demonstrated *Klal Yisrael's* famous "stiff neck," but in the most positive sense. They were as stiff as a palm tree! Yechezkel agreed with this plan but told them that Hashem would not save them, and they would die. As the Midrash explains, Hashem told Yechezkel that He would actually save them but did not want them to know this in advance. The reason: Hashem wanted them to receive extra reward due to their willingness to give up their lives for His sake. Indeed, they did not bow with everyone else, and were thrown into the fire. A miracle took place, and they were saved! But the fire was so intense that those who threw them in, as well as the wicked ministers who encouraged the decree and were gleefully watching, were all burned to death!

Let us now put this into the perspective of the entire verse. *Klal Yisrael* is likened to the date palm tree which does not sway in the wind. This means that the many righteous

---

89   We saw earlier that "breasts" alludes to the leaders (4:5).

people of *Klal Yisrael* did not sway under the pressure of Nevuchadnetzar and chose to hide rather than bow down to his statue. But the verse goes on to speak of "her breasts, beautiful like grape clusters." This is an allusion to the fact that Chanayah, Mishael, and Azaryah were more than just an immovable palm tree — they put their lives in jeopardy by standing up to Nevuchadnetzar in order to teach the world that there is no none like our God. They are like grape clusters in the sense that they provided spiritual nourishment and stimulation, like wine that comes from grape clusters: their public declaration and conduct strengthened the world's belief in Hashem.

SUCH IS YOUR STATURE, LIKENED TO A PALM TREE

We can gain added insight into this image by turning to the Vilna Gaon's discussion of the Midrash[90] that likens *Klal Yisrael* to a date tree. The Midrash notes that every part of the date tree can be used for mitzvos. The branches are used for *lulavim*, the fruit (one of the *shivas haminim*) serves as a measure for many Torah laws,[91] and the leaves can be used for *schach*. So, too, no member of *Klal Yisrael* is superfluous. The Midrash explains that every Jewish person is valuable: if he learns Gemara, then his Gemara is valuable; if only Mishnah or Chumash, then that, too, is valuable; if he does *chessed* or gives charity, then that is valuable.

The Vilna Gaon applies this concept to a righteous person. Even when he is not learning, praying, or performing *chessed*, none of his actions are "wasted" since everything he does is intended to serve Hashem. Because he eats and sleeps to have energy to serve Hashem, he is rewarded for even these actions. This is an important lesson for all of us. A person can change all that he does from being, God forbid, worthless to being extremely valuable. It all depends on his intentions. Even a vacation, if taken with the intention of refreshing oneself so that he will be able to better serve Hashem, is viewed as a valuable action. A person will be rewarded for that as well. The palm tree teaches us that all of one's actions can be used to serve Hashem if one has the right intentions. But if a person never really thinks about his actions, many of them go to waste.

The metaphor of the palm tree, then, alludes to three aspects of *Klal Yisrael*'s greatness. The straightness of the palm tree symbolizes *Klal Yisrael*'s honesty. Its ability to withstand strong winds symbolizes their steadfastness. And the fact that all of it is used for serving Hashem teaches that all of *Klal Yisrael*, and all their actions, have value.

---

90 *Bamidbar Rabbah* 3:1.
91 *Berachos* 41b.

אָמַרְתִּי אֶעֱלֶה בְתָמָר, אֹחֲזָה בְּסַנְסִנָּיו; וְיִהְיוּ נָא שָׁדַיִךְ כְּאֶשְׁכְּלוֹת הַגֶּפֶן, וְרֵיחַ אַפֵּךְ כַּתַּפּוּחִים.

ט

9

I [Hashem] said, "I shall be exalted through [Klal Yisrael, who are likened to] the palm tree,[92] and I shall grasp its branches. So, now,[93] let your breasts be like the grape clusters of the vine, and the fragrance of your forehead like apples."

Allegorical Translation — I, Hashem, say that I am exalted, and My Name sanctified, through you *Klal Yisrael*[94] who are like the date tree (as described in the previous verse). I attach Myself to your branches (i.e., to all your components).[95] I therefore beg of you to justify My confidence in you by continuing your steadfastness and ensuring that the righteous among you exert a positive influence such that even your young people resist all temptations.

Subject of the Verse — Hashem is asking *Klal Yisrael* to justify His praise of them.

Mashal — After the husband praises his wife profusely, he looks forward to seeing how her conduct justifies his admiration of her and how all his praises are borne out.

Nimshal — In this verse, Hashem is speaking to *Klal Yisrael*. Hashem proclaims that He is exalted through the Jewish People. He asks them to be true to their values and not to let Him down so that He will have reason to be proud of them and so that His praise will be justified.

---

92   Literally, "I shall be exalted through the palm tree," but the meaning is, "I shall be exalted through *Klal Yisrael*." Since *Klal Yisrael* is compared to the date tree (as explained in the previous verse) so the date tree is now simply another name for *Klal Yisrael*. This same symbol is used in the *Hoshanah* prayers: "Hashem, please save *Klal Yisrael*, who are likened to the date palm tree [דמתה לתמר]."

93   The word "נא" means "now" (*Targum*). Alternatively, it can mean "please" (*Devash V'Chalav*).

94   *Klal Yisrael*'s mission is to sanctify the Name of Hashem in this world. That is the underlying message of the *Kaddish* prayer. The children of a deceased parent thus recite *Kaddish* for him or her during the year after his or her death to, *ki'veyachol*, make up for the diminished sanctification of Hashem's Name that has resulted from the loss of one more Jew to sanctify it.

95   "Branches" alludes either to the great individuals, who stand out like branches, or to the children, who are like branches of a tree.

HASHEM SAID

Rashi tells us that Hashem boasts to the angels about the Jewish People. Hashem says: I am sanctified and exalted through My nation, *Klal Yisrael*, who serve Me regardless of all the influences of the other nations.

This can be likened to a loving father who tells everyone how wonderful his children are. If the children subsequently misbehave, it is extremely upsetting to the father and makes him look like a liar. Similarly, if we sin, this indicates that Hashem's praise was unwarranted and puts Hashem in a bad light, *ki'veyachol*. This verse repeats much of the earlier verse because Hashem is telling us here that the heathen nations' praise of *Klal Yisrael* echoes Hashem's own praise of our people in front of the angels.

Although this is all to be understood metaphorically, we should be filled with joy and pride that Hashem, *ki'veyachol*, boasts about His people, *Klal Yisrael*, to the angels. How much love greatness and delight this demonstrates![96]

Rashi tells us that the second part of this verse is to be understood against the background of the efforts of the heathen nations to seduce *Klal Yisrael* to serve idols. Hashem, together with all the angels to whom He has "boasted," is watching to see how *Klal Yisrael* will respond. Hashem "begs us," *ki'veyachol*: "Please don't let Me down, and make sure your response to the heathen nations justifies My praises and belief in you! Let Me see a great display of your wonderful behavior and faith!" Thereby even the "branches," which symbolize either the children of *Klal Yisrael* or their weak members (since a branch is weaker than the main trunk of the tree), will be attached to Hashem, enabling Hashem to justly say, "I shall grasp [even] its branches."[97]

The "fragrance of your forehead" alludes to the positive aspect of *Klal Yisrael*'s stubbornness.[98] In *lashon* hakodesh, a brazen person is called "עז פנים" ("a brazen forehead").[99] In this verse, Klal Yisrael's brazenness and stubbornness in standing up to the heathen nations is being highlighted.

Hashem's call, at the end of the verse, for *Klal Yisrael* to give off a fragrant smell of

---

[96] Imagine parents hearing a great tzaddik proudly describing the good behavior of their child. How happy this would make them!
One of the most precious of the "*HaRachaman*" prayers recited at the conclusion of *Birkas HaMazon* is this: "הרחמן הוא ישתבח לדוד דורים, ויתפאר בנו לעד ולנצח נצחים, ויתהדר בנו לעד ולעולמי עולמים — May the Compassionate One be praised for all generations, and may He be glorified *through us* forever and ever, and may He be honored *through us* forever and all eternity." This is an ideal place to contemplate our privilege and responsibility in seeing to it that Hashem is honored through us.

[97] Rashi.
The Gemara interprets the "branches" as an allusion to the individuals who stand out and sanctify Hashem's Name publicly (*Sanhedrin* 93a).

[98] See earlier 7:5.

[99] *Avos* 5:20.

apples[100] alludes to the impression *Klal Yisrael* will make. As we know, some precious things that do not give off a nice smell are very off-putting until we look at them intently and see their value. But a good smell is noticed quickly and easily. The Jewish People, which the world knows to be Hashem's nation and a source of pride to Him, must make sure to give off a nice smell so that all the other nations will appreciate its greatness. Hashem is telling us that not only must we withstand all the pressures of the nations and behave correctly, but we must also smell and look good. This means, for example, that we must make sure our actions do not leave a negative impression, even if there is nothing wrong with them. To an outsider, who only takes a cursory look, that would be a *chillul Hashem*. It is for this reason that Rav said, "If I buy food on credit, it is a *chillul Hashem*."[101] Of course, there is nothing wrong with buying on credit. But Rav feared that an outsider seeing him take something without paying for it would arouse suspicions. It does not "smell" good. We, of course, must make an effort to "smell good" as well.

According to this interpretation, the verse reads this way:

> "I [Hashem] said, "I shall be exalted through [*Klal Yisrael*, who is likened to] the palm tree, [honest, steadfast, and valuable], and I shall grasp its branches [since even the individuals in *Klal Yisrael* who are not exceptionally great will be inspired to serve Me]. So let [Me and the angels see] now [how indeed it is true that] your [*Klal Yisrael*'s] breasts [leaders] are like the grape clusters of the vine [providing spiritual nourishment as in the verse above], and the fragrance of your forehead [steadfastness] like apples [giving off a pleasant and attractive smell to all those who come in contact with you.]"

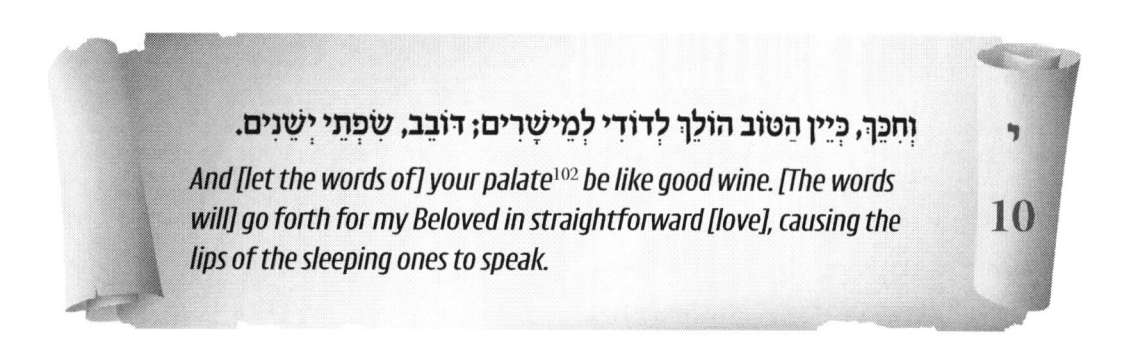

וְחִכֵּךְ, כְּיֵין הַטּוֹב הוֹלֵךְ לְדוֹדִי לְמֵישָׁרִים; דּוֹבֵב, שִׂפְתֵי יְשֵׁנִים.

And [let the words of] your palate[102] be like good wine. [The words will] go forth for my Beloved in straightforward [love], causing the lips of the sleeping ones to speak.

10

---

100 The smell of Gan Eden is like the smell of an apple orchard. (See *Bereishis* 27:27 with Rashi.)

101 *Yoma* 86a.

102 The word "חִכֵּךְ," translated here simply as "palate," can also mean "your waiting" (לפדות מחכי קץ means "to redeem those who *wait* for redemption"). But how can waiting be like good wine? Generally, as things get older, they spoil. The exception is wine, which gets better and better with age. We are waiting for Hashem — waiting for the Redemption. Our waiting is like fine wine in the sense that the longer we wait for Hashem without losing our trust in Him and without ceasing to serve Him, the greater our reward will be (*Migdal Dovid*).

Allegorical Translation — Hashem continues to exhort *Klal Yisrael*: "Make sure that your response to the temptations of the nations is one that brings pride and joy."

Klal Yisrael reply to Hashem: "We will indeed speak in a way that displays our true love for You; and our words will even cause the Avos to rejoice and offer praise that they have such good descendants."

Subject of the Verse — There are two speakers in this verse. In the first part, Hashem continues his call (from the previous verse) to *Klal Yisrael* to live up to the praise He has heaped on them, and not let Him down. In the second part, *Klal Yisrael* promise to indeed give Hashem cause for pride.

Mashal — The husband urges his wife to make sure her response to the ones who try to seduce her proves her loyalty to him.

The wife replies that her words will always prove her love and adds that they will cause joy even to those who normally are lethargic and sleepy, much as wine does.

Nimshal — This is a continuation of Hashem urging the Jewish People to live up to His praises of them. Hashem exhorts *Klal Yisrael* not to let Him down. He tells them that when the nations test *Klal Yisrael*, pressing them to stop serving Hashem, their reply should be like good wine — a reply that brings joy both to Hashem and to people.[103]

That *Klal Yisrael*'s words should be like good wine hints at purity of speech. Although wine is a precious beverage, it can be unpalatable when not filtered due to sediment and other impurities. In this verse, we are urged to make our words like fine wine: pure and clean, without any blemished or dirty words mixed in.

In the second part of the verse, *Klal Yisrael* promise to speak and behave as befitting the nation of Hashem. They say: "[My words will] go forth for my Beloved in straightforward [love]." This means that their words will go forth in front of Hashem and honor Him because, as mentioned earlier, Hashem looks on with pride as we reject the overtures of the heathen nations. Furthermore,

---

103 In *Shoftim* (9:13), we learn that wine, *ki'veyachol*, brings joy to Hashem as well as to people. That is because wine is used for any number of mitzvos, such as the *nesachim* (pouring wine on the *mizbe'ach*). Therefore, Hashem tells us that our reply should be like good wine. When *Klal Yisrael* reject the influence of the heathen nations, and serve Hashem, it brings joy both to Hashem and to people since those who serve Him ultimately feel great joy.

our reply will demonstrate that our love comes straight from the heart. It is a straightforward and honest love without a hidden agenda.[104] Rashi renders *Klal Yisrael*'s reassurance to Hashem in these touching words: "I am careful to reply to the nations that I will stand steadfast in my faith, and thus my words go forth to my Beloved as a straightforward love directly from the heart, without deceit and trickery."

"Causing the lips of the sleeping ones to speak" means that when *Klal Yisrael* serve Hashem properly, their ancestors and forefathers rejoice. Even when they are lying in their graves [resembling sleeping], they sing and praise Hashem over their good fortune that they have such wonderful descendants. The conclusion of the verse is therefore to be understood as follows: "evoking [through our good behavior] speech [words of joy and praise] from the lips of the sleeping ones [the departed ancestors]."

This dramatic image of how much joy and delight our forefathers and ancestors feel when we do mitzvos should motivate us to be the kind of descendants that elicit their praise.[105]

LET YOUR PALATE BE LIKE GOOD WINE

As explained above, this means that the *words* of the palate should be pure, like good wine. But the explicit focus of the verse is the palate itself. This teaches us that not only our speech, but our mouth itself should be pure. As the Chafetz Chaim writes,[106] a person must realize that even *after* he utters negative words, his mouth remains blemished. He should not imagine that the words have left, and now his mouth has returned to being naturally clean and pure. On the contrary, bad words ruin the mouth such that even pure words of Torah and prayer that come afterward are ruined. The verse reminds us to keep our mouth clean and pure.

CAUSING THE LIPS OF THE SLEEPING ONES TO SPEAK

The Gemara[107] tells us that when words of Torah are repeated in the name of a righteous person who has passed away, his lips miraculously murmur them in the grave. This is derived from our verse: "…causing the lips of the sleeping [the dead] to speak." The

---

104 See earlier 1:4.
105 In his discussion of *kibbud av va'eim* (honoring parents), the Pele Yo'etz writes that observing mitzvos oneself is the very best way to honor one's parents because this brings them reward and honor in the World to Come!
106 *Shemiras HaLashon, Shaar HaZechirah*, ch. 7.
107 *Yevamos* 97a.

dead are described as only sleeping because they will "wake up" at the time of *techiyas hameisim* (the resurrection of the dead). What causes the dead to bring forth speech? *Chazal* tell us that this is through Torah repeated in their name. Indeed, our great leaders were careful to remind their students that their *divrei Torah* should be repeated in their name in order that they should merit this special murmuring.[108]

Here we see the awesome power of Torah. We know that a person is rewarded for all his righteous deeds, and any ripple effects which were caused by his acts of kindness or other mitzvos will increase his reward. The seeds of righteousness that a person plants in his lifetime yield great reward forever. But here we see that this concept goes even further. When we give voice to the deceased person's words of Torah, not only does this give him reward, but it causes him to speak. Why does Hashem make this miracle? The answer is that when a person learns Torah, Hashem gives him the ability to "acquire" it, *ki'veyachol*.[109] Not only do the words of Torah become his, but they become part of him. When the words of Torah which this person learned and taught are repeated, it is *his* words that are being repeated. *Part of him* is being stirred, and that is why his lips murmur. This teaches us the very deep and unique connection a person develops with the Torah that he learns.

AND [LET THE WORDS OF] YOUR PALATE…

The Toras Chessed sees this verse alluding to those who speak words of Torah to others to encourage them to serve Hashem and stay on the straight path. It adjures them to speak words that will cause people to be excited about serving Hashem, and thereby merit *techiyas hameisim*. According to this interpretation, the verse would read this way:

> "Let your admonishing words be like good wine [that stirs emotion and excitement thereby causing others to] go forth to my Beloved [in service] in a straightforward path [of righteousness], thus causing speech to the lips of the sleeping ones." (This last piece means that by serving Hashem, they will merit *techiyas hameisim* whereby they will ultimately awaken from their "sleep" and will once again be able to speak). Encouraging others to serve Hashem and reminding them of the great reward in store for them if they do, is the greatest act of kindness a person can perform.

---

108 *Yevamos*, ibid.

109 *Kiddushin* 32a, from the verse in *Tehillim*: "On [the words of] *his* Torah, he will meditate, day and night" (1:2).

> אֲנִי לְדוֹדִי, וְעָלַי תְּשׁוּקָתוֹ.
>
> I belong to my Beloved, and His desire is for me.
>
> **יא**
> **11**

Allegorical Translation — *Klal Yisrael* declare: "I belong to Hashem, and His desire is for me."

Subject of the Verse — *Klal Yisrael* is declaring their devotion.

Mashal — The wife lives up to her husband's praise. When she is enticed by those who wish to separate her from her husband, she declares loyally: "I belong to my beloved, and his desire is for me."

Nimshal — *Hashem* had exhorted *Klal Yisrael* in the previous verse to speak words that bring joy. In response, *Klal Yisrael* promised that their response to the enticement of the heathen nations will make Hashem and their own ancestors proud. Here we have their response: "I belong to Hashem, and His desire is for me!"

In this verse, *Klal Yisrael* declare their great devotion to Hashem: "I am faithful to Him, and His desire is for me." With this awesome declaration, they demonstrate how all the praise Hashem heaped upon them is well deserved (as explained in v. 9), and they bring tremendous joy and honor to their ancestors (as explained in the previous verse).

I BELONG TO MY BELOVED, AND HIS DESIRE IS FOR ME

Rabbeinu Bachaye presents a fascinating observation that relates to Hashem's desire for *Klal Yisrael*.[110] He points out that the word חשק (*cheshek*) — which does not have a precise English equivalent, but can be translated loosely as "absolute desire" — is never used to describe the Jewish People's relationship to Hashem, but only the other way around.[111] Hashem desires the Jewish People, but we are never commanded to desire Him. We are commanded to love Hashem,[112] to attach ourselves to Hashem,[113] but never to feel *cheshek*. Why not? Rabbeinu Bechaye answers that "*cheshek*" connotes a total and

---

110 *Devarim* 6:5.
111 See *Devarim* 7:7.
112 *Devarim* 6:5.
113 Ibid. 10:20.

constant craving and bonding with that which one desires. A human being is incapable of being in such a relationship with Hashem because he has to eat and sleep, which is impossible to do while he is consumed with desire. Therefore, he can only be commanded to love Hashem, but not to feel this complete desire. When a very righteous person dies, we are taught that the death occurs through a "kiss" from Hashem.[114] Rabbeinu Bechaye explains that the kiss creates an intense desire to cleave to Hashem that is so powerful that the person's physical body is overcome and his soul leaves it to join Hashem.[115] But while a person is alive, he is unable to have this overwhelming bond with Hashem. Hashem, however, who is unlimited and unhindered by any physical constraints, is able to truly desire the Jewish People. Therefore, it is appropriate to describe His love for the Jewish People as *cheshek* (absolute desire).

We must marvel over the love that Hashem has for the Jewish People. It is so powerful that we human beings are unable to reciprocate it because, as Rabbeinu Bechaye explains, such a love would make us incapable of doing anything else. Yet this is the love that Hashem has for us all the time. This awareness should make us feel tremendous joy and gratitude to Hashem.

I BELONG TO MY BELOVED, AND HIS DESIRE IS FOR ME

This verse touches on another even deeper aspect of the love between Hashem and *Klal Yisrael*. Normally, when a person loves someone passionately, the love grows calmer when he is with that person because it is readily available and right in front of him. However, in this verse *Klal Yisrael* declare: I am with my Beloved, and (while I am with Him), His desire for me grows even stronger and more passionate.[116] Rabbi Elisha Galiko points out that this holds true in both directions: Not only does Hashem's desire for us increase, *ki'veyachol*, the more we are with Him, but the closer we get to Hashem, the more we realize His greatness, and the more we desire His closeness and love. Unlike other relationships where the desire diminishes the closer one gets, the love for Hashem grows stronger and stronger. The relationship between *Klal Yisrael* and Hashem has a spiraling effect: As *Klal Yisrael* is drawn closer to Hashem, they desire Him more, and as they desire Him more, He wishes to bring them closer to Him. This is the deeper meaning of our verse: Because I am close to my Beloved, my desire for His

---

114 *Bava Basra* 17a.

115 This is why all of the Jewish people died when they heard the voice of Hashem at Har Sinai and needed to be revived (*Shabbos* 88b). The voice of Hashem was so appealing that their souls left them. This gives us some small idea of just how exciting *Ma'amad Har Sinai* was (see further, 7:2).

116 *Toras Chessed*. It should be noted that this rendering of the verse differs slightly from our translation given above (which is based on Rashi).

love grows even stronger and more passionate — and vice versa.

I BELONG TO MY BELOVED, AND HIS DESIRE IS FOR ME

The Hebrew word for "I," *ani*, also connotes importance, as in Pharaoh's declaration, "*Ani Pharaoh* — I am Pharaoh!"[117] In the context of our verse, "*ani*" means the essence of who I am, and what makes me truly "me." *Klal Yisrael* is thus proclaiming: I am important only because I belong to Hashem… "and [because of this acknowledgement,] His desire is for me." Some people derive their feeling of importance from their job, some from their financial success, some from their family, etc., but the true importance one can acquire is through our relationship with Hashem. Indeed, this is one of the main messages of *Shir HaShirim*: Our greatness and our pride stem from Hashem's love for us. When we feel this and declare this to be the sole definition of who we are, we find favor in the eyes of Hashem.

The Torah Temimah takes a similar approach in citing the passage in the Gemara[118] where Hashem says: I so much desire the Jewish People because when they attain importance, they subjugate themselves to Me, humbling themselves and not taking credit for their own greatness. Rather, they proclaim that all their success belongs to Me. In contrast, whenever the heathen nations attain greatness, they immediately become arrogant and boastful, claiming that their own power and success brought them this.

The Gemara[119] then provides a long list of examples of their arrogance, such as Sancheirev, who declared, "No God can stop me,"[120] and Chiram, who proclaimed, "I dwell among the gods."[121] In contrast, the humble Jewish People become even more humble when they achieve greatness, as we see from the words of our Patriarchs and forefathers. Avraham Avinu, the first Patriarch of *Klal Yisrael* and prince of the world,[122] described himself as "dust and ashes."[123] Moshe Rabbeinu and Aharon HaKohen declared, "What importance do we have?!"[124]

In light of the above, *Klal Yisrael*'s declaration in this verse can be paraphrased this way: "I [my success] belongs to my Beloved, Hashem; and [because *Klal Yisrael* proclaim this,] His desire is for me."

---

117 *Bereishis* 41:44 and *Midrash Rabbah* there.
118 *Chullin* 89a.
119 Ibid.
120 *Melachim II* 18:5.
121 *Yechezkel* 28:2.
122 Rashi on *Bereishis* 14:17, *s.v. eimek hamelech*.
123 *Bereishis* 18:27.
124 *Shemos* 16:7.

לְכָה דוֹדִי נֵצֵא הַשָּׂדֶה, נָלִינָה בַּכְּפָרִים.

יב

12 Come,[125] my Beloved, let us go out to the fields; let us stay the night in the villages.

נַשְׁכִּימָה לַכְּרָמִים, נִרְאֶה אִם פָּרְחָה הַגֶּפֶן פִּתַּח הַסְּמָדַר, הֵנֵצוּ הָרִמּוֹנִים; שָׁם אֶתֵּן אֶת דֹּדַי לָךְ.

יג

13 Let us arise early [to go] to the vineyards, and see if the vine has blossomed, if the young grapes have begun to appear, and if the pomegranates are in bloom. There I shall show You my love.

הַדּוּדָאִים נָתְנוּ רֵיחַ, וְעַל פְּתָחֵינוּ כָּל מְגָדִים; חֲדָשִׁים גַּם יְשָׁנִים, דּוֹדִי צָפַנְתִּי לָךְ.

יד

14 The baskets [of figs][126] have produced a fragrance, and on our doorsteps are all [kinds of] sweet delicacies, both new and old. I put them aside for You, My Beloved.

Allegorical Translation

12 *Klal Yisrael* ask Hashem: "Come out with me to see the hard-working people in the fields and villages who serve You despite their poverty; and compare them to the wicked people who have so much wealth, yet rebel against You."

13 Come and see those who frequent shuls and places of learning, and meet those who have just started learning, and thus only understand Chumash. View with love how others have already grown and are already learning Mishnah and admire those who have matured and learn Gemara.

14 There I will proudly show You my descendants who, through their behavior,

---

125 The word "לכה" is usually translated as "go." But it can also be an expression of encouragement to arouse oneself to come (see Metzudas Tzion and Radak on *Bereishis* 19:31).

126 The word "דודאים" is translated by Rashi as "baskets" (or "pans") filled with figs. We have followed this rendering throughout the *mashal* and the *nimshal* here. It should be noted, however, that the Midrash and many other *meforashim* explain that דודאים are a kind of flower, the same type that Reuven plucked for his mother, Leah, who gave them to Rachel on condition that she allow Yaakov to spend the night with her (as described in *Bereishis* 30:14-16). Yissachar was conceived that night, and a great many *talmidei chachamim* were descended from Yissachar (Rashi on *Devarim* 33:18, s.v. *ve'Yissachar*). Since the previous verse describes the greatness of *talmidei chachamim* (as will be explained), here we praise those דודאים that brought about the birth of so many worthy Torah scholars. Its fragrance spreads throughout the world through the *talmidei chachamim* who learn and teach Torah around the world (*Avodas HaGeirshuni*).

demonstrate our greatness. Both those who are good and those who are bad seek Your Presence and are full of merits which can be seen immediately upon arriving at their gateway. I have stored in my heart for You, my Beloved, both the new mitzvos (i.e., newly ordained Rabbinical decrees) as well as the original mitzvos of the Torah."

Subject of the Verses — These three verses depict *Klal Yisrael* speaking to Hashem at a time of exile. They are asking Hashem to rejuvenate the relationship between them and to help them find favor in His eyes.

Mashal — Continuing the basic *mashal* of *Shir HaShirim* about a husband and his beloved wife, these three verses contain the wife's request to her husband at a time when their relationship is strained. The young woman declared her loyalty in the previous verse, but she wants more: she wants their relationship to be optimal. She therefore asks her husband to try to rebuild their relationship, and she spells out how it should be done:

12 Come, my beloved husband, let us go "out of town," and stay out in the fields. Let us stay the night in the beautiful, tranquil holiday villages.

13 We will arise early to go to the soothing vineyards, and enjoy seeing the blossoming vines, the beautiful young grapes which have begun to appear, and the blooming pomegranates. There, in such a pleasant and tranquil setting, I will be able to truly display my love to you.

14 We will enjoy the fragrance of the figs and all kinds of sweet delicacies at our door (i.e., Immediately upon stepping through the door, you will find it pleasant). My beloved husband, new gifts [that I have never given you before] and old ones [that I have given you in the past], I have saved to show you and make you happy.[127]

Nimshal — Each of the metaphors and symbols in these verses will be explained individually

---

[127] It should be noted that, as a rule, it is healthy for husband and wife to make time to go out and be with each other in a new and pleasant setting, thereby refreshing their relationship. But there is more to it than that. Sometimes, when a relationship has been severely challenged, breaking the everyday routine, making an effort to exchange gifts, finding new ways to display love, and going to a different setting can reignite the spouses' love for one another. This is especially true if the new location helps bring out the spouses' merits, as in the *mashal* here. The essence of the *mashal* is that the wife asks her husband to go out of their daily routine so that under the influence of the beauty of nature, she can really show him her love which was hidden when they were in the busy and harsh city. She then mentions appealing delicacies that she has saved for him, with the aim of increasing his love for her.

Rashi (on *Mishlei* 1:6) informs us that when a great person tells a *mashal*, we can learn not only from the *nimshal*, but also from the *mashal* itself, as here.

in the following pages,[128] but it is helpful to first understand the essence of these verses.

After *Klal Yisrael* declare their loyalty in the previous verse, and reject the heathen nations attempt to pull them away from Hashem in their long and bitter exile, they seek a way to cause Hashem to want to redeem them. As in the *mashal*, *Klal Yisrael* ask Hashem to find a way, *ki'veyachol*, to see them favorably, to love them even more, and to choose surroundings which will be conducive to reignite His love for them. These verses are a continuation of the verses in which *Klal Yisrael* is in exile. Although they hear the praises of Hashem, they have not yet been redeemed. They therefore look to find favor in Hashem's eyes by urging Him to see what is good about them and recall why He loved them so much in the past so that He will wish to redeem them.

"Come, my Beloved, let us go out to the fields" is a plea to Hashem, whom we love, to come with us and see firsthand that which we wish to show Him. "The fields" represents poverty. In contrast to the city, where there were many opportunities for business, the fields offered little financial opportunity, and people tended to struggle and be poor. Since, during the exile, Jewish scholars are typically poor, this "metaphor within a metaphor" is about going to see the Torah scholars who are committed to their learning even while they are suffering from poverty. They struggle financially like those who work in the field.

"Let us stay the night in the *kefarim* [villages]." The word "*kefarim*" in this verse hints at the word "*kofrim*" (disbelievers).[129] In stark contrast to the Torah scholars, they are blessed with abundance, as those living in the villages were generally wealthier. "Despite their affluence, they do not serve You." In a broader sense, *Klal Yisrael* want to contrast the conduct of the righteous, who serve Hashem despite their poverty, with the conduct of the wicked, who do not serve Hashem despite their wealth.

"Let us stay the *night*..." By asking Hashem to observe the wicked at night, *Klal Yisrael* is also hinting that for the heretics and the wicked, it is constantly night.[130] There are three reasons for this. Firstly, night is a time when one sleeps, and the wicked are always "sleeping" in the sense that they never exert themselves to serve Hashem properly. Second of all, night is a time when one cannot see properly, and the wicked are always "walking in the dark," in the sense that they do not see the truth. They are blind

---

128 Based on *Eruvin* 21b, where these verses are addressed at length.
129 Depending on the vowels the word "*kefarim*" can mean either "villages" or "disbelievers" (*kofrim*).
130 As we will see shortly, day is associated with the righteous.

to Hashem's existence and His awesome power, and they are blind in the sense that they are unable to distinguish between good and bad. Finally, night is symbolic of gloom and doom, and the wicked are generally unhappy and gloomy.

"Let us arise early [to go] to the vineyards." The vineyards represent places of learning since the Torah scholars based there sit in rows like the vines in a vineyard.[131] "Arise early" hints at the fact that for the righteous, it is always "day." Daytime is a time for working. The righteous are constantly exerting themselves to serve Hashem. Furthermore, for the righteous, there is bright daylight because they have the light of Hashem leading them. They do not fumble in darkness and are able to see the truth clearly. Finally, day is associated with the righteous because they are filled with light and joy.

"Arise early" alludes to the righteous also because they get up early to serve Hashem. Unlike the wicked, they do not fritter away their day. The study halls that they frequent fill up very early in the day with dedicated Torah scholars. By asking Hashem to, *ki'veyachol*, "arise early to see," we are proudly telling Him that from early in the day, He would find the places of learning filled with *talmidei chachamim*.

"See if the vine has blossomed... if the young grapes have begun to appear... if the pomegranates are in bloom." These three metaphors allude to progressively higher (and more advanced) levels of Torah learning: Chumash, Mishnah and Gemara.[132] Thus, *Klal Yisrael* is saying that they wish to display to Hashem their entire array of Torah students and scholars. The different stages of developing and blooming are metaphors for different levels of progressing in Torah. First of all, there are those who have just started out, and are thus learning Chumash. They are likened to the vines that have not yet produced anything edible — just a flower. In a loosely similar sense, those learning only Chumash cannot teach any laws.[133] Then *Klal Yisrael* want to show those who are already learning Mishnah. They are likened to young grapes because they are almost able to provide food, i.e., teach laws. Finally, they want to highlight those who are learning Gemara. These scholars are likened to ripened pomegranates, providing food that can be eaten. Let us note parenthetically that by likening fledgling scholars to budding plants, the verse is reminding us that they are not like other flawed items that will always

---

131 *Eiduyos* 2:4. See earlier 6:11.
132 Rashi.
133 Vilna Gaon.
  In this context, "learning Chumash, Mishnah, etc." refers not to the material being learned, but to levels of learning. "Learning Chumash" represents those who have learned and absorbed wisdom but have not yet learned the underlying reasons and explanations. In contrast, those who "learn Mishnah" understand the reasons behind the learning. And those who "learn Gemara" are able to apply the wisdom they have learned to new and unfamiliar cases and situations. (Rashi on *Berachos* 5a and *Sotah* 44a, *s.v.* Gemara)

be lacking. Even though they have not yet reached a high level, these Torah scholars are on the way there. Given time, they will develop, mature, and eventually ripen.[134]

"There I shall show my love to You" means that by displaying these wonderful, budding righteous young men, I am showing my honor and my good attributes[135] and hope You will enjoy seeing my display of love for You.[136]

"The baskets of figs have produced a fragrance." Figs are a sweet and nourishing food, but they also spoil easily.[137] Figs therefore represent both the righteous (sweet) and the sinful (spoiled) Jews.[138] (Unlike the *kofrim* mentioned earlier, these sinners are part of the Jewish People and actually aspire to become righteous. They are therefore included in the praises of *Klal Yisrael*.) Because figs spoil easily, a large basket of sweet figs (i.e., the righteous) will always contain some bad figs as well. The verse thus alludes to the mixture of the righteous and the wicked. By likening sinful Jewish people to spoiled figs, the verse is emphasizing that they are not intrinsically bad, like thorns,[139] or poisonous, like hemlock. On the contrary, they are good fruit which has gotten spoiled because it has not been looked after and stored properly. Similarly, the wicked among *Klal Yisrael* are not inherently evil, but they have not been taken proper care of and have therefore spoiled. The basket alludes to the Jewish community that contains some good and some spoiled Jews. They all still give off a pleasant "fragrance" because even the sinful have good deeds, and they all seek the Presence of Hashem.[140] Furthermore, from the whole "basket" comes a wonderful "fragrance," i.e., the many wonderful accomplishments which the community as a whole achieve.

"On our doorsteps are all [kinds of] sweet delicacies." "The doorstep" symbolizes

---

134 The Gemara (*Ta'anis* 4a) uses the symbol of a sapling to describe a Torah scholar. It comments that just as we know that when a small plant sprouts, it will continue to grow, so too with a Torah scholar. This is a beautiful image. Instead of seeing a budding Torah scholar as someone who is insufficiently knowledgeable or deficient, we see him as a small plant. Given time and nurturing, a sapling will grow to be huge tree. All the potential is already there. Similarly, once a person dedicates himself to Torah, even if he is now only a small sapling, all the potential is there to enable him to grow to be a great Torah scholar.

135 Rashi.

136 We see that a basic way to show our love for Hashem is by showing Him how our young serve Him. If a person does not dedicate himself to the *chinuch* (education) of the young, he is showing a lack of love for Hashem. As the Chafetz Chaim point out, when Hashem speaks of His special love for Avraham, He says: "...because I know that he instructs his children and his household after him to follow the way of Hashem..." (*Bereishis* 18:19). Out of all the great deeds Avraham performed, nothing made him beloved to Hashem as much as his dedication to ensuring that his children served Hashem. There is no greater way to show love for Hashem than making sure that one's future generations serve Him (*Chafetz Chaim al HaTorah*). When a person loves a cause, he not only dedicates himself to it, but also encourages his children to do so as well.

137 As the Gemara notes in *Bava Metzia* 21b.

138 Based on the Midrash here.

139 To which the wicked nations were compared earlier (2:2).

140 Rashi. See earlier 4:3.

our readiness and willingness — just as something placed at the entranceway is readily available, and just as guests will be greeted warmly by their host at the doorstep and will not have to wait for a welcome until they reach the living room. "The doorstep" thus symbolizes enthusiasm as well. Our enthusiasm is to do many mitzvos, represented by the sweet delicacies on the doorstep. There is nothing sweeter than Torah and mitzvos.[141]

"Both new and old, I put away for You, My Beloved." Not only do we observe the original ("old") mitzvos that Hashem gave us, but we have taken upon ourselves ("new") Rabbinical mitzvos and prohibitions as well. Through Rabbinic law, powered by the desire to stay away from evil and do more than the barest minimum, *Klal Yisrael* has generated many new mitzvos. This, too, shows their greatness. A worker generally does only what he is told and no more. A loving son, however, deduces from his father's few requests what his father truly desires and then takes it upon himself to do more than what his father asked. A loving son is constantly innovating new ways to please his father. Similarly, the "new" alludes to our ongoing efforts to innovate ways to please Hashem. Very often, the extra effort that a person makes — one that he is not obligated to — prove that everything he is doing is out of true love. When we do more than what Hashem tells us, we show our true love for Him. This is very precious to Hashem.[142]

"I put them aside (i.e., stored and treasured them) for You." *Klal Yisrael* has been storing Torah and mitzvos in their mind and heart so as not to forget them. The memory of *Klal Yisrael* is vast, storing millions upon millions of Torah ideas, knowledge and laws.[143] Furthermore, the word "צפנתי" (translated here as, "I put aside") can also mean,

---

141 *Tehillim* 19:11.

142 *Mesillas Yesharim*, Chaps. 18 and 19.
The concept of doing even more than required by Rabbinical decree is a major subject in its own right and is beyond the scope of this *sefer*. But I would like to take this opportunity to offer a few observations. Although such conduct is highly commendable and is the basis of *chassidus*, one must be careful with it since one can easily cause more harm than good (as *Mesillas Yesharim* discusses (ch. 20). The Emes L'Yaakov (end of *Nezikin*) offers a *mashal* which sheds light on this potential pitfall. A father asks his son to bring him a drink of water. The loving son realizes that his father would prefer a coffee but does not wish to trouble him and therefore asks only for water. Wishing to be especially helpful and show his love, the son gets coffee. But if by getting the preferred drink, he keeps his thirsty father waiting a long time, he has actually caused his father discomfort. To get it right, the son must have a very clear understanding of what the father truly wants. This is a simple illustration, but there can obviously be much more complicated scenarios. Similarly, in *avodas Hashem*, one has to be very clear about what Hashem really wants before attempting to do more. There is another facet to taking on "new" mitzvos: a person must constantly look for new ways to serve Hashem in accordance with his own circumstances and nature. The Magen Avos writes that if, for example, a person gets angry after eating certain foods, he has a mitzvah to avoid them. If a person knows that going to a certain place may cause him to look at things he should not, he has a mitzvah to avoid going there. *Klal Yisrael* is praised for the "new" because an essential part of being a Jew is cultivating a constant freshness and renewal in our service of Hashem.

143 Despite the many expulsions, massacres, book-burnings, and never-ending persecution of the Jewish people over thousands of years, *Klal Yisrael* has retained such vast amounts of Torah knowledge there is almost no area in the Torah about which tens and even hundreds of *sefarim* have not been written. If we think about this a bit, we will begin to appreciate the praise inherent in this verse.

"I hid away."[144] This alludes to the fact that *Klal Yisrael* hide their mitzvos and acts of righteousness from public eye, preferring to do them in private. This shows that they do them only for Hashem, and not for glory, as the verse concludes, "For You." *Klal Yisrael* observe the mitzvos *only* for the sake of Hashem.

In light of the above, these three verses should be understood as follows:

12 (*Klal Yisrael* say to Hashem): Come, my Beloved, let us go out together — to reconnect with one another — to the places of poverty, and see the dedication of those poor people learning Torah. And then let us contrast them with the wicked, and observe the laziness, blindness, and gloominess of those who reject You.

13 We will then observe the greatness of righteous Jews, seeing the alacrity with which they serve You and follow Your guiding light with great happiness. We will go to the places of Torah learning and humility and see the young who learn Chumash, the young who learn Mishnah, and the young who learn Gemara. There I shall show my love to You by displaying how my youth all serve You due to the way I raised them.

14 I will also show You, Hashem, the mixture of my community, some good and some bad, but all wishing to serve You. I am ready, waiting, and available to "give" You the mitzvos I fulfill, both those You commanded a long time ago as well as those the Rabbis instituted more recently. My Beloved, I treasured them in the privacy of my heart for You.

LET US GO OUT TO THE FIELDS; LET US STAY THE NIGHT IN THE VILLAGES...

As explained above (in the *Nimshal* section), *Klal Yisrael* ask that Hashem should compare them with the other nations, that He should notice the difference between the dedicated *talmidei chachamim* who serve Hashem despite their poverty and the wicked who ignore Hashem even though they are wealthy. Besides being a prayer to Hashem, this verse is also a reminder to us about how to view *Klal Yisrael*. If a person should, God forbid, feel a certain lack of appreciation for the greatness of *Klal Yisrael*, he can restore his appreciation by comparing and contrasting them to the other nations. Compared to them, *Klal Yisrael*'s greatness shines like a beacon. We, *Klal Yisrael*, invest our money in the education of our children while they waste it on frivolities. We greet the new year with prayer, repentance, and charity, while they usher in their new year with drinking parties, etc. The qualitative difference between our life and their lives is so great that, by comparison, we are very righteous. We must remember this and always

---

144 From the root of the word "צפן," meaning "hidden" (as on Seder Night, eating the hidden *afikoman* is referred to as "צפון").

judge the Jewish People favorably.

I PUT THEM ASIDE FOR YOU

As the Midrash tells us, Hashem responds to *Klal Yisrael*'s statement that they have stored mitzvos for Him by saying: "You have filled your storehouses with righteous deeds; I have filled My storehouses with reward and treasures for you." The Midrash continues that Hashem's storehouses are far, far greater and superior to our storehouses, but since we do what we can for Him, He does the maximum for us. When we try our best to observe the mitzvos and "store" them so as not to forget them, Hashem stores and safeguards our rewards. Of course, His rewards are infinitely greater than our efforts. Yet, in His kindness, He rewards our efforts in this wonderfully disproportionate manner. We should be full of excitement knowing that Hashem's reward for every single mitzvah will be so great — much, much more than we can possibly grasp or even imagine.

The Gemara[145] says that if a person gives his full handful of food to the poor, Hashem responds by giving the person His full handful of payment as a reward. Now, how great is Hashem's "handful"?! The Gemara tells us that we can calculate this from the fact He measured all of the heavens with His Hand, *ki'veyachol*. Who can possibly handle such vast amounts of reward? The Gemara explains that Hashem will provide special miraculous capabilities to take in this reward. If we meditate on this remarkable passage, we can develop overwhelming excitement about serving Hashem.

I PUT THEM ASIDE FOR YOU

As mentioned above, the word "*tzafanti*" here in verse 14, translated as "I put aside" or "I stored", can also mean "I hid." The Midrash explains that *Klal Yisrael* "hide" their mitzvos. The verse continues "for You," meaning that when a mitzvah is done in private, this shows that it is being done for the sake of Hashem, and not to gain honor and praise from others. There is great value in hiding one's mitzvos.[146] *Sefer Shiras Dovid* quotes the Rambam's statement that to get the complete reward, one must do a mitzvah only for Hashem's sake.[147] The Rambam explains that Hashem commanded many different mitzvos so that during a person's lifetime, he will have many different opportunities to do a mitzvah. This way, he will surely perform one of them privately, correctly, and with the right intentions and will thus be properly rewarded.

Let us underscore the connection between the two Midrashim that we are discussing:

---

145 *Sanhedrin* 100a.

146 See our commentary on 7:2.

147 *Peirush al HaMishnah, Makkos*, end of ch. 3.

the one that describes the great reward given for the mitzvos and the one that teaches us to hide our mitzvos.[148] Hiding the mitzvos, as *Klal Yisrael* do, shows that they are doing them purely for Hashem's sake. It is for such mitzvos that Hashem stores away great reward for *Klal Yisrael* since such a reward is given only for mitzvos done for the sake of Hashem.

The humility implicit in hiding one's mitzvos actually connects with the metaphor of going out into the vineyards as going to see the righteous (in the previous verse, v. 13). The Midrash comments that just as the branches of a heavily laden vine tend to stoop lower, so a righteous person laden with good deeds and wisdom stoops lower, i.e., is more humble. By the same token, those who hold their heads up high often do so out of arrogance, not because they have more than others, but just as lighter branches tend to be found higher off the ground because they carry less fruit. This is a beautiful symbol. The more precious the vine's load, the more it is bent and humbled. And Moshe Rabbeinu, the greatest leader and teacher of Torah, was the most humble person in all of *Klal Yisrael*.

True stories abound about the tremendous humility of our righteous leaders. Rabbi Yitzchak Zilberstein[149] retells the following story from Rabbi Zvi Hirsh Palei:

When Rabbi Shalom Schwadron published *Lev Eliyahu*, a collection of Rabbi Eliyahu Lopian's *mussar* teachings, Rabbi Palei was surprised to see his own name listed as one of the editors of this wonderful *sefer*. He found out that Rabbi Schwadron had not felt worthy of taking full credit for compiling and editing his rebbe's teachings. Therefore, shortly before publishing, he sent a number of paragraphs for review to several rabbis. He then went ahead and added their names, as if they had participated equally in the editing. Even though he actually put out the *sefer* himself, he added other names! Let us recall how much effort it takes to put out a *sefer* and how much Rabbi Schwadron had sacrificed to make sure everything came out correctly. Very often, a person is inclined to take full credit for things which he only had a hand in. Here, Rabbi Schwadron gave away credit to others for effort that he himself had invested. What an amazing expression of humility!

---

148 Both are from *Shir HaShirim Rabbah*.
149 In *Aleinu L'Shabeiach, Bamidbar, Parashas Beha'aloscha*.

פרק ח'
CHAPTER 8

INTRODUCTION TO CHAPTER EIGHT

According to many *meforashim*, this final and climactic chapter of *Shir HaShirim* is about the end of the exile, the coming of Mashiach, and the final day of reckoning. This interpretation follows naturally from the fact that the whole of *Shir HaShirim* is about Hashem's love for *Klal Yisrael*. In those days, Hashem's love will become most noticeable and evident. Hashem will then bring us back to Him, and all the nations will appreciate how fortunate we are for being His nation. It is axiomatic that the conclusion of *Shir HaShirim* should describe the "final episodes" which demonstrate the love of Hashem for *Klal Yisrael*.

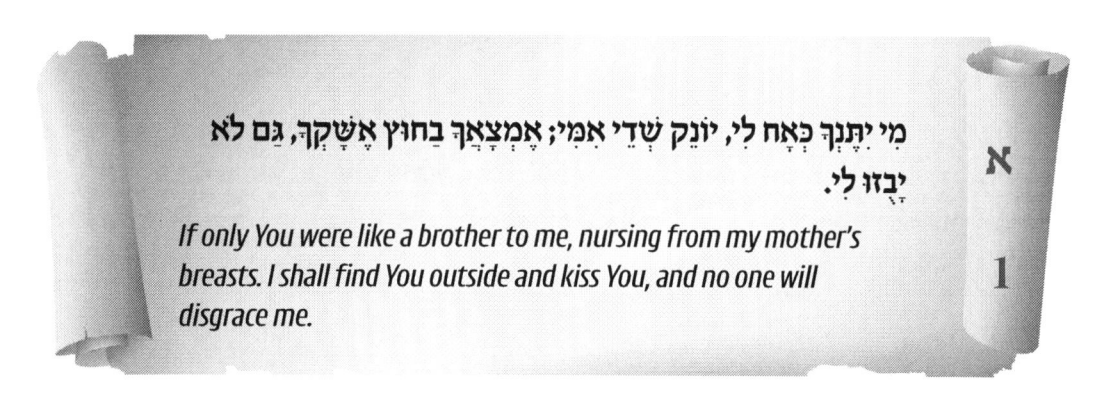

> מִי יִתֶּנְךָ כְּאָח לִי, יוֹנֵק שְׁדֵי אִמִּי; אֶמְצָאֲךָ בַחוּץ אֶשָׁקְךָ, גַּם לֹא יָבֻזוּ לִי.
>
> If only You were like a brother to me, nursing from my mother's breasts. I shall find You outside and kiss You, and no one will disgrace me.
>
> **א / 1**

Allegorical Translation

Klal Yisrael say to Hashem: "If only You will treat us as a brother treats his siblings — with mercy, forgiveness, and comfort — and bring us back to You! Then we will meet the prophets who speak in Your Name and will hug and kiss them publicly. The other nations will not disgrace us for behaving this way because they will understand that Your love is so precious that it is well worth seeking."

8:1 ETERNAL LOVE

Subject of the Verse — *Klal Yisrael* is begging Hashem for His love and beseeching Him to redeem them.

Mashal — In the *mashal*, the wife wants to be even closer to her husband. She says that she wishes their relationship could be like that of a sister and her little brother. Obviously, the relationship between husband and wife is far greater than the relationship between a sister and her younger brother. But there are several aspects of the sibling relationship that transcend that of a marital relationship. The wife is asking for these aspects to be part of their marriage as well. For example, one kisses a little brother in public without shame and interference. Similarly, the wife wishes nothing should stop them from displaying their love for each other. Furthermore, the relationship can never be terminated.

Nimshal — Up to this point, the megillah has generally described Hashem's love for the Jewish People as the love of a husband for his wife. Now, a new allegory is introduced to augment the description of this relationship: the love between a brother and a sister.[1] In this verse, the "dear one"[2] expresses her wish that the Beloved, i.e., Hashem, would be her baby brother who is still nursing from their mother. This way, she could kiss Him publicly. Even though a baby brother's love is not as strong as a spouse's love, it is much more innocent, and has the advantage of not being grounded in the physical. Therefore, one does not feel the shame one should feel in expressing marital love in public. It does not require privacy.[3] The Jewish People wants to be able to express their love for Hashem publicly and thus speaks of her love as the love of a sister for her little brother whom she can hug and kiss in public.[4] This is essentially a prayer that the relationship between Hashem and the Jewish People rise to a level where we are able to feel so confident in our relationship that we are not embarrassed about it at all, and that Hashem's love for us will be expressed in the most public way.

---

1 As discussed in the Introduction, *Shir HaShirim* uses a variety of analogies to describe our loving relationship with Hashem. Here we see an example of how the Megillah takes the best aspects of certain key relationships to augment the central parable of husband and wife.

2 As *Klal Yisrael* is called earlier in *Shir HaShirim*.

3 It is actually forbidden to show affection for one's wife in public (*Even Ha'ezer* 21:5, Rema).

4 The Midrash illustrates this with the account of a young boy living alone in a house in Miron that caught fire. His sister, who lived in the nearby town of Gush Chalav, came rushing over to see what happened. When she perceived that her younger brother was safe, she hugged, kissed, and embraced him all over. She commented that no one would disturb them because they understand how she felt. Similarly, we ask Hashem to save us from exile and embrace us with that level of intensity and purity.

Metzudas Dovid explains that this is also a prayer that the heathen nations will stop interfering with our way of life and allow us to serve Hashem without hindrance. Those who watch a couple kissing are violating their intimacy. (Incidentally, a couple should not kiss in public, nor should one watch a couple who are kissing in private. Justifiably, people view a couple who actually kiss in public as disgraceful.) But when a big sister kisses her younger brother, no one disturbs them, and there is no disgrace attached to it. We are therefore asking that our relationship with Hashem should not be disgraced or hindered by the other nations. Indeed, the Torah promises that when Mashiach comes, not only will the nations not scorn us,[5] but they will praise us and admire us for our devotion to Hashem: "All the people of the earth will see that Hashem's Name is upon you, and they will be afraid of you."[6]

Another unique facet of the sibling relationship is that it cannot be severed because both siblings share the same mother and father. Theirs is a blood relationship. This is emphasized here in our verse through the words "nursing from my mother's breasts." Because the foundation of this relationship is so deep, the bond can never be terminated — unlike in marriage, where a couple can get divorced. In this verse, we express a desire that our love of Hashem, which has the intensity of marriage, should also be indissoluble, like the bond between siblings.[7]

These three aspects in which a sibling relationship trumps a marital relationship — being indissoluble, publicly expressed, and unhindered — will all come to fruition when Mashiach comes. Once the Final Redemption arrives, Hashem will never send us away again. Even though it may seem that Hashem has rejected us in our present exile, this will never recur. Our relationship will be indissoluble, like a sibling relationship. Our relationship will be public and clearly evident (as we will explain in more detail later). Finally, the heathen nations will admire us for this relationship, and not show scorn for us as they do when we are in exile.

---

5 As they have done throughout the exile, as exemplified by the verse: "They [the heathen nations] mocked their [the Jewish People's] observance of the festivals" (*Tzror HaMor* citing *Eichah* 1:7).

6 *Tzror HaMor* citing *Devarim* 28:10.

7 The Netziv points out that a while a husband and wife must put a lot of nurturing and effort into their relationship, two siblings, even if they have not seen each other for years, can pick up quickly and easily because they are familiar with each other and have a very deep family bond. This verse then, conveys our desire that our relationship with Hashem should be readily available and that He should never be aloof or withdrawn even if we have not invested correctly in our relationship with Him.

Accordingly, this verse should be understood as follows: "If only You [Hashem] were like a brother to me, nursing from my mother's breasts [i.e., connected to me in a blood relationship that can never be severed]. I shall find you outside [i.e., our relationship can be displayed even in public] and kiss you, and no one would disgrace me [i.e., there would be no interference in our relationship]."

IF ONLY YOU WERE LIKE A BROTHER TO ME.

We ask that Hashem should be like the most wonderful of all brothers to us.[8] Just as when we liken *Klal Yisrael* to a flower, we invoke the rose, the most precious flower, and when we liken them to a plant, we invoke the vine, the most valuable plant, when we liken the relationship to that of siblings, we think of the best possible sibling. Thus, the verse is alluding to Yosef. The ultimate level of this bond of brotherhood was reached by Yosef. Yosef not only forgave his brothers for their sinful treatment of him, which included selling him into slavery, but even comforted them, was pleasant to them, looked after all their needs, and supported them for years.[9] He did all this even though he had been living apart from them for the previous twenty-two years. We ask Hashem to treat us like Yosef treated his brothers. Even though we sinned and caused His "home," the Beis HaMikdash, to be destroyed, we ask that He forgive us and comfort us, and take us out of this long exile. Even though we have been separated from Hashem for so long because of our sins, we ask that He be close to us.

The Midrash[10] describes how *Klal Yisrael*, when pleading with Hashem to forgive them, invoke the merit of Yosef. We ask Hashem to treat us in the same way that Yosef treated those who had wronged him terribly. We say to Him: "Even though we disobeyed all Your commands, please grant us forgiveness and show us kindness just as Yosef did [to his brothers]."[11] The Midrash is saying that not only do we invoke Yosef as an exemplar of the love we ask from Hashem, but we also call on his merit: "Since he was able to do this for his undeserving brothers, please do this for us as well!"[12]

According to *Midrash Tanchuma*, this verse is recalling the brotherhood shown by

---

8   Rashi.

9   *Bereishis* 47:12 and 50:21.

10 *Pesikta D'Rav Kahana*, ch. 29.

11 We would do well to contemplate Yosef's tremendous greatness in granting forgiveness to those who badly mistreated him. We should try to emulate this behavior and forgive all those who have hurt us.

12 Similar to the prayer said after reciting the Akeidah passage in the morning. We beseech Hashem: just as Avraham Avinu conquered his will in order to carry out Your will, please "conquer" Your anger (*ki'veyachol*) and forgive us.

Moshe and Aharon.¹³ Moshe cared so deeply for Aharon that he initially turned down Hashem's offer to go to Egypt to save *Klal Yisrael*. He hesitated for fear that Aharon, his older brother would be hurt. Similarly, Aharon loved Moshe so much that even though Moshe, the younger brother, became the nation's leader — thus taking the position away from him (as until then Ahron had been the leader) — Aharon was not jealous at all. Instead, he rejoiced at his younger brother's success. Indeed, when he first met Moshe in the desert after the latter was appointed leader, he kissed him.¹⁴ We pray that in the merit of their brotherhood and unity, Hashem should treat us kindly. And even though we are undeserving, and it is thus difficult, *ki'veyachol*, for Hashem to forgive us, He should be kind to us just as Aharon was kind to Moshe despite the difficulty involved.

I WILL FIND YOU OUTSIDE AND KISS YOU, AND NO ONE WILL DISGRACE ME.

The verse expresses our desire to be able to feel and express our love of Hashem even "outside" places of Torah learning and prayer. Even when we are not actively serving Hashem, we want our minds and focus to be directed to Him and want to be constantly ready to kiss Him.¹⁵

The Brisker Rav¹⁶ interprets the "kiss of Hashem" as prophecy. Usually, to receive prophecy, one needed to be in solitude following many demanding preparations.¹⁷ When Mashiach comes, however, prophecy will be so common and widespread that even outside in the marketplace one will be able to receive this "kiss of Hashem." This is foretold by the prophet Yoel: והיה אחרי כן אשפוך את רוחי על כל בשר ונבאו בניכם ובנותיכם זקניכם ... וגם על העבדים ועל השפחות בימים ההמה אשפוך את רוחי — "Then it will be that I will pour My Spirit on all flesh, and your sons your daughters and your elders will all prophesize ... Even on your servants and maidservants, I will pour My Spirit in those days."¹⁸ This vision of *Klal Yisrael* being so close to Hashem is both wonderful and amazing! We have no real appreciation of how special prophecy is.¹⁹ Even just understanding the greatness of what prophecy entails is beyond our grasp. Yet, when Mashiach comes we will all actually merit to become prophets.

The great tzaddik Rabbi Shmuel of Lubavitch, *zt"l*, used to quote this verse in

---

13　*Shemos* 27.
14　*Shemos* 4:27.
15　Seforno.
16　*Gryz al HaTorah*.
17　The Rambam enumerates the preparations and qualifications needed to be worthy of receiving prophecy (*Hilchos Yesodei HaTorah* 7:1-4).
18　*Yoel* 3:1-2.
19　The Rambam (ibid.) does describe some aspects of how special prophecy is.

exhorting his disciples to think holy thoughts even while they worked in business. He explained the verse this way: "I shall find You, Hashem, outside the *beis midrash* and *shul* and "kiss" You there by thinking about You."[20]

He was once challenged, "How do you expect us to be able to do this?"

He replied, "If people are able, without any effort, to think mundane thoughts while in the middle of praying, then why can't they think holy thoughts while working!"

The approach of the *Targum* is that this entire chapter alludes to the Final Redemption. The *Targum* translates and explains this verse as follows. (For ease of understanding, the translation of the words upon which the *Targum* is based have been put in bold print.) "At that time, the King Mashiach will reveal himself to *Klal Yisrael*. They will say to him: '**Be to us as a brother,** and we will go up to Yerushalayim and will suckle the wisdom of Torah like a **baby suckles from its mother**. While we, *Klal Yisrael*, were **outside** in exile, we would **find** and remember Hashem, and sacrifice ourselves for Him [i.e., be devoted to Him as if we were **kissing** Him], and the heathen nations **did not belittle us** [for our devotion]."

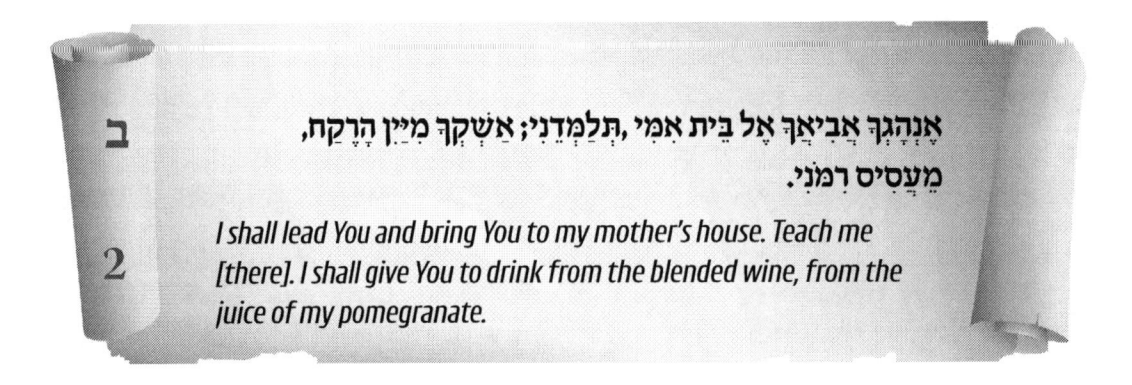

> ב אֶנְהָגְךָ אֲבִיאֲךָ אֶל בֵּית אִמִּי, תְּלַמְּדֵנִי; אַשְׁקְךָ מִיַּיִן הָרֶקַח, מֵעֲסִיס רִמֹּנִי.
>
> 2 I shall lead You and bring You to my mother's house. Teach me [there]. I shall give You to drink from the blended wine, from the juice of my pomegranate.

Allegorical Translation *Klal Yisrael* continue speaking: "By virtue of our good deeds, we will then lead You, Hashem, to the Beis HaMikdash.[21] There, You will teach us the Torah, and we will pour libations of wine for You on the *Mizbe'ach*. You will find them as sweet and as pleasing as pomegranate juice."[22]

Subject of the Verse *Klal Yisrael* is speaking to Hashem about the Final Redemption.

---

20 See our commentary on 1:2.

21 Hashem will ultimately save and lead *Klal Yisrael* out of exile. But because this will be in the merit of our good deeds, it is as if we are leading Him (*Divrei Yedidyah*; see our commentary on 1:9).

22 *Devash V'Chalav*, following Rashi. Since pomegranate juice is never poured on the *Mizbe'ach*, this must mean that it will be as sweet as pomegranate juice.

Mashal   Having expressed the wish that their relationship be similar (in a sense) to that of siblings, the wife goes on to ask that they go back to their "parents' house" to strengthen their relationship. When meeting in their parents' house, siblings usually feel closer to each other because that is where their first memories start. In other words, the wife is saying to her husband: "I would like to take you back to where our relationship began in order to rekindle those original good feelings. There you can teach me how to be kind to you." There she will please her beloved with tasty drinks.

Nimshal   Continuing to address Hashem, *Klal Yisrael* ask to go back to where their relationship with Him was first cemented. Following on from the metaphor of siblings used in the previous verse, they speak now of "the mother's house." Just as siblings can improve their relationship just by being in the place where they originally grew up together, *Klal Yisrael* ask Hashem to go with them to the place where their relationship took root in order to rekindle their love. The "mother's house" alludes either to the Beis HaMikdash[23] or Har Sinai.[24] Coming to the Beis HaMikdash or remembering the events of Har Sinai rekindle the love that we, *Klal Yisrael*, have for Hashem, and Hashem has for us, thus strengthening our relationship. Furthermore, those places are where we felt most loved and protected by Hashem.

In saying "Teach me [there]," *Klal Yisrael* express the hope that when they go back, Hashem will then teach them Torah and how to conduct themselves, reawakening in them a desire to serve Him.[25]

As earlier, "grapes" (here in the form or wine) allude to the righteous among the Jewish People,[26] while "pomegranates" allude to the wicked, who are nevertheless full of merits like a pomegranate is full of seeds.[27] When our commitment to Hashem is renewed, we will give Him to drink "blended wine and the juice of my pomegranate." This means that the entire nation — including the wicked — will do their utmost to produce and bring forth good deeds and merits that are pleasing to Hashem — just as pleasing wine and juice

---

23   Rashi. This metaphor is explained in our commentary on 3:4 at greater length.

24   Midrash.

25   The Brisker Rav notes that there will be a renewal of understanding the Torah when Mashiach comes. He explains this entire verse accordingly (*Gryz al HaTorah*).

26   See verse 7:8.

27   See verse 4:3.

are produced from grapes and pomegranates. When the Final Redemption comes, the entire Jewish People will do only deeds that are pleasing to Hashem.

The *Targum* understands that *Klal Yisrael* is addressing Mashiach, not Hashem: "I shall **lead you**, Mashiach,[28] **and bring you** to the Beis HaMikdash (symbolized by "**my mother's house**"). **Teach me there** how to fear Hashem and to follow His ways. There, we will eat from the meal of the *leviason*, **drink** from the old **wine** which Hashem preserved for the righteous from the time of Creation,[29] and eat from the **pomegranates** and other fruit prepared for the righteous in the Garden of Eden."

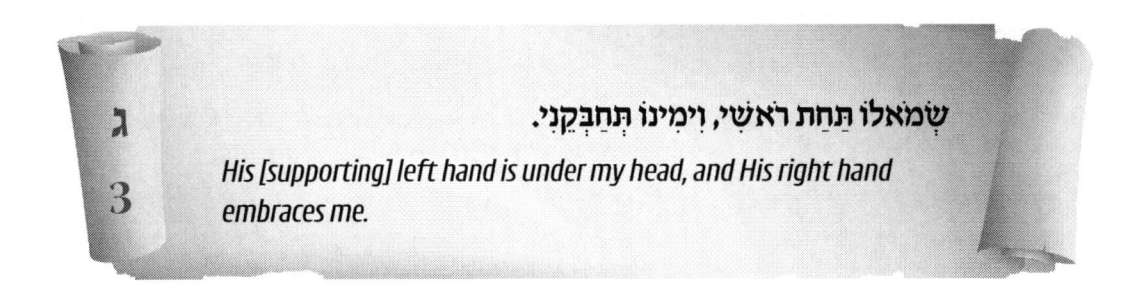

> ג
> 3
> שְׂמֹאלוֹ תַּחַת רֹאשִׁי, וִימִינוֹ תְּחַבְּקֵנִי.
>
> *His [supporting] left hand is under my head, and His right hand embraces me.*

Allegorical Translation — Hashem supports me and shows His love to me.

Subject of the Verse — *Klal Yisrael* is expressing how Hashem shows them His love and support.

Mashal — The wife describes how her husband is loving and supporting, embracing her and holding her up.

Nimshal — *Klal Yisrael* speak of how Hashem loves them and protects them.

HIS [SUPPORTING] LEFT HAND IS UNDER MY HEAD...

This verse is a repetition of a verse in Chapter Two. It describes the intense love and kindness that Hashem has shown for the Jewish People. Let us summarize what we explained there.[30] The two "hands" represent the two modes of conduct that Hashem uses in relating to us. The stronger and predominant "right hand" represents Hashem's

---

28 We know that Mashiach will lead us. If so, why does this verse speak of our leading him? Mashiach — the Redeemer — will call out to us that it the time of our redemption has arrived, but in our eagerness to go to the Beis HaMikdash, it will seem as if we are leading or pushing him to take us there.

29 This is one of the sources that tell us that already at the time of Creation, Hashem prepared a special meal of *leviason* and wine for the righteous to be served when Mashiach comes.

30 See our commentary on 2:6.

constant kindness and mercy. This is the principal way in which He relates to us. The weaker "left hand" represents His judging and punishing us when we sin. The kindness of Hashem is an embrace, making us feel loved. The right hand is thus said to be "embracing" us. The punishment of Hashem ensures that we do not stumble and fall into sin. Hence it is described in the verse as the hand that "[supports] our head."

The repetition of this verse here teaches us that whether in a time of redemption (as in the earlier verse) or in a time of exile (as here), Hashem always loves us, treats us with kindness, and protects us with the same vigor. The Vilna Gaon adds that the earlier verse describes the beginning of our people's relationship with Hashem at *yetzias Mitzrayim*, and this verse describes the culmination of the relationship when Mashiach comes. This teaches us that just as we experienced His love at the time of the Exodus, so too will we experience it again when Mashiach comes. There has never been an interruption or change in His love for *Klal Yisrael*. Our perspective can, perhaps, be likened to that of a person who managed to hear only the beginning and end of a speech. If he hears the same message both at the beginning and end, he knows what the speech was about. So, too, even if we do not understand every stage of Jewish history, since we saw His great love in the beginning and will see it again in the End of Days, we know it was always there.

According to the *Targum* which, as mentioned earlier, understands that this entire chapter is about the Final Redemption, *Klal Yisrael* is now saying: "We are the nation chosen from among all the others because we are the only ones to wear His tefillin on our **left** arm and on our **head,** and place the mezuzah on the **right**-hand side of the doors, a third of the way from the top. Thus, no one can come to harm us (because Hashem **supports** us and keeps us safe in His **embrace**)."

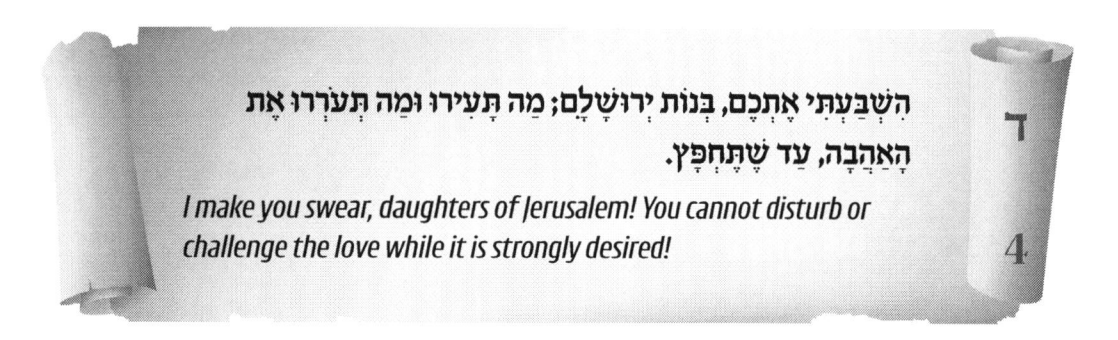

> הִשְׁבַּעְתִּי אֶתְכֶם, בְּנוֹת יְרוּשָׁלָ͏ִם; מַה תָּעִירוּ וּמַה תְּעֹרְרוּ אֶת הָאַהֲבָה, עַד שֶׁתֶּחְפָּץ.
>
> *I make you swear, daughters of Jerusalem! You cannot disturb or challenge the love while it is strongly desired!*
>
> ד 4

Allegorical Translation — We (*Klal Yisrael*) promise the heathen nations that their efforts to undermine our relationship with Hashem are for naught. They will never be able to undermine the love between us and Hashem since He still loves us.

Subject of the Verse — *Klal Yisrael* is telling the nations that they cannot weaken their relationship with Hashem.

Mashal — The wife tells her competitors that they will never be able to cause a rift between her and her husband since their relationship is very strong.

Nimshal — *Klal Yisrael* tell the heathen nations that even though they are suffering in the exile, it is not because Hashem has stopped loving them. Their relationship is still very strong, and Hashem is still supporting them.[31] Therefore, they will never be able to cause conflict between Hashem and *Klal Yisrael*.

I MAKE YOU SWEAR…

This verse, too, is almost an exact repetition of an earlier verse.[32] But there is one substantial difference. Here, we tell the nations that they cannot challenge or try to destroy our relationship with Hashem, but we do this without threatening them with dire consequences. Earlier, we said that if they even attempt it, they will be destroyed. Why the difference? The answer is that at the beginning of the relationship, we wanted to frighten them into not causing harm during the long exile because we feared that they might succeed. But since our relationship is now so well established, we are confident that they simply cannot cause harm. So, all we do now is inform them: Don't waste your time trying; you will get nowhere![33]

In a similar vein, the Vilna Gaon explains that during the exile, it may seem that Hashem has stopped loving us. We have to warn the nations sternly because they think they have a chance of supplanting us. But when the time of the Redemption comes, Hashem's love will be so continuously open and intense[34] that the nations will clearly see that they cannot spoil it. We will not need to warn them. We will simply be able to boast that our relationship is unshakable.

This verse is far more formidable because we do not say only that they will be punished for ruining our relationship. Rather, we assert that they are *unable* to ruin the

---

31 Rashi.

32 See verse 2:7 and commentary for an elucidation of this verse. This verse is actually repeated in different forms several times in *Shir HaShirim* because it reflects the intensity of the love between Hashem and *Klal Yisrael* (see also verse 3:5). The Midrash makes the following pithy comment about this verse: "Who would be foolish enough to get between a lion and a lioness at the time when they desire to mate together?" If a person would dare to intervene at this time, his fate would be sealed. The Midrash provides a vivid example of how intense the love between Hashem and *Klal Yisrael* is, and how foolish it would be to disturb it.

33 Rabbi Yosef Kimchi.

34 The Vilna Gaon quotes the words of the Prophet that Hashem will ultimately make a new promise of love to *Klal Yisrael*, a promise that will never be abrogated in any way (*Yirmeyahu* 31:30-21).

relationship. Describing something as being impossible is a far greater deterrent than saying it is doable but subject to punishment.³⁵

The *Targum*, which interprets this entire chapter as being about the Final Redemption, explains this verse as follows: "Mashiach will then make Klal Yisrael ["the daughters of Yerushalayim"] **promise not to start up** with the nations and **not to rebel** against Gog and Magog in order to break free from exile. Rather, he insists that they wait a short while until the nations who come to attack Yerushalayim are destroyed. Then Hashem will remember the **love** of their righteous people and will **desire** to redeem them."

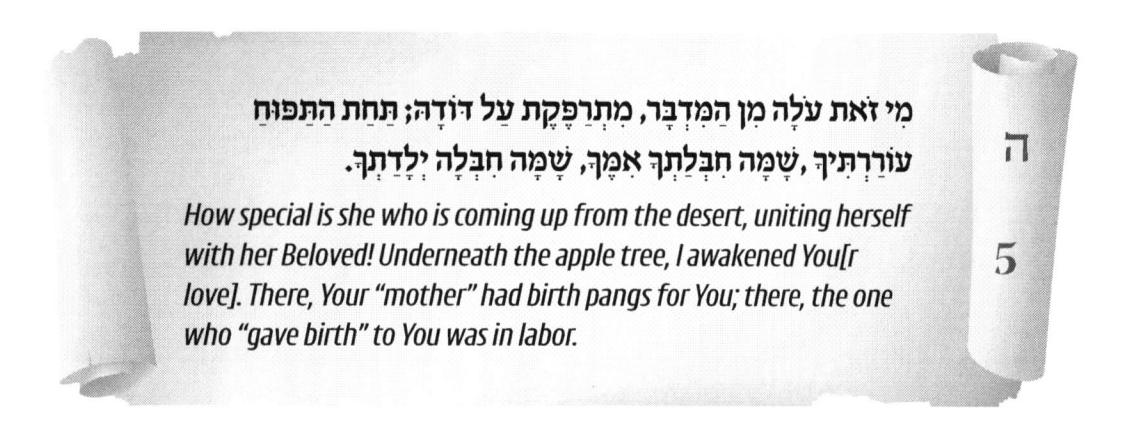

> מִי זֹאת עֹלָה מִן הַמִּדְבָּר, מִתְרַפֶּקֶת עַל דּוֹדָהּ; תַּחַת הַתַּפּוּחַ עוֹרַרְתִּיךָ, שָׁמָּה חִבְּלַתְךָ אִמֶּךָ, שָׁמָּה חִבְּלָה יְלָדַתְךָ׃
>
> How special is she who is coming up from the desert, uniting herself with her Beloved! Underneath the apple tree, I awakened You[r love]. There, Your "mother" had birth pangs for You; there, the one who "gave birth" to You was in labor.
>
> ה 5

Allegorical Translation — Hashem says to *Klal Yisrael*: "How important are you who became exalted in the *midbar*, bonding with your Beloved! And you [*Klal Yisrael*] say to Me: 'Remember how, at the foot of Har Sinai, we awakened Your love for us, and accepted Your mitzvos. There, we thus gave birth to Your Name [i.e., made Your Name known in this world].³⁶'"

Subject of the Verse — Hashem and the Heavenly Court of the angels praise *Klal Yisrael*, and *Klal Yisrael*, who is seeking Hashem's love, interjects and recalls their devotion.

Mashal — Praising his wife, the husband first exclaims about the wondrous sight of his beloved coming out of the difficult desert, yet still looking beautiful and devoted to him. All of her travails do not cause her to abandon her devotion. He then praises her for the wonderful way in which she aroused his love for her.

---

35   This is how we should view all sins. Stealing is not just forbidden, but it is impossible because that which one is not supposed to have, one cannot ultimately acquire. Thinking that punishment is the only consequence of a sin gives the mistaken impression that it is an option. The reality, however, is that going against the command of Hashem is impossible.

36   *Devash V'Chalav* in explanation of Rashi.

As Rashi notes, a devoted wife can awaken the love and interest of her sleeping husband by hugging and kissing him at night or under a beautiful tree.[37] There she "gave birth" to the love and the union and became almost like a mother to her husband in the sense she gave him a new lease on life.

Nimshal Hashem speaks in this verse, exclaiming about the greatness of *Klal Yisrael*.

In the first part of this verse, Hashem expresses His amazement, *ki'veyachol*, at the greatness of the Jewish People in coming out of the "desert" beautiful and united with Him, where others would have come out dirty and weakened. Not only did *Klal Yisrael* not come out weaker, but they actually developed and became a greater nation in the "desert" of exile. "How special is she who is coming up from the desert..." is an expression of surprise: "Who is this great nation that became uplifted in the desert!?" Hashem goes on to characterize *Klal Yisrael*'s relationship with Him as "uniting herself with her Beloved."[38]

In the second part of the verse, *Klal Yisrael* interjects: "Under the apple tree, I awakened You."[39] This alludes to the beginning of their relationship with Hashem in Mitzrayim and at Har Sinai, places where their love for Hashem was plainly evident. They do so in order to "remind" Hashem of their devotion and thereby reawaken His love for them.[40] The word "תפוח," translated here as "apple tree," also means "pile" or "mound/mountain."[41] Thus, *Klal Yisrael* is saying metaphorically that under the mountain of Har Sinai, they accepted the Torah, thereby awakening Hashem's love. The Midrash adds that just as an apple tree produces fruit in the month of Sivan, so too, *Klal Yisrael* accepted the Torah in the month of Sivan.

"There, Your 'mother' had birth pangs for You; there, the one who 'gave birth' to You was in labor." *Klal Yisrael* is referred to as the "mother" in this context

---

37   Rashi uses this kind of explicit language to create a vivid picture of awakening love, and thereby convey *Klal Yisrael*'s greatness in doing this for Hashem.

38   The word "מתרפקת," translated here as "uniting," implies more than just unity. It connotes loving closeness, cleaving to the beloved and enjoying his company. This is how *Klal Yisrael* has bonded with Hashem throughout history.

39   This verse begins with Hashem's praise, but suddenly changes to the words of *Klal Yisrael*. This is because *Klal Yisrael* wish to earn additional praise from Hashem. When He speaks of their greatness, they interject with an additional aspect of their devotion. Another approach to this verse is that Hashem is extolling *Klal Yisrael* throughout (see *Devash V'Chalav*). After describing their coming out of the desert and cleaving to Him, Hashem adds the kind of words would *Klal Yisrael* say. This is a new kind of praise, wherein one says about another that this is the kind of amazing thing that I would expect to hear from him.

40   Midrash. See our commentary on 2:3 regarding the significance of the apple tree.

41   See Rashi on *Bamidbar* 20:22 and *Mishnayos Avodah Zarah*, 4:3.

because they are as beloved, cared for, and precious in the eyes of Hashem as a person's mother.[42] Also, it is as if *Klal Yisrael*, *ki'veyachol*, "gave birth" to Hashem. By accepting Hashem's Torah and mitzvos, they, *ki'veyachol*, "empowered" Hashem. Like a devoted wife gives a new lease on life to her husband, we "gave" Hashem joy and energy by promising to be devoted to Him. Obviously, Hashem does not need *Klal Yisrael* or their mitzvos, but Hashem made it seem as if they gave Him power.[43] Furthermore, *Klal Yisrael* made His name known to the world and taught humanity that they must serve Hashem. They "gave birth" to the idea of serving Hashem. The verse, then, is to be understood this way: "There [at Har Sinai], Your "mother" [*Klal Yisrael*] had birth pangs for You [in the sense that they took upon themselves all the hardships of serving You]; there, she [*Klal Yisrael*] who gave birth to You was in labor." The repetition evident in this verse is often used in a song as an outpouring of emotion describing a momentous event. The repetition communicates the speaker's excitement.

HOW SPECIAL IS SHE WHO IS COMING UP FROM THE DESERT...

This is a repetition of an earlier verse where the nations say the very same thing.[44] It is an expression of wonder at the greatness of the Jewish People in coming out of the harsh desert both exalted and beautiful. As Rashi elaborates, "How distinguished is this nation that came out of the desert with all kinds of good gifts! There, she became exalted through *Matan Torah* and attachment to the Shechinah, and her love was revealed to all." According to this explanation, this verse conveys Hashem's praise of *Klal Yisrael*.

The Metzudas Dovid, however, understands that *Klal Yisrael* is speaking throughout, trying to elicit her Beloved's favor. She does so by praising herself and reminding Hashem that she was the only nation willing to follow Him faithfully into the desert, where she was united with Him in love by being the only nation to accept His Torah. According to this interpretation, the beginning of the verse reads thus: "Who [else besides us us] came through the desert [for You]?!" The continuation of the verse, "uniting

---

42 See earlier 3:11.

43 See earlier 1:9 and commentary, and *Nefesh HaChaim*, *shaar* 1.
    The *Sidduro Shel Shabbos* (*Drush* 8, 2:11) quotes the *Zohar* (*Bechukosai* 113a) on the words in *Vayikra* (26:3) "וַעֲשִׂיתֶם אֹתָם," meaning, "You shall fulfill them (i.e., mitzvos)." But the *Zohar*, relating to these words on a deeper level, explains them to mean, "You shall create 'Heavenly Power,'" as if the words were written ועשיתם אַתֶּם. The *Sidduro Shel Shabbos* asks: in light of the fact that nothing truly exists except Hashem, what does this mean? It answers that when one proclaims the name of Hashem and teaches the world to serve Him, it is as if one is "creating" the existence of Hashem because only through these efforts is Hashem known and served.

44 See verse 3:6 and our commentary there.

herself with her Beloved," follows beautifully. We followed Hashem because we wanted to cleave to, and unite with, our Beloved (Hashem.)

According to this approach, the reference is to the desert that *Klal Yisrael* went through upon coming out of Egypt, just as in the earlier appearance of this verse (3:6). The Brisker Rav, however, explains that the earlier verse is alluding to the wonder of the Jewish People coming out of the desert after forty years, during which time they became beautiful with Torah and the Mishkan (as explained earlier). This verse, however, refers to the times of Mashiach, when Hashem is going to take us out of the "desert" of exile.[45] As the prophets Yechezkel and Hoshea both prophesized that before the Final Redemption, Hashem will take the Jewish People through a "desert," whereupon He will judge them. Those who are found worthy will bond with Hashem and receive many types of blessing.[46] This metaphorical desert that Hashem takes us through symbolizes the dangers and challenges of exile where we are in the midst of hostile nations, unprotected and vulnerable like someone in a desert.[47] Before the Redemption finally comes, Hashem will lead *Klal Yisrael* through very challenging times in order to determine who really wants to get through and who is strong enough to survive. Then those who come out of the desert uplifted will merit to cleave to Hashem. This verse exclaims that *Klal Yisrael* will not just get through and survive but will flourish. As history testifies, the Jewish People has not succumbed to exile but has carried on with much beauty and with profound loyalty to Hashem. Indeed, our nation has so many accomplishments to be proud of even in exile.[48]

UNDER THE APPLE TREE, I AWAKENED YOU ...

Rashi explains that this alludes to *Klal Yisrael* lovingly accepting the Torah under Har Sinai. But how does this accord with the Gemara's teaching[49] that Hashem held the mountain of Sinai above *Klal Yisrael* and warned them of their imminent demise if they refuse the Torah? Seemingly, this was an act of coercion on Hashem's part and not an act of love on *Klal Yisrael*'s part!? The answer is that even before Hashem "forced" *Klal Yisrael*, they had already joyfully and eagerly promised to accept the Torah. The threat was intended only to underscore both the grave responsibility they had taken on, and also the importance of the Torah itself. They were being made to understand that once they have the Torah, they cannot survive without it. This can be likened to a person who volunteers to join the army and when he is inducted, he is told that from now on,

---

45 Quoted in *Haggadah MiBeis Brisk*.
46 *Yechezkel* 20:35; *Hoshea* 2:16.
47 Rashi and the Malbim, ibid.
48 This fact has been recognized even by non-Jewish scholars and historians.
49 *Shabbos* 88a.

disobedience or going AWOL could cost him dearly.

Here we see both the greatness of *Klal Yisrael* and their love for Hashem in willingly taking upon themselves the acceptance of Torah despite the responsibility and possible grave consequences that this entailed. *Klal Yisrael* was willing to bind themselves to a commitment that could cost them their lives. Our verse, then, justly praises *Klal Yisrael* for "awakening" Hashem's love through the acceptance of Torah.[50]

The Gemara interprets this verse as alluding to the righteousness of Jewish women in Mitzrayim.[51] During that bitter exile — and with the terrible decree that all newborn boys were to be drowned — many men gave up on trying to have a family and lost their desire for their wives. Their wives, whose trust in Hashem was greater than that of the men, never gave up. They went out into the fields, taking food and drink with them for their weary husbands. They would wash their husbands and reignite their husbands' desire until they wished to be with them.[52] When the time came, these righteous women gave birth in secret in the apple orchards to avoid getting caught by the Egyptians. Hashem sent angels to help these mothers and their new babies. Because the mothers feared being discovered, they had to leave their babies with the angels. The angels would feed them miraculously and take care of them. When the children were old enough, they rejoined their family. Having seen and experienced Hashem's protection, they later proclaimed (after the miracle of the Splitting of the Sea), "This is my God,"[53] meaning, "I recognize Him from when He saved me as a baby."

"Under the apple, tree I awakened my beloved" is, according to the Gemara, an allusion to these great women who gave birth under the apple tree. The Gemara understands the word "עוררתיך" to mean "stirring." There, they "stirred" the newborns in the sense that they brought them into life.[54] The continuation of the verse, "There, your mother had birth pangs for you; there, she who gave birth to you was in labor," alludes to how a nation was born "there" under the apple tree out in the open, exposed to the

---

50   See Tosafos, ibid., *s.v. kafa alieyhen*; Maharal, ibid.; Rashi on *Devarim* 33:3; *Devash V'Chalav* (here).

51   *Sotah* 11b. See also *Shemos Rabbah* 1 at greater length.

52   Among the techniques these righteous women used was the following: they would take out mirrors, and show themselves and their husbands in the mirrors, pointing out how beautiful they were. These mirrors were later donated to the Mishkan. As Rashi notes (*Shemos* 38:8), Moshe Rabbeinu was reluctant to use them since mirrors are used primarily for beauty and the *yetzer ha'ra*. Hashem told him that, on the contrary, these are the most precious items of all since they were used to strengthen marriages. Moshe thus took them and used them for the *Kiyor* (the washing vessel in the Mishkan and the Beis HaMikdash). A woman suspected of infidelity would have to drink from the *Kiyor*, which was made out of these mirrors, thus reminding her of the importance of her marriage.

53   *Shemos* 15:2.

54   Rashi, *Sotah* 11b, *s.v. orarticha*. This phrase also hints at how the women "awakened" their husbands' love in the fields, as explained above. When a husband and wife are together, the *Shechinah* is also there (*Sotah* 17a). Thus, the wives actually awakened Hashem's Presence under the apple tree.

elements. It is a further evocation of the greatness of these women. They were willing to give birth, itself a traumatic experience, in the worst of circumstances and under the harshest of conditions in their determination that the Jewish People survive and flourish.[55] The Gemara praises these women highly for this, and for their tremendous faith in Hashem's eventual salvation. Also, they showed great loyalty, love, and faithfulness to their husbands by making so much effort to keep their marriage alive. In short, this verse is a paean of praise for these righteous women. The Gemara tells us that salvation eventually came in the merit of these righteous women.

As we continue to learn about the loyalty between *Klal Yisrael* and Hashem here in *Shir HaShirim*, it would be well to remember that the parable itself is also edifying. True devotion of husband and wife to one another is highly praised and rewarded by Hashem.

BIRTH PANGS

In this world, if we find something difficult, we know that doing more of it will be even more difficult. If we struggle to swim a mile, then swimming ten miles will be much, much harder. But when it comes to serving Hashem, this is not the case. If we struggle, it is only in the beginning. As we keep at it, we find it easier.[56] Rabbi Moshe Shmuel Shapiro, *zt"l*, the Rosh Yeshivah of Be'er Ya'akov, touched on this point when he chided the *bachurim* that they find it hard to keep learning because they are always starting! He meant that instead of just continuing to learn, *bachurim* tend to switch off completely when they stop to eat, etc. Then, when they start learning again, they need to make a new start. They are thus always struggling with the beginning.

As explained earlier, *Klal Yisrael* describe their acceptance of Torah and serving Hashem in terms of giving birth.[57] However demanding the job of nurturing a baby, the difficulty and pain of giving birth are never repeated. Similarly, while one must constantly seek to serve Hashem, the main challenge is only in the beginning. Once one gets into it, it is much easier.[58]

---

55 This has been true throughout Jewish history. Even during the Holocaust, the women of *Klal Yisrael* showed great faith and determination, and continued to be loyal to their husbands and also determined to have children under the most unimaginably difficult circumstances.

56 Rashi (on *Shemos* 19:5) says that with regard to serving Hashem, it is always the beginning that is difficult.

57 This is Rashi's explanation. As mentioned earlier, the Gemara explains that it is alluding to the women giving birth in Egypt.

58 This metaphor of giving birth is multi-dimensional. It also communicates that just as giving birth is very painful and difficult, so *Klal Yisrael* has faced much pain and difficulty in serving Hashem faithfully despite persecution and oppression. Furthermore, *Klal Yisrael* gave birth to the idea — and have taught the world — to serve Hashem. This has been extremely challenging, just as giving birth is.

This insight changes one's view of the entire service of Hashem. If one starts a project and finds the first half hour extremely difficult and is told that this will continue all day, one will easily give up. Similarly, if one begins serving Hashem, and finds it very difficult, it can be disheartening if one mistakenly thinks this is how it will always be. One could, God forbid, give up. But with this new insight, one realizes that with regard to serving Hashem, it is different. The difficult beginning does not reflect on how it will be later. If one just gets into it, one finds it not just "not painful," but actually very pleasant. Those who serve Hashem continuously find it smoother and more satisfying than those who serve Hashem only on occasion.[59]

The *Targum*, which understands this entire chapter to be about the Final Redemption (as noted earlier), reads this verse as follows: When *techiyas hameisim* (the resurrection of the dead) occurs, Har Zeisim (the Mount of Olives in Yerushalayim) will split open, and all the righteous who have died will come to life again and emerge from it. Even those righteous people who are buried abroad will come through tunnels under Eretz Yisrael and emerge from Har Zeisim. At the same time, all the wicked buried in Eretz Yisrael will be thrown out like a stone from a catapult. The people of the world will then declare: "**What is** the merit of this nation now coming up from the ground in its tens upon tens of thousands, like the day it **came out of the desert** to go to Eretz Yisrael. It is **savoring the love of its Beloved** Master, like the day its myriads went **under the mountain** to receive the Torah." Then their **mother** Tzion **will give birth** to her children[60] and Yerushalayim will gather in all of her exiles.

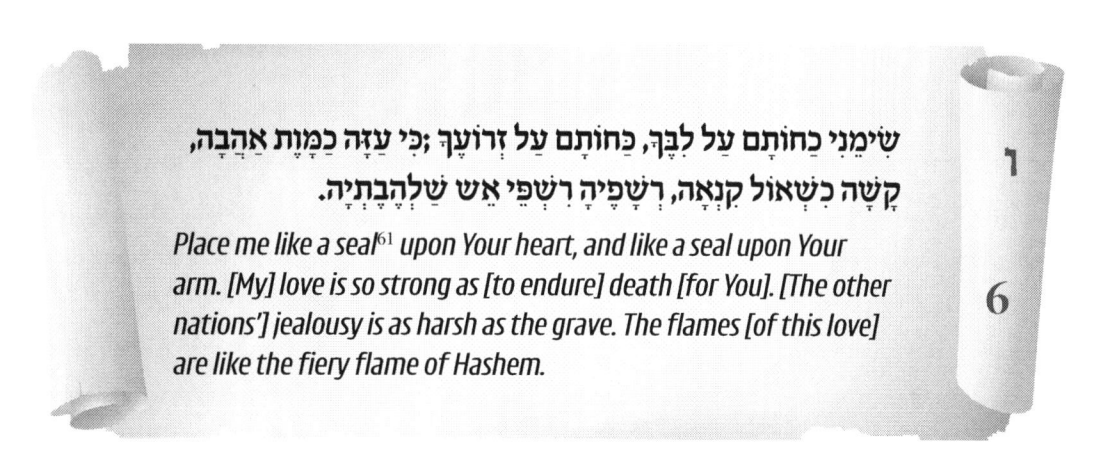

שִׂימֵנִי כַחוֹתָם עַל לִבֶּךָ, כַּחוֹתָם עַל זְרוֹעֶךָ ;כִּי עַזָּה כַמָּוֶת אַהֲבָה, קָשָׁה כִשְׁאוֹל קִנְאָה, רְשָׁפֶיהָ רִשְׁפֵּי אֵשׁ שַׁלְהֶבֶתְיָה.

Place me like a seal[61] upon Your heart, and like a seal upon Your arm. [My] love is so strong as [to endure] death [for You]. [The other nations'] jealousy is as harsh as the grave. The flames [of this love] are like the fiery flame of Hashem.

6

---

59   *Ohr Yechezkel.*

60   This alludes to the fact that when Mashiach comes, it will seem as if an entire nation is born almost instantaneously, as is vividly described in *Yeshayahu* 66:8.

61   In former times, a king would often have a private seal or stamp bearing his coat of arms or signature with which he would authorize important documents and was a mark of his approval. The "seal" in this verse is thus intended as a badge of honor.

Allegorical Translation

Klal Yisrael beseech Hashem: Please, never forget us! See how our love for You is so strong that we have even sacrificed our lives for it. Our love for You has not diminished despite the other nations being very jealous of us, and our having to endure all their cruelty. Our love for You burns as strong and as bright as the most powerful of all fires — the fires of Gehinnom.

Subject of the Verse

Klal Yisrael is speaking to Hashem, describing their love for Him.[62]

Mashal The wife expresses feelings of intense love to her husband. She does not want her husband to ever forget her, so she asks that he place reminders of her on his heart and as a seal on his arm. She continues that she deserves to be treated ever so lovingly by him because her love for him has been very strong despite the great personal price she has had to pay. She has had to endure great suffering and the cruel jealousy of all her opponents. Despite this, her love for him burns within her like a great fire.

Nimshal The *nimshal* is clear from the allegorical translation above. *Klal Yisrael* is asking Hashem to remember them and to keep them close to Him. They feel they deserve this because of the heavy price they have paid for loving Hashem: death, persecution, and intense jealousy from all the other nations. Despite all this, their love for Hashem is as strong and as intense as ever. It burns within them bright and strong, like a very powerful fire.

PLACE ME LIKE A SEAL UPON YOUR HEART, AND LIKE A SEAL UPON YOUR ARM

Klal Yisrael ask that Hashem remember them like a seal or stamp on His heart and arm. Let us take a moment to elaborate on this metaphor, one we have not yet encountered in *Shir HaShirim*. We know that similar emblems, badges, epaulets (which indicates one's rank), insignias, and medals, are universally worn on the arms and on the chest near the heart. The rationale for this would seem to be that the heart represents thought and emotion, while the arm represents action. When one places a badge or the like on his *heart*, he is announcing that what the badge symbolizes is in his *thoughts* and *emotions* and makes him proud. "This is what makes me special." If the insignia or medal is worn on his *arm*, he is announcing that his *actions* revolve around this area or achievement — both in the past and in the future. Therefore, on a certain level, he is announcing: "All that I have done in the past with my arms and thought about with my heart was for this

---

62   Alternatively, this is Hashem and the *beis din* of the angels testifying to the greatness of *Klal Yisrael* that this is how they speak to Hashem. They say, "Place me like a seal..." (as explained in the previous verse).

achievement. The medal representing my triumph that I place on my heart defines my greatness now in the present. When people see me, I want that them to see my medal(s) because this is who I am. Furthermore, what I hope to achieve in the future through my actions and my passions will revolve around the symbols and successes that I place on my arm and heart."

In a similar way, we ask Hashem that we should be His medal, His emblem, and Hashem indeed complies. The Gemara[63] tells us that Hashem, *ki'veyachol*, wears *tefillin* on His "arm," near His "heart." Inside Hashem's *tefillin* are verses describing the greatness of the Jewish People. This is one of the ways in which Hashem keeps *Klal Yisrael* as a "seal" on His heart and on His arm, as *Klal Yisrael* asks Him to here in this verse.

Our coat of arms, our medal, and our prominence is our *tefillin*. It is a symbol of our love for Hashem, and (our arm-*tefillin*) is also positioned near our heart. We place our tefillin, containing verses describing Hashem's greatness, on our heart and our arm. In symbolic terms, this means that all our thoughts and actions are devoted to Hashem.

As explained regarding medals, by wearing *tefillin* on our arms and opposite our hearts, we are proclaiming that all our past efforts were made in the service of Hashem. This is our identity and pride, as well as our future goal.

In this verse, we pray that Hashem, *ki'veyachol*, does likewise for for us, that, *ki'veyachol*, all His efforts, identity and pride is *Klal Yisrael*, and indeed He does![64]

PLACE ME LIKE A SEAL UPON YOUR HEART...

Chazal tell us that the prophets informed *Klal Yisrael* that their request for Hashem to place the seal of His love on His arm and heart, *ki'veyachol*, falls short of the true depth of His love for them.[65] This is because the arm and heart, despite their great importance, are often covered. Whatever is situated there can thus be forgotten. Therefore, they should ask that Hashem "remember" them by means of a diamond-studded crown. A crown is worn in the open, never covered over, and impossible to forget, as the Prophet Yeshayahu says, "You [the Jewish People] will be as a crown of royalty in the hand of your King [Hashem]."[66] Even so, Hashem told the prophets that they too fell short in their request because a crown can fall off or be taken off and then temporarily disregarded. Therefore, Hashem promised that besides wearing a seal showing His love for the Jewish People on His arm opposite His heart, and besides wearing a crown of

---

63 *Berachos* 6a; *Zohar, Bamidbar* 120b.
64 *Ayeles Ahuvim*.
65 *Ta'anis* 4a, *Midrash Rabbah* here.
66 *Yeshayahu* 62:3.

Klal Yisrael, He will engrave their remembrance on the palm of His hand. Thereby it is never covered and can never fall off ensuring that He will not forget His love for them even for a moment.[67] As the verse says, "Behold, you are engraved on the palm of (My) hands."[68]

Hashem ultimately adopts all three methods of remembering *Klal Yisrael*. *Klal Yisrael* is Hashem's badge of honor on His Heart, they are His crown of glory, and are prominently etched on His hands. Obviously, this is all to be understood figuratively. Hashem has no physical body and does not need anything to remind Him of His love for us. This teaching is meant only to help us gain some understanding of the depth of Hashem's love. If we meditate on this, we will be moved by the intensity of Hashem's desire to make us feel remembered by Him.

BECAUSE [MY] LOVE IS SO STRONG AS [TO ENDURE] DEATH,

Klal Yisrael go on to point out to Hashem that they deserve His deep and abiding love because of their devotion to Him. They have demonstrated how precious this love is to them by the personal price they have paid for it. Indeed, they have paid for this love with their lives over and over again.[69] We see how valuable something is to a person by the price he is willing to pay for it. If someone pays a fortune for a painting, this tells us that he finds the painting very precious. The more one is willing to pay for something, the more precious that item is for that person. Hashem's love is so precious that we have paid the ultimate price for it. There is nothing more precious to us.

JEALOUSY IS AS HARSH...

The "jealousy" here in this verse is that of the heathen nations. The cruel and constant persecution has been very difficult for *Klal Yisrael*, but they have endured it because of their love for Hashem. They thus deserve that Hashem keep them close to Him on His heart. As the Gemara teaches, since the time we received the Torah at Har Sinai, the nations have been jealous of us, and this is the real reason for their ongoing persecution.[70] Their tremendous hatred stems from one source only: jealousy of our Torah observance.

---

67 Midrash.

68 *Yeshayahu* 49:16.

69 Metzudas Dovid takes a slightly different approach. He explains not that we, *Klal Yisrael*, have died because of Your love, but that we would rather die than lose Your love. Therefore, it is only proper that You do not remove Your love from us. The message is similar: Hashem's love is more precious than our physical life.
   Tzror HaMor adds that we are implicitly requesting that Hashem forgive us for all our sins. Even if we deserve to be punished, the tremendous suffering we have endured for Him should obviate the need for any other punishment. So, we are asking that — in the merit of our suffering — Hashem bring the Final Redemption and absolve us of any punishment we might otherwise deserve.

70 *Shabbos* 89a.

Indeed, the name "Sinai" comes from the word "שנאה," meaning "hatred." They may not consciously realize this, but their deep hatred comes from a feeling that we have something very special that they will never have.

Rabbi Aharon Yehuda Leib Steinman once drove home this point about how special our Torah is in a particularly memorable fashion. A businessman came to Rabbi Steinman with the following question. He was doing well in business and wanted to buy a beautiful new car since he needed to travel a lot and could afford to do so in style. His wife, however, was concerned that such a purchase might arouse jealousy among their neighbors since they lived in a community where a car was considered a luxury — and an expensive car was very rare. Rabbi Steinman asked the businessman if he knew the Talmud Bavli by heart. When he replied in the negative, Rabbi Steinman asked him if he knew one tractate by heart. When the businessman once again answered in the negative, Rabbi Steinman proceeded to ask him if he knew at least one chapter by heart? Again, the businessman had to answer in the negative. "If that is the case," said Rabbi Steinman, "then go home and tell your wife that you may buy the car. You have absolutely nothing of value that someone will be jealous of!" The person took the message to heart and came back to Rabbi Steinman a few months later to tell him that he had succeeded in learning a chapter of Gemara by heart!

Obviously, each case should be assessed on an individual basis. What the *gadol* was trying to teach, though, was that people are jealous only of something valuable — and only the Torah is truly valuable.

THE FLAMES [OF THIS LOVE] ARE LIKE THE FIERY FLAME OF HASHEM

The word "שלהבתיה" here is a combination of two words: "שלהבת" (flame) and "י-ה" (Hashem). *Klal Yisrael* is saying that love burns within them as intensely and as greatly as the greatest fire of all, the flame of Hashem. Rashi sees this as an allusion to the fire of Gehinnom. The fire of Gehinnom is sixty times stronger than our fires[71] and will never die out.[72] In contrast, the Midrash sees this as an allusion to the fire with which Hashem created the heavens. The heavens were created with fire and water.[73] Normally fire will be extinguished by water, but this fire of the heavens is so powerful that it still remains after thousands of years.[74] According to both interpretations, however, *Klal Yisrael* is speaking of the intense love for Hashem burning inside them, which is as powerful as

---

71 *Berachos* 57b.
72 *Yeshayahu* 66:23.
73 The word "שמים" (heavens) is a combination of the words for "fire" and "water" (Rashi on *Bereishis* 1:8, *s.v. vayikra*).
74 The Netziv explains that this is the fire of the *Shechinah* which, the Gemara tells us, is so powerful that it actually consumes other fires (*Yoma* 21b).

these heavenly fires.

If we follow the Metzudas Dovid's understanding of "רשפיה" as "glowing coals," *Klal Yisrael* likens their love to hot coals in order to emphasize that the heat and passion of their love for Hashem will go on and on. While a flame is easily extinguished and provides little heat, glowing coals are very difficult to extinguish and go on providing heat even after the actual fire goes out. The love that *Klal Yisrael* has for Hashem is not easily extinguished!

PLACE ME...

According to the Netziv, this entire verse portrays *Klal Yisrael* asking to be very close to Hashem. He thus reads the verse as follows:

> "Place me like a seal upon Your heart [such that we will feel any 'emotion' flowing through You, like two people who are so close that they are aware of each other's feelings. And since Your primary emotion is the love You have for us, we will feel this, and thus come to love You]. [And place me] like a seal upon Your Arm [such that we will notice anything You do, and since all Your actions are for our good, we will thus be aware of Your kindness]. Because [our] love is so strong, [the nations ardently desire to undermine it and eliminate it as if it is] death [because their] jealousy is as harsh as the grave. Our love for You burns like the fiery coals of Heaven."

The Netziv adds that it is easy to rekindle a fire from burning hot coals even after their flame has gone out. So, too, we ask that our love should always simmer and be easily rekindled.[75]

The *Targum*, which (as we have noted) interprets this entire chapter as being about the Final Redemption, reads this verse as follows. *Klal Yisrael* say to Hashem on that day of salvation: "Please **place me like a seal upon Your Heart and like a seal upon Your Arm** so that You will never again send us away into exile."[76] **Because my love is so strong as** [to endure] **death** for You, **the jealousy** of the nations is as harsh as the

---

[75] The Netziv derives from here that when one needs to take a break from actively serving Hashem (e.g., to eat or rest), one should make sure that his feelings of love for Hashem remain simmering. Afterwards, it will not require much effort to rekindle the passion to serve Hashem.

[76] Although *Klal Yisrael* is thrilled to be redeemed, they wish to be reassured that there will never be another exile. They ask that just as the arm and the heart are always connected to the body, so too, they should always be connected to Hashem.

grave and their hatred is like the **fiery flames** of Gehinnom, which Hashem created on the second day to consume those who serve idols.

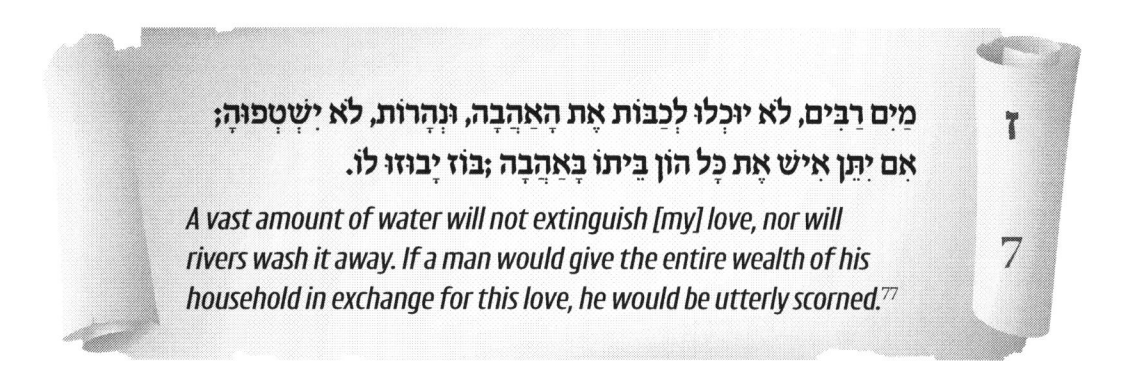

> מַיִם רַבִּים, לֹא יוּכְלוּ לְכַבּוֹת אֶת הָאַהֲבָה, וּנְהָרוֹת, לֹא יִשְׁטְפוּהָ;
> אִם יִתֵּן אִישׁ אֶת כָּל הוֹן בֵּיתוֹ בָּאַהֲבָה; בּוֹז יָבוּזוּ לוֹ.
>
> *A vast amount of water will not extinguish [my] love, nor will rivers wash it away. If a man would give the entire wealth of his household in exchange for this love, he would be utterly scorned.*[77]
>
> ז
>
> 7

Allegorical Translation — *Klal Yisrael* declare: "All the nations will never be able to weaken our love for Hashem, and all their kings and ministers cannot force us to stop serving Him. Even if they would offer all their wealth to entice us to sin, they would be scorned because they have no chance at all of succeeding."

Subject of the Verse — Hashem and the Heavenly Court testify to the greatness of *Klal Yisrael* in having boundless devotion to Hashem.

Mashal — In the previous verse, the wife described her love for her husband as a fire within. In this verse, she continues in the same vein by declaring that there is no way to weaken or extinguish this love. She adds that she would not trade this love for any amount of money. If someone tried to make this exchange, she would scorn him because of the foolishness of the notion.

Nimshal — *Klal Yisrael* dramatically declare that nothing can extinguish their love of Hashem. Having compared Hashem's love to fire, they develop their metaphor. They speak of a fire so powerful that a river cannot extinguish it. That is the fire of love that burns in our hearts. "A vast amount of water" and "rivers" represent

---

77 While a Jew is obligated to use up all of his resources to save himself from committing an *aveirah*, he is obligated to give up his life only to avoid committing one of the three cardinal sins: idol worship, murder, or illicit sexual relationships. These three mitzvos are the second, sixth, and seventh of the Ten Commandments: "Do not worship idols," "Do not murder," and "Do not engage in illicit sexual relationships." The word "בוז" in this verse, whose letters have the *gematria* [numerical equivalent] of 2, 6, and 7, corresponds to these three special commandments. Picking up on this correspondence, the Ben Yehoyada offers a brilliant interpretation of this verse: "A man should give up the entire wealth of his household in exchange for this love, [i.e., to be saved from sinning, which is hateful to Hashem, one should give up all his wealth], [but] for 'ב.ו.ז' [i.e., the three cardinal sins] he should 'give away' himself." The Ben Yehoyada understands the phrase "יבוזו לו" as "giving away himself" because, as we will see, "יבוזו" can be read as a form of the verb "to plunder." Here, then, it would mean: "allowing oneself to be plundered/killed for Hashem."

the various desires and major difficulties that pull one away and block one from serving Hashem. *Klal Yisrael* overcome them all. Furthermore, no amount of money can come close to being worth giving up on that love. It would be ludicrous to even suggest such an exchange.

A VAST AMOUNT OF WATER...

This dramatic verse speaks of our intense love for Hashem and how nothing can diminish it. We would do well to consider it very carefully.

"A vast amount of water" symbolizes the numerous nations of the world who are as vast as the ocean. "Rivers" symbolize the mighty kings who have the power to devastate everything in their way like a raging river that sweeps away everything in its path. The verse tells us that the heathen nations and their kings are unable to quell the love we have for Hashem. Nothing can stop us from serving Him.

The converse is true as well. Nothing will take away Hashem's love from us. The Ramban[78] points out that it would seem more fitting that Hashem should have the heathen nations, who are great in number, as His people. It is surely a far greater honor for a king to have many subjects,[79] and Hashem created this world to be populated by His servants. Yet Hashem chose *Klal Yisrael* because He loves them. This love overrides all calculations. The "vast waters" in this verse, according to this explanation, allude to the nations arguing that since they are numerous, they ought to deserve Hashem's love. But they are unable to get Hashem to redirect His love from us to them. The "rivers," as mentioned above, symbolize powerful kings. Seemingly, they can do more for Hashem than *Klal Yisrael*. Yet Hashem rejects their efforts because He prefers that which *Klal Yisrael* do.

The verse concludes: "If a man would give the entire wealth of his household in exchange for this love..." This means that one cannot "buy" the love of Hashem. But how could we even think that one can buy the love of Hashem?! The Netziv explains that if the heathen nations would pool all their resources and give everything away for the sake of Hashem — to serve Him — He would still love *Klal Yisrael* more. Hashem's love for *Klal Yisrael* is like that of a parent for his or her child. Even if a stranger would give the parent all his money and do everything the parent wants, the parent will still love his or her child more than the stranger.

The Netziv sees this connecting with the first part of the verse in the following way.

---

78 *Devarim* 7:7.

79 He quotes the well-known verse/principle "ברוב עם הדרת מלך — The greater the crowd, the greater the honor to the king." This verse from *Mishlei* (14:28) has halachic ramifications. See *Rosh Hashanah* 32b.

This verse declares that Hashem's love for *Klal Yisrael* is unshakeable. Regardless of whether the nations try to accomplish more than *Klal Yisrael* (as in the first half of the verse) or to expend more (as in the second half of the verse), Hashem will still choose *Klal Yisrael*.

The Netziv considers this verse to be the last verse of the main body of *Shir HaShirim*. He sees the verses that follow as an addendum (as will be explained later). He points out that this verse is the culmination of the main thrust of *Shir HaShirim*: to show just how powerful Hashem's love for *Klal Yisrael* is. This verse tells us that it is absolutely impossible for the love between Hashem and *Klal Yisrael* to be terminated, regardless of our adversaries and adverse circumstances. Even if the heathen nations would do everything perfectly and do much more than *Klal Yisrael* could ever do — giving away everything they have for Hashem — He would nevertheless choose *Klal Yisrael*.[80] Hashem's great love for us, and our great love for Him, is eternal. This verse should fill us with tremendous joy, pride, and confidence.[81]

A VAST AMOUNT OF WATER WILL NOT EXTINGUISH (MY) LOVE

According to the Shiras Dovid, the "vast amount of water" and the "river" in this verse allude to the twin dangers faced by *Klal Yisrael*. One danger is assimilation. Since there are so many non-Jewish people in the world, we could easily get lost in their midst, as have so many Jews in America. Indeed, there are other small ethnic groups that have lost their unique identity in the larger society in which they find themselves. This is symbolized by "a vast amount of water," like an ocean. Even if the ocean is calm, something small will easily get lost in it. The other danger is devastation, i.e., the destruction and persecution directed against us by other nations, as happened in Communist Russia. This is symbolized by a powerful river that can overturn and destroy everything in its path. This verse teaches us that neither of these will wipe out *Klal Yisrael* and that our relationship with Hashem will last forever.[82]

A VAST AMOUNT OF WATER WILL NOT EXTINGUISH (MY) LOVE

The Torah commands us to love Hashem with all of our heart/desire, all of our life, and

---

80 The fact that Hashem loves *Klal Yisrael* regardless of all calculations was the subject of Rabbi Yerucham's talks on Simchas Torah in Yeshivas Mir. He would bring the *bachurim* to a state of ecstasy by explaining this concept in great detail. (See *Bemichitzasam*, vol. II, p. 39 and *Zerichah mipa'asei kedem*).

81 The Shem MiShmuel (*Bamidbar*, p. 56) expresses this in the strongest words possible: "It is better to be sinful and a failure as a Jew than righteous and a success as a non-Jew."

82 Rashi explains the twin water metaphors in this verse similarly: Neither "the harshness and fear [of the nations] nor their seduction and temptation [will cause us to exchange His love]."

all of our resources.[83] This means that our love for Hashem should be so great that it fills our heart and even takes precedence over our life and all financial considerations.

At this point in *Shir HaShirim*, explains the Brisker Rav, we declare how we truly love Hashem as commanded. The "vast amount of water" represents the great enticements/desires that threaten to weaken our love,[84] but because we love Hashem with all our hearts, it fails to do so. The raging "rivers," which represent the dangers and life-threatening situations the nations put us through because of our commitment to Hashem, prove that we love Hashem with all of our life — even at the risk of losing our life. Finally, no amount of money can entice us away from loving Hashem since we have been commanded to love Him with all of our money — even at the risk of losing all of our wealth.

UTTERLY SCORNED

Someone who would offer *Klal Yisrael* all of his money in exchange for Hashem's love would be "utterly scorned." We can better understand this expression through a simple *mashal*. There are marketplaces where the prices of items are not fixed but can be negotiated. People often go there hunting for a bargain, and much bargaining indeed takes place. Imagine a naïve person going to such a market and offering twenty cents for a diamond ring. He would obviously be scorned for not recognizing the worth of this item. Similarly, even if one would offer all the money in the world to buy away the love of Hashem, he would deserve to be scorned for offering a ridiculously low price.[85]

HE WOULD BE UTTERLY SCORNED

While many commentators understand the words "בּוֹז יָבוּזוּ" here in our verse as relating to "scorn," the Ramban connects them with the word "בִּיזָה,"[86] meaning "booty" and "spoils."[87] He thus interprets this phrase as follows: When one gives away all of his wealth for the love of Hashem (בּוֹז), then he will receive Hashem's bountiful spoils (יָבוּזוּ לוֹ). And what are these spoils? They are, says the Ramban, having the Shechinah, Hashem's Presence, dwell with him.

The Chovos HaLevavos points out that the love of Hashem and the love of worldly

---

83 *Devarim* 6:5; *Berachos* 54a.

84 Desire is often symbolized by water because just as one thirsts for water, one thirsts to fulfill one's desires. (See *Iyov* 15:16 and *Resisei Layla*, ch. 58.)

85 This reminds us that undervaluing mitzvos should be the greatest cause for scorn.

86 *Esther* 9:10.

87 As the *Targum*, cited below, explains as well.

indulgences are two opposing forces.[88] One cannot fill his heart with both of these loves at the same time. Even if there is nothing intrinsically wrong with wanting a beautiful house and a luxury vacation, these desires make it more difficult to truly desire the Presence of Hashem, even if one wishes to have that desire. This is loosely similar to a husband who is married to two wives. Any devotion he shows to one amounts to a rejection of the other, even if it is not meant that way. Similarly, the devotion and attachment that one shows to the mundane is a kind of a rejection of the spiritual — and vice versa. We may think that only sin pushes us away from Hashem, but that indulgence — which is permitted — does not. The Chovos HaLevavos tells us that this is a mistake. Indulging oneself in this world automatically distances one from Hashem. Conversely, as one keeps away from indulgence for the sake of Hashem, one become closer to Him. Our verse, as the Ramban explains it, makes this very point. When a person gives away all the wealth of his home for the love of Hashem because only the love of Hashem is precious to him, he will be greatly rewarded. He will automatically become very close to Hashem and feel His Presence.

The Midrash relates the following episode that illustrates the practical application of this verse. Rabbi Yochanan was walking with his student Rabbi Chiya when they passed a certain field. Rabbi Yochanan informed his student that this field had once been his, but that he had sold it to be able to devote himself to the study of Torah. They then passed a vineyard, and Rabbi Yochanan said that this, too, had once belonged to him, but that he sold it to be able to learn Torah. They then passed an olive press, which also had been sold by Rabbi Yochanan to enable him to learn Torah. At this point, his student, Rabbi Chiya, began crying. "Why are you weeping?" Rabbi Yochanan asked? Rabbi Chiya replied, "I am weeping because I am concerned about how you will manage in your old age!" He realized that Rabbi Yochanan was now left penniless and would be reduced to privation for the rest of his life. Rabbi Yochanan answered that there was nothing to be upset about. On the contrary, he should rejoice that he had sold that which had been created in six days (this world) in exchange for that which had been given in forty days (the Torah). When Rabbi Yochanan died, the people of the generation[89] said of him,

---

88 *Shaar HaAhavah*, ch. 5.

89 It is noteworthy that it was not just his friends and students who said this about Rabbi Yochanan. His love of Torah was so renowned that everyone felt way this about him.
Rabbi Elazar Menachem Man Shach, *zt"l*, embodied this love of Torah, as countless stories bear witness. Here is just one example, related by Rabbi Yoel Kluft. He once met Rabbi Shach who told him sadly that he had just lost his only copy of *Shut MaHarit* and was extremely upset that he would no longer be able to learn from this *sefer*. To Rabbi Kluft's question about where he lost it, Rabbi Shach answered that it was in a suitcase together with all his personal items that

citing this verse: "If a man would give the entire wealth of his household in exchange for this love [of Torah that Rabbi Yochanan possessed], he would be utterly scorned." They recognized Rabbi Yochanan's love for Torah was so great that no price would be too great to pay for, and it would be silly to offer anything else in exchange.[90]

IF A MAN WOULD GIVE THE ENTIRE WEALTH OF HIS HOUSEHOLD IN EXCHANGE FOR THIS LOVE...

The Gemara[91] applies this verse to Shevna, the brother of Hillel. The Gemara relates that Azaryah was the brother of the great Rabbi Shimon. Azaryah supported Rabbi Shimon who devoted his life to Torah. He thus merited sharing the great reward that Rabbi Shimon received for learning Torah, as per the famous Yissachar-Zevulun arrangement.[92] He even earned the honor of being mentioned in connection with his brother's Torah learning. The great Rabbi Shimon is quoted as "Rabbi Shimon, the brother of Azaryah."

Hillel did not have anyone to support him but devoted himself to learning Torah despite his extreme poverty.[93] After learning Torah for many years, his brother Shevna offered to give him half of his total wealth in exchange for Hillel's reward for learning Torah up to that point. Regarding this offer, the Gemara draws on our verse to comment disparagingly: "If a man would give the entire wealth of his household in exchange for this (Torah of Hillel), he should be utterly scorned." These two people, Azaryah and Shevna, may seem similar but they were actually worlds apart. There is nothing greater than supporting someone who is learning Torah, but trying to buy the merit of Torah that has already been learned is futile and foolish. The merit of Torah is far too precious to be bought and sold. The important message of the Gemara here is that one cannot

---

got lost on a bus. "And where are all the other items?" asked Rabbi Kluft. "Oh," said Rabbi Shach, "those were also lost, but that doesn't bother me!" His love for Torah overshadowed all other concerns.

90   The Radal explains that the people of Rabbi Yochanan's generation would mock him for selling all his property just to learn Torah. We see that Rabbi Yochanan not only used up all of his resources to be able to learn Torah, but also had to cope with widespread disparagement. Nevertheless, he ignored it all because of his great determination to learn Torah. According to the Ramban and the *Targum*, who understand that "בּוֹז יָבוּזּוּ" refers to spoils, the people recognized that Rabbi Yochanan achieved his greatness only because he was ready to give up all of his resources for Torah. By applying our verse to him, they were praising him, saying in effect: "If one would give away all of his resources to study Torah, like Rabbi Yochanan, then he would receive the spoils of Torah," – great reward in the World to Come and true knowledge of Torah here in this world.

91   *Sotah* 21a.

92   Rashi (*Devarim* 33:18) tells us that they made a partnership. Yissachar would share the merit of his Torah learning, and Zevulun would share his profits in business.

93   As described in *Yoma* 35b. The Gemara recounts how Hillel once learned Torah on the roof of the *beis midrash* on a freezing, snowy winter night because he could not afford the entrance fee.

buy the merit of Torah learning, but one can *earn* it by using his money to support those who are learning so that they are able to continue learning.

Rabbi Eliezer Yazeresky, the father-in-law of Rabbi Yitzchak Elchanan Spector, *zt"l*, the Rav of Kovno, truly appreciated and exemplified the virtue of supporting Torah study. When his daughter got married to the young Rabbi Spector, he gave him a generous dowry. Rabbi Yitzchak Elchanan turned this money over to an investor. After a few months, the investor stopped paying him the monthly earnings that he had promised. Rabbi Spector's wife, Sarah Reizel, went to the investor and protested. He arrogantly told her that since her husband was the one who had given him the money, he would only answer to him. She went and told her husband, who responded that he did not wish to sacrifice precious time from his Torah learning to chase after this investor. One day she cried out to her husband that this money would be lost forever. Her father heard the commotion and asked what was wrong. When she told him, instead of standing up for her, he gave her this rebuke: "Don't you realize that a minute of your husband's learning is more precious in my eyes than the entire dowry?!"[94] Interestingly, Sarah Reizel often repeated this amazing story to others to teach them, and to show the greatness of her father and husband.[95]

The distinction between earning Torah and buying Torah emerges clearly from another episode in the life of Rabbi Yitzchak Elchanan. He once related that when he was a *bachur* in yeshivah, he could not afford a pair of shoes. At one point, he approached a wealthier *bachur* who was buying new shoes before his upcoming wedding, and asked if he would give him his old, worn-out shoes. This *chassan* refused, preferring to throw out his old shoes. He also told Yitzchak Elchanan that if he had no money, he should go to work instead of sitting around learning. Years later, when Rabbi Yitzchak Elchanan became a world-famous halachic authority, this man came to him and offered him money to publish his *sefarim* and for other expenses. Rabbi Yitzchak Elchanan refused him, however, and reminded him that he once had the opportunity to support Torah but threw it away. Rabbi Spector added that because he did not have shoes at that time, he ended up catching pneumonia and losing hours of learning. In short, he communicated that this man did not deserve to buy this merit. The distinction between earning Torah and buying Torah is a fine one, but it is fundamental. One who has the opportunity to earn this merit should be overjoyed, and one who loses the opportunity should be devastated.

---

94 The fact that it was his own money in jeopardy and his own daughter who was upset, yet he defended his son-in-law, makes this account all the more extraordinary.

95 This account appears in *Toldos Yitzchak*, a biography of Rabbi Yitzchak Elchanan Spector, *zt"l*.

IF A MAN WOULD GIVE THE ENTIRE WEALTH OF HIS HOUSEHOLD IN EXCHANGE FOR THIS LOVE...

Based on this verse, the Midrash teaches that all the money in the world cannot buy the love that Hashem has for *Klal Yisrael*. And if one were to try to use money to harm *Klal Yisrael*, he would be mocked. The Midrash offers the story of Haman as an illustration of this. He offered ten thousand talents (*kikaros*) of silver, a truly astronomical sum, to *buy* the right to destroy *Klal Yisrael*.[96] "If a man would give the entire wealth of his household in exchange for this love," his plan would come to nothing, as Haman's did, and "he would be utterly scorned," as Haman was. He became an object of ridicule and shame when he led Mordechai around on the king's horse, and when he was hanged.

The *Targum*, mentioned earlier, reads our verse as Hashem reassuring *Klal Yisrael*: "If all of the numerous nations who are likened to **great amounts of water** would gather together, they still would not be able **to extinguish My love** for you. And if all their kings, likened to raging **rivers** that wash away everything, would gather together, they would be unable to **sweep you out** of this world. **If a man would give the entire wealth of his household** to acquire the wisdom of Torah [a true measure of how much a person **loves** Hashem] while still in exile, he will receive it back twofold[97] in the World to Come. And **all the spoils** from the camp of Gog will be **his**."

INTRODUCTION TO VERSES 8-14

The last seven verses in *Shir HaShirim* are considered by many *meforashim* to be a chapter in their own right — more like an addendum to *Shir HaShirim*.[98] This approach is supported by the break here in *Shir HaShirim* when written as a scroll. These verses encapsulate the theme of *Shir HaShirim* — the wonderful relationship between *Klal Yisrael* and Hashem — but through a different *mashal* and with a different structure. No longer are *Klal Yisrael* likened to a wife, and no longer is the relationship described in terms of marriage. Here, *Klal Yisrael* is brought before the Heavenly Court for their fate and the fate of their oppressors to be decided. In this way, we get an even better sense of the limitless love between Hashem and *Klal Yisrael*.

---

96   Although we may not understand what Haman was thinking, we understand that his offer was a truly great threat to *Klal Yisrael* (as seen in *Megillah* 13b and the commentaries there).

97   This is hinted at by the doubled verb in our verse "בוז יבוזו."

98   See the Netziv on the previous verse (as noted in our commentary above) and the Malbim on this verse.

The events alluded to in these verses will take place towards the end of history as we know it: when Mashiach comes and Hashem judges the entire world.[99] At that time, the love between Hashem and *Klal Yisrael* will reach its zenith, and all will see how great *Klal Yisrael* is, and that, despite our long exile, Hashem never rejected us.

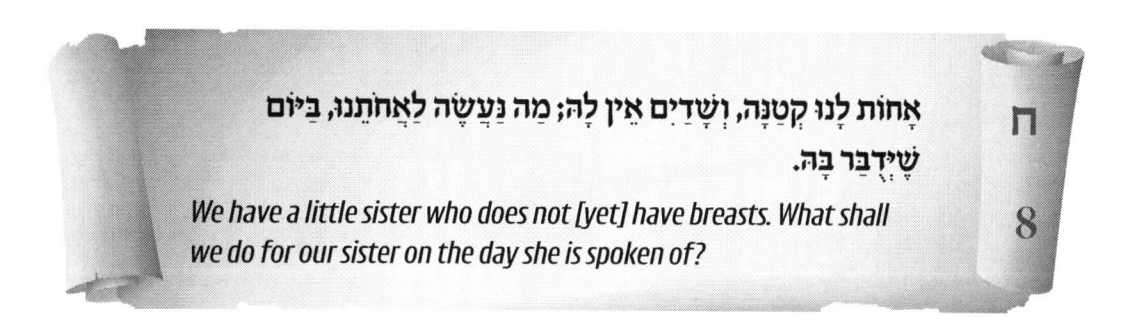

> אָחוֹת לָנוּ קְטַנָּה, וְשָׁדַיִם אֵין לָהּ; מַה נַּעֲשֶׂה לַאֲחֹתֵנוּ, בַּיּוֹם שֶׁיְּדֻבַּר בָּהּ.
>
> **ח 8**
>
> *We have a little sister who does not [yet] have breasts. What shall we do for our sister on the day she is spoken of?*

Allegorical Translation — Hashem says: "We[100] have a humble and modest nation below that wishes to bond with Me. They are not fully matured (i.e., they are not completely ready for salvation). What fate should We decree on it when the nations come to assault it?"

Subject of the Verse — Hashem and the Heavenly court are deciding the fate of *Klal Yisrael*.

Mashal — A kindly and protective older brother is concerned regarding the fate of his helpless little sister who is not fully matured and is facing judgment.

Nimshal — These next few verses introduce a new scenario in which Hashem and the Heavenly Court look with caring concern upon *Klal Yisrael* at the time of their struggles and "discuss" what should happen to them. This verse describes the circumstances of *Klal Yisrael*'s judgment. It begins with a declaration by Hashem and His Court regarding the situation of *Klal Yisrael* on the day of judgment, just before the Final Redemption.

As Rashi explains, *Klal Yisrael* is the "little sister" in the positive sense that they always humble themselves and make themselves small. Because they are a humble nation, they are called "little."[101] The Midrash takes a different approach: just as one does not grow angry or blame little children when they

---

99 As mentioned earlier, the *Targum* understands this entire chapter to be alluding to the time of Mashiach. From the perspective of the *Targum*, then, this is a continuation of the theme of the chapter.

100 The next few verses are cast in the plural because they refer to Hashem judging together with His Heavenly Court (*Devash V'Chalav*).

101 See *Devarim* 7:7 (with Rashi) where the Torah itself tells us that Hashem loves *Klal Yisrael* because of their humility.

do something, so Hashem will not punish *Klal Yisrael* for their past sins when the Final Redemption comes. Shiras Dovid explains that just as little children are not held accountable for their misdeeds because they are easily influenced — and thus their actions do not reflect their essence — so too *Klal Yisrael* does not really want to sin but is influenced by the other nations to sin. This verse can also be read as communicating that just as one wants to be very protective of a younger sister, so Hashem and the angels want to be very protective of *Klal Yisrael*.

Klal Yisrael is referred to lovingly as a "sister" because the angels who sit in judgment together with Hashem see *Klal Yisrael* as their compatriots and equal.[102]

Picking up on another meaning of the word *achos*, meaning "sewn or melded together,"[103] Rashi explains that *Klal Yisrael* is being referred to here as the one with whom Hashem bonds. Let us try to appreciate the power of this expression. *Klal Yisrael* and Hashem are so closely attached to each other that it is as if they are sewn or bonded together — not just pinned together.

The Midrash, using the same translation that *achos* means to bond, explains that *Klal Yisrael* is the nation that "bonds" the world with Hashem by teaching them to serve only Him. We, *Klal Yisrael*, cause the world to serve Hashem and cleave to Him through our example and through our teachings. We are thus the ultimate "repairers" of the world.

Either way, "little sister/repairer," is an expression of loving endearment for *Klal Yisrael*. Furthermore, it hints at the unique care and concern that a brother feels for a younger sister.[104] Hashem cares for us in that same loving way.

The verse continues, "...but she does not [yet] have breasts." *Klal Yisrael* has not yet reached full maturity. They are missing something that they need in order to be perfect. There are a number of explanations for exactly what this is.

The *Targum* explains that *Klal Yisrael* lack kings. Just as breasts provide nurture and support, so these kings will be needed to help and support *Klal*

---

102 *Targum*. In other words, the great angels see *Klal Yisrael* as those they feel close to — as if our people were on par with them. When they look at this world, they feel an affinity only with *Klal Yisrael* because they are the only nation who serves Hashem. This is a wonderful description of how we are viewed "Upstairs."

103 As in *Moed Katan* 26a.

104 See earlier 8:1.

Yisrael in their war against all of the nations in the time of Mashiach. In a similar vein, the *Tzror HaMor* explains that "breasts" are symbolic of good, strong leaders who nurture the nation. Another explanation is that the time of the Final Redemption has not arrived yet, so it is if *Klal Yisrael* is too young to be redeemed. This is symbolized by their "undeveloped breasts."[105] *Akeidas Yitzchak* explains that at the time of Redemption, *Klal Yisrael* will still be lacking full Torah knowledge. The two breasts allude to the Written Torah and the Oral Torah which nurture the world.[106]

The verse concludes with a further expression of Hashem's love for *Klal Yisrael*: "What shall we do for our sister on the day she is spoken of?" Understood simply, this means: "What rules of justice should we apply to *Klal Yisrael* [or how should we treat *Klal Yisrael*] on the day that she is judged?" On a deeper level, however, Hashem is asking: "How can we help *Klal Yisrael* get through the judgment unscathed?" Even though there must be justice, because Hashem loves *Klal Yisrael*, He seeks ways to find them worthy, and thereby enable them to succeed in the judgment.[107]

WE HAVE A LITTLE SISTER...

Relating to the word "*achos*" as "bonding,"[108] the Midrash interprets this as an allusion to Avraham Avinu who brought humanity together to serve Hashem. He was "little" in that he was extremely humble. The "undeveloped breasts" mentioned in the verse — i.e., the lack of maturity — allude to the fact that this all happened when Avraham was young, and he had not yet performed very many mitzvos. "What shall we do…on the day she is spoken of?" is Hashem's response to Nimrod's declaration that he was going to throw Avraham into the furnace. According to the Midrash, the next verse continues this theme, as we will see shortly.

The *Targum* explains our verse as follows: At that time, the angels in Heaven will say to each other: "**We have** one nation in the land whose merits are **few.** It also lacks kings

---

105 Rashi. The verse in *Yechezkel* (16:7) which we recite in the Haggadah on Seder Night depicts *Klal Yisrael* as a young maiden whose breasts *are* developed. This means that she is mature and ready for redemption.

106 As explained in our commentary on 4:5.

107 This is similar to the judgment on Rosh Hashanah. While Hashem judges the world according to the laws of justice, He always finds *Klal Yisrael* as a nation worthy, and enables them to triumph in judgment (see *Vayikra Rabbah* 29:1).

108 Rashi adopted this approach, as mentioned above.

and leaders to wage war against its enemies, the camp of Gog. **What can we do for our sister on the day** the nations **will speak** about going up against her in battle?"

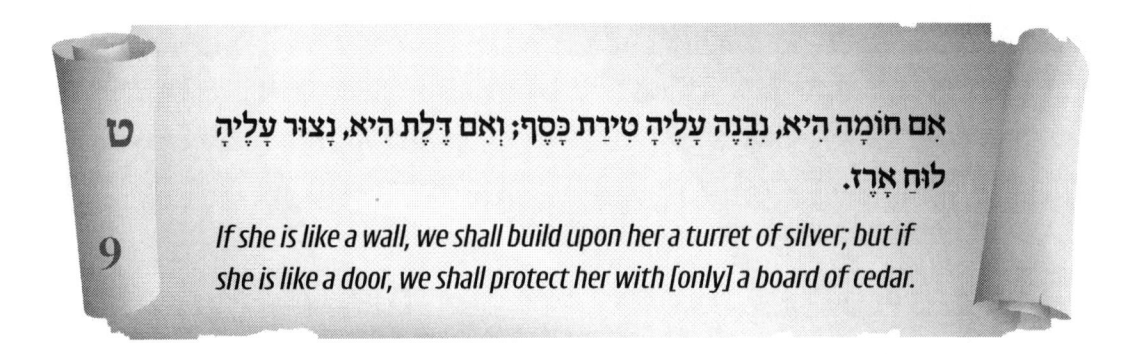

> **ט** אִם חוֹמָה הִיא, נִבְנֶה עָלֶיהָ טִירַת כָּסֶף; וְאִם דֶּלֶת הִיא, נָצוּר עָלֶיהָ לוּחַ אָרֶז.
>
> **9** *If she is like a wall, we shall build upon her a turret of silver; but if she is like a door, we shall protect her with [only] a board of cedar.*

Allegorical Translation — Hashem declares: "If *Klal Yisrael* is as strong in their faith as a wall and do not intermingle and intermarry with the other nations, we will build for them a Beis HaMikdash. But if they are like a door, ready to open up to the other nations, they will get only a weak, temporary, wooden fence."

Subject of the Verse — Hashem and the Heavenly court outline how they will decide the fate of *Klal Yisrael*.

Mashal — The older brother decides that if his younger sister is like a wall, i.e., impregnable to wicked people, he will build her a silver palace. But if she is open to all influences, like a flimsy door, then she will get only a weak, wooden fence as protection. Such a fence is susceptible to rotting and being eaten by worms.

Nimshal — This verse tells us the basis of the judgment mentioned in the previous verse. The judgment hinges on whether or not *Klal Yisrael* is firm in their commitments. If *Klal Yisrael* is found to be as firm as a wall, they will be judged favorably and will receive extra protection — the equivalent of silver, which does not rot and cannot be eaten by worms. But if they are found to be as flexible as a door that opens and closes, they will get minimal protection that will eventually give out.

Rashi says that the underlying question here is whether or not *Klal Yisrael* will allow foreign nations to intermarry with them. If she is like a wall and does not marry out of the faith, she will be given a sterling building, the Beis HaMikdash. If she allows other nations to join with her, she will be surrounded only by a wooden fence which is weak like a rotting and highly vulnerable wooden door. In other words, if they are susceptible to the influences of the heathen nations, they do not deserve the ultimate salvation. While they will still receive temporary protection, they will not merit complete redemption until they repent fully.[109]

This is *middah k'negged middah* – measure for measure. If *Klal Yisrael* is steadfast and firm, they will be rewarded with a strong building that does not give out. But if their conduct resembles a flimsy door, which is sometimes open and sometimes closed, they will be punished with protection that is temporary as well.

IF SHE IS LIKE A WALL

The Vilna Gaon understands that this verse is alluding to the two kinds of righteous people: those who are not influenced by the wicked and those who are. If the righteous are "wall-like," and thus not susceptible to negative influences, they can be made into a "silver palace." Everyone will come to them and learn from their ways, like a beautiful palace that everyone comes to admire and study. When someone is not influenced by others, he can have the public come to him, and can teach them without fear of being weakened. But if he is like a door which opens up and is affected by the pressure of every person, he must be protected and "enclosed with a board of cedar." Otherwise, when he goes out into society, people will change him for the worse instead of him changing them for the better.

As discussed above in connection with the previous verse, the Midrash says that these few verses allude to Avraham Avinu. In Heaven, they are asking: Is he like a wall, uninfluenced and firm? If so, he will be saved from Nimrod. But if he is flimsy like a door, he will not be saved. As the next verse testifies that Avraham was indeed like a wall. Indeed, *Chazal* teach us that he was called "Avraham HaIvri[110] — Avraham of the other side," because he was on one side of the world in his thinking, while everyone else was on the other. Avraham Avinu had the strength to reject the way the entire world thought, and he choose another way. His wall was so strong that the entire world could not trample it down. Therefore, as this verse says (according to the Midrash), he was graced with a "silver turret" or "palace." Humanity admired him and learned how to behave from him. In fact, Avraham was crowned as the king of the world, deserving of a palace.[111] Noach, in contrast, was considerably less strong in his beliefs.[112] Because he

---

109 Even if *Klal Yisrael* is unworthy, Hashem will not leave them unprotected because of His love for them.
110 *Bereishis* 14:13.
111 *Bamidbar Rabbah* 15:14.
112 See Seforno on *Bereishis* 6:8.

could have been influenced by others, he was therefore enclosed in a wooden ark for his protection and safety. He was literally surrounded by the "wooden boards" of this verse. Indeed, the world never learned from him, and he did not influence others. These two men, then, illustrate the two different levels of righteousness. This verse underscores the tremendous difference between the two levels.[113]

This verse is therefore to be understood on a national level and on an individual level. If *Klal Yisrael* is as strong as a wall, they will merit the Final Redemption and be deserving of a "beautiful palace," i.e. the Beis HaMikdash. On an individual level, one who is as firm as a wall, he will be held up as an example for others and will be worthy of being a leader. He will also be deserving of a "beautiful palace," a base from which he can teach the many how to conduct themselves.

The Gemara sees this verse alluding to a disappointing era in our history.[114] When Darius granted permission for Jews to go back to Eretz Yisrael to rebuild the Beis HaMikdash, only a relatively small portion of the nation took advantage of this opportunity. Hashem said about this: "Had you been a wall [in the sense of going en masse] then I would have built you a beautiful Beis HaMikdash in all its glory, never to be destroyed. But since you were only like a doorway [which often has one door open and one door closed,[115] meaning that only some of you went], the Beis HaMikdash will only be like a wooden structure, lacking permanence and vulnerable to worms and rot. And it will eventually be destroyed."[116]

According to the *Targum*, the angel Michael, the heavenly minister of *Klal Yisrael*, will say: "**If she** [*Klal Yisrael*] stands strong and upright like **a wall** among the nations, and gives away her money for the sake of her belief in the Oneness of Hashem, then we and you [other angels], together with her leaders, will **encompass her like fortifications of silver**. The other nations will then have no power to rule over her, just as worms cannot affect silver. And even if **she is destitute**[117] in terms of mitzvos, we will beg for mercy for her from Hashem. **He will remember to her credit**[118] the merit accruing from the

---

113 *Sefer Shiras Dovid*.
114 *Yoma* 9b.
115 Rashi ibid., *s.v. ke'delasos*.
116 See commentary on 5:5.
117 The *Targum* understands the word "דלת" to mean "being poor," from the root "דל," meaning "pauper."
118 The *Targum* understands the word "נצור" as "retaining/remembering." This is another meaning of the word, as in *Shemos* 34:7 and *Tehillim* 34:14.

Torah learning of her young, from the fact that it [Torah] is inscribed on the hearts of her young, and from her readiness to stand up to the heathen nations like a **cedar**."

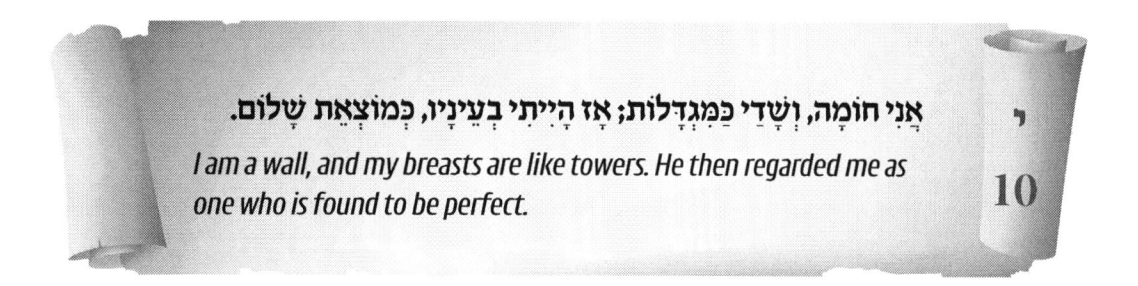

> אֲנִי חוֹמָה, וְשָׁדַי כַּמִּגְדָּלוֹת; אָז הָיִיתִי בְעֵינָיו, כְּמוֹצְאֵת שָׁלוֹם.
>
> *I am a wall, and my breasts are like towers. He then regarded me as one who is found to be perfect.*
>
> **י 10**

Allegorical Translation — *Klal Yisrael* proudly and confidently reply: We are as impregnable as a wall in our love and devotion to Hashem, and our places of learning nurture us with Torah and protect us like towers. When we say this, we are found perfect in the eyes of Hashem.

Subject of the Verse — *Klal Yisrael* proudly replies that they are a wall.

Mashal — The younger sister proudly replies that she is as firm and dependable as a wall. When she says this, she finds favor in the eyes of those who are judging her.

Nimshal — With great joy and pride, *Klal Yisrael* respond to the question by declaring their strength and virtue: "I am [as firm as] a wall, and my breasts [meaning, my places of learning or Torah scholars who nurture and sustain Klal Yisrael] are like towers." What is the difference between a wall and a tower? Although both offer protection, a wall protects only those who are behind it. In contrast, a tower protects all those in the vicinity of the tower. This is because a tower is as strong as a wall, but it is much more than that due to its height and fortification. It is also a place of power and protection for all the surroundings. Castles and fortresses were built not only as protection for those living there, but to enhance the security of the entire country.

In other words, *Klal Yisrael*, on the whole, are like a wall: firm in their observance of the Torah and safe in their conduct. But *Klal Yisrael* also harbor places of learning and *talmidei chachamim* who learn Torah. They are even better than walls. They are like towers, bringing strength and staying power to the whole of *Klal Yisrael*.

The verse concludes, "He then regarded me as one who is found to be perfect." When we, *Klal Yisrael*, respond that we are firm in observing the Torah, and when Hashem sees that this is indeed the case, we find favor in His eyes. Then we are to Him like a perfect nation.

I AM A WALL…

Besides teaching us that *Klal Yisrael* is firm and unshakable, the "wall" metaphor hints that their strength lies in their unity. A wall is made up of many bricks packed tightly together. If a lack of "unity" in a wall would develop, i.e., the bricks would separate from one another, the wall would crumble. *Klal Yisrael* say: We are like a wall made up of myriad individuals, attached to one another in perfect unity. We know that if we lose our unity, we lose our strength and our existence. But in this verse, we declare that we do not need to worry about such an eventuality because we are strongly united. We have the great strength of an imposing wall.[119]

Furthermore, towers built on city walls rely on ramparts on top of ramparts. They require even more unity than a wall. If they are just a bit out of joint, they will come tumbling down. Similarly, Torah scholars build on each other to grow together to great heights. They learn from each other and develop together and thus build towers of Torah learning.

MY BREASTS ARE LIKE TOWERS

These "towers" are the places of Torah learning and Torah scholars. A nursing baby's joy and nourishment are dependent on its continuing to nurse.[120] Its dependence on its mother's breasts can be compared to the Torah scholar's need for Torah. For him, the thought of his leaving Torah is as worrying as the thought of an infant stopping to nurse. Furthermore, just as an infant who stops nursing (in the age before baby formula) dies, so those who separate from *talmidei chachamim* die a spiritual death.[121]

Towers are tall buildings upon which watchmen would stand and warn of any approaching dangers. Torah scholars are very great personalities standing spiritually tall, and like watchmen on a tower, they are able to see far into the future and warn of any dangers to *Klal Yisrael*. Therefore, they are likened to towers. Just as only a fool would disregard the watchmen, so only a fool would disregard the warnings of the great Torah scholars.

I AM A WALL…

In declaring their commitment to Hashem, *Klal Yisrael* say that they are like immovable walls when it comes to observing the mitzvos. We, *Klal Yisrael*, are not willing to budge even one inch when it comes to the mitzvos. We have not compromised on our values and ideals despite being in exile for thousands of years, and despite the endless persecution and attempts by so many nations to weaken our resolve. We still

---

119 *Sar Shalom*.

120 See commentary on 4:5.

121 See *Pesachim* 112a, where the Gemara likens learning and teaching Torah to a mother nursing her baby. Just as a baby cannot live without the one, Torah scholars cannot live without the other.

say the same *Shema*, wear the same *tefillin*, and observe the same mitzvos that Moshe Rabbeinu taught us so many centuries ago. This uncompromising stance is the essence of the power of *Klal Yisrael*, and what has kept them true to their faith. When Hashem sees this, we are "perfect in His eyes."

This uncompromising dedication to Hashem is something we should be very proud of. *Klal Yisrael* is praised just for this virtue alone. Since we embody this trait it has become synonymous with *Klal Yisrael* as we say in the *Hoshanos* on Sukkos: Please save אום אני חומה ("The nation that declares: 'I am a wall!'"). We are identified as the nation that is strong in principles.[122]

Rabbi Moshe Feinstein was a living example of this "wall-like" steadfastness. His commitment to halachah was absolute, with no attempt to skirt it even a tiny bit. Here is one of the many stories that illustrate this virtue:

It happened once that Rabbi Moshe finished davening *Shemoneh Esrei* but could not take the concluding steps backwards because someone was still davening behind him. Quite some time passed, but Rabbi Moshe did not move. Even though he was supposed to leave the shul promptly in order to give a keynote speech at an Agudah convention, he did not budge because this would have involved passing in front of this man. When asked why he waited when he was expected elsewhere, he answered simply, with an amazed look: "How could I move? If there would have been a wall behind me, would you have expected me to walk through it?! For me, halachah is like a wall!"

Years earlier, Rabbi Moshe's steadfastness saved his community from disaster.[123] In the town of Lyuban, Russia, where he was the Rav before he came to America, there was an infamous *moser* ("informer"). This evildoer would regularly badmouth his fellow Jews in front of the Communist authorities and thus cause his brethren a great deal of trouble. On his deathbed, however, he announced that he wished to do *teshuvah* for all the harm he had caused by having his body buried face down in a disrespectful manner. When the time came to bury this man, the *Chevrah Kaddisha* asked Rabbi Moshe what to do. They were afraid of this person whose family still had powerful connections and wished to fulfill his last instructions. Rabbi Moshe ruled that he be interred like everyone else: face up. He said that no matter what the man had requested or what his reason was, we must follow the halachah.

A few weeks after the burial, which was carried out as Rabbi Moshe had ruled, government officers appeared in town with a court order demanding that the *moser*'s body be exhumed. When asked for an explanation, they said that before he died, this man

---

122 As described in *Bava Basra* 8a.
123 Adapted from Rabbi Yissachar Frand's Commuter Chavrusa Tapes on the weekly Torah portion, # 821.

had sent a letter to the Russian government saying that the Jews hated the government and did terrible things to anyone who helped the government. As proof of this, he predicted that the Jews would disgrace him by burying him face down. However, when they dug up the grave, the officers found that all was in order. Due to Rabbi Moshe's unwillingness to bend the halachah, the community was saved from the *moser's* scheme!

I AM A WALL…

The main subject of these few verses is the virtue of being firm and immovable in observing mitzvos. The previous verse tells us that the Heavenly Court bases its judgment of *Klal Yisrael* on how firm they are. And in this verse, *Klal Yisrael* declare their commitment. We must remain true to this commitment, and make sure that we always continue to be like a wall, and not like a door. A door swings back and forth according to every person's whim. A wall does not move even if one bangs on it continuously. Our success depends on our continuing to be like a wall because both the *yetzer ha'ra* and the heathen nations will continue to try to move us away from mitzvah observance. Only by being like a wall can we sustain our *avodas Hashem*.

Rabbi Yerucham Levovitz, *zt"l*, *mashgiach* of the pre-war Mir Yeshivah, discusses this fundamental concept a number of times in his *Da'as Torah*.[124] The truth is that commitment is needed to succeed in anything. Without wall-like firmness, there can be no stability and no success. A person who stops and starts different endeavors on a whim will not succeed in anything. But when it comes to learning Torah and observing mitzvos, this is even more important because of the wiles of the *yetzer ha'ra* as well as the myriad distractions and influences that militate against our commitment. It is no accident that after a person dies, his soul is asked: Did you set aside fixed times for Torah learning?[125] Learning Torah at random times is not enough. One must make a commitment to Torah. Our great leaders were able to do this with great commitment for most of the day. We should try to emulate them at least regarding the time slots during which we can learn.

It is not always easy to be firm like a wall. Rabbi Yerucham says that we should start on a small scale, and practice until we become used to it. He says that a relatively easy way to start being like a wall is to keep strictly to one's schedule of learning and davening.

---

124 One of the times he talks about this is in his discussion of *Parashas Nitzavim*. The word "*nitzavim*" actually means "to stand firm." The verse there describes *Klal Yisrael* joining Hashem in a covenant and begins by saying "אתם נצבים — You stand firm." We see that the Torah itself already introduces this concept that *Klal Yisrael* has to stand firm in their commitment to Torah.

125 *Shabbos* 31a.

Even if one has a very limited amount of time in which to learn, he should make sure that at least that time is absolutely fixed, and not flexible.

In *Tenuas HaMussar*,[126] Rabbi Dov Katz, *zt"l*, describes how Rabbi Simcha Zissel Ziv of Kelm would learn for twelve hours at a time without distraction. In the summer, he would learn from 9:00 a.m. to 9:00 p.m. since *Minchah* there in the town of Grobin, Lithuania, was very late. Once, a very wealthy man came to Rabbi Simcha Zissel Ziv's Talmud Torah to speak to him at 8:30 in the morning. The *mashgiach*, Rabbi Eliyahu Dov Leizerovitz, *zt"l*, told the man to make sure to approach Rabbi Simcha Zissel right away because his daily learning session was going to begin in half an hour. The wealthy man ignored the advice, thinking that for an important person like himself, an exception would be made. But by the time he got around to it, Rabbi Simcha Zissel had already started learning. The wealthy man knocked and banged on the door with increasing intensity but was completely ignored! Despite the many reasons Rabbi Simcha Zissel could have had to open the door, his commitment was like a wall — and that is how he succeeded!

I AM A WALL...

Until this point, we have been discussing the "high end of the spectrum," so to speak – the greatness of someone who is committed to Torah like an immovable wall. But the "wall" in this verse also symbolizes the barriers and protection that one must put in place when one is not yet fully committed to Torah. They help ensure that one does not, *chas v'shalom*, stumble and fall even lower.

Rabbi Mordechai Gifter, *zt"l*, once had occasion to explain this to an anti-religious Jewish professor when the latter sat down next to him on an airplane. Rabbi Gifter feared that he would soon be facing numerous questions and accusations against Torah in general, and religious Jews in particular. These are usually trotted out as questions, but actually serve the Jewish questioner as an answer to the gnawing question within him as to why he is not observant.

Rabbi Gifter decided to preempt the professor by asking him a personal question. He first noted that everyone sets boundaries in their lives which they hold sacred and which they will not overstep under any circumstances. Even most of those citizens who are not especially patriotic would never spy on their own country because that crosses a red line in their minds. Even unethical people may decide never to cheat those who are very poor. Rabbi Gifter then asked him: "I see that you are not religious, but do you have any boundaries at all in your Jewish life?"

The professor thought for a few moments, and then answered that he would never

---

[126] Vol. 2, p. 31.

have married out of the faith, and it would disturb him if his children did. Rabbi Gifter was at first disturbed to hear that Shabbos, Yom Kippur, and all the other mitzvos were expendable to this professor, but at least he did have some values that he treasured.

Rabbi Gifter then commented that one does not wait until he gets to the edge of a cliff before stopping himself. Rather, he keeps a good distance back, and builds good fences to keep himself from even coming close to falling off. If a person would wait until reaching the edge of the cliff before stopping himself, there would be a real danger that in a moment of forgetfulness or loss of balance, he would actually fall off. Similarly, if a person waits until he is actually standing at the edge of the cliff of intermarriage, who knows if he will be able to avoid falling off?! "Since you appreciate that intermarriage is absolutely wrong," Rabbi Gifter now challenged the professor, "what fences are you building for your children to ensure that they never fall off this cliff?!" With this question hanging in the air, Rabbi Gifter proceeded to open up a *sefer*, thus indicating that he meant to give the professor some important food for thought.

Needless to say, it would be best to be like a wall, and never budge regarding any part of Torah. But if one is unable to do this, he should, at the very least, build barriers that protect him from falling lower. These barriers have to be as firm as walls because once they can be moved like doors, they are not safe anymore. A door that sometimes can be opened will, as we have seen, eventually be opened. There will always be another excuse why it has to be opened again. If a person has strong barriers, then even when he is not at his best and even when he is being strongly tempted, he will still stay safe.[127]

MY BREASTS ARE LIKE TOWERS

Two verses earlier, *Klal Yisrael* is described as not yet having breasts. How, then, can they suddenly claim, "My breasts are like towers"? The answer is that *Klal Yisrael* is correcting a misapprehension here: "You mistakenly think that we have not yet fully developed [i.e., we are not ready for redemption],[128] but you are wrong. We do have breasts [i.e., We are fully matured and ready for salvation]."[129]

The Shiras Dovid cites the *Targum*'s explanation that the absence of "breasts" means

---

127 This is part of the reason why one must have strong barriers and safety nets if he is forced to go online. Without them, one could easily fall to perilous depths, *chas v'shalom*, in a moment of temptation.

128 Alternatively, "We do not have suitable leaders," as explained above.

129 Rashbam. He adds that where there is greater maturity, there is usually a greater desire for independence. But *Klal Yisrael* always remains subservient to Hashem. So included in *Klal Yisrael*'s reply is the acknowledgment that even though we have matured, we remain completely under Your authority. We have not moved away one iota, like a wall that does not move. According to this approach, the verse should be understood this way: "I am a wall [in the sense that I have not moved away from You, even though] my breasts are like towers [meaning that I am fully matured. That is] perfection in the eyes of Hashem."

that *Klal Yisrael* lack kings to help them fight their battles and achieve redemption. According to the Shiras Dovid, the meaning of *Klal Yisrael*'s reply would then be: "We have breasts in the sense of having Torah scholars." Torah is so powerful that it can help save *Klal Yisrael* even under the most difficult circumstances, and even without kings to lead them in battle. This dovetails with the *Ohr HaChaim*'s statement that when *Klal Yisrael* has Torah, they are able to come out of even the darkest exiles, relying completely on the merit of learning Torah.[130]

HE THEN REGARDED ME AS ONE WHO IS FOUND TO BE PERFECT

"He *then* regarded me as one who is found to be perfect"[131] When was this? It happens when *Klal Yisrael* declare that they are a "wall," firm in their service of Hashem. This declaration alone — before *Klal Yisrael* has done anything else — causes Hashem to find them perfect. And this also applies on the individual level. There is tremendous value in declaring one's faithfulness and steadfastness to Hashem. The statement itself makes a very deep impression on oneself (and on those around him if made in public) and shows how a person really wishes to behave. We must never underestimate the value of declaring our faith. Even if we feel that our declaration goes beyond our present spiritual level, it is still valuable.[132]

The *Targum* explains this verse as follows. The Jewish People reply: "**I am** strong in words of Torah like a **wall**, and my children are as sturdy **as towers**." **At that time,** the Jewish People **will find favor in the eyes** of its Master, and all the people of the world will seek its **welfare**."

---

130 *Shemos* 3:8.

131 The word "שלום" can mean "peace" (as in *Bamidbar* 6:26) and can also mean "completion" or "perfection" (*Bereishis* 15:16). Rashi finds both meanings reflected in the verse. He says that when *Klal Yisrael* speak this way, she is "like a bride who was found *perfect* and also finds *peace* in her husband's home." Both perfection and peace are the rewards for those who proclaim their faith in Hashem.

132 The biography of Rabbi Amnon, the author of the famous *Unesaneh Tokef* prayer is well worth mentioning in this connection. A certain Christian nobleman respected Rabbi Amnon greatly but kept trying to convince him to convert to Christianity. He kept telling him how much money, honor, and power he would gain by doing so. On one occasion, Rabbi Amnon told the nobleman he would consider it. Although Rabbi Amnon had absolutely no intention of forsaking his faith — and said this just to get the man off his back — he immediately regretted his words. He fasted and prayed to Hashem for forgiveness and stayed away from the nobleman. But this cruel nobleman eventually caught up with Rabbi Amnon and tortured him in an attempt to get him to forsake his beliefs. Although the nobleman cut off all his limbs, Rabbi Amnon remained steadfast in his faith, and composed the *Unesaneh Tokef* prayer with his last breaths. We see how greatly distressed Rabbi Amnon was that his words did not display his convictions even though they were said under great duress. How much more so are words which *do* declare our faith in Hashem and display our devotion worthy of being praised.

> יא כֶּרֶם הָיָה לִשְׁלֹמֹה בְּבַעַל הָמוֹן, נָתַן אֶת הַכֶּרֶם לַנֹּטְרִים; אִישׁ יָבִא בְּפִרְיוֹ, אֶלֶף כָּסֶף.
>
> The Master of Peace had a vineyard at Ba'al Hamon. He entrusted the vineyard to the guardians; each one garnered a thousand pieces of silver through the fruit.

Allegorical Translation — *Klal Yisrael* was under the protection of Hashem in Yerushalayim, the city of multitudes. When they sinned, He handed them over to harsh masters and nations. Each nation plundered *Klal Yisrael* as much as they could.

Subject of the Verse — This is a description of exile and the heathen nations' conduct vis-à-vis *Klal Yisrael*.

Mashal — A king told a group of guardians to look after his beautiful vineyard. Instead of faithfully looking after the vineyard, they abused their position of power, and helped themselves to whatever they fancied from the vineyard.

Nimshal — Following the judgment of *Klal Yisrael* in the previous verses, this verse and the next move on to the final judgment of the nations. That judgment revolves around only one thing: how they treated *Klal Yisrael*.[133] The entire world was created for *Klal Yisrael*. Consequently, the ultimate success or failure of any nation hinges upon how they treated *Klal Yisrael*. These verses also summarize symbolically the whole process of our nation's exile and its consequences.

In these verses, *Klal Yisrael* is likened to Hashem's vineyard, as they often are in *Tanach*. Part of what lies behind this metaphor is the fact that a vineyard requires a great deal of tending. Even a small amount of frost or too much heat can damage the vines because they do not have a hardy trunk and branches. They need much pruning, watering, etc. Also, a vineyard is very precious because it produces grapes, a prized commodity. Both because of the vineyard's many

---

133 See *Avodah Zarah* 2b.
The Tiferes Shlomo (on *Parashas Noach*) explains that, originally, all mankind were created to serve Hashem. After Adam HaRishon failed his test, Hashem choose one nation to accept the Torah and observe its mitzvos. When *Klal Yisrael* took on that role, the rest of the world's mission became to assist them. This can be likened to the units of the army whose job is to make sure that the front-line soldiers have what they need to carry out their mission. If the heathen nations do their job properly, they will be rewarded. But if they do not, even if they find other important missions to perform, they have failed in their *tafkid* (role), and will be punished. That Hashem judges the other nations only in terms of whether or not they have done their duty to *Klal Yisrael* also illustrates the greatness of our People.

needs and because of its high value, it is looked after very well. This is how we want Hashem to look after us, showering us with great care and attention and cherishing us because of our preciousness.

Furthermore, the pedigree of the grapes makes a major difference in the quality of the wine. Indeed, it is common to find the pedigree ("*yichus*") of the grapes mentioned on the label of good bottles of wine. Similarly, *Klal Yisrael*'s greatness stems from their lineage, from their great forefathers: Avraham, Yitzchak and Yaakov.[134]

"The Master of Peace" is an allusion to Hashem, to whom all peace belongs.[135] The verse tells us that the Master of Peace had a vineyard (*Klal Yisrael*) in a place called "Ba'al Hamon." This is an allusion to Yerushalayim. "Ba'al Hamon" literally means "place of the multitude." Yerushalayim was a place filled with a vast multitude of people.[136] Yerushalayim is given this title here because it miraculously held so many people. Because of its large population, it was also a multi-faceted place. Indeed, Yerushalayim was the most multi-dimensional place in the world. Our verse speaks as if *Klal Yisrael* lived in Yerushalayim despite the fact that they were spread out all over Eretz Yisrael. This is because Yerushalayim was the capital, and the most important and central part of the country.

The Midrash points out that the word "*hamon*" can mean "desired."[137] Therefore, "Ba'al Hamon" means "the land that is desired." All the kings and nations wished to possess at least a part of Eretz Yisrael because of its beauty and greatness. It was a place desired by everyone.[138]

---

134 The Gemara (*Ta'anis* 31a) describes how the young Jewish men and women would go to the vineyards to find a *shidduch*. The Ben Yehoyada (ibid.) notes that the vine cannot be grafted with other types of plants. Its "lineage" therefore remains pure. This reminded the young men and women that they, too, should make sure to marry only within the pure lineage of the Jewish People. The "vine" thus represents the purity of the Jewish People, and how they have not intermarried. Not surprisingly, then, a good *shidduch* is described in the Gemara (*Pesachim* 49a) this way: ענבי הגפן בענבי הגפן, דבר נאה ומתקבל — Fruit of the vine with fruit of the vine: something pleasant and appropriate.")

135 As explained in our commentary on 1:1.

136 The Midrash describes how millions upon millions of people used to live in Yerushalayim (beginning of *Eichah*).

137 From the word "הומה" (desire), as in *Shir HaKavod*: הומה לבי אל דודיך (my heart *desires* Your love).

138 Owning property in certain places in the world is a sign of great wealth and a badge of prestige. Eretz Yisrael has this virtue in the extreme. Everyone wanted to have some little part of the land of Eretz Yisrael. (See Rashi on *Devarim* 33:17, *s.v. afsei*, who explains that this is why Yehoshua and the Jewish People had to defeat no fewer than thirty-one kings before they could take over Eretz Yisrael. Many kings had come from around the world to take over a portion of Eretz Yisrael.)

When *Klal Yisrael* sinned, Hashem put them under the supervision of other nations. Metaphorically, "He entrusted the vineyard to the guardians." But instead of looking after them, they betrayed the trust Hashem had put in them. They exploited *Klal Yisrael* for their own gain, plundering their wealth and taking from them whatever they could through taxation, theft, expulsion, and various other methods. This is the meaning of the conclusion of the verse: "Each one garnered a thousand pieces of silver through the fruit."

A VINEYARD

As we have seen, *Shir HaShirim* uses many symbols to describe *Klal Yisrael* in their relationship with Hashem. The most common one is "wife." *Klal Yisrael* is the "wife" of Hashem because their relationship is one of love. But *Klal Yisrael* is also likened to a "sister," a "flower," a "vineyard," etc. We should understand that *Klal Yisrael* is all of these things together. Hashem loves us with the passion of a spouse, the caring of an older brother, the tenderness shown to a flower, and now with the regard shown to a precious vineyard.

THE GUARDIANS

When *Klal Yisrael* sinned, Hashem sent them into exile. In this verse, this is symbolized by the vineyard being handed over to other caretakers. But isn't this puzzling? Why does the verse speak of the calamity of exile in such mild terms?!

The answer is that we are now being shown a new perspective on exile. In *Shir HaShirim*, which describes Hashem's love for *Klal Yisrael*, we do not see Hashem rejecting *Klal Yisrael* and sending them away. Rather, we see how Hashem wants the best for *Klal Yisrael*. Since *Klal Yisrael* need special treatment due to their sins and also need to recognize the error of their ways, Hashem appoints other nations to "educate" them. The role of these guardians is to stop *Klal Yisrael* from sinning by showing them how painful the punishment for sin is.[139] When they administer punishment, and thus cause *Klal Yisrael* to regret sinning, they are effectively *guarding* them from sin. This aspect of exile is not immediately obvious. Exile is a process that *Klal Yisrael* must go through in order to become a better nation.[140]

The Midrash on this verse offers a short parable about a disobedient prince that

---

[139] This can be likened to father who takes his sick son to a surgeon for an operation. Even though the surgeon may hurt the patient in the course of the operation, the father understands that the doctor is doing what is best for his son so that he will return to good health. The father is in pain to see his son suffering, but he knows that the boy needs this treatment. Similarly, Hashem sends us to receive painful treatments for our own good.

[140] As explained in our commentary on 5:7.

illustrates this idea. In an attempt to educate his son, the king decided to have the prince educated by one of his servants. The servant started hitting the prince, and telling him, "You must disobey your father!" The prince responded: "Stupid fool! My father, the king, handed me over to you because I did not obey him. And now you tell me: 'Don't listen to your father!'"

Similarly, says the Midrash, when *Klal Yisrael* was taken into exile by Nevuchadnetzar, he commanded them to serve idols. *Klal Yisrael* responded: "We were put under your control because we served idols, and now you are telling us to do that very same thing!?"

We see from the Midrash that *Klal Yisrael* need to view the exile as a special type of education that they must have because of their sins. However, the heathen nations failed to do their job. Instead of ensuring that *Klal Yisrael* learn to act better, thus guarding them from sin, they tried to persuade them to sin even more. They selfishly used their power over *Klal Yisrael* for their own gain and took everything they could.[141] We must therefore be careful never to listen to them when they try to deter us from serving Hashem. That would totally defeat the purpose of exile.

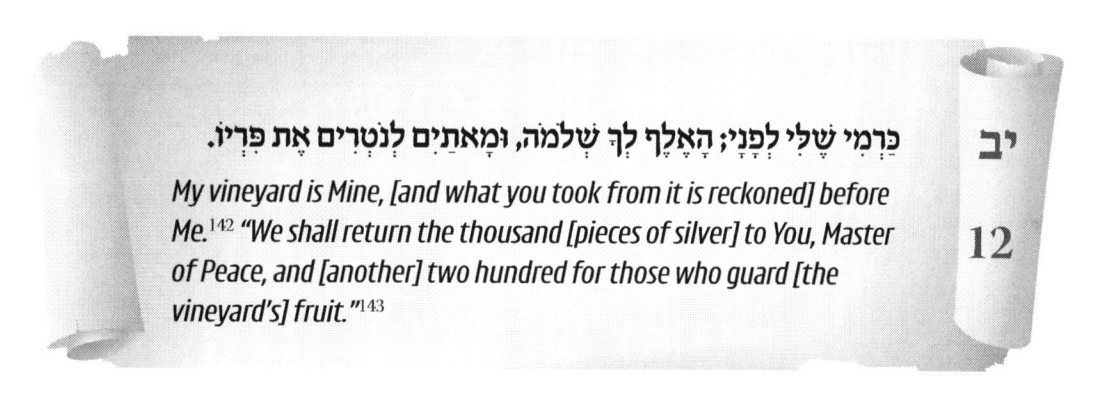

> **יב** כַּרְמִי שֶׁלִּי לְפָנָי; הָאֶלֶף לְךָ שְׁלֹמֹה, וּמָאתַיִם לְנֹטְרִים אֶת פִּרְיוֹ.
>
> **12** My vineyard is Mine, [and what you took from it is reckoned] before Me.[142] "We shall return the thousand [pieces of silver] to You, Master of Peace, and [another] two hundred for those who guard [the vineyard's] fruit."[143]

---

141 The Netziv tells us that the expression in our verse "a thousand pieces of silver" was commonly used to indicate an extremely large sum (as in *Bereishis* 20:16). This is loosely similar to the way a "million dollars" is used nowadays. This means that the nations took and stole from *Klal Yisrael* the most they could.

142 Rashi explains Hashem's words "כרמי שלי לפני" (literally, "It is My vineyard before Me") as two statements: "It is My vineyard" (i.e., *Klal Yisrael* belong to Me); and "[What you took from it is reckoned] before Me" (i.e., You heathen nations must give an account before Me for that which you took).

The Divrei Yedidyah explains more simply that Hashem is saying that the vineyard is Mine, and I want it back before Me. That is, "*Klal Yisrael* is My nation, and I want them back before Me." In the translation and commentary, we have incorporated both approaches.

143 In his *Chomas Anach*, the Chida offers a remarkable homiletical explanation of this verse based on the mitzvah to recite a hundred blessings daily (*Orach Chaim* 46:3). On a weekday, because of the longer *Shemoneh Esrei*, one fulfils this requirement as a matter of course — without making any special effort. But on Shabbos, it is much harder to get to the required hundred blessings because each *Shemoneh Esrei* consists of only seven blessings. The *Shulchan Aruch* (ibid. 284:3 and 290:1) and *Mishnah Berurah* (46:14) write that since there are approximately twenty blessings missing on Shabbos, one should eat more fruit (and, of course, recite the blessings over them) in order to reach a hundred. But *talmidei chachamim*, who are busy learning Torah and have no time to eat fruit, should listen to other blessings with the intention of being included — as if they had recited the blessings themselves. Now, we know that a blessing is worth

Allegorical Translation On the day of judgment, Hashem tells the nations: "*Klal Yisrael* is Mine, and I want them back since you are not looking after them properly! And that which you have taken from them is calculated before Me." They reply, "We will return all that we have plundered, and will even give back more to the leaders and *talmidei chachamim*."

Subject of the Verse Justice is demanded from the nations.

Mashal The king now calls in the guardians to whom he had entrusted his vineyard and demands it back since they have been negligent in taking care of it. The guardians recognize their wickedness and promise to pay back everything they took. They also promise to pay fines and compensation and give them to those who truly look after the vineyard.

Nimshal Continuing the symbolism of the previous verse, this verse alludes to the time when Hashem will take *Klal Yisrael* back and hold the nations responsible for all the suffering they caused them.

The king reclaiming his vineyard symbolizes Hashem wanting *Klal Yisrael* back from the nations at the time of the Final Redemption. After Hashem takes *Klal Yisrael* back, He tells the nations that He has calculations "before [Him]." This means that He has careful records of all that they took from *Klal Yisrael*, and He demands that they repay them. The nations agree to repay all that they took. In addition, they promise to pay an extra fine which they will give to the Torah leaders who truly looked after *Klal Yisrael*.

TWO HUNDRED FOR THOSE WHO GUARD ITS FRUIT

Hashem determines that they owe "the thousand pieces of silver [they stole, plus] another two hundred..." Rashi explains that in addition to repaying their debt, the nations will have to pay another "two hundred" as a fine and as compensation for the harm they caused. As Yeshayahu[144] prophesizes, "For the copper [we nations took from the Jewish People], we will [have to] pay back gold; for the iron [we stole], we will pay

---

ten coins since one who "stole" a blessing (by reciting a blessing that someone else was supposed to recite) must pay ten coins to the person he deprived (*Chullin* 87a).

In light of the above, our verse can be understood as follows: "Master of Peace, the thousand that You have [i.e., the thousand coins Hashem 'pays' every person for the hundred daily blessings] and two hundred [ten coins each for the twenty missing blessings that Hashem 'pays'] for those who 'guard' its fruit [i.e., eat fruit in order to recite a hundred blessings on Shabbos]..." [The next verse continues:] "Friends who sit in the gardens" [the *talmidei chachamim* learning Torah in the *batei midrash*] "listen to the voice..." they will be rewarded for the blessings they complete by listening.

144 60:17.

back silver; for the wood [we stole], we will pay back copper; and for the stones [we stole], we will pay back iron." Whatever the nations seized, they will have to repay — and much more. This, they promise to do.

Considering how much they have plundered during the thousands of years of exile, and how many times they dealt treacherously with *Klal Yisrael*, the enormous compensation they owe us is beyond anything we can imagine.

However, even this added payment does not adequately compensate us for the harm they have inflicted. Their promise to give back more does not comfort us. As the Gemara[145] poignantly asks: What about the precious lives of the righteous, like Rabbi Akiva and his colleagues, which they took?! How can they possibly repay us for this loss?! They can, perhaps, repay us with interest for the material wealth which they deprived us of, but how can they possibly repay us for the precious spiritual lives of towering Torah scholars and the myriad Jewish souls that they deprived us of?! Since they cannot possibly compensate for all the losses we have incurred throughout the bitter exile, they will always be guilty of having defaulted on their obligations. Indeed, as the Gemara concludes, only Hashem can do justice in our case because only He is capable of compensating us and punishing them for this.

Rashi offers another interpretation of the fine of "two hundred" silver pieces. This can be seen as the exact amount of the fine levied on one who steals from consecrated property. The rule is that someone who gets illicit benefit from items that have been sanctified for use in the Beis HaMikdash (הנהנה מן ההקדש) has to pay back, besides the principal, an extra fifth as a penalty. *Klal Yisrael* is also sanctified, consecrated to Hashem.[146] Therefore, the nations have to pay, besides the principal of one thousand pieces of silver (the symbolic "value" of *Klal Yisrael*), an extra two hundred pieces of silver, which is one fifth of a thousand, as a penalty.[147]

Even if we do not understand its full depth, we, *Klal Yisrael*, ought to be inspired by the thought that we are considered to be like holy objects. It as if our bodies were actually consecrated and sanctified to Hashem, like the Altar or the other vessels in the Beis HaMikdash. The sin of misusing a Jewish person is as grave as misusing any holy item. If one does, one deserves a penalty. *Klal Yisrael* is a holy nation to Hashem and may not

---

145 *Rosh Hashanah* 23a.

146 As expressed by the Prophet Yirmiyahu, *Klal Yisrael* is "holy unto Hashem" (*Yirmiyahu* 2:3).

147 The Gemara records a halachic disagreement as to whether the fine is one-fifth of the original sum or one-fifth of the final sum (*Bava Metzia* 54a). The halachah follows the second opinion. One-fifth of the final sum is really one-quarter of the original sum. Thus, the fine here should be 250, not 200. The *Rinas Yitzchak* poses the question: How are we to understand the fact that Rashi's explanation is not in accord with the established halachah?

be misused by the other nations. We are intrinsically holy, like sanctified objects, and remembering this should influence how we feel about ourselves and behave.

The Midrash sees "two hundred" not as an addition sum, but as a multiplication factor. For everything the nations stole from us throughout our very long and bitter exile, they will have to pay us back two-hundredfold! Hashem will reward us in a manner much, much greater than the manner in which He punished us. Despite their differences, the various calculations give us a completely new appreciation of just how great our eventual reward will be, and how terrible the punishment of the nations will be. May it happen speedily, in our lifetime!

TWO HUNDRED FOR THOSE WHO GUARD ITS FRUIT

As we learned, when Hashem redeems *Klal Yisrael*, the heathen nations will be forced to pay back what they took, plus a fine. To whom will the payment be made? It will go to those "who [truly] guard the fruit." This is an allusion to the *talmidei chachamim*, the Torah leaders of *Klal Yisrael* who are our nation's true guardians.[148]

In light of the understanding of the exile discussed in connection with the previous verse, we can understand that the punishment is appropriate to the crime. Originally, Hashem gave the nations power over *Klal Yisrael* to motivate them to repent. Had the nations done so, they could even have requested payment for doing that which Hashem asked of them: to be the guardians of *Klal Yisrael*. But the nations used the power Hashem gave them for their own benefit and did not help *Klal Yisrael* return to Hashem at all. Who then proved to be the true guardians of *Klal Yisrael*? Who saved *Klal Yisrael* from sin, and who actually deserve the payment? The answer is: the Torah leaders who ensured that *Klal Yisrael* continued to observe the Torah. They were the true guardians. They saved *Klal Yisrael* from extinction during the exile by teaching them Torah and enacting new laws to protect them from sin. Therefore, Hashem justifiably tells the nations who had neglected their job of guarding *Klal Yisrael* that they must give back whatever they took, plus they must pay an extra fine to the true guardians, i.e., the Torah leaders.

This verse actually contrasts two types of guardians: the false guardians (i.e., the nations who abused their power for their own benefit and who will therefore be severely punished) and the true guardians (i.e., the Torah scholars who will be richly rewarded because they seek the good of the nation, and not their own benefit).

This is true to a lesser extent for every Jewish person who gets a position. Even a very minor position brings with it a certain amount of power. There are two ways to relate to

---

148 Rashi.

it: 1) How can I benefit myself? 2) How can I benefit *Klal Yisrael*? Ultimately Hashem will reward those who chose to use their power to help others and will punish those who use their power only for their own selfish purposes. If we think about it, we will realize that each of us has a "position." Being a parent or a spouse is also a position. Indeed, these are positions with tremendous power and opportunities. But even being a son or daughter, or a friend or neighbor, is a position of sorts. A person must ask himself: Am I using the position for my own gain or to help others? As this verse teaches us, Hashem handsomely rewards those who use their power for others and severely punishes those who behave selfishly.

> יג הַיּוֹשֶׁבֶת בַּגַּנִּים, חֲבֵרִים מַקְשִׁיבִים לְקוֹלֵךְ, הַשְׁמִיעִנִי.
>
> 13 You who sit in the gardens, [your] friends are listening to your voice. "Let Me hear it!"

Allegorical Translation — Hashem says to *Klal Yisrael*: "You, My nation sitting in the scattered shuls in exile, the angels who are your friends have come to listen to your voice. I ask you to lift up your voice in prayer so that We can hear it. Only then will the angels be allowed to praise Me."

Subject of the Verse — Hashem is calling on *Klal Yisrael* to pray to Him.

Mashal — The husband calls out to his wife and says that even though she is lost in the gardens of others, he and her other friends want to hear her voice so that she should find favor in their eyes. This will inspire him to come and redeem her and bring her back as his wife. He urges her to lift up her voice and call out to him loudly.

Nimshal — These are Hashem's last words to the Jewish People in *Shir HaShirim*. He tells them that the angels, their "friends," are listening to them. They should thus raise their voice in praise and prayer to Hashem so that He and the angels will hear, and they will thereby find favor in their eyes. Hashem will then redeem them.[149]

In this verse, Hashem refers to *Klal Yisrael* as "you who sit in the gardens." As

---

149 Rashi.

explained earlier, "gardens" represent the shuls that are so central to the life of *Klal Yisrael*.[150]

"Gardens" also allude to exile. *Klal Yisrael* is a nation "sitting in the garden of exile." A "garden" symbolizes exile for a number of reasons.[151] A garden is not suitable for an extended stay. Unlike a home, a garden offers no protection from the elements or the surroundings. If it rains, one gets drenched there, and if the summer sun is beating down, one quickly grows hot, and sometimes faint. There, one is vulnerable not only to the flies but to all kinds of horrible people as well. Similarly, in exile, we are vulnerable to horrible nations and terrible dangers all around. We are uncomfortable and out of our element there. We hope to come out of the exile quickly and go back home to the Beis HaMikdash. We are only there because we are "homeless" — without the Beis HaMikdash, our true home.

On the other hand, in the garden, one can see things that one cannot see at home. This can be good for a person. Indeed, sometimes a person goes intentionally into the garden to see new sights and get a new perspective. As explained in the Introduction, in *Shir HaShirim*, we see everything in a positive light with the "lens" of love. Therefore, the pertinent verses do not speak about Hashem sending us away but just sending us into the garden to wait for Him. Here, we can rethink our conduct and come back as better people.

The angels are called "friends" either because they are friends of *Klal Yisrael*[152] or because they are friends with one another in the sense that there is no fighting among themselves.[153]

Rashi notes that the angels must wait until they hear *Klal Yisrael* praising Hashem before they themselves can praise Him.[154] The verse thus presents the angels waiting in anticipation for *Klal Yisrael*'s voice so that they can begin to praise Hashem after them.[155]

---

150 See our commentary on 6:2.
151 Rashi interprets "gardens" in this verse to mean "other people's gardens" because in exile, we are under the jurisdiction of other nations.
152 Rashi.
153 Midrash.
154 See *Chullin* 91b.
155 Even when we are in exile, the angels have to wait for *Klal Yisrael* before they can praise Hashem. This is because *Klal Yisrael*'s praise is more important, and thus the angels have to wait out of respect — similar to the practice of not beginning to eat until the most important person at the table has started eating (*Berachos* 47a). This shows the tremendous

LISTENING TO YOUR VOICE

As mentioned above, these are Hashem's final words to *Klal Yisrael* in *Shir HaShirim*. They communicate a key message of the entire megillah: that Hashem waits to hear *Klal Yisrael*'s prayers, and He asks them to pray to Him.

Klal Yisrael's most powerful weapon is their ability to pray to Hashem. The Midrash puts it this way: Why is *Klal Yisrael* likened to a worm? Just as all of a worm's power lies in its mouth, so all of *Klal Yisrael*'s power lies in their mouths (via prayer).[156] We must remember that the only way we will come out of exile is through prayer.[157] Hashem loves to hear our prayers. Each one of them is heard and treasured, and none are ignored.

The whole of *Shir HaShirim* teaches us how much Hashem loves *Klal Yisrael*. This has any number of practical applications,[158] but the most significant one is the importance of prayer. We see this several times in *Shir HaShirim*,[159] and it is the final message from Hashem in this megillah of love.

There is a famous story of a little boy on the beach that can help us appreciate the power of prayer. While his friends are playing in the sand, the boy is waving a small toy flag. A man goes up to him and says: "My dear boy, why are you not playing with your friends? What are you doing?" The boy explains that there is a ship in the distance, and he is waving to the captain of the ship. "You silly little boy," the man says, "why are you wasting your time? Do you think the captain of an enormous ship is going to notice your little flag?! Go and play with your friends!" As he is speaking a huge flag is raised from the ship, and the sound of the ship's horn is sounded. All of the sailors, together with the captain, stand on deck and wave to the boy. The man is astonished! How did anyone even notice the boy, and why would they stop everything to wave to him? The boy explains, "The captain of the ship is my father!"

A person sits at home and speaks to Hashem. He may wonder: "Will the Captain of the world listen to my voice when He has so many important things to attend to?" The answer is that since the Captain is his Father, he will definitely listen. Hashem is our Father, and He listens to every word we say to Him.

When we fully absorb the message of *Shir HaShirim* — that Hashem loves us ever so much — we will easily understand and appreciate that Hashem wants to hear our

---

importance of *Klal Yisrael* and the importance of their praise.

156 *Shemos Rabbah* 21:6. The Midrash adds that Hashem promises: Whenever you pray to Me, I listen and accept your prayers.

157 The Midrash (*Vayikra Rabbah* 38:4) says that Hashem declares: Just as I redeemed your forefathers through their prayers, so I will redeem you through your prayers.

158 As explained in the Introduction.

159 See earlier 2:14 and 6:2.

prayers, praises, and thanks. Indeed, the most important result of appreciating Hashem's love is a renewed enthusiasm and appreciation for all aspects of davening. It is no accident that the final words of Hashem to us are, "Let Me hear it!" — let Me hear your voice speaking to Me.

YOU WHO SIT IN THE GARDENS, THE FRIENDS...

The Divrei Yedidyah understands that the "friends" here are not the angels, but the other nations.[160] They are listening to hear if *Klal Yisrael* is praying well or are remiss in their prayers. The nations pay careful attention because they know that when *Klal Yisrael* is praying well, they cannot harm them. If they stop praying well, however, they are at the mercy of the nations who can pillage and destroy them.[161] According to this interpretation, the verse is to be understood as follows: "You [*Klal Yisrael*] who sit in the gardens [exile], [know that] the friends [other nations] are listening to your voice [to see if you pray properly]. Let Me hear it [raised in sincere prayer so that they will be incapable of harming you]." Hashem wants to save *Klal Yisrael*, but is powerless, *ki'veyachol*, to help us unless we are davening well. He thus begs us to raise our voices in sincere prayer. This is a very powerful message regarding the importance of *tefillah*.

THE FRIENDS

Of all the terms available to denote the holy spiritual angels, the verse here calls them, simply, "friends." Wouldn't a greater and more honorable term have been more appropriate?![162]

The Midrash explains that angels are called "friends" because they live together in unity and harmony. In contrast, our world is full of conflict. It is rare to have a relationship without any jealousy, something that can lead to hatred.[163] Since the angels have no jealousy, they live in complete harmony.

The Midrash here also says that when *Klal Yisrael* daven, Hashem responds this way:

> Raise your voices in learning and prayer so that the angels may hear you. But make sure that there is no hatred, no jealousy, no competition, and no embarrassing one another going on between you. If there

---

160 Similar to Rashi's interpretation of this same word *"chaveirim"* in 1:7.

161 The Midrash also states this in connection with the verse, "הקול קול יעקב והידים ידי עשיו" — The voice is the voice of Yaakov, but the hands are the hands of Eisav" [*Bereishis* 27:22]): When the voice of Yaakov (symbolizing *Klal Yisrael*) is raised in true prayer, Eisav cannot harm them (*Bereishis Rabbah* 65:16).

162 Elsewhere in *Tanach*, they are referred to as "holy beings" and "members of the Heavenly Court." See *Iyov* 1:6, *Daniel* 3:25 (with Metzudas Tzion) and 4:14 above.

163 *Shaarei Kedushah* 2:4.

is, the angels will say to Me that *Klal Yisrael* is not observing the Torah that You, Hashem, gave them. Therefore, make sure to observe the Torah with unity among you.

Even if we perform the mitzvos, if we do so amidst discord, the angels are convinced that we are not really observant. For the angels, discord among us is a proof that we are not observing the Torah because they cannot imagine serving Hashem without harmony.[164] Let us note that the angels' "conclusion" applies both to "interpersonal" mitzvos (בין אדם לחברו) and to the mitzvos between us and our Creator (בין אדם למקום). Obviously, when there is conflict, there is something very wrong with the way we are observing the interpersonal mitzvos. But one might mistakenly think that the mitzvos between us and Hashem can be done even when there is no harmony. Here we learn that when there is antagonism among us, even these mitzvos are tainted. As we see from the Midrash, this applies to the mitzvah of davening as well. Although we might have thought that davening has no connection to how we act towards one another, the angels reveal to us that even davening, if done while there is infighting, is no good.

This concept, that without unity there is no real service of Hashem, can be understood on a number of levels. On a very basic level, if *Klal Yisrael* is being unpleasant to each other, this shows that they have not developed the traits needed to serve Hashem. Serving Hashem requires that a person be grateful for His kindness, as well as obedient, humble, sincere, able to practice self-control, etc. All these traits produce a kind and grateful person. If a person is unpleasant, he lacks the characteristics needed to make him a servant of Hashem.

On a deeper level, if we cannot cultivate a spiritual connection between us and our fellow Jews, then we cannot possibly find it between us and Hashem. This is because, as the *Zohar* puts it, "Hashem, *Klal Yisrael*, and the Torah are all one."[165] There is a spiritual unity between Hashem and *Klal Yisrael*, and the same type of unity exists among all members of *Klal Yisrael* and between *Klal Yisrael* and the Torah.[166] Only when we are aware of this spiritual connection, are in touch with our spiritual dimension, and unite with each other through this spiritual connection are we really able to connect to Hashem. The essence of our connection to Hashem and Torah is a spiritual one. It is in that identity of our spirituality that we are one with Hashem, His Torah, and the rest of

---

164 The angels' service of Hashem is performed with complete harmony, and without any jealousy (*Mesillas Yesharim*, ch. 11).

165 *Zohar, Acharei Mos* 73a. See *Nefesh HaChaim*, 4:11, which elaborates on this concept from the *Zohar*.

166 This is the reason why Hashem (as quoted in the Midrash) singles out davening and learning. These are the times when one has to concentrate on the unity of Hashem, *Klal Yisrael*, and the Torah.

Klal Yisrael. If we are in conflict with one another, this spiritual connection and spiritual identity is evidently missing, and thus we cannot connect to Hashem either. This is why those who love *Klal Yisrael*, love Hashem, and why those who hate *Klal Yisrael*, hate Hashem.[167] It is understandable, then, that the angels conclude that if we are in conflict with one another, we are not really serving Hashem.

The whole of *Shir HaShirim* describes the spiritual connection between *Klal Yisrael* and Hashem. In order for us to have perfect unity with Hashem, we have to have unity with each other. It is to this that we aspire. The angels are called "friends" because they are on this level. In view of the theme of *Shir HaShirim*, this is the most elevated title of all. It communicates that they are in perfect unity with each other and that their spiritual relationship is perfect. The essence of *Shir HaShirim* is the spiritual unity that exists between Hashem, His Torah, and *Klal Yisrael*. This is displayed through Hashem's love for us and our love for Him. The angels, who demonstrate unity, teach us that the unity must be within our People as well. Otherwise, our bond with Hashem will also be defective.

At the same time, let us not forget that the angels are called "friends" because they are *our* friends. It should fill us with great pride that the angels see us as friends and compatriots. Imagine a person who has a *gadol* (great Torah scholar and leader) as a close friend. How much pride and joy that would give him! Every Jew has holy angels as friends![168]

יד / 14

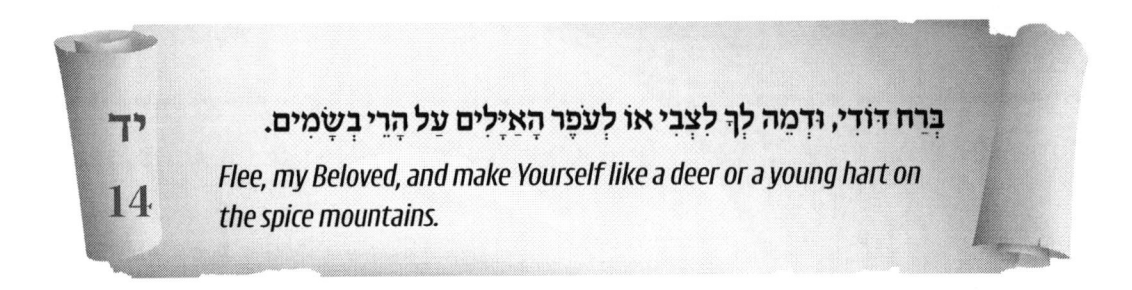

בְּרַח דּוֹדִי, וּדְמֵה לְךָ לִצְבִי אוֹ לְעֹפֶר הָאַיָּלִים עַל הָרֵי בְשָׂמִים.

Flee, my Beloved, and make Yourself like a deer or a young hart on the spice mountains.

Allegorical Translation: *Klal Yisrael* plead with Hashem to escape this exile (together with them) and to be as fast as a deer in speedily redeeming them and causing His Presence to dwell on Mount Moriah, where the Beis HaMikdash will be built.

Subject of the Verse: *Klal Yisrael* pleas with Hashem to quickly take them out of exile.

---

167 Rashi on *Bamidbar* 10:35.

168 As explained in our commentary on 8:8.

Mashal The wife asks her husband to run away from the place where he has hidden himself, and come back to her as soon as possible, with the speed of a swift animal. She asks him to accompany her to the most beautiful mountain where they can live together without interference, happily ever after.

Nimshal In this last verse of *Shir HaShirim*, *Klal Yisrael* ask Hashem to take them out of exile and redeem them. This is the natural conclusion and culmination of *Shir HaShirim*, a book devoted to describing how much *Klal Yisrael* love Hashem and how much Hashem loves *Klal Yisrael*.

In the verse, *Klal Yisrael* ask Hashem to "run away" from the exile. They ask Hashem to come to them as quickly as possible. Then they ask Hashem to join them on the mountains of spice. This is an allusion to the Beis HaMikdash, which stands on Mount Moriah. "Moriah" comes from the root "*mor*," meaning "spice." The Beis HaMikdash spreads Hashem's fame like pleasant spices that spread a good smell. Therefore, it is called "Mount Moriah." Alternatively, the name is an allusion to the spices offered up daily in the Beis HaMikdash, the *ketores*.

FLEE, MY BELOVED

This phrase, "Flee, my Beloved," was incorporated in many *piyutim*, especially those recited on Pesach. Here we ask Hashem to leave the exile and run away to us. Interestingly, the standard verb used by someone asking another person to come to him, "come," is replaced in this verse, by "Flee!" — in the sense of "Escape!" This implies that Hashem is stuck, and needs to flee, when in actuality, it is us, *Klal Yisrael*, who are trapped in exile!

The reason for the unexpected expression is as follows: When we have been in exile for so long, we may start thinking that this is the way Hashem wants things to be. We perceive that we have to beg Him to take us out. The truth, however, is that Hashem wants to come and save us, but He is, *ki'veyachol*, so to speak, stuck in exile because of our sins.

To make sense of this, we need a better understanding of what exile is. On a superficial level, exile is a punishment for our sins. Seen from this perspective, it is *us*, not Hashem, who has to "flee." We have to "flee" and escape our sins in order to come out of exile. But from the "*Shir HaShirim* perspective," we can see more deeply. We see that exile causes Hashem to suffer, *ki'veyachol*, as well. As *Chazal* tell us, when we are in exile, it is as if Hashem is in exile as well.[169] Indeed, every bit of pain that we suffer, He

---

169 *Megillah* 29a. See earlier 4:8.

"suffers" as well!¹⁷⁰ From this perspective, exile is like a relationship that has gotten stuck and needs help. Both parties are equally distressed that they are in this mess!

After learning all of *Shir HaShirim*, we reach the level of understanding that our exile causes Hashem to "suffer." We thus ask Hashem to tear Himself away ("flee") from the exile and come to save us. The underlying message of this verse is most beautiful: we are aware that Hashem is suffering our pain in exile along with us and that He is as distressed as we are that we are in exile. Because this phrase, "Flee, my Beloved," shows just how much Hashem loves us — to the extent that our pain is His pain. Many *paytanim* chose to include it in their liturgical poems to remind us of this truth.¹⁷¹

LIKE A DEER

The Midrash informs us that when a deer sleeps at night, it still keeps one eye open to see if there is any danger approaching. In this verse, we, *Klal Yisrael*, ask Hashem to be like a deer in the sense that He should watch over us even during the "night" of exile.

Commenting on the Midrash, the Sar Shalom suggests that the request that Hashem be like a "deer" (with its one eye open and one eye closed) is symbolically a plea that Hashem see only our good deeds and ignore all our bad deeds. He adds that the further request that Hashem be like a hart relates to this animal's constant practice of looking back (to see if predators are chasing it). We are thus asking Hashem to look back at the deeds of previous generations — our forefathers and righteous tzaddikim of earlier times — even if we are not worthy of being saved on our own merits.

ON THE SPICE MOUNTAINS

Mount Moriah is referred to here in this verse in the plural: "spice *mountains*." Why is this? The Midrash¹⁷² explains that in the time of Mashiach, Hashem will bring the mountains of Sinai, Tavor, and Carmel together on top of Mount Moriah. As a result, the mountain upon which Hashem will build the Beis HaMikdash will be extremely high and grand. It will be a mountain that is really "*mountains*," upon which the Presence of Hashem will dwell.¹⁷³

Why will Hashem perform this miracle? Since all of these mountains contributed to

---

170 As the verse in *Yeshayahu* (63:9) tells us, "All their [*Klal Yisrael*'s] pain is His pain."

171 Rabbi Elisha Galiko offers a very different explanation of the phrase, "Flee, my Beloved." He notes that in the Heavens, Hashem gets tremendous honor, while here in this world, His Name is not treated as it should be. Therefore, He might be more "comfortable," *ki'veyachol*, so to speak, in the Heavens. We thus we beg Him to leave the Heavens and come to us.

172 *Pesikta de Rav Kahana, Yalkut Shimoni, Yeshayahu* 391.

173 *Shiras Dovid, Devash V'Chalav*, and others.

glorifying Hashem's name,[174] they all deserve to be part of the final, great celebration of redemption and the true revelation of Hashem's glory. Similarly, anyone who has contributed to glorifying Hashem's Name will also be a part of the final salvation and glory. Hashem will reckon every effort on His behalf and combine them together to bring forth the light of eternal salvation.

To better appreciate this miracle of the mountains, let us recall a bit of history. When Hashem wished to give the Torah, the mountains began arguing with one another, each one wanting the Torah to be given on it. Each one boasted that because of its grandeur, the Torah should be given on it. Mount Sinai humbly kept quiet, and Hashem chose it.[175] This is known even to schoolchildren and indeed teaches the important lesson of humility.

What is less well known, unfortunately, is that Hashem declared that since all these mountains desired to glorify His Name, they will all be compensated beyond what they lost. This promise was fulfilled when Mount Tavor played host to the miracle of Sisra. There, Devorah sang a song in which the word "*anochi*" appears twice (whereas it appears only once in the Ten Commandments given on Mount Sinai). And the promise was also fulfilled when Mount Carmel played host to the miracle wrought for Eliyahu. There, *Klal Yisrael* twice declared, "Hashem is God" (whereas the equivalent declaration, "I am Hashem, your God," was made only once on Mount Sinai).

While arrogance is disliked by Hashem, we must remember that all our efforts and desires to serve Hashem — even if tainted – will be greatly rewarded. Ultimately, they will all be brought together and "piled up" in glorification of Hashem's Name. Every such act that we do, however small, and every feeling of wanting to serve Hashem that we have, even if it is small and not perfect, is treasured by Hashem. It will never be lost. Eventually, Hashem will use it to aggrandize His Glory and to bring about the Final Redemption.

The image of Hashem "piling up" the mountains and putting the Beis HaMikdash on top of them helps us understand that the glory of Hashem is raised higher and higher through the cumulative efforts of *Klal Yisrael* all through history. This is a very important message and is also part of the essence of *Shir HaShirim*. Every Jew is precious to Hashem. This can be likened to parents using their children's artwork to decorate their home or sukkah. Regardless of the talent reflected in the work, they find their children's

---

[174] The Torah was given on Mount Sinai, the battle of Sisra took place on Mount Tavor (*Shoftim* 4), and the miracle performed for Eliyahu took place on Mount Carmel (see verse 7:6).

[175] *Midrash Tehillim* 68.

efforts beautiful. So, too, Hashem utilizes all the efforts of every single Jew, and they will all be celebrated when Mashiach comes.

ON THE SPICE MOUNTAINS

"Spice mountains" also hint at the *ketores* (incense offering) which was part of the service in the Beis HaMikdash. Now, we might wonder why this particular offering is alluded to here. As we know from the Gemara, the different offerings and sacrifices atoned for different sins (see *Yoma* 44a). The *ketores* atoned for *lashon hara* (badmouthing and relating negative information about others). The Second Beis HaMikdash was destroyed due to our sin of *lashon hara*, and until this sin is atoned for, we will not be redeemed.[176] We therefore allude to Mount Moriah ("as spice mountains") to remind Hashem of the *ketores* which atones for this sin. More than any other sin, *lashon hara* is the one thing holding back Mashiach. We pray that Hashem remove this obstacle to our redemption in the merit and atonement generated by the incense offering. We must take to heart this reminder of how to merit to see the fulfillment of this verse with the Final Redemption. This means putting ceaseless efforts into eradicating the sin of *lashon hara*.

What follows is the *Targum*'s poignant rendering of the final verse of *Shir HaShirim*.

> At that time, the elders of the Jewish People will plead with Hashem: "Our Beloved Master of the world, flee from the land which has been contaminated by sin, and let Your Presence dwell in the High Heavens. And in times of trouble, when we pray to You, be like a deer which always — even when sleeping — keeps an eye open to see our troubles; or be like a gazelle which, when it runs, always looks back over its shoulder. So, too, look back and observe our pain; see our afflictions from the High Heavens until such time as You will be pleased with us, and redeem us. Then You will deliver us to the mountain of Yerushalayim, and there the *Kohanim* will offer up before You the sweet-smelling spices.

May it happen very soon, in our lifetime!

---

176 *Yoma* 9a; Introduction to *Sefer Chafetz Chaim*.

CONCLUSION

The Mishnah tells us that Hashem loves *Klal Yisrael* and then goes on to say: חבה יתירה נודעת להם — An extra love was *made known to them*. This means that not only does Hashem love us, but He also made it known to us that He loves us. The Maharal asks: Why did Hashem make it known to us that He loves us, and what is the difference between a love that one reveals/expresses and a love that one does not?[177] He answers that the purpose of revealing one's love to another person is in order that the other person wish to become closer and enjoy the love. One who does not want the other person to become close to him does not reveal his love. Hashem does not just love *Klal Yisrael*, He lets us know that He loves us so that we will wish to draw closer to Him and enjoy that love even more.[178]

We can say that this is essentially why we learn *Shir HaShirim*. Discovering how much Hashem loves us will make us want to draw closer to Him. And that is the entire purpose of our lives: to become closer to Hashem and to revel in His Presence. As Dovid HaMelech put it: **"One thing I request of Hashem, only that do I seek: that I [be able to] sit in the house of Hashem all the days of my life, to behold the pleasantness of Hashem and to frequent His Sanctuary."**[179]

---

177 *Avos* 3:14.
178 *Derech HaChaim*, ibid.
179 *Tehillim* 27:4, as explained in *Mesillas Yesharim*, ch. 1.

RECITING SHIR HASHIRIM

RECITING SHIR HASHIRIM ON EREV SHABBOS AND ON OTHER OCCASIONS

There is a custom to recite *Shir HaShirim* on Erev Shabbos, as Rabbi Akiva did.[1] If one did not manage on Erev Shabbos, one can recite it on Shabbos.[2] This custom is based on the Midrash that Shabbos is a partner with *Klal Yisrael*,[3] just as *Klal Yisrael* is a "partner" with Hashem. Shabbos is also like a matchmaker, bringing *Klal Yisrael* closer to Hashem. Since *Shir HaShirim* describes the intimate relationship between *Klal Yisrael* and Hashem, it is fitting to be reviewed then.[4]

There is another reason for this custom rooted in the fact that the halachic status of an item on Shabbos is defined at the time when Shabbos comes in. For example, if an item is forbidden as *muktzeh* at the onset of Shabbos, it is forbidden the entire Shabbos;

---

1. See Introduction. The Taz (288:2) adds that Rabbi Akiva used to weep copious tears while reciting it because he truly understood how great the words are, and how far they go. Rabbi Shalom Schwadron helps us understand this with an illustration. A person writing a letter to a friend will not be especially careful about how he phrases each point. If, however, he is writing something intended for his teacher's eyes or for those of a king or the *gadol ha'dor*, he will spend a great deal of time composing it carefully. Because Rabbi Akiva understood the loftiness of the words of *Shir HaShirim* and how far they go in the Heavenly spheres, he recited it with tremendous devotion.

2. *Kaf HaChaim* 260:27-28; *Yesod V'Shoresh HaAvodah*, ch. 8, where the author urges readers to recite it with tremendous devotion and great concentration and joy, and without interruption; *Yesodei Yeshurun*, p. 260. Shelah HaKadosh adds that one should already be wearing Shabbos clothes when reciting it. The Midrash mentions that Rabbi Eliezer taught *Shir HaShirim* on Erev Shabbos (see our Introduction). See also *Yalkut Yosef*, *Orach Chaim*, vol. 8, p. 233.

3. *Bereishis Rabbah* 11:8. See also *Pri Megadim*, *Orach Chaim* 490:8.

4. This concept of the "intimate" relationship between *Klal Yisrael* and Hashem is also based on the *Zohar* (*Parashas Pinchas*) which says that on Shabbos, *Klal Yisrael* become bonded with Hashem in the most intimate manner, like a husband and wife at their time of greatest intimacy. (The author of *Tomer Devorah* learns from this passage of the *Zohar* how a person should conduct himself on Shabbos [ch. 9].) The song *Lecha Dodi* is based on this concept as well. Therefore, it is a fitting introduction to Shabbos to delve into the relationship between *Klal Yisrael* and Hashem.

but if it is permitted, it is permitted the entire Shabbos.[5] By reciting *Shir HaShirim* as Shabbos comes in, we ensure that we are in an elevated state, thus defining the character of our entire Shabbos.[6]

There are many who recite *Shir HaShirim* regularly since it brings one closer to Hashem. This is also a *segulah*, protecting one from Gehinnom[7] and from illness.[8] The Yeshuas Yisrael adds that it is a *segulah* for health, wealth and good children. Furthermore, reciting *Shir HaShirim* with concentration can bring many blessings into a person's life.[9]

There are many *segulos* associated with reciting *Shir HaShirim*, some of whose sources are difficult to verify. However, there is no greater blessing, achievement, or success than to gain a love for Hashem and become closer to Him. Any method that one uses to become closer to Hashem is to be commended, and *Shir HaShirim* is certainly one of the best. For those who wish to recite *Shir HaShirim* regularly and understand it readily, I have provided a running allegorical translation below.[10]

Before reciting *Shir HaShirim*, some recite the following prayer:

יְהִי רָצוֹן מִלְּפָנֶיךָ יְהֹוָה אֱלֹהֵינוּ וֵאלֹהֵי אֲבוֹתֵינוּ הַבּוֹחֵר בְּדָוִד עַבְדּוֹ וּבְזַרְעוֹ אַחֲרָיו וְהַבּוֹחֵר בְּשִׁירוֹת וְתִשְׁבָּחוֹת שֶׁתֵּפֶן בְּרַחֲמִים אֶל קְרִיאַת שִׁיר הַשִּׁירִים שֶׁאֶקְרָא כְּאִלּוּ הִשַּׂגְנוּ כָּל הַסּוֹדוֹת הַנִּפְלָאִים וְהַנּוֹרָאִים אֲשֶׁר הֵם חֲתוּמִים בּוֹ. וְנִזְכֶּה לְחַבֵּר אֵשֶׁת נְעוּרִים עִם דּוֹדָהּ בְּאַהֲבָה וְאַחֲוָה וְרֵעוּת וּלְיַחֵד אַרְבַּע אוֹתִיּוֹת שֶׁל שִׁמְךָ הַגָּדוֹל וְכָל הָעוֹלָמוֹת עַל יְדֵי קְרִיאַת וְלִמּוּד שִׁיר הַשִּׁירִים שֶׁהוּא קֹדֶשׁ קָדָשִׁים: יָחִיד וּמְיֻחָד מִשְׂגַּבֵּנוּ וּמְאוֹרֵנוּ. אַהֲבָתְךָ וְיִרְאָתְךָ תִּקְבַּע בְּלִבֵּנוּ. הָאֵר פָּנֶיךָ אֵלֵינוּ בִּישׁוּעָתֶךָ. דֶּרֶךְ פִּקּוּדֶיךָ הֲבִינֵנִי וְאָשִׂיחָה בְּנִפְלְאוֹתֶיךָ. וּבְחַיִּים אֲרוּכִים וְהַצְלָחָה וּבְבָנִים טוֹבִים וְכָל טוּב תְּבָרְכֵנוּ. וְתִבְנֶה בֵּית הַמִּקְדָּשׁ בִּמְהֵרָה בְיָמֵינוּ. נָא הָקֵם מַלְכוּת שְׁכִינַת עֻזֶּךָ וְתָבִיא מָשִׁיחַ וְאֵלִיָּהוּ לְעַמֶּךָ. הִגָּלֶה נָא וְתָאִיר אֶרֶץ מִכְּבוֹדֶךָ וַהֲשִׁיבֵנוּ לִירוּשָׁלַיִם עִיר קָדְשֶׁךָ וְשַׂמַּח נַפְשֵׁנוּ בִּישׁוּעָתֶךָ. יָחִיד תִּיחֵד מְדוֹתֶיךָ וְנִרְאֶה מְאוֹרוֹת. וְטַהֵר לִבֵּנוּ לְעָבְדְּךָ בֶּאֱמֶת. וּכְשֵׁם שֶׁנֶּאֱמַר בִּימֵי שְׁלֹמֹה עַבְדֶּךָ יְהוּדָה וְיִשְׂרָאֵל רַבִּים כַּחוֹל אֲשֶׁר עַל הַיָּם

---

5   *Sukkah* 46b.

6   Introduction to *Kesser HaShabbos*.

7   *Ma'ase Rokeiach*, beginning of *Hilchos Shabbos*. *Shaar Bas Rabim* (beginning of *Shir HaShirim*) explains this in Kabbalistic terms based on how many hours a week one prays. (See *Zohar, Noach* 62b and *Siddur Derech HaChaim* p. 223.) The 117 verses of *Shir HaShirim* are also considered to be Shlomo HaMelech's personal atonement for violating three prohibitions specifically relating to the king spelled out in *Devarim* (ch. 17): having too many wives, too many horses, and too much gold and silver. For each sin, he deserved thirty-nine lashes, for a total of 117. By writing the 117 verses of *Shir HaShirim*, he was atoning for these sins (*Beis Yisrael Shemos* 17).

8   *Ahavas Chaim*, vol. I, p. 282. *Sidduro Shel Shabbos* 3:2 says it protects one from all harm.

9   *Binas HaShir*, p. 17.

10   This translation is designed for those who recite *Shir HaShirim*, and wish to have a meaningful, yet simplified, explanation of the text in front of them. It is not literal, and not based solely on the main body of this *sefer*.

לָרוֹב אוֹכְלִים וְשׁוֹתִים וּשְׂמֵחִים. כֵּן תּוֹשִׁיעֵנוּ גַּם עַתָּה לְגַדֵּל בָּנֵינוּ וּבְנוֹתֵינוּ לְכָל טוֹב וְהַצְלָחָה. וְיִתְרַבּוּ צֶאֱצָאֵיהֶם עַד סוֹף כָּל הַדּוֹרוֹת. וְהוֹשִׁיעֵנוּ שֶׁנִּהְיֶה בְּרִיאִים וַחֲזָקִים לֶאֱכֹל וְלִשְׁתּוֹת וְלִשְׂמֹחַ בְּלִמּוּד תּוֹרָתֶךָ וּבְקִיּוּם מִצְוֹתֶיךָ: וְאַל תַּצְרִיכֵנוּ לִידֵי מַתְּנַת בָּשָׂר וָדָם וְלֹא לִידֵי הַלְוָאָתָם. כִּי אִם לְיָדְךָ הַמְּלֵאָה וְהָרְחָבָה וּמֵאוֹצַר מַתְּנַת חִנָּם תְּחָנֵּנוּ. וּכְשֵׁם שֶׁנֶּאֱמַר בִּימֵי שְׁלֹמֹה עַבְדֶּךָ וַיֵּשֶׁב יְהוּדָה וְיִשְׂרָאֵל לָבֶטַח אִישׁ תַּחַת גַּפְנוֹ וְתַחַת תְּאֵנָתוֹ. כֵּן תּוֹשִׁיעֵנוּ גַּם עַתָּה לֵישֵׁב כָּל אִישׁ עִם בְּנֵי בֵיתוֹ בְּשַׁלְוָה וְהַשְׁקֵט בְּבְרִיאוּת וְהַצְלָחָה וְכָל טוּב: וּכְשֵׁם שֶׁבִּימֵי שְׁלֹמֹה עַבְדֶּךָ הוֹפִיעַ כְּבוֹד מַלְכוּתְךָ עַל כָּל יוֹשְׁבֵי תֵבֵל אַרְצֶךָ. כֵּן תּוֹשִׁיעֵנוּ גַּם עַתָּה. וּמְלֹךְ עַל כָּל הָעוֹלָם כֻּלּוֹ בִּכְבוֹדֶךָ. וִיקַבְּלוּ כֻלָּם אֶת עֹל מַלְכוּתְךָ וְתִמְלֹךְ עֲלֵיהֶם מְהֵרָה לְעוֹלָם וָעֶד:

(בחול ישאל פה בקשתו בלשון הקדוש, כל אחד לפי מה שצריך)

חַיִּים אֲרֻכִּים וְטוֹבִים תִּסְמְכֵנוּ. יְרוּשָׁלַיִם עִירְךָ תִּבְנֶה וְתִגְאָלֵנוּ. שְׁכִינַת עֻזְּךָ תְּרוֹמֵם בִּמְהֵרָה בְיָמֵינוּ. עָזְרֵנוּ וְחָנֵּנוּ וַאֲמָצֵנוּ יְהוָה אֱלֹהֵינוּ. יָחִיד תְּיֻחַד מְדוֹתֶיךָ וְנִרְאֶה בְרָכוֹת וִישׁוּעוֹת. הַבֵּט נָא לְעַמְּךָ בְּפָנִים מְאִירוֹת. וּתְפִלָּתֵנוּ הַאֲזִינָה פּוֹעֵל יְשׁוּעוֹת. כַּוָּנַת הֲגִיגֵנוּ נָא קַבֵּל בְּרָצוֹן אֱלֹהֵי הַפְּלָאוֹת. וּבְכֵן תִּתְהַדַּר בְּכָל שִׁיר. תִּתְנַשֵּׂא בְּכָל פְּאֵר. תִּתְקַדֵּשׁ לַעֲדֵי עַד. כַּכָּתוּב בְּתוֹרָתֶךָ יְהוָה יִמְלֹךְ לְעוֹלָם וָעֶד. בָּרוּךְ יְהוָה לְעוֹלָם אָמֵן וְאָמֵן:

May it be Your will, Hashem our God and the God of our forefathers, who chose Dovid, His servant, and his offspring after him, and who chose songs and praises, that You turn with mercy to the recitation of *Shir HaShirim* that I shall recite, as if we have grasped all the wondrous and awesome secrets that are concealed within it. May we merit to unite the bride of youth with her Beloved in love, brotherhood, and companionship, and to unite the four letters of Your Great Name with all the worlds through the reciting and studying of *Shir HaShirim*, which is Holy of Holies.

One and Only [God], our strength and our light, establish Your love and fear in our hearts. Shine Your face upon us with Your salvation. Teach me the path of Your mitzvos, and I will speak of Your wonders. Bless us with long life, success, good children and all good. Build the Beis HaMikdash soon, in our lifetime. Please establish the Kingdom of Your Powerful Presence and bring Mashiach and Eliyahu to Your nation. Reveal Yourself and light up the world with Your Honor. Bring us back to Yerushalayim, Your Holy City, and let us rejoice in Your salvation. Display Your Oneness, and we will see the true light. Purify our hearts to serve You in truth.

Just as it is written about the time of Shlomo, Your servant, that [the people of] Yehudah and Yisrael were as numerous as the [grains of] sand at the seashore, and that they ate and drank and rejoiced. Save us now, too, so that we can bring up our children to all good and to success. May our offspring continue to increase until the end of all generations. Save us so that we will be healthy and strong, and thus able to eat and drink and to rejoice in the study of Your Torah and observance of Your mitzvos. Let us not be needful of the gifts of human beings nor of their loans, but only of Your full and generous hand. Grace us from [Your] storehouse of gifts.

It is written about the time of Shlomo, Your servant, that [the people of] Yehudah and Yisrael dwelled in peace, each person under his vine and fig tree. Redeem us now too, so that each person, together with his household, can dwell in peace and tranquillity, in good health, success, and with all good. And just as it was in the days of Shlomo, Your servant, when the glory of Your Kingdom revealed itself to everyone on Your earth, save us too, now, and rule over the entire world in Your glory. And may everyone accept upon themselves the yoke of Your Kingdom, and may You soon rule over them forever and ever!

(Here on a weekday one can add one's personal prayers and requests according to one's needs.)

Grant us a good, long life. Rebuild Yerushalayim, Your city, and redeem us. Raise up Your Powerful Presence soon, in our lifetime. Help us, favor us, and give us strength, Hashem our God. Display Your Oneness, and we will experience blessing and salvation. Please view Your nation with a shining face and listen to our prayers, You who effect salvation. God of wonder, accept with favor the intent of our thoughts. Be lauded with every song, exalted with all glory, sanctified forever and ever, as it is written in Your Torah: "Hashem will reign for eternity." Blessed is Hashem forever! *Amen, Amen!*

Some say this prayer before reciting *Shir HaShirim*

לְשֵׁם יִחוּד קוּדְשָׁא בְּרִיךְ הוּא וּשְׁכִינְתֵּיהּ, לְיַחֲדָא שֵׁם יוֹד קֵ"י בְּוָא"ו קֵ"י בִּדְחִילוּ וּרְחִימוּ, בְּיִחוּדָא שְׁלִים בְּשֵׁם כָּל יִשְׂרָאֵל. הִנֵּה אֲנַחְנוּ בָּאִים לְשׁוֹרֵר בְּקוֹל נָעִים שִׁיר

הַשִּׁירִים, לְתַקֵּן אֶת שָׁרְשָׁהּ בְּמָקוֹם עֶלְיוֹן, לַעֲשׂוֹת נַחַת רוּחַ לְיוֹצְרֵנוּ וְלַעֲשׂוֹת רְצוֹן בּוֹרְאֵנוּ. וִיהִי נֹעַם אֲדֹנָי אֱלֹהֵינוּ עָלֵינוּ. וּמַעֲשֵׂה יָדֵינוּ כּוֹנְנָה עָלֵינוּ. וּמַעֲשֵׂה יָדֵינוּ כּוֹנְנֵהוּ:

For the sake of the unification of the Holy Name, Blessed is He and His Presence, to unify the Name, *yud-kei* with *vav-kei*, in fear and love, in perfect unity, on behalf of all *Klal Yisrael*.

We are about to recite *Shir HaShirim* in a pleasant voice to rectify its source on High, to create a spirit of contentment for our Maker, and to fulfill the will of our Creator.

May the pleasantness of Hashem, our God, be upon us. May He establish our handiwork for us. May He establish our handiwork!

RUNNING ALLEGORICAL TRANSLATION OF SHIR HASHIRIM

CHAPTER 1 - פרק א

1. A song composed of two songs: *Klal Yisrael*'s song of praise to Hashem for His kindness and His giving us the Torah, and Hashem's song of praise to *Klal Yisrael* for being devoted to His Torah and mitzvos despite their suffering. The song which is the most precious of all songs dedicated to Hashem, to whom peace belongs.

א. שִׁיר הַשִּׁירִים אֲשֶׁר לִשְׁלֹמֹה:

Klal Yisrael express their longing for Hashem in exile

2. "I desire Your closeness, Hashem, because Your love is more precious to me than all other worldly pleasures.

ב. יִשָּׁקֵנִי מִנְּשִׁיקוֹת פִּיהוּ כִּי טוֹבִים דֹּדֶיךָ מִיָּיִן:

3. The beautiful fragrances from Your Presence are sweet to me like flowing perfume. I therefore love You with constantly renewed energy.

ג. לְרֵיחַ שְׁמָנֶיךָ טוֹבִים שֶׁמֶן תּוּרַק שְׁמֶךָ עַל כֵּן עֲלָמוֹת אֲהֵבוּךָ:

4. You drew me near, and I hurried to follow You. The revelation of Your most hidden secrets brings me delight and joy. The memory of Your love gives me great pleasure. We love you with true love!"

ד. מָשְׁכֵנִי אַחֲרֶיךָ נָּרוּצָה הֱבִיאַנִי הַמֶּלֶךְ חֲדָרָיו נָגִילָה וְנִשְׂמְחָה בָּךְ נַזְכִּירָה דֹדֶיךָ מִיַּיִן מֵישָׁרִים אֲהֵבוּךָ:

Klal Yisrael to the heathen nations:

5. "Unfortunately, I have become sullied by sin, but I am pure in my relationship with Hashem. Although I look dirty like Bedouin tents, I am easily cleaned to look as beautiful as the curtains of Hashem.

ה. שְׁחוֹרָה אֲנִי וְנָאוָה בְּנוֹת יְרוּשָׁלָיִם כְּאָהֳלֵי קֵדָר כִּירִיעוֹת שְׁלֹמֹה:

6. Do not examine and condemn my deficiencies because they are caused by the terrible exile. Foreign nations enslaved me in order to fulfill their desires. I was therefore unable to dedicate myself to serving Hashem as I wanted to."

ו. אַל תִּרְאוּנִי שֶׁאֲנִי שְׁחַרְחֹרֶת שֶׁשְּׁזָפַתְנִי הַשָּׁמֶשׁ בְּנֵי אִמִּי נִחֲרוּ בִי שָׂמֻנִי נֹטֵרָה אֶת הַכְּרָמִים כַּרְמִי שֶׁלִּי לֹא נָטָרְתִּי:

Klal Yisrael ask Hashem:

7. "Please tell me Hashem, whom I love, how can I find the correct way to withstand this harsh exile? Why should I have to hide in shame among the nations who surround me?!"

ז. הַגִּידָה לִּי שֶׁאָהֲבָה נַפְשִׁי אֵיכָה תִרְעֶה אֵיכָה תַּרְבִּיץ בַּצָּהֳרָיִם שַׁלָּמָה אֶהְיֶה כְּעֹטְיָה עַל עֶדְרֵי חֲבֵרֶיךָ:

Hashem replies:

8. "If you, the most beautiful nation, do not know how to flourish, follow in the footsteps of your teachers, and learn from your forefathers who chose to dwell in My Presence.

ח. אִם לֹא תֵדְעִי לָךְ הַיָּפָה בַּנָּשִׁים צְאִי לָךְ בְּעִקְבֵי הַצֹּאן וּרְעִי אֶת גְּדִיֹּתַיִךְ עַל מִשְׁכְּנוֹת הָרֹעִים:

Hashem declares to Klal Yisrael:

9. "I revealed My love to you through the horses and chariots of Pharaoh.

ט. לְסֻסָתִי בְּרִכְבֵי פַרְעֹה דִּמִּיתִיךְ רַעְיָתִי:

10. I displayed My love by gifting you with rows of gems to adorn your cheeks and with necklaces to beautify yourself.

י. נָאווּ לְחָיַיִךְ בַּתֹּרִים צַוָּארֵךְ בַּחֲרוּזִים:

11. I then gave you an even greater amount of spoils following the Splitting of the Sea than you received when you left Egypt."

יא. תּוֹרֵי זָהָב נַעֲשֶׂה לָּךְ עִם נְקֻדּוֹת הַכָּסֶף:

Klal Yisrael say to Hashem:

12. "Even while You, Hashem, were still at Mount Sinai, I sinned through the Golden Calf, and let out a bad smell.

יב. עַד שֶׁהַמֶּלֶךְ בִּמְסִבּוֹ נִרְדִּי נָתַן רֵיחוֹ:

13. Nevertheless, You, Hashem, not only forgave me, but You agreed to dwell with me in the Mishkan.

יג. צְרוֹר הַמֹּר דּוֹדִי לִי בֵּין שָׁדַי יָלִין:

14. Again and again, You forgave me, providing me with numerous bundles of sweet-smelling myrrh."

יד. אֶשְׁכֹּל הַכֹּפֶר דּוֹדִי לִי בְּכַרְמֵי עֵין גֶּדִי:

Hashem replies:

15. "You, *Klal Yisrael*, are so beautiful! Your teachers and leaders are clean and pure!"

טו. הִנָּךְ יָפָה רַעְיָתִי הִנָּךְ יָפָה עֵינַיִךְ יוֹנִים:

Klal Yisrael respond:

16. "You, Hashem, have made us beautiful by forgiving us and giving us Your Torah and mitzvos.

טז. הִנְּךָ יָפֶה דוֹדִי אַף נָעִים אַף עַרְשֵׂנוּ רַעֲנָנָה:

17. And You have gathered us around Your holy Mishkan, built from sacred wood and fresh beams."

יז. קֹרוֹת בָּתֵּינוּ אֲרָזִים רַהִיטֵנוּ בְּרוֹתִים:

CHAPTER 2 - פרק ב

Klal Yisrael describe themselves:

1. "I am like a beautiful, fresh rose which flourishes only in a fertile land. I, too, only flourish in the Presence of Hashem."

א. אֲנִי חֲבַצֶּלֶת הַשָּׁרוֹן שׁוֹשַׁנַּת הָעֲמָקִים:

Hashem replies:

2. "You, *Klal Yisrael*, are like a precious rose among the worthless thorns, the nation chosen from among the discarded nations."

ב. כְּשׁוֹשַׁנָּה בֵּין הַחוֹחִים כֵּן רַעְיָתִי בֵּין הַבָּנוֹת:

Klal Yisrael declare:

3. "Like a lush apple tree among trees that have no fruit, so is Hashem. Unlike all the other worthless gods, He provides protection and sustenance. I desire to dwell in the shade of Hashem, and I get much joy from fulfilling His mitzvos.

ג. כְּתַפּוּחַ בַּעֲצֵי הַיַּעַר כֵּן דּוֹדִי בֵּין הַבָּנִים בְּצִלּוֹ חִמַּדְתִּי וְיָשַׁבְתִּי וּפִרְיוֹ מָתוֹק לְחִכִּי:

4. You, Hashem, brought me close to You at Mount Sinai, and, with love, gave me the treasure of Torah.

ד. הֱבִיאַנִי אֶל בֵּית הַיָּיִן וְדִגְלוֹ עָלַי אַהֲבָה:

5. Now that I am in exile, I ask You to sustain me and console me with comforting words of Torah and prophecies of salvation.	ה. סַמְּכוּנִי בָּאֲשִׁישׁוֹת רַפְּדוּנִי בַּתַּפּוּחִים כִּי חוֹלַת אַהֲבָה אָנִי:
6. You, Hashem, support me with Your left hand and embrace me with Your right."	ו. שְׂמֹאלוֹ תַּחַת לְרֹאשִׁי וִימִינוֹ תְּחַבְּקֵנִי:

Klal Yisrael to the nations:

7. "A terrible punishment awaits you, nations, if you attempt to uproot or disturb the eternal love between Hashem and us! You will be as terrified as deer and harts who run away from the wild animals of the field!"	ז. הִשְׁבַּעְתִּי אֶתְכֶם בְּנוֹת יְרוּשָׁלַם בִּצְבָאוֹת אוֹ בְּאַיְלוֹת הַשָּׂדֶה אִם תָּעִירוּ וְאִם תְּעוֹרְרוּ אֶת הָאַהֲבָה עַד שֶׁתֶּחְפָּץ:

Klal Yisrael remember:

8. "Hashem announced to us the wonderful news that the time of our salvation from Egypt had arrived. He shortened the time of exile and brought the salvation more quickly in the merit of our Patriarchs and Matriarchs.	ח. קוֹל דּוֹדִי הִנֵּה זֶה בָּא מְדַלֵּג עַל הֶהָרִים מְקַפֵּץ עַל הַגְּבָעוֹת:
9. Indeed, Hashem was swift like a deer. We realized that He had always been right nearby, standing behind our wall and watching us through the windows, peeping through the cracks, and waiting for our time of redemption.	ט. דּוֹמֶה דוֹדִי לִצְבִי אוֹ לְעֹפֶר הָאַיָּלִים הִנֵּה זֶה עוֹמֵד אַחַר כָּתְלֵנוּ מַשְׁגִּיחַ מִן הַחֲלֹּנוֹת מֵצִיץ מִן הַחֲרַכִּים:
10. Hashem then called out to us: 'Prepare yourselves My beloved My beautiful one and get ready to be freed from exile.	י. עָנָה דוֹדִי וְאָמַר לִי קוּמִי לָךְ רַעְיָתִי יָפָתִי וּלְכִי לָךְ:
11. [Do so] because the time of exile has passed, the years of suffering have ended.	יא. כִּי הִנֵּה הַסְּתָו עָבָר הַגֶּשֶׁם חָלַף הָלַךְ לוֹ:
12. The righteous, who are likened to blossoms, have appeared in the world, and the time of singing praises to Hashem has arrived. The voice of Moshe Rabbeinu announcing the redemption is ready to be heard in the land.	יב. הַנִּצָּנִים נִרְאוּ בָאָרֶץ עֵת הַזָּמִיר הִגִּיעַ וְקוֹל הַתּוֹר נִשְׁמַע בְּאַרְצֵנוּ:

13. The wicked have departed and the remainder have repented. Therefore, rise My beloved, My beautiful one, and leave the exile!'"

יג. הַתְּאֵנָה חָנְטָה פַגֶּיהָ וְהַגְּפָנִים סְמָדַר נָתְנוּ רֵיחַ קוּמִי לָךְ רַעְיָתִי יָפָתִי וּלְכִי לָךְ:

Hashem describes the events at the Splitting of the Sea:

14. "My faithful one, *Klal Yisrael*, was trapped between the Egyptians and the sea. I called out to them: 'Display your beautiful deeds of faith and express your words of prayer because the sound of your prayer is pleasant and the sight of you doing mitzvos is beautiful.'

יד. יוֹנָתִי בְּחַגְוֵי הַסֶּלַע בְּסֵתֶר הַמַּדְרֵגָה הַרְאִינִי אֶת מַרְאַיִךְ הַשְׁמִיעִינִי אֶת קוֹלֵךְ כִּי קוֹלֵךְ עָרֵב וּמַרְאֵיךְ נָאוֶה:

15. Then I, Hashem, will instruct the sea to seize and destroy the wicked Egyptians who are like little foxes attempting to ruin a vineyard when it has only just begun to blossom."

טו. אֶחֱזוּ לָנוּ שׁוּעָלִים קְטַנִּים מְחַבְּלִים כְּרָמִים וּכְרָמֵינוּ סְמָדַר:

Klal Yisrael proclaim:

16. "Hashem is mine. He supplies all my needs, and I fulfill all His *mitzvahs*. He looks after me with kindness...

טז. דּוֹדִי לִי וַאֲנִי לוֹ הָרֹעֶה בַּשּׁוֹשַׁנִּים:

17. Until my sins blew away Hashem's friendship and protection. I then begged Him, 'Come quickly with the speed of the deer who dashes across the mountains. Please return and have Your Presence dwell among us.'"

יז. עַד שֶׁיָּפוּחַ הַיּוֹם וְנָסוּ הַצְּלָלִים סֹב דְּמֵה לְךָ דוֹדִי לִצְבִי אוֹ לְעֹפֶר הָאַיָּלִים עַל הָרֵי בָתֶר:

CHAPTER 3 - פרק ג

Klal Yisrael muse painfully:

1. "Even when I am in the dark and bitter exile, I have not stopped seeking my Beloved and praying for His return. Yet my prayers have not been answered.

א. עַל מִשְׁכָּבִי בַּלֵּילוֹת בִּקַּשְׁתִּי אֵת שֶׁאָהֲבָה נַפְשִׁי בִּקַּשְׁתִּיו וְלֹא מְצָאתִיו:

2. I have risen up and gathered my people in the city centers to pray for the One I love to return, but our prayers have still not been answered.

ב. אָק֣וּמָה נָּ֗א וַאֲסוֹבְבָ֣ה בָעִ֔יר בַּשְּׁוָקִים֙ וּבָ֣רְחֹב֔וֹת אֲבַקְשָׁ֕ה אֵ֥ת שֶׁאָהֲבָ֖ה נַפְשִׁ֑י בִּקַּשְׁתִּ֖יו וְלֹ֥א מְצָאתִֽיו:

3. I met with the righteous leaders who protect their cities and asked them: 'When will the salvation come?'

ג. מְצָא֙וּנִי֙ הַשֹּׁ֣מְרִ֔ים הַסֹּבְבִ֖ים בָּעִ֑יר אֵ֛ת שֶׁאָהֲבָ֥ה נַפְשִׁ֖י רְאִיתֶֽם:

4. They encouraged me to repent, and thereby find His love, to seek His closeness and to go to His shuls and places of learning. There I will feel His Presence."

ד. כִּמְעַט֙ שֶׁעָבַ֣רְתִּי מֵהֶ֔ם עַ֣ד שֶֽׁמָּצָ֔אתִי אֵ֥ת שֶׁאָהֲבָ֖ה נַפְשִׁ֑י אֲחַזְתִּיו֙ וְלֹ֣א אַרְפֶּ֔נּוּ עַד־שֶׁ֤הֲבֵיאתִיו֙ אֶל־בֵּ֣ית אִמִּ֔י וְאֶל־חֶ֖דֶר הוֹרָתִֽי:

Klal Yisrael to the nations:

5. "You nations will receive a terrible punishment if you attempt to uproot or disturb the eternal love between Hashem and us. You will be as terrified as deer and harts who run away from the wild animals of the field!"

ה. הִשְׁבַּ֨עְתִּי אֶתְכֶ֜ם בְּנ֤וֹת יְרוּשָׁלִַ֙ם֙ בִּצְבָא֔וֹת א֖וֹ בְּאַיְל֣וֹת הַשָּׂדֶ֑ה אִם־תָּעִ֧ירוּ ׀ וְֽאִם־תְּע֥וֹרְר֛וּ אֶת־הָאַהֲבָ֖ה עַ֥ד שֶׁתֶּחְפָּֽץ:

The nations declare in wonder:

6. "How awesome is the Jewish People coming up through the desert, led by pillars of cloud and fire, and having received so many precious gifts from Hashem!"

ו. מִ֣י זֹ֗את עֹלָה֙ מִן־הַמִּדְבָּ֔ר כְּתִֽימֲר֖וֹת עָשָׁ֑ן מְקֻטֶּ֤רֶת מוֹר֙ וּלְבוֹנָ֔ה מִכֹּ֖ל אַבְקַ֥ת רוֹכֵֽל:

Klal Yisrael explain:

7. "Behold, the source of this greatness is the Presence of Hashem dwelling in the Mishkan which travels with *Klal Yisrael*. It is surrounded by twenty-four groups of *Kohanim*, and twenty-four groups of *Levyim*, and by the encampment of the Twelve Tribes, the multitudes of *Klal Yisrael*.

ז. הִנֵּ֗ה מִטָּתוֹ֙ שֶׁלִּשְׁלֹמֹ֔ה שִׁשִּׁ֥ים גִּבֹּרִ֖ים סָבִ֣יב לָ֑הּ מִגִּבֹּרֵ֖י יִשְׂרָאֵֽל:

8. All of them are Torah scholars ready to engage in Torah learning. They all guard themselves so that they do not forget the Torah during the dark exile.

ח. כֻּלָּם אֲחֻזֵי חֶרֶב מְלֻמְּדֵי מִלְחָמָה אִישׁ חַרְבּוֹ עַל יְרֵכוֹ מִפַּחַד בַּלֵּילוֹת:

9. The Mishkan is made for Hashem from the finest wood.

ט. אַפִּרְיוֹן עָשָׂה לוֹ הַמֶּלֶךְ שְׁלֹמֹה מֵעֲצֵי הַלְּבָנוֹן:

10. Its pillars are made of silver, its supports of gold, and its curtains of precious, purple wool. Within it is to be found the perfect love between Hashem and His most precious nation.

י. עַמּוּדָיו עָשָׂה כֶסֶף רְפִידָתוֹ זָהָב מֶרְכָּבוֹ אַרְגָּמָן תּוֹכוֹ רָצוּף אַהֲבָה מִבְּנוֹת יְרוּשָׁלָיִם:

11. May we all merit to see this beautiful sight and to participate in this wonderful joy when He returns His Presence to us at the time of the Final Redemption and the building of the third Beis HaMikdash!"

יא. צְאֶינָה וּרְאֶינָה בְּנוֹת צִיּוֹן בַּמֶּלֶךְ שְׁלֹמֹה בָּעֲטָרָה שֶׁעִטְּרָה לּוֹ אִמּוֹ בְּיוֹם חֲתֻנָּתוֹ וּבְיוֹם שִׂמְחַת לִבּוֹ:

CHAPTER 4 - פרק ד

Hashem gives voice to His love and praise of Klal Yisrael:

1. "You, *Klal Yisrael*, are beautiful; your eyes are pure. All of your people, even the weakest, follow the straight path directed by your wise leaders.

א. הִנָּךְ יָפָה רַעְיָתִי הִנָּךְ יָפָה עֵינַיִךְ יוֹנִים מִבַּעַד לְצַמָּתֵךְ שַׂעְרֵךְ כְּעֵדֶר הָעִזִּים שֶׁגָּלְשׁוּ מֵהַר גִּלְעָד:

2. You eat appropriately, without indulgence. Your food is untainted by sin or theft, and there is no imperfection in any aspect of your conduct.

ב. שִׁנַּיִךְ כְּעֵדֶר הַקְּצוּבוֹת שֶׁעָלוּ מִן הָרַחְצָה שֶׁכֻּלָּם מַתְאִימוֹת וְשַׁכֻּלָה אֵין בָּהֶם:

3. Your speech is uplifting, and your words are pleasant and kind. Your thoughts are devoted to how to fulfill the mitzvos, and you do so modestly.

ג. כְּחוּט הַשָּׁנִי שִׂפְתוֹתַיִךְ וּמִדְבָּרֵיךְ נָאוֶה כְּפֶלַח הָרִמּוֹן רַקָּתֵךְ מִבַּעַד לְצַמָּתֵךְ:

4. Your citadels of learning are powerful and strong such that thousands can come and learn there in the shadow of the Torah scholars. In this way, they [also] learn how to control their *yetzer ha'ra*.

ד. כְּמִגְדַּל דָּוִיד צַוָּארֵךְ בָּנוּי לְתַלְפִּיּוֹת אֶלֶף הַמָּגֵן תָּלוּי עָלָיו כֹּל שִׁלְטֵי הַגִּבּוֹרִים:

5. Together, your leaders, Moshe and Aharon, nurtured you and taught you the Living Torah. They led you with compassion.	ה. שְׁנֵי שָׁדַיִךְ כִּשְׁנֵי עֳפָרִים תְּאוֹמֵי צְבִיָּה הָרוֹעִים בַּשּׁוֹשַׁנִּים:
6. You wait for the yoke of exile to be removed and the darkness of the nations to be eliminated. Then the Presence of Hashem will return to Yerushalayim, and the service of the Beis HaMikdash will be reestablished.	ו. עַד שֶׁיָּפוּחַ הַיּוֹם וְנָסוּ הַצְּלָלִים אֵלֶךְ לִי אֶל הַר הַמּוֹר וְאֶל גִּבְעַת הַלְּבוֹנָה:
7. [Then it will be clear that] you *Klal Yisrael*, are completely beautiful, and have no blemishes.	ז. כֻּלָּךְ יָפָה רַעְיָתִי וּמוּם אֵין בָּךְ:
8. Just as I went into exile with you, I will return with you to the Beis HaMikdash. You will then sing in gratitude for all the miracles that I have done for you in the past, starting from the redemption from Egypt slavery, and for all the times I saved you from your dangerous enemies.	ח. אִתִּי מִלְּבָנוֹן כַּלָּה אִתִּי מִלְּבָנוֹן תָּבוֹאִי תָּשׁוּרִי מֵרֹאשׁ אֲמָנָה מֵרֹאשׁ שְׂנִיר וְחֶרְמוֹן מִמְּעֹנוֹת אֲרָיוֹת מֵהַרְרֵי נְמֵרִים:
9. You, *Klal Yisrael*, have captivated My heart. I would love you for even just one aspect of your good attributes, for just one good act that you have done.	ט. לִבַּבְתִּנִי אֲחֹתִי כַלָּה לִבַּבְתִּנִי בְּאַחַת מֵעֵינַיִךְ בְּאַחַד עֲנָק מִצַּוְּרֹנָיִךְ:
10. How beautiful is your love and your faith! How good is your devotion, especially when you sacrifice all other desires to cling to Me!	י. מַה יָּפוּ דֹדַיִךְ אֲחֹתִי כַלָּה מַה טֹּבוּ דֹדַיִךְ מִיַּיִן וְרֵיחַ שְׁמָנַיִךְ מִכָּל בְּשָׂמִים:
11. Your words of prayer are as sweet as honey, My beloved bride. Your words of learning are as nourishing as milk. Your mitzvos are as glorious as flourishing trees.	יא. נֹפֶת תִּטֹּפְנָה שִׂפְתוֹתַיִךְ כַּלָּה דְּבַשׁ וְחָלָב תַּחַת לְשׁוֹנֵךְ וְרֵיחַ שַׂלְמֹתַיִךְ כְּרֵיחַ לְבָנוֹן:
12. You are clean and pure because you guard yourself from being contaminated by strangers.	יב. גַּן נָעוּל אֲחֹתִי כַלָּה גַּל נָעוּל מַעְיָן חָתוּם:

13. Even your young offspring observe all the mitzvos. They are so exceptional in their good *middos* that they make a good impression even from a distance.

יג. שְׁלָחַיִךְ פַּרְדֵּס רִמּוֹנִים עִם פְּרִי מְגָדִים כְּפָרִים עִם נְרָדִים:

14. Like a mixture of many beautiful and sweet-smelling spices emitting a wonderful fragrance, so all the different parts of your nation give off a good smell.

יד. נֵרְדְּ וְכַרְכֹּם קָנֶה וְקִנָּמוֹן עִם כָּל עֲצֵי לְבוֹנָה מֹר וַאֲהָלוֹת עִם כָּל רָאשֵׁי בְשָׂמִים:

15. Your good deeds flow like a sparkling spring which continually gives forth pure water.

טו. מַעְיַן גַּנִּים בְּאֵר מַיִם חַיִּים וְנֹזְלִים מִן לְבָנוֹן:

16. When the Final Redemption takes place, I, Hashem, will command that all the nations from the north and the south gather you, *Klal Yisrael*, to Yerushalayim and bring you as a gift to Me. Then your good name will spread like the smell of perfume."

טז. עוּרִי צָפוֹן וּבוֹאִי תֵימָן הָפִיחִי גַנִּי יִזְּלוּ בְשָׂמָיו יָבֹא דוֹדִי לְגַנּוֹ וְיֹאכַל פְּרִי מְגָדָיו:

Klal Yisrael beg Hashem

"Please come to Your Beis HaMikdash and accept our sacrifices once again!"

CHAPTER 5 - פרק ה

Hashem replies:

1. "I came to your Mishkan in the past. There, I ate from all your sacrifices — even those that were unusual. I rejoiced and celebrated its inauguration together with Aharon and his sons, and all of *Klal Yisrael*."

א. בָּאתִי לְגַנִּי אֲחֹתִי כַלָּה אָרִיתִי מוֹרִי עִם בְּשָׂמִי אָכַלְתִּי יַעְרִי עִם דִּבְשִׁי שָׁתִיתִי יֵינִי עִם חֲלָבִי אִכְלוּ רֵעִים שְׁתוּ וְשִׁכְרוּ דּוֹדִים:

Klal Yisrael reminisce regretfully:

2. "When I was lazy and detached, Hashem tried to arouse within me feelings of love for Him by saying: 'Please open up to Me, My beloved, My faithful, My partner! I am waiting outside for you in the wet and windy night.'

ב. אֲנִי יְשֵׁנָה וְלִבִּי עֵר קוֹל דּוֹדִי דוֹפֵק פִּתְחִי לִי אֲחֹתִי רַעְיָתִי יוֹנָתִי תַמָּתִי שֶׁרֹאשִׁי נִמְלָא טָל קְוֻצּוֹתַי רְסִיסֵי לָיְלָה:

3. I then replied to Him, 'I have forsaken the robe of mitzvos, and I have no wish to wear it again. I have prepared myself for rest and have no wish to get up and walk towards You.'	ג. פָּשַׁטְתִּי אֶת כֻּתָּנְתִּי אֵיכָכָה אֶלְבָּשֶׁנָּה רָחַצְתִּי אֶת רַגְלַי אֵיכָכָה אֲטַנְּפֵם:
4. Hashem then tried to stretch His hand through the lock, begging me to reach out to Him. Eventually, my interest in Him was partially reawakened.	ד. דּוֹדִי שָׁלַח יָדוֹ מִן הַחֹר וּמֵעַי הָמוּ עָלָיו:
5. I got up to open the door. My fingers opening the lock were perfumed with the smell of my devotion to Him.	ה. קַמְתִּי אֲנִי לִפְתֹּחַ לְדוֹדִי וְיָדַי נָטְפוּ מוֹר וְאֶצְבְּעֹתַי מוֹר עֹבֵר עַל כַּפּוֹת הַמַּנְעוּל:
6. I then attempted to become closer to Hashem, my beloved, but Hashem hid His face from me. I felt like fainting in sorrow, wishing I could see Him, but I was unable to. I prayed and called out to Him, but He did not reply.	ו. פָּתַחְתִּי אֲנִי לְדוֹדִי וְדוֹדִי חָמַק עָבָר נַפְשִׁי יָצְאָה בְדַבְּרוֹ בִּקַּשְׁתִּיהוּ וְלֹא מְצָאתִיהוּ קְרָאתִיו וְלֹא עָנָנִי:
7. When I was in exile, the various nations hurt me and wounded me. Claiming to be my guardians, they stole my precious ornaments."	ז. מְצָאֻנִי הַשֹּׁמְרִים הַסֹּבְבִים בָּעִיר הִכּוּנִי פְצָעוּנִי נָשְׂאוּ אֶת רְדִידִי מֵעָלַי שֹׁמְרֵי הַחֹמוֹת:

Klal Yisrael declare to the heathen nations:

8. "I make you promise that when my Beloved asks you about me, you will tell Him that I am sick with longing for His love."	ח. הִשְׁבַּעְתִּי אֶתְכֶם בְּנוֹת יְרוּשָׁלָ͏ִם אִם תִּמְצְאוּ אֶת דּוֹדִי מַה תַּגִּידוּ לוֹ שֶׁחוֹלַת אַהֲבָה אָנִי:

The heathen nations ask Klal Yisrael:

9. "What is so special about your relationship with Hashem that you, the most beautiful of nations, have sacrificed so much for Him?"	ט. מַה דּוֹדֵךְ מִדּוֹד הַיָּפָה בַּנָּשִׁים מַה דּוֹדֵךְ מִדּוֹד שֶׁכָּכָה הִשְׁבַּעְתָּנוּ:

Klal Yisrael reply:

10. "Hashem, who is my beloved, is both kind and just. He has tens of thousands of angels who fulfill His every command.	י. דּוֹדִי צַח וְאָדוֹם דָּגוּל מֵרְבָבָה:

11. He gave us the Torah, which is like a precious diamond. From its every black letter and quill stroke, one can learn mountains of laws.	יא. רֹאשׁוֹ כֶּתֶם פָּז קְוֻצּוֹתָיו תַּלְתַּלִּים שְׁחֹרוֹת כָּעוֹרֵב:
12. His eyes constantly watch over those who fear Him, those who are pure and clean and who are perfect in the fulfillment of His mitzvos.	יב. עֵינָיו כְּיוֹנִים עַל אֲפִיקֵי מָיִם רֹחֲצוֹת בֶּחָלָב יֹשְׁבוֹת עַל מִלֵּאת:
13. His words are as pleasant and distinct as a flower garden, His speech kind and sweet, smelling like perfume.	יג. לְחָיָו כַּעֲרוּגַת הַבֹּשֶׂם מִגְדְּלוֹת מֶרְקָחִים שִׂפְתוֹתָיו שׁוֹשַׁנִּים נֹטְפוֹת מוֹר עֹבֵר:
14. His tablets of stone are like gold studded with sapphire that spreads goodness throughout the world. His Torah is organized with clear laws like a diamond-filled ornament.	יד. יָדָיו גְּלִילֵי זָהָב מְמֻלָּאִים בַּתַּרְשִׁישׁ מֵעָיו עֶשֶׁת שֵׁן מְעֻלֶּפֶת סַפִּירִים:
15. The pillars of His Torah are as strong as marble pillars embedded with precious stones. Those who seek Him constantly discover new aspects of wonder.	טו. שׁוֹקָיו עַמּוּדֵי שֵׁשׁ מְיֻסָּדִים עַל אַדְנֵי פָז מַרְאֵהוּ כַּלְּבָנוֹן בָּחוּר כָּאֲרָזִים:
16. His words are all sweet, He is totally pleasant! You nations should appreciate that this is just a partial description of Hashem, who is my Beloved and my Friend."	טז. חִכּוֹ מַמְתַקִּים וְכֻלּוֹ מַחֲמַדִּים זֶה דוֹדִי וְזֶה רֵעִי בְּנוֹת יְרוּשָׁלָם:

CHAPTER 6 - פרק ו

The heathen nations derisively inquire:

1. "Where has your precious Beloved gone? Now that He has forsaken you, let us go together and search for Him."	א. אָנָה הָלַךְ דּוֹדֵךְ הַיָּפָה בַּנָּשִׁים אָנָה פָּנָה דוֹדֵךְ וּנְבַקְשֶׁנּוּ עִמָּךְ:

Klal Yisrael reply:

2. "Hashem has gone to the places of learning to hear the words of Torah and to gather precious deeds.	ב. דּוֹדִי יָרַד לְגַנּוֹ לַעֲרוּגוֹת הַבֹּשֶׂם לִרְעוֹת בַּגַּנִּים וְלִלְקֹט שׁוֹשַׁנִּים:

SHIR HASHIRIM

3. I alone am for Hashem, and He dwells only with me and looks after me with mercy."

Hashem interjects:

4. "You, *Klal Yisrael*, are beautiful when You try to please Me. You are as beautiful as Yerushalayim, as awesome as the angels.

5. Turn your eyes away from Me because when I see you, I become overwhelmed, and inclined to give you more than what is good for you. Even your common people are wonderful when they follow their righteous leaders.

6. Your warriors are prefect in deeds, without blemish of sin.

7. The merits of even the least worthy among you are as many as the seeds of a pomegranate.

8. Sixty nations are descended from Avraham, and eighty from Noach, and from them, many more nations.

9. But there is only one whom I love: only you, *Klal Yisrael*. You are faithful to Me, and faithful to your forefathers. The other nations see how beloved you are and praise you.

10. This is what they say, 'Which other nation besides you is as bright as the morning sun, as beautiful as the moon, as dazzling as the sun, and as awesome as the angels?!'

11. I, Hashem, go to your holy homes and your shuls to hear your youth learning and to see your children observing the mitzvos."

ג. אֲנִי לְדוֹדִי וְדוֹדִי לִי הָרֹעֶה בַּשּׁוֹשַׁנִּים:

ד. יָפָה אַתְּ רַעְיָתִי כְּתִרְצָה נָאוָה כִּירוּשָׁלָ͏ִם אֲיֻמָּה כַּנִּדְגָּלוֹת:

ה. הָסֵבִּי עֵינַיִךְ מִנֶּגְדִּי שֶׁהֵם הִרְהִיבֻנִי שַׂעְרֵךְ כְּעֵדֶר הָעִזִּים שֶׁגָּלְשׁוּ מִן הַגִּלְעָד:

ו. שִׁנַּיִךְ כְּעֵדֶר הָרְחֵלִים שֶׁעָלוּ מִן הָרַחְצָה שֶׁכֻּלָּם מַתְאִימוֹת וְשַׁכֻּלָה אֵין בָּהֶם:

ז. כְּפֶלַח הָרִמּוֹן רַקָּתֵךְ מִבַּעַד לְצַמָּתֵךְ:

ח. שִׁשִּׁים הֵמָּה מְלָכוֹת וּשְׁמֹנִים פִּילַגְשִׁים וַעֲלָמוֹת אֵין מִסְפָּר:

ט. אַחַת הִיא יוֹנָתִי תַמָּתִי אַחַת הִיא לְאִמָּהּ בָּרָה הִיא לְיוֹלַדְתָּהּ רָאוּהָ בָנוֹת וַיְאַשְּׁרוּהָ מְלָכוֹת וּפִילַגְשִׁים וַיְהַלְלוּהָ:

י. מִי זֹאת הַנִּשְׁקָפָה כְּמוֹ שָׁחַר יָפָה כַלְּבָנָה בָּרָה כַּחַמָּה אֲיֻמָּה כַּנִּדְגָּלוֹת:

יא. אֶל גִּנַּת אֱגוֹז יָרַדְתִּי לִרְאוֹת בְּאִבֵּי הַנָּחַל לִרְאוֹת הֲפָרְחָה הַגֶּפֶן הֵנֵצוּ הָרִמֹּנִים:

ETERNAL LOVE

Klal Yisrael comment:

12. "I did not watch over myself, and thereby caused myself to be enslaved by other nations."

יב. לֹא יָדַעְתִּי נַפְשִׁי שָׂמַתְנִי מַרְכְּבוֹת עַמִּי נָדִיב:

CHAPTER 7 - פרק ז

The heathen nations try to persuade Klal Yisrael:

1. "Turn away from Hashem, and we will appoint you to powerful positions"

א. שׁוּבִי שׁוּבִי הַשּׁוּלַמִּית שׁוּבִי שׁוּבִי וְנֶחֱזֶה בָּךְ מַה תֶּחֱזוּ בַּשּׁוּלַמִּית כִּמְחֹלַת הַמַּחֲנָיִם:

Klal Yisrael reply:

"What can you offer that compares with what Hashem gave me in allowing me to encircle Him with the angels at Mount Sinai?!"

The heathen nations praise Klal Yisrael:

2. "How wonderful are your footsteps on the way to the Beis HaMikdash! One sees that you are a nation of nobility. You are like an ornament made by an expert craftsman.

ב. מַה יָּפוּ פְעָמַיִךְ בַּנְּעָלִים בַּת נָדִיב חַמּוּקֵי יְרֵכַיִךְ כְּמוֹ חֲלָאִים מַעֲשֵׂה יְדֵי אָמָּן:

3. Your essence is filled with Torah scholars who do not sin. They feed and nourish the world with their Torah knowledge.

ג. שָׁרְרֵךְ אַגַּן הַסַּהַר אַל יֶחְסַר הַמָּזֶג בִּטְנֵךְ עֲרֵמַת חִטִּים סוּגָה בַּשּׁוֹשַׁנִּים:

4. Your two leaders are like twin deer working together in harmony.

ד. שְׁנֵי שָׁדַיִךְ כִּשְׁנֵי עֳפָרִים תָּאֳמֵי צְבִיָּה:

5. The Beis HaMikdash standing high is as strong as an ivory tower. From there, the leaders gaze out to oversee all the needs of the nation. Your head anticipates the final salvation.

ה. צַוָּארֵךְ כְּמִגְדַּל הַשֵּׁן עֵינַיִךְ בְּרֵכוֹת בְּחֶשְׁבּוֹן עַל שַׁעַר בַּת רַבִּים אַפֵּךְ כְּמִגְדַּל הַלְּבָנוֹן צוֹפֶה פְּנֵי דַמָּשֶׂק:

6. Hashem dwells among all your people, and even your poorest in deeds are like royalty. The King is bonded with you.

ו. רֹאשֵׁךְ עָלַיִךְ כַּכַּרְמֶל וְדַלַּת רֹאשֵׁךְ כָּאַרְגָּמָן מֶלֶךְ אָסוּר בָּרְהָטִים:

7. How beautiful are you, and how pleasant! All your love is pleasurable.

ז. מַה יָּפִית וּמַה נָּעַמְתְּ אַהֲבָה בַּתַּעֲנוּגִים:

8. Your steadfastness is tall and unbending, like a tall palm tree. You thereby educate your children to have faith."

ח. זֹאת קוֹמָתֵךְ דָּמְתָה לְתָמָר וְשָׁדַיִךְ לְאַשְׁכֹּלוֹת:

Hashem declares:

9. "I boast about you that I am exalted through your conduct. I therefore ask that your teachers strengthen the nation and bring out the best in you even from the weakest ones.

ט. אָמַרְתִּי אֶעֱלֶה בְתָמָר אֹחֲזָה בְּסַנְסִנָּיו וְיִהְיוּ נָא שָׁדַיִךְ כְּאֶשְׁכְּלוֹת הַגֶּפֶן וְרֵיחַ אַפֵּךְ כַּתַּפּוּחִים:

10. And [I ask] that your speech should be wonderful, like sweet wine, thereby justifying my boasts."

י. וְחִכֵּךְ כְּיֵין הַטּוֹב הוֹלֵךְ לְדוֹדִי לְמֵישָׁרִים דּוֹבֵב שִׂפְתֵי יְשֵׁנִים:

Klal Yisrael interject;

"I shall heed Your plea, and my words shall be pleasing to You as well as a source of pride for my forefathers. And this is what I say:

11. 'I am devoted only to Hashem, and His desire is only for me.'

יא. אֲנִי לְדוֹדִי וְעָלַי תְּשׁוּקָתוֹ:

Klal Yisrael continue:

12. "Hashem, please come with me, and I will show You some of my precious deeds. I will contrast the behavior of my righteous, who serve You even in poverty, with the wicked deeds of the other nations who disobey You even though You have given them abundance.

יב. לְכָה דוֹדִי נֵצֵא הַשָּׂדֶה נָלִינָה בַּכְּפָרִים:

13. I will take You to the shuls and places of learning. There, You will see my young flourishing in Torah, developing in mitzvos, and becoming spiritually fruitful.

יג. נַשְׁכִּימָה לַכְּרָמִים נִרְאֶה אִם פָּרְחָה הַגֶּפֶן פִּתַּח הַסְּמָדַר הֵנֵצוּ הָרִמּוֹנִים שָׁם אֶתֵּן אֶת דֹּדַי לָךְ:

14. You will see how both the good and the weak people of my nation all wish to attach themselves to You. I will display to You all the mitzvos that we have done, both those You commanded and the ones that were newly ordained by the Torah leaders. We observe all of these for Your sake."

יד. הַדּוּדָאִים נָתְנוּ רֵיחַ וְעַל פְּתָחֵינוּ כָּל מְגָדִים חֲדָשִׁים גַּם יְשָׁנִים דּוֹדִי צָפַנְתִּי לָךְ:

CHAPTER 8 - פרק ח

Klal Yisrael turn to Hashem and plead:

1. "If only I could be as close to you as a sister to her young brother whom she can hug and kiss even in public without anyone shaming her.

א. מִי יִתֶּנְךָ כְּאָח לִי יוֹנֵק שְׁדֵי אִמִּי אֶמְצָאֲךָ בַחוּץ אֶשָּׁקְךָ גַּם לֹא יָבֻזוּ לִי:

2. I will go with You to the Beis HaMikdash where You can teach me Torah, and I will merit to discover Your most innermost secrets.

ב. אֶנְהָגְךָ אֲבִיאֲךָ אֶל בֵּית אִמִּי תְּלַמְּדֵנִי אַשְׁקְךָ מִיַּיִן הָרֶקַח מֵעֲסִיס רִמֹּנִי:

3. Your left hand will support me while Your right hand will embrace me."

ג. שְׂמֹאלוֹ תַּחַת רֹאשִׁי וִימִינוֹ תְּחַבְּקֵנִי:

Klal Yisrael tell the heathen nations:

4. "You are unable to uproot or disturb the eternal love between Hashem and us."

ד. הִשְׁבַּעְתִּי אֶתְכֶם בְּנוֹת יְרוּשָׁלָ͏ִם מַה תָּעִירוּ וּמַה תְּעֹרְרוּ אֶת הָאַהֲבָה עַד שֶׁתֶּחְפָּץ:

Hashem and the Heavenly Court praise Klal Yisrael:

5. How important is *Klal Yisrael* who came out of the desert having bonded with Hashem; at *Matan Torah* they committed themselves to observing His Torah. There, they were reborn.

ה. מִי זֹאת עֹלָה מִן הַמִּדְבָּר מִתְרַפֶּקֶת עַל דּוֹדָהּ תַּחַת הַתַּפּוּחַ עוֹרַרְתִּיךָ שָׁמָּה חִבְּלַתְךָ אִמֶּךָ שָׁמָּה חִבְּלָה יְלָדַתְךָ:

Klal Yisrael plead with Hashem;

6. "Please, Hashem, remember me and place me on Your 'heart' and on Your 'arm' because I have sacrificed my life for you. And regardless of all our troubles, I have always loved You and served You.

ו. שִׂימֵנִי כַחוֹתָם עַל לִבֶּךָ כַּחוֹתָם עַל זְרוֹעֶךָ כִּי עַזָּה כַמָּוֶת אַהֲבָה קָשָׁה כִשְׁאוֹל קִנְאָה רְשָׁפֶיהָ רִשְׁפֵּי אֵשׁ שַׁלְהֶבֶתְיָה:

7. All the nations have been unable to extinguish the love I have for You, and all their tactics to distance me have not succeeded. For all the money in the world, I have not traded in my love for You!"

ז. מַיִם רַבִּים לֹא יוּכְלוּ לְכַבּוֹת אֶת הָאַהֲבָה וּנְהָרוֹת לֹא יִשְׁטְפוּהָ אִם יִתֵּן אִישׁ אֶת כָּל הוֹן בֵּיתוֹ בָּאַהֲבָה בּוֹז יָבוּזוּ לוֹ:

Hashem and the Heavenly court decide:

8. "Our young partner, *Klal Yisrael*, has not fully matured. What can we do to help her on her day of judgment?

ח. אָחוֹת לָנוּ קְטַנָּה וְשָׁדַיִם אֵין לָהּ מַה נַּעֲשֶׂה לַאֲחוֹתֵנוּ בַּיּוֹם שֶׁיְּדֻבַּר בָּהּ:

9. If she is as firm in her convictions as a wall, we will build for her a silver tower to protect her. But if she is flimsy like a door, we will provide her only with temporary, wooden protection."

ט. אִם חוֹמָה הִיא נִבְנֶה עָלֶיהָ טִירַת כָּסֶף וְאִם דֶּלֶת הִיא נָצוּר עָלֶיהָ לוּחַ אָרֶז:

Klal Yisrael reply proudly:

10. "I am as firm as a wall, and my teachers are like towers!" When we say this, we find favor in Hashem's eyes.

י. אֲנִי חוֹמָה וְשָׁדַי כַּמִּגְדָּלוֹת אָז הָיִיתִי בְעֵינָיו כְּמוֹצְאֵת שָׁלוֹם:

Shlomo HaMelech summarizes:

11. Hashem chose *Klal Yisrael* and brought them into His precious land. He entrusted them, His treasured vineyard, to the nations for safeguarding. But they stole from the vineyard.

יא. כֶּרֶם הָיָה לִשְׁלֹמֹה בְּבַעַל הָמוֹן נָתַן אֶת הַכֶּרֶם לַנֹּטְרִים אִישׁ יָבִא בְּפִרְיוֹ אֶלֶף כָּסֶף:

Hashem reprimands the heathen nations:

12. "The vineyard is Mine, and your theft is clear to Me!"

יב. כַּרְמִי שֶׁלִּי לְפָנָי הָאֶלֶף לְךָ שְׁלֹמֹה וּמָאתַיִם לְנֹטְרִים אֶת פִּרְיוֹ:

The nations reply:

"We will return all that we stole. Besides that, we will give additional compensation to the true guardians."

Hashem instructs Klal Yisrael:

13. "Those who are scattered in exile, call out to Me so that I and the angels can hear your voice which I desire so much."

יג. הַיּוֹשֶׁבֶת בַּגַּנִּים חֲבֵרִים מַקְשִׁיבִים לְקוֹלֵךְ הַשְׁמִיעִינִי:

Klal Yisrael pray:

14. "Please, Hashem, run away from this exile as fast as a deer, and return Your holy Presence to the Beis HaMikdash."

יד. בְּרַח דּוֹדִי וּדְמֵה לְךָ לִצְבִי אוֹ לְעֹפֶר הָאַיָּלִים עַל הָרֵי בְשָׂמִים:

May it happen very soon, in our lifetime. Amen!

If one is unable to recite the entire *Shir HaShirim*, one should recite the following four verses:[11]

[פרק א פסוק ב] יִשָּׁקֵנִי מִנְּשִׁיקוֹת פִּיהוּ, כִּי טוֹבִים דֹּדֶיךָ מִיָּיִן.

[1:2] If only He would kiss me with the kisses of His mouth, for Your love is better than wine.

[פרק ד פסוק טז] עוּרִי צָפוֹן וּבוֹאִי תֵימָן, הָפִיחִי גַנִּי יִזְּלוּ בְשָׂמָיו; יָבֹא דוֹדִי לְגַנּוֹ, וְיֹאכַל פְּרִי מְגָדָיו.

[4:16] Stir yourself, north [wind]; and south [wind], come; blow [across] My garden so that its perfumes flow forth. Let my Beloved enter His garden and eat His luscious fruit.

[פרק ב פסוק ח] קוֹל דּוֹדִי, הִנֵּה זֶה בָּא; מְדַלֵּג עַל הֶהָרִים, מְקַפֵּץ עַל הַגְּבָעוֹת.

[2:8] The sound of my Beloved! Behold, He is coming, leaping over the mountains, springing over the hills.

[פרק ה פסוק א] בָּאתִי לְגַנִּי, אֲחֹתִי כַלָּה; אָרִיתִי מוֹרִי עִם בְּשָׂמִי, אָכַלְתִּי יַעְרִי עִם דִּבְשִׁי, שָׁתִיתִי יֵינִי עִם חֲלָבִי; אִכְלוּ רֵעִים, שְׁתוּ וְשִׁכְרוּ דּוֹדִים.

[5:1] I entered My garden, My sister, [My] bride, I gathered My myrrh with My perfume; I [even] ate My honeycomb with My honey. I drank My wine with My milk. Eat, friends; drink, and become intoxicated, [My] loved ones!

---

11 *Siddur Beis Yaakov.* These verses are not in order. When combined, the initial letters of these four verses spell out the name of Yaakov Avinu. Rabbi Yaakov Emden explains that since *Chazal* (*Shabbos* 118b) tell us that observing Shabbos brings us the blessings that Hashem promised Yaakov, we should recite verses that spell out his name.

After completing *Shir HaShirim*, some recite this prayer:

רִבּוֹן כָּל הָעוֹלָמִים, יְהִי רָצוֹן מִלְּפָנֶיךָ יְהֹוָה אֱלֹהַי וֵאלֹהֵי אֲבוֹתַי, שֶׁבִּזְכוּת שִׁיר הַשִּׁירִים אֲשֶׁר קָרֵיתִי וְלָמַדְתִּי, שֶׁהוּא קֹדֶשׁ קָדָשִׁים, בִּזְכוּת פְּסוּקָיו, וּבִזְכוּת תֵּבוֹתָיו, וּבִזְכוּת אוֹתִיּוֹתָיו, וּבִזְכוּת נְקֻדּוֹתָיו, וּבִזְכוּת טְעָמָיו, וּבִזְכוּת שְׁמוֹתָיו וְצֵרוּפָיו וּרְמָזָיו וְסוֹדוֹתָיו הַקְּדוֹשִׁים וְהַטְּהוֹרִים הַנּוֹרָאִים הַיּוֹצְאִים מִמֶּנּוּ, שֶׁתְּהֵא שָׁעָה זוֹ שְׁעַת רַחֲמִים, שְׁעַת הַקְשָׁבָה, שְׁעַת הַאֲזָנָה, וְנִקְרָאֲךָ וְתַעֲנֵנוּ, נַעְתִּיר לְךָ וְהֵעָתֵר לָנוּ, שֶׁיִּהְיֶה עוֹלֶה לְפָנֶיךָ קְרִיאַת וְלִמּוּד שִׁיר הַשִּׁירִים כְּאִלּוּ הִשַּׂגְנוּ כָּל הַסּוֹדוֹת הַנִּפְלָאוֹת וְהַנּוֹרָאוֹת אֲשֶׁר הֵם חֲתוּמִים בּוֹ בְּכָל תְּנָאָיו, וְנִזְכֶּה לְמָקוֹם שֶׁהָרוּחוֹת וְהַנְּשָׁמוֹת נֶחְצָבוֹת מִשָּׁם, וּכְאִלּוּ עָשִׂינוּ כָּל מַה שֶּׁמֻּטָּל עָלֵינוּ לְהַשִּׂיג בֵּין בְּגִלְגּוּל זֶה, בֵּין בְּגִלְגּוּל אַחֵר, וְלִהְיוֹת מִן הָעוֹלִים וְהַזּוֹכִים לְעוֹלָם הַבָּא, עִם שְׁאָר צַדִּיקִים וַחֲסִידִים. וּמַלֵּא כָּל מִשְׁאֲלוֹת לִבֵּנוּ לְטוֹבָה, וְתִהְיֶה עִם לְבָבֵנוּ וְאִמְרֵי פִינוּ בְּעֵת מַחְשְׁבוֹתֵינוּ, וְעִם יָדֵינוּ בְּעֵת מַעְבָּדֵינוּ, וְתִשְׁלַח בְּרָכָה, וְהַצְלָחָה וְהַרְוָחָה, בְּכָל מַעֲשֵׂי יָדֵינוּ, וּמֵעָפָר תְּקִימֵנוּ, וּמֵאַשְׁפּוֹת דַּלּוּתֵנוּ תְּרוֹמְמֵנוּ, וְתָשִׁיב שְׁכִינָתְךָ לְעִיר קָדְשֶׁךָ בִּמְהֵרָה בְיָמֵינוּ, אָמֵן:

Master of all worlds, may it be Your will, Hashem, my God and the God of my forefathers, that in the merit of *Shir HaShirim* which I have read and studied, and which is "holy of holies," in the merit of its verses, words, letters, vowels, and cantillation symbols, and in the merit of the holy, pure, awesome Names, combinations, allusions and secrets that emanate from it, that this be an hour of compassion, attention, and listening [on Your part]. Then we will call to You, and You will answer us; we will entreat You, and You will allow Yourself to be prevailed upon by us.

May the recitation and learning of *Shir HaShirim* rise before You, as if we have grasped all the wondrous and awesome secrets that are sealed and hidden in it with all its requirements. And may we be worthy of [ultimately reaching] the place from where the spirits and the souls are hewn, as if we have accomplished all that is required of us, whether in this *gilgul* (incarnation) or in another *gilgul*. And may we be among those who rise and merit the World to Come along with other righteous and pious ones.

Fulfil all the requests of our hearts for the good. Be with our hearts and the words of our mouth at the time of our thoughts, and with our hands at the time of our actions. And [please] send blessings, success, and salvation to all our handiwork. Stand us up out of the dust; raise us up out of the trash heap of our poverty; and return Your Presence to Your Holy City very soon, in our lifetime. *Amen!*

BIBLIOGRAPHY OF SOME OF THE LESSER - KNOWN WORKS CITED IN OUR COMMENTARY:

Avodas Hageirshuni, by Rabbi Gershon, son of Rabbi Avraham, the brother of the Vilna Gaon; d. 5591 (1831).

Devash V'Chalav, by Rabbi Chaim Samuel, *shlita*, of Lakewood.

Divrei Yedidyah, by Rabbi Aryeh Leib Lipkin, chief Rabbi of Kartinga, Lithuania. Nephew of Rabbi Yisrael Salanter; d. 5662 (1902).

Rabbi Elisha Galiko, disciple of Rabbi Yosef Karo. Lived in Tzefas; d. 5338 (1578).[12]

Rina Shel Torah by Rabbi Naftali Tzvi Yehudah Berlin, better known as the Netziv. Rosh Yeshivah in Volozhin; d. 5653 (1893).

Rinas Dodim by Rabbi Eliyahu Luenz, disciple of the Maharal. Lived in Prague; d. 5396 (1636).

Rinas Yitzchak, by Rabbi Yitzchak Sorotzkin, *shlita*, of Lakewood.

Shiras Dovid, by Rabbi Dovid Goldberg, *shlita*, Rosh Yeshivah of the Telz Yeshivah.

Tzror HaMor by Rabbi Yaakov Lisa, the famous author of *Nesivos HaMishpat* and *Chavos Da'as*; d. 5592 (1832).

---

12 Rabbi Galiko's work does not bear a name.

DETAILED TABLE OF CONTENTS

As emphasized above, *Shir HaShirim* is intended to teach us how much Hashem loves us, the entire Jewish People. Those who do not understand *Shir HaShirim* properly may find the many different expressions of Hashem's love for us repetitive. But the truth is that even after absorbing *Shir HaShirim*, we cannot fathom Hashem's great love for us because it is infinite. Indeed, we should try to enhance our understanding of the various aspects of this love throughout our lifetime. Furthermore, a concept that a person appreciates and understands in one scenario can be forgotten in another. Therefore, it is necessary to describe this love in many different ways. Each one speaks to a different state of mind.[1]

Unfortunately, we often lose sight of the nature of the relationship between Hashem and *Klal Yisrael*. Hashem loves us more than we can imagine and much more than we even love ourselves.[2] Remembering this is also insufficient. We need to live with this awareness and feel this love constantly.

---

1 This very important idea can be better understood by considering Rashi's comment on the Torah's instructions to soldiers on the battlefield not to be fainthearted and not to panic (*Devarim* 20:3). Rashi elaborates: When we go to battle, we should trust in Hashem and not fear the enemies' screams, the banging of their weapons, and the pounding of their horses' hooves. The question is: if one trusts in Hashem regarding the enemies' screams, why does he need to be told once again to trust in Hashem regarding the horses, etc. The answer is that one may find one thing challenging but another not. One may trust in Hashem regarding health, but not regarding finances or difficult neighbors, etc. Therefore, we are taught again and again, in any number of different ways and regarding various different challenges, to trust in Hashem. Similarly, one may feel Hashem's love in one area, but not in another. We therefore need to be taught this in every way and regarding every situation.

2 This point was driven home by the Chazon Ish after World War II (as retold in *Ma'aseh Ish*, vol. 2). When the sister of the Chazon Ish heard the news of the horrible destruction that had befallen the Jews of Europe, she came to the Chazon Ish and started crying. She asked him how such a terrible thing could have happened. The Chazon Ish answered: "Do not think for a moment that you have more love or mercy for *Klal Yisrael* than Hashem! Hashem's love for *Klal Yisrael* is far greater than we can comprehend. If what happened pains us, then it certainly pained Hashem. Therefore, Hashem must have had a very good reason for doing as He did." The Chazon Ish then went on with a parable. He said that when we see a tailor cutting up a small piece of valuable cloth, we know that he has a small job to do with it. But when we see a tailor cutting up a huge roll of very valuable cloth, we know that there is a very important reason for this. Similarly, when Hashem, so to speak, cut up such a huge part of *Klal Yisrael*, we know there must have been extremely important reasons for it.

Even though this is something we always need to remember, there are times when this lesson is even more important. When a tragedy strikes or when we commit a sin, it is much harder to believe that Hashem truly still loves us. Therefore, it is at times like these that we need to remind ourselves of Hashem's love and be keenly aware of its great intensity.

As we have seen, *Shir HaShirim* contains many different expressions of love in many different forms. This is because Shlomo HaMelech wished to convey this message for every kind of person in every kind of situation. He understood that at different times and in different situations, a person needs to hear the message of love differently. When *Klal Yisrael* is in exile, they need to hear this love expressed in a way that is different from how they would need to hear it in the Beis HaMikdash — with its array of daily miracles. Again, after a person sins, he needs to hear the love expressed in an yet another way. Shlomo HaMelech wrote *Shir HaShirim* in such a way that there is a lesson for everybody at any time that will speak to them. The message does not change, but our ability to appreciate the message and be aware of Hashem's love — and feel it all the time — does change.[3]

My father, *shlita*, who read parts of this *sefer*, recommended adding a detailed table of contents containing a summary of each verse,[4] which will enable every reader to locate the verse that is appropriate for them in their present situation and stage in life. Thus, a reader who wishes to be inspired by Hashem's love when he is going through his own challenges does not need to page through the entire *sefer*. In addition, there is a limit to how many times a person responds to hearing that Hashem loves *Klal Yisrael* without there being a more specific point to it. Therefore, there is value in being able to see at a glance, from different perspectives and in specific ways, how the relevant verses touch on Hashem's love for us.

---

3   When we convey information, such as "two plus two equals four," it makes no difference what the situation is. But when we try to teach others how to feel, such as that one should always trust in Hashem, the way the lesson must be taught will vary according to the various listeners' circumstances. This is why the Torah tells us that when we retell the account of *yetzias Mitzrayim*, we should first ascertain what type of son we have, and then proceed with the recounting (and the lessons that emerge from it) in accordance with the child's personality.

4   Because of the complexity of *Shir HaShirim*, it is very difficult to define a verse and say that this verse is describing Hashem's love in such and such a way. But on a broader level, it is possible to say that each verse has its own particular topic.

Central theme of *Shir HaShirim*, (Foreword) 22
The difficulties in understanding *Shir HaShirim*, (Foreword) 23
Every person will understand *Shir HaShirim* somewhat differently, (Foreword) 24
A Yid should make sure that his relationship with Hashem is constantly growing, (Foreword) 24
The worst thing a Yid can do is forget that he is a Yid, (Foreword) 24
How knowing about Hashem's love can change our lives, (Introduction) 28
Our relationship with Hashem is the most important relationship in our life, (Introduction) 28
The message of *Ahavas Olam* (Introduction) 29
The tremendous love that Hashem has for every Jew, (Introduction) 30
The importance of recognizing how much Hashem loves us, (Introduction) 30
The greatness of *Klal Yisrael*, (Introduction) 31
Why is *Klal Yisrael* so criticized, (Introduction) 31
Klal Yisrael is "betrothed" to Hashem, (Introduction) 31
The *mashal* of *Shir HaShirim*, (Introduction) 32
The story of *Shir HaShirim*, (Introduction 33
The many explanations to every verse in *Shir HaShirim*, (Introduction) 34
The language of the heart, (Introduction) 35
Shir HaShirim's song, symbolism, and perspective, (Introduction) 36
The meaning of the symbols, (Introduction) 37
Klal Yisrael as one unified, unique entity, (Introduction) 38
The new perspective that *Shir HaShirim* provides, (Introduction) 39
The multifaceted relationship between Hashem and *Klal Yisrael*, (Introduction) 40
Anthropomorphism (representing G-d as physical), (Introduction) 41
The Torah wants us to have a real relationship with Hashem, (Introduction) 42
Not using *Shir HaShirim* as an excuse, (Introduction) 43
The important balance between love and fear of Hashem, (Introduction) 43
The author and timeframe of *Shir HaShirim*, (Introduction) 44
When the relationship is strong then one should prepare for challenges, (Introduction) 45

Living without *korbanos*, (Introduction) 45
Even in exile, it is possible to feel Hashem's love, (Introduction) 46
The importance of Torah in our relationship with Hashem, (Introduction) 46
The great vision of *Shir HaShirim*, (Introduction) 47
Why *Shir HaShirim* is written as a seemingly mundane parable, (Introduction) 47
Even the simplest Jew must know that Hashem loves him, (Introduction) 48
One's perspective is shaped by one's desires, (Introduction) 48
True friendship is with Hashem, (Introduction) 49
This world is a mashal for the spiritual world, (Introduction) 50
Hashem created all love because of His love for us, (Introduction) 51
Our relationship with Hashem is the root of all our relationships, (Introduction) 51
Marriage is also a lesson how to relate to Hashem, (Introduction) 52
The importance of *Shir HaShirim*, (Introduction) ... 54
All that happens in this world is designed to facilitate our becoming closer to Hashem, (Introduction) 55
The great reward for those who thank Hashem for His love, (Introduction) 56
Shir HaShirim and Pesach, (Introduction) 57
Shir HaShirim and shalom bayis, (Introduction) 58
The chapters of *Shir HaShirim*, (Introduction) 60
Meaning of the phrase "song of songs", (1:1) 65
A song that we are able to sing, (1:1) 66
The love of Hashem for *Klal Yisrael* will last forever — even when people doubt it, (1:1) 66
Why in *Shir HaShirim* is Hashem referred to as Shlomo, (1:1) 68
True harmony and peace exist only in serving Hashem, (1:1) 68
How Hashem's love is like the love of husband for his wife, (1:2) 70
Torah creates the greatest closeness to Hashem, (1:2) 71
Klal Yisrael wish to become as close as possible to Hashem, (1:2) 71
When one makes an effort to become close to Hashem, He responds immediately and draws the person closer, (1:2) 72
One must consistently focus his thoughts to Hashem, (1:2) 73

To become close to Hashem, one has to distance himself from other interests, (1:2) ... 74

Nothing is more precious than Hashem's love, (1:2) 75

Through Torah one revives the feelings of Har Sinai, (1:2) ... 75

The preciousness of the words of *Chazal*, (1:2) ... 76

The entire world will come to love Hashem by seeing the greatness of *Klal Yisrael*, (1:3) ... 77

How our service of Hashem differs from that of the Avos, (1:3) ... 78

Our lives demonstrate the greatness of serving Hashem, (1:3) ... 79

Klal Yisrael's unique relationship and devotion to Hashem is not compromised by ulterior motives, (1:4) ... 81

The greatness of *Klal Yisrael* in following Hashem into the desert (1:4) ... 81

The value of true devotion, (1:4) ... 82

Klal Yisrael remains loyal to Hashem even when He seems to be ignoring them, (1:4) ... 83

What is unique about our relationship to Hashem, (1:4) ... 84

Klal Yisrael remains loyal to Hashem even when others try to seduce them away, (1:4) ... 85

The tremendous beauty of *Klal Yisrael*, (1:5-6) ... 88

Klal Yisrael's greatness and true beauty even when they look sullied and appear to have sinned terribly, (1:5-6) ... 88

Klal Yisrael have aspects of beauty even in their ugliness, (1:5) ... 90

Klal Yisrael is easily aroused to repent and cleanse themselves from sin, (1:5) ... 91

Klal Yisrael sins only due to the influence of the other wicked nations, (1:6) ... 92

Klal Yisrael sins only because the nations force them into it, (1:6) ... 92

Klal Yisrael must stop wasting their efforts and focus them exclusively to serve Hashem, (1:6) ... 94

Hashem's devotion and care for *Klal Yisrael* is like a shepherd's tending of his sheep, (1:7) ... 96

The ravages of exile, (1:7) ... 97

The honor of Hashem is entwined with the honor of *Klal Yisrael*, (1:7) ... 97

Klal Yisrael is the most beautiful of all nations, (1:8) 98

The safest path is the one our forefathers chose for us, (1:8) ... 99

Hashem's guidance to *Klal Yisrael* in exile, (1:8) ... 100

Our pride is that we follow our *mesores* (tradition), (1:8) ... 101

Hashem's love for *Klal Yisrael* as displayed through *Kriyas Yam Suf*, (1:9-11) ... 102

Our loyalty must be only for Hashem, (1:9) ... 105

Hashem taught *Klal Yisrael* to be loyal to Him at *Kriyas Yam Suf*, (1:9-11) ... 106

Hashem's love for *Klal Yisrael* as displayed through *Matan Torah*, (1:9-11) ... 106

Hashem entrusted the destiny of the world to *Klal Yisrael*, (1:9-11) ... 107

Klal Yisrael, ki'veyachol, "feed" Hashem, (1:9-11) ... 107

Hashem constantly forgives *Klal Yisrael* for their sins — even major sins, (1:12-14) ... 111

The forgiveness of Hashem displays His love, (1:12-14) ... 112

After forgiving *Klal Yisrael*, Hashem relates to them with warmth and closeness, (1:12-14) ... 112

Hashem's Presence dwelling in the Mishkan is a sign of His love and forgiveness, (1:12-14) ... 113

Klal Yisrael is always devoted to Hashem, even when it is difficult, (1:12-14) ... 115

Klal Yisrael displayed their love to Hashem from the very beginning, (1:12-14) ... 115

Klal Yisrael recognizes the friendship and love of Hashem even when He seems distant, (1:12-14) ... 116

Klal Yisrael's beauty both internally and externally, (1:15) ... 118

Aspects of the beauty of *Klal Yisrael* reflected in the beauty of their "eyes", (1:15) ... 118

Klal Yisrael follow their righteous leaders, (1:15) .. 120

Klal Yisrael greatness is their perseverance, (1:15) 121

The greatness of *Klal Yisrael* in never moving completely away from Hashem, (1:15) ... 122

Hashem loves *Klal Yisrael* and wishes to have His Presence dwell among them in the Mishkan, (1:16-17) ... 123

Hashem and *Klal Yisrael* bring out the best, *ki'veyachol*, in one another, (1:16-17) ... 124

Even in anger, Hashem is always pleasant, (1:16-17) ... 125

Hashem forgives *Klal Yisrael* completely so that the relationship is not harmed in any way, (1:16-17) ... 125

Because Hashem is the source of life, the Beis HaMikdash was a vibrant source of life, (1:16-17). 126

The beauty of *Klal Yisrael* is likened to flowers, solely love and beauty, (2:1) ... 129

Hashem loves *Klal Yisrael* even when they have done nothing to deserve it, (2:1) ... 129

Even when *Klal Yisrael* is pricked, they remain beautiful, (2:2) ... 131

Suffering brings out *Klal Yisrael*'s beauty, (2:2) 131
Klal Yisrael is like a rose amongst thorns – chosen from all other nations, (2:2) 132
Torah has many dimensions of greatness, (2:3) 134
Klal Yisrael's ability to delay gratification is the source of their success, (2:3) 134
Klal Yisrael notice Hashem's love and power, (2:3) 135
Klal Yisrael's greatness in accepting the Torah and recognizing its sweetness, (2:3) 136
Klal Yisrael acceptance of Torah with *Na'aseh* ("We will do") before *Nishma* ("We will understand") displays their greatness and their trust in Hashem, (2:3) 137
Torah's various pleasures likened to wine, (2:4) 139
Even when *Klal Yisrael* makes mistakes, Hashem loves their efforts, (2:4) 141
Torah can be explained in a variety of different ways, (2:4) 143
Hashem loves the discussion of Torah, (2:4) 143
The gathering of *Klal Yisrael* at Hashem's behest displays His love for them, (2:4) 144
Hashem's love and care for *Klal Yisrael* continue during the exile (even when He seems distant), (2:5-9) 144
Torah sustains *Klal Yisrael* and gives them hope, (2:5) 145
Hashem loves *Klal Yisrael* even at their worst, (2:5) 146
Klal Yisrael love for Hashem is overwhelming, (2:5) 147
The symbolism of the right and left hands, (2:6) 148
Hashem deals with *Klal Yisrael* both with mercy and with strict judgment — all for their own good, (2:6) 149
The heathen nations will never be able to disrupt the relationship between Hashem and *Klal Yisrael*, (2:7)... 151
Klal Yisrael must wait for Hashem to redeem them, (2:7) 152
Hashem breaks through all boundaries in His eagerness to redeem *Klal Yisrael*, (2:8) 154
In the past, *Klal Yisrael*'s salvation came swiftly, (2:8) 155
The Future Redemption can arrive at any moment, (2:8) 155
Hashem is always right next to us even in exile, (2:9)... 157
The surprising speed of the redemption from Egypt, (2:9) 158
Our anticipation of Mashiach should be immediate, (2:9) 159
Only our sins keep us away from Hashem, (2:9) 160
The two ways in which Hashem watches over us: hidden and revealed, (2:9) 161
Hashem is our *mashgiach*, (2:9) 162
Hashem's love for *Klal Yisrael* is displayed in the way He redeems them, (2:10-13) 163
The two fundamental mitzvos, (2:10) 164
The perfect timing of the Redemption, physically and spiritually, (2:11-12) 165
How Hashem encourage us to serve Him, (2:11-12) 168
Exile and Redemption are important processes, (2:11-12) 169
The various stages of Redemption, (2:13) 170
Hashem loves *Klal Yisrael* and waits for their prayers, (2:14) 173
Hashem loves the sight of *Klal Yisrael*, (2:14) 173
Hashem's awesome power and His infinite ability to look after us, (2:14) 174
The importance of prayer, (2:14) 175
Hashem loves the songs of *Klal Yisrael*, (2:14) 176
The evil of the Egyptians, (2:15) 178
Hashem is devoted to *Klal Yisrael*, (2:16) 179
The close, unique, and multifaceted relationship between *Klal Yisrael* and Hashem, (2:16) 179
The gentleness of Hashem and Torah leaders, (2:16..... 180
Exile is a deviation, an unpleasant situation causing distance between Hashem and *Klal Yisrael* who truly love each other, (2:17) 181
The yearning of *Klal Yisrael* for Hashem in exile, (3:1-2) 183
Like a person longing in bed, *Klal Yisrael* long for Hashem, (3:1) 184
Our deepest yearning are actually a desire for closeness to Hashem, (3:1) 185
Klal Yisrael search for Hashem, (3:2) 186
Hashem is found by doing mitzvos, (3:2) 187
Klal Yisrael determination to find Hashem, (3:3) .. 188
Love breaks through all normal boundaries, (3:3) . 188
Keeping hold of our closeness to Hashem, (3:4) 190
Preserving our closeness to Hashem with all our might, (3:4) 191
Remaining close to Hashem requires effort, (3:4) .. 192
True spiritual growth requires effort, (3:4) 192
The nations will never be able to disrupt the relationship between Hashem and *Klal Yisrael*,

especially after exile, (3:5) 194

Klal Yisrael's tremendous greatness in the desert, (3:6) 195

Klal Yisrael flourish even under harsh circumstances, (3:6) 196

Through troubles, *Klal Yisrael* grow, (3:6) 197

The greatness of *Birkas Kohanim*, (3:7) 197

The greatness of the Mishkan, (3:7-8) 198

The greatness of Torah scholars and righteous people, (3:7-8) 198

The true battles of life, (3:7-8) 200

The pride of the Mishkan, (3:7-8) 202

The beauty and love reflected in the Mishkan, (3:9-11) 203

Hashem chose to dwell in the Mishkan to demonstrate His love, (3:9-11) 205

The inside of the Mishkan was sanctified through love, (3:9-11) 206

The sense in which Hashem sees us as a "mother", (3:9-11) 207

The amazing rebuke of Batsheva, the mother of Shlomo HaMelech, (3:9-11) 208

The praise from Hashem elicited by *Klal Yisrael*'s wonderful deeds and good attributes, (Chapter Four in its entirety) 210

Every aspect of the greatness of *Klal Yisrael* reflects well on the entire nation, (Introduction to Chapter Four) 211

Klal Yisrael is unparalleled, (4:1) 213

Even the weakest among *Klal Yisrael* is unique, (4:1) 214

The importance of staying within the fold, (4:1) 214

The greatness of every "hair" in the Torah, (4:1) 215

The importance of *yeshivos*, (4:1) 215

The greatness of even the warriors of *Klal Yisrael*, (4:2) 217

The honesty of *Klal Yisrael*, (4:2) 218

The greatness of the Torah scholars of *Klal Yisrael*, (4:2) 219

The nations can never really harm *Klal Yisrael*, (4:2) 219

Klal Yisrael always keep their word, (4:3) 221

The greatness of even the "empty ones" among *Klal Yisrael*, (4:3) 222

The metaphor of the pomegranate, and how it pertains to even the "empty" Jews, (4:3) 223

The importance of the Sanhedrin, (4:4) 224

The importance of the Beis HaMikdash, (4:4) 225

The "neck" of *Klal Yisrael*, (4:4) 225

The symmetry and unity of the leaders of *Klal Yisrael*, (4:5) 227

The nurturing provided by the leaders of *Klal Yisrael*, (4:5) 227

The symmetry of the two *Luchos*, and how all mitzvos are interconnected, (4:5) 228

One must observe all of Torah and not just certain parts, (4:5) 230

The leaders of *Klal Yisrael* work together for the sake of the nation, (4:5) 231

Hashem speaks gently regarding the sins of *Klal Yisrael*, (4:6) 233

Coming to the Beis HaMikdash to reunite with Hashem, (4:6) 233

Once the merits of the heathen nations have been consumed they will be like chaff, (4:6) 234

Klal Yisrael is perfectly beautiful in absolutely every way, (4:7) 235

The beauty of the unity of *Klal Yisrael*, (4:7) 235

The Beis HaMikdash cleanses us from sin, (4:8) 237

Hashem goes into exile with *Klal Yisrael*, (4:8) 237

Klal Yisrael is like a new bride to Hashem; how kindly one must treat a new bride, (4:8) 239

The great reward Hashem gives to those who have faith in Him, (4:8) 240

The great faith of *Klal Yisrael*, (4:8) 240

Singing when Mashiach comes, (4:8) 240

Hashem loves modesty, (4:9) 241

Each individual aspect of *Klal Yisrael* is precious to Hashem, (4:9) 241

One complete mitzvah is enough to bring ultimate reward, (4:9) 242

Any love for Hashem that *Klal Yisrael* displays is greatly treasured by Him, (4:10) 244

Klal Yisrael is more precious than all the other nations, (4:10) 245

Klal Yisrael's praise of Hashem is more precious to Him than the praise of the angels, (4:10) 245

The spirituality of the sense of smell, (4:10) 246

Everything about *Klal Yisrael* is loved by Hashem, (4:11) 247

The sweetness of the speech of *Klal Yisrael*, (4:11) 248

All of Torah is sweet, (4:11) 249

The symbolism of honey and milk, (4:11) 249

We are proud to express our love for Hashem outwardly as well as inwardly, (4:11) 251

The sweetness of prayer, (4:11) 251
The modesty of *Klal Yisrael* (men, women, and girls), (4:12) 253
Modesty vs privacy, (4:12) 254
Klal Yisrael do a great variety of many great deeds, (4:13-14) 256
The greatness of the young and simple Jews and their great potential, (4:13-14) 257
Modesty brings forth the beauty and kindness of *Klal Yisrael*, (4:13-14) 257
All the various components of *Klal Yisrael* are precious and bring forth beauty for Hashem, (4:13-14) 258
The beauty of the purification of *Klal Yisrael*, (4:15) 259
The Jewish mother's influence on the home, (4:15) 260
Hashem "longs for" salvation in order to see the full beauty of *Klal Yisrael*, (4:16) 261
There is nothing more precious than a Jewish child, (4:16) 262
Klal Yisrael is open only to Hashem, (4:16) 262
Only *Klal Yisrael* may eat from the *korbanos* in the Beis HaMikdash, (4:16) 263
Only *Klal Yisrael* elevate the mundane, (4:16) 264
The joy of the *Chanukas HaMishkan*, (5:1) 265
Just as Hashem's Presence dwelled among us in the past, it will in the future as well, (5:1) 266
Love of Hashem breaks the normal rules, (5:1) 267
Excitement about when the Beis HaMikdash will be built, (5:1) 267
Hashem searches for *Klal Yisrael* and invests a great deal in order to bring us back to Him, (5:2-6) 268
Hashem searches for each and every Jew and constantly sends "messages" to bring them closer, (Introduction to 5:2-6) 269
A son who neglects his father shamefully, *mashal* to *Klal Yisrael*, (5:2) 270
The heart of *Klal Yisrael*, (5:2) 272
Klal Yisrael is never completely asleep, (5:2) 272
If one repents, Hashem opens up opportunities for him, (5:2) 273
The words of love that Hashem uses to call to *Klal Yisrael* and their meanings, (5:2) 274
The four kinds of love and all apply to Hashem, (5:2)... 275
Reward and punishment, to awaken our repentance, (5:2) 276
Three methods of encouragement, (5:2) 276

Hashem never forgets us at all, (5:2) 277
The desperate call of Hashem to awaken us, (5:2) . 278
Klal Yisrael's disturbing laziness, (5:3) 279
Middos and measurements, (5:3) 280
Hashem helps us get clean and stay clean, (5:3) 280
Hashem resorts to punishment to awaken us, (5:4)281
Hashem begs us to repent, (5:4) 281
Every feeling of repentance is effective, (5:4) 283
Klal Yisrael's feeble attempt to repent, (5:5) 284
The danger of haughtiness and laziness when repenting, (5:5) 285
One must grab the opportunity to return to Hashem lest it be lost, (5:5) 285
Klal Yisrael's constant search to revive their closeness to Hashem, (5:6) 287
The pain of *Klal Yisrael* because they miss Hashem, (5:6) 287
The five things missing from the Second Beis HaMikdash, (5:6) 287
One must not waste his speech, (5:6) 288
The yearning for Hashem is precious, (5:6) 288
The inner desire of a Jew is to serve Hashem, (5:6) 289
The true suffering of exile, (5:7) 290
The purpose of the heathen nations is to guard us from sin, (5:7) 291
Hashem never gives up on *Klal Yisrael*, (5:7) 292
Accepting suffering protects us from harm, (5:7) .. 292
Klal Yisrael's greatest declaration of love for Hashem, (5:8) 293
The nations will testify regarding *Klal Yisrael*'s devotion, (5:8) 294
Lovesick, (5:8) 294
Nothing disturbs *Klal Yisrael* like the loss of Hashem's love, (5:8) 296
The innermost yearning of a Jew is to become close to Hashem, (5:8) 296
The great sacrifices *Klal Yisrael* has made for their love for Hashem, (5:8) 296
Klal Yisrael is obsessed with love for Hashem, (5:8) 297
The desire to serve Hashem is most precious of all, (5:8) 297
The nations are awe-struck by *Klal Yisrael*'s declaration, (5:9) 298
The nations question *Klal Yisrael*, (5:9) 298
Klal Yisrael constantly seek to bring Hashem closer to them, (Introduction to 5:10-16) 301

As much as we praise Hashem, we have no grasp of Him, (Introduction to 5:10-16) ... 301

Klal Yisrael's great praises of Hashem, (5:10-16) 301

Hashem is both very merciful and very strict, (5:10) 302

Hashem's strictness is for our good, (5:10) 303

Hashem's wide range of powers, (5:10) 303

Hashem's words are as bright as gold, (5:11) 304

Every hair-like protrusion from the letters of the Torah has great depths, (5:11) 304

Hashem embodies greatness, (5:11) 305

Hashem's actions are incomprehensible to a mere human, (5:11) 305

Torah is both clear and complicated, (5:11) 306

Acquiring Torah requires sacrifice, (5:11) 307

Through Torah, one connects to Hashem, (5:11) .. 307

One "sees" Hashem through Torah and His Creation, yet Torah is superior, (5:11) 308

Praise of the clarity of Hashem, His Torah, and its scholars, (5:12) 309

The good "smell" that Hashem sends forth, (5:13) 311

The preciousness of the *Luchos*, (5:14) 312

Hashem's hidden deeds are all absolutely just, (5:14) ... 314

That Hashem allows evil displays His greatness, (5:14) ... 314

Only the righteous truly discern Hashem's deeds, (5:14) 315

Torah is like a well-built building, (5:15) 316

Hashem watches carefully over this world, (5:15) . 317

The forest as a metaphor of how difficult it is to truly see Hashem, (5:15) 317

Hashem is extremely sweet, (5:16) 319

Hashem rewards us for doing mitzvos that benefit ourselves, (5:16) 319

From the little we know of Hashem, we understand He is completely kind, (5:16) 320

Our relationship with Hashem is unique and He is unique, (5:16) 321

The nations taunt *Klal Yisrael* that Hashem has left them, (6:1) 322

The nations wish to interfere with our relationship with Hashem, (6:1) 323

Klal Yisrael inspire the nations to want to help them serve Hashem, (6:1) 324

The unique relationship between *Klal Yisrael* and Hashem, (6:2-3) 325

Klal Yisrael replies confidently to the nations that Hashem loves them and has not completely left them, (6:2-3) 325

Hashem's Presence dwells in our shuls, (6:2-3) 326

When *Klal Yisrael* is in exile, Hashem's Presence is still in their midst, albeit in a different manner, (6:2-3) 326

Mitzvos in exile are extremely precious, (6:2-3) 327

"I belong to my Beloved, and my Beloved to me", (6:2-3) 328

The order of the elements in the verse above, and why the order differs from a similar verse earlier in *Shir HaShirim*, (6:2-3) 328

In good times and bad times, *Klal Yisrael* is devoted to Hashem, (6:2-3) 328

As we become closer to Hashem, Hashem becomes closer to us, (6:2-3) 328

All of Hashem's efforts are for *Klal Yisrael* and vice versa, (6:2-3) 329

The goal of Ellul is to reach the level of "I belong to Hashem", (6:2-3) 329

When one serves Hashem, Hashem fulfills his desires, (6:2-3) 330

How special is the one who remembers to serve Hashem when everyone neglects to, (6:2-3) 330

Converts are added to *Klal Yisrael* through exile, (6:2-3) 332

Even when *Klal Yisrael* is in exile, Hashem treasures the good things that they do, (6:2-3) 333

Even when *Klal Yisrael* is not at their best, Hashem finds plenty to praise, (Introduction to 6:4-10) 334

Hashem describes His love for *Klal Yisrael*, (6:4-12) 334

Klal Yisrael knows how to please Hashem, (6:4) 335

Klal Yisrael is awe-inspiring, (6:4) 335

The greatest rally is for Hashem, (6:4) 336

Shimon HaTzaddik victorious, (6:4) 336

Hashem treasures the Second Beis HaMikdash, (6:4) ... 337

Klal Yisrael's desire to serve Hashem is most pleasing, (6:4) 338

Klal Yisrael is always very kind, (6:4) 338

Hashem is "overwhelmed," *ki'veyachol*, by His love for *Klal Yisrael*, (6:5) 340

Hashem loves all parts of *Klal Yisrael*, (6:5) 341

Klal Yisrael has the ability to sway Hashem, (6:5) .. 342

Even when one is close to Hashem, one must be careful with halachah, (6:5) 342

The greatness of even the warriors of *Klal Yisrael*, (6:6-

7) 344	The constant enticement of the *yetzer ha'ra*, (7:1) . 365
The greatness of even the empty among *Klal Yisrael*, (6:6-7) 345	*Klal Yisrael* is *shulamis* (perfect and beautiful), (7:1) 365
Klal Yisrael's eating and thinking is devoted to Hashem, (6:6-7) 346	The four exiles are all tests for *Klal Yisrael*, (7:1) 366
A Jew utilizes everything for Hashem, (6:6-7) 346	Various tactics used by the *yetzer ha'ra*, (7:1) 367
Even though Hashem could choose any nation, He loves only *Klal Yisrael*, (6:8-9) 348	The authenticity of Torah as proven at Har Sinai, (7:1) 367
The *temimus* of Klal Yisrael, (6:8-9) 349	*Klal Yisrael's* steadfastness because nothing compares to what they have, (7:1) 368
The unity of *Klal Yisrael*, even when they argue *halachicly*, (6:8-9) 349	The encouragement offered by the Rambam in his *Iggeres Teiman*, (7:1) 369
The symbolism of the dove, (6:8-9) 349	*Klal Yisrael* withstands all the temptations of the nations, (7:1) 370
Hashem chose to dwell specifically among *Klal Yisrael*, (6:8-9) 350	The purpose of *Ma'amad Har Sinai*, (7:1) 370
Forefathers get *nachas* from their descendants, (6:8-9) 350	*Klal Yisrael* sees serving Hashem as the greatest joy, (7:1) 371
All the other nations admit the superiority of *Klal Yisrael*, (6:8-9) 350	Nothing compares to the importance of *Klal Yisrael* in Hashem's eyes, (7:1) 371
The purity of *Klal Yisrael* as seen in their children, (6:8-9) 350	The prophets exhort *Klal Yisrael* to repent, (7:1) ... 371
The greatness of Esther HaMalkah, (6:8-9) 351	The greatness of *Klal Yisrael* which even the nations notice, (Introduction to 7:2-14) 372
Klal Yisrael is the most superior nation, (6:8-9) 351	The prophets try to bring about a reconciliation, *ki'veyachol*, between *Klal Yisrael* and Hashem, (Introduction to 7:2-14) 373
The Beis HaMikdash is the "highest place", (6:10) .. 352	
Klal Yisrael continually grows and flourishes, (6:10) 352	The greatness of *Klal Yisrael*, (7:2-14) 373
Klal Yisrael is destined for greatness, (6:10) 353	*Aliyah l'regel*: a description of its grandeur, (7:2) 375
Klal Yisrael possesses beauty, warmth, and awe, (6:10) 354	The footsteps of *Klal Yisrael* as they performed *aliyah l'regel*, (7:2) 375
The symbolism of nuts, (6:11) 356	The pride of *aliyah l'regel*, (7:2) 376
Klal Yisrael is always clean, (6:11) 356	Humility is not a sense of worthlessness, (7:2) 376
Torah brings out the goodness of *Klal Yisrael*, (6:11) 357	As descendants of Avraham Avinu, we are a "daughter of nobility", (7:2) 376
Torah is the ultimate purpose of everything, (6:11) 357	The pipes of the *Mizbe'ach*, (7:2) 377
Like nuts, *Klal Yisrael* is filled with goodness, (6:11) 358	Yearning to become close to Hashem, (7:2) 378
	Hidden service of Hashem is most valuable, (7:2) . 378
Klal Yisrael is modest and reticent, (6:11) 357	Locked into serving Hashem, (7:2) 378
Klal Yisrael is precious like nuts, (6:11) 358	The Sanhedrin and its unimaginable greatness, (7:3) 380
The vitality of *Klal Yisrael*, (6:11) 358	
Conflict destroys *Klal Yisrael*, (6:12) 359	A fence of roses, (7:3) 382
Klal Yisrael regrets their sins, especially the sin of internal strife, (6:12) 359	*Klal Yisrael's* self-control, (7:3) 382
Klal Yisrael regrets their lack of response to Hashem, (6:12) 360	*Klal Yisrael* appreciates the greatness of the fences of Torah, (7:3) 383
Klal Yisrael is amazed by their own greatness, (6:12) 361	The twin leadership of *Klal Yisrael*, (7:4) 385
	The "nose" of *Klal Yisrael*, (7:5) 386
The salvation of *Klal Yisrael* often takes people by surprise — even themselves, (6:12) 362	The *Mizbe'ach*: a conduit between Heaven and earth, (7:5) 387
The nations try to lure *Klal Yisrael*, (7:1) 364	Purity of the leaders of *Klal Yisrael*, (7:5) 388

The greatness of the calendric calculations, (7:5)... 388
Mental perseverance of *Klal Yisrael*, (7:5) 389
The ivory neck, life-giving and strong, as a symbol of *Klal Yisrael*, (7:5).. 389
The ivory neck, life-giving and strong, as a symbol of Torah leaders, (7:5) 389
The *nazir*, (7:6) 391
Klal Yisrael's every mitzvah has a great effect, (7:6) 392
Eliyahu on Mount Carmel, (7:6) 392
Purity and strength of thought, (7:6) 393
Even the lowly and poor are special, (7:6) 394
Hashem is bound to the love of *Klal Yisrael*, (7:6) . 394
All sectors of *Klal Yisrael* are special, (7:6) 395
It is a pleasure to be with *Klal Yisrael*, (7:7) 396
Loving Hashem is completely enjoyable, (7:7) 396
Only spirituality truly satisfies a person, (7:7) 396
Accepting suffering with love, (7:7)............................. 397
In Eretz Yisrael we can truly enjoy Hashem's love, (7:7) 397
Tall and firm like a date tree, (7:8) 398
The honesty of *Klal Yisrael*, (7:8) 398
Chananyah, Mishael, and Azaryah demonstrate faith to the world, (7:8) 399
A righteous person's every action is for Hashem, (7:8) 400
Hashem is proud of *Klal Yisrael* and "boasts" about them, (7:9) 401
Klal Yisrael make a very good impression on everyone, (7:9) 403
Hashem wants *Klal Yisrael* to respond with faith to justify His pride in them, (7:10) 404
Our forefathers thank Hashem for their good children, (7:10) 405
One must keep one's mouth clean, (7:10) 405
When repeated in their name, words of Torah enliven the dead, (7:10)... 405
The value of speaking words of rebuke, (7:10) 406
Klal Yisrael justify Hashem's pride in them, (7:11) 407
Klal Yisrael is completely devoted to Hashem, (7:11) 407
Hashem's attachment to *Klal Yisrael* is all-consuming, (7:11) 407
As one becomes attached to Hashem, the passion becomes stronger, (7:11) 408
Klal Yisrael's importance is their relationship to Hashem, (7:11) 409
Hashem loves the humility of *Klal Yisrael*, (7:11) .. 409

Klal Yisrael seek to rejuvenate their relationship with Hashem, (7:12-14) 411
The righteous serve Hashem even in poverty, while the wicked rebel even in prosperity, (7:12-14) 412
For the righteous, it is always light; for the wicked, it is always dark, (7:12-14)... 412
The righteous are always ready to serve Hashem; the wicked always wish to rest, (7:12-14).......................... 413
The righteous see the truth, while the wicked are blind, (7:12-14) 413
Torah scholars are constantly developing and rising higher and higher, (7:12-14) 413
The wicked of *Klal Yisrael* are not intrinsically bad; they just need better care, (7:12-14)............................. 414
Klal Yisrael is always ready to serve Hashem, (7:12-14) 414
Klal Yisrael is always looking for new and additional ways to serve Hashem, (7:12-14).................................. 415
Klal Yisrael conceal and store their good deeds, (7:12-14) 415
Contrasting *Klal Yisrael* with the nations shows the former's greatness, (7:12-14) 416
Hashem fills His immense storehouses with reward, (7.12-14) 417
Mitzvos done only for Hashem are especially precious, (7:12-14) 417
The humility of Torah scholars, (7:12-14) 418
The conclusion of *Shir HaShirim* refers to the days of *Mashiach* (Introduction to chapter Eight), ... 419
Klal Yisrael seek brotherhood with Hashem, (8:1)........ 420
The special relationship between siblings and how it relates to *Klal Yisrael*'s relationship with Hashem, (8:1) 420
Klal Yisrael seek to have their relationship with Hashem publicly, (8:1)... 420
Klal Yisrael seek to have an unhindered relationship with Hashem, (8:1) 421
Klal Yisrael seek to have a relationship with Hashem that does not end, (8:1) 421
Yosef's righteousness towards his brothers, (8:1) 422
Aharon's devotion to Moshe, (8:1).............................. 423
Abundant prophecy in the days of Mashiach, (8:1) 423
Connecting to Hashem always, (8:1) 424
Klal Yisrael seek to go to where their relationship with Hashem was first cemented, (8:2).............................. 425
Har Sinai and the Beis HaMikdash are where our relationship with Hashem matured, (8:2) 425
The whole of *Klal Yisrael* look to serve Hashem, (8:2)

- 425
- Hashem always supports and protects *Klal Yisrael*, (8:3) 425
- *Klal Yisrael*'s relationship with Hashem is constant, (8:3) 426
- The nations are unable to disrupt *Klal Yisrael*'s relationship with Hashem, (8:4) 428
- The grave danger of getting in between *Klal Yisrael* and Hashem, (8:4) 428
- Hashem exclaims in wonder over the greatness of *Klal Yisrael*, (8:5) 429
- "Under the apple tree" symbolism, (8:5) 430
- *Klal Yisrael* taught the world to serve Hashem, and thereby it is as if they "gave birth" to Him, (8:5) 431
- *Klal Yisrael* remind Hashem of their devotion, (8:5) 431
- The final test for those who cleave to Hashem, (8:5) 432
- *Klal Yisrael*'s greatness in accepting the Torah, (8:5) 432
- The righteousness of the Jewish women in Egypt, (8:5) 433
- At the outset, serving Hashem is very difficult, but it gets easier, (8:5) 434
- The very intense love and pride that Hashem has for *Klal Yisrael*, (8:6) 435
- *Klal Yisrael* are Hashem's medals, (8:6) 436
- The symbolism of a medal, and why it is placed on the heart and arm, (8:6) 436
- Hashem remembers *Klal Yisrael* and always keeps them before Him, (8:6) 437
- *Klal Yisrael* has paid with their lives for their love of Hashem, (8:6) 438
- Because jealousy clarifies what is valuable, one should only be jealous of Torah, (8:6) 439
- The burning love of *Klal Yisrael*, (8:6) 439
- *Klal Yisrael* is linked to Hashem, (8:6) 440
- All the nations with all their tactics cannot usurp Hashem's love for *Klal Yisrael*, (8:7) 441
- Even if the nations would sacrifice everything for Hashem, He would love only *Klal Yisrael*, (8:7) 443
- Neither friendliness nor threats will sway *Klal Yisrael*, (8:7) 443
- *Klal Yisrael* love Hashem with all their heart, being, and resources, (8:7) 444
- It would be ludicrous to try to buy the love of *Klal Yisrael*, (8:7) 444
- What one sacrifices for Hashem, one receives back tenfold, (8:7) 444
- Earthly pleasures and spiritual pleasures are always in competition, (8:7) 445
- Rabbi Yochanan's dedication to Torah, (8:7) 445
- The love of Torah by great Torah scholars, (8:7) 445
- Torah learning cannot be bought, but its merit can be earned, (8:7) 446
- The amazement of people who see this love of Torah, (8:7) 446
- Rabbi Yitzchak Elchanan's family's great love of Torah, (8:7) 447
- Haman's wealth did not help him harm *Klal Yisrael*, (8:7) 448
- The fate of *Klal Yisrael* and the nations is settled (Introduction to 8:8-14) 448
- Hashem watches over *Klal Yisrael* with compassion, as an older brother watches over a little sister, (8:8) 449
- Hashem's and the angels' concern for *Klal Yisrael* on the day of their judgment, (8:8) 449
- *Klal Yisrael* are the friends and compatriots of the angels, (8:8) 450
- *Klal Yisrael* bonds the world to Hashem, (8:8) 450
- *Klal Yisrael* need additional protection, (8:8) 450
- Avraham Avinu's dedication to Hashem, (8:8) 451
- *Klal Yisrael* is judged based on their commitment to Hashem, (8:9) 452
- Those who are strong in their service to Hashem deserve strong protection, (8:9) 452
- Only one who is not influenced by others can truly teach the world, (8:9) 453
- The difference between Avraham and Noach, (8:9) 453
- If one does not grab a mitzvah, one may lose it altogether, (8:9) 454
- *Klal Yisrael* is a wall, (8:10) 455
- *Klal Yisrael*'s absolute firmness, (8:10) 455
- *Klal Yisrael*'s unity, (8:10) 456
- Torah scholars are like fortresses, (8:10) 456
- Teachers of Torah are like nursing mothers, (8:10) 456
- Rabbi Moshe Feinstein's unbending commitment to halachah, (8:10) 457
- Becoming a wall, (8:10) 458
- Creating strong barriers, (8:10) 459
- Torah will save us from exile, (8:10) 461
- Declaring one's faith is priceless, (8:10) 461
- The judgment of the nations centers on how they treat *Klal Yisrael*, (8:11) 462

Klal Yisrael is precious and vulnerable, like a vineyard, (8:11) 463

Klal Yisrael's excellent pedigree, (8:11) 463

Yerushalayim is a place of multitudes, (8:11) 463

Eretz Yisrael is a place everyone desires, (8:11) 463

The nations plunder *Klal Yisrael*, (8:11) 464

Even the exile is due to Hashem's care of *Klal Yisrael*, (8:11) 464

The main task of the nations is to help *Klal Yisrael*, (8:11) 464

The importance of the hundred daily blessings, (8:12) 465

The great compensation the nations owe *Klal Yisrael*, (8:12) 466

Hashem will compensate *Klal Yisrael* for everything that they suffered, (8:12) 467

Klal Yisrael is like holy vessels, (8:12) 467

Since the heathen nations did not guard *Klal Yisrael*, they will not be rewarded, (8:12) 468

The true guardians of *Klal Yisrael*, the Torah leaders, will be richly rewarded, (8:12) 468

One must use one's position to further Hashem's goals, (8:12) 468

Hashem wants our prayers, (8:13) 469

Exile as a garden, (8:13) 470

The angels have to wait for *Klal Yisrael* to praise Hashem, (8:13) 470

The importance and power of prayer, (8:13) 471

Because *Klal Yisrael* is so close to Hashem, He truly hears their prayers, (8:13) 471

The nations check to see if *Klal Yisrael* is serving Hashem in order to know whether or not they can harm them, (8:13) 472

The friendship of the angels, (8:13) 472

All service of Hashem requires unity, (8:13) 472

The closeness of *Klal Yisrael* to Hashem and the angels, (8:13) 473

The spiritual unity between Hashem, Torah, and *Klal Yisrael*, (8:13) 473

Shir HaShirim describes the spiritual connections, (8:13) 474

Klal Yisrael's deepest desire is to get out of exile, (8:14) 475

Hashem must also "escape" the exile, (8:14) 475

When *Klal Yisrael* is in exile, it is as if Hashem is in exile as well, (8:14) 475

Hashem watches *Klal Yisrael* like a deer, always alert and seeing only the good, (8:14) 476

All the mountains will be part of Mount Moriah, (8:14) 476

Every effort a person makes for Hashem, even if mistaken, is treasured, (8:14) 477

Mashiach can only come when the sin of *lashon hara* is eradicated, (8:14) 478

Hashem wants *Klal Yisrael* to know that He loves them, (Conclusion) 479

Reciting *Shir HaShirim* on Erev Shabbos, (Reciting *Shir HaShirim*) 481

Shabbos is a partner of *Klal Yisrael*, (Reciting *Shir HaShirim*) 481

How one starts Shabbos lays the foundation for the whole Shabbos, (Reciting *Shir HaShirim*) 481

Just how far does *Shir HaShirim* go?, (Reciting *Shir HaShirim*) 481

The *segulos* of reciting *Shir HaShirim*, (Reciting *Shir HaShirim*) 482

One needs to absorb the message of *Shir HaShirim* in all of its aspects, (Detailed Table of Contents) 505

In every situation, one must remember that Hashem loves *Klal Yisrael*, (Detailed Table of Contents) 506

INDEX BY TOPIC
FOR THOSE WHO WANT REINFORCEMENT
AND GUIDANCE IN FEELING HASHEM'S LOVE

(Subtitles according to the Detailed Table of Contents)

Why it is important to know that Hashem loves us

Foreword: Worst thing a Yid can do 24

Introduction: How knowing about Hashem's love can change our lives..................28

Introduction: The importance of recognizing how much Hashem loves us..................30

Introduction: Even the simplest Jew must know that Hashem loves him..................48

Introduction: The great reward for those who thank Hashem for His love..................56

2:14: Hashem loves *Klal Yisrael* and waits for their prayers 173

4:11: The sweetness of prayer.................. 251

4:16: Hashem "longs for" salvation in order to see the full beauty of *Klal Yisrael*.................. 261

7:1: *Klal Yisrael's* steadfastness because nothing compares to what they have 368

7:1: *Klal Yisrael* sees serving Hashem as the greatest joy 371

8:13: Because *Klal Yisrael* is so close to Hashem, He truly hears their prayers 471

8:13: The spiritual unity between Hashem, Torah, and *Klal Yisrael* 473

8:13: Shir HaShirim describes the spiritual connections 474

Conclusion: Hashem wants *Klal Yisrael* to know that He loves them 479

Detailed Table of Contents: In every situation, one must remember that Hashem loves *Klal Yisrael*........................505

Every Yid's personal relationship with Hashem

Foreword: A Yid should make sure that his relationship with Hashem is constantly growing 24

Introduction: Our relationship with Hashem is the most important relationship in our life 28

Introduction: The Torah wants us to have a real relationship with Hashem 42

1:2: When one makes an effort to become close to Hashem, He responds immediately and draws the person closer 72

1:2: To become close to Hashem, one has to distance himself from other interests 74

2:9: Hashem is our *mashgiach* 162

3:1: Our deepest yearning are actually a desire for closeness to Hashem 185

6:5: Hashem loves all parts of *Klal Yisrael* 341

6:6-7: A Jew utilizes everything for Hashem 346

7:7: Loving Hashem is completely enjoyable.... 396

7:11: As one becomes attached to Hashem, the passion becomes stronger 408

7:12-14: *Klal Yisrael* is always looking for new and additional ways to serve Hashem 415

7:12-14: Mitzvos done only for Hashem are especially precious 417

8:1: Connecting to Hashem always 424

Detailed Table of Contents: One needs to absorb the message of Shir HaShirim in all of its aspects ..
.... 506

One who feels unworthy of Hashem's love because of his sins or his failure to fulfill enough mitzvos

One who feels that Klal Yisrael is unworthy of Hashem's love because of their sins

1:5: *Klal Yisrael's* greatness and true beauty even

when they look sullied and appear to have sinned terribly 88

1:5: *Klal Yisrael* have aspects of beauty even in their ugliness 90

1:5: *Klal Yisrael* is easily aroused to repent and cleanse themselves from sin 91

1:6: *Klal Yisrael* sins only due to the influence of the other wicked nations 92

1:6: *Klal Yisrael* sins only because the nations force them into it 92

1:12-14: Hashem constantly forgives *Klal Yisrael* for their sins — even major sins 111

1:16-17: Hashem forgives *Klal Yisrael* completely so that the relationship is not harmed in any way 125

2:1: Hashem loves *Klal Yisrael* even when they have done nothing to deserve it 129

2:4: Even when *Klal Yisrael* makes mistakes, Hashem loves their efforts 141

2:5: Hashem loves *Klal Yisrael* even at their worst 146

4:1: Even the weakest among *Klal Yisrael* is unique 214

4:3: The greatness of even the "empty ones" among *Klal Yisrael* 222

4:3: The metaphor of the pomegranate, and how it pertains to even the "empty" Jews 223

4:6: Hashem speaks gently regarding the sins of *Klal Yisrael* 233

4:9: One complete mitzvah is enough to bring ultimate reward 242

4:13-14: *Klal Yisrael* do a great variety of many great deeds 256

5:2: If one repents, Hashem opens up opportunities for him 273

5:3: Hashem helps us get clean and stay clean .. 280

5:4: Every feeling of repentance is effective 283

5:8: The innermost yearning of a Jew is to become close to Hashem 296

5:8: The desire to serve Hashem is most precious of all 297

6:2-3: Mitzvos in exile are extremely precious 327

Introduction to 6:4-10: Even when *Klal Yisrael* is not at their best, Hashem finds plenty to praise 334

6:12: The salvation of *Klal Yisrael* often takes people by surprise — even themselves 362

7:6: Even the lowly and poor are special 394

7:6: All sectors of *Klal Yisrael* are special 395

7:12-14: The wicked of *Klal Yisrael* are not intrinsically bad; they just need better care 414

8:14: Hashem watches *Klal Yisrael* like a deer, always alert and seeing only the good 476

8:14: Every effort a person makes for Hashem, even if mistaken, is treasured 477

One who doubts if Hashem loves him because he feels that Hashem has punished him severely

One who doubts if Hashem loves Klal Yisrael because of the suffering of the exile

Introduction: Even in exile, it is possible to feel Hashem's love 46

Introduction: The great vision of *Shir HaShirim* 47

1:1: The love of Hashem for *Klal Yisrael* will last forever — even when people doubt it 66

2:6: Hashem deals with *Klal Yisrael* both with mercy and with strict judgment — all for their own good 149

2:9: Hashem is always right next to us even in exile 157

2:5-9: Hashem's love and care for *Klal Yisrael* continue during the exile (even when He seems distant) 144

2:9: The two ways in which Hashem watches over us: hidden and revealed 161

2:11-12: Exile and Redemption are important processes 169

3:1-2: The yearning of *Klal Yisrael* for Hashem in exile 183

3:6: Through troubles, *Klal Yisrael* grow 197

4:8: Hashem goes into exile with *Klal Yisrael* ... 237

5:6: The inner desire of a Jew is to serve Hashem 289

5:7: The true suffering of exile 290

5:7: The purpose of the heathen nations is to guard us from sin 291

5:10: Hashem is both very merciful and very strict 302

5:10: Hashem's strictness is for our good 303

5:11: Hashem's actions are incomprehensible to a mere human 305

5:14: Hashem's hidden deeds are all absolutely just 314

6:1: The nations taunt *Klal Yisrael* that Hashem has left them 322

6:2-3: Even when *Klal Yisrael* is in exile, Hashem treasures the good things that they do 333

8:11: Even the exile is due to Hashem's care of *Klal Yisrael* 464

8:11: The main task of the nations is to help *Klal Yisrael* 464

8:12: Hashem will compensate *Klal Yisrael* for everything that they suffered 467

8:13: Exile as a garden............................ 470

8:14: Hashem must also "escape" the exile......... 475

8:14: When *Klal Yisrael* is in exile, it is as if Hashem is in exile as well 475

One who desires to feel the intensity of Hashem's love

Introduction: The message of *Ahavas Olam* 29

Introduction: The tremendous love that Hashem has for every Jew 30

Introduction: *Klal Yisrael* are "betrothed" to Hashem 31

Introduction: True friendship is with Hashem ... 49

Introduction: Hashem created all love because of His love for us... 51

Introduction: All that happens in this world is designed to facilitate our becoming closer to Hashem 55

1:1: How Hashem's love is like the love of husband for his wife 70

1:2: Nothing is more precious than Hashem's love 75

1:9-11: Hashem entrusted the destiny of the world to *Klal Yisrael* 107

1:12-14: The forgiveness of Hashem displays His love 112

1:16-17: Hashem and *Klal Yisrael* bring out the best, *ki'veyachol*, in one another 124

2:4: The gathering of *Klal Yisrael* at Hashem's behest displays His love for them 144

2:16: The close, unique, and multifaceted relationship between *Klal Yisrael* and Hashem 179

2:16: Hashem is devoted to *Klal Yisrael* 179

3:9-11: Hashem chose to dwell in the Mishkan to demonstrate His love 205

3:9-11: The sense in which Hashem sees us as a "mother" 207

4:8: *Klal Yisrael* is like a new bride to Hashem; how kindly one must treat a new bride 239

4:9: Each individual aspect of *Klal Yisrael* is precious to Hashem 241

4:10: Any love for Hashem that *Klal Yisrael* displays is greatly treasured by Him 244

4:10: *Klal Yisrael*'s praise of Hashem is more precious to Him than the praise of the angels.. 245

4:11: Everything about *Klal Yisrael* is loved by Hashem 247

5:1: Love of Hashem breaks the normal rules 267

5:2: The words of love that Hashem uses to call to *Klal Yisrael* and their meanings............................ 274

5:2: Hashem never forgets us at all 277

6:2-3: As we become closer to Hashem, Hashem becomes closer to us.. 328

6:5: Hashem is "overwhelmed," *ki'veyachol*, by His love for *Klal Yisrael* 340

6:5: *Klal Yisrael* has the ability to sway Hashem...... 342

6:8-9: Hashem chose to dwell specifically among *Klal Yisrael* 350

7:11: Hashem's attachment to *Klal Yisrael* is all-consuming 407

8:1: The special relationship between siblings and how it relates to *Klal Yisrael*'s relationship with Hashem 420

8:1: *Klal Yisrael* seek to have their relationship with Hashem publicly 420

8:3: *Klal Yisrael*'s relationship with Hashem is constant.. 426

8:4: The nations are unable to disrupt *Klal Yisrael*'s relationship with Hashem 428

8:5: Hashem exclaims in wonder over the greatness of *Klal Yisrael* 429

8:5: *Klal Yisrael* taught the world to serve Hashem, and thereby it is as if they "gave birth" to Him... 431

8:5: *Klal Yisrael* remind Hashem of their devotion 431

8:5: The final test for those who cleave to Hashem 432

8:6: The burning love of *Klal Yisrael* 439

8:6: *Klal Yisrael* is linked to Hashem................ 440

8:7: It would be ludicrous to try to buy the love of *Klal Yisrael* 444

8:8: Hashem watches over *Klal Yisrael* with compassion, as an older brother watches over a little sister.. 449

8:8: *Klal Yisrael* are the friends and compatriots of the angels 450

8:12: *Klal Yisrael* is like holy vessels 467

8:13: The angels have to wait for *Klal Yisrael* to praise Hashem 470

One who feels little self-worth

2:1: The beauty of *Klal Yisrael* is likened to flowers,

solely love and beauty 129

2:4: Even when *Klal Yisrael* makes mistakes, Hashem loves their efforts 141

5:6: The yearning for Hashem is precious 288

6:2-3: How special is the one who remembers to serve Hashem when everyone neglects to 330

6:4: *Klal Yisrael*'s desire to serve Hashem is most pleasing 338

7:2: The pride of *aliyah l'regel* 376

7:2: Humility is not a sense of worthlessness 376

7:11: *Klal Yisrael* justify Hashem's pride in them 407

8:14: Every effort a person makes for Hashem, even if mistaken, is treasured 477

One who wants to see Klal Yisrael's good qualities

One who wishes to appreciate how Klal Yisrael is more beloved by Hashem than any other nation

Introduction: The Greatness of *Klal Yisrael* 31

Introduction: Why are *Klal Yisrael* so criticized 31

Introduction: The multifaceted relationship between Hashem and *Klal Yisrael* 40

1:2: *Klal Yisrael* wish to become as close as possible to Hashem 71

1:3: The entire world will come to love Hashem by seeing the greatness of *Klal Yisrael* 77

1:3: Our lives demonstrate the greatness of serving Hashem 79

1:3: *Klal Yisrael*'s unique relationship and devotion to Hashem is not compromised by ulterior motives 81

1:4: What is unique about our relationship to Hashem 84

1:4: *Klal Yisrael* remains loyal to Hashem even when others try to seduce them away 85

1:5: The tremendous beauty of *Klal Yisrael* 88

1:7: The honor of Hashem is entwined with the honor of *Klal Yisrael* 97

1:8: *Klal Yisrael* is the most beautiful of all nations 98

1:9-11: *Klal Yisrael*, *ki'veyachol*, "feed" Hashem 107

1:15: *Klal Yisrael*'s beauty both internally and externally 118

1:15: Aspects of the beauty of *Klal Yisrael* reflected in the beauty of their "eyes" 118

1:15: *Klal Yisrael* follow their righteous leaders 120

1:15: *Klal Yisrael* greatness is their perseverance 121

1:15: The greatness of *Klal Yisrael* in never moving completely away from Hashem 122

1:16-17: Hashem loves *Klal Yisrael* and wishes to have His Presence dwell among them in the Mishkan 123

2:2: *Klal Yisrael* is like a rose amongst thorns – chosen from all other nations 132

3:2: *Klal Yisrael* search for Hashem 186

3:6: *Klal Yisrael* flourish even under harsh circumstances 196

Chapter Four in its entirety: The praise from Hashem elicited by *Klal Yisrael*'s wonderful deeds and good attributes 210

4:7: *Klal Yisrael* is perfectly beautiful in absolutely every way 235

4:1: *Klal Yisrael* is unparalleled 213

4:4: The importance of the Sanhedrin 224

4:8: The great faith of *Klal Yisrael* 240

4:10: *Klal Yisrael* is more precious than all the other nations 245

4:13-14: *Klal Yisrael* do a great variety of many great deeds 256

4:13-14: The greatness of the young and simple Jews and their great potential 257

4:13-14: All the various components of *Klal Yisrael* are precious and bring forth beauty for Hashem 258

4:16: There is nothing more precious than a Jewish child 262

4:16: Only *Klal Yisrael* may eat from the *korbanos* in the Beis HaMikdash 263

5:8: Nothing disturbs *Klal Yisrael* like the loss of Hashem's love 296

5:8: *Klal Yisrael* is obsessed with love for Hashem 297

5:9: The nations are awe-struck by *Klal Yisrael*'s declaration 298

Introduction to 5:10-16: *Klal Yisrael* constantly seek to bring Hashem closer to them 301

5:16: Our relationship with Hashem is unique and He is unique 321

6:1: *Klal Yisrael* inspire the nations to want to help them serve Hashem 324

6:4: *Klal Yisrael* knows how to please Hashem 335

6:4: *Klal Yisrael* is awe-inspiring 335

6:4: *Klal Yisrael* is always very kind 338

6:8-9: Even though Hashem could choose any nation, He loves only *Klal Yisrael* 348

6:8-9: All the other nations admit the superiority of *Klal Yisrael* 350

6:8-9: The purity of *Klal Yisrael* as seen in their children 350

6:8-9: *Klal Yisrael* is the most superior nation . 351

6:10: *Klal Yisrael* continually grows and flourishes, (6:10) 352

6:10: *Klal Yisrael* is destined for greatness 353

6:10: Like nuts, *Klal Yisrael* is filled with goodness 358

6:11: *Klal Yisrael* is modest and reticent 357

6:11: *Klal Yisrael* is precious like nuts 358

7:1: Nothing compares to the importance of *Klal Yisrael* in Hashem's eyes 371

Introduction to 7:2-14: The greatness of *Klal Yisrael* which even the nations notice 372

7:2-14: The greatness of *Klal Yisrael* 373

7:8: Tall and firm like a date tree 398

7:8: The honesty of *Klal Yisrael* 398

7:8: Chananyah, Mishael, and Azaryah demonstrate faith to the world 399

7:8: A righteous person's every action is for Hashem 400

7:9: Hashem is proud of *Klal Yisrael* and "boasts" about them 401

7:9: *Klal Yisrael* make a very good impression on everyone 403

7:10: Our forefathers thank Hashem for their good children 405

7:11: *Klal Yisrael* justify Hashem's pride in them 407

7:11: *Klal Yisrael* is completely devoted to Hashem 407

7:12-14: The righteous are always ready to serve Hashem; the wicked always wish to rest 413

8:1: *Klal Yisrael* seek to have an unhindered relationship with Hashem 421

8:1: *Klal Yisrael* seek to have a relationship with Hashem that does not end 421

8:1: The whole of *Klal Yisrael* look to serve Hashem 425

8:8: *Klal Yisrael* bonds the world to Hashem ... 450

8:11: *Klal Yisrael's* excellent pedigree 463

Selected times when Hashem displayed His special love for Klal Yisrael

1:7: Hashem's devotion and care for *Klal Yisrael* is like a shepherd's tending of his sheep 96

1:9-11: Hashem's love for *Klal Yisrael* as displayed through *Kriyas Yam Suf* 102

1:9-11: Hashem's love for *Klal Yisrael* as displayed through *Matan Torah* 106

1:12-14: After forgiving *Klal Yisrael*, Hashem relates to them with warmth and closeness 112

1:12-14: Hashem's Presence dwelling in the Mishkan is a sign of His love and forgiveness .. 113

1:12-14: *Klal Yisrael* recognizes the friendship and love of Hashem even when He seems distant.. 116

2:8: Hashem breaks through all boundaries in His eagerness to redeem *Klal Yisrael* 154

2:10-13: Hashem's love for *Klal Yisrael* is displayed in the way He redeems them 163

5:2: The four kinds of love and all apply to Hashem 275

5:2: The desperate call of Hashem to awaken us 278

5:4: Hashem begs us to repent 281

5:4: Hashem resorts to punishment to awaken us 281

5:2-6: Hashem searches for *Klal Yisrael* and invests a great deal in order to bring us back to Him ... 268

5:7: Hashem never gives up on *Klal Yisrael* 292

5:16: Hashem rewards us for doing mitzvos that benefit ourselves 319

6:2-3: The unique relationship between *Klal Yisrael* and Hashem 325

6:2-3: All of Hashem's efforts are for *Klal Yisrael* and vice versa, (6:2-3) 329

6:4-12: Hashem describes His love for *Klal Yisrael* 334

7:6: Hashem is bound to the love of *Klal Yisrael* 394

8:1: Abundant prophecy in the days of Mashiach 423

8:3: Hashem always supports and protects *Klal Yisrael* 425

8:6: The very intense love and pride that Hashem has for *Klal Yisrael* 435

8:6: *Klal Yisrael* are Hashem's medals 436

8:6: Hashem remembers *Klal Yisrael* and always keeps them before Him 437

8:7: All the nations with all their tactics cannot usurp Hashem's love for *Klal Yisrael* 441

Occasions when Klal Yisrael displayed their greatness

1:4: The greatness of *Klal Yisrael* in following

Hashem into the desert 81

1:4: *Klal Yisrael* remains loyal to Hashem even when He seems to be ignoring them 83

1:8: Our pride is that we follow our *mesores* (tradition) 101

1:9-11: Hashem entrusted the destiny of the world to *Klal Yisrael* 107

1:12-14: *Klal Yisrael* is always devoted to Hashem, even when it is difficult 115

1:12-14: *Klal Yisrael* displayed their love to Hashem from the very beginning 115

2:2: Even when *Klal Yisrael* is pricked, they remain beautiful 131

2:2: Suffering brings out *Klal Yisrael*'s beauty ... 131

2:3: *Klal Yisrael* acceptance of Torah with *Na'aseh* ("We will do") before *Nishma* ("We will understand") displays their greatness and their trust in Hashem 137

2:3: *Klal Yisrael*'s ability to delay gratification is the source of their success 134

2:3: *Klal Yisrael* notice Hashem's love and power 135

2:3: *Klal Yisrael*'s greatness in accepting the Torah and recognizing its sweetness 136

2:5: *Klal Yisrael* love for Hashem is overwhelming 147

3:3: *Klal Yisrael* determination to find Hashem) 188

3:3: Love breaks through all normal boundaries 188

3:6: *Klal Yisrael*'s tremendous greatness in the desert 195

3:7-8: The greatness of Torah scholars and righteous people 198

Introduction to Chapter Four: Every aspect of the greatness of *Klal Yisrael* reflects well on the entire nation 211

4:2: The honesty of *Klal Yisrael* 218

4:2: The greatness of even the warriors of *Klal Yisrael* 217

4:2: The greatness of the Torah scholars of *Klal Yisrael* 219

4:3: *Klal Yisrael* always keep their word 221

4:4: The "neck" of *Klal Yisrael* 225

4:12: The modesty of *Klal Yisrael* (men, women, and girls) 253

4:16: *Klal Yisrael* is open only to Hashem 262

4:16: Only *Klal Yisrael* elevate the mundane 264

5:2: The heart of *Klal Yisrael* 272

5:2: *Klal Yisrael* is never completely asleep 272

5:8: *Klal Yisrael*'s greatest declaration of love for Hashem 293

5:8: The nations will testify regarding *Klal Yisrael*'s devotion 294

6:2-3: *Klal Yisrael* replies confidently to the nations that Hashem loves them and has not completely left them 325

6:2-3: "I belong to my Beloved, and my Beloved to me" 328

6:2-3: In good times and bad times, *Klal Yisrael* is devoted to Hashem 328

6:6-7: The greatness of even the warriors of *Klal Yisrael* 344

6:6-7: The greatness of even the empty among *Klal Yisrael* 345

6:6-7: *Klal Yisrael*'s eating and thinking is devoted to Hashem 346

6:8-9: The *temimus* of Klal Yisrael 349

6:10: *Klal Yisrael* possesses beauty, warmth, and awe 354

6:11: *Klal Yisrael* is always clean 356

6:11: The vitality of *Klal Yisrael* 358

6:12: *Klal Yisrael* is amazed by their own greatness 361

7:1: *Klal Yisrael* is *shulamis* (perfect and beautiful) 365

7:1: *Klal Yisrael* withstands all the temptations of the nations 370

7:2: *Aliyah l'regel*: a description of its grandeur 375

7:2: As descendants of Avraham Avinu, we are a "daughter of nobility" 376

7:3: The Sanhedrin and its unimaginable greatness 380

7:3: *Klal Yisrael*'s self-control 382

7:3: *Klal Yisrael* appreciates the greatness of the fences of Torah 383

7:5: The "nose" of *Klal Yisrael* 386

7:5: The *Mizbe'ach*: a conduit between Heaven and earth 387

7:5: Purity of the leaders of *Klal Yisrael* 388

7:5: The greatness of the calendric calculations 388

7:5: Mental perseverance of *Klal Yisrael* 389

7:5: The ivory neck, life-giving and strong, as a symbol of *Klal Yisrael* 389

7:6: *Klal Yisrael*'s every mitzvah has a great effect 392

7:6: Eliyahu on Mount Carmel 392
7:6: Purity and strength of thought 393
7:7: It is a pleasure to be with *Klal Yisrael* 396
7:11: *Klal Yisrael's* importance is their relationship to Hashem 409
7:11: Hashem loves the humility of *Klal Yisrael* 409
7:12-14: The righteous serve Hashem even in poverty, while the wicked rebel even in prosperity 412
7:12-14: For the righteous, it is always light; for the wicked, it is always dark 412
7:12-14: Torah scholars are constantly developing and rising higher and higher 413
7:12-14: *Klal Yisrael* is always ready to serve Hashem 414
7:12-14: *Klal Yisrael* conceal and store their good deeds 415
7:12-14: Contrasting *Klal Yisrael* with the nations shows the former's greatness 416
7:12-14: The humility of Torah scholars 418
8:1: Yosef's righteousness towards his brothers 422
8:1: Aharon's devotion to Moshe 423
8:5: *Klal Yisrael's* greatness in accepting the Torah 432
8:5: The righteousness of the Jewish women in Egypt 433
8:6: *Klal Yisrael* has paid with their lives for their love of Hashem 438
8:7: Even if the nations would sacrifice everything for Hashem, He would love only *Klal Yisrael* 443
8:7: Neither friendliness nor threats will sway *Klal Yisrael* 443
8:7: *Klal Yisrael* love Hashem with all their heart, being, and resources 444
8:10: *Klal Yisrael* is a wall 455
8:10: *Klal Yisrael's* absolute firmness 455
8:11: The judgment of the nations centers on how they treat Klal Yisrael 462
8:11: *Klal Yisrael* is precious and vulnerable, like a vineyard 463

The importance of Torah, the greatness of those who learn it and how Torah is the main foundation in creating our bond with Hashem

Introduction: The importance of Torah in our relationship with Hashem 46
1:2: Through Torah one revives the feelings of Har Sinai 75
1:6: *Klal Yisrael* must stop wasting their efforts and focus them exclusively to serve Hashem 94
1:8: Our pride is that we follow our mesores (tradition) 101
1:9-11: Hashem's love for *Klal Yisrael* as displayed through Matan Torah 106
2:3: Torah has many dimensions of greatness .. 134
2:3: *Klal Yisrael's* greatness in accepting the Torah and recognizing its sweetness 136
2:4: Torah's various pleasures likened to wine ... 139
2:4: Hashem loves the discussion of Torah 143
2:5: Torah sustains *Klal Yisrael* and gives them hope 145
3:2: Hashem is found by doing mitzvos 187
3:7-8: The greatness of Torah scholars and righteous people 198
4:1: The greatness of every "hair" in the Torah. 215
4:1: The importance of yeshivos 215
4:5: One must observe all of Torah and not just certain parts 230
4:11: All of Torah is sweet 249
5:11: Every hair-like protrusion from the letters of the Torah has great depths 304
5:11: Torah is both clear and complicated 306
5:11: Through Torah, one connects to Hashem 307
5:11: One "sees" Hashem through Torah and His Creation, yet Torah is superior 308
5:15: Torah is like a well-built building 316
6:2-3: Hashem's Presence dwells in our shuls 326
6:11: Torah brings out the goodness of *Klal Yisrael* 357
6:11: Torah is the ultimate purpose of everything 357
7:10: When repeated in their name, words of Torah enliven the dead 405
7:12-14: Torah scholars are constantly developing and rising higher and higher 413
7:12-14: The humility of Torah scholars 418
8:5: *Klal Yisrael's* greatness in accepting the Torah 432
8:7: Rabbi Yochanan's dedication to Torah 445
8:7: The love of Torah by great Torah scholars 445
8:7: Torah learning cannot be bought, but its merit can be earned 446
8:7: The amazement of people who see this love of Torah 446

8:7: Rabbi Yitzchak Elchanan's family's great love of Torah 447

8:10: Torah scholars are like fortresses 456

8:10: Teachers of Torah are like nursing mothers 456

8:10: Rabbi Moshe Feinstein's unbending commitment to halachah 457

8:10: Torah will save us from exile 461

8:12: The true guardians of *Klal Yisrael*, the Torah leaders, will be richly rewarded 468

8:13: The spiritual unity between Hashem, Torah, and *Klal Yisrael* 473

Why Klal Yisrael's greatness lies in their unity

Introduction: *Klal Yisrael* as one unified, unique entity 38

4:5: The symmetry and unity of the leaders of *Klal Yisrael* 227

4:5: The leaders of *Klal Yisrael* work together for the sake of the nation 231

4:7: The beauty of the unity of *Klal Yisrael* 235

6:4: The greatest rally is for Hashem 336

6:8-9: The unity of *Klal Yisrael*, even when they argue *halachicly* 349

6:12: Conflict destroys *Klal Yisrael* 359

6:12: *Klal Yisrael* regrets their sins, especially the sin of internal strife 359

8:10: *Klal Yisrael*'s unity 456

8:13: The spiritual unity between Hashem, Torah, and *Klal Yisrael* 473

8:13: All service of Hashem requires unity 472

Printed in Great Britain
by Amazon

3c6a49e4-a85a-46fa-b84c-6fb599670377R01